HISTORY OF SYRIA

A restoration by John Dibs, Beirut

MODEL OF THE TEMPLE OF BA'LABAKK, HELIOPOLIS

This temple of Jupiter was enlarged and completed by members of the Syrian dynasty of Roman emperors in the second and third Christian centuries

Frontispiece

See below, pp. 310-316

HISTORY OF SYRIA

INCLUDING
LEBANON AND PALESTINE

BY

PHILIP K. HITTI
PROFESSOR OF SEMITIC LITERATURE ON THE
WILLIAM AND ANNIE S. PATON FOUNDATION
PRINCETON UNIVERSITY

Volume Two

GORGIAS PRESS
2002

First Gorgias Press Edition, 2002.

ISBN 1-931956-60-X (volume 1)
ISBN 1-931956-61-8 (volume 2)

GORGIAS PRESS
46 Orris Ave., Piscataway, NJ 08854 USA
www.gorgiaspress.com

Printed and bound in the United States of America.

CONTENTS

PART I

THE PRE-LITERARY AGE

CHAPTER I

PAGE

Place in History 3

CHAPTER II

Cultural Background: Stone Implements . . 7

The earliest relics: stone implements — Earliest human skeletons — Late Palaeolithic — Fire: charcoal — Language — The middle Stone Age — The Naṭūfian culture — Domestication of animals — Agriculture — Settled life — Higher life — Art — Neolithic culture — Pottery.

CHAPTER III

Metal Implements 23

Chalcolithic — The Ghassūlian culture — Irrigation agriculture — Ethnic relationship — Aesthetic development.

CHAPTER IV

The Setting of the Stage 30

Maritime plain — The western range — Lebanon — Home of the lost cause — Galilee — Caves — The median depression — Al-Biqā' — Earthquakes, volcanoes — The eastern range: Anti-Lebanon — Ḥawrān — Syrian Desert.

CHAPTER V

Physical Environment 45

Climate — Erosion — Vegetation — The olive tree — The cedar — Fauna — The horse — The camel.

PART II

ANCIENT SEMITIC TIMES

CHAPTER VI

PAGE

The Advent of the Semites 57

Nomenclature — Determining historical factors — The great international highway — Tent-dwellers versus house-dwellers — Who were the Semites? — Arabia, the cradle of the Semites.

CHAPTER VII

The Amorites: First Major Semitic Community in Syria 65

Enter the Amorites — The archives of Mari — The Syrian Saddle — Amorite centre shifts south — International double dealing — The Amorites in Palestine — Amorite religion.

CHAPTER VIII

The Canaanites: Second Major Semitic People in Syria 79

Canaan — City-states — Island cities — Leagues — Economy: agriculture — Industry — Metallurgy — Ivory — Glass — Cloth industry — Purple.

CHAPTER IX

Maritime Activity and Colonial Expansion . . 97

Sea routes — Navigation — Circumnavigation of Africa — Colonies — In Spain — Carthage.

CHAPTER X

Literature, Religion and Other Aspects of Cultural Life 109

The alphabet — Phoenician inscriptions — Ugarit — Fertility cult — Gods — Temples — Idols — "High places" — Burial customs.

CHAPTER XI

International Relations: Egypt 126

The Old Kingdom — Middle Kingdom — Tale of Sinuhe — Syria incorporated in the empire — Battle of Megiddo — Qadesh — Naharin — Decline of Egyptian control — Syrian influence on Egypt — Relations with Mesopotamia: Sumer — Babylon — Assyria — Chaldaean hegemony — Cultural penetration — Hyksos — In Egypt — Avaris — Hurrians — Kingdom of Mitanni — The Hurrian language — Hurrian remains — Hittites — The old kingdom — The new kingdom — Treaty with Egypt — In Palestine — Organization — Language — Religion — Who were the Khabiru?

CHAPTER XII

PAGE

THE ARAMAEANS: THE THIRD MAJOR SEMITIC PEOPLE . 162

Early beginnings in Mesopotamia — Spread into North Syria — Aramaean states in Mesopotamia — Aram Damascus — The battle of Qarqar — Hazael — Aramaean merchants — Aramaic — Inscriptions — Material culture — Hadad the Thunderer — Atargatis.

CHAPTER XIII

THE HEBREW PEOPLE 176

Hebrew origins — The Patriarchal age — The Exodus — Settlement — The Judges — The Philistines — Their five cities — Iron.

CHAPTER XIV

THE HEBREW MONARCHY 186

The united monarchy — David — Solomon in all his glory —Ezion-geber — The divided monarchy — The kingdom of Israel — Israel's end — The Samaritans — The kingdom of Judah — Hezekiah — Josiah's reforms — Last days of Judah — Fall of Jerusalem.

CHAPTER XV

ASPECTS OF CULTURAL AND SPIRITUAL LIFE: MONOTHEISM 203

Borrowed ritual — Art — Domestic affairs — Coinage — Religious teachers — The prophets — Amos, the first monotheist — Isaiah and the holiness of God — Jeremiah and the new covenant — Other prophetic contributions.

CHAPTER XVI

UNDER PERSIAN RULE — FROM THE SEMITIC ERA TO THE INDO-EUROPEAN 217

Neo-Babylonian suzerainty — The fall of new Babylon — A new world power: the Persians — The organization of the empire — The restoration — In Phoenicia — Tripoli, Phoenician capital — Sidon in ashes — Cultural aspects.

PART III

THE GRECO-ROMAN PERIOD

CHAPTER XVII

ALEXANDER AND HIS SUCCESSORS, THE SELEUCIDS . . 231

Battle of Issus — Tyre resists — Egypt reduced — The decisive battle near Arbela — Fusion of East and West — The break-up of the empire — Seleucus, founder of the Syrian monarchy — The Maccabean revolt — A Jewish commonwealth — Last convulsions of the Seleucid kingdom — The Romans annex Syria.

CHAPTER XVIII

PAGE

THE HELLENISTIC AGE 251

Greek settlements — Cities re-colonized — Degrees of Hellenization — Persistence of Aramaic — Literary activity — Posidonius the historian — Greco-Syrian poets — Meleager.

CHAPTER XIX

SELEUCID INSTITUTIONS 262

The royalty — The court — Army — War elephants — The fleet — Government of the provinces — Cities — Taxes.

CHAPTER XX

TRADE AND INDUSTRY 270

Seleucid policy — India — Dura-Europus — Gerrha — Trade with the West — New Phoenician colonies — Agricultural products — Industry — Coinage — Manifestations of luxury — Population.

CHAPTER XXI

SYRIA AS A ROMAN PROVINCE: THE PRE-EMPIRE PERIOD . 280

Proconsuls — In the days of Herod the king — Roman Hellenism.

CHAPTER XXII

UNDER THE EARLY ROMAN EMPERORS 286

Provincial government — Local government — Roman contribution — Syria at its height — Economic productivity — Agriculture — Gardening — Industry — Trade.

CHAPTER XXIII

CITY AND COUNTRY LIFE 299

The villages — The well-to-do — Social conditions — Antioch and Daphne — Laodicea and Apamea — Emesa — Damascus — Berytus — Heliopolis — South Syria.

CHAPTER XXIV

INTELLECTUAL ACTIVITY 319

History — Geography — Rhetoricians — Philosophy — The law school of Berytus — Papinian — Ulpian.

CHAPTER XXV

THE RISE OF CHRISTIANITY 328

Its progress — Persecution — Mystery religions — Centres of Syrian Christianity — Church Fathers.

CHAPTER XXVI

PAGE

Syrianizing versus Romanizing 337

Romanization through citizenship — Through military service — Jewish resistance — Titus destroys Jerusalem — Syrian dynasty at Rome — The Syrian sun-god installed in Rome — Philip the Arab — Economic penetration.

CHAPTER XXVII

Byzantine Syria 349

The later Roman Empire — Constantinople, the new capital — Christianity, the new religion — Administrative divisions — Trade — Emigrant artisans — Literature and education — Libanius — Ammianus Marcellus — John Chrysostom — Eusebius — Gaza — Berytus as a scientific centre — Student life.

CHAPTER XXVIII

An Ecclesiastical Age 363

Monasticism — Church buildings — Christian art — Aramaic revived — Edessa — Religious schisms — Apollinaris — The Nestorian Church — The Jacobite Church — The Persian peril.

CHAPTER XXIX

Pre-Islamic Syro-Arab States 375

1. The Nabataeans — From herders to tillers — From tillers to traders — The monarchy — The kingdom at its height — The last monarchs — Commercial and industrial contacts — Cultural aspects — Religion — Art and architecture — 2. The Palmyrenes — Tadmur — Centre of trans-desert trade — A vassal of Rome — The family of Udaynath — Zenobia — Last days of Palmyra — Monumental ruins — Language — Longinus — Palmyrene gods — The Ghassānids — Al-Ḥārith ibn-Jabalah — Al-Mundhir — Anarchy — The grandeur of the Ghassānid court.

PART IV

THE ARAB ERA

CHAPTER XXX

Syria in the Embrace of Islam 409

On the eve of Islam — Preliminary raids — The invasion begins — Khālid's perilous crossing — Damascus surrenders — Jerusalem and Caesarea reduced — " Easy conquest " — The administrator replaces the warrior — Significance of the conquest — Interpretation of the Islamic conquests.

CHAPTER XXXI

PAGE

Arab Administration 422

'Umar's covenant — Military districts — The plague of 'Amwās — Mu'āwiyah as governor — First navy built — The Byzantine fleet almost annihilated.

CHAPTER XXXII

The Orthodox Caliphate 428

A patriarchal period — 'Ali's case — 'Ali's caliphate — Mu'āwiyah enters the arena — The second civil war — Arbitration.

CHAPTER XXXIII

Mu'āwiyah Establishes the Umayyad Caliphate . 435

The anti-caliph out of the way — Al-'Irāq temporarily pacified — Second wave of conquests — Other achievements — A crown prince nominated — Mu'āwiyah the model king.

CHAPTER XXXIV

Hostile Relations With the Byzantines . . . 442

Syrian marches — Constantinople reached — Second siege of Constantinople — Last Umayyad attack on Constantinople — Mardaites in Lebanon.

CHAPTER XXXV

Domestic Disturbances: Shī'ites, Medinese, Persians . 450

The tragedy of al-Ḥusayn — Another pretender — Al-Ḥajjāj, energetic viceroy.

CHAPTER XXXVI

The Glory that was Damascus 457

Subjugation of Transoxiana — "Beyond the river" incorporated — Conquest in India — Against the Byzantines — North Africa — Conquest of Spain — Ṭāriq crosses the strait — A decisive victory — Mūsa follows — A triumphal procession — Explanation of the conquest — The Pyrenees crossed — The battle of Tours — Damascus the capital — Nationalizing the state — Postal service — Fiscal and other reforms.

CHAPTER XXXVII

Political and Social Conditions under the Umayyads 477

Provincial government — Bureau of registry — Military organization — Royal life — Innocent pastimes — Royal harem — The capital — Society — Clients — Dhimmis — Disabilities imposed by 'Umar — Slaves — General state of economy.

CHAPTER XXXVIII

PAGE

Higher Aspects of Life under the Umayyads . . 490

Grammar and lexicography — Religious tradition and canon law — Historiography — Oratory — Correspondence — Poetry — Education — Science: medicine — Alchemy — Schools of thought — St. John of Damascus — Murji'ites — Khārijites — The Shīʻah — Music — Painting — Palaces in the desert — Qaṣr al-Ḥayr — Mosques: the Dome of the Rock — The Aqṣa Mosque — The Umayyad Mosque.

CHAPTER XXXIX

The Syrian Christian Church 517

The East Syrian Church — The West Syrian Church — The Maronites — The Melkites — Interaction with Islam — Loan words — Orthography.

CHAPTER XL

Fall of the Umayyad Dynasty 527

A devout caliph — The last able Umayyad — Four incompetent caliphs — ʻAlids and ʻAbbāsids — The Khurāsānians — Revolt breaks out — Final blow — A dramatic escape.

CHAPTER XLI

Syria an ʻAbbāsid Province 534

A new era — Traitors and suspects disposed of — Unrest in Syria, Lebanon and Palestine — A veiled rebel — Damascus a temporary capital — Anti-Christian legislation — Islamization — The conquest of Arabic.

CHAPTER XLII

Syrian Contribution to Arab Renaissance . . . 548

Translations from Greek — Ḥunayn ibn-Isḥāq — Ṣābians — Original contribution — Moslem contribution: abu-Tammām — Al-Buḥturi — Dīk al-Jinn — Al-Awzāʻi.

CHAPTER XLIII

Syria an Adjunct of Minor States 557

The Ṭūlūnids — Khumārawayh — The Qarmaṭians — The Ikhshīdids — A Negro ruler — Fall of the Ikhshīdids — The Ḥamdānids: Sayf-al-Dawlah — The glamorous circle of Sayf-al-Dawlah — Al-Mutanabbi' — Abu-Firās — Other than poets — Al-Fārābi — Al-Maqdisi, geographer — Dark ages begin.

CHAPTER XLIV

PAGE

Between Saljūqs and Fāṭimids 573

Ṭughril in Baghdād — The Saljūqs of Syria — The Atābegs — The Fāṭimids established — Their vast domain — Precarious hold — The Mirdāsids — A blind poet-philosopher: al-Ma'arri — The Druzes — The Nuṣayrīyah — Persecution of Christians.

CHAPTER XLV

Meeting of East and West: The Crusades . . 590

Complexity of motivation — The first Crusade — The first Latin principality — Antioch, the second principality — Along the coast — Jerusalem seized — Baldwin, first king — Expansion in the north — Moslem reaction: Zangi — Nūr-al-Dīn — Enter Ṣalāḥ-al-Dīn — The decisive encounter: Ḥiṭṭīn — 'Akka, centre of activity — After Ṣalāḥ-al-Dīn's death — St. Louis — Baybars, leader of the counter-Crusade — The Assassins — The last of the Crusading colonies.

CHAPTER XLVI

Cultural Interaction 614

The impact on the West: science and literature — Military art — Architecture — Agriculture and industry — International exchange — Social contacts — Usāmah's testimony — Effects on Syria — Feudalism — Missionary activity.

CHAPTER XLVII

Ayyūbids and Mamlūks 627

Ayyūbids supplanted by Mamlūks — Baḥri Mamlūks — Mongol invasions — Burji Mamlūks — Administration of Syria — Famine and plague — Trade and industry — In Lebanon — Cultural activity: hospitalization — Medicine — Madrasahs — Mamlūk architecture and decoration — Intellectual endeavour — Illuministic Sufism — Ibn-'Arabi — Biography — History and geography — Tīmūr — Ottomans against Mamlūks and Ṣafawids — Marj Dābiq: a decisive victory — Mamlūk rule abolished.

PART V

UNDER THE OTTOMAN TURKS

CHAPTER XLVIII

Syria a Turkish Province 661

The Ottoman state — Administrative divisions of Syria — Special position of Lebanon — Al-Ghazāli — The system of administration — Abuses and attempts at reform — Abortive constitutional measures — Social and economic aspects — Cultural aspects — The printing press.

CHAPTER XLIX

PAGE

THE MAʻNS AND THE SHIHĀBS: LORDS OF LEBANON . 678

Fakhr-al-Dīn II — Period of anarchy — The Shihābs succeed the Maʻns — Al-Shaykh Ẓāhir al-ʻUmar — Aḥmad Pasha al-Jazzār — Bashīr II — An internationally recognized autonomous Lebanon.

CHAPTER L

THE CONTEMPORARY SCENE 697

Political penetration — The Ḥamīdian régime — Union and Progress — Cultural penetration — Nationalism and the struggle for independence — Democracy.

INDEX 707

PART IV

THE ARAB ERA

CHAPTER XXX

SYRIA IN THE EMBRACE OF ISLAM

On the eve of Islam

Two episodes of late ancient times stand out in significance: the migration of the Teutonic tribes which resulted in the destruction of the Roman Empire in the West, and the eruption of the Moslem Arabian tribes which annihilated the empire of the Persians and stripped the Byzantine of its fairest provinces. Of the two the Arabian episode was the more phenomenal. At the time of its occurrence Persia and Byzantium were the only two world powers; the Arabians were nobody. Who living then could have guessed that such a happening was within the realm of possibility?

In 628, after six years of war with several reverses, Heraclius, whose ancestral home was Edessa (al-Ruhā') in North Syria, succeeded in recovering Syria, which had passed into Persian hands. Chosroes II had swept over the country (611–14) carrying plunder and destruction wherever he passed. He pillaged Damascus and decimated its people by murder and captivity. The Church of the Holy Sepulchre he left in ruins; its treasures, including the true cross, he carried off as booty. On September 14, 629, the triumphant Byzantine emperor restored this cross to Jerusalem [1] and was hailed deliverer of Christendom and restorer of the unity of the Eastern Empire.

Preliminary raids

Meantime a band of 3000 Arabians was carrying a raid into a town east of the southern end of the Dead Sea called Mu'tah.[2] The leader was Zayd ibn-Ḥārith, adopted son of Muḥammad. The object was ostensibly to avenge the murder, by a Ghassānid, of an emissary sent by the Prophet to Buṣra, actually to gain for the new converts rich booty including the coveted Mashrafīyah swords manufactured in that neighbourhood.[3] The policy of

[1] The occasion is still celebrated with bonfires by the Christians of Lebanon.

[2] In Transjordan, two hours' journey south of al-Karak; visited by Alois Musil; see his *Arabia Petraea*, vol. i (Vienna, 1907), p. 152.

[3] Consult Yāqūt, vol. iv, p. 536; M. J. de Goeje, *Mémoire sur la conquête de la Syrie* (Leyden, 1900), p. 5.

attacking border countries thus inaugurated by Muḥammad was calculated to make the new religion popular among the believers. Zayd fell on the battlefield. The remnant of his army was led back to Medina by young Khālid ibn-al-Walīd,[1] soon to become the champion of militant Islam. To the natives the attack on Mu'tah was but another of the frequent Bedouin raids to which they had long been accustomed. In reality it was the first shot in a struggle that was not to cease until Byzantium itself had surrendered and the name of the Arabian Prophet substituted for that of Christ on its cathedrals.

In the following year (630) Muḥammad led in person an expedition against the oasis of Tabūk [2] in northern al-Ḥijāz, whence he opened negotiations with neighbouring settlements which led to their submission. The people were granted security and the right to retain their property and profess their religion on condition that they paid an annual tribute. First among those settlements was Aylah (Aila) at the head of the Gulf of al-ʿAqabah,[3] whose population was Christian. South of it on the gulf stood Maqna,[4] with a Jewish population mostly engaged in weaving and fishing. Another was Adhruḥ, with a population of about a hundred families, which lay between Petra and Maʿān. An hour's journey to the north of Adhruḥ, on the ancient Roman road from Buṣra to the Red Sea, lay al-Jarbā', whose people were also Christians. The site later played a part in the Crusades. These were the only places in Syria with which Islam established contact in the lifetime of the Prophet. The terms of their capitulation [5] are suggestive of what was to come. The attempt on these settlements in southern Syria by Muḥammad was but a rehearsal for what was to follow under his successors.

The year after the death of the Prophet, the stage was set for

[1] Ṭabari, vol. i, p. 1610; cf. Theophanes, p. 336; J. Wellhausen, *Skizzen und Vorarbeiten*, vol. vi (Berlin, 1899), p. 52.

[2] On the pilgrimage road and now the railroad between Damascus and Medina. Al-Wāqidi, *al-Maghāzi*, ed. A. von Kremer (Calcutta, 1855–6), pp. 425-6; Yāqūt, vol. i, pp. 824-5; Balādhuri, p. 59; tr., p. 92; Caetani, vol. ii, pp. 238 *seq.* For a description of the modern village consult Jaussen and Savignac, pp. 57-64; Alois Musil, *The Northern Ḥeǵâz* (New York, 1926), pp. 234-7, 318-19.

[3] See above, p. 190; Caetani, vol. ii, pp. 253-5.

[4] Yāqūt, vol. iv, p. 610. For a modern description of this oasis consult Musil, *Northern Ḥeǵâz*, pp. 114-16, 312.

[5] Balādhuri, pp. 59-60; tr., pp. 92-4.

a full-dress invasion of neighbouring lands. Arabia had just concluded its so-called wars of apostasy [1] and was consolidated and unified under the leadership of one man, the first caliph abu-Bakr (632–4). The momentum acquired in these internal wars had to seek new outlets, especially since the new religion had supposedly converted its adherents into one brotherhood. The martial spirit of the tribes, to whom raids [2] were a sort of national sport from time immemorial, could not but assert itself in some form after Islam. Then there was the expectation of collaboration on the part of the Arabian tribes domiciled in southern Syria. These tribes, such as the Judhām and Quḍā'ah,[3] were by this time Christianized but not satisfied. The annual subsidy which for years they had been receiving for guarding the frontiers had recently been suspended by Heraclius as a measure of economy.[4] The forts along that southern border had also been neglected and stripped of their garrisons to enable concentration in the north in face of the Persian danger. Syria was the nearest arena.

The invasion begins

To it three detachments were led in 633 by 'Amr ibn-al-'Aṣ, Yazīd ibn-abi-Sufyān and Shuraḥbīl ibn-Ḥasanah.[5] 'Amr, future hero of the Egyptian campaign, was to be the commander-in-chief in case of unified operation. The standard-bearer in Yazīd's army was his brother Mu'āwiyah, future founder of the Umayyad dynasty in Damascus. The route followed by Yazīd and Shuraḥbīl was the much-frequented Tabūk-Ma'ān one, that by 'Amr was the coast route via Aylah. The detachments were later augmented from about 3000 to some 7500 each. Abu-'Ubaydah ibn-al-Jarrāḥ, who later became generalissimo, probably came at the head of one of the reinforcements.

The first engagement took place at Wādi al-'Arabah,[6] the great depression south of the Dead Sea. There Sergius, patrician of Palestine with headquarters at Caesarea, suffered a defeat at the hands of Yazīd. His retreating army was overtaken at Dāthin,

[1] *riddah*; Hitti, *History of the Arabs*, pp. 140-42; C. H. Becker in *The Cambridge Medieval History* (New York, 1913), vol. ii, pp. 334-6.

[2] *ghazw*, whence English razzia.

[3] The Salīḥ (above, p. 401) were a clan of Quḍā'ah. The 'Āmilah were at this time settled a little farther north, whence they later spread into southern Lebanon, still called Jabal (mountain of) 'Āmil — 'Āmilah in abu-al-Fidā', *Taqwīm*, p. 228.

[4] Theophanes, p. 335.

[5] Balādhuri, pp. 107-8; tr., p. 165; de Goeje, pp. 21-4.

[6] See above, p. 36 map.

near Gaza, and almost annihilated (February 4, 634).[1] Sergius himself lost his life. The way was now temporarily clear. Yazīd and 'Amr raided the entire southern part of Palestine. Even Caesarea was threatened. Jerusalem was cut off from the sea.[2]

Khālid's perilous crossing

On receiving the news Heraclius, who was still in Emesa (Ḥimṣ), where reportedly he had received a message from the Prophet summoning him to Islam, hastened to organize and dispatch a fresh army under his brother Theodorus. Meantime Khālid ibn-al-Walīd received orders from abu-Bakr to rush from al-'Irāq to the reinforcement of the army on the Syrian front. The raid on al-'Irāq began shortly before that on Syria, but Syria being closer to al-Ḥijāz was of greater concern.

Khālid probably started his perilous march across the desert from al-Ḥīrah, which with other places had capitulated to him. The track he followed was presumably the south-westward one leading to Dūmat[3] al-Jandal (modern al-Jawf), midway between the two countries. Once in Dūmah he could have continued through Baṭn al-Sirr (Wādi al-Sirḥān) to Buṣra, eastern gateway of Syria; but forts lay on the way. He, therefore, followed the north-western route to Qurāqir (Qulbān Qarāqir) on the eastern boundary of the Baṭn. Thence he pushed northward to Suwa,[4] a journey of five days in almost waterless desert. Water for the troops, who numbered five to eight hundred, was carried in bags; but for the horses the paunches of camels served as reservoirs. This camel water could also be used by men in case of emergency. The horses were led alongside and intended for use only at the time of the encounter. The guide, one Rāfi' ibn-'Umayr of the Ṭayyi' tribe, was at one point so dazzled by the rays of the sun that he could not spot the expected sign for underground water. So he besought the troops to look for a box-thorn (*'awsaj*) and as they dug near it, they struck damp soil with water. Thus was the

[1] Yāqūt, vol. ii, pp. 514-15; Balādhuri, p. 109; tr., pp. 167-8; de Goeje, pp. 31-4; Caetani, vol. ii, pp. 1141-54.

[2] The Arabic records of the war of conquest, compiled two to three centuries after the events, are confused in chronology, fact and evaluation. The reconstruction followed here is based on Caetani, de Goeje, Wellhausen, Becker and other modern critical scholars.

[3] Mentioned in Gen. 25:14; Is. 21:11.

[4] Near modern Sab' Biyār (seven wells), north-east of Damascus.

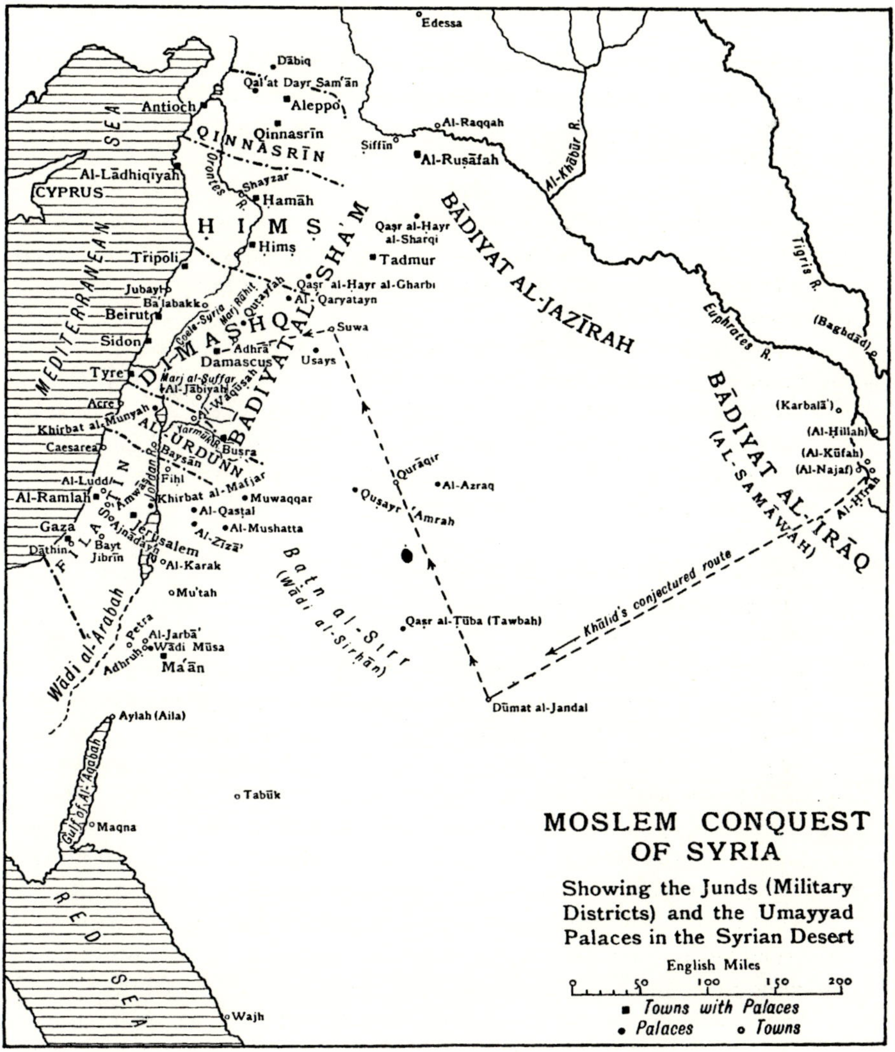
MOSLEM CONQUEST OF SYRIA
Showing the Junds (Military Districts) and the Umayyad Palaces in the Syrian Desert
English Miles
0
50
100
150
200
Towns with Palaces
Palaces
Towns
Edessa
Dābiq
Qal'at Dayr Sam'ān
Aleppo
Antioch
Qinnasrīn
QINNASRĪN
Ṣiffīn
Al-Raqqah
Al-Ruṣāfah
Al-Khābūr R.
Al-Lādhiqīyah
CYPRUS
Orontes R.
Shayzar
Ḥamāh
ḤIMṢ
Ḥimṣ
Qaṣr al-Ḥayr al-Sharqi
Tadmur
BĀDIYAT AL-JAZĪRAH
BĀDIYAT AL-SHA'M
Tigris R.
Euphrates R.
(Baghdād)
MEDITERRANEAN SEA
Tripoli
Jubayl
Ba'labakk
Beirut
Sidon
Tyre
Acre
Qaṣr al-Ḥayr al-Gharbi
Al-Qaryatayn
Suwa
Usays
Adhra'
Damascus
DIMASHQ
Marj al-Ṣuffar
Al-Jābiyah
Al-Wāqūṣah
Yarmūk R.
Buṣra
AL-URDUNN
Khirbat al-Munyah
Caesarea
Baysān
Faḥl
Al-Ludd
Al-Ramlah
Amwās
Jordan R.
Khirbat al-Mafjar
Muwaqqar
Al-Qasṭal
Al-Mushatta
Al-Zīzā'
Gaza
Ajnādayn
Jerusalem
Bayt Jibrīn
Dāthin
FILASTĪN
Al-Karak
Mu'tah
Wādi al-'Arabah
Petra
Al-Jarbā'
Wādi Mūsa
Adhruḥ
Ma'ān
Quraqir
Al-Azraq
Quṣayr 'Amrah
Baṭn al-Sirr (Wādi al-Sirḥān)
Qaṣr al-Ṭūba (Tawbah)
Dūmat al-Jandal
Khālid's conjectured route
BĀDIYAT AL-'IRĀQ (AL-SAMĀWAH)
(Karbalā')
(Al-Ḥillah)
(Al-Kūfah)
(Al-Najaf)
Al-Ḥīrah
Aylah (Aila)
Gulf of Al-'Aqabah
Tabūk
Maqna
RED SEA
Wajh

army saved and an unparalleled feat in the desert saga achieved.[1]

With dramatic suddenness Khālid made his appearance (April 24, 634), after only eighteen days' journey, north-east of Damascus and directly in the rear of the improvised Byzantine army. His first encounter, a successful one, was with the Christian Ghassānid forces on Easter at a place near 'Adhrā' in Marj Rāhiṭ.[2] Shrewd strategist that he was, Khālid pressed southward through Transjordan aiming at effecting a junction with the harassed army of his fellow-generals; desire for neither self-aggrandizement nor booty could sidetrack him.

Damascus surrenders

The combined forces, perhaps with Khālid in chief command, won a bloody victory at Ajnādayn[3] (July 30, 634). All Palestine now lay open before the invader. For six months random raids were carried on in all directions. Buṣra yielded with but little resistance. Fiḥl,[4] commanding the eastern crossing of the Jordan, followed suit; so did Baysān on the other side of the river. The new Byzantine general Baanes fared no better than his predecessor. A month later the Byzantine army was again encountered and routed at Marj al-Ṣuffar,[5] whence it sought safety behind the walls of Damascus. Khālid pursued it. He laid siege to the future capital of the Moslem empire which simply meant that he endeavoured to isolate it, as the Arabians had not yet acquired the technique of the siege or implements. After six months the city surrendered (September 635) through treachery. The negotiators were the bishop and Manṣūr ibn-Sarjūn, grandfather of St. John the Damascene and high official in the finance department of the government. The traditional report that the city was conquered half by force (*'anwatan*) and

[1] Khālid's itinerary in Arabic sources presents many historical and geographical problems; cf. Balādhuri, pp. 110-12; tr., pp. 169-72; Ṭabari, vol. i, pp. 2111-13, 2121-4; ibn-al-Athīr, vol. ii, pp. 312-13; al-Ya'qūbi, *Ta'rīkh*, ed. M. Th. Houtsma (Leyden, 1883), vol. ii, pp. 150-51; ibn-'Asākir, *al-Ta'rīkh al-Kabīr* (Damascus), vol. i, p. 130; al-Baṣri, *Futūḥ al-Sha'm*, ed. W. N. Lees (Calcutta, 1854), pp. 63-5. The itinerary conjectured here is based on Musil, *Arabia Deserta*, pp. 553-73; Caetani, vol. ii, pp. 1220-36.

[2] A plain 15 miles from Damascus. Balādhuri, p. 112; tr., p. 172; Yāqūt, vol. iv, p. 1016.

[3] This otherwise unknown place should perhaps be emended to Jannābatayn, between al-Ramlah and Bayt Jibrīn (Eleutheropolis) on the Gaza-Jerusalem road. Caetani, vol. iii, pp. 176-87; Wellhausen, *Skizzen*, vol. vi, pp. 57-8; Dussaud, *Topographie*, p. 318.

[4] Or Faḥl, Gr. Pella, Bi-hi-lim of the 'Amārnah tablets (above, p. 71), now Kkirbat Faḥil. Caetani, vol. iii, pp. 187-211; Abel, vol. ii, pp. 34, 405.

[5] A plain 20 miles south of Damascus.

half by capitulation (*ṣulḥan*) has all the earmarks of being a late one intended to justify the partition of the cathedral by the Umayyads.[1] The terms of surrender embodied the same principles as those exacted by the Prophet[2] and established a precedent for dealing with other Syrian towns:

In the name of Allah, the compassionate, the merciful. This is what Khālid ibn-al-Walīd would grant to the inhabitants of Damascus if he enters therein: he promises to give them security for their lives, property and churches. Their city wall shall not be demolished, neither shall any Moslem be quartered in their houses. Thereunto we give to them the pact of Allah and the protection of His Prophet, the caliphs and the believers. So long as they pay the poll tax, nothing but good shall befall them.[3]

With the fall of the Syrian metropolis, total victory was assured. Before the end of the year abu-ʿUbaydah had occupied Ḥimṣ. All neighbouring towns — Baʿlabakk, Ḥimṣ, Ḥamāh — opened their gates. In some cases, as that of Shayzar,[4] "The people went out to meet him accompanied by players on the tambourines and singers and bowed down before him". Only Jerusalem, Caesarea and certain coastal towns held out in expectation of aid from Heraclius.

Heraclius did not intend to disappoint them. Having mustered from the vicinity of Antioch and Aleppo an army of some fifty thousand, mostly Armenian and Arab mercenaries, he put it again under the command of his brother Theodorus assisted by Baanes.[5] Realizing the superiority of this army in numbers, Arabian generalship immediately relinquished Ḥimṣ, even Damascus and other strategic towns, and concentrated about 2500 men at the valley of the Yarmūk,[6] whence retreat to the desert would be assured if forced. Heraclius' army took the Coele-Syria-Transjordan route. After a period of skirmishing, in the course of which Baanes was declared emperor by the troops, the battle was joined. The locale was at the juncture of the Yarmūk with its tributary al-Ruqqād near al-Wāqūṣah (modern al-Yāqūṣah). The climax came on a hot day (August,

[1] Caetani, vol. iii, pp. 359-92. See below, pp. 513-15.

[2] See above, p. 410.

[3] Balādhuri, p. 121; tr., p. 187.

[4] Larissa, modern Sayjar, on the Orontes, 15 miles north-west of Ḥamāh. See below, pp. 621-2.

[5] Theophanes, p. 337; Ṭabari, vol. i, p. 2125.

[6] Hieromax, now Sharīʿat al-Manādhirah (after a Bedouin tribe; Abel, vol. i, p. 171), tributary of the Jordan; not to be confused with Jarmuth of Josh. 10:3, modern Khirbat Yarmūk, near Ajnādayn.

20, 636) with a dust storm before which the Arabians were at a decided advantage. The Byzantine troops were manœuvred into a tight position between the two streams. On the west the bridge of al-Ruqqād was occupied by the Arabians; on the east the line of communication was also cut off. All chances of retreat were thus nullified. The chants and prayers of the priests and the use of the crosses were of no avail.[1] Before the onslaught of the sons of the desert Armenian and Syro-Arab mercenaries could not hold their own. Some were slaughtered then and there. Others were driven relentlessly into the river. Still others deserted and were caught and annihilated on the other side. Theodorus was one of the victims. The fate of Syria was sealed. Even Heraclius admitted it. "Farewell, O Syria", were his last words, "and what an excellent country this is for the enemy!"[2]

In the autumn of the same year a contingent, probably under abu-'Ubayadah, reoccupied Damascus. All other cities previously occupied now received the conqueror with open arms. "We like your rule and justice", declared the natives of Ḥimṣ, "far better than the state of tyranny and oppression under which we have been living."[3] Farther north Aleppo and Antioch were soon reduced. Only Qinnasrīn put up some resistance. Finally the Taurus Mountains, natural boundary of Syria, put a stop to the uninterrupted advance of Arabian arms.

Jerusalem and Caesarea reduced

Other generals were operating with equal success in the interior and along the coast. Shuraḥbīl reduced Acre and Tyre.[4] Yazīd and his brother Mu'āwiyah acquired Sidon, Beirut, Jubayl and Tripoli.[5] In the south Jerusalem and Caesarea (Qaysārīyah), both Hellenized, persisted in their resistance. Jerusalem held out against 'Amr till 638, when its people stipulated that 'Umar, who was then visiting in al-Jābiyah, receive the capitulation in person.[6] The problem of Caesarea was complicated by the fact that the city was accessible to naval aid. At last it fell in 640, after seven years of intermittent attacks climaxed by a

[1] Ibn-'Asākir, vol. i, p. 163; Baṣri, p. 197.

[2] Balādhuri, p. 137; tr., p. 210; cf. Ṭabari, vol. i, pp. 2395-6.

[3] Balādhuri, p. 137; tr., p. 211. Almost the same sentiments were attributed to the natives of Fiḥl; Baṣri, p. 97.

[4] Balādhuri, p. 116; tr., p. 179; de Goeje, p. 133.

[5] Balādhuri, p. 126; tr., p. 194; Caetani, vol. iii, p. 801.

[6] Ṭabari, vol. i, pp. 2402 *seq.*; Balādhuri, pp. 138-9; tr., pp. 213-14; Ya'qūbi, vol. ii, pp. 167-8; de Goeje, pp. 152 *seq.*

siege conducted by Muʿāwiyah.[1] The treachery of a Jew inside its walls contributed to the final fall. In those seven years (633–40) the entire country from south to north was subdued.

" Easy conquest "

This " easy conquest "[2] of a strategic province of the Byzantine empire is not difficult to explain. The military structure of that empire had been as effectively undermined by the Persian incursions of the early seventh century as the spiritual unity of its society had been disrupted by the Monophysite schism of the middle fifth. Heraclius' last minute effort (638) to bridge the religious gap by offering a compromise was as fruitless as earlier ones. The compromise was devised by his patriarch Sergius, a Syrian of Jacobite lineage, and aimed at glossing over the controversial issue of the nature of Christ and emphasizing his one will (*thelēma*). The new formula satisfied neither the Byzantine orthodox nor the Syrian dissenters. In fact it resulted in the creation of a new sect, the Monothelites, who maintained that Christ had but one will, the divine. The bulk of the Syrians held on to their Church. To them it was more than a religious institution; it was an expression of a submerged, semi-articulate feeling of nationality.

At no time since Alexander's conquest, as we learned before,[3] did the people of Syria, as a people, lose their national character, their native tongue, their Semitic religion, and identify themselves wholeheartedly with the Greco-Roman way of life. At its thickest Hellenistic culture was only skin-deep, affecting a crust of intelligentsia in urban settlements. The bulk of the population must throughout that millennium have considered the rulers aliens. The alienation between rulers and ruled was no doubt aggravated by misrule and high taxation. To the masses of seventh century Syria the Moslem Arabians must have appeared closer ethnically, linguistically and perhaps religiously than the hated Byzantine masters.

The administrator replaces the warrior

Now that all Syria is conquered, the general must give way to the administrator. Khālid, whose brilliant military record in Arabia, al-ʿIrāq and Syria had entitled him to the appellation " the sword of Allah ", was replaced on orders from the Caliph

[1] Balādhuri, pp. 140-42; tr., pp. 215-19; de Goeje, pp. 166-9; Caetani, vol. iv, pp. 156-63.

[2] Balādhuri, p. 16, l. 18, p. 126, ll. 13, 19; tr., p. 179, l. 17, p. 193, l. 22, p. 194, l. 7.

[3] Above, pp. 254, 256-7, 281, 287-8.

'Umar by abu-'Ubaydah, distinguished Companion of the Prophet, and member of the triumvirate which had monopolized Islamic authority.[1] The two other members were abu-Bakr and 'Umar. 'Umar had succeeded abu-Bakr as caliph shortly after the battle of Ajnādayn in 634 and evidently harboured ill feeling against Khālid, but did not entrust the supreme command to his friend abu-'Ubaydah until after the Yarmūk battle. Khālid withdrew from public life to Ḥimṣ. There he died in oblivion (642) to live in tradition as a miracle worker. His shrine and mosque were built in 1908 in Turkish style. His wife Faḍā' was buried with him.

When in 638 'Umar visited the Moslem camp in al-Jābiyah to solemnize the conquest and determine the status of the conquered, he not only confirmed abu-'Ubaydah in his position as generalissimo but appointed him governor-general and vice-regent. The aged caliph's entry into Jerusalem riding on a camel and wearing shabby raiment did not leave a favourable impression.[2] He was received by the patriarch and "honey-tongued defender of the church" Sophronius, who is said to have turned to an attendant and remarked in Greek,[3] "Truly this is the abomination of desolation spoken of by Daniel the Prophet as standing in the holy place".[4]

Significance of the conquest

The conquest of Syria transcended local and temporary considerations. It gave the nascent power of Islam prestige before the world and confidence in itself.

With Syria as a base an Arab army under 'Iyāḍ ibn-Ghanm operated north-east and between 639 and 646 subjugated all Mesopotamia.[5] The way was thence open to north-west Persia and lands beyond; full advantage was taken thereof. Another army under 'Amr and other veterans of the Syrian campaign operated south-westward and between 640 and 646 subdued Egypt.[6] From Egypt operations were easily continued with the

[1] H. Lammens, "Le Triumvirat Aboû Bakr, 'Omar et Aboû 'Obaidah" *Mélanges de la faculté orientale*, vol. iv (Beirut, 1910), pp. 113 *seq.*

[2] De Goeje, p. 157; cf. Ṭabari, vol. i, p. 2407.

[3] Theophanes, p. 339; Constantine Porphyrogenitus, "De administrando imperio" in J.-P. Migne, *Patrologia Graeca*, vol. cxiii (Paris, 1864), col. 109. Sophronius was probably of Maronite origin.

[4] Dan. 9:27; 11:31; 12:1; quoted in Matt. 24:15; Mk. 13:14. The reference in Dan. is to Antiochus Epiphanes; see above, p. 244.

[5] Balādhuri, pp. 172 *seq.*; tr., pp. 269 *seq.*; Ṭabari, vol. i, pp. 2505-8.

[6] Hitti, *History of the Arabs*, pp. 160 *seq.* The same term *ghazw*, formerly used for petty tribal raids, was used for the national Moslem campaigns.

collaboration of Syrians into north-west Africa and ultimately into Spain. From northern Syria, Asia Minor was vulnerable to attacks which were carried on intermittently for almost a century.

Interpretation of the Islamic conquests

All these conquests, however, belong to the category of systematic campaigning rather than the casual raiding to which the earlier conquests belonged.[1] The initial campaigns into al-ʿIrāq and Syria were not the result of purposeful and far-sighted planning. Neither abu-Bakr nor ʿUmar, under whom most of these victories were achieved, held a war council, worked out a strategy or even dreamed — at least in the initial stages — of ever establishing a permanent foothold in the conquered territories. But the logic of events forced such an outcome. The armies were first not allowed to settle in cities; a camp near al-Jābiyah served as initial capital. In fact there is reason to believe that some of the early operations, like Khālid's campaign into al-ʿIrāq, may have been undertaken not only without caliphal orders but perhaps against them.

Nor should the Moslem conquests be viewed as primarily or mainly religious crusades. The classical interpretation of Moslem historians follows the theological interpretation by the Hebrews of their national history and by the medieval Christians of the expansion of the Church; it makes the movement predominantly religious and providentially determined. In reality the Arabian Islamic expansion had underlying economic causes.[2] This economic aspect did not fully escape the attention of judicious Arab historians like al-Balādhuri,[3] who declares that, in recruiting for the Syrian campaign, abu-Bakr " wrote to the people of Mecca, al-Ṭā'if, al-Yaman and all the Arabians in Najd and al-Ḥijāz summoning them to a holy war and arousing their desire for it and for the booty to be got from the Greeks ".

Viewed in its proper perspective the Islamic expansion was one in a series of migrations, " waves ", which carried a surplus population from a barren peninsula to a bordering fertile region with a more abundant life. In fact it was the last stage in the age-long process of infiltration which had begun with the Babylonians some four thousand years before.[4] The Islamic move-

[1] Hitti, *History of the Arabs*, pp. 160, 167-8.

[2] Worked out by Caetani, vol. ii, pp. 831-61, followed by Becker, Lammens and other modern critical scholars.

[3] P. 107; tr., p. 165.

[4] Consult above, pp. 62, 64.

ment, however, did possess one distinctive feature — religious impulse. Combined with the economic, this made the movement irresistible and carried it far beyond the confines of any preceding one. Islam admittedly provided a battle cry, a slogan comparable to that provided by " democracy " in the first and second world wars. More than that it served as a cohesive agency cementing tribes and heterogeneous masses never united before. But while the desire to spread the new faith or go to Paradise may have been the motivating force in the lives of some of the Bedouin warriors, the desire for the comforts and luxuries of settled life in the Fertile Crescent was the driving force in the case of many of them.

A corresponding and equally discredited hypothesis held by Christians portrays the Arabian Moslems as going around with the offer of the Koran in one hand and the sword in the other. In the case of *ahl al-kitāb* (people of the Book),[1] there was a third choice offered — tribute. " Make war . . . upon such of those to whom the Book has been given until they pay tribute offered on the back of their hands,[2] in a state of humiliation ".[3] It is important to remember that from the conquerors' point of view tribute was more desirable. Once a non-Moslem professes Islam tribute should no more be paid.

In historical significance the Moslem conquests of the first century rank with those of Alexander. The two stand out as the principal landmarks in the political and cultural history of the ancient Near East. For a thousand years after Alexander's conquest the civilized life of Syria and its neighbouring lands was oriented westward, across the sea; now the orientation changed eastward, across the desert. The last links with Rome and Byzantium were severed; new ones with Mecca and Medina were forged. Strictly the orientation was a reversion to an old type, for the Arab Moslem civilization did not introduce many original elements. It was rather a revivification of the ancient Semitic culture.[4] Thus viewed Hellenism becomes an intrusive phenomenon between two cognate layers.

In about a decade the Moslem conquests changed the face of

[1] See below, p. 422, n. 3.

[2] *'an yadin*, differently rendered ' out of hand ", " readily ", " by right of subjection ".

[3] Sūr. 9 : 29.

[4] Consult Hitti, *History of the Arabs*, pp. 174-5.

the Near East; in about a century they changed the face of the civilized world — something more than Alexander's conquests could claim. Far from being peripheral, the victories of Islam proved to be a decisive factor in the evolution of medieval society. They changed *mare nostrum* to a Moslem lake. Contact by sea between East and West was thus broken. This, coupled with the occupation of the eastern, the western and the southern shores of the Mediterranean, created a new world, that in which Charlemagne (768–814) and his contemporaries lived. Thereby ancient times ended and the Middle Ages began.[1]

[1] This is the thesis of Henri Pirenne, *Mahomet et Charlemagne*, 7th ed. (Brussels, 1935); do., *Histoire de l'Europe* (Paris, 1936), pp. 18-24.

CHAPTER XXXI

ARAB ADMINISTRATION

HOW to administer the new domain was the next question. The Arabians awoke after the intoxication of the great victory to find themselves confronted with a new and colossal problem for which they were ill prepared. There was nothing in their past experience on which they could draw. Clearly the laws of their primitive Medinese society were not adequate and those of their new Islamic society were not applicable, as the conquered people were not yet Moslems.

'Umar's covenant

'Umar was the first man to address himself to this problem. On the "day of al-Jābiyah", as it is called, a three-week conference was held in which he and his generals took up the question. What exactly transpired there is not known. Nor does anybody precisely know the terms of the so-called covenant (*'ahd*) of 'Umar.[1] Different versions [2] have been handed down and they all clearly contain enactments that belong to later times. 'Umar could not have legislated for situations that had not yet risen.

It may be assumed, however, that certain principles in the covenant represent 'Umar's policy. First among these was that Arabian Moslems in conquered lands should constitute a sort of religio-military aristocracy, keeping their blood pure and unmixed, living aloof and abstaining from holding or cultivating any landed property. The conquered peoples were given a new status, that of *dhimmis* (or *ahl al-dhimmah*),[3] people of the covenant or obligation. As Dhimmis they were subject to a tribute which comprised both land-tax (later *kharāj*) and poll-

[1] A. S. Tritton, *The Caliphs and their Non-Muslim Subjects* (Oxford, 1930), p. 12.

[2] Consult ibn-'Asākir, vol. i, pp. 178-80, pp. 150-51; al-Ibshīhi, *al-Mustaṭra* (Cairo, 1314), vol. i, p. 99.

[3] Originally meant to apply only to the "people of the Book", i.e. Jews, Christians and Ṣābians (of Mesopotamia), the term was later widened to include Zoroastrians and others.

tax (later *jizyah*) but enjoyed the protection of Islam and were exempt from military duty. Only a Moslem could draw his sword in defence of the land of Islam. Thus was established the principle of inequality between victor and vanquished as a permanent basis of policy.

Another principle said to have been enunciated by 'Umar was that moveable property and prisoners won as booty constituted *ghanīmah* and belonged to the warriors as hitherto, but not the land. The land belonged to the Moslem community and, with all moneys received from subjects, constituted *fay'*. Those who cultivated *fay'* lands continued to pay land-tax even with the adoption of Islam.

The tax legislation traditionally ascribed to the initiative of 'Umar is clearly the result of years of practice. The first caliphs and provincial governors could not have devised and imposed a system of taxation and finance administration ; it was easier for them to continue in Allah's name the system of Byzantine provincial government already established in Syria and Egypt. In the Moslem empire tribute varied from place to place according to the nature of the soil and the previously prevailing system (Byzantine or Persian) and not according to whether the Moslem acquisition of the land was by capitulation (*ṣulḥan*) or by force (*'anwatan*). This explanation of tax variation on the basis of the type of conquest, which is the one ordinarily given in Arabic sources,[1] is clearly a late legal fiction. Even the distinction between *jizyah* as poll-tax and *kharāj* (from Gr. *chorēgia* or Aramaic) as land-tax could not have arisen at so early a date as that of 'Umar. The two terms must have been used in that early period interchangeably, both meaning tribute in general. In the Koran (9 : 29) *jizyah* occurs only once and in no legal sense ; *kharāj* likewise occurs once (23 : 74) and in a sense different from land-tax. In fact no differentiation between the terms *jizyah* and *kharāj* was made till late Umayyad days.

Poll-tax was an index of lower status and was exacted in a lump sum. It was generally four dinars [2] for the well-to-do, two

[1] Al-Māwardi, *al-Aḥkām al-Sulṭānīyah*, ed. M. Enger (Bonn, 1853), pp. 253-6 ; abu-Yūsuf, *Kitāb al-Kharāj* (Cairo, 1346), p. 46 ; Balādhuri, pp. 120-21 ; tr., pp. 186-7.

[2] Ar. *dīnār*, from Gr.-Latin *denarius* ; the unit of gold currency in the caliphate, weighing approximately 4 grams. In 'Umar's time the dinar was equivalent to 10 dirhams, later 12.

for the middle-class and one for the poor. Women, children, beggars, the aged and the diseased were exempt except when with independent income. Land-tax was paid in instalments and in kind from the cattle and the produce of the land, but never in the form of pigs, dead animals or wine, the use of which was prohibited in the Koran. In addition the subject people were liable to special exactions in support of Moslem armed forces.

Military districts

At the Jābiyah conference, Syria was divided for administrative purposes into four military districts (sing. *jund*), corresponding to Byzantine provinces found at the time of the conquest. These were Dimashq (Damascus), Ḥimṣ, al-Urdunn (Jordan) and Filasṭīn (Palestine). The Urdunn covered Galilee and extended eastward to the desert. Filasṭīn comprised the region south of the plain of Esdraelon (Marj ibn-ʿĀmir). Later the Caliph Yazīd, Muʿāwiyah's son, formed a new district, Qinnasrīn, detached from Ḥimṣ and embracing Anṭākiyah (Antioch), Manbij (Hierapolis) and al-Jazīrah (Mesopotamia).[1] The Caliph ʿAbd-al-Malik separated al-Jazīrah and made it a district by itself. The camp at al-Jābiyah was, for the time being, maintained as capital. Other military camps soon grew near Ḥimṣ, ʿAmwās,[2] Ṭabarīyah [3] (for the Urdunn district) and al-Ludd (Lydda, for Filasṭīn). Later al-Ramlah replaced al-Ludd.

To these camps the Arabian soldiers, soon to become the new citizenry of the conquered province, brought their families; many of their wives or concubines were no doubt captured native women. As warriors and defenders (*muqātilah*) they enjoyed rights and privileges which later immigrants from Arabia could not enjoy. At their head stood the commander-in-chief and governor-general who combined in his person all the executive, judiciary and military functions. The governmental framework of the Byzantine system was preserved; even the local officials who did not withdraw from the country at the time of conquest were left in their positions. The Arabians had no trained personnel to replace such officials. Besides, their paramount interest was to keep the captured province under

[1] Yāqūt, vol. i, p. 136; Balādhuri, pp. 131-2; tr., pp. 302-3; cf. Yaʿqūbi, vol. ii, p. 176; consult p. 413, map.

[2] Or ʿAmawās, ancient Emmaus; Lk. 24:13.

[3] Tiberias, modern Ṭabarayyah.

control and to collect the taxes due from its people.[1] In its primitive stage the Arabian provincial government, whether in Syria, Egypt or al-'Irāq, was purely military with a financial end in view.

The plague of 'Amwās

Before the year of the Jābiyah conference (639) was over, a terrible plague, which had its start at 'Amwās, spread and played havoc among the troops. Some 20,000 of them are said to have thus perished. The commander-in-chief himself, abu-'Ubaydah,[2] was carried off, as was his successor Yazīd.[3] 'Umar thereupon appointed Yazīd's younger brother Mu'āwiyah. This was in the year 640. For twenty years after this Mu'āwiyah dominates the scene in Syria as its governor; for twenty more he dominates the world of Islam as its caliph. When Syria under him became the seat of the caliphate, it entered upon an era of leadership and pre-eminence which lasted for almost a century.

Mu'āwiyah as governor

The policies initiated by Mu'āwiyah the governor were themselves pursued by Mu'āwiyah the caliph and resulted in giving him a permanent and prominent niche in the Arab hall of fame. He made the starting-point of his policy the cultivation of his new Syrian subjects, who were still Christians, as well as the Arab tribes, such as the Ghassānids, who were domiciled in the country since pre-Islamic days and were Christianized. Many of these tribes were of South Arabian origin as opposed to the new emigrants, who were North Arabians. For wife Mu'āwiyah chose a Jacobite Christian, Maysūn, daughter of Baḥdal of the Kalb, a South Arabian tribe. She retained her religion and became the mother of Yazīd. Both his personal physician and his court poet were also Christians.[4] For financial controller of the state Mu'āwiyah retained Manṣūr ibn-Sarjūn.[5] Arab chronicles dilate on the sense of loyalty which the Syrians cherished toward their new chief consequent upon his enlightened and tolerant policy.[6]

[1] J. Wellhausen, *Das arabische Reich und sein Sturz* (Berlin, 1902), pp. 18, 20-21; tr. Margaret G. Weir, *The Arab Kingdom and its Fall* (Calcutta, 1927), pp. 28, 32.

[2] His memory, like that of other early Moslem conquerors, lives today as that of a saint.

[3] Ya'qūbi. vol. ii, p. 172; Ṭabari, vol. i, pp. 2516-20; ibn-'Asākir, vol. i, pp. 175-7.

[4] See below, pp. 439, 494, 497.

[5] Mentioned above, p. 414.

[6] Ṭabari, vol. i, pp. 3409-10; Mas'ūdi, vol. v, pp. 80, 104; cf. '*Iqd*, vol. i, p. 207, l. 31.

Muʿāwiyah then proceeded to organize the province on a stable basis. The raw material which constituted the Arab army he now whipped into the first ordered, disciplined military force in Islam. Its archaic tribal organization, a relic of patriarchal days, was abolished. There was no interference from Medina especially since the new caliph ʿUthmān (644–56), ʿUmar's successor, was a relative of Muʿāwiyah, both being members of the aristocratic Umayyad branch of the Quraysh. Muḥammad belonged to another clan of the same tribe. The army was kept in fit condition by seasonal raids into the "land of the Romans" (*bilād al-Rūm*, Asia Minor).

First navy built

For the defence of a province bordering on the sea, Muʿāwiyah realized that a body of disciplined, loyal troops did not suffice. In Acre he found fully equipped Byzantine shipyards.[1] These he now put into such use that this arsenal became second only to that of Alexandria. The forests of Lebanon were still there ready to provide the necessary wood for construction. Later Umayyads transferred the dockyards to Tyre.[2] The new Moslem fleet was doubtless manned by Greco-Syrians, who had a long seafaring tradition.

From Acre the first naval expedition was conducted in 649 against Cyprus (Qubrus), which pointed like a dagger against the heart of Syria. So close was the island, wrote Muʿāwiyah to the Caliph ʿUthmān, that people in Syria "could hear the dogs of the Greeks bark and their roosters crow".[3] The expedition received the half-hearted assent of ʿUthmān, who stipulated that Muʿāwiyah take his wife along as evidence of the proximity of the island and the contemplated ease of its subjugation.[4] This expedition made Muʿāwiyah the first admiral [5] in Arab annals. ʿUthmān's predecessor, ʿUmar, had flatly refused to authorize this naval campaign, as he had also done in the case of Africa. His instructions to ʿAmr ibn-al-ʿĀṣ indicate the terror that a man of the desert instinctively feels toward the sea: "Let no water intervene between me and thee, and camp not in any place which

[1] Ar. *dār al-ṣināʿah*, whence "arsenal". Balādhuri, p. 117; tr., p. 180.

[2] Balādhuri, pp. 117-18; tr., p. 181; Guy Le Strange, *Palestine under the Moslems* (Boston, 1890), p. 342.

[3] Ṭabari, vol. i, pp. 2820-21.

[4] Balādhuri, pp. 152-3; tr., pp. 235-6.

[5] This word, from Ar. *amīr al-[baḥr]*, commander of the sea, was not introduced into European languages until the Arab-Spanish period, when it was confused with L. *admirabilis*, admirable.

I cannot reach riding on my mount ".[1]

The Byzantine fleet almost annihilated

The first naval expedition in the history of Islam netted Cyprus; the second (654) reached Rhodes (Rūdis). Two years later the remains of its colossus, the statue of Apollo which rose to a height of a hundred and twenty feet and was considered one of the seven wonders of the ancient world, were sold for old metal to a junk dealer who reportedly employed nine hundred camels to carry them away. In the year 655 the Syrian fleet under Busr ibn-abi-Arṭāh, in conjunction with the Egyptian fleet, encountered the Byzantine navy commanded by the Emperor Constans II (Heraclius' son) at Phoenix (modern Finike) on the Lycian coast. This marked the first great naval victory of Islam. Arabic chroniclers named the battle dhu (or dhāt)-al-Ṣawāri (that of the masts),[2] either because the place was rich in cypress trees or because of the large number of masts of the many boats engaged. By tying each Arab ship to a Byzantine one the Arabs converted the sea fight into a hand-to-hand encounter, to which they were accustomed. This battle did for the Byzantine naval forces what the Yarmūk had done for their land forces, virtually annihilated them.[3] The historian al-Ṭabari[4] asserts that the water of the sea was saturated with blood.

Muʿāwiyah, however, could not take full advantage of these exploits by his admirals and generals. Domestic disturbances leading to civil war were convulsing the Moslem world. In 658 or 659 he even found it expedient to purchase a truce from Constans II at the price of a yearly tribute mentioned by Theophanes[5] and referred to in passing by al-Balādhuri.[6] But the tribute was soon repudiated and hostilities were pressed against the eternal enemy to the north by land and by sea.

[1] Yaʿqūbi, vol. ii, p. 180; cf. ibn-al-Ṭiqṭaqa, *al-Fakhri*, ed. H. Derenbourg (Paris, 1894–5), p. 114.

[2] Ibn-ʿAbd-al-Ḥakam, *Futūḥ Miṣr wa-Akhbāruha*, ed. Charles C. Torrey (Leyden, 1920), pp. 189-90; Ṭabari, vol. i, pp. 2865, 2927.

[3] Theophanes, pp. 332, 345-6.

[4] Vol. i, p. 868.

[5] P. 347.

[6] P. 159, l. 1; tr., p. 245.

CHAPTER XXXII

THE ORTHODOX CALIPHATE

On June 16, 656, Islam witnessed the first murder of a caliph[1] by Moslem hands. This was ʿUthmān, third among the four orthodox (*rāshidūn*) caliphs, so called because all four were closely related to and associated with the Prophet, and in the conduct of state affairs largely tried to act in accordance with his behests and precedent. The awe inspired by Muḥammad's personality and behaviour was still a dominant force in their lives. All of them but ʿUthmān were early believers. Medina was their capital.

Orthodox Caliphs

1.	Abu-Bakr	632–4
2.	ʿUmar	634–44
3.	ʿUthmān	644–56
4.	ʿAli	656–61

None of these caliphs passed the caliphate on to his son; none founded a dynasty. Each was elected by a process termed *bayʿah* (sale), whereby the leaders of the people and shaykhs of tribes would literally or figuratively take the hand of the candidate as a token of homage.

A patriarchal period

The orthodox caliphs lived in patriarchal simplicity but achieved on a grand scale. Abu-Bakr, who was Muḥammad's father-in-law and three years his senior, conquered and pacified Arabia and by the sterling qualities of his character won the title al-Ṣiddīq (veracious). ʿUmar had to his credit the fixing of the year of the *hijrah* (Hegira, 622) as the commencement of the Moslem era, the supervision of the conquest of large portions of the then known world, the institution of the state register

[1] Ar. *khalīfah*, successor, successor to Muḥammad in all but his prophetic function. As the last ("seal") of the prophets Muḥammad could have no successor. The caliphal office is therefore purely secular. With no priesthood and no hierarchy Islam could have no correspondent to the pope at its head. The contrary and utterly false notion was not given wide currency until the late eighteenth century. See Hitti, *History of the Arabs*, pp. 185-6.

(*dīwān*)[1] and the organization of the government of captured provinces. Struck down by the poisoned dagger of a Christian Persian slave,[2] he left a name that has lived in tradition as the greatest in early Islam after Muḥammad's.

'Uthmān introduced a discordant element into an otherwise harmonious series. He was a member of the Umayyad aristocracy of Quraysh which held out until Mecca fell into Muḥammad's hands in 629–30, two short years before his death. As custodians of the Ka'bah, which by attracting pilgrims was an important source of income, the Umayyads had much more at stake than other converts. In 'Uthmān's reign the compilation and canonization of the Koran was accomplished. Thereby was the word of Allah given an unalterable form, which it has preserved until the present. In his reign the conquest of Persia, Ādharbayjān and a part of Armenia was completed. But 'Uthmān's record was not free from blemish. He appointed a foster brother of his, who was one of the ten proscribed by Muḥammad at the conquest of Mecca, governor over Egypt; a half-brother, who had spat in Muḥammad's face over al-Kūfah; a cousin,[3] over the important financial bureau of the state register. The caliph himself accepted presents from his governors or their partisans; one came to him in the form of a beautiful maid from al-Baṣrah. Charges of nepotism and irregularity were circulated, and feelings of dissatisfaction were fanned by three aspirants to the caliphate. All three were Qurayshites. 'Ali stood first among them.[4]

'Ali's case

'Ali had from the outset a devoted following which religiously maintained that he and no one else should have succeeded Muḥammad in 632. By virtue of his being first cousin [5] of the Prophet, second or third believer in him, husband of his only surviving daughter (Fāṭimah) and father of the two (al-Ḥasan and al-Ḥusayn) who were the only descendants of Muḥammad,

[1] This public register of state receipts and expenditures was evidently borrowed from the Persian system as the word itself (Persian *dīwān*) indicates; *Fakhri*, p. 116; Māwardi, pp. 343-4; Hitti, *History of the Arabs*, p. 172.

[2] Ṭabari, vol. i, pp. 272-3; Ya'qūbi, vol. ii, p. 183.

[3] Marwān ibn-al-Ḥakam, a future Umayyad caliph; see below, p. 446, table.

[4] The other two were Ṭalḥah ibn-'Ubaydullāh and al-Zubayr ibn-al-'Awwām, early converts and Companions of the Prophet and counted among the ten to whom he had promised Paradise (*mubashsharah*).

[5] The subjoined tree shows the genealogical relationship between 'Ali, 'Uthmān, Mu'āwiyah and Muḥammad: [*contd. on p.* 430

ʿAli — so his partisans argued — was entitled to first consideration. More than that these partisans (*shīʿah*) of ʿAli held that elevation to the highest office in Islam could not have been left to the whims and predilections of an electorate, that it was something for which Allah and Muḥammad must have made provision and that ʿAli was the one designated for that office by them. This would make ʿAli the only legitimate successor to Muḥammad and relegate his predecessors to the position of usurpers. After ʿAli, these legitimists maintained, his descendants were entitled to the successorship by the right of heredity.

The ʿAlids organized a strong party in al-Kūfah. There the uprising against ʿUthmān had its inception. Thence it spread to Egypt, which sent some five hundred rebels to Medina. This was in April 655. The aged caliph was shut in his residence and as he read the copy of the Koran [1] which he had once canonized, one of the insurgents, son of his friend, abu-Bakr, laid the first violent hand on him ʿAli was then (June 24, 656) and there proclaimed caliph.

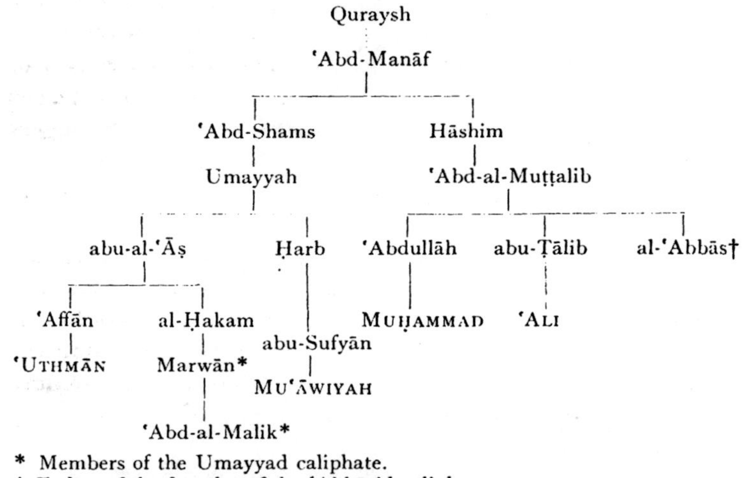

* Members of the Umayyad caliphate.
† Father of the founder of the ʿAbbāsid caliphate.

[1] Different cities claim the honour of having preserved this copy with ʿUthmān's blood staining the page on which this verse occurs: "And if they believe even as ye believe, then are they rightly guided. But if they turn away, then are they in schism, and Allah will suffice (as a protection) for thee against them. And He is the hearer, the knower" (2 : 131). A mosque in al-Baṣrah claimed the copy when ibn-Baṭṭūṭah visited it about 1326; see his *Tuḥfat al-Nuẓẓar fi Gharāʾib al-Amṣār wa-ʿAjāʾib al-Asfār*, ed. and tr. C. Defrémery and B. R. Sanguinetti, vol. ii (Paris, 1894), pp. 10-11.

'Ali's caliphate

The caliphate of 'Ali was beset with trouble from beginning to end. The first problem was how to dispose of the two remaining claimants, Ṭalḥah and al-Zubayr, who with their followers in al-Ḥijāz and al-'Irāq had refused to recognize his succession. The dissidents' position was reinforced when 'Ā'ishah, favourite wife of the Prophet, joined their ranks. 'Ā'ishah harboured a lifelong grudge against 'Ali; for when she once in her youthful days loitered behind her husband's caravan, 'Ali cast doubt upon her fidelity, necessitating intervention in her favour by Allah through a revelation.[1] The battle was joined December 9, 656, outside of al-Baṣrah and was styled "the battle of the camel", after the camel on which 'Ā'ishah rode. Both rivals of 'Ali fell.[2] 'Ā'ishah was captured and treated with the consideration befitting "the mother of the believers". Thus came to an end the first civil war in Islam. 'Ali established himself in his new capital al-Kūfah as the seemingly undisputed caliph. The second civil war, however, was not far off.

Mu'āwiyah enters the arena

Only one provincial governor denied the new caliph the usual oath of fealty. That was Mu'āwiyah. The governor of Syria and kinsman of 'Uthmān now came out as the avenger of the martyred caliph. Dramatically he exhibited in the Damascus mosque the blood-stained shirt of 'Uthmān and the fingers chopped from the hands of his wife Nā'ilah, originally like Mu'āwiyah's wife a Syro-Arab of the Kalb tribe, as she tried to defend her husband.[3] Carefully keeping his own interests under cover Mu'āwiyah publicly confronted 'Ali with this dilemma: punish the assassins or accept the position of an accomplice. Punishing the culprits was something 'Ali neither would nor could do. But the issue at bottom transcended personalities. It involved the question as to whether al-'Irāq or Syria, al-Kūfah or Damascus, should head the Islamic world. Medina clearly was out of the race. The far-flung conquests had shifted the centre of gravity to the north and relegated the former capital to a marginal position.

The second civil war

On the plain of Ṣiffīn [4] the two armies — that of al-'Irāq led

[1] Sūr. 24: 11-20. [2] Ṭabari, vol. i, pp. 3218 *seq.* [3] *Fakhri*, pp. 125, 137.

[4] South of al-Raqqah on the west bank of the Euphrates; "Sapphin" in Theophanes, p. 347. Ṭabari, vol. i, pp. 3256 *seq.*; Ya'qūbi, vol. ii, pp. 218 *seq.*; al-Dīnawari, *al-Akhbār al-Ṭiwāl*, ed. Vladimir Guirgass (Leyden, 1888), pp. 178 *seq.*

by ʿAli and that of Syria led by Muʿāwiyah — at last met. After weeks of skirmishing the battle was joined on July 26, 657. ʿAli's forces were on the point of achieving complete victory after three days of bloody fighting when lo and behold manuscripts of the Koran, fastened to lances, were lifted high in the air. The gesture, contrived by the shrewd and wily ʿAmr ibn-al-ʿĀṣ, Muʿāwiyah's lieutenant, was interpreted as meaning an appeal from the decision of arms to the decision of the Koran — whatever that might mean. Hostilities stopped. ʿAli, pious and simple-hearted, accepted Muʿāwiyah's proposal to arbitrate "according to the word of Allah" and thus spare Moslem blood.[1]

Arbitration

For the arbitration ʿAli appointed as his personal representative abu-Mūsa al-Ashʿari, a man of undoubted piety but of dubious loyalty to the ʿAlid cause. Muʿāwiyah matched him with ʿAmr ibn-al-ʿĀṣ, one of "the four Arabian political geniuses (*duhāt*) of Islam".[2] Muʿāwiyah himself was counted among the four.[3] The two arbiters (sing. *ḥakam*), each accompanied by four hundred witnesses, held a public session in January 659 at Adhruḥ, on the main caravan route between Damascus and Medina.

The classical view is that the two umpires privately agreed to depose both principals, thus clearing the way for a "dark horse"; but after abu-Mūsa, as the elder of the two, had stood up and publicly declared the caliphate of his chief null and void, ʿAmr stood up and confirmed his chief, thus double-crossing his associate.[4] Modern critical scholars, however, are inclined to believe that what really happened was that both referees deposed both principals, which meant practically that ʿAli was the one deposed, as Muʿāwiyah was not yet a caliph.[5] Of course the fact of the arbitration itself had raised Muʿāwiyah's position to the level of that of ʿAli, or lowered ʿAli's position to the level of Muʿāwiyah's; but the sentence of the judges deprived ʿAli of

[1] For the arbitration document consult Dīnawari, pp. 206-8.

[2] Masʿūdi, vol. iv, p. 391; ibn-Ḥajar, *al-Iṣābah fi Tamyīz al-Ṣaḥābah*, vol. v (Cairo, 1907), p. 3.

[3] For the other two see below, p. 436.

[4] Cf. *Fakhri*, pp. 127-30; Yaʿqūbi, vol. ii, pp. 220-22; Ṭabari, vol. i, pp. 3340-3360; Masʿūdi, vol. iv, pp. 392-402.

[5] H. Lammens, "Études sur le règne du calife Omaiyade Moʿawia 1er", *Mélanges de la faculté orientale*, vol. ii (1907), pp. 17-32; Wellhausen, pp. 57-9; tr., pp. 89-93; Caetani, vol. x, pp. 6-76.

a real office and Mu'āwiyah of a fictitious claim which he had not yet dared publicly assert. In fact not until two years after the arbitration did Mu'āwiyah proclaim himself caliph; by that time 'Ali was dead.

Early on January 24, 661, as 'Ali was on his way to the mosque at al-Kūfah, he was struck on the forehead with a poisoned dagger wielded by a Khārijite. The Khārijites (seceders) were alienated followers of 'Ali who adopted as slogan *la ḥukma illa lillāh* [1] and turned to be his deadly enemies. Their organization constituted the first sect in Islam. The murderer, though, was actuated by purely personal motives.[2] The lonely spot outside of al-Kūfah where 'Ali was interred was kept secret throughout the Umayyad and early 'Abbāsid periods until Hārūn al-Rashīd in 791 fell upon it by chance.[3] This is the present Mashhad [4] (shrine of) 'Ali in al-Najaf, one of the great centres of pilgrimage in Islam and the greatest in al-Shī'ah.

'Ali dead proved to be more influential than 'Ali living. To his Shī'ite partisans he soon became the patron saint, the *wali* (friend and vice-regent) of Allah. Deficient in the traits that make a politician, he was rich in those that, from the Arab point of view, constitute a perfect man. Eloquent in speech, sage in counsel, valiant in battle, true to his friends, magnanimous to his foes, tradition raised him to the position of paragon of Moslem chivalry (*futūwah*). Enough proverbs, orations, wise sayings, verses and anecdotes have clustered around his name to make another Solomon of him. The sabre he wielded, dhu-al-Faqār (cleaver of vertebrae), supposedly the one first used by Muḥammad on the memorable battlefield of Badr,[5] has been immortalized in an oft-quoted verse: *La sayfa illa dhu-l-Faqā — ri wa-la fatan illa 'Ali* (no sword can match dhu-al-Faqār and no youth can compare with 'Ali). The youth (*fityān*) move-

[1] *Fakhri*, p. 130; cf. Koran 12:70.

[2] Al-Mubarrad, *al-Kāmil*, ed. William Wright (London, 1864), pp. 548-51.

[3] For the earliest detailed account of the tomb consult ibn-Ḥawqal, p. 163.

[4] Ar. *mashhad* means place of a *shāhid*, one who bears witness to the oneness of God but not necessarily by dying for it as a *shahīd*, martyr. As an architectural term it replaces Syr. *shahdē*. Ar. *maqām*, literally place of standing or sojourn, technically means a commemorative monument over a spot where once a holy man stopped. It corresponds to Heb. *māqōm* (Gen. 28:11). Loosely it is used interchangeably with *mashhad*.

[5] On this battle consult Hitti, *History of the Arabs*, pp. 116-17.

ment in Islam, which developed later along lines parallel to those of the medieval orders of chivalry, took ʿAli for its model. Many dervish fraternities have likewise considered him their ideal exemplar and patron. To most of his partisans he has remained through the ages infallible ; to the extremists (*ghulāh*) among them he even became the incarnation of the deity.[1]

[1] See below, pp. 577-8, 586, 610.

CHAPTER XXXIII

MU'ĀWIYAH ESTABLISHES THE UMAYYAD CALIPHATE

EARLY in 661 [1] Mu'āwiyah was proclaimed caliph at Īliyā' (Jerusalem), but he chose Damascus for capital. Jerusalem was closer to the Bedouins and Arabians than the ancient capital of the Aramaeans and the recent seat of the provincial Byzantine government. The seaports were open to naval attack. Medina and al-Kūfah had the desert for a background.

The anti-caliph out of the way

His first problem was to get rid of the claimants to the caliphate, pacify the empire and consolidate it. In this he was fortunate in having the collaboration of a group of lieutenants the like of which Islam thereafter seldom produced. His right-hand man, 'Amr, had already (658) wrested Egypt from 'Alid rulers, which made him the double conqueror of that land, and was now holding it in Mu'āwiyah's name.[2] This he continued to do until his death in 663.[3] Al-Ḥijāz was naturally lukewarm in its loyalty to the new caliph. Mecca and Medina never forgot that the Umayyads were late believers and that their belief was one of convenience rather than conviction. But for the time being the cradle of Islam gave no serious trouble. Al-'Irāq openly and immediately declared for al-Ḥasan, eldest son of 'Ali and Fāṭimah. To its people he was the one and only legitimate successor of his assassinated father. In the course of a swift campaign (661) Mu'āwiyah secured from the claimant definite renunciation of all claims. Al-Ḥasan, as a matter of fact, was more at home in the harem than in the court. In consideration of a handsome subsidy, the amount of which he himself fixed, he abdicated in favour of Mu'āwiyah and retired to a life of ease and luxury in Medina. The subsidy was for life

[1] Shawwāl, A.H. 41 in Mas'ūdi, vol. v, p. 14; A.H. 40 in Ṭabari, vol. ii, p. 4, and Ya'qūbi, vol. ii, p. 256.

[2] Ibn-al-Athīr, vol. iii, pp. 295 *seq.*

[3] Ya'qūbi, vol. ii, pp. 262-3; Ṭabari, vol. i, pp. 3401-11.

and consisted of five million dirhams [1] from the Kūfah state treasury and the revenue of a Persian district, plus a two-million-dirham pension for his younger brother al-Ḥusayn.[2] About eight years later al-Ḥasan died in Medina, aged forty-five, after having made and unmade no less than a hundred marriages, which earned him the title *miṭlāq* (great divorcer). He was evidently consumptive, but his death was possibly caused by poisoning [3] connected with some harem intrigue; his followers blamed it on Muʻāwiyah and raised al-Ḥasan to the rank of a *shahīd* (martyr), in fact the "*sayyid* (lord) of all martyrs".

Al-ʻIrāq temporarily pacified

Over jealous, humiliated and turbulent al-Kūfah Muʻāwiyah appointed (661) al-Mughīrah ibn-Shuʻbah, a native of al-Ṭā'if in al-Ḥijāz who had been dismissed by the Caliph ʻUmar from the governorship of al-Baṣrah because of lax morality.[4] Al-Mughīrah was described as "one who if shut behind seven doors his cunning would find a way to burst all the locks". In the confusion following ʻAli's assassination, he had forged a diploma of appointment from Muʻāwiyah over the annual pilgrimage to al-Ḥijāz. As governor he pitted Khārijite against Shīʻite and Shīʻite against Khārijite, suppressed ʻAlid opposition and established Umayyad prestige in his domain. Thereby he won his place among the four political geniuses of Islam.[5]

Al-Mughīrah was succeeded by his protégé Ziyād ibn-Abīh, the fourth political genius. Ziyād had unfurled the ʻAlid flag in Persia but, recognizing in him a man of unusual ability, Muʻāwiyah by a bold and shameless stroke accorded him official acknowledgment as half brother, son of his father abu-Sufyān and a prostitute in al-Ṭā'if.[6] Because of the doubt which clouded the identity of his father, he was nicknamed ibn-Abīh (son of his father). Ziyād's appointment over al-Kūfah was extended to include, besides al-ʻIrāq, Persia and the dependent

[1] From Per. *diram*, from Gr. *drachme*, the unit of silver coinage in the Arab monetary system. It was generally $\frac{1}{10}$ or $\frac{1}{12}$ of a dinar (see above, p. 425, n. 1), but its real value varied greatly.

[2] Ṭabari, vol. i, p. 3; Dīnawari, p. 231; ibn-Ḥajar, vol. ii, pp. 12-13.

[3] Yaʻqūbi, vol. ii, p. 266.

[4] Balādhuri, pp. 256, 344-5; tr., p. 410; ibn-al-Athīr, *Usd al-Ghābah*, vol. iv (Cairo, 1286), p. 407.

[5] See above, p. 432.

[6] This legitimization (*istilḥāq*) is reported in Masʻūdi, vol. v, pp. 20-22; Ṭabari, vol. ii, pp. 69-70; ibn-ʻAsākir, vol. v, pp. 409-10.

parts of Arabia. This made him viceroy over the eastern half of the empire. With an open eye on all happenings in this vast domain, sharp ear close to the ground and firm hand on the sword, the illegitimate son of abu-Sufyān held the turbulent realm within the Sufyānid orbit. The problem of troublesome Arabians and Bedouins from al-Baṣrah and al-Kūfah he solved by transplanting 50,000 of them to eastern Persia.[1]

Second wave of conquests

With the territory of Islam temporarily pacified Mu'āwiyah's extraordinary energies sought new outlets in the form of campaigns into foreign territory by land and sea. The naval campaigns were entirely against the Byzantines.[2] Mu'āwiyah's conquests constitute the second wave of Moslem expansion after an interruption by the two civil wars,[3] the first wave having been initiated by abu-Bakr and having culminated under 'Umar.

On land the expansion under Mu'āwiyah took two courses, one eastward and the other westward. Al-Baṣrah of Ziyād served as headquarters of the eastern campaigns, which resulted in completing the subjugation of Khurāsān (663–71), crossing the Oxus [4] and raiding Bukhāra in far-away Turkestan (674).[5] Marw (Merv), Balkh, Harāt (Herat) and other cities which developed into brilliant centres of Islamic culture were captured. The army returned to al-Baṣrah laden with booty from the wandering Turkish tribes of Transoxiana. The first contact between Arabs and Turks, destined to play a major rôle in later Islam, was established.

The hero of westward expansion was 'Uqbah ibn-Nāfi', whose mother was a sister of 'Amr's mother, conqueror and governor of Egypt.[6] In 663 'Uqbah was appointed by his cousin over Ifrīqīyah (now Ifrīqiyah).[7] There he established (670) al-Qayrawān [8] as a military base against the Berbers. The new camp was built partly with material taken from the ruins of

[1] Balādhuri, p. 410; Ṭabari, vol. ii, pp. 81, 155-6. For earlier cases of transplantation in the Near East consult above, pp. 196-7, 202.

[2] To be treated in the next chapter.

[3] See above, pp. 430, 431.

[4] See below, pp. 458 *seq.*

[5] Ya'qūbi, vol. ii, p. 258; Balādhuri, pp. 409-10; Ṭabari, vol. ii, pp. 166 *seq.*

[6] Ibn-Khaldūn, *Kitāb al-'Ibar*, vol. iii, pp. 10-11.

[7] Africa Minor, Tunis, modern Tunisia; corruption of Latin Africa. The name was borrowed by the Arabs from the Romans and given to the eastern part of Barbary, the word Maghrib being reserved for the western part.

[8] From Per. *kārwān*, whence English caravan. For 'Uqbah's campaigns consult ibn-'Abd-al-Ḥakam, pp. 171, 194-9.

near-by Carthage, of which it became a Moslem successor. As the Berbers were Islamized, they were pressed into the Arab army and served as relays for its further conquests in North Africa and later in Spain. With their aid ʿUqbah chased the Byzantines out of a large part of North Africa. The place where he fell in battle (683) is still known after him as Sīdi (Sayyidi, my lord) ʿUqbah, a few miles south-east of Biskra in Algeria,[1] where his tomb stands as a national shrine. Brilliant as it was, ʿUqbah's military advance in Algeria, like that of his contemporary in Central Asia, was of no lasting significance, because it was not followed up by occupation. Here as in Transoxiana the work had to be done over again.[2]

Other achievements

These campaigns, colossal as they were, did not make the commander-in-chief neglect domestic affairs. The financial administration of the state was left in the hands of the capable and experienced Sarjūnids, of whom St. John was a descendant.[3] Such was the revenue that Muʿāwiyah could double the pay of the soldiers, strengthen the Syrian frontier fortresses against the northern enemy, undertake projects of agriculture and irrigation in al-Ḥijāz — the province least favoured by nature — and appease through subsidy ʿAlids and Hāshimites. The Hāshimites included the ʿAbbāsids, who were closer of kin to the Prophet than the Umayyads. This technique of "reconciling the hearts" (*ta'līf al-qulūb*)[4] was introduced by the Prophet himself. In Syria Muʿāwiyah instituted a bureau of registry and laid the basis of a postal service (*barīd*).[5]

Throughout his undertakings, peaceful or military, he was sustained by the unflinching loyalty of his Syrian subjects, natives and Arabian immigrants. The Syro-Arabs were mostly of Yamanite, not Ḥijāzite, origin and, as we learned before, had been Christianized. His wife Maysūn was one of them, but he is said to have divorced her because of poems attributed to her in which she expressed her yearning for the desert and her preference for a different type of a husband:

A tent with rustling breezes cool
  Delights me more than palace high,
And more the cloak of simple wool
  Than robes in which I learned to sigh.

[1] Ibn-al-Athīr *Kāmil*, vol. iv, p. 91.
[2] See below, pp. 458 *seq.*
[3] See above, p. 425.
[4] Consult Koran 9:60.
[5] *Fakhri*, p. 148. Cf. below, p. 474.

The crust I ate beside my tent
Was more than this fine bread to me;
The wind's voice where the hill-path went
Was more than tambourine can be.[1]

His Christian physician ibn-Uthāl he appointed financial administrator over the district of Ḥimṣ — an unprecedented appointment for a Christian in Moslem annals.[2] His poet laureate, al-Akhṭal,[3] belonged to the Christian tribe of Taghlib. Maronites and Jacobites brought their religious disputes before Muʿāwiyah.[4] In Edessa he reportedly rebuilt a Christian church that had been demolished by an earthquake.[5] By such acts of tolerance and magnanimity Muʿāwiyah fastened his hold upon the hearts of the Syrians and firmly established the hegemony of their country in the Moslem empire.

But perhaps his most prominent quality was what his Arab biographers term *ḥilm*,[6] that *finesse politique* which made him unerring in doing the right thing at the right time. This supreme statesmanship he himself defined in these words: "I apply not my sword, where my lash suffices; nor my lash, where my tongue is enough. And even if there be one hair binding me to my fellowmen, I do not let it break. When they pull, I loosen; and if they loosen, I pull."[7] The letter he sent to al-Ḥasan inducing him to abdicate further illustrates this trait: "I admit that because of thy blood relationship thou art more entitled to this high office than myself. And if I were sure of thy greater ability to fulfil the duties involved, I would unhesitatingly swear allegiance to thee. Now then, ask what thou wilt." Enclosed was a blank already signed by Muʿāwiyah.[8] This *ḥilm* made his personal relations with his contemporaries frank and friendly. His opponents would call him the bastard's brother and express their devotion to ʿAli even in his presence, and his friends would tease him about his name, which meant "a barking bitch", and

[1] Nicholson, *A Literary History of the Arabs*, p. 195; abu-al-Fidā', vol. i, p. 203.
[2] Yaʿqūbi, vol. ii, p. 265; Wellhausen, p. 85, considers the report fictitious.
[3] See below, p. 494.
[4] Wellhausen, p. 84. This is the first mention of Maronites in Arab history.
[5] Theophanes, p. 356.
[6] *Fakhri*, p. 145; *ʿIqd*, vol. ii, p. 304; Masʿūdi, vol. v, p. 40; Lammens in *Mélanges*, vol. i, pp. 66-108.
[7] Yaʿqūbi, vol. ii, p. 283; *ʿIqd*, vol. i, p. 10.
[8] Ṭabari, vol. ii, p. 5.

about his huge buttocks. His family name was a diminutive of *amah*, bondwoman.

A crown prince nominated

In 679,[1] six months before his death (April 680) at the age of eighty, Mu'āwiyah nominated his son Yazīd as his successor, an unprecedented procedure in Islam. Yazīd had been brought up by his mother partly in the *bādiyah* (desert), more particularly Palmyrena, where her Christian tribe roamed.[2] In the capital he also associated with Christians and counted among his boon companions St. John, when still a layman, and the poet al-Akhṭal. In the desert the youthful prince became habituated to the chase, rough riding and hard life; in the city, to wine-bibbing and verse-making. Al-Bādiyah from this time on became the open-air school to which the young royal princes of the dynasty resorted for vacationing, acquiring the pure Arabic [3] — unadulterated with Aramaicisms — and incidentally escaping the recurring city plagues. That the caliph had had in mind for some time the nomination of his son may be inferred from his sending him as early as 668 against Constantinople,[4] where Yazīd's success served to dispel any doubts that the puritans might have entertained regarding his qualifications. And now Mu'āwiyah, after being sure of the capital, summoned deputations from the provinces and took from them the oath of allegiance (*bay'ah*) to his favourite son. Unsympathetic 'Irāqis were cajoled, coerced or bribed.[5]

This master stroke was a landmark in Islamic history. It introduced the hereditary principle,[6] which was followed thereafter by the leading Moslem dynasties. It established a precedent enabling the reigning caliph to proclaim as his successor him among his sons or kinsmen whom he considered competent and to exact for him an anticipatory oath of allegiance. The designation of a crown prince tended to promote stability and continuity and discourage ambitious aspirants to the throne.

Mu'āwiyah the model king

Despite his unparalleled contributions to the cause of the Arabs and Islam, Mu'āwiyah was no favourite with the Arab Moslem historians. Nor were his "tyrannical" lieutenants.

[1] Mas'ūdi, vol. v, pp. 69-73; cf. Ṭabari, vol. ii, pp. 174-7, and ibn-al-Athīr, vol. iii, pp. 416-17, where the date is made three years earlier.
[2] Lammens in *Mélanges*, vol. iii, pp. 189-226.
[3] *'Iqd*, vol. i, p. 293, l. 30. [4] See below, p. 444.
[5] *'Iqd*, vol. ii, pp. 306-9; ibn-'Asākir, vol. iv, pp. 327-8.
[6] For succession in the orthodox caliphate see above, p. 428.

The explanation is not difficult to find. Most of those writers were Shī'ites or members of the 'Irāqi-Persian and Medinese schools.[1] As historians they reflect the puritanical attitude which resented the fact that he was the man who secularized Islam and transformed the *khilāfat al-nubū'ah* (the prophetic, i.e. theocratic, caliphate) into a *mulk* [2] (a temporal sovereignty). Mu'āwiyah, they emphasized, was the first *malik* (king) in Islam, a title so abhorrent to Arabians that they applied it almost exclusively to non-Arab potentates. He is blamed for several profane innovations, including the *maqṣūrah*,[3] a sort of bower inside the mosque reserved for the exclusive use of the caliph, the delivering of the Friday noon sermon (*khuṭbah*) while seated,[4] and the use of a royal throne (*sarīr al-mulk*).[5] The fact remains that such was the example of energy, tolerance and astuteness he set before his successors that while many of them tried to emulate it [6] few came near succeeding.

[1] Of the Syrian school only one major representative, ibn-'Asākir of Damascus (1105-76), has survived.

[2] Ibn-Khaldūn, *Muqaddamah* (Cairo), pp. 169 *seq.*; Ya'qūbi, vol. ii, p. 257.

[3] Ya'qūbi, vol. ii, p. 265; Dīnawari, p. 229; Ṭabari, vol. ii, p. 70, l. 20; Mubarrad, p. 552. The bower was built as a protection after an unsuccessful attempt on the life of the caliph while praying.

[4] Ibn-al-'Ibri, *Mukhtaṣar al-Duwal*, ed. Anṭūn al-Ṣāliḥāni (Beirut, 1890), p. 188. Mu'āwiyah's excuse was that he had become in his late years excessively corpulent and pot-bellied.

[5] Ibn-Khaldūn, *Muqaddamah*, p. 217; al-Qalqashandi, *Ṣubḥ al-A'sha*, vol. iv (Cairo, 1914), p. 6.

[6] Mas'ūdi, vol. v, p. 78. Mu'āwiyah's tomb in the cemetery of [al-] Bāb al-Ṣaghīr at Damascus is still visited.

CHAPTER XXXIV

HOSTILE RELATIONS WITH THE BYZANTINES

Syrian marches

IN the Umayyad period, as in the 'Abbāsid down to about the middle of the twelfth century, the frontier between Arab and Byzantine lands was formed by the great ranges of the Taurus and Anti-Taurus. As the two hostile states stood face to face across this line, they first sought to keep each other off by turning the intervening stretch of land into a desolate terrain. Mu'āwiyah contributed to the creation of this unclaimed waste zone.[1] Later Umayyads pursued a different policy aiming at establishing a footing there by rebuilding as fortresses abandoned or destroyed towns and building new ones. Thus grew a cordon of Moslem fortifications stretching from Tarsus in Cilicia to Malaṭyah (Malaṭīyah, Melitene) by the upper Euphrates and including Adhanah, al-Maṣṣīṣah (Mopsuesta) and Mar'ash (Germanicia). These units were strategically situated at the intersections of military roads or the entrances of narrow passes. The term *'awāṣim* (defences) was rightly applied to them. The same term was used in a narrow sense for only the inner, the southern, line of fortresses in contradistinction to the outer, the northern, called *thughūr*.[2] The *thughūr* zone stretched across the Syrian and Mesopotamian marches. The part guarding Syria was styled *al-thughūr al-Sha'mīyah*; that guarding Mesopotamia *al-thughūr al-Jazīrīyah*.[3]

Under the 'Abbāsids the *thughūr* zone shrank to the limits of the area extending from Awlās on the Mediterranean, past Tarsus to Sumaysāṭ (Samosata) on the Euphrates.[4] As the city commanding the southern entrance of the celebrated pass across the Taurus known as the Cilician Gates, Tarsus served as a base

[1] Balādhuri, pp. 164-5; called *ḍawāḥi*, outer land, in Ṭabari, vol. ii, p. 1317, and ibn-al-Athīr, vol. iv, p. 250.

[2] Pl. of *thaghr*, fissure, opening. Cf. Guy Le Strange, *The Lands of the Eastern Caliphate* (Cambridge, 1930), p. 128.

[3] Balādhuri, pp. 183 *seq.*, 163 *seq.*

[4] Iṣṭakhri, pp. 67-8.

for the major military campaigns against the territory of the Romans. In it a good-sized army of horse and foot was stationed. A less-frequented path across the Taurus led from Marʿash to Abulustayn [1] and was called Darb al-Ḥadath. All these strongholds changed hands again and again as the tide of war ebbed or flowed. Under the Umayyads and ʿAbbāsids almost every foot was contested repeatedly and fiercely. It was a real " no man's land ". Its soil was soaked with more blood than perhaps any other piece of land in Asia.

In Muʿāwiyah's time as well as that of ʿAbd-al-Malik and other successors a greater campaign in summer (*ṣā'ifah*) and a smaller one in winter (*shātiyah*) [2] were undertaken year by year as a matter of routine. The campaigns served as a training school. The objective, as in the case of the traditional Bedouin raids, was booty, though the dim spectacle of Byzantium may have beckoned from beyond in the distant background. Constantinople lay four hundred and fifty miles from Tarsus in a direct line. At no time did the Arabs establish a firm foothold in Asia Minor. Their main military energy followed the line of least resistance and was directed eastward and westward. The lofty ranges of the Taurus and Anti-Taurus seem to have been eternally fixed by nature as the boundary line. Then there was the climate of Anatolia, too rigorous for the sons of the desert. The Arabic language froze on the southern slopes of those ranges. No part of Asia Minor ever became Arabic speaking. Since earliest times, those of the Hittites, its basic population has been non-Semitic.

Constantinople reached

The recurring raids into Asia Minor did at last reach the capital. That was in 668,[3] only thirty-six years after Muḥammad's death. It was then for the first time that eyes of Arab warriors opened to see the mighty and proud city on the Bosphorus. The leader was Faḍālah ibn-ʿUbayd al-Anṣāri.[4] The army wintered in Chalcedon (the Asiatic suburb of Constantinople), where it suffered severely from want of provisions and

[1] Yāqūt, vol. i, pp. 93-4; cf. Le Strange, p. 133. The Byzantine name was Ablastha, the Greek Arabissus, late Arabic al-Bustān (cf. below, p. 552, n. 6).

[2] Balādhuri, p. 163, l. 1.

[3] Ibn-al-Athīr, vol. iii, p. 381; Ṭabari, vol. ii, pp. 86, 111, cf. p. 27, where a report about an earlier naval attack on Constantinople by Busr ibn-abi-Arṭāh is questioned.

[4] Of the *anṣār*, helpers; technically the believers of Medina who received and assisted the Prophet after his migration from Mecca in 622.

from smallpox and other diseases.[1] Muʿāwiyah sent, in the spring of 669, his pleasure-loving son Yazīd, much against his will, with reinforcements.[2] Yazīd and Faḍālah laid siege to Constantinople with its high triple wall. The fleet no doubt supported this enterprise. But the siege was raised that summer; Byzantium had found a new and energetic emperor, Constantine IV (668–85).

In the legendary account of this siege Yazīd distinguished himself for bravery and fortitude. He thereby earned the title *fata al-ʿArab* (the champion of the Arabs). As the pendulum of victory swung from one side to the other, alternate shouts of jubilation were heard from two Byzantine tents — so the *Aghāni*[3] reports. One was occupied by the daughter of the king of the Rūm (Romans); the other by the daughter of the ex-king of Ghassān, Jabalah ibn-al-Ayham.[4] The prospect of seizing the Arab princess spurred Yazīd to extraordinary activity. But Yazīd's legendary fame was eclipsed by that of the aged abu-Ayyūb al-Anṣāri, once the standard-bearer of the Prophet and his first host in Medina at the time of the hijrah.[5] In the course of the siege abu-Ayyūb died of dysentery. His tomb outside the city walls soon became for the Christian Greeks a shrine where prayer was considered especially efficacious for bringing rain in time of drought.[6] In later times when Constantinople was besieged by other Moslems, Ottoman Turks, the tomb was miraculously discovered by rays of light — reminiscent of the discovery of the "holy lance" at Antioch by the first Crusaders.[7] A mosque was built on the site; and the Medinese gentleman became a saint for three nations.

Second siege of Constantinople

Twice did Muʿāwiyah stretch his mighty arm across the territory of the Romans into the capital itself The second time was five years after the first. This was the so-called seven years' war (674–80), waged mainly between the two fleets in the Bosphorus and the Sea of Marmora. What made such a long operation possible was the early occupation of the peninsula

[1] *Aghāni*, vol. xvi, p. 33; al-Nuwayri, *Nihāyat al-Arab fi Funūn al-Adab* (Cairo, 1925), vol. iv, p. 91.

[2] Lammens in *Mélanges*, vol. iii, pp. 306-12; J. Wellhausen, "Die Kämpfe der Araber mit den Romäern in der Zeit der Umaijiden", *Nachrichten von der Königlichen Gesellschaft der Wissenschaften zu Göttingen, philologisch-historische Classe* (Göttingen, 1902), pp. 423 *seq*.

[3] Vol. xvi, p. 33.

[4] See above, p. 404.

[5] Balādhuri, p. 5.

[6] Ibn-al-Athīr, vol. iii, p. 382.

[7] See below, pp. 592-3.

projecting from Asia Minor into Marmora and styled Cyzicus by the Greeks and " the isle of Arwād " by the Arabs.[1] Cyzicus served as winter headquarters for the invading army and a base for spring and summer attacks. Arab and Byzantine accounts of these campaigns do not tally and are in themselves badly confused. The city was saved supposedly by the use of Greek fire, a newly invented highly combustible compound which would burn even on or under water. The inventor was a Syrian refugee from Damascus named Callinicus. This was perhaps the first time this " secret weapon " was used. The Byzantines kept its formula unrevealed for several centuries after which the Arabs acquired it; but it has since been lost. Greek accounts dilate on the disastrous effects of this fire on enemy ships. What was left of the Arab fleet was wrecked on the return journey,[2] necessitated by the death of Muʻāwiyah.

To this period also belong several naval attacks on islands in the Aegean and eastern Mediterranean waters. Cyprus was already secure in the Moslem fold. Rhodes, which had been pillaged by Muʻāwiyah's fleet as early as 654,[3] was temporarily occupied in 672.[4] Two years later Crete (Iqrīṭish) was treated to the same operation. Sicily (Ṣiqillīyah), destined to become later a flourishing appanage of the Arab Aghlabid dynasty which conquered it from Africa, was also reached about 664 and repeatedly attacked thereafter.[5] Under a successor of Muʻāwiyah, Sulaymān, Rhodes was again temporarily occupied (717–18).

Last Umayyad attack on Constantinople

For thirty-five years after Muʻāwiyah's death lull characterized the hostile relations between Arabs and Byzantines. His son's short reign (680–83) was occupied by domestic disturbances,[6] and his grandson Muʻāwiyah II's reign lasted only three months. This Muʻāwiyah was a weak and sickly youth, and Yazīd was no worthy successor of his father — what genius' son is? It was not until Sulaymān (715–17), a member of the Marwānid branch of the Umayyad family,[7] that expeditions

[1] Theophanes, pp. 353-4; Ṭabari, vol. ii, p. 163; ibn-al-Athīr, vol. iii, p. 413; Balādhuri, p. 236.

[2] Theophanes, pp. 353 *seq.*

[3] See above, p. 427.

[4] Balādhuri, p. 236; cf. Ṭabari, vol. ii, p. 157.

[5] Balādhuri, p. 235.

[6] See below, pp. 450-52.

[7] The subjoined tree shows the relation between the Sufyānid and the Marwānid branches of the family: [*contd. on p.* 446

were resumed. A current *ḥadīth* (saying attributed to the Prophet) claimed that the caliph to conquer Constantinople would bear the name of a prophet. Sulaymān (Arabic for Solomon, whom the Moslems considered a prophet) took the *ḥadīth* to refer to himself. No sooner, therefore, had he been installed than he began to expedite the equipment and departure of the expedition which his great brother al-Walīd had started. Another brother, Maslamah, late in 715 led the expedition through Asia Minor. The land forces were supported by sea forces. Neither met initial success. While the fleet was in Cilicia on its way, Byzantine sailors landed on the Syrian coast and burned al-Lādhiqīyah. In Phrygia Amorium (Amorion, ʿAmmūrīyah, modern Assar Qalʿah) was passed by after an unsuccessful siege. Farther west, however, Pergamum and Sardis were taken. Finally the Dardanelles were crossed at Abydos and on August 25, 716, Constantinople was blockaded on the land side and two weeks later on the sea side. The Arab armada anchored by the walls of the city along the coast of Marmora and the Bosphorus. Entrance to the Golden Horn was barred by a chain, the first historical reference to such a barrier.

Of all the Arab attacks on the capital this was unquestionably the most threatening and the best recorded. The besiegers received aid from the Egyptian fleet. They used naphtha and siege artillery.[1] But the city was fortunate in having for defender Emperor Leo[2] the Isaurian (717–40), a soldier of humble Syrian origin from Marʿash, who was probably born a subject of the caliph and knew Arabic as perfectly as Greek.[3]

- Umayyah
  - abu-al-ʿĀṣ
    - al-Ḥakam
      - 4. Marwān (683–5)
        - 5. Abd-al-Malik (685–705)
          - 6. Al-Walīd I (705–15)
          - 7. Sulaymān (715–17)
  - Ḥarb
    - abu-Sufyān
      - 1. Muʿāwiyah I (661–80)
        - 2. Yazīd I (680–83)
          - 3. Muʿāwiyah II (683)

[1] *Al-ʿUyūn w-al-Ḥadāʾiq*, ed. de Goeje (Leyden, 1871), pt. 3, p. 24.
[2] Ilyūn of Arabic sources; Ṭabari, vol. ii, p. 1315.
[3] *ʿUyūn*, pt. 3, p. 25.

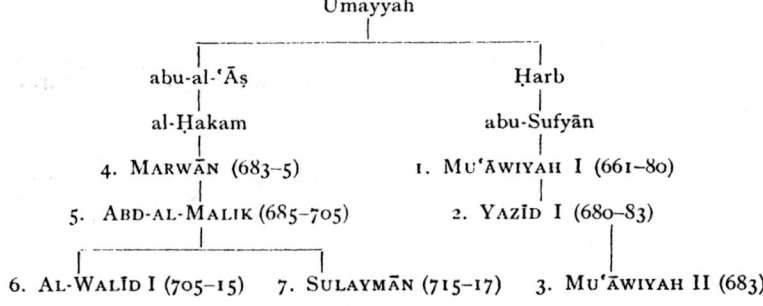

While the besieged were hard pressed, the besiegers were equally harassed. Pestilence, Greek fire, scarcity of provisions and attacks from Bulgars wrought havoc among them.[1] The rigours of an unusually severe winter added its share. But Maslamah stubbornly persisted. Neither such hardships nor the death of the caliph[2] seemed to deter him. But the order of the new caliph, 'Umar ibn-'Abd-al-'Azīz (717-20), he had to heed. The army withdrew in a pitiful state. The fleet, or what was left of it, was wrecked by a tempest on its way back; out of the 1800 vessels, if Theophanes' figures[3] are credible, only five survived to reach port in Syria. The Arab armada was gone. The Syrian founder of the Isaurian dynasty was hailed the saviour of Christian Europe from Moslem Arabs.

Only on one other occasion after this did an Arab host reach Constantinople; but that was not under the Umayyads. The leader was the 'Abbāsid Hārūn al-Rashīd, when still a crown prince, and the date was 782.[4] Hārūn encamped at Scutari (Chrysopolis) and exacted tribute from the Empress Irene.[5] The "city of Constantine" was no more to witness a Moslem invader at its gate until about seven centuries thence, when a new ethnic element, the Central Asian Turks, had adopted the religion of the Arabs and became its world champions.

Though a failure in itself the determined and energetic campaign by Maslamah fired the imagination of Moslem reporters and left many a legendary souvenir. Maslamah may have built a mosque at Abydos,[6] where he encamped, and dug a fountain that became known by his name; but that he was the first to erect a mosque in Constantinople,[7] stipulate the erection

[1] Consult Theophanes, pp. 386–99; ibn-al-Athīr, vol. v, pp. 17-19.

[2] Sulaymān died at Dābiq, the base of military operations against Asia Minor, which he had taken an oath not to leave until Constantinople was captured; Ṭabari, vol. ii, pp. 1315-16, 1336.

[3] Pp. 395, 399.

[4] Balādhuri, p. 168.

[5] Ṭabari, vol. iii, pp. 503-5; ibn-al-Athīr, vol. vi, 44-5. See below, p. 540.

[6] Ar. Abdus, corrupted into Andus in Yāqūt, vol. i, p. 374, and in ibn-al-Faqīh, *al-Buldān*, ed. M. J. de Goeje (Leyden, 1885), p. 104, l. 1, and into Andalus in Mas'ūdi, vol. ii, p. 317; cf. ibn-Khurdādhbih, *al-Masālik w-al-Mamālik*, ed. de Goeje (Leyden, 1889), p. 104.

[7] Ibn-al-Athīr, vol. x, p. 18; al-Dimashqi, *Nukhbat al-Dahr fi 'Ajā'ib al-Barr w-al-Baḥr*, ed. A. F. Mehren (Saint Petersburg, 1865), p. 227. Ibn-Taghri-Birdi, *al-Nujūm al-Zāhirah fi Mulūk Miṣr w-al-Qāhirah*, ed. W. Popper, vol. ii, pt. 2 (Berkeley, 1909–12), p. 40, ll. 12-13, claims that a Faṭimid *khuṭbah* (Friday noon sermon) was pronounced in this mosque. Consult ibn-al-Qalānisi, *Dhayl Ta'rīkh Dimashq*, ed. H. F. Amedroz (Beirut, 1908), p. 68, ll. 27-8.

of a special house for Arab prisoners near the imperial court and enter on horseback into Santa Sophia is pure fiction. The Syrian geographer al-Maqdisi [1] enthusiastically writes in 985: "When Maslamah ibn-ʿAbd-al-Malik invaded the land of the Romans and penetrated into their territory, he stipulated that the Byzantine dog should erect by his own palace in the Hippodrome (*maydān*) a special building [2] to be occupied by [Moslem] notables and noblemen when taken captives". The chief of Maslamah's guard, ʿAbdullāh al-Baṭṭāl, stood next to Maslamah in legendary distinction. He won the title of champion of Islam. Killed in a later campaign (740),[3] he became a Turkish national hero under the title Sayyid Ghāzi (lord conqueror). At his grave in Eski-Shehr (medieval Dorylaeum) a Baktāshi *takīyah* (monastery) has risen. Local Greek Christians likewise canonized him. His was another instance of "an illustrious Moslem for whom Christians have raised a statue in one of their churches".[4]

Mardaites in Lebanon

An earlier and less spectacular campaign of Maslamah was directed against an obscure semi-independent people who occupied the rugged regions of North Syria. From their fastnesses in the Amanus (al-Lukkām) and the Taurus, these Mardaites (Maradah [5]), as they were called, had furnished recruits and irregular troops to the Byzantines and proved a thorn in the side of the Arabs. They were also called Jurājimah (Jarājimah) after their chief city al-Jurjūmah in the Amanus.[6] Entrenched on the Arab-Byzantine border they formed a "brass wall" [7] in defence of Asia Minor. Christians they were, but whether Monothelites or Monophysites is undetermined. As rebels, adventurers and warriors they offered their services to the highest bidder. When the Arab Moslems seized Antioch, the Jurājimah agreed to serve as scouts and guardians of the passes in their neighbourhood.[8] About 666 the Byzantine emperor dispatched bands of them, with his cavalry and regular

[1] *Aḥsan al-Taqāsīm*, p. 147.

[2] Known as al-Balāṭ, mentioned in Yāqūt, vol. i, p. 709, as being in use at the time of Sayf-al-Dawlah al-Ḥamdāni (944–67, see below, p. 564). *Balāṭ* is a loan word through Syriac from Latin or Greek *platea*, *palatium*.

[3] Ṭabari, vol. ii, p. 1716.

[4] Masʿūdi, vol. viii, p. 74.

[5] From an ancient Semitic stem *mrd*, to rebel, to resist. Cf. Dīnawari, p. 130 l. 3, where *mard* is erroneously made Persian for "man".

[6] Yāqūt, vol. ii, p. 55; Balādhuri, p. 159.

[7] Theophanes, p. 364.

[8] Balādhuri, p. 159.

troops, which penetrated into the heart of Lebanon and occupied its chief strategic points as far as Palestine. Mount Lebanon then must have been very sparsely populated [1] and thickly wooded; only the part bordering on the maritime plain was fairly settled. Around these Mardaites as nucleus, fugitives and malcontents gathered. In northern Lebanon they were fused with the Maronites.[2] At that time Muʿāwiyah had his hands full with ʿAlid and other domestic problems and agreed to the payment of a heavy annual tribute to the emperor in consideration of his withdrawal of support from this internal enemy, to whom the caliph also agreed to pay a tax. Mountainous warfare, be it remembered, was never palatable to the Arabs. Ibn-Khaldūn's [3] observation that Arab facile domination is limited to plain lands is not without historic justification.

Evidently to counteract these Jurājimah Muʿāwiyah in 669 transported fresh people from al-ʿIrāq to the maritime coast and Antioch.[4] Earlier (662 or 663) he had transplanted many from Persia to replace the Greeks who left after the Moslem conquest and as a measure of protection against Byzantine naval raids. The Persians were settled in Sidon, Beirut, Jubayl, Tripoli, ʿArqah, Baʿlabakk and other towns.[5]

The Jurājimah caused as much trouble to the early Marwānids as they had done to the Sufyānids. Around 689 ʿAbd-al-Malik accepted the terms of Justinian II and agreed to pay a thousand dinars weekly to the Jurājimah. The emperor had loosed fresh bands of these highlanders on Syria. Thereby ʿAbd-al-Malik followed "the precedent established by Muʿāwiyah" [6]

At last in the days of ʿAbd-al-Malik's son al-Walīd (705–15) it was resolved to put an end to this Mardaite peril. Maslamah attacked the troublesome people in their own headquarters and demolished their capital al-Jurjūmah. Some perished, others migrated to Anatolia, and of those who remained some joined the Syrian army and fought under the banner of Islam. In the days of Yazīd II they co-operated in suppressing rebellions in al-ʿIrāq.[7]

[1] Cf. above, p. 82. [2] See below, pp. 521-2. [3] *Muqaddamah*, p. 125.
[4] Balādhuri, p. 162. [5] Yaʿqūbi, p. 327; Balādhuri, p. 148.
[6] Balādhuri, p. 160, l. 8; do. *Ansāb al-Ashrāf*, ed. S. D. F. Goitein, vol. v (Jerusalem, 1936), p. 300.
[7] For more on the Mardaites consult Lammens in *Mélanges*, vol. i, pp. 14-22; do. *Tasrīḥ al-Abṣār fi Ma Yaḥtawi Lubnān min al-Āthār*, vol. ii (Beirut, 1914), pp. 41-8.

CHAPTER XXXV

DOMESTIC DISTURBANCES: SHI'ITES, MEDINESE, PERSIANS

The tragedy of al-Husayn

As long as the rule of powerful Mu'āwiyah lasted, no 'Alids dared dispute his authority in an overt act; but the accession of frivolous Yazīd (680) was an invitation to secession. In response to urgent and reiterated appeals from 'Irāqis, al-Ḥusayn, younger son of 'Ali and Fāṭimah, now declared himself the legitimate caliph after his elder brother and father.[1] At the head of a weak escort of devoted followers and relatives, including his harem, al-Ḥusayn, who had hitherto resisted the solicitations of his 'Irāqi partisans and lived in retirement in Medina, set out from Mecca for al-Kūfah. 'Ubaydullāh, son of Ziyād whom Mu'āwiyah had found convenient to acknowledge as brother,[2] was now his father's successor in the governorship of al-'Irāq. Having received advance news of al-Ḥusayn's move, 'Ubaydullāh planted outposts on all roads leading from al-Ḥijāz to al-'Irāq. In Karbalā', twenty-five miles north-west of al-Kūfah, 'Ubaydullāh's cavalry patrol closed in on the pretender and when he refused to surrender, 'Umar, son of Sa'd ibn-abi-Waqqāṣ, famous conqueror of al-'Irāq and founder of al-Kūfah, attacked with his 4000 men. Al-Ḥusayn was slaughtered, his band of 200 was cut down.[3] The head of the Prophet's grandson was sent to Yazīd in Damascus. The caliph turned it over to al-Ḥusayn's sister and son, who had accompanied it to the capital, and it was buried in Karbalā'.[4]

The day on which al-Ḥusayn fell, Muḥarram 10, A.H. 61 (October 10, 680), has since become a national day for mourning in Shī'ah Islam. Annually a passion play is enacted on this "tenth day" (*'āshūrā'*) portraying the "heroic" struggle and tragic suffering of the martyred leader (*imām*). The more

[1] *Fakhri*, p. 59; Dīnawari, pp. 243-4.
[2] See above, p. 436.
[3] Cf. Ya'qūbi, vol. ii, p. 289; Mas'ūdi, vol. v, p. 143.
[4] Ibn-Ḥajar, vol. ii, p. 17; ibn-'Asākir, vol. iv, pp. 332-5; ibn-al-Athīr, vol. iv pp. 67-75; Dīnawari, pp. 264, 267.

violent of the Persian mourners would, until recent times, walk in the streets almost naked with blood gushing from wounds inflicted on their bodies by themselves as acts of love, anguish and mortification. The names of Yazīd, 'Ubaydullāh and 'Umar have ever since been held accursed by all Shī'ites, to whom Karbalā' became the holiest place in the world. Pilgrimage to it is still considered more meritorious than to Mecca. In it Shī'ism was born. Al-Ḥusayn's blood, even more than 'Ali's, proved to be the seed of the new "church". From then on leadership and successorship in 'Ali's progeny became as fundamental a dogma in Shī'ite creed as that of the prophethood of Muḥammad in Sunnite Islam.[1] The "day (*yawm*) of Karbalā'" and "vengeance for al-Ḥusayn" became the battle cry of the Shī'ite camp, a camp that never ceased its activity even after it had made its contribution to the undermining of the Umayyad throne.

Another pretender

The elimination of al-Ḥusayn did not end the struggle for the caliphate, as it was a three-cornered struggle. 'Abdullāh ibn-al-Zubayr, whose father had fruitlessly disputed the caliphate with 'Ali,[2] now came out openly against Yazīd. In fact, he was one of those who had encouraged al-Ḥusayn in his perilous adventure,[3] and now al-Ḥijāz proclaimed him commander of the believers (*amīr al-mu'minīn*). Quick to act, Yazīd dispatched against the Medinese dissidents a disciplinary force in which many Christian Syrians served. The leader was the one-eyed Muslim ibn-'Uqbah, whose old age necessitated his carriage in a litter.[4] The battle was joined August 26, 683, and won by the Syrians. That for three days unchecked Damascene soldiery pillaged the city of the Prophet[5] is apocryphal. Ibn-al-Zubayr took refuge in Mecca, whose soil was considered inviolable, and Muslim pursued him.[6] *En route* the Syrian general died and was succeeded by al-Ḥuṣayn ibn-Mumayr al-Sakūni, one of whose arrows had pierced the mouth of al-Ḥusayn at Karbalā' as he was drinking.[7] Al-Ḥuṣayn had no scruples in directing his catapults against the Ḥaram (holy mosque).[8] The Ka'bah itself caught fire and was burned to

[1] See below, p. 502.
[2] See above, p. 431.
[3] Mas'ūdi, vol. v, p. 131; Dīnawari, pp. 256-7.
[4] Not related to 'Uqbah, above, p. 437.
[5] Dīnawari, pp. 274-5.
[6] *Ansāb*, vol. iv B, p. 40.
[7] Ṭabari, vol. i, p. 2220; Ya'qūbi, vol. ii, p. 299; Dīnawari, p. 269.
[8] *Ansāb*, vol. iv B, pp. 47-9.

the ground. The Black Stone, a fetish of pre-Islam and the holiest relic of Islam, was split in three.[1] The house of Allah looked " like the torn bosoms of mourning women ".[2] Meantime Yazīd had died and the operations which had begun September 24, 683, were suspended on November 27.

The death of Yazīd and the sudden withdrawal of Syrian troops from Arabian soil improved ibn-al-Zubayr's chances. He was thereupon proclaimed caliph not only in his home al-Ḥijāz but in al-ʿIrāq, South Arabia and even parts of Syria. Over al-ʿIrāq he appointed as his representative his brother Muṣʿab.[3] In Syria he appointed as provisional regent al-Ḍaḥḥāk ibn-Qays al-Fihri, leader of the Qaysite (North Arabian) party, which had always been anti-Umayyad.[4] The Yamanites (South Arabians), who included the Kalbites, rallied to the support of the aged legitimate caliph Marwān ibn-al-Ḥakam [5] and inflicted a crushing defeat on al-Ḍaḥḥāk and his party. This was on July 684 at Marj Rāhiṭ, a plain north-east of Damascus.[6] Rāhiṭ was another Ṣiffīn for the Umayyads. It marked the end of the third civil war in Islam which, like the second between Muʿāwiyah and ʿAli, was a dynastic war.[7] As for the internal feud between the Qays, representing the new emigrants from North Arabia, and the Kalb, staunch supporters of the Umayyad cause, it lingered and finally precipitated the fall of the Umayyad dynasty. The Qaysi and Yamani parties figured even in the modern politics of Lebanon and Syria.[8]

The crushing of the anti-Umayyad party in Syria amputated the limb but the head was still animate in al-Ḥijāz. There the anti-caliphate of ibn-al-Zubayr continued to exist until Marwān's son and successor ʿAbd-al-Malik sent against it his iron-handed general al-Ḥajjāj ibn-Yūsuf, formerly a schoolmaster in al-Ṭāʾif. Al-Ḥajjāj belonged to the same tribe, Thaqīf, to which al-Mughīrah belonged.[9] He was then thirty-one years old. His army had reportedly 20,000 men.[10] For six and a half months beginning March 25, 692, al-Ḥajjāj pressed the siege against

[1] Yaʿqūbi, vol. ii, pp. 309-11; *Ansāb*, vol. iv B, pp. 52, 55. For a Nabataean black stone and kaʿbah see above, p. 385.

[2] Ṭabari, vol. ii, p. 427.

[3] Yaʿqūbi, vol. ii, p. 314.

[4] See above, p. 425.

[5] Cited above, pp. 429, n. 3, 446, table.

[6] *ʿIqd*, vol. ii, pp. 320-21; Masʿūdi, vol. v, p. 201; *Ansāb*, vol. v, pp. 136 *seq.* See above, p. 414.

[7] See above, pp. 431-2.

[8] See below, pp. 686-7.

[9] See above, p. 436.

[10] Yaʿqūbi, vol. ii, p. 318.

Mecca. He had no more hesitancy than al-Ḥuṣayn in using his catapults effectively against the Holy City. Inspired by the heroic exhortations of his mother Asmā', daughter of abu-Bakr and sister of ʿĀ'ishah, ibn-al-Zubayr fought valiantly but hopelessly.[1] At last he was slain. His head was sent to Damascus. His body, after hanging upside down on a cross, was delivered to his mother.[2] This is the first recorded crucifixion in Islam.

With the death of ibn-al-Zubayr the last champion of primitive Islam passed away. ʿUthmān was avenged. The Anṣār's (supporters') power was forever broken. The new orientation in Islam was secure; the ascendancy of the political over the religious in state authority was complete. Henceforth Mecca and Medina take back seats, and the history of Arabia begins to deal more with the effect of the outer world on the peninsula and less with the effect of the peninsula on the outer world. The mother "island" had spent itself.

ʿAbd-al-Malik committed to al-Ḥajjāj the government of al-Ḥijāz. This he held for a couple of years in the course of which he pacified not only that region but al-Yaman and even al-Yamāmah in the east. In 694 he was called to an equally, if not more, difficult task in the government of al-ʿIrāq.

Al-Ḥajjāj, energetic viceroy

Al-ʿIrāq was still a seething cauldron of discontent. Its people were "men of schism and hypocrisy".[3] In addition to Zubayrites and regular Shīʿites there were Khārijites[4] and those of the ʿAlids who after al-Ḥusayn's death had proclaimed a half-brother of his, Muḥammad ibn-al-Ḥanafīyah, as their imām and *mahdi*.[5] This Muḥammad was a son of ʿAli and was so called after his mother. Especially troublesome were the Khārijites. They kept the east in constant turmoil. From al-ʿIrāq they spread into Persia, split into several fanatic, theocratic sects, overran al-Ahwāz and Karmān, took al-Rayy, besieged Iṣbahān and ravaged wherever they went. In Persia their movement

[1] Ṭabari, vol. ii, pp. 845-8.

[2] Yaʿqūbi, vol. ii, pp. 319-20; Dīnawari, p. 321; *Aghāni*, vol. xiii, p. 43; *Ansāb*, vol. v. pp. 368-9.

[3] Masʿūdi, vol. v, p. 295; Yaʿqūbi, vol. ii, p. 326.

[4] See above, p. 433. For their tenets of belief consult al-Baghdādi, *Mukhtaṣar al-Farq bayn al-Firaq*, ed. Philip K. Hitti (Cairo, 1924), pp. 65-94.

[5] The divinely guided one. In Shīʿite circles the *mahdi* came to mean some forthcoming leader who would restore true Islam, conquer the world and, Messiah-like, usher in a period of peace and prosperity before the end of all things; Hitti, *History of the Arabs*, p. 441.

allied itself with the rising of the *mawālī*,[1] clients, against the Arabian masters. These were Persians who had accepted Islam on the assumption that it equalized all those within its fold and were now disappointed and disillusioned.

No sooner had al-Ḥajjāj received his appointment than he set out from Medina with a small mounted escort, crossed the desert by forced marches and arrived at al-Kūfah disguised and unannounced. It was early dawn, time of prayer. Accompanied by only twelve cameleers and with his bow on his shoulder and sword on his side, he entered the mosque, removed the heavy turban which veiled his stern features and delivered a fiery oration that has ever since formed one of the most favoured and dramatic themes in Arabic literature:

> "I am he who scattereth darkness and climbeth summits.
> As I lift the turban from my face, ye will know me."
>
> O people of al-Kūfah. Certain am I that I see heads ripe for cutting, and verily I am the man to do it. Methinks I see blood flowing between the turbans and the beards. . . . Verily the commander of the believers has ordered me to distribute among you the military stipends and enroll you under al-Muhallab ibn-abi-Ṣufrah [2] against the enemy. He of you who in three days after receiving his allowance does not depart, I swear by Allah that I will decapitate him.[3]

Saying this, al-Ḥajjāj commanded the caliph's rescript to be read aloud. It opened with: "In the name of God, the merciful, the compassionate. From the slave of God 'Abd-al-Malik, the commander of the believers, to those of al-Kūfah who are Moslems. Peace be unto you!" But there was no response. "Stop", shouted al-Ḥajjāj in anger to the reader. "Has it come to such a pass that ye respond not to the greeting of the commander of the believers? By Allah I will teach you soon to mend your ways. Begin again, young man." The reader did and when he repeated the caliphal salutation not one of the terrified congregation failed to join in the loyal

[1] Pl. of *mawla*, a non-Arab embracing Islam and affiliating himself with an Arabian tribe. His ill-defined rank placed him below the Moslem Arabians. See below, pp. 474, 485.

[2] This was the general who early in Mu'āwiyah's days (664–5) had undertaken a campaign as far as India and raided Kābul and Multān; cf. above, pp. 474, 485. Al-Ḥajjāj was his son-in-law.

[3] Mubarrad, pp. 215-16; cf. Ya'qūbi, vol. ii, p. 326; Mas'ūdi, vol. v, p. 294. The verse introducing the oration was a quotation from an earlier poet.

response: "And peace be unto the commander of the believers!"[1]

The new viceroy who had laid down the teacher's rod and taken up the warrior's sword was as good as his word. No neck proved too high for him to reach, no head too strong to crush. His task was to establish the ascendancy of the state over all elements within its framework — cost what it may. This he did. Human lives to the number of 120,000 are said to have been sacrificed by him; 50,000 men and 30,000 women were found held in prison at his death.[2] These undoubtedly exaggerated figures with the equally exaggerated reports about the tyranny of this Arab Nero, his blood-thirstiness, gluttony and impiety indicate that what the historians — mostly Shī'ites or Sunnites of the 'Abbāsid régime — have left us is a caricature rather than a portrayal of the man.

Reading between the lines, one can detect a number of constructive administrative achievements to the credit of al-Ḥajjāj. He dug old canals and opened new ones. He built a new capital Wāsiṭ (medial), so called from its half-way position between the two key cities of al-'Irāq — al-Baṣrah and al-Kūfah.[3] He introduced regulations to reform currency, taxes and measures.[4] The corruption of the Koran with which he was charged was evidently limited to a slight critical revision and to the introduction of orthographical signs designed to prevent incorrect reading of the sacred text.[5] Justifiable or not the repressive measures he took restored order in al-Kūfah and al-Baṣrah, hotbeds of discontent and opposition. The state authority was likewise firmly established along the eastern coast of Arabia, including hitherto independent 'Umān. His vice-royalty embraced also Persia. Here his general al-Muhallab practically eliminated that sect of the Khārijites most dangerous to Moslem unity, al-Azraqis. These got their name from their first leader, Nāfi' ibn-al-Azraq (the blue one), whose teaching went as far as considering all non-Khārijites — even if Moslems — infidels, whose blood with their wives' and

[1] Mubarrad, p. 216.

[2] Ibn-al-'Ibri, p. 195; cf. Mas'ūdi, vol. v, p. 382; do., *al-Tanbīh w-al-Ishrāf*, ed. M. J. de Goeje (Leyden, 1893), p. 318; Ṭabari, vol. ii, p. 1123.

[3] Ibn-Khallikān, *Wafayāt al-A'yān* (Cairo, 1299), vol. i, p. 221; al-Dhahabi, *Duwal al-Islām* (Ḥaydarābād, 1337), vol. i, p. 42; Ṭabari, vol. ii, p. 1125.

[4] See below, pp. 474.

[5] See below, p. 476.

children's was lawful.[1] By this time the Azraqis had, under the leadership of Qaṭar ibn-al-Fujā'ah, acquired mastery over Karmān,[2] Fāris and other eastern provinces. Beyond Persia al-Ḥajjāj's generals penetrated into the valley of the Indus, as we shall see in the next chapter. In his capital al-Ḥajjāj depended upon the faithful support of his garrison of Syrian troops, in whom his confidence — like his loyalty to the Umayyad house — knew no bound.

[1] Al-Shahrastāni, *al-Milal w-al-Niḥal*, ed. William Cureton (London, 1846), pp. 89-90; Baghdādi, pp. 72-6; Ṭabari, vol. ii, pp. 1003 *seq*.

[2] Or Kirmān, Yāqūt, vol. iv, p. 263; ibn-Khallikān, vol. ii, pp. 184-5.

CHAPTER XXXVI

THE GLORY THAT WAS DAMASCUS

DURING the reigns of ʿAbd-al-Malik and his four sons [1] the Umayyad dynasty in Damascus reached the meridian of its power and glory. Under al-Walīd (705–15) and his brother Hishām (724–43) the Islamic empire attained its greatest expansion, from the shores of the Atlantic and the Pyrenees to the Indus and the confines of China — an extent greater than that of the Roman empire at its height. At no time before or after did the Arab empire reach such dimensions. It was in this period of glory that the final and definite subjugation of Transoxiana, the reconquest and pacification of North Africa and the acquisition of the Iberian peninsula were accomplished. To this era also belong the nationalization or Arabicization of the state administration, the introduction of the first purely Arab coinage, the development of a system of postal service and the erection of such monuments of architecture as the Dome of the Rock in Jerusalem, the holiest sanctuary in Islam after those of Mecca and Medina.

The acquisition of Syria, al-ʿIrāq, Persia and Egypt under ʿUmar and ʿUthmān brought to an end the first stage in the history of Moslem conquest. The extension of the Moslem frontier under Muʿāwiyah to Khurāsān and Central Asia in

[1] The subjoined tree shows the genealogical relationship of the Marwānid branch of the Umayyad dynasty:

- 4. MARWĀN (683–5)
  - Muḥammad
    - 14. MARWĀN II (744–50)
  - 5. ʿABD-AL-MALIK (685–705)
    - 6. AL-WALĪD I (705–15)
      - 12. YAZĪD III (744)
      - 13. IBRĀHĪM (744)
    - 7. SULAYMĀN (715–17)
    - 9. YAZĪD II (720–24)
      - 11. AL-WALĪD II (743–4)
    - 10. HISHĀM (724–43)
  - ʿAbd-al-ʿAzīz
    - 8. ʿUMAR II (717–20)

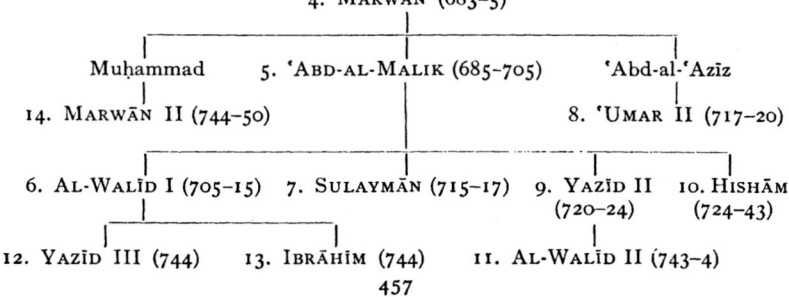

the east and to Ifrīqiyah in the west marked the second stage.[1] The definitive reduction of Transoxiana and the Indus valley under ʻAbd-al-Malik and his immediate successors signalize the third stage.

Subjugation of Transoxiana

It was the generals of al-Ḥajjāj who brought about the final reduction of the regions now called Turkestan, Afghanistan, Baluchistan and the Panjāb. One of these was ʻAbd-al-Raḥmān ibn-Muḥammad ibn-al-Ashʻath, governor of Sijistān and scion of the old royal family of Kindah in Central Arabia. His sister had married a son of al-Ḥajjāj. In 699–700 ʻAbd-al-Raḥmān marched against the *Zunbīl*,[2] Turkish (Iranian?) king of Kābul (Afghanistan), who had refused to pay the customary tribute. The dynasties and armies of these and other kingdoms in Central Asia were Turkish, but the subjects were mostly Iranians. So magnificently equipped was ʻAbd-al-Raḥmān's army that it was styled "the army of peacocks". ʻAbd-al-Raḥmān's successful campaign was cut short by his rebellion against al-Ḥajjāj, which resulted in the downfall of the general. In 704 he threw himself from the top of a tower and was killed,[3] one of the rare recorded cases of suicide in Islam.

The exploits of ʻAbd-al-Raḥmān pale before those of Qutaybah ibn-Muslim al-Bāhili, who in 704 on the recommendation of al-Ḥajjāj was appointed governor over Khurāsān, which he held as a subordinate of the viceroy.[4] From his capital Marw Qutaybah in a decade conducted a series of brilliant military campaigns into the lands "beyond the river" (*ma warā' al-nahr*). The river was the Oxus,[5] which until then had formed the traditional, though not historical, boundary line between "Īrān and Tūrān", i.e. between the Persian- and the Turkish-speaking peoples. In this period, the caliphate of al-Walīd, a permanent Moslem foothold was established there. Qutaybah's army comprised 40,000 Arab troops from al-Baṣrah, 7000 from al-Kūfah and 7000 clients.[6] In his first campaign

[1] See above, pp. 437-8.

[2] Wellhausen, *Reich*, p. 144, n. 3; less correctly Rutbīl, Ṭabari, vol. ii, pp. 1042 *seq.*; *Tanbīh*, p. 314.

[3] Ṭabari, vol. ii, p. 1135.

[4] Ibn-Khallikān, vol. ii, p. 180; Masʻūdi, vol. viii, p. 321.

[5] Modern Āmu Darya, Ar. and Per. Jayḥūn, adaptation of Gihon of Gen. 2 : 13. Sayḥūn for its sister river, Jaxartes, modern Sīr Darya, is an adaptation of Pison of Gen. 2 : 11.

[6] Balādhuri, p. 423; Ṭabari, vol. ii, pp. 1290-91.

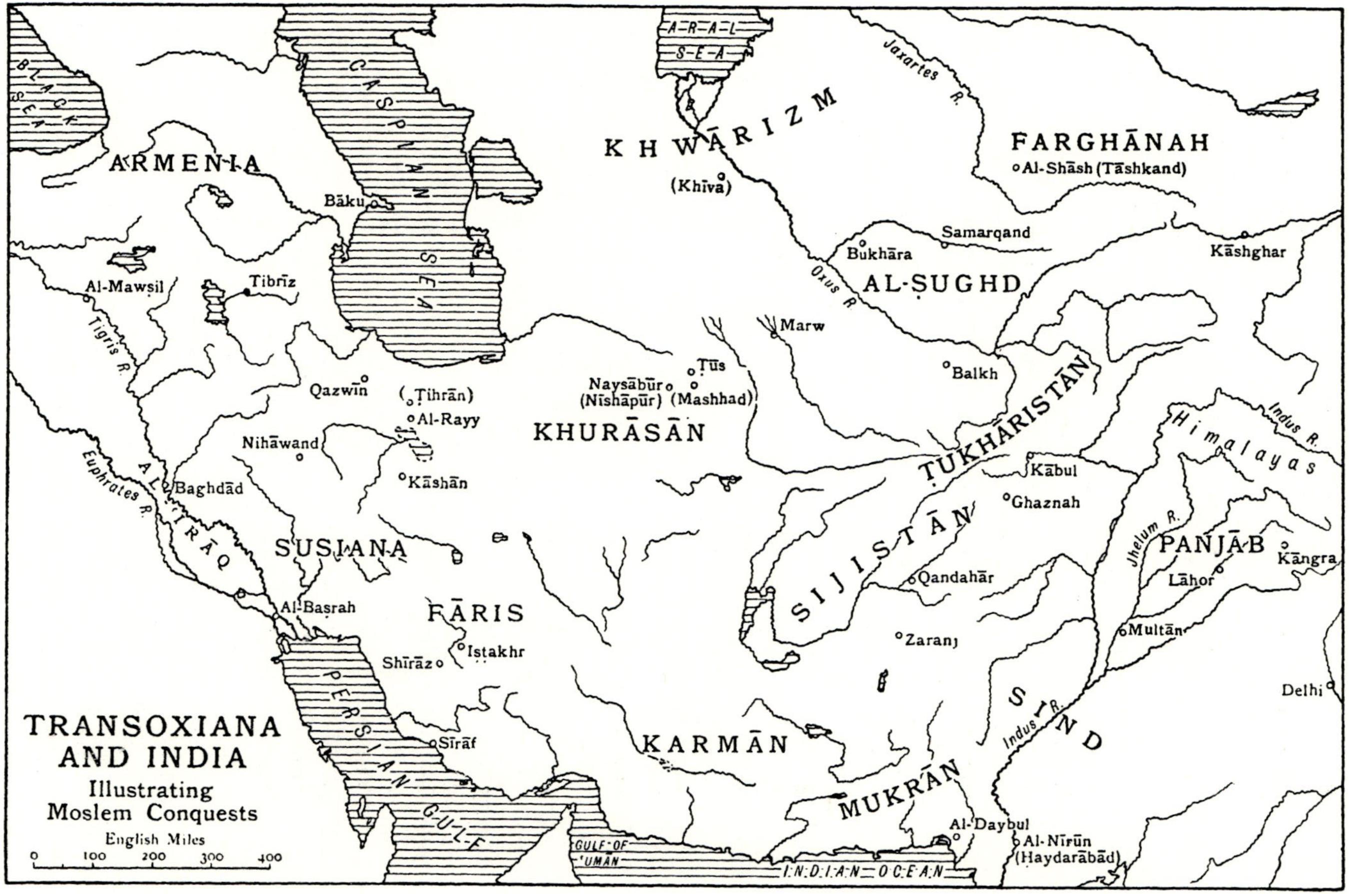
TRANSOXIANA
AND INDIA
Illustrating
Moslem Conquests
English Miles
0 100 200 300 400
BLACK SEA
ARMENIA
CASPIAN SEA
ARAL SEA
KHWĀRIZM
FARGHĀNAH
Al-Shāsh (Tāshkand)
Jaxartes R.
(Khīvā)
Bāku
Samarqand
Bukhāra
Kāshghar
AL-ṢUGHD
Oxus R.
Al-Mawṣil
Tibrīz
Tigris R.
Marw
Balkh
Qazwīn
(Tihrān)
Al-Rayy
Naysābūr
(Nīshāpūr)
Ṭūs
(Mashhad)
KHURĀSĀN
ṬUKHĀRISTĀN
Nihāwand
Kāshān
Euphrates R.
Baghdād
AL-ʿIRĀQ
Kābul
Ghaznah
Himalayas
Indus R.
SUSIANA
SIJISTĀN
Qandahār
Jhelum R.
PANJĀB
Kāngra
Lāhor
Al-Baṣrah
FĀRIS
Iṣṭakhr
Shīrāz
Zaranj
Multān
Delhi
SIND
Sīrāf
KARMĀN
PERSIAN GULF
MUKRĀN
Al-Daybul
Al-Nīrūn
(Ḥaydarābād)
GULF OF ʿUMĀN
INDIAN OCEAN

Qutaybah recovered lower Ṭukhāristān with its capital Balkh.[1] In 706–9 he conquered Bukhāra in al-Ṣughd (Sogdiana) and the adjoining territory. In 710–12 he reduced Samarqand (also in al-Ṣughd) and Khwārizm (modern Khīva) west of it. In the following two years he led an expedition into the Jaxartes provinces, particularly Farghānah, thus establishing nominal Moslem rule in what were known until recently as the Central Asian Khānates. Many of the communities in that entire region were nomadic. The pattern followed there was the same as in North Africa and other regions: raids, followed by more raids and tribute, refusal to continue to pay, attacks and conclusion of peace.

The crossing of the Jaxartes was an epoch-making event, as this river, rather than the Oxus, formed a natural political and racial frontier between Iranians and Turks. Its crossing constituted the first direct challenge by Arabs to Mongoloids and by Islam to Buddhism. Bukhāra, Balkh and Samarqand[2] had Buddhist monasteries. In Samarqand Qutaybah fell upon a number of idols to which he set fire with his own hand, resulting in a number of conversions from among devotees who had expected instant destruction to him who dared outrage the images. In Bukhāra the fire temple was likewise demolished. Bukhāra, Samarqand and Khwārizm were soon to become nurseries of Islam in Central Asia and to develop into centres of Arabic culture corresponding to Marw and Naysābūr (Per. Nīshāpūr) in Khurāsān, and to al-Baṣrah and al-Kūfah in al-ʿIrāq.

"Beyond the river" incorporated

The work of Qutaybah was continued by his lieutenant Naṣr ibn-Sayyār[3] and his successors. Appointed by the Caliph Hishām (724–43) as the first governor over Transoxiana, Naṣr used first Balkh and then Marw as capital. From Marw he had to reconquer (738–40) most of the territory overrun earlier by Qutaybah. Qutaybah was presumably satisfied with plant-

[1] Baktra of the Greeks. Balādhuri, p. 419.

[2] The ruler of Sogdiana resided at Samarqand and bore a Persian title *ikhshīd*, also borne by the king of Farghānah. The native rulers of these as well as Khwārizm and al-Shāsh, who too bore Persian titles (*khudāh, shāh, dihqān*), were perhaps related by marriage to the khān or khāqān of the Western Turks. The Arabs applied "Turk" to any non-Persian north-east of the Oxus. See ibn-Khurdādhbih, pp. 39-40; Yaʿqūbi, vol. ii, p. 479.

[3] Ibn-al-Athīr, vol. iv, p. 416; W. Barthold, *Turkestan down to the Mongol Invasion*, 2nd ed. (Oxford, 1928), p. 192.

ing Arab military agents who collected taxes and functioned side by side with native rulers. Kāshghar in Chinese Turkestan, allegedly conquered by Qutaybah (715),[1] was not reached until this time. When al-Walīd II ascended the throne (743), he recalled Naṣr and ordered him to come to Damascus with all kinds of strange hunting birds and musical instruments; but the caliph was assassinated while his governor was still on the way. By 751 Naṣr's successors had occupied al-Shāsh (Tāshkand), north-east of Samarqand, thus definitely establishing the supremacy of Islam in Central Asia, a supremacy that was not to be disputed any further by the Chinese. What lies "beyond the river" was at last fully incorporated into the extensive empire of the caliphs.

Conquest in India

While Qutaybah and Naṣr were conducting their successful campaigns in the eastern theatre of war, another general was moving southward into India. This was Muḥammad ibn-al-Qāsim al-Thaqafi, son-in-law of al-Ḥajjāj. His column comprised 6000 Syrian troops.[2] In 710 Muḥammad subdued Mukrān, pushed on through what is now called Baluchistan and in 711–712 reduced Sind, the lower valley and delta of the Indus. There he captured the seaport al-Daybul, which had a statue of the Buddha (Ar. Budd) "rising to a height of forty cubits",[3] and al-Nīrūn (modern Ḥaydarābād). In the following year the conquest was extended north as far as Multān, in south Panjāb, and the foot of the Himalayas. Multān was the seat of a national Buddhist shrine at which the invaders fell upon a large number of priests and pilgrims whom they took captive. So vast was the wealth plundered from this shrine that it became known by the name "the house of gold".[4] Multān served for years as the capital of Arab India and the outpost of Islam there.

Against the Byzantines

It was also in this period that some of the most determined attacks against the Byzantines were undertaken. In his early reign and while ibn-al-Zubayr was contesting the caliphate, ʿAbd-al-Malik paid tribute (A.H. 70/689–90) to the "tyrant of the Romans", as well as to his Christian allies, the Jurājimah, who had by that time established themselves in Lebanon.[5] But

[1] Ibn-al-Athīr, vol. v, p. 2.
[2] Balādhuri, p. 436.
[3] Yaʿqūbi, vol. ii, p. 346.
[4] Balādhuri, p. 440.
[5] See above, pp. 448-9.

shortly after that ʿAbd-al-Malik was in a position to take the offensive against the eternal enemy. In 692 his troops defeated those of Justinian II at the Cilician Sebastopolis. ʿAbd-al-Malik's successor, al-Walīd, pressed the offensive. About 707 his army occupied Tyana (al-Ṭawānah), the strongest fortress of Cappadocia. After capturing Sardis and Pergamum the way was open to Constantinople, to which Sulaymān's brother and general Maslamah laid his memorable but futile siege, August 716 to September 717.[1] Armenia, which had been overrun (644–5) while Muʿāwiyah was still governor of Syria but had taken advantage of ibn-al-Zubayr's debacle to revolt, was again reduced under ʿAbd-al-Malik.[2]

North Africa

Likewise Ifrīqiyah had to be reconquered at this time. So precarious was the hold of Muʿāwiyah's general ʿUqbah [3] on the land that it had to be evacuated by his successor. In ʿAbd-al-Malik's caliphate Ḥassān ibn-al-Nuʿmān al-Ghassāni (693–*ca.* 700) put an end to Berber resistance and Byzantine authority. With the aid of a Moslem fleet he drove the Byzantines from Carthage (698) and other coast towns. He then pursued and defeated their ally the Berber leader, a prophetess (Ar. *kāhinah*) [4] who held a mysterious control over her followers. The heroine was killed in the Awrās Mountain (Algeria) near a well that still bears her name, Bīr al-Kāhinah.

Ḥassān was followed by the celebrated Mūsa ibn-Nuṣayr. Under him the government of Ifrīqiyah, administered from al-Qayrawān, was divorced from Egypt and held directly from the caliphate in Damascus. Mūsa was born near Beirut. His father was a Syrian Christian captive who fell into the hands of Khālid ibn-al-Walīd with other boys while studying the Gospels at a church in ʿAyn al-Tamr in al-ʿIrāq.[5] It was Mūsa who extended the boundaries of the province westward as far as Tangier (Ṭanjah).

The conquests of Ḥassān and Mūsa brought the Berbers [6] permanently within the fold of Islam. Most of the Berbers who

[1] See above, p. 446. [2] Balādhuri, p. 160. [3] See above, p. 437.

[4] Balādhuri, p. 229; ibn-Khaldūn, vol. vii, pp. 8-9; ibn-ʿIdhāri, *al-Bayān al-Mughrib fi Akhbār al-Maghrib*, ed. R. Dozy (Leyden, 1848), vol. i, pp. 20-24.

[5] Others maintain that Mūsa was a Lakhmid, still others a Yamanite. Cf. Balādhuri, p. 230; ibn-ʿIdhāri, vol. i, p. 24.

[6] Eng. "Berber" and Ar. *Barbar* presumably come from L. *barbari* (originally Gr.), barbarians, a term applied by the Latinized cities of Roman Africa to all natives who did not adopt the Latin tongue.

were then on the fertile strip of land bordering on the sea were Christians. Among them Tertullian, Cyprian, Augustine and other saints and princes of the early Christian Church had flourished. The Byzantine settlers, as well as the Roman before them, were confined to the coastal towns. They represented a culture that remained alien to these nomads and semi-nomads of North Africa. Toward the Moslem Arabs the Berbers felt more affinity. As Hamites they were closer of kin to the Semites. Then they were all on the same cultural level. Moreover, the ancient Phoenician conquest and colonization of that region must have had its facilitating effects. Arabic tradition makes the majority of Berbers of Canaanite origin.[1] Punic, like Arabic a Semitic tongue, was still used in out-of-the-way places until shortly before the Moslem conquest. This explains the seemingly inexplicable miracle of so speedy and complete an Islamization and Arabicization of the Berbers. No sooner were they conquered than they were pressed into service, used as fresh relays in the continued forward march of Islam.

Conquest of Spain

The subjugation of North Africa as far as the Atlantic[2] opened the way for the conquest of south-western Europe. The momentous step was taken in 710, when the thirteen-mile strait was crossed by an Arab army for the first time. Plunder was the immediate objective. The raid developed into a conquest, the conquest of the entire Iberian peninsula.[3] The conquest was followed by occupation and control which lasted in part or in full for almost eight centuries. This successful campaign into the south-western part of Europe was the last and one of the most sensational military operations undertaken by the Arabs. It marked the acme of the Africo-European expansion, just as the conquest of Turkestan marked the height of the Asiatic expansion.

Ṭāriq crosses the strait

In its swiftness of execution and completeness of success this expedition into Spain holds a unique place not only in Arab but in medieval European annals. In July 710 a Berber band of four hundred foot and one hundred horse, under a client of Mūsa named Ṭarīf, landed on the tiny peninsula which

[1] Ṭabari, vol. i, p. 516; Mas'ūdi, vol. iii. pp. 239-40; ibn-al-Faqīh, p. 83. See above, p. 103.

[2] Ibn-'Abd-al-Ḥakam, pp. 203-5.

[3] Ar. al-Andalus, from Vandals, the German tribe that had overrun Spain.

formed almost the southernmost tip of the European continent. Whether Ṭarīf was a Berber or an Arab is still uncertain.[1] The peninsula has since borne the name of the general Jazīrat (isle of) Ṭarīf (Sp. Tarifa).[2] Encouraged by Ṭarīf's success and by the dynastic trouble in the Visigothic kingdom of Spain, Mūsa dispatched in 711 another freedman of his, Ṭāriq ibn-Ziyād. At the head of 7000 men, most of whom were, like him, Berbers, Ṭāriq landed near the mighty rock which has since immortalized his name, Gibraltar.[3] The ships, tradition asserts, were provided by a semi-legendary person, Julian,[4] Byzantine count of Ceuta.[5] The motive for his co-operation is not determined. The story of the violation of his beautiful daughter by the Visigothic usurper Roderick, offered in explanation, is apocryphal. In fact the entire story of the conquest has been richly embellished by both Arab and Spanish reporters.

A decisive victory

Reinforced, Ṭāriq at the head of 12,000 men encountered on July 19, 711, the army of Roderick at the mouth of the Barbate River[6] on the shore of the lagoon of the Janda.[7] Treachery in the Visigothic camp, instigated by relatives of the dethroned king, a son of Witiza,[8] contributed to the routing of the Spaniards, who numbered 25,000. Roderick himself disappeared and was heard of no more.

This turned out to be a decisive victory. The march of Moslem arms throughout the peninsula went on unchecked. Ṭāriq with the bulk of the army headed toward the capital Toledo. On his way he sent detachments against neighbouring

[1] Cf. al-Maqqari, *Nafḥ al-Ṭīb min Ghuṣn al-Andalus al-Raṭīb*, ed. Dozy, Wright *et al.* (Leyden, 1855), vol. i, p. 159; ibn-Khaldūn, vol. iv, p. 117; ibn-'Idhāri, vol. ii, p. 6; tr. Fagnan, vol. ii, p. 7; *Akhbār Majmū'ah fi Fatḥ al-Andalus*, ed. Lafuente y Alcántara (Madrid, 1867), p. 6 (text), p. 20 (tr.).

[2] Mentioned by al-Idrīsi, *Dhikr al-Andalus* (extracts from *Nuzhat al-Mushtāq*), ed. and tr. Don Josef A. Conde (Madrid, 1799), pp. 11, 35, 44.

[3] Ar. Jabal (mount of) Ṭāriq. Idrīsi, p. 36.

[4] Ulyān in Balādhuri, p. 230; Yulyān in *Akhbār*, vol. i, p. 4; ibn-'Idhāri, vol. ii, p. 6; Maqqari, vol. i, p. 159; ibn-'Abd-al-Ḥakam, p. 206; Yūliyān in ibn-al-Athīr, vol. iv, p. 444. Perhaps his real name was Urban or Olban.

[5] Sp. from Ar. Sabtah, ultimately from L. Septem Fratres (seven brothers). Idrīsi, p. 12.

[6] Now called Salado. Ar. Wādi Bakkah (Lakkah) corrupted into Sp. Guadilbeca and confused with Guadelete. Cf. Stanley Lane-Poole and Arthur Gilman, *The Moors in Spain* (New York, 1911), pp. 14, 23.

[7] Ar. al-Buḥayrah (the lake).

[8] Ar. Ghayṭasah, Ghīṭishah, etc. Roderick is Ar. Ludhrīq, Lazrīq, Rudhrīq. Maqqari, vol. i, pp. 160, 161; ibn-'Abd-al-Ḥakam, p. 206; ibn-'Idhāri, vol. ii, p. 8; ibn-Khaldūn, vol. iv, p. 117; *Akhbār*, p. 8; Mas'ūdi, vol. i, p. 359.

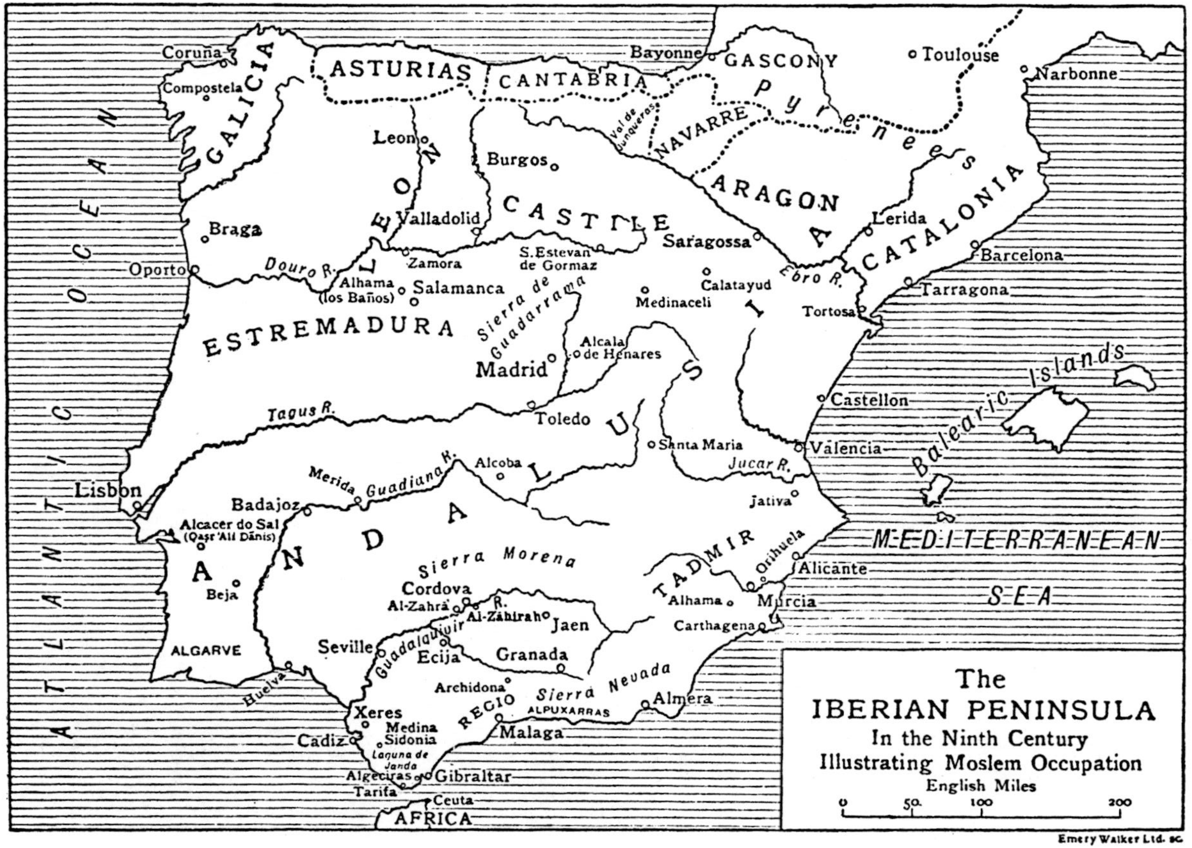

From Hitti, " History of the Arabs "

towns. Seville, a strongly fortified city, was by-passed. Cordova, future resplendent capital of Moslem Spain, fell through treachery on the part of a shepherd, so the story goes, who pointed out a breach in the wall.[1] Malaga offered no resistance. Toledo was betrayed by Jewish citizens. That was toward the end of the summer of 711. In less than half a year the Berber raider found himself master of half of Spain. He had destroyed a whole kingdom.

Mūsa follows

In June of the following year Mūsa with 10,000 Arabians and Syrians [2] rushed to the scene. He did not relish the idea of having all the honour and booty go to his lieutenants. For objective he chose those towns avoided by Ṭāriq. In or near Toledo he caught up with his former slave, whom he whipped and chained for refusing to obey a halt order early in the campaign.[3] The triumphal march was then resumed. Soon Saragossa in the north was reached and occupied. The highlands of Aragon, Leon and Galicia would have come next but for a caliphal order from al-Walīd in distant Damascus. The caliph charged his viceroy with the same offence for which the viceroy had disciplined his subordinate — acting independently of his superior.

A triumphal procession

Mūsa left his son 'Abd-al-'Azīz in command and slowly made his way overland toward Syria. His princely train comprised, besides his staff, 400 of the Visigothic royalty and aristocracy, wearing their crowns and girdled with gold belts, followed by a long retinue of slaves and captives [4] loaded with treasures of booty. The triumphal passage through North Africa and South Syria forms a favourite theme with Arab chroniclers.[5] On reaching Tiberias, Mūsa received orders from Sulaymān, brother and heir of the sick al-Walīd, to delay his arrival at the capital so that it might synchronize with his accession to the caliphal throne.[6]

[1] Ibn-'Idhāri, vol. ii, pp. 10-11; *Akhbār*, p. 10. Cf. Maqqari, vol. i, pp. 164-5.

[2] Ṭabari, vol. ii, p. 1253.

[3] Ibn-'Idhāri, vol. ii, pp. 17-18; ibn-'Abd-al-Ḥakam, p. 210.

[4] 30,000 (!) according to Maqqari, vol. i, p. 144; cf. ibn-al-Athīr, vol. iv, p. 448.

[5] Ibn-'Abd-al-Ḥakam, pp. 210-11; ibn-'Idhāri, vol. ii, pp. 21-2; ibn-al-Qūṭīyah, *Ta'rīkh Iftitāḥ al-Andalus* (Madrid, 1868), p. 10; pseudo-ibn-Qutaybah, *Qiṣṣat Fatḥ al-Andalus* (taken from *al-Imāmah w-al-Siyāsah* and issued as supplement to ibn-al-Qūṭīyah), pp. 138, 140 *seq.*

[6] Cf. al-Marrākushi, *al-Mu'jib fi Talkhīṣ Akhbār al-Maghrib*, R. Dozy, 2nd ed. (Leyden, 1881), p. 8; tr. E. Fagnan, *Histoire des Almohades* (Algiers, 1893), p. 10.

Evidently Mūsa ignored the orders. In February 715 he made his impressive entry into Damascus and was received by al-Walīd, though some say by the newly installed caliph Sulaymān. The royal reception was held with great dignity and pomp in the courtyard of the newly and magnificently built Umayyad mosque, adjoining the caliphal palace. What a memorable day in the history of triumphant Islam! No such numbers of Western princes and fair-haired European captives were ever seen offering homage to the commander of the believers. If any single episode can exemplify the zenith of Umayyad glory, it is this. Foremost among the trophies Mūsa offered the caliph was the priceless table (*mā'idah*) which Ṭāriq had seized from the Toledo cathedral. Gothic kings had vied with each other in embellishing this table with precious stones. Legend assigns the original workmanship to jinn in the service of King Solomon, from whose temple it was carried away by Romans into their capital and thence by Goths into Spain. Ṭāriq, so the story goes, had secreted one of its legs when Mūsa wrested it from him in Toledo, and now dramatically produced the missing part as proof of his own exploit.[1]

Al-Walīd's successor disciplined Mūsa and humiliated him. After making him stand until exhausted in the sun, he dismissed him from office and confiscated his property. Mūsa met the same fate that many a successful general and administrator in Islam had met. The conqueror of Africa and Spain was last heard of begging for sustenance in a remote village of al-Ḥijāz.[2]

Spain was now incorporated in the Syrian empire. Mūsa's successors carried on the work of rounding out the conquered territory in the east and north. Half a dozen years after the landing of the first Arab troops on Spanish soil, their successors stood facing the towering and mighty Pyrenees.

Explanation of the conquest

Such seemingly unprecedented conquest would not have been possible but for internal weakness and dissension. The population of the country was Spanish-Roman; the rulers were

[1] Maqqari, vol. i, pp. 167, 172; ibn-'Abd-al-Ḥakam, p. 211; ibn-al-Athīr, vol. iv, pp. 448-9; ibn-Khallikān, vol. iii, pp. 26-7; *Nabdhah min Akhbār Fatḥ al-Andalus* (ext. *al-Risālah al-Sharīfīyah ila al-Aqṭār al-Andalusīyah*, supplement to ibn-al-Qūṭīyah, Madrid, 1868), pp. 193, 213. See *Arabian Nights*, No. 272.

[2] Maqqari, vol. i, p. 180; cf. ibn-Khallikān, vol. iii, p. 27.

Teutonic Visigoths (West Goths) who had occupied the land in the early fifth century. They ruled as absolute, often despotic, monarchs. For years they professed Arian Christianity and did not adopt Catholicism, the denomination of their subjects, until the latter part of the following century. The lowest stratum of the society was held in serfdom and slavery and, with the persecuted Jews, contributed to the facility with which the conquest was achieved.

The Pyrenees crossed

In 717 or 718 Mūsa's third successor, al-Ḥurr ibn-'Abd-al-Raḥmān al-Thaqafi [1] crossed the mountains that separate Spain from France. These were raids and they were continued by his successor al-Samḥ ibn-Mālik al-Khawlāni. The object was to seize the reputed treasures of convents and churches. In 720, under the Caliph 'Umar II, al-Samḥ captured Narbonne (Ar. Arbūnah), to be later converted into a huge citadel with an arsenal. In the following year an unsuccessful attempt was made on Toulouse, seat of Duke Eudes of Aquitaine, in which al-Samḥ was killed. Thereby the first victory by a Germanic prince over Arabs was registered.

The battle of Tours

Twelve years later 'Abd-al-Raḥmān ibn-'Abdullāh al-Ghāfiqi, al-Samḥ's successor as amīr over Spain, undertook the last and greatest expedition across the Pyrenees. Having vanquished Duke Eudes on the banks of the Garonne, he stormed Bordeaux and pushed northward to Poitiers, outside of whose walls he set a basilica on fire. Thence he headed toward Tours. Tours held the shrine of St. Martin, apostle to the Gauls. Its votive offerings provided the chief attraction to the invader.

Between Poitiers and Tours 'Abd-al-Raḥmān's way was intercepted by Charles, mayor of the palace at the Merovingian court. Not a king in name, Charles was a king in fact. His valour had subdued many enemies and forced Eudes to acknowledge the sovereignty of the northern Franks.

After seven days of skirmishing the battle raged. It was an October Saturday in 732. The Frankish warriors, mostly foot, knew how to protect themselves against the cold weather with wolfskins. In the thick of the battle they stood shoulder to shoulder, forming a hollow square, firm as a rock and inflexible as a block of ice — to use the words of a Western historian.[2]

[1] Ibn-'Idhāri, vol. ii, pp. 24-5; ibn-al-Athīr, vol. v, p. 373.
[2] André Duchesne, *Historiae Francorum scriptores*, vol. i (Paris, 1936), p. 786.

Without giving way they hewed down the light cavalry of the enemy as it attacked them. ʿAbd-al-Raḥmān fell. Darkness separated the combatants. Under cover of night the invaders stole away and vanished. It was not until the morning that Charles realized what he had done. He had won a victory. His surname then became Martel (hammer).

To the Moslems this battlefield was simply a *balāṭ*[1] *al-shuhadā'*,[2] a pavement of martyrs, a martyr being anyone killed in war against non-Moslems. To the Christians, however, it marked a turning-point in the military career of their eternal foe. European historians would see in Paris and London mosques, where cathedrals now stand, and fezes where hats are worn, had the outcome of the battle been otherwise.[3] In reality nothing was decided on the battlefield of Tours. The Moslem wave, already about a thousand miles from its starting-point in Gibraltar — to say nothing about its base in al-Qayrawān — had already spent itself and reached a natural limit. Moreover, the army's morale had been lowered by internal discord. Jealousy thrived between Arabs and Berbers. The Berbers complained that they were allotted the arid central plateau while the Arabs appropriated for themselves the most smiling provinces of Andalusia, this despite the fact that the Berbers had carried the brunt of the battle. The Arabs themselves were far from being united by common feeling and purpose. The old feud between North Arabians (Muḍarites)[4] and South Arabians (Yamanites) was reasserting itself. And now sectarian differences were adding their contribution. The Muḍarites were Sunnites, but some of the Yamanites were now Shīʿites or Shīʿite sympathizers. The Berbers expressed their difference by espousing another doctrine, the Khārijite.[5]

Damascus the capital

Though checked at Tours the Arab raids in other directions did not cease. In 734 Avignon was captured; nine years later Lyons was pillaged. The fact, however, remains that Tours does indicate the extreme limit of the victorious march of Islam. Its year 732 marks the centennial of the Prophet's death. A

[1] See above, p. 448, n. 2.

[2] *Akhbār*, p. 25; Maqqari, vol. i, p. 146. The battle was fought on a paved Roman road. Cf. John 19:13.

[3] Gibbon, *Decline and Fall*, vol. vi, pp. 15 *seq.* See also Lane-Poole, pp. 29-30.

[4] The Muḍar and Rabīʿah, both of North Arabian origin, were often included under the collective term Maʿadd. Cf. above, p. 452.

[5] See above, p. 433.

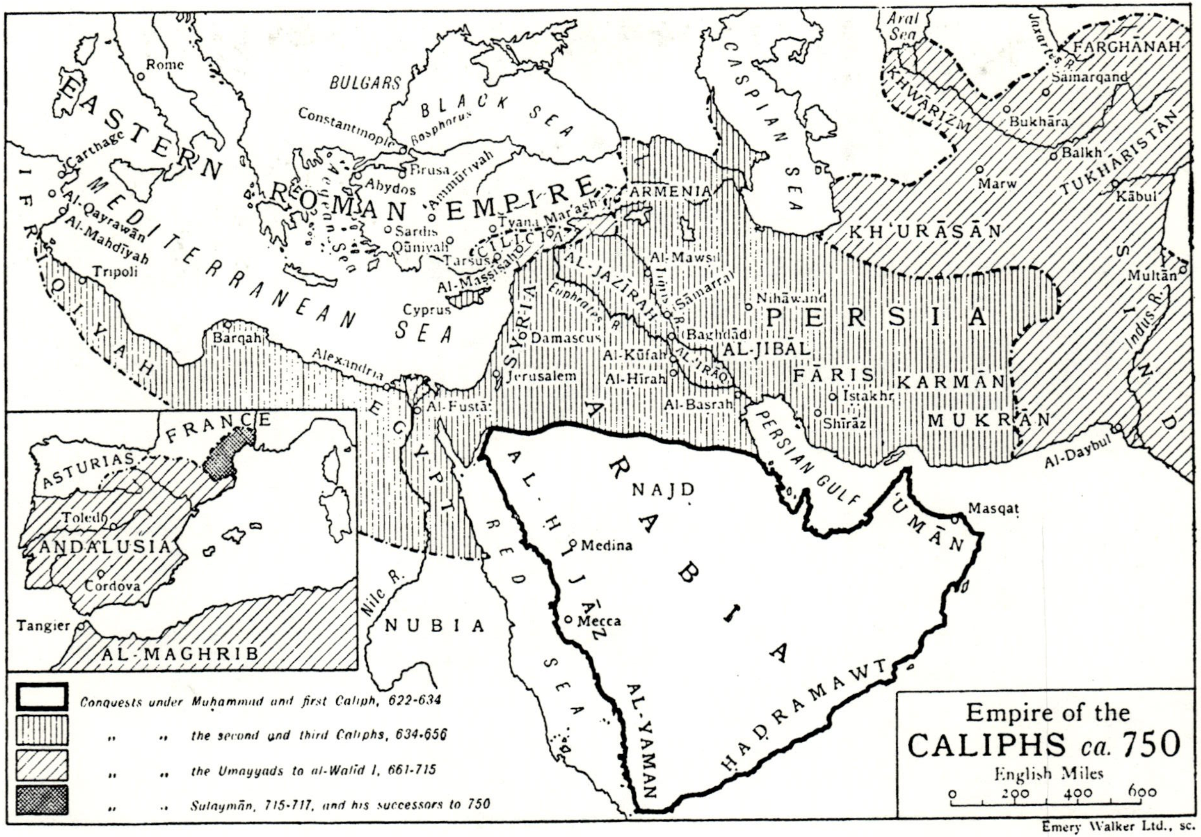

From Hitti, "History of the Arabs"

pause here and now to survey the entire situation may be worth while. A hundred years after the death of the founder of Islam,

From J. Sauvaget, J. Weulersse and M. M. L. Écochard, "Damas et la Syrie Sud" (Damascus)

DAMASCUS FROM THE MINARET OF THE UMAYYAD MOSQUE

In the foreground is the tomb of Salāḥ-al-Dīn, in the rear the citadel and behind it Mount Qāsiyūn cut by the gorge of Barada

his followers were the masters of an empire greater than that of Rome at its zenith — an empire extending from the Bay of Biscay to the Indus and the confines of China and from the

Aral Sea to the cataracts of the Nile. The capital of this huge domain was Damascus, the oldest living city, the one which reportedly Muḥammad hesitated to enter, because he wished to enter paradise but once.[1] The city was set like a pearl in an emerald girdle of gardens (*ghūṭah*). Through the ages these gardens relied upon snow-fed brooks from Anti-Lebanon for their existence From the north rushes Barada to fling tassels of silver streams across the outstretched plain. From the south comes Pharpar (Abana) laden with tribute from the copious springs of Mount Hermon. Yāqūt,[2] the great geographer of the early thirteenth century, claims that he visited all four spots considered earthly paradises and found Damascus the first among them. "To sum up," he continues, "nothing attributed by way of description to the heavenly paradise is not found in Damascus."[3] The city overlooked a plain stretching southwestward to that venerable patriarch of Lebanon crests, Mount Hermon, called by the Arabs al-Jabal al-Shaykh (the grey-haired peak),[4] because of its turban of perpetual snow. In the centre of the city stood the Umayyad mosque, a gem of architecture that still attracts lovers of beauty. Near by lay the caliphal palace, called al-Khaḍrā', because of its green dome.[5] In his palace the caliph held his formal audiences. Dressed in gorgeous flowing robes, he would sit, cross-legged, on a square throne covered with richly embroidered cushions. Paternal relatives, arranged according to seniority, stood on the right side; maternal relatives on the left; courtiers, poets and petitioners behind.

Nationalizing the state

It was only natural for the state on attaining maturity to Arabicize its administration and nationalize its institutions. Until now Greek had persisted in Syria as the language of the public registers; Pahlawi and certain local dialects had survived in al-'Irāq and the eastern provinces. There was no choice in the matter. The Moslem conquerors, fresh from the desert and ignorant of book-keeping and finance, had to retain in the exchequer Greek-, Pahlawi- and other non-Arabic-writing officials. By this time, however, some of these secretaries had undoubtedly mastered Arabic, and some Arab officials had

[1] For other traditions extolling Damascus see ibn-'Asākir, vol. i, pp. 46 *seq.*
[2] *Buldān*, vol. ii, p. 589. [3] *Buldān*, vol. ii, p. 590. [4] See above, p. 41, n. 6.
[5] Ibn-Jubayr, *Riḥlah*, ed. William Wright (Leyden, 1907), p. 269, l. 3; *Aghānī*, vol. vi, p. 159.

mastered the intricacies of secretarial details. It was time for Arabic to replace all other languages as the official language of the bureaus. The transition was necessarily slow, beginning under ʿAbd-al-Malik and continuing during the reign of his son. That may be inferred from the fact that certain authorities

From "Katalog der orientalischen Münzen, Königliche Museen zu Berlin" (Walter de Gruyter & Co., Berlin)

AN IMITATION IN GOLD OF A BYZANTINE COIN WITH ARABIC INSCRIPTION

Retaining on the obverse the figures of Heraclius, Heraclius Constantine, and Heracleonas, and on the reverse a modified Byzantine cross

ascribe the change to the father, others to the son.[1] Thus in the course of a millennium three written languages succeeded each other in Syria: Aramaic, Greek and Arabic. In al-ʿIrāq and its dependencies the Umayyad viceroy al-Ḥajjāj substituted

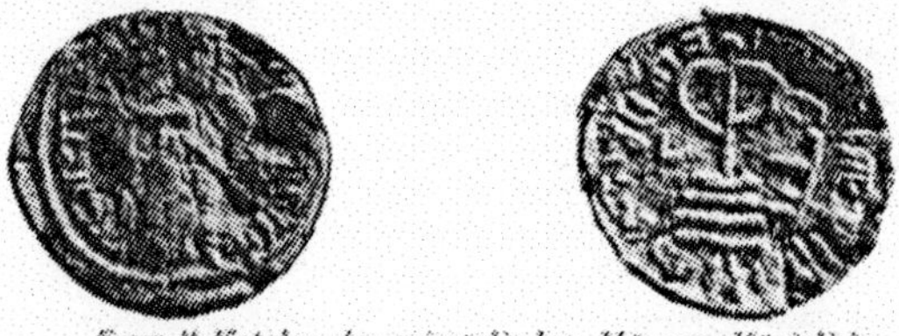

From "Katalog der orientalischen Münzen, Königliche Museen zu Berlin" (Walter de Gruyter & Co., Berlin)

COPPER COIN OF ʿABD-AL-MALIK

Bearing on the obverse his image and his name and on the reverse φ on four steps together with the *shahādah* and the mint name, Baʿlabakk. An imitation of the Byzantine dinar

Arabic for the dialects in the chancellery. As to the extent to which the population was Arabicized, that will be treated in the next chapter.[2]

With the change of language went a change in coinage. Hitherto the Byzantine coinage, found current in Syria at the time of conquest, was left undisturbed.[3] In certain cases

[1] *ʿIqd*, vol. ii, p. 322; Māwardi, pp. 349-50; Balādhuri, pp. 193, 300-301. Balādhuri naïvely ascribes the cause to a trivial occurrence, urination of a Greek clerk in an inkwell. [2] Pp. 484-5. [3] Balādhuri, pp. 465-6.

koranic superscriptions were stamped on the coins. A few gold and silver pieces were struck in imitation of Byzantine and Persian types. Muʿāwiyah issued some copper pieces on which the portrait of the king holding a cross was replaced by that of the caliph brandishing a sword. But it was not until the time of ʿAbd-al-Malik (695) that the first purely Arabic dinars and dirhams [1] were struck.[2] In the following year al-Ḥajjāj minted silver in al-Kūfah.[3]

Postal service

Moreover, ʿAbd-al-Malik developed a regular postal service (*barīd*) [4] designed primarily to meet the needs of government officials and their correspondence. In this he built on the foundation laid by his great predecessor Muʿāwiyah.[5] ʿAbd-al-Malik promoted the service through a well-organized system knitting together the various parts of his far-flung empire. To this end relays of horses were used between Damascus and the provincial capitals. Postmasters were installed, charged among other duties with the task of keeping the caliph posted on all important happenings in their respective territories. Al-Walīd made use of the system for his building operations.

Fiscal and other reforms

Other changes in this period involved taxes and fiscal matters. In theory the only tax incumbent on a Moslem, no matter what his nationality might be, was the alms-tax (*zakāh*); but in practice only the Moslem of Arabian origin usually enjoyed this privilege. Taking advantage of the theory, new converts to Islam, particularly from al-ʿIrāq and Khurāsān, began under the Umayyads to desert their farms and villages in favour of the cities with the hope of joining the Arab army as *mawāli* (singular *mawla*, client). This term was used later for freedmen but at this time bore no connotation of inferior status. From the standpoint of the treasury the movement constituted a double loss, for at conversion the taxes were supposedly reduced and upon joining the army a special subsidy was due. As a measure of remedy al-Ḥajjāj ordered such men restored to their farms [6] and reimposed the high tribute origin-

[1] See above, p. 436, n.

[2] Ṭabari, vol. ii, p. 939; Balādhuri, pp. 240, 466-70.

[3] Cf. Yāqūt, *Buldān*, vol. iv, p. 886.

[4] Al-ʿUmari, *al-Taʿrīf bi-al-Muṣṭalaḥ al-Sharīf* (Cairo, 1312), p. 185. Ar. *barīd* is an ancient Semitic word from *brd*, "to send" Cf. Esth. 8: 10; Iṣfahāni, *Taʾrīkh*, p. 39.

[5] *Fakhri*, p. 148.

[6] Mubarrad, p. 286.

ally paid, the equivalent of the land-tax (*kharāj*) and poll-tax (*jizyah*).

Al-Ḥajjāj's enactment resulted in so much dissatisfaction among Neo-Moslems, that the pious caliph ʿUmar II (717–20) considered it wise to re-establish the old principle ascribed to his earlier namesake [1] — that a Moslem, whether Arabian or *mawla*, need pay no tribute whatsoever.[2] When an official in Khurāsān objected that the numerous conversions were adversely affecting the treasury and suggested testing the new converts by ascertaining whether they had gone through

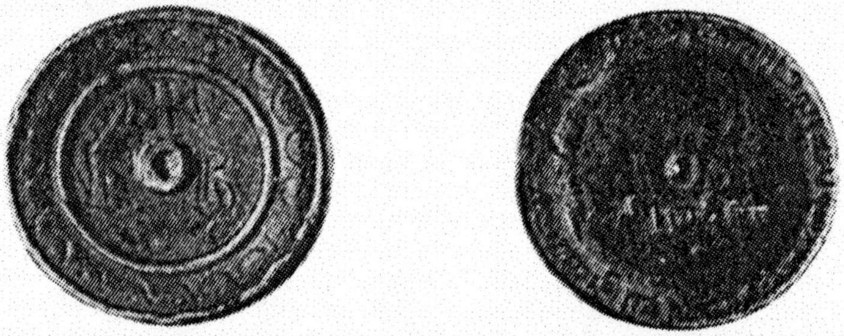

By courtesy of E. T. Newell
From "Numismatic Notes and Monographs", No. 87 (New York, 1939)

A BYZANTINE WEIGHT VALIDATED BY AL-WALĪD (d. 715)

Bearing on the obverse a cross with the inscription ΓB, i.e. two ounces, and on the reverse a Kufic inscription stating that the caliph has recognized this as equivalent to two *waqīyahs*. Probably the earliest inscribed Moslem weight thus far found

circumcision, ʿUmar replied: "Verily God sent His Prophet as a missionary and not as a circumciser".[3] ʿUmar insisted, however, that the land for which *kharāj* was paid should, on the conversion of its owner, be considered joint property of the Moslem community, with the understanding that the original owner might continue to use it as a leaseholder.[4] Since the poll-tax was a comparatively low item, the treasury thus continued to receive its main income from the land-tax.

ʿUmar's policy was not successful. It diminished the state revenue in proportion as it increased the number of city clients.[5] Berbers, Persians and others flocked to Islam for the pecuniary

[1] See above, pp. 422-3.
[2] Balādhuri, p. 426.
[3] Ṭabari, vol. ii, p. 1354; ibn-al-Athīr, vol. v, p. 37.
[4] Ibn-ʿAsākir, vol. iv, p. 80; Yaʿqūbi, vol. ii, p. 362; ibn-al-Jawzi, *Sīrat ʿUmar ibn-ʿAbd-al-ʿAzīz* (Cairo, 1331), pp. 88-9.
[5] Ibn-al-Jawzi, pp. 99-100.

privileges that accrued. Later practice reverted to the system of al-Ḥajjāj with minor modifications.

Other reforms undertaken by al-Ḥajjāj relate to Arabic orthography. To distinguish such similarly written letters as *bā'*, *tā'* and *thā'*, *dāl* and *dhāl* he introduced diacritical marks, and to remove ambiguity in vocalization he adapted from Syriac certain signs (*ḍammah* (*u*), *fatḥah* (*a*) and *kasrah* (*i*)) to be inserted above and below the letters.

The architectural monuments which stand out among the great achievements of this period will be treated in a later chapter (XXXVIII).

CHAPTER XXXVII

POLITICAL AND SOCIAL CONDITIONS UNDER THE UMAYYADS

THE administrative divisions of the Umayyad empire followed in the western provinces the Byzantine pattern and in the eastern provinces the Persian. The main provinces were nine: (1) Syria-Palestine; (2) al-Kūfah, which included al-'Irāq; (3) al-Baṣrah with Persia, Sijistān, Khurāsān, al-Baḥrayn, 'Umān and probably Najd and al-Yamāmah; (4) Armenia; (5) al-Ḥijāz; (6) Karmān and the frontier districts of India; (7) Egypt; (8) Ifrīqiyah; (9) al-Yaman and the rest of South Arabia. Out of these, five vice-royalties developed: that of al-'Irāq, which included most of Persia and eastern Arabia with al-Kūfah as capital; that of al-Ḥijāz, which embraced al-Yaman and Central Arabia; the vice-royalty of al-Jazīrah (the northern part of the Tigro-Euphrates region), with which went Armenia, Ādharbayjān and parts of eastern Asia Minor; that of Egypt, which combined both Upper and Lower; and finally Ifrīqiyah, whose capital was al-Qayrawān and which comprised northern Africa west of Egypt, together with Spain and the Mediterranean islands.

Provincial government

The threefold governmental function of political administration, tax collection and religious ministry was directed by three types of officials. The viceroy (*amīr*, *ṣāḥib*) had under him provincial governors (sing. *'āmil*), whom he appointed and for whose conduct he was responsible. As viceroy he had full charge of the political as well as military administration of his domain. In certain cases revenues were collected by a special officer (*ṣāḥib al-kharāj*) responsible directly to the caliph. The chief source of income was tribute from subject peoples. All provincial expenses were met from local income; only the balance went to the caliphal treasury.

The first purely judicial officials in the provinces received their appointments from the governors. Many such judges[1]

[1] Sing. *qāḍi*, Anglicized kazy, kasi, cadi and in six other forms.

were installed in the Umayyad period, recruited as a rule from among scholars learned in the Koran and Islamic tradition. Their jurisdiction was limited to Moslem citizens; non-Moslems were allowed autonomy under their own religious heads, especially in personal matters relating to marriage, divorce and inheritance. Besides judging cases these officials administered pious foundations (sing. *waqf*) and estates of orphans and imbeciles.

Bureau of registry

Created by Mu'āwiyah, the bureau of the seal (*dīwān al-khātim*) was a sort of state chancery charged with the duty of making and preserving one copy of each official document before sealing and dispatching it.[1] The first part of the Arabic name suggests Persian origin.[2] By 'Abd-al-Malik's time a whole state archive had developed in Damascus.[3]

Military organization

Like the Byzantine army, after which it was modelled, the Umayyad army was divided into five corps: centre, two wings, vanguard and rearguard. The last Umayyad caliph Marwān II (744–50) abandoned this formation in favour of the small compact body termed *kurdūs* (cohort).[4] In outfit and armour the Arab warrior was hard to distinguish from his Greek counterpart. The cavalry used plain, rounded saddles like the ones still in fashion in the Near East. The heavy artillery comprised the ballista (*'arrādah*), mangonel (*manjanīq*) and battering-ram (*kabsh*, *dabbābah*). Such heavy engines together with the baggage were transported on camels behind the army.

The core of the army at Damascus consisted of Syrians and Syrianized Arabs. The Sufyānid caliphs maintained a standing army of 60,000, entailing a yearly expenditure of 60,000,000 dirhams.[5] Yazīd III (744) reduced all annuities by ten per cent, which won him the sobriquet of *nāqiṣ* (diminisher, also deficient). Under his successor, the last of the dynasty, the army probably numbered not more than 12,000.[6]

The Arab fleet was likewise an imitation of the Byzantine model and was manned mostly by Syrians.[7] The galley, with

[1] Ṭabari, vol. ii, pp. 205-6; *Fakhri*, p. 149.

[2] Cf. Balādhuri, p. 464.

[3] Mas'ūdi, vol. v, p. 239.

[4] Ṭabari, vol. ii, p. 1944; ibn-al-Athīr, vol. v, p. 267, ll. 7-8; ibn-Khaldūn, vol. iii, p. 165, l. 16 (cf. p. 195, ll. 25-7).

[5] Mas'ūdi, vol. v, p. 195.

[6] Erroneously given as 120,000 in *Fakhri*, p. 197; abu-al-Fidā', vol. i, p. 222. See below, p. 531.

[7] See above, p. 426.

a minimum of twenty-five seats on each of the two lower decks, was the fighting unit. Each seat held two rowers; the hundred or more rowers in each ship were armed. Those who specialized in fighting took up their positions on the upper deck.

Caliphal life in Damascus was fully regal in contrast with **Royal life** that of Medina, which had been on the whole simple and patriarchal.[1] Relations with the Umayyad caliphs began to be regulated by protocol. Ceremonial clothes with the name of the caliph and religious sentences embroidered on their borders came into use possibly in ʻAbd-al-Malik's days. The cloth was manufactured by Copts in Egypt, who also prepared the papyrus scrolls [2] for writing purposes. This caliph ordered that Moslem formulas replace the cross and the Trinity at the head of the scrolls. The Persian word *ṭirāz*, applied to embroideries, brocades, robes of honour and other material manufactured for the sole use of the royalty, suggests that in this the caliphs followed Iranian rather than Byzantine models.

The evenings of the caliph were set apart for entertainment and social intercourse. Muʻāwiyah's pastime was listening to tales. He imported a story-teller, ʻAbīd (ʻUbayd ?) ibn-Sharyah, all the way from al-Yaman to relate to him deeds of the heroes of the past.[3] Rose sherbet, still enjoyed in Damascus and other Eastern towns, was a favourite drink.

Some, however, desired a stronger beverage. Muʻāwiyah's son Yazīd was the first confirmed drunkard among the caliphs. His intemperance won him the sobriquet Yazīd *al-khumūr* (of wines).[4] Among those who participated in his drinking bouts was a pet monkey, abu-Qays, whom he trained to drink with him. Yazīd is said to have drunk daily, whereas al-Walīd I drank every other day; Hishām once every Friday; and ʻAbd-al-Malik only once a month, but then so heavily as to necessitate the use of emetics.[5] Most of this information about the lighter side of the caliphs' lives comes from the *ʻIqd*, *Aghānī* [6] and similar literary works which should not be taken too literally. Yazīd II's weakness was for singing girls as well as wine. Most

[1] See above, p. 428. [2] Sing. *qirṭās*, from Gr.; Balādhuri, p. 240.
[3] See below, pp. 492-3.
[4] *Ansāb*, vol. iv B, p. 30; *ʻIqd*, vol. iii, p. 403; Nuwayri, *Nihāyah*, vol. iv, p. 91.
[5] Cf. *ʻIqd*, vol. iii, p. 404.
[6] Vol. i, p. 3, gives as criterion for the choice of data: "elegance that pleases the onlooker and entertains the hearer"

of his time he spent with his two favourite songstresses, Sallāmah and Ḥabābah. And when Ḥabābah was choked on a grape which he had playfully thrown into her mouth, the passionate young caliph fretted himself to death.[1] But the prize in drinking should be awarded to his son al-Walīd II (743–4), an incorrigible libertine (*khalī'*), whose favourite pastime reportedly was to go swimming in a pool of wine of which he would gulp enough to lower the surface.[2] He is said to have once opened the Koran and as his eyes fell upon the passage "And every froward potentate was brought to naught",[3] he was so enraged that he shot the sacred book to pieces with his bow and arrow.[4] The *Aghāni*[5] has preserved an eye-witness's report of one of this caliph's debauched parties, some of which were held in his desert palace by al-Qaryatayn, midway between Damascus and Palmyra. Those among the caliphs who maintained reasonable self-respect would screen themselves behind curtains which separated them from the entertainers; but not this al-Walīd.[6]

Innocent pastimes

Several caliphs and courtiers engaged in more innocent pastimes such as hunting, dicing and horse-racing. Polo (*jūkān*, from Per. *chawgān*) was introduced from Persia probably toward the end of the Umayyad period and soon became a favourite and fashionable sport with the 'Abbāsids. Cock-fights at that time were not infrequent. The chase was one of the early sports of Arabia, where the saluki (*salūqi*, from Salūq in al-Yaman) dog was at first exclusively used. The cheetah (*fahd*) was used later. The Persians and Indians had trained this animal long before the Arabians. Yazīd I was the first great hunter in Islam; he trained the cheetah to ride on the croup of his horse. His hunting dogs wore gold anklets and each had a special slave assigned to it.[7] Al-Walīd I was one of the first caliphs to institute and patronize public horse-races.[8] His brother Sulaymān had planned a national competition in horse-racing when death overtook him.[9] In a course organized by their brother Hishām, 4000 racers from the royal and other stables took part, "which finds no parallel in pre-Islamic or

[1] *Al-'Uyūn w-al-Ḥadā'iq* (1865), pp. 40-41; cf. *Aghāni*, vol. xiii, p. 165.
[2] Al-Nawāji, *Ḥalbat al-Kumayt* (Cairo, 1299), p. 98.
[3] Sūr. 14:18.
[4] *Aghāni*, vol. vi, p. 125.
[5] Vol. ii, p. 72.
[6] Al-Jāḥiẓ, *al-Tāj fi Akhlāq al-Mulūk*, ed. Aḥmad Zaki (Cairo, 1914), p. 32.
[7] *Fakhri*, p. 76.
[8] Mas'ūdi, vol. vi, pp. 13-17
[9] Ibn-al-Jawzi, *Sīrat*, p. 56.

Islamic annals ".[1] A daughter of this caliph evidently kept a stud.[2]

The harem of the caliphal household apparently enjoyed a relatively large measure of freedom. They undoubtedly appeared veiled in public, veiling (*ḥijāb*) being an ancient Semitic custom sanctioned by the Koran.[3] 'Ātikah, the beautiful daughter of Mu'āwiyah, was the subject of love poems addressed to her by a Meccan poet who happened to catch a glimpse of her face through the lifted veils and curtains as she was on a pilgrimage. The poet did not hesitate to follow her to her father's capital. Here the caliph found it expedient to " cut off the poet's tongue " by the usual procedure of offering a subsidy. He, moreover, found him a suitable wife.[4] A granddaughter of Mu'āwiyah, also named 'Ātikah, reportedly locked the door of her room when angry with her husband-caliph, the powerful 'Abd-al-Malik, and refused to open it until a favourite courtier rushed weeping and falsely announced that one of his two sons had killed the other and that the caliph was on the point of executing the fratricide.[5] Another poet, Waḍḍāḥ al-Yaman, ventured to make love to a wife of al-Walīd I in Damascus, the caliphal threats notwithstanding. For his audacity he finally paid with his life.[6] This poet and other good-looking men veiled themselves on festive occasions as a protection against the evil eye.[7] The harem system, with its concomitant auxiliary of eunuchs, was not fully instituted until the days of al-Walīd II.[8] The eunuch institution was based on the Byzantine model; most of the early eunuchs were Greeks.[9] Royal harem

The city of Damascus cannot have changed much in character and tone of life since its Umayyad days. Then, as now, in its narrow covered streets the Damascene with his baggy trousers, heavy turban and red pointed shoes rubbed shoulders with the sun-tanned Bedouin in his flowing gown surmounted The capital

[1] Mas'ūdi, vol. v, p. 466. [2] *Al-'Uyūn w-al-Ḥadā'iq* (1865), p. 69, l. 12.
[3] See above, pp. 174, 388, fig.; Sūr. 33:53, 55.
[4] *Aghāni*, vol. vi, pp. 158-61.
[5] Mas'ūdi, vol. v, pp. 273-5.
[6] *Aghāni*, vol. vi, pp. 36 *seq.*; vol. xi, p. 49.
[7] *Aghāni*, vol. vi, p. 33.
[8] *Aghāni*, vol. iv, pp. 78-9.
[9] J. B. Bury, *The Imperial Administrative System in the Ninth Century* (London, 1911), pp. 120 *seq.*; Charles Diehl, *Byzance: grandeur et décadence* (Paris, 1919), p. 154.

by the *kūfīyah* (head shawl) and *'iqāl* (head band). Occasionally a European-dressed *Ifranji* [1] passed by. A few women, all veiled, crossed the streets; others stole glimpses through the latticed windows of their homes overlooking the bazaars and public squares. There was no right or left rule of way, no part of the passage reserved for riders or pedestrians. Amidst the confused crowd an aristocrat might be seen on horseback cloaked in a silk *'abā'* and armed with a sword. The screaming voices of sherbet sellers and sweetmeat vendors competed with the incessant tramp of passers-by and of donkeys and camels laden with the varied products of the desert and the sown. The entire city atmosphere was charged with all kinds of smell. The demand on eye, ear and nose was overwhelming.

As in Ḥimṣ, Aleppo (Ḥalab) and other towns the Arabians lived in separate quarters of their own according to their tribal affiliation. These quarters (sing. *ḥārah*) are still well marked. The door of the house usually opened from the street into a courtyard. In the centre of the courtyard stood a large basin with a flowing jet emitting intermittently a veil-like spray. An orange or citron tree flourished by the basin. It was the Umayyads who, to their eternal glory, supplied Damascus with a water system unexcelled in its day and still functioning. The name of one of them, Yazīd I, is still borne by a canal from the Barada which he dug or more probably widened.[2] The luxurious gardens outside of Damascus, al-Ghūṭah, owe their very existence to this river, which sends off other canals to spread freshness and fertility throughout the city. About sixty remaining public baths, some with mosaics and decorated tiles, testify to the richness and distribution of its water supply.[3]

Society

The population of the empire was divided into four social classes. At the top stood the ruling Moslems, headed by the caliphal family and the aristocracy of Arabian conquerors. Down to the 'Abbāsid period the Arabs constituted a social hereditary caste. How numerous was this class cannot be exactly ascertained. It should be borne in mind that few of

[1] A Frank, a word used for all Europeans, especially common during the Crusades.

[2] Iṣṭakhri, p. 59; cf. H. Sauvaire, "Description de Damas: 'Oyoûn et-Tawârîkh, par Mohammed ebn Châker", *Journal asiatique*, ser. 9, vol. vii (1896), p. 400.

[3] For more consult M. Écochard, *Les Bains de Damas* (Beirut. 1942).

the Arabs and Bedouins were interested in agriculture and that they mostly congregated in cities. Lebanon was naturally avoided. The mountain does not seem to have received an influx of Arabs till the ninth and succeeding centuries. According to a late tradition the Tanūkh, who figured prominently in the political affairs of Lebanon, did not enter it till the early ninth.[1] The Tanūkh were not very numerous and, like other feudal families, left no descendants.[2] The banu-ʻĀmilah spread to its southern part after the eleventh.[3] In Syria the banu-Ḥamdān, who established a dynasty in Aleppo,[4] did not reach there until the middle of the tenth. The banu-Mirdās,[5] who succeeded them, reached Aleppo in the early eleventh. It is interesting to note that none of these tribes came directly from the desert; they were all previously domesticated in the Ḥīrah or some other region of the Fertile Crescent. As for the Bedouin tribes today in control of the Syrian Desert, their migration there is comparatively recent. The ʻAnazah did not figure prominently till the second half of the seventeenth century, succeeding the Shammar, who had come from Najd. The Ruwalah are a branch of the ʻAnazah. These were the last great Bedouin migrations to Syria.[6]

Some Arabians, even Bedouins, no doubt drifted into country places and established villages. The village development followed a clear line of transition from a temporary settlement to a semi-permanent pastoral-agricultural unit to the permanent village establishment. Most villages had as nucleus a spring of water with due consideration to ease of defence and fertility of soil. Traits of tribal life and organization, such as family solidarity, exaltation of individual prowess, hospitality, predominance of personal touch in all human relations, are still manifest and highly prized in the Syrian and Lebanese society.

[1] Al-Shidyāq, *Ta'rīkh al-Aʻyān fi Jabal Lubnān* (Beirut, 1859), p. 224; cf. Ṣāliḥ ibn-Yaḥya, *Ta'rīkh Bayrūt*, ed. L. Cheikho (Beirut, 1902), p. 65, where Tanūkh from whom the Buḥtur were descended is not made a member of the Tanūkh tribe but a descendant of the Lakhmid al-Mundhir ibn-Mā'-al-Samā'.

[2] Cf. Fu'ād Ḥamzah, *Qalb Jazīrat al-ʻArab* (Cairo, 1933), p. 233.

[3] See above, p. 411, n. 3.

[4] See below, pp. 564 *seq*.

[5] See below, pp. 580-81.

[6] Consult Waṣfi Zakarīya, *ʻAshā'ir al-Sha'm*, vol. i (Damascus, 1945), pp. 117-118.

The Arabian army which conquered Syria numbered some 25,000.[1] Under Marwān I the number of Arabian Moslems in the military registers of Ḥimṣ and its district (*jund*) was 20,000. Under al-Walīd I, Damascus and its district, which included the Phoenician coast, had 45,000 registered. On this basis the number of Moslems in Syria toward the end of the first century after the conquest could not have exceeded 200,000 out of an estimated population of 3,500,000.[2] As for the population of Lebanon the bulk remained Aramaicized Phoenicians. A small minority in all conquered lands, the Arabians were the same minority everywhere; and that is why they were able to play the important rôle they did in the unifying of the vast majority.

The Arab concentration in cities was such that Arabic by that time had become the urban language. As the country folk came to these cities to sell their products or practise their crafts, they acquired the new tongue without necessarily forsaking the old one. The indigenous intellectuals also found it convenient to acquire Arabic in order to qualify for government posts.

The number of country people who readily accepted the new faith must have been fewer than those who accepted the new language, mainly because the Umayyad caliphs, with the exception of the pious ʿUmar II,[3] did not favour conversion especially from among owners of arable land. Umayyad liberalism was not only political but religious and intellectual also. The capital and the large cities may by the end of the Umayyad era have presented the aspect of Moslem towns, but the other places, more particularly the mountain regions, preserved their native features and ancient culture pattern. Umayyad Syria reared one of the greatest theologians and hymnologists of the Eastern Church, St. John of Damascus, and her sons gave Christendom five popes; two of whom were canonized.[4] Lebanon remained Christian in faith and Syriac in speech for centuries after the conquest. Indeed, what came to an end with the conquest was the physical conflict; the

[1] See above, pp. 415-16.

[2] Lammens, *La Syrie*, vol. i, pp. 119-20; cf. above, pp. 279, 292.

[3] See above, pp. 475-6.

[4] John V (685-6), St. Sergius (687-701), Sisinnius (708), Constantine (708-15), St. Gregory III (731-41); see below, p. 499.

religious, ethnic, social and above all linguistic conflicts had just begun.

Next below the Arabian Moslems stood the Neo-Moslems. Those were natives who because of force, pressure or persuasion professed Islam and were thereby in theory, though not in practice, admitted to the full rights of Islamic citizenship. Such converts usually attached themselves as clients (*mawāli*) to some Arabian tribe and became members thereof. **Clients**

As clients the neophytes formed the low stratum of Moslem society, a status which they bitterly resented. Their espousal of the Shīʿite cause in al-ʿIrāq and the Khārijite in Persia was one way in which they expressed their dissatisfaction. Some of them, however, embraced the new faith with such zeal that they became its fanatic exponents ready to persecute their former co-religionists. Clients were naturally the first within the Moslem society to devote themselves to learned studies and the fine arts. They mediated their old traditions and culture to their new co-religionists. As they demonstrated their superiority in the intellectual field, they began to contest with them political leadership. And as they intermarried with them they diluted the Arabian stock and ultimately made the term *ʿArab* applicable to all Arabic-speaking Moslems regardless of the original ethnic relationship.

The third class consisted of members of tolerated sects, professors of revealed religions, i.e. Christians, Jews and Ṣābians (*Ṣābi'ah*), with whom the Moslems had entered into a covenant relationship. The tolerated status was granted to Christians and Jews as *ahl al-kitāb* (people of the book, Scripturaries) by Muḥammad himself [1] and was partly due to the esteem in which the Prophet held the Bible and partly to the fact that a number of Arabian tribes on the Syro-ʿIrāqi border, like the Ghassān, Bakr, Taghlib, Tanūkh, were already Christianized. The Ṣābians were granted this privilege [2] on the assumption that they were monotheists. These people were identical with the Mandeans, the so-called Christians of St. John, and still survive in the marshes at the mouth of the Euphrates. In Arabia proper, however, consequent to an alleged statement by Muḥammad, no non-Moslems were tolerated, the only exception being a small Jewish community **Dhimmis**

[1] Koran 9:29; 2:99, 103; 3:62-5, etc. [2] Koran 2:59; 5:73; 22:17.

in al-Yaman. This recognition of tolerated sects was predicated on disarming their devotees and exacting tribute from them in return for Moslem protection (*dhimmah*). This was Islam's solution of the minority problem.

In this status dhimmis enjoyed, against the payment of land and capitation tax, a measure of toleration. Not being members of the dominant religious community they held an inferior position socially and politically. In matters of civil and criminal judicial procedure they were left under their own spiritual heads (unless a Moslem was involved).[1] Moslem law was considered too sacred to be applicable to non-Moslems. Essential parts of this system survived through the Ottoman era and the mandatory régimes. The theory of inseparability between religion and nationality was an ancient Semitic one and not a Moslem invention.

The tolerated status was, after Muḥammad, extended to the fire-worshipping Zoroastrians (Magians, *Majūs*), the star worshippers of Ḥarrān (pseudo-Ṣābians), the heathen Berbers and others. Though not devotees of a revealed religion and technically outside the pale of Islam, these were offered by the Moslem invaders the three choices: Islam, the sword or tribute, rather than the first two only. Abu-Yūsuf,[2] the distinguished judge under Hārūn al-Rashīd, expressly states that — in addition to Scripturaries — polytheists, fire-worshippers and idolaters may be accepted as protected citizens of a Moslem state.

In Syria the dhimmis were well treated until the days of ʻUmar II. One conspicuous exception was the case of the chief of the Christian tribe of Taghlib who was put to death by al-Walīd I for refusing to profess Islam.[3] Evidently the Moslems were less tolerant of Christians who were descended from Arabian stock, as illustrated by this case and the case of the Tanūkh. The Tanūkh of the neighbourhood of Qinnasrīn were summoned to Islam at the time of the conquest of Syria and some of them responded;[4] others, of the neighbourhood of Aleppo, were forced to adopt Islam by the ʻAbbāsid al-Mahdi (775–85), who demolished their churches. In Egypt the Copts, after expressing their individuality by several risings against their Moslem overlords, finally succumbed in the days of the

[1] Consult Koran 5:47-52.
[2] *Kharāj*, p. 79, ll. 15-17.
[3] *Aghāni*, vol. x, p. 99.
[4] Balādhuri, pp. 144-5.

'Abbāsid al-Ma'mūn (813–33).[1] Christians and Jews pursued their usual means of livelihood though some, such as the manufacture and sale of wine and the conduct of gambling games, were taboo to Moslems. Drinking and gambling houses, where dicing was a favourite pastime, continued to flourish and were patronized even by Moslems. Monks were experts in wine-making and in honey, fruit and flower raising. In connection with the monasteries, some of them must have maintained special guest rooms for entertainment and pleasure. Al-'Umari, himself a Damascene (d. 1349), cites many cases in which caliphs and other Moslems patronized monasteries and convents for drinking and pleasure, not all of the innocent variety. This was especially true of al-Walīd ibn-Yazīd.[2] In one instance this caliph so much appreciated the wine of a monastery that he filled the stone basin, which he with the collaboration of his brother had emptied, with silver pieces. From Lebanon wine was exported as far as Medina. A Ḥijāzi poet who attended so many all-night parties that his wife's suspicion was aroused, explained to her, " Deprive me not of an honourable companion who ne'er speaks ill of others. . . . It is wine from the villages of Beirut,[3] pure, faultless, or from the land of Baysān. Forsooth we drank it until it caused us to stagger." [4]

Dis-abilities imposed by 'Umar

'Umar's fame does not rest primarily on his piety or his remission of taxes on neophyte Moslems. He was the first caliph in Islam to impose humiliating restrictions on his Christian subjects — measures wrongly ascribed to his earlier namesake.[5] He issued regulations excluding Christians from public offices, forbidding their wearing turbans and requiring them to cut their forelocks, don distinctive clothes with girdles of leather, ride without saddles, erect no places of worship and pray in subdued voices. The penalty for a Moslem's killing of a Christian, he further decreed, was only a fine, and a Christian's testimony against a Moslem was not acceptable in court. It may be assumed that such legislation was enacted in response to popular demand. In administration, business and industry the Arabian

[1] Al-Kindi, *Ta'rīkh Miṣr wa-Wulātuha*, ed. Rhuvon Guest (Leyden, 1912), pp. 73, 81, 96, 116, 117; al-Maqrīzi, *al-Mawā'iẓ w-al-I'tibār bi-Dhikr al-Khiṭaṭ w-al-Āthār* (Būlāq, 1270), vol. ii, p. 497.

[2] Ibn-Faḍl-Allāh al-'Umari, *Masālik al-Abṣār fi Mamālik al-Amṣār*, ed. Aḥmad Zakī, vol. i (Cairo, 1924), pp. 321-22, 349, 351-2, 355-6.

[3] Cf. above, pp. 97, 297-8.

[4] *Aghāni*, vol. ii, pp. 86, 88.

[5] See above, p. 422. Ibn-'Abd-al-Ḥakam, pp. 151-2.

Moslems, still predominantly illiterate, could offer no competition to the indigenous Christians. The Jews, who were fewer than Christians and often held meaner jobs, were evidently included under some of these restrictions and excluded from government posts. It should be noted that wearing distinctive dress to designate differing peoples was somewhat practised before Islam in the Near East and that some of these enactments were not enforced after ʿUmar's day.

Slaves

At the bottom of the social ladder stood the slaves. Slavery was an ancient Semitic institution the legality of which the Old Testament admitted. Islam accepted the institution and legislated to ameliorate the condition of the slave [1] (*ʿabd*). Canon law forbade the Moslem to enslave his co-religionist, but did not guarantee liberty to an alien slave on adopting Islam.

In early Islam, slaves were recruited by purchase, kidnapping, raiding and from unransomed prisoners of war, including women and children. Soon the slave trade became brisk and lucrative in all Moslem lands. East and Central Africa supplied black slaves; Farghānah and Chinese Turkestan yellow ones, the Near East and south-eastern Europe white ones. The institution was a self-perpetuating one. Islamic law considers the offspring of a female slave by another slave, by any man other than her master, or by her master in case he does not admit the fatherhood of the child, likewise a slave. But the offspring of a male slave by a free woman is considered free.

Between master and female slave concubinage was made permissible by koranic legislation. The children of such a union belong to the master and are therefore free. The status of the concubine is then raised to that of "child's mother" (*umm walad*). In this state the husband-master can neither sell her nor give her away; at his death she is declared free. The liberation of a slave has always been looked upon as a good work (*qurbah*) bringing the master nearer to God. A liberated slave enjoyed the status of a client (*mawla*) to his former master and was entitled to inherit his patron's estate in case of death without heirs.

In the melting-pot process which resulted in the amalgamation of Arabians and non-Arabians, slaves, no doubt, played a

[1] Koran 4:40, 29-30; 24:33.

significant rôle. This was true of the royalty as well as the commonalty. In Yazīd III the proud tradition of pure-blooded Arab caliphs was broken. Yazīd's mother was a royal Persian princess captured in Khurāsān and sent by al-Ḥajjāj as a present to al-Walīd; whereas Yazīd's brother-successor, Ibrāhīm, was the son of an obscure concubine, perhaps a Greek.[1] The mother of Ibrāhīm's successor, Marwān II, was a Kurdish slave.[2] According to one report, she was already pregnant with Marwān when his father acquired her,[3] which would make the last Umayyad not an Umayyad at all. This encroachment by slave females on the position of the free-born Arab woman continued and increased steadily in the 'Abbāsid period.[4]

General state of economy

Syria's severance from the Byzantine empire considerably reduced her maritime trade, but that was somewhat compensated for by new markets opened by the acquisition of Persia and Central Asia. The ships plying the Mediterranean had their decks fastened with iron nails and covered with tar to prevent leakage, but those in the Persian Gulf and eastern waters had decks bound with cords prior to the time of al-Ḥajjāj, who ordered the Mediterranean model followed.[5] Al-Ḥajjāj's ships reached distant Ceylon and were at times attacked by Indian pirates.[6] In addition to the shipbuilding factory of Mu'āwiyah at Acre,[7] 'Abd-al-Malik founded one in Tunis.[8] His son Hishām transferred the factory from Acre to Tyre, where it remained till the days of the 'Abbāsid al-Mutawakkil.[9] Under one of the last Umayyad governors of al-Baṣrah the canals in that city and its precincts numbered "120,000", on which small boats plied, a number which was doubted by the tenth century geographer al-Iṣṭakhri,[10] who visited the place in person.

These canals, like those of Damascus, were mainly for irrigation. Agriculture on the whole did not suffer in Syria in spite of the greed of the exchequer. Islamic prohibition against wine was not, except to a limited extent, detrimental to viticulture, a flourishing activity since remote antiquity.

[1] *'Iqd*, vol. ii, pp. 333, 352; Ya'qūbi, vol. ii, pp. 401, 403; Ṭabari, vol. ii, p. 1874; Mas'ūdi, vol. vi, pp. 31-2.
[2] Ya'qūbi, vol. ii, p. 404; Ṭabari, vol. iii, p. 51.
[3] *Ansāb*, vol. v, p. 186.
[4] See below, p. 535.
[5] Ibn-Rustah, *al-A'lāq al-Nafīsah*, ed. M. J. de Goeje (Leyden, 1891), pp. 195-196.
[6] Balādhuri, p. 435.
[7] See above, p. 426.
[8] Ibn-Khaldūn, *Muqaddamah*, p. 211.
[9] Balādhuri, p. 118.
[10] P. 80.

CHAPTER XXXVIII

HIGHER ASPECTS OF LIFE UNDER THE UMAYYADS

As Syrians, 'Irāqis, Persians, Copts and Berbers joined the bandwagon of Islam and intermarried with Arabians, the gap between Arabians and non-Arabians was bridged. The follower of Muḥammad, no matter what his original nationality might have been, would now adopt the Arabic tongue and pass for an Arab. The Arabians themselves brought no science, no art, no tradition of learning, no heritage of culture from the desert. The religious and linguistic elements were the only two novel cultural elements they introduced. In everything else they found themselves dependent upon their subjects. In Syria and the other conquered lands they sat as pupils at the feet of the conquered. Theirs was another case of the victors led captive by the vanquished. What Greece was to the Romans Syria was to the Arabians. When, therefore, we speak of Arabian medicine or philosophy or mathematics what we mean is not something that was necessarily the product of the Arabian mind or cultivated by the inhabitants of the Arabian peninsula but the learning that was enshrined in Arabic books written by men who were themselves Syrians, Persians, 'Irāqis, Egyptians or Arabians — Christians, Jews or Moslems — who drew their material from Greek, Aramaean, Indo-Persian and other sources.

Intellectual life in the Umayyad period was not on a high level. In fact the whole period was one of incubation. Its closeness to the dark pre-Islamic age (*jāhilīyah*), the frequence of its civil and foreign wars and the instability of its economic and social conditions militated against the possibility of high intellectual attainment. But in it the seeds were sown to come into full bloom in the 'Abbāsid caliphate.

Grammar and lexicography

The study of Arabic grammar was one of the first disciplines cultivated in this period. It was necessitated by the linguistic needs of Neo-Moslems eager to learn the Koran, hold government positions and push ahead with the conquering class. It is significant that the first scientific study of the Arabic language was begun in al-Baṣrah, near the Persian border, and was conducted mainly for foreign converts and partly by them. It was in this city that the legendary founder of Arabic grammar, abu-al-Aswad al-Du'ali (d. 688) flourished. The noted biographer ibn-Khallikān [1] naïvely explains the origin of this science in these words: "'Ali laid down for al-Du'ali the basic principle that the parts of speech are three: noun, verb and particle, and then asked him to found a complete treatise thereon". In fact Arabic grammar went through a process of slow, long development and bears striking marks of the influence of Greek logic and Sanskrit linguistics.

Another Baṣrite scholar, al-Khalīl ibn-Aḥmad (d. *ca.* 786), compiled the first Arabic dictionary, *Kitāb al-'Ayn*. In it he seems to have followed the Sanskrit system, which begins with the guttural *'ayn*. Biographers ascribe to al-Khalīl the discovery of Arabic prosody and the formulation of its rules,[2] still followed today.

Religious tradition and canon law

The twin sciences of lexicography and philology arose as a result of the study of the Koran and the necessity of expounding it. The same is true of the most characteristically Moslem literary activity, the science of tradition, *ḥadīth* (narrative), technically a saying or act attributed to the Prophet or to one of his Companions. The Koran and tradition lay at the foundation of theology and *fiqh* (law), the obverse and reverse of sacred law. Of this period, from which hardly any literature has come down to us, we know only a few traditionists and jurists. Most renowned among them were al-Ḥasan al-Baṣri (d. 728) and ibn-Shihāb al-Zuhri (d. 742). Al-Baṣri was believed to have personally known more than seventy Companions. Orthodox Sunnis never tire of quoting his devout sayings, and Sufis never shook off the influence of his ascetic piety.[3] Al-Zuhri was so deeply absorbed in his study of tradition that his wife once remarked, "By Allah, these books of yours are worse to me than three rival wives could be".[4] Al-Kūfah, which rivalled al-Baṣrah as an intellectual centre, produced 'Āmir ibn-Sharāḥīl al-Sha'bi

[1] Vol. i, pp. 429-30.
[2] Ibn-Khallikān, vol. i, p. 307.
[3] For more on him consult ibn-Khallikān, vol. i, pp. 227-9.
[4] Ibn-Khallikān, vol. ii, p. 223; abu-al-Fidā', vol. i, pp. 215-16.

(d. *ca.* 728), who is said to have heard traditions from some hundred and fifty Companions [1] which he related from memory without putting down a single line in black and white. Al-Sha'bi was sent by 'Abd-al-Malik on an important mission to the emperor in Constantinople.

Roman law, directly or through the Talmud and other media, did undoubtedly affect certain phases of Islamic law, especially in Umayyad Syria and Egypt. Those phases were contractual transactions (*mu'āmalāt*) [2] and state monopolies such as coinage, official seals, papyrus for documents and other public utilities. The Arabs followed the Byzantine precedent in regarding these commodities and utilities as state monopolies, in considering it the state duty to protect its citizens against forgery, counterfeit, contraband and other abuses connected with them, and in administering heavy punishments.[3] The channels of transmission were the administrative departments inherited by the Arab state and Moslem converts from former Byzantine subjects. In Arabic legal vocabulary no loan words from Greek or Latin are met, though certain terms in Arabic have the same meaning as corresponding Latin ones.[4] Nor do we know of any book on Roman law translated into Arabic. All the major schools of Moslem jurisprudence, it should be remembered, flourished in non-Byzantine territory, al-'Irāq and al-Ḥijāz.[5] One minor school founded by a Syrian, al-Awzā'i (d. 774), did not survive.[6]

Historiography

History writing started in the form of tradition (*ḥadīth*) and was one of the earliest disciplines cultivated by Arab Moslems. The stimuli for historical research were provided by the interest of the believers in collecting old stories about the Prophet and his Companions, the necessity of ascertaining the genealogical relationship of each Moslem Arab in order to determine the amount of state stipend to be received and the desire of the early caliphs to scan the proceedings of kings and rulers before them. 'Abīd ('Ubayd),[7] who was summoned to Damascus to inform Mu'āwiyah about "the early kings of the Arabians and

[1] Al-Sam'āni, *al-Ansāb*, ed. Margoliouth (Leyden, 1912), fol. 334 recto; cf. ibn-Khallikān, vol. i, p. 436.

[2] M. Ḥamīdullāh, "Influence of Roman on Moslem Law", *Hyderabad Academy Studies*, No. 6 (1943), pp. 43 *seq.*

[3] Balādhuri, pp. 262-70.

[4] See below, p. 556.

[5] See below, p. 556.

[6] See below, p. 555.

[7] See above, p. 479.

their races ",[1] composed for his royal patron *Kitāb al-Mulūk wa-Akhbār al-Māḍīn* (the book of kings and the history of the ancients), which was still in wide circulation at the time of the historian al-Mas'ūdi [2] (d. 956). Another one of those versed in the "science of origins" (*'ilm al-awā'il*) was Wahb ibn-Munabbih (d. *ca.* 728), a Yamanite Jew who probably professed Islam. One of his works (*al-Tījān*), dealing with the kings of Ḥimyar, has recently been published.

Oratory

Public speaking in its varied forms attained in the Umayyad epoch heights unsurpassed in later times. It was employed by the *khaṭīb* as an instrument of religion in the Friday noon sermons, resorted to by the general as a means for arousing military enthusiasm and depended upon by the governor for instilling patriotic feeling in his subjects. The sermonettes of al-Ḥasan al-Baṣri, delivered in the presence of 'Umar II and partly preserved in the latter's biography,[3] the patriotic speeches of Ziyād ibn-Abīh [4] and the fiery orations of al-Ḥajjāj [5] are among the most prized literary treasures handed down to us from that early age.[6]

Correspondence

Early official correspondence must have been brief, concise and to the point. It was not till the days of the last Umayyads that the flowery, long-drawn-out style was introduced. Ibn-Khallikān [7] ascribes its introduction to the court secretary 'Abd-al-Ḥamīd al-Kātib (i.e. the scribe, d. 750). Its conventional, polite phraseology betrays Persian patterns. Persian literary influence may also be detected in the many early wise sayings and proverbs.

Poetry

The strenuous period of conquest and expansion produced no poet in a nation that had a long tradition of poetry. Nor was Islam favourable to the chief of the Muses.[8] But with the accession of the worldly Umayyads, the old contacts with the goddesses of wine, song and poetry were re-established. The greatest measure of literary progress was then achieved in the field of poetical composition.

[1] *Fihrist*, p. 89, l. 26; Wahb ibn-Munabbih, *al-Tījān fi Mulūk Ḥimyar* (Ḥaydarābād, 1347), pp. 312-13; ibn-Khallikān, vol. ii, p. 365.

[2] Vol. iv, p. 89.

[3] Ibn-al-Jawzi, *Sīrah*, pp. 121-6.

[4] See above, p. 436.

[5] See above, p. 454.

[6] For other specimens consult ibn-Qutaybah, *'Uyūn al-Akhbār*, vol. ii (Cairo, 1928), pp. 231-52; al-Jāḥiẓ, *al-Bayān w-al-Tabyīn*, vol. i (Cairo, 1926), pp. 177 *seq.*, vol. ii (1927), pp. 47 *seq.*; *'Iqd*, vol. ii, pp. 172 *seq.*

[7] Vol. i, p. 350; cf. Mas'ūdi, vol. vi, p. 81.

[8] Koran 26:24-7; 36:69; 69:41.

One of the earliest of Umayyad poets was Ka'b ibn-Ju'ayl (d. *ca.* 705) of the Taghlib tribe, which was then partially Islamized. Though a Moslem, Ka'b takes oaths by the Lord of the Christians and Moslems and holds the readers of the Evangels and the Koran in the same high esteem.[1] In his poetry Christian influence is more apparent than in that of his fellow Taghlibite the Christian al-Akhṭal.

Al-Akhṭal [2] (*ca.* 640–*ca.* 710) was the poetical champion of the Umayyad cause against the theocratic party. He had no hesitancy in satirizing the Companions when requested by Yazīd, whereas Ka'b had.[3] As poet of the court he would enter Mu'āwiyah's palace with a cross dangling from his neck. But Christianity must have sat lightly on the heart of this wine-bibbing, licentious poet who addressed these words to his pregnant wife as she rushed to touch the garment of a passing bishop and succeeded only in reaching the tail of the donkey he was riding: "He and the tail of his ass — there is no difference!" [4]

Al-Akhṭal was one of a trio which dominated the poetical scene of the age. The other two were the vitriolic Jarīr (d. *ca.* 729), court poet of al-Ḥajjāj,[5] and the dissolute al-Farazdaq (640–732), the poet laureate of 'Abd-al-Malik and his sons al-Walīd, Sulaymān [6] and Yazīd. All three poets were satirists as well as panegyrists. In their panegyrics, on which they lived, they performed the same function as that of the party press today. Their satires were often directed against each other. As poets they stand among those with whom Arabic criticism has found none to compare since their time.

Under the Umayyads the poet of love makes his first full appearance. The peninsular school had for its chief exponent 'Umar ibn-abi-Rabī'ah (d. *ca.* 719), prince of Arabic erotic poetry. A Qurayshite,[7] 'Umar specialized in making love to

[1] Khalīl Mardam, "Ka'b ibn-Ju'ayl al-Taghlibi", *Majallat al-Majma' al-'Ilmi al-'Arabi*, vol. xix (1944), pp. 15-24, 104-12.

[2] Two collections of his poems have been published as *Shi'r al-Akhṭal*, ed. A. Ṣāliḥāni (Beirut, 1891, 1905).

[3] Ibn-Qutaybah, *Kitāb al-Shi'r w-al-Shu'arā'*, ed. M. J. de Goeje (Leyden, 1902–4), pp. 301-4.

[4] *Aghāni*, vol. vii, p. 183.

[5] Ibn-Qutaybah, *Shi'r*, p. 287. For other samples of his poetry see his *Dīwān* (Cairo, 1313), vol. i.

[6] Ibn-Qutaybah, *Shi'r*, pp. 297-8. For Farazdaq's eulogies of his patrons see his *Dīwān*, ed. R. Boucher (Paris, 1875), *passim*. Consult also *Aghāni*, vol. viii, pp. 186-97; vol. xix, pp. 2-52; ibn-Khallikān, vol. iii, pp. 136-46.

[7] *Aghāni*, vol. i, p. 32. On his life and works see Jibrā'īl Jabbūr, *'Umar ibn-abi-Rabī'ah*, 2 vols. (Beirut, 1935–9).

beautiful damsels pilgrimaging in the Holy Cities. In language of intense passion and exquisite felicity he immortalized his feeling toward the fair sex.

If 'Umar represented free love in poetry, his contemporary Jamīl al-'Udhri (d. 701) stood for innocent love of the platonic type. His people, the banu-'Udhrah, were a Christian tribe settled in al-Ḥijāz. His verses addressed to Buthaynah, of the same tribe,[1] breathe a spirit of tenderness unmatched in that age. As a representative of the lyric type of poetical composition Jamīl had a rival in the semi-legendary Majnūn Layla [2] (he who is crazy because of Layla, d. *ca.* 699 [3]). Qays ibn-al-Mulawwaḥ, for that is supposedly his name, was infatuated with a woman of the same tribe who reciprocated his love but was forced by her father to marry another. Crazed with despair, Qays passed the rest of his life wandering half naked among the hills and vales of his native Najd singing the beauty of his beloved and yearning for a glimpse of her. Only when her name was mentioned would he return to his senses. Majnūn Layla became the hero of numberless romances, Arabic, Turkish and Persian, extolling the power of undying love.

Besides love poetry political poetry makes its debut at this time. The occasion was the historic nomination of Yazīd to the caliphate,[4] when Miskīn al-Dārimi was requested to compose and publicly recite appropriate verses.[5] This type of poetry culminated in the odes of ibn-Qays al-Ruqayyāt [6] (d. 704) addressed to 'Abd-al-Malik. In this period also the first attempt to compile ancient pre-Islamic poetry was made and that by Ḥammād al-Rāwiyah (i.e. the transmitter, *ca.* 713-72). Of Persian origin, Ḥammād spoke Arabic with an accent. He was one of those famed in Arabic annals for their phenomenal memories. Once, so the story goes, he offered to recite to al-Walīd II — himself a poet [7] — of the pre-Islamic poems alone, rhyming in each of the letters of the alphabet, one hundred different odes for each letter. After listening in person and by

[1] Ibn-Qutaybah, *Shi'r*, pp. 260-68; *Aghāni*, vol. vii, pp. 77-100.
[2] *Aghāni*, vol. i, p. 169, quoted by ibn-Khallikān, vol. i, p. 148.
[3] Al-Kutubi, *Fawāt al-Wafayāt* (Būlāq, 1283), vol. ii, p. 172.
[4] See above, p. 440.
[5] *Aghāni*, vol. xviii, pp. 71-2; cf. ibn-Qutaybah, *Shi'r*, p. 347.
[6] See his *Dīwān*, ed. N. Rhodokanakakis (Vienna, 1902), pp. 67 *seq.*
[7] Consult his *Dīwān*, ed. F. Gabrieli (Damascus, 1937), in which *khamrīyāt* (wine odes) are prominent.

proxy to 2900 odes, the caliph felt satisfied and ordered 100,000 dirhams to the reciter.[1]

The closeness of Umayyad poetry to Islam and to Jāhilīyah poetry endowed it with purity of style, strength of expression and natural dignity that raised it to the position of a model for all generations to come. Its techniques and motifs set the pattern and provided the mould into which the Arabic poet's individual feeling and composition has since been cast. His inability since then to dissociate himself from his literary heritage and produce a composition which belongs to timeless humanity has been well marked. Grammar text-books have always drawn their illustrations mostly from pre-Islamic and Umayyad poetry.

Education

Education of the formal type was not common in those days. The Umayyads sent their young sons to the *bādiyah*,[2] the eastern desert, where they could acquire the pure Bedouin Arabic, practise riding and learn the chase. The precedent was set by Muʿāwiyah, who sent there his son and future successor. The public considered him educated who could read and write, use the bow and arrow and swim. Indeed he was more than educated who mastered these skills; he was *kāmil*, a perfect man.[3] Swimming as an educational ideal must have evolved through life on the Mediterranean coast. The ethical ideals of education, as gleaned from literature, tried to preserve values highly prized in Bedouin life: courage, endurance in face of trouble (*ṣabr*), regard to the rights and obligations of neighbourliness (*jiwār*), manliness (*murū'ah*), generosity, hospitality and fulfilment of solemn promises.

Beginning with the caliphate of ʿAbd-al-Malik the private tutor (*mu'addib*) becomes a standing figure in the court. One of the instructions the tutor of this caliph's sons received from the father was: "Teach them to swim and accustom them to little sleep".[4] ʿUmar II was inclined to resort to corporal punishment in case his children violated the rules of Arabic grammar.[5] The piety of this caliph is reflected in the official instructions he handed to their tutor: "Let the first moral

[1] Ibn-Khallikān, vol. i, p. 292; *Aghāni*, vol. v, pp. 164-5. See *ʿIqd*, vol. iii, pp. 137-8.

[2] See above, p. 440.

[3] Ibn-Saʿd, vol. iii, pt. 2, p. 91, ll. 10-11, cf. vol. v, p. 309, ll. 7 *seq.*; *Aghāni*, vol. vi, p. 165, l. 9.

[4] Mubarrad, p. 77, ll. 6-7.

[5] Yāqūt, *Muʿjam al-Udabā'*, ed. Margoliouth, vol. i (Leyden, 1907), pp. 25-6.

lesson impressed upon them be hatred of means of amusement, whose initiative is from the devil and whose consequence is God's wrath ".[1]

From the rise of Islam the only schools that the masses desirous of education could attend were the mosque schools. These had their curricula centred on the Koran and ḥadīth. Their teachers were Koran readers (*qurrā'*). The Koran readers were thus the earliest teachers in Islam: they are still the only teachers in country and out-of-the way places. 'Umar I as early as 638 sent such teachers in all directions and ordered the people to meet with them in mosques on Fridays. The first man to distinguish himself as teacher in Egypt was a judge sent there in 746 by 'Umar II.[2] In al-Kūfah, al-Ḍaḥḥāk ibn-Muzāḥim (d. 723), mentioned among the tutors of 'Abd-al-Malik's sons,[3] conducted an elementary school (*kuttāb*) where no tuition fees were charged.[4]

Arab science was based on the Greek and had its start with medicine. Moslem regard for medical science is echoed in a tradition ascribed to the Prophet: " Science is twofold: That which relates to religion and that which relates to the body ". Science: medicine

At the Arab conquest of Western Asia, Greek science was no longer a living force. It was rather a tradition in the hands of Greek- or Syriac-writing commentators and practitioners. To this category belonged the physicians of the Umayyads. Outstanding among them were ibn-Uthāl, the Christian doctor of Mu'āwiyah,[5] and Tayādhūq, the Greek doctor of al-Ḥajjāj.[6] A Jewish physician of Persian origin, Māsarjawayh of al-Baṣrah translated in 683, in the days of Marwān ibn-al-Ḥakam, a Syriac medical treatise originally composed in Greek by a Christian priest in Alexandria named Ahrūn.[7] This was the first scientific book in the language of Islam. Marwān's grandson al-Walīd is credited with segregating persons afflicted with leprosy, blindness and other chronic diseases and making special provision for their treat-

[1] Ibn-al-Jawzi, *Sīrah*, pp. 257-8. Consult Jāḥiẓ, *Bayān*, vol. ii, pp. 138-143.

[2] Kindi, *Wulāh*, p. 89; al-Suyūṭi, *Ḥusn al-Muḥāḍarah fi Akhbār Miṣr w-al-Qāhairh* (Cairo, 1321), vol. i, p. 154.

[3] Jāḥiẓ, *Bayān*, vol. i, p. 175.

[4] Ibn-Sa'd, vol. vi, p. 210.

[5] Ibn-abi-Uṣaybi'ah, '*Uyūn al-Anbā' fi Ṭabaqāt al-Aṭibbā'* (Cairo, 1882), vol. i, p. 116.

[6] Ibn-abi-Uṣaybi'ah, vol. i, p. 121.

[7] Ibn-al-'Ibri, p. 192.

ment.[1] This was the first institution for the sick in Islam. ʿUmar II is said to have transferred the schools of medicine from Alexandria, where the Greek tradition flourished, to Antioch and Ḥarrān.[2]

Alchemy

Closely related to medicine was alchemy, one of the earliest disciplines cultivated by Arabs. In it as in medicine the later Arabs made a distinct contribution. Khālid (d. 704 or 708), son of Yazīd I, is credited by legend with being the first scientist and philosopher (*ḥakīm*) of Islam. He, according to the *Fihrist*,[3] was the first to undertake translating Greek and Coptic works on alchemy, medicine and astrology. The element of truth in this allegation is that the Arabs received their earliest impulses and their scientific knowledge from Greek sources. Legend goes on to associate the name of this Umayyad prince with that of Jābir ibn-Ḥayyān (Latinized Geber). Jābir flourished long after this time (*ca.* 776) and will be treated later. Likewise the alchemical and astrological treatises ascribed to Jaʿfar al-Ṣādiq (700–65),[4] one of the twelve Shīʿite imāms, have been proved spurious by modern scholarship.[5]

Schools of thought

The Umayyad period also saw the beginnings of several religio-philosophical movements often referred to as sects. Contact with Christianity in Syria provoked theological speculation that led to the rise of some of these schools. One of them was the Muʿtazilah, a school of rationalism founded in al-Baṣrah by Wāṣil ibn-ʿAṭā' (d. 748). The major doctrine of the Muʿtazilites (seceders) was that he of the Moslems who commits a mortal sin (*kabīrah*) secedes from the ranks of believers but does not thereby become an unbeliever; he then occupies a medial position between the two.[6] A pupil of al-Ḥasan al-Baṣri, who for a time leaned toward this doctrine, Wāṣil made it a cardinal point in Muʿtazilite belief. Another cardinal

[1] Ibn-al-ʿIbri, p. 195; Ṭabari, vol. ii, p. 1196; Maqrīzi, *Khiṭaṭ*, vol. ii, p. 405.

[2] Ibn-abi-Uṣaybiʿah, vol. i, p. 116, ll. 25-6.

[3] Pp. 242, 354. Cf. Julius Ruska, *Arabische Alchemisten*, I. *Chālid Ibn Jazīd Ibn Muʿāwija* (Heidelberg, 1924), pp. 8 *seq.*

[4] *Fihrist*, p. 317, l. 25; ibn-Khallikān, vol. i, p. 300; Ḥājji Khalfah, *Kashf al-Ẓunūn ʿan Asāmi al-Kutub w-al-Funūn*, ed. Fluegel, vol. ii (Leipzig, 1837), pp. 581, 604; vol. iii (London, 1842), pp. 53, 128.

[5] J. Ruska, *Arabische Alchemisten*, II. *Ǧaʿfar Alṣādiq, der sechste Imām* (Heidelberg, 1924), pp. 49-59.

[6] Masʿūdi, vol. vi, p. 22; vii, p. 234; cf. Shahrastāni, p. 33; al-Baghdādi, *Uṣūl al-Dīn* (Istanbul, 1928), vol. i, p. 335; do., *Mukhtaṣar*, p. 98; al-Nawbakhti, *Firaq al-Shīʿah*, ed. H. Ritter (Istanbul, 1931), p. 5.

doctrine was a denial of the co-existence with God of the divine attributes, such as power, wisdom, life, on the ground that such conceptions tend to destroy the unity of God, Islam's basic and most important dogma. Moreover, they weakened the conception of God's omnipotence in favour of the demands of justice. Hence the Mu'tazilites' favourite description of themselves: "the partisans of justice and unity". Their movement attained its height under the 'Abbāsid al-Ma'mūn [1] in Baghdād, which began intellectually where al-Baṣrah and al-Kūfah ended.

The doctrine of free will was at this time held by another group called Qadarites (from *qadar*, power), as opposed to the Jabrites (from *jabr*, compulsion).[2] The Qadarīyah arose as a reaction against the harsh predestination of Islam, a corollary of God's almightiness as stressed in the Koran,[3] and betrays Christian influence. To them man was the author of his own acts. This was the earliest philosophical school in Islam and claimed an extensive membership including two caliphs, Mu'āwiyah II and Yazīd III.[4]

St. John of Damascus

Chief among the agents through whom Christian lore and Greek thought found their way into Islam was St. John of Damascus (*ca.* 676–*ca.* 748). Joannes Damascenus, surnamed Chrysorrhas (golden stream) on account of his oratorical gifts, wrote in Greek but was a Syrian who no doubt spoke Aramaic at home and knew, in addition, Arabic. His debates with Moslems on free will and predestination inaugurated the short-lived movement toward rationalism in Islam.[5] He taught that God created the world and then let it go on with its momentum.[6] John began his career as a boon companion to Mu'āwiyah's son Yazīd and then succeeded to the high position in the government held by his father as councillor. Early in Hishām's caliphate (*ca.* 724) he retired to a life of asceticism and devotion in the monastery of St. Sāba, south-east of Jerusalem.

St. John produced several monumental works [7] chief among which was the *Fountain of Wisdom*, in which he collated and

[1] See below, p. 541.
[2] Cf. al-Īji, *Kitāb al-Mawāqif*, ed. Th. Soerensen (Leipzig, 1848), pp. 334, 362.
[3] Sūrs. 3:25-26; 15:21; 42:26; 43:10.
[4] Cf. ibn-Ḥazm, *al-Fiṣal fi al-Milal w-al-Ahwā' w-al-Niḥal*, vol. iii (Cairo, 1347), p. 31.
[5] See below, p. 541.
[6] See his "Exposition of the Orthodox Faith", in *Nicene and Post-Nicene Fathers*, ser. 2, vol. ix, p. 39.
[7] Migne, *Patrologia Graeca*, vols. xciv-xcvi.

epitomized the ideas of the leading ecclesiastical writers who preceded him. The first *summa theologica* that has come down to us, this work was used by Peter Lombard and Thomas Aquinas and became the standard for the great Scholastics that followed. Many of John's works were translated into Latin; he was regarded as a saint by both the Greek and the Latin Churches. Of special interest to us are the two dialogues between a Christian and a Saracen which he wrote and which emphasize the divinity of Christ and the freedom of human will.[1] The work was intended as an apology for Christianity, a manual for the guidance of Christians in their arguments with Moslems. It was probably based on debates in the caliph's presence in which John himself took part and shows that he was at home in both the Koran and the ḥadīth.[2] As for the story of the ascetic Barlaam and the Hindu prince Josaphat,[3] perhaps the most famous religious romance of the Middle Ages, its ascription to St. John is erroneous. The real author was an obscure monk by the name of John who had lived in St. Sāba a couple of centuries earlier. The story is a Christian version of the life of the Buddha, who under the name of Josaphat (or Iosaph), was, strangely enough, made a saint and canonized by both the Latin and the Greek Churches.

From S. Joannes Damascenus, "Opera", ed. J. Billium (Paris, 1619)

ST. JOHN OF DAMASCUS

[1] Migne, vol. xciv, cols. 1585-98; vol. xcvi, cols. 1335-48.
[2] Cf. above, p. 439.
[3] Migne, vol. xcvi, cols. 857-1250.

One conspicuous activity in St. John's life was his defence of images as an instrument of worship, emphasizing that what is worshipped is not the material of the image but that which is imaged.[1] This was the time when Emperor Leo the Isaurian, perhaps with an eye to currying favour with the Moslems, was making strenuous efforts to suppress icons. John thereby incurred imperial wrath. Shortly before his death he toured Syria fighting the iconoclasts and even visited Constantinople at the risk of his life. Ritual in its varied aspects was of vital significance in his estimation. He himself composed hymns (some of which are still used in Protestant hymnals) which mark the highest attainment of beauty in Church poetry. He was the last of the Greek Fathers. As theologian, orator, apologist, polemicist, codifier of Byzantine art and hymnologist, St. John stands out as an ornament to the body of the Church under the caliphate.

Murji'ites

The Qadarite-Mu'tazilite movement was the first step on the way to weakening universal Moslem orthodoxy. The Murji'ite was the second. The fundamental article of faith in this sect consisted in the suspension (*irjā'*) of judgment against believers who commit sins and in not declaring them infidels.[2] To the Murji'ites works were irrelevant to faith. This doctrine arose in justification of the position of the Umayyad caliphs, who were accused of suppressing the religious law. To the followers of this doctrine the fact that the Umayyads were nominally Moslems sufficed; as the *de facto* political leaders of Islam homage was due them from all. 'Ali as well as Mu'āwiyah were both servants of God and by God alone must they be judged. In the tolerant atmosphere of this school was reared the great divine abu-Ḥanīfah (d. 767), founder of the first of the four orthodox schools of jurisprudence in Islam.[3]

Khārijites

Like the Murji'ite the Khārijite was a religio-political school of thought. It dates from earlier times when certain followers of 'Ali became indignant on his submittal of his claim to the caliphate to arbitration.[4] Once supporters of 'Ali, the Khārijites became his deadly enemies. They aimed at maintaining the

[1] *Nicene and Post-Nicene Fathers*, ser. 2, vol. ix, p. 88.
[2] Cf. Baghdādi, *Mukhtaṣar*, pp. 122-3; ibn-Ḥazm, vol. ii, p. 89.
[3] See below, p. 555.
[4] See above, p. 433.

primitive democratic principles of puritanical Islam and in pursuit of their aim caused rivers of blood to flow in the first three centuries of Islam. They opposed the prerogative conferred on the Quraysh that the caliph should be one of their number,[1] forbade the cult of saints with its attendant local pilgrimages and prohibited Sufi fraternities. Today they survive as Ibāḍites (commonly Abāḍites), after ibn-Ibāḍ [2] of the second half of the first Moslem century, and are scattered in Algeria, Tripolitania, 'Umān and Zanzibar.

The Shī'ah

More important than all these was the Shī'ah, one of the two hostile camps into which early Islam was split on the all-important issue of the caliphate. The other camp was the Sunnite.[3] It was in the Umayyad period that the Shī'ah took its definite form. The differentiating element between Shī'ites (partisans of 'Ali) and Sunnites (orthodox) was the imāmship, successorship to Muḥammad and leadership of Islam. The Shī'ites cling to the belief in 'Ali and 'Ali's sons as the only true imāms with the same persistence with which Catholics cling to the belief in the successorship of Peter. The Prophet made a revelation, the Koran, the intermediary between God and man; the Shī'ites made a person, the imām,[4] the intermediary. To the Sunnite "I believe in Allah the one God" and "I believe in the revelation of the Koran, which is uncreated from eternity", the Shī'ites added another article of faith: "I believe that the imām especially chosen by Allah as the bearer of a part of the divine being is the leader to salvation"

The Sunnite view makes the caliph secular head of the Moslem community, leader of the believers and protector of the faith, but bestows no spiritual authority on him.[5] In opposition to that the Shī'ite view confines the imāmate to the

[1] Ibn-al-Jawzi, *Naqd al-'Ilm w-al-'Ulamā'* (Cairo, 1340), p. 102.

[2] Baghdādi, *Mukhtaṣar*, pp. 87-8; Īji, p. 356; Shahrastāni, p. 100.

[3] From *sunnah*, custom, use; technically the theory and practice of the catholic Moslem community.

[4] Koran 2:118; 15:79; 25:74; 36:11, where the word occurs in its basic, non-technical meaning, he who precedes or leads. It is ordinarily applied to the person who in the canonical services indicates the ritual movements. Originally the Prophet, and after him the caliphs or their delegates, fulfilled this function. Ibn-Khaldūn, *Muqaddamah*, pp. 159-60.

[5] Īji, pp. 296 *seq.*; Māwardi, pp. 23-4; al-Nasafi, *'Umdat 'Aqīdat Ahl al-Sunnah*, ed. W. Cureton (London, 1843), pp. 28-9.

family of ʿAli and makes the imām not only the sole legitimate head of the Moslem society but also the spiritual and religious leader whose authority is derived from a divine ordinance (*naṣṣ*). As such the lineal descendant of Muḥammad through ʿAli and Fāṭimah becomes endowed with a mysterious power transmitted to him by heredity.[1] He then stands above any human being and enjoys impeccability (*ʿiṣmah*). Later Sunnite tradition ascribed in varying degrees immunity from sin and error to the prophets only, especially to Muḥammad.[2] Extremists among Shīʿites went so far as to consider the imām the incarnation of the Deity. The Mahdi hypothesis developed later and held out the expectation of a saviour-leader who would usher in a new era of liberty and prosperity, undoubtedly a reflex of Messianic and allied ideas.

Of all Moslem lands al-ʿIrāq proved to be the most fertile soil for the germination of ʿAlid doctrines. After the beginning of the sixteenth century Persia became the bulwark of Shīʿism. In all there are today some 35,000,000 Shīʿites, about 12 per cent of the Moslem body.[3] In Lebanon and Syria, where they go by the name Matāwilah (i.e. partisans of ʿAli), they number roughly 130,000. Within the Shīʿah itself an almost unlimited number of minor sects arose, including heterodoxies and extremists who are no longer acknowledged as Shīʿites. Like a magnet Shīʿism attracted to itself all sorts of non-conformists and malcontents — economic, social, political and religious. Some of the heterodoxies which arose in early Islam were in reality veiled protests against the victorious religion of the Arabians and gradually gravitated to the bosom of the Shīʿah as the strongest representative of opposition to the established order. The Ismāʿīlites, the Qarmaṭians, the Druzes, the Nuṣayris and the like, with whom we shall deal later, were all historical offshoots of the Shīʿah.

Music

Muḥammad may have looked with disfavour upon music, as he did upon poetry,[4] only because of the association with pagan religious rites. A ḥadīth makes him declare all musical

[1] Shahrastāni, pp. 108-9; Masʿūdi, vol. i, p. 70.
[2] Ibn-Ḥazm, vol. iv, pp. 2-25; Īji, pp. 218 *seq.*; I. Goldziher in *Der Islam*, vol. iii (1912), pp. 238-45.
[3] If Shīʿite heterodoxies, such as Yazīdis, Assassins and ʿAli-Ilāhis, are added the total would reach approximately 45,000,000, 15 per cent of the Moslem body.
[4] Sūr. 26: 224-6.

instruments the devil's muezzin, serving to call men to his worship.[1] Most Moslem legists and theologians frowned on music and musicians, but the masses expressed their view in the adage: " Wine is as the body, music as the soul, and joy is their offspring ".[2]

No sooner had the awe inspired by Islam worn off than male and female professional singers and musicians began to make their appearance. In the Umayyad era Mecca, and more particularly Medina, became a nursery of song and a conservatory of music.[3] They attracted gifted artists from outside and supplied the Damascus court with an ever-increasing stream of talent. The second Umayyad caliph, Yazīd I, himself a composer, introduced singing and musical instruments into the court.[4] It was he who initiated the practice of holding grand festivities in the royal palace which featured wine and song. ʻAbd-al-Malik patronized Saʻīd ibn-Misjaḥ (Musajjaḥ ?, *ca.* 714) of the Ḥijāz school, perhaps the greatest musician of the entire Umayyad age. Saʻīd was a Meccan negro client. He reportedly toured Syria and Persia and put Byzantine and Persian songs into Arabic.[5] In addition, he is credited with the systematization of Arabian musical theory and practice of classical times. Al-Walīd I, the patron of art and architecture, summoned ibn-Surayj (d. *ca.* 726), regarded as one of the four great singers of Islam,[6] and Maʻbad (d. 743), a Medinese mulatto, to the capital, where the caliph received them with great honour. Maʻbad continued to be a court favourite under Yazīd II and al-Walīd II.[7] This Yazīd reinstated poetry and music as an adjunct to royal life after a lapse during the caliphate of the austere and puritanical ʻUmar II. His episodes with the songstresses Ḥabābah and Sallāmah are well known.[8] The licentious al-Walīd II, himself a lute player and song composer, welcomed to his court a host of musician singers.

[1] Consult Nuwayri, *Nihāyah*, vol. iv, pp. 132-5; al-Ghazzāli, *Iḥyā' ʻUlūm al-Dīn* (Cairo, 1334), vol. ii, pp. 238 *seq.*; A. J. Wensinck, *A Handbook of Early Muhammadan Tradition* (Leyden, 1927), p. 173; Henry G. Farmer, *A History of Arabian Music to the Thirteenth Century* (London, 1929), pp. 24-5.

[2] Nawāji, p. 178. Consult Nuwayri, vol. iv, pp. 136 *seq.*

[3] *ʻIqd*, vol. iii, p. 237.

[4] *Aghāni*, vol. xvi, p. 70; cf. Masʻūdi, vol. v, pp. 156-7.

[5] *Aghāni*, vol. iii, p. 84.

[6] *Aghāni*, vol. i, p. 98.

[7] *Aghāni*, vol. ii, pp. 19 *seq.*; Masʻūdi, vol. vi, p. 4

[8] See above, pp. 479-80.

Notes were then known but transmitted by word of mouth from one generation to another. The *Aghānī* is replete with verses set to music in Umayyad days, but not a solitary note has been preserved in it. Hishām bestowed his patronage on an artist from al-Ḥīrah, Ḥunayn by name. So widely spread was the cultivation of musical art under the Umayyads that it provided their rivals, the ʻAbbāsid party, with an effective argument in their propaganda aimed at undermining the house of the " ungodly usurpers ".

Painting

Moslem hostility toward representational art does not manifest itself until early ʻAbbāsid times. It evidently reflects views of converted Jews and a residue of the primitive notion that he who holds the likeness of another is in a position to exercise magical influence on that person.

Most theologians have since ʻAbbāsid days maintained that the representation of animate objects is the prerogative of the deity. Words were put into the mouth of the Prophet to the effect that those to be most severely punished on the judgment day are the *muṣawwirūn*, portrayers (painters and sculptors).[1] Since then no representation of human beings has occurred anywhere on mosques, though it did in a few cases on palaces and in manuscripts. Practically all decorative motifs have been derived from geometry and from the vegetable kingdom.

The frescoes of Quṣayr ʻAmrah, the Transjordanian hunting lodge of al-Walīd I, are the earliest illustrations of Moslem pictorial art. They betray workmanship of Christian painters. The walls depict six royal personages including the caliph himself and his Visigothic adversary Roderick.[2] Other figures are symbolic, representing Victory, Philosophy, History and Poetry. A hunting scene depicts a lion attacking a wild ass. Other pictures portray nude dancers, musicians and merrymakers. Nowhere else have ancient Moslem murals been preserved in such perfect condition.

The recent excavations at Khirbat al-Mafjar,[3] three miles north of Jericho, revealed an elaborate Umayyad winter palace with walls decorated with human and animal motifs. Work-

[1] Al-Bukhāri, *al-Jāmiʻ al-Ṣaḥīḥ* (Būlāq, 1296), vol. vii, p. 61.

[2] See above, p. 464.

[3] Work begun in 1935 by the Palestine Department of Antiquities. Consult " Excavations at Khirbet el Mefjer ", *Quarterly of the Department of Antiquities in Palestine*, vol. v (1936), pp. 132-8; vol. vi (1937), pp. 157-68.

men's graffiti mention the name of Hishām (724–43), leaving no doubt as to the identity of its builder. A statue in the round represents a girl carrying a bouquet of flowers. A panel displays a group of plump dancing girls with lipstick and with finger and

Department of Antiquities, Amman

A MOSAIC FLOOR AT KHIRBAT AL-MAFJAR

A stylized pomegranate tree has two gazelles grazing under it, while a third is attacked by a lion. Brilliantly hued, the mosaic is surrounded by a border which gives it a tapestry-like effect

toe nails painted scarlet. A whole menagerie of birds, rabbits and other animals is exhibited. The art displays an unmistakable ultimate relation to that of the Hellenized Nabataeans The palace was evidently destroyed by earthquake in 746, before its completion.

Palaces in the desert

The Umayyad caliphs, as we learned before,[1] had country places to which they resorted to escape contagious diseases,[2]

[1] P. 440. [2] Ṭabari, vol. ii, p. 1784.

lead rural life and satisfy their nostalgia for the desert. The fringes of the Syrian Desert (al-Bādiyah), especially in its southern part, are strewn with remains of palaces and hunting lodges, either erected by Umayyad architects on Byzantine and Persian patterns or restored by them. Some no doubt were originally Roman fortresses.[1]

'Amrah and al-Mafjar are but two samples of such palaces. Both names, as well as the names of most of the others, are modern, not occurring in classical literature. On account of its extraordinary mural paintings Quṣayr [2] is the best known among them. Built by al-Walīd I between 712 and 715 it was discovered for the learned world in 1898.[3]

Another well-known palace in this region is al-Mushatta (Bedouin pronunciation Mshatta, winter resort),[4] built by al-Walīd II, who was addicted to the chase and less innocent pastimes. The magnificently carved façade of this beautiful chateau is now in a Berlin museum.[5] The newly discovered Khirbat al-Munyah (garden), to the north-west of Lake Tiberias, was also built by this caliph. Two excavated dinars agree in their dating with an inscription which declares him the one who ordered the building.[6] This caliph also occupied al-Qasṭal,[7] about twenty miles south of 'Ammān. Al-Qasṭal is said by an early historian [8] to have been built by the Ghassānid al-Ḥārith ibn-Jabalah.[9] If correct, the palace would be pre-Islamic. Al-Walīd made use of another villa in that neighbourhood, al-Azraq [10] (the blue one). His father Yazīd II either built or restored Muwaqqar,[11] of which few remains are left. Nothing

[1] See above, p. 289.

[2] Diminutive of *qaṣr*, castle; from L. *castrum* through Syriac.

[3] Alois Musil, *Ḳuṣejr 'Amra und andere Schlösser östlich von Moab*, pt. I (Vienna, 1902), pp. 5 *seq.*; do., *Ḳuṣejr 'Amra*, I. *Textband* (Vienna, 1907). Musil thought al-Walīd II built it.

[4] Cf. Musil, *Arabia Deserta*, p. 408; do., *Palmyrena*, p. 279, where he makes this and other palaces summer, rather than winter, resorts.

[5] Consult Brünnow and Domaszewski, *Provincia Arabia*, vol. ii, pp. 105-70; B. Schulz and J. Strzygowski, "Mschatta", *Jahrbuch der Königlich-preuszischen Kunstsammlungen*, vol. xxv (1904), pp. 205-373.

[6] "Khirbat Minya", *Quarterly of the Department of Antiquities in Palestine*, vol. vi (1937), pp. 215-16; vol. vii (1938), pp. 49-51.

[7] From Latin *castellum*, castle, through Syriac. *Yāqūt*, vol. iv, p. 95; Ṭabari, vol. ii, p. 1784.

[8] Ḥamzah al-Iṣfahāni, p. 117.

[9] Cited above. p. 402.

[10] Ṭabari, vol. ii, p. 1743.

[11] Yāqūt, vol. iv, p. 687. Al-Balqā', where Muwaqqar, al-Qasṭal and other structures stood, was the eastern Jordan district comprising Moab.

From B. Moritz, "Bilder aus Palästina, Nord-Arabien und dem Sinai" (Dietrich Reimer Verlag, Berlin)

FAÇADE OF AL-MUSHATTA

is known about Qaṣr al-Ṭūba (Tawbah?), south-east of Muwaqqar.

Farther north on the Bādiyah border lie in ruins other castles, some of which have not yet been studied. Most important among these is Usays [1] (modern Says), lying eighty-

Department of Antiquities, Amman

QUṢAYR 'AMRAH, AN UMMAYYAD HUNTING LODGE IN THE SYRIAN DESERT

three miles east of Damascus. This is a fortified site with an irrigation system dependent on winter rain. It is perhaps the work of al-Walīd I and one of the earliest surviving structures of its kind.

Two other palaces in that region go by the name Ḥayr (Ḥair [2]). Many caliphal residences evidently had walled gardens in which wild game was kept for hunting. Forty miles north-east of Tadmur lies the first of these Ḥayrs dis- Qaṣr al-Ḥayr

[1] Yāqūt, vol. i, p. 271; Musil, *Palmyrena*, p. 282; J. Sauvaget, "Les Ruines omeyyades du Djebel Seis", *Syria*, vol. xx (1939), pp. 239-56.

[2] "Ḥā'ir" in Miskawayh, *Tajārib al-Umam*, ed. D. S. Margoliouth, vol. i (Cairo, 1914), p. 159, l. 15. The word comes from Syriac and means enclosed area. It is related to *ḥīrah*, camp; see above, p. 404.

covered, Qaṣr al-Ḥayr al-Sharqi (the eastern) to distinguish it from al-Gharbi (the western), lying between Tadmur and al-Qaryatayn. Its enclosure is about five miles long and almost a mile wide. Built by Hishām in 729, it has recently been supposed by one scholar to be the Ruṣāfah [1] ascribed to this caliph.[2] Hishām was attached to al-Ruṣāfah, where he died and was buried.[3] The machicolation (*saqqāṭah*), known in Syria in pre-Islam and in Europe at the end of the twelfth century, was employed at this Qaṣr.

About forty miles south-west of Tadmur lies Qaṣr al-Ḥayr al-Gharbi, built in 727 by the same caliph, as an extant inscription declares. It was evidently the residence of Hishām before he moved to al-Ruṣāfah. This al-Ḥayr may have been al-Zaytūnah of Arab historians,[4] originally a Byzantine or Roman castle. Its remarkable decorations include statues of two women at the entrance which reflect Palmyrene art. Among the pictures are two songstresses, one of whom is using a five-stringed lute.[5]

The decorations of this Qaṣr, now in the Syrian National Museum at Damascus, fill a gap between the Byzantine and the Islamic art. They combine and harmonize Sāsānid, Byzantine and Syrian elements. The motifs begun here were carried into al-Maghrib and developed to their highest possibilities in Cordova and Granada. The ʿAbbāsids followed the Umayyads in building Ḥayr gardens. Their temporary capital Sāmarra had one described by the geographer al-Yaʿqūbi,[6] who says that it held " wild animals : gazelles, wild asses, deer, hares and ostriches kept in by an enclosing wall in a fine open tract ". The Romans showed no interest in zoological gardens till the imperial period, which suggests Eastern influence.[7]

[1] See above, p. 391.

[2] J. Sauvaget in *Bulletin d'études orientales*, vol. v (1935), pp. 136-7 ; do., " Remarques sur les monuments omeyyades ", *Journal asiatique*, vol. ccxxxi (1939), pp. 1-13. For more on this structure consult Henri Seyrig, *Antiquités syriennes*, ser. 1 (1934), pp. 1-3 ; ser. 2 (1938), pp. 1-9 ; K. A. C. Creswell, *Early Muslim Architecture*, pt. 1 (Oxford, 1932), p. 330.

[3] Ṭabari, vol. ii, p. 1729.

[4] Ṭabari, vol. ii, p. 1467.

[5] This would discredit the ascription of the fifth string to the celebrated Ziryāb, who died *ca.* 852 ; see Hitti, *History of the Arabs*, p. 598.

[6] *Buldān*, p. 263.

[7] For more on this palace consult D. Schlumberger, " Les Fouilles de Qasr el-Heir el-Gharbi ", *Syria*, vol. xx (1939), pp. 195-238, 324-73 ; Jaʿfar al-Ḥasani, " Qaṣr al-Ḥayr ", *Majallat al-Majmaʿ al-ʿIlmi al-ʿArabi*, vol. viii (1941), pp. 337-45.

The Caliph Sulaymān (715–17) took up his residence in a city which he built, al-Ramlah in Palestine. This is the only town established by the Arabs in Syria.[1] Traces of the caliphal palace could be seen there until the early twentieth century and the minaret of his White Mosque, as rebuilt by the Mamlūks, is still standing. This mosque, after the Umayyad Mosque of Damascus and the Dome of the Rock in Jerusalem, became the third leading sanctuary of Syria.

Mosques: the Dome of the Rock

For fully half a century after the conquest of Syria Moslems worshipped in converted churches and erected no special mosques. In Damascus they divided not the church itself, as tradition states, but the sacred enclosure. Damascene worshippers entered through the same gate; the Christians turned left and the Moslems right.[2] At the occupation of Ḥamāh its church, styled "the greater" by a local historian,[3] was converted into the Great Mosque (*al-Jāmi' al-Kabīr*). The east and west façades of the church are still intact.[4] Likewise the Great Mosque of Ḥimṣ [5] and that of Aleppo [6] were originally Christian places of worship. Christian relics and Roman columns are still visible in the Ḥimṣ sanctuary.

First among the mosques built in Syria was the Dome of the Rock [7] (Qubbat al-Ṣakhrah) in Jerusalem. The Dome was erected by 'Abd-al-Malik in 691 on a site which once held the Temple of Solomon and represents the earliest Moslem monument surviving. To the right of the Rock Muḥammad halted on his nocturnal journey and thence he was translated heavenward on his miraculous mount.[8] As the Prophet's halting station and the first *qiblah* in Islam (the point toward which the first believers turned in prayer), Jerusalem acquired early sanctity in Moslem eyes. Then there were weighty political considerations. The Umayyads aimed at a sumptuous place of worship to divert the current of Syrian pilgrimage from Mecca, then in an anti-caliph's hands,[9] and to outshine the Church of

[1] *Al-'Uyūn w-al-Ḥadā'iq fi Akhbār al-Ḥaqā'iq*, ed. T. G. J. Juynboll (Leyden, 1853), p. 40.

[2] Creswell, pt. 1, p. 134.

[3] Abu-al-Fidā', vol. i, p. 168.

[4] Creswell, p. 14.

[5] Balādhuri, p. 131; Maqdisi, p. 156.

[6] Balādhuri, pp. 146-7.

[7] Wrongly called by Europeans the Mosque of 'Umar, who in 638 on visiting Jerusalem (see above, p. 418) may have erected a simple place of worship of timber or brick.

[8] Hitti, *History of the Arabs*, p. 114.

[9] Ya'qūbi, vol. ii, p. 311; see above, pp. 452-3.

the Holy Sepulchre and Christian cathedrals of Syria.[1] To this end ʿAbd-al-Malik employed native architects and artisans trained in the Byzantine school. The edifice was modelled after that of the cathedral of Buṣra.[2] Its bronze doors, decorated with incrustation in silver, a distinguished achievement of Byzantine artists, are among the oldest dated ones of their

From C. A. Raven, "Palestine in Pictures" (Cambridge)

THE DOME OF THE ROCK AND THE DOME OF THE CHAIN

kind. Qāshāni and mosaic decoration was lavishly used in the original structure and later in its renovation. Qāshāni involves the use of square or hexagonal glazed tiles, sometimes figured with floral or geometrical designs, and goes back to Persian origin as the name indicates.[3] The mosaic technique can be traced to Babylonian days. ʿAbd-al-Malik left a Kufic inscription around the inside of the dome which represents one of the oldest Islamic writings extant. About a century and a quarter later the structure underwent restoration by the ʿAbbāsid al-

[1] Maqdisi, p. 159.

[2] Dussaud, *Syrie antique*, p. 10; cf. M. S. Briggs, *Muhammadan Architecture in Egypt and Palestine* (Oxford, 1924), p. 37.

[3] Kāshān, a city in Media; Yāqūt, *Buldān*, vol. iv, p. 15.

Ma'mūn, who unscrupulously substituted his own name for that of 'Abd-al-Malik's but fortunately failed to change the date.[1]

East of this edifice stands an elegant little cupola called Qubbat al-Silsilah (dome of the chain), which served as a treasure house (*bayt al-māl*) of the Rock. Its structure and decoration belong to the same period. To make the place inviolable Moslem tradition manufactured a chain which Solomon stretched across and which a truthful witness could grasp without producing any effect on the chain, but not a perjurer.

The Aqṣa Mosque

Close to the Dome 'Abd-al-Malik erected another mosque, the Aqṣa,[2] of which the Dome is in reality the shrine. In local usage al-Masjid [3] al-Aqṣa includes the entire sacred area of some thirty-four acres with its dervish monasteries (sing. *takīyah*, *zāwiyah*) and public fountains (sing. *sabīl*), some of which were built later by Mamlūk and Ottoman sultans. Al-Ḥaram al-Sharīf (the noble sanctuary) is another designation for this area, where once stood a Jewish temple, a Christian church and a heathen (Roman) sanctuary, making it one of the most hallowed places on the surface of the earth. On the site of al-Aqṣa there was a church dedicated to St. Mary by Justinian; its ruins were utilized in the construction of the mosque. Rebuilt by the 'Abbāsid al-Manṣūr, following an earthquake, the Aqṣa was modified by the Crusaders and restored to Islam in 1187 by Ṣalāḥ-al-Dīn (Saladin).

The Umayyad Mosque

Next in chronology and importance was the Umayyad Mosque of Damascus. It was not until 705 that 'Abd-al-Malik's son al-Walīd seized from his Christian subjects the Cathedral of St. John the Baptist and converted it into this mosque,[4] one of the sublimest places of worship in the world. After the three Ḥarams of Mecca, Medina and Jerusalem, the

[1] Following is a literal translation: HATH BUILT THIS DOME THE SERVANT OF GOD 'ABD[ULLĀH AL-IMĀM AL-MA'MŪN CO]MMANDER OF THE BELIEVERS IN THE YEAR TWO AND SEVENTY.—MAY GOD ACCEPT OF HIM AND FAVOUR HIM! AMEN.

[2] "The farther mosque", from a supposed reference in the Koran (17:1) to the site. It was this passage that gave rise to the story of Muḥammad's nocturnal journey. According to *Fakhri*, p. 173, al-Walīd was the builder. For the earliest description consult ibn-al-Faqīh, pp. 100-101, written *ca.* 903, and Maqdisi, pp. 169-171, *ca.* 985.

[3] "Place of bowing down", whence "mosque" through Italian and French.

[4] Ibn-'Asākir, vol. i, p. 200; abu-al-Fidā', vol. i, pp. 209-10.

Umayyad Mosque is still considered the fourth holiest place in Islam. The cathedral stood on the site of a temple consecrated

From J. Sauvaget, J. Weulersse and M. M. L. Écochard "Damas et la Syrie Sud" (Damascus)

THE UMAYYAD MOSQUE OF DAMASCUS

to Jupiter Damascenus, originally the Syrian Hadad,[1] and modelled after the temple of the Sun at Palmyra. To justify

[1] See above, p. 172.

the seizure by the Moslems, who until then had shared with its Christian owners a part of the temenos, tradition claimed that at the time of conquest the two contingents led respectively by Khālid and abu-'Ubaydah [1] entered the city simultaneously, one coming from the east by force and the other from the west by capitulation, and met unknowingly in the middle of the cathedral. The resting-place of the head of St. John is still shown under a richly gilded dome in the mosque. Another Christian relic is a Greek inscription over the lintel of the southern portal of the enclosure: "Thy kingdom, O Christ, is an everlasting kingdom, and Thy dominion endureth throughout all generations".[2]

For seven years, we are told, al-Walīd pursued the project, expending on it the entire land revenue from Syria.[3] Not satisfied with local talent he drafted Persian and Indian craftsmen and requested a hundred Greek artisans from the Byzantine emperor.[4] Multicoloured mosaics and rare marbles adorned its upper walls and ceiling. Murals of gold and precious stones representing trees and cities, and witnessed by the Syrian geographer al-Maqdisi,[5] were plastered later by some pious ruler, to be rediscovered in 1928.[6] A comparative study of the decorations reveals native Syrian, rather than Greek Byzantine, workmanship.

On the north side of the mosque al-Walīd constructed a minaret [7] which was used as a beacon tower and became a model for similar structures in Syria, North Africa and Spain, to which it was introduced by 'Abd-al-Raḥmān I. This is the oldest purely Moslem minaret still standing. The two minarets on the south side stand on earlier church towers.[8] Al-Ghazzāli (d. 1111) tells us that he isolated himself in the north minaret

[1] See above, p. 414.

[2] Cf. Ps. 145 : 13; Heb. 1 : 8.

[3] Maqdisi, p. 158; cf. *al-'Uyūn w-al-Ḥadā'iq*, p. 7.

[4] Ibn-'Asākir, vol. i, p. 202; *al-'Uyūn* raises the figure to 100,000, of whom some were used in Mecca and Medina. Cf. Ṭabari, vol. ii, p. 1194; abu-al-Fidā', vol. i, p. 210; ibn-Jubayr, p. 261.

[5] P. 157; cf. Iṣṭakhri, p. 57; ibn-Rustah, p. 326; *al-'Uyūn*, pp. 8-9.

[6] E. de Lorey and M. van Berchem, *Les Mosaïques de la mosquée des Omayyades à Damas* (Paris, 1930); Creswell, pp. 119-20.

[7] From Arabic *manārah*, lighthouse; also called *ṣawma'ah* (ibn-'Asākir, vol. i, p. 200), monk's cell; *mi'dhanah*, place from which the muezzin calls to prayer, came later into general use.

[8] Cf. Yāqūt, vol. ii, p. 593.

for daily contemplation and devotion.[1] The Syrian type of minaret, a plain square structure, is clearly descended from the watch or church tower. The slender, tapering, round style, reminiscent of classical Roman columns, was a later adoption by the Turks, who introduced it into Syria as exemplified in the Mosque of Khālid at Ḥimṣ.

The Damascus mosque enjoys the further distinction of being the first one in which the semicircular niche for prayer (*miḥrāb*) appears. In it the horseshoe arch is also evident. Burned in 1069 and again in 1400 (by Tamerlane) and for the last time in 1893, the edifice still holds its place in Moslem eyes as the fourth wonder of the world.[2]

Al-Walīd, greatest among Umayyad builders, was also responsible for rebuilding the Mosque of Medina, enlarging and beautifying that of Mecca, erecting in Syria a number of schools, hospitals [3] and places of worship and for removing a dome of gilded brass from a church in Ba'labakk to the mosque built by his father in Jerusalem. In his reign, peaceful and opulent, whenever people in Damascus got together fine buildings formed the chief topic of conversation.[4]

In the palaces and mosques left by the Umayyads the harmonization of Arabian, Persian, Syrian and Greek elements is accomplished and the resultant synthesis called Moslem art makes its start. The Arabian element is endless repetition of small units to which one could add or from which he could subtract without materially affecting the whole. The columns of the Cordova Mosque illustrate the point. The motif suggests the monotony of the desert, the seemingly endless rows of trunks of date palms in an oasis or the legs of a caravan of camels. The Persians contributed delicacy, elegance, multicolour. In Umayyad Syria the ancient Semitic and the intruding Greek elements and motifs were reconciled and pressed into the permanent service of Islam.

[1] Al-Ghazzāli, *al-Munqidh min al-Ḍalāl* (Cairo, 1936), p. 27; cf. ibn-Khallikān, vol. ii, p. 246.

[2] Ibn-al-Faqīh, p. 106; ibn-'Asākir, vol. i, p. 198; Yāqūt, vol. ii, p. 591.

[3] See above, pp. 497-8.

[4] Ṭabari, vol. ii, pp. 1272-3.

CHAPTER XXXIX

THE SYRIAN CHRISTIAN CHURCH

The East Syrian Church

BEFORE the rise of Islam the Syrian (*Suryānī*) Christian Church had split into several communities. There was first the East Syrian Church or the Church of the East. This communion, established in the late second century, claims uninterrupted descent in its teachings, liturgy, consecration and tradition from the time the Edessene King Abgar allegedly wrote to Christ asking him to relieve him of an incurable disease and Christ promised to send him one of his disciples after his ascension.[1] This is the church erroneously called Nestorian, after the Cilician Nestorius,[2] whom it antedates by about two and a half centuries. The term Nestorian was applied to it at a late date by Roman Catholics to convey the stigma of heresy in contradistinction to those of its members who joined the Catholic Church as Uniats and received the name Chaldaeans. The first patriarch of the Chaldaean rite was the metropolitan of Diyār Bakr consecrated in 1681.

With its God-and-man doctrine of Christology,[3] its protest against the deification of the Virgin Mary and its unusual vitality and missionary zeal, this Church at the rise of Islam was the most potent factor in Syrian culture which had impressed itself upon the Near East from Egypt to Persia. Members of this community from the fourth century onward had studied and translated Greek philosophical works and spread them throughout Syria and Mesopotamia. From Edessa the Church extended eastward into Persia. Toward the end of the fifth century the bishop of the Sāsānid capital Seleucia-Ctesiphon declared himself patriarch of the Eastern Church. In 762,

[1] For copies of the correspondence consult Sa'īd ibn-Baṭrīq (Eutychius), *al-Ta'rīkh al-Majmū' 'ala al-Taḥqīq w-al-Taṣdīq* (Beirut, 1909), pp. 263-4.

[2] For more on him consult Assemani (al-Sam'āni), *Bibliotheca Orientalis*, vol. iii, pt. 1 (Rome, 1725), pp. 35-7 ; see above, p. 371.

[3] In contrast to the orthodox doctrine which held that while in Christ two natures existed, these were moulded into one person ; cf. above, pp. 371-2.

when Baghdād was founded, the patriarchate moved to the ʿAbbāsid capital, where it enjoyed caliphal favour. Even under Islam this Church had an unparalleled record of missionary activity. Sepulchral and other evidences attest the existence of Syrian churches in Marw, Harāt (Herat), Samarqand and other places of Central Asia going back to the mid-sixth century.

About the same time missionaries of this " Protestantism of the East " had penetrated south to India, where Christianity had struck root a couple of centuries earlier. Syrian churches arose on the west coast of India, especially Malabar, and in Ceylon. Members of the Syrian rite in India acquired the name " Christians of St. Thomas ", after the apostle whom unreliable tradition makes the first teacher of Christianity in India. Christian immigrants from Baghdād and other Moslem cities reinforced in the eighth and ninth centuries this community, whose fame spread to the West, resulting in an embassy which King Alfred of England sent to that distant land.

But the crowning missionary achievement was in the Far East. In the seventh to the ninth centuries, and again in the twelfth and fourteenth, Syrian monks penetrated to China. The first missionaries arrived at Sian Fu in 635, when the Moslem army was conquering Persia. A stele commemorating in Chinese and Syriac the names and labours of sixty-seven missionaries was erected " on the seventh of the first month of 781 of the Christian era " and now stands in that city.[1] Not far from this place a Nestorian monastery, now a Taoist temple, can still be seen. After an existence of over seven hundred years (635–1367) this Syrian Church in China, cut off from a mother which because of Islam was becoming too weak to reinforce it, was swallowed up by local cults, Taoist sects and Moslem communities. It lives in the Chinese records as the " luminous religion ".[2] Its cultural traces are still visible in the Syriac characters in which Mongol and Manchu were written [3] and in the technique and decoration of bookbinding in Turkestan, which are related to the style used by the Copts in Egypt and were presumably transmitted by these Syrian Christians.[4]

[1] P. Y. Saeki, *The Nestorian Documents and Relics in China* (Tokyo, 1937), pp. 35, 68.

[2] Saeki, pp. 65, l. 15, 457, l. 7 ; cf. 449, l. 10.

[3] See above, p. 371.

[4] Mehmet Aga-Oglu, *Persian Bookbindings of the Fifteenth Century* (Ann Arbor, 1935), p. 1. For more on the Nestorians consult Assemani, vol. iii, pt. 2.

The East Syrian Church was represented at the beginning of the first world war by 190,000 members domiciled around Urmiyah, al-Mawṣil (Mosul) and Central Kurdistan.[1] Those who survived have since drifted into al-ʿIrāq and Syria. As an ethnic group they would rather be called Assyrians, an appellation that does not seem inappropriate when the physical features of many of them are compared with the Assyrian type as portrayed on the monuments.

From P. Y. Saeki, "The Nestorian Documents and Relics in China" (Tokyo)

THE SYRIAN MONUMENTAL COLUMN IN SIAN FU, DATED A.D. 781

THE SYRIAC AND CHINESE INSCRIPTIONS ON THE LOWER PART OF THE MONUMENT

The West Syrian Church

The western branch of the Syrian Church, with its God-man Christology[2] and its exaltation of the Virgin to celestial rank, was comparatively lacking in missionary endeavour. Its theology was Monophysite, giving prominence to the unity of Christ at the expense of the human element. In Syria the Monophysite communion was called by hostile Greeks Jacobite after Jacob

[1] A. Yuhanan, *The Death of a Nation* (New York, 1916), pp. 8-9.

[2] Cf. above, p. 371.

Baradaeus, bishop of Edessa in the mid-sixth century.[1] The Ghassān and other Syrian Arabs adopted this creed before the advent of Islam.[2] The so-called Jacobite Church was preponderant in Syria as the miscalled Nestorian was preponderant in Persia. Syriac [3] was and has remained the language of both Churches ; but Greek was also taught in the cloisters, and the Jacobites seconded the efforts made by the Nestorians in transmitting Greek thought to Syria and then to Islam. Qinnasrīn was a great centre in North Syria for disseminating Monophysite doctrine and Greek knowledge. Jacobite scholars were depositories of whatever sciences were cultivated or transmitted in those days.

Some two hundred thousand communicants of this venerable Church survived until the early twentieth century in the neighbourhood of Mārdīn, Diyār Bakr and Armenia.[4] Since then they have been decimated, the remnant taking refuge in Syria and Lebanon. The patriarchate has its present seat at Ḥimṣ. They object to the term Jacobite, to which they prefer the designation Orthodox or Old Syrians (*Suryān*). Those of them who in recent times adopted the Roman Catholic rite form the Syrian Catholic Church with its patriarchal seat in Lebanon. This is a Uniat offshoot corresponding to the Chaldaean.

Besides the Jacobite Church of Syria, the Armenian Church and the Coptic-Ethiopic Church are independent descendants of the Monophysite rite. The triumph of the Church of the Syrians over those of Armenia, Egypt and Ethiopia was another conspicuous achievement of Syrian society and culture. With all their interest in Greek learning the two sister Syrian Churches of the East and of the West, be it remembered, arose and developed as a reaction of the Syrian society against the Hellenizing influences of Byzantium and Rome. Treated as " heresies " by these two Christian capitals, both Jacobitism and Nestorianism were basically protests against foreign intrusion and against the process of syncretism that was turning Christianity, a Syrian religion, into a Greco-Roman institution.

[1] See above, pp. 371-2. Assemani devotes most of his *Bibliotheca Orientalis*, vol. ii, to a study of the Monophysites and Jacobites.

[2] See above, p. 403.

[3] This term after the Aramaeans were Christianized was considered by them preferable to the term Aramaic. See above, pp. 170-71.

[4] Yuhanan, p. 9.

Both Churches " survive today as fossils of an extinct Syriac society ".[1]

The Maronites

Another offshoot of the ancient Church of Syria was the Maronite, which owes its origin to its patron saint Mārūn (Maron, Maro [2]). An ascetic monk about whose life not much is known, Mārūn lived between Antioch and Qūrus (Qūrush, Cyrrhus), where he died about 410. He is presumably the " Maron, the monk priest " to whom John Chrysostom on his way to exile addressed an epistle soliciting his prayers and news.[3] After his death, so tradition asserts, Mārūn's disciples carried his remains to a place near Apamea (Afāmiyah) on the Orontes, where a monastery was erected in his memory. Conflict with Jacobites led to a massacre in this monastery of three hundred and fifty monks, whose memory is still celebrated in the Maronite calendar. Lebanon offered a better refuge and the new sect struck root in its northern soil. There the amalgamation took place with the Mardaites, who had also filtered from the north.[4]

If Mārūn was the saint of the new sect, Yūḥanna Mārūn (Joannes Maro, d. *ca.* 707) was the hero and founder of the new nation. He is probably the Mārūn from whom the congregation received its name. Born at Sarūm, near Antioch, Yūḥanna studied Syriac and Greek in Antioch before joining the monastery on the Orontes. He pursued his studies in Constantinople and was consecrated bishop of al-Batrūn in Lebanon. His headquarters were first in Samār Jubayl and later in Kafarḥayy, where he established a monastery and was buried. Under him the Maronite community developed into an autonomous nation which with one arm kept the Moslem caliph [5] at a distance and with the other the Byzantine emperor. When in 694 Justinian II desired to subdue the Maronites, his troops, after destroying the monastery on the Orontes, were routed by Yūḥanna at Amyūn.[6] Since then the Maronites have isolated themselves and developed the kind of individualism that characterizes mountaineers. For a time Qannūbīn,[7] carved in

[1] Toynbee, vol. v, p. 127. [2] From Syriac meaning " the small lord "

[3] For Arabic translation consult al-Duwayhi, *Ta'rīkh al-Ṭā'ifah al-Mārūnīyah*, (Beirut, 1890), pp. 19-20. [4] See above, p. 448. [5] See above, p. 449.

[6] For more on him see Assemani, vol. i, pp. 496-520.

[7] Syr. from Gr. for monastery; one of the few Greek place names surviving in Lebanon.

the solid rock of rugged Lebanon, provided a seat for the Maronite patriarchate, which has since moved into Bakirki in the neighbourhood of Beirut.

The Maronite leaders of the mid-seventh century were friendly with the Emperor Heraclius, and the entire sect has been charged with espousing his Monothelite cause.[1] Sa'īd ibn-Baṭrīq (fl. *ca.* 931) was one of the first to make this assertion.[2] His Moslem contemporary al-Mas'ūdi [3] held the same views. Sa'īd was followed by William of Tyre,[4] historian of the Crusades, who states that "the heresy of Maro and his followers is and was that in our Lord Jesus Christ there exists, and did exist from the beginning, one will and one energy only". William estimates their number at forty thousand and goes on to say that in 1180 they repudiated their heresies and returned to the Catholic Church; but Maronite apologists, beginning with al-Duwayhi [5] (d. 1704) and ibn-Namrūn [6] (d. 1711), have claimed continued orthodoxy for their Church throughout the ages.[7] A modern Maronite author [8] claims that there was another Maron, a Monothelite of Edessa, who died about 580 and whose followers these authors confused with the Lebanese Maronites. There is no doubt that in this period of the Crusades the Maronites attracted the attention of Rome but union was not effected till the eighteenth century. Their Church, which may be considered the national Church of Lebanon, has retained till the present day its Syriac liturgy and non-celibate priesthood and Rome has failed to include in its list of saints either of its reputed eponymous founders. The 1942 census gives the number of Maronites in Lebanon as 318,211, more than any other religious body in that republic. Recent Maronite emigrants have carried their rite into Italy, France, North and South America, Australia and other parts of the civilized world.

The Melkites

The East and the West Syrian Churches with their ramifica-

[1] See above, p. 417. [2] Ibn-Baṭrīq, p. 12. [3] *Tanbīh*, p. 154.

[4] *History*, tr. Emily A. Babcock and A. C. Krey, vol. ii, p. 459.

[5] Pp. 292 *seq.*

[6] Fausto (Murhij) Naironi, *Dissertatio de origine, nomine, ac religione Maronitharum* (Rome, 1679).

[7] Among the recent apologists Afrām al-Dayrāni, *al-Muḥāmāh 'an al-Mawārinah wa-Qiddīsīhim* (Beirut, 1899); Yūsuf al-Dibs, *Ta'rīkh Sūrīyah*, vol. v (Beirut, 1900), pp. 156 *seq.*

[8] Bernard G. al-Ghazīri, *Rome et l'Église syrienne-maronite* (Paris, 1906), pp. 31-3, 44-5.

tions did not comprise all Syrian Christians. There remained a small body which succumbed under the impact of Greek theology from Antioch and Constantinople and accepted the decrees of the Council of Chalcedon (451). Thereby this community secured orthodoxy and not only escaped excommunication but obtained protection, even patronage, from the state church and the imperial city. By way of reproach their opponents centuries later nicknamed them Melkites,[1] royalists. Melkite ranks must have been recruited mainly from city-dwellers and descendants of Greek colonists. Gradually Greek replaced Syriac as the language of ritual and the Syriac liturgy gave place to the Byzantine. Hundreds of manuscripts in European and Oriental libraries indicate that the victory of Greek was not complete till the early seventeenth century.[2] Though supported by the ruling state the Melkite community remained comparatively weak and was confined to North Syria, Palestine and Egypt. Their Syrian descendants maintain one patriarchate in Damascus and another in Jerusalem and are now known as Greek Orthodox.[3]

In recent years, strangely enough, "Melkite" has been exclusively employed to designate Christians drawn from the Orthodox Church and attached to Rome. They, however, claim old and uninterrupted communion with the Roman Catholic Church. At present they number about one-half of the Orthodox community estimated at about 230,000. Their patriarch maintains a residence in Egypt and another in Lebanon. The majority of the Greek Catholics and of the Greek Orthodox live in Syria, rather than in Lebanon.

Inter-action with Islam

To the Syrian Christian, infant Islam could not have appeared as entirely alien or exotic; in fact it must have appeared more like a new Judaeo-Christian sect than a new religion. In general, Islam's hostility to Christianity was one of rivalry rather than of conflicting ideology. Writing immediately after the conquest, a patriarch of the Eastern Church[4] describes the new masters in the following glowing terms: "The Arabs, to whom God at this time has granted dominion

[1] Less corectly Melchites, from Syr. *malka*, king.

[2] Isḥāq Armalah, *al-Malakīyūn: Baṭriyarkīyatuhum al-Anṭākīyah* (Beirut, 1936), pp. 102, 104-15; Ḥabīb al-Zayyāt in *al-Mashriq*, vol. xxxvii (1939), p. 174.

[3] For a list of the patriarchs consult Armalah, pp. 26 *seq.*

[4] Išo'yahb III, "Liber epistularum", in *Scriptores Syri*, ser. II, vol. lxiv, ed. Rubens Duval (Paris, 1904–5), text p. 251, ll. 13-19, cf. p. 252, ll. 8-12, tr. p. 182.

over the world, are, as you know, among us. But they are not enemies of Christianity. On the contrary they praise our faith and honour the priests and saints of the Lord and confer benefits upon the churches and monasteries." Certain Orientalists [1] go as far as making Islam in many respects an heir of Syrian Christianity. John of Damascus regarded Muḥammad as a heretic rather than the founder of a new faith and confounded Islam with Arianism, which discounted the divinity of Christ.[2] John tells his Moslem opponents, "When you call us associators (*mushrikūn*), we call you mutilators", and asks why should Christians be blamed for bowing before the cross when the Moslems do the same before the Black Stone. So supercilious an attitude was no doubt encouraged by his being a cleric writing in a foreign tongue. 'Umar II evidently considered it easy to convert Leo the Isaurian by addressing a theological epistle to him, which the emperor attempted to refute by correspondence.[3]

The oneness of God and the last judgment were favourite themes equally in koranic literature and in the Apocryphal gospels and ascetic writings.[4] St. Ephraim (d. *ca.* 373), revered by both branches of the Syrian Church as the greatest preacher they produced, depicts the abode of bliss in these materialistic colours :

> I witnessed the dwelling places of the just and the just themselves, dripping with ointments, giving forth pleasant odours, wreathed in flowers and adorned with fruits. . . . When the just lie at the table, the trees offer them shade in the clear air. Flowers grow beneath them and fruits above. . . . Swift winds stand before the blessed, ready to do their will. One of the winds wafts appeasement, another causes drink to flow. One wind is filled with oil, another with ointment. . . . Whoever has abstained from wine on earth, for him do the vines of Paradise yearn. Each one of the trees holds out to him a bunch of grapes. And if a man has lived in chastity, females receive him in a pure bosom.[5]

[1] E.g. Carl H. Becker, *Islamstudien*, vol. i (Leipzig, 1924), pp. 16-18, 386 *seq.*

[2] Migne, *Patrologia Graeca*, vol. xciv, cols. 763-74. See above, p. 371.

[3] Theophanes, *Chronographia*, p. 399; Maḥbūb (Agapius of Manbij), "Kitāb al-'Unwān", in *Patrologia Orientalis*, vol. viii (Paris, 1912), p. 503.

[4] Consult William Wright, *Apocryphal Acts of the Apostles*, 2 vols. (London, 1871).

[5] Sancti Ephraem Syri, *Opera omnia* (Rome, 1743), p. 563; cf. Tor Andrae, tr. Theophil Menzil, *Mohammed: the Man and his Faith* (New York, 1936); Koran 88:4-16; 55:46-78.

The distinction between obligatory and supererogatory works was common to both religions. In the practice of ritual and adoration there were many resemblances. The Syrian Church had recognized three canonical prayers in the daytime and two at night long before the five Moslem prayers were instituted. Night vigils described in the Koran (73 : 1-8, 20) recall monastic practice and ascetic piety. Monks observed fixed bodily postures in time of prayer, involving genuflections and touching the ground with the forehead. The hair of the head of a monk fell off in front from the number of times he hit it on the ground in supplication.[1] A pre-Islamic poem describes a monk with a callous on the forehead comparable to that on a goat's knee.[2]

As Christians turned Moslem, they naturally carried over with them old ideas and practices, some of which were perpetuated in the sects and heterodoxies. The gap was further bridged as early narrators of ḥadīth borrowed events from the life of the founders of Christianity and ascribed them to the founder of Islam. Muḥammad is reported to have commended " him who gives alms only in secret, so that his left hand knows not what his right hand does " [3] and proclaimed that God said : " I have prepared for my righteous servants what eye hath not seen, nor ear heard, nor hath it entered into the heart of man ".[4] Even a version of the Lord's Prayer is put in Muḥammad's mouth.[5] Through the Sufi institution of later days Christian ascetic piety opened another channel into the heart of Islam.

The Syriac-speaking Christian readily recognized many key words in Islamic vocabulary. Arabic *furqān* (salvation,[6] Koran 8 : 29, 42), *āyah* (sign, 2 : 37 ; 3 : 9), *kāhin* (soothsayer, priest, 52 : 29 ; 69 : 42), *sujūd* (prostration, 2 : 19 ; 68 : 42, 43), *sifr* (book, 62 : 5), *qissīs* [7] (monk, 5 : 85), *ṣalāh* (ritual prayer, 2 : 2, 40 ; 24 : 57), *zakāh* (alms, 2 : 40, 77, 104) and many others were loan words from Syriac or Aramaic.[8] Many other church and ecclesiastical terms from Syriac were Arabicized, as illustrated Loan words

[1] John of Ephesus in *Patrologia Orientalis*, vol. xvii, p. 40.
[2] L. Cheikho, *al-Naṣrānīyah wa-Ādābuha* (Beirut, 1919), p. 178.
[3] Cf. Matt. 6 : 3-4.
[4] Cf. 1 Cor. 2 : 9.
[5] Hitti, *History of the Arabs*, p. 396.
[6] In sūr. 25 used as a synonym of Koran.
[7] This word and the preceding occur in the Koran only in plural.
[8] For other words consult Arthur Jeffery, *The Foreign Vocabulary of the Qur'ān* (Baroda, 1938).

by *ishbīn* (godfather), *burshān* (wafer), *tilmīdh* (disciple), *shammās* (deacon), *'imād* (baptism), *kanīsah* (church), *kārūz* (preacher), *nāqūs* (gong). The Greek loan words were not quite so numerous and included : *ṭaqs* (rite), *qandalaft* (sexton), *injīl* (Evangel), *usquf* (bishop), *shidyāq* (subdeacon), *abrashīyah* (parish), *zunnār* (girdle).[1] Several Greek words found their way into Arabic through Syriac: *khūri* (priest), *baṭriyark* (patriarch), *iskīm* (monk's hood), *harṭūqi* (heretic).

Orthography

In one other respect did Syriac make a significant contribution to Arabic, orthography. The Arabic characters themselves, as we learned before,[2] were derived from Nabataean, a sister of Syriac.

In its earliest form Arabic writing entirely lacked the diacritical points which now serve to distinguish letters formerly written alike. It was also destitute of vocalization, all its characters being consonantal. In the course of the first Moslem century diacritical points, of possible Nabataean origin, as well as vowel signs were introduced and put into limited use. A single dot over the letter was employed to indicate the *a* sound ; a dot below the letter to indicate the *i* sound.[3] But that was precisely what the East Syrians had been doing for a long time. Toward the end of that century, and following again the Syriac practice, the dots were elongated into the supralinear and infralinear dashes still in use. These are the reforms ascribed by tradition to al-Ḥajjāj.[4] The same Syriac system of vowel pointing lies at the basis of the Hebrew system, which the Masorites borrowed after A.D. 750.[5]

[1] For more consult Georg Graf in *Zeitschrift für Semitistik und verwandte Gebiete*, vol. vii (1929), pp. 225 *seq.*; vol. ix (1939), pp. 234 *seq.*; see below, p. 547.

[2] Pp. 169, 384.

[3] The sign for the *u* sound was evidently borrowed from the letter *w*.

[4] See above, p. 476.

[5] Frank R. Blake in *Journal, American Oriental Society*, vol. lx (1940), pp. 391-413.

CHAPTER XL

FALL OF THE UMAYYAD DYNASTY

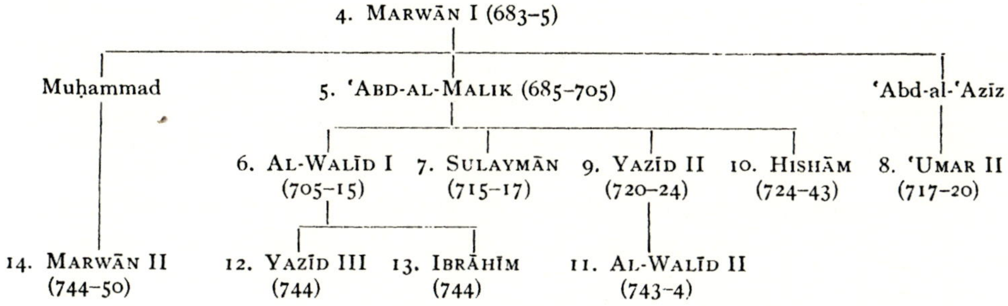

Tree showing the genealogical relationship of the Marwānid caliphs of the Umayyad dynasty

THE Umayyad power passed its zenith with the reign of al-Walīd (705–15). Only two distinguished rulers may be noted after him, 'Umar II and Hishām.

A devout caliph

'Umar (717–20) stood out as the only pious caliph in a reputedly worldly régime. His ideal was to follow in the footsteps of his maternal grandfather, the second orthodox caliph, whose namesake he was. His devotion, frugality and simplicity are emphasized by his biographer, who asserts that the caliph wore clothes with so many patches and mingled with his subjects so freely that when one came to petition him he found it difficult to recognize him.[1] During his reign the theologians had their day. Hence the saintly reputation he acquired in Moslem history. 'Umar abolished the practice introduced by Mu'āwiyah of cursing 'Ali from the pulpit at the Friday prayers.[2] He introduced fiscal reforms which failed of survival but nevertheless substantially contributed toward the equal treatment of Arab and non-Arab Moslems and the ultimate fusion of the sons of conquerors and conquered.[3]

The last able Umayyad

Hishām (724–43) was rightly considered by Arab historians

[1] Ibn-al-Jawzi, pp. 173-4, 145 *seq.* [2] *Fakhri*, p. 176. [3] See above, p. 475.

as the last statesman of the house of Umayyah.[1] His four successors were incompetent if not dissolute and degenerate. When his son, Muʿāwiyah, ancestor of the Spanish Umayyads, met his death while hunting, the father remarked, "I brought him up for the caliphate and he pursues a fox!"[2] His governor over al-ʿIrāq, who appropriated for himself 13,000,000 dirhams after squandering of the state revenue nearly thrice that sum, was apprehended and forced to make repayments.[3] His case was one of many, proving widespread corruption in the body politic. The eunuch system, an inheritance from Byzantium and Persia, was now assuming large proportions and facilitating the harem institution. Increased wealth brought in its wake a superabundance of slaves, and both resulted in general indulgence in luxurious living. Nor was the moral turpitude limited to high classes. The vices of civilization, including wine, women and song, had evidently seized upon the sons of the desert and were now beginning to sap their vitality.

Four incompetent caliphs

Hishām's successor al-Walīd II, a physically strong and handsome man, was more of a virtuoso in music and poetry than an adept in state affairs.[4] He took time from his life of pleasure in the desert to be enthroned in the capital and then resumed his usual career. The ruins of his palaces still adorn the desert.[5] More serious, however, were the mistakes he made in designating his two minor sons, whose mother was a freedwoman, as heirs to the caliphate and then in alienating the Yamanites (South Arabians), who formed the bulk of the Arab population of Syria. The principle of heredity in the caliphate, introduced by Muʿāwiyah,[6] conflicted with the time-honoured tribal principle of seniority in succession. The problem was further complicated when the founder of the Marwānid branch designated two of his sons, ʿAbd-al-Malik and ʿAbd-al-ʿAzīz, as his consecutive successors.[7] The lack of an accepted clear-cut principle of caliphal succession was, of course, not conducive to stability and continuity. As for the Yamanites they were the party on whose shoulders the Syrian throne was raised. Their feud with the Qaysites (North Arabians) was deep-rooted and

[1] Masʿūdi, vol. v, p. 479; cf. Yaʿqūbi, vol. ii, p. 393; ibn-Qutaybah, *Maʿārif*, p. 185.

[2] Ṭabari, vol. ii, pp. 1738-9.

[3] Ṭabari, vol. ii, p. 1642; Yaʿqūbi, vol. ii, p. 387.

[4] *Aghāni*, vol. vi, pp. 101 *seq*.

[5] See above, p. 507.

[6] See above, p. 440.

[7] Yaʿqūbi, vol. ii, p. 306.

destined to last till recent times.[1] A conspiracy headed by Yazīd, cousin of al-Walīd, used Yamanite insurgents to track the caliph and murder him south of Palmyra.[2]

The reign of Yazīd III (744), first caliph born of a slave mother,[3] was marked by disturbances in the provinces. His brother and successor Ibrāhīm, after a reign of only two months, was obliged to abdicate in favour of a distant cousin, Marwān II (744–50), who, like his two predecessors, was the son of a slave concubine.[4]

When Marwān was installed, anarchy was already on the march throughout the whole domain. An Umayyad claimant arose in Syria, a Khārijite one rebelled in al-ʿIrāq and leaders in Khurāsān refused to acknowledge the caliph's authority. Marwān moved his seat of government to Ḥarrān, where he could rely upon Qaysite support and deal more effectively with his two worst enemies — the ʿAlids and the ʿAbbāsids.

ʿAlids and ʿAbbāsids

To the Shīʿites the Umayyads were but ungodly usurpers who had perpetrated an unforgivable, unforgettable wrong against ʿAli and his descendants. The unswerving devotion of the Shīʿites to the house of the Prophet made them the focus of popular interest and sympathy. Their camp gradually became the rallying point of the dissatisfied, politically, socially and economically. Since ʿAli had chosen al-Kūfah for capital, al-ʿIrāq had been their stronghold. The ʿIrāqis, moreover, nurtured a grudge against the Syrians for depriving them of the seat of the caliphate. Sunnite pietists joined the band of critics who charged the house of Umayyah with worldliness, secularism and neglect of koranic law.

Like the Shīʿites the ʿAbbāsids took advantage of the general chaotic condition to press their own claim to the throne. Their claim was based on the proposition that as descendants of an uncle of the Prophet[5] they had a prior claim on the

[1] See above, p. 452. [2] Yaʿqūbi, vol. ii, p. 400; *Fakhri*, p. 182.
[3] Ṭabari, vol. ii, p. 1874; Masʿūdi, vol. vi, pp. 31-2.
[4] Yaʿqūbi, vol. ii, pp. 403, 404; Masʿūdi, vol. vi, p. 47.
[5] Hāshim
|
ʿAbd-al-Muṭṭalib
|
ʿAbdullāh — Abu-Ṭālib — AL-ʿABBĀS
|
MUḤAMMAD (son of ʿAbdullāh); ʿALI + Fāṭimah (son of Abu-Ṭālib)

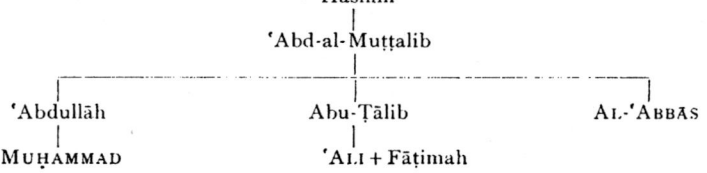

caliphate as compared with the banu-Umayyah.

The Khurāsānians

Another factor that entered into the situation was the discontent felt by non-Arabian Moslems in general and Persian Moslems in particular because of the treatment accorded them by Arabian Moslems. Far from being granted the equality promised by Islam, these neophytes were actually reduced to the status of clients (*mawāli*).[1] In certain cases they were not even granted exemption from the capitation tax paid by them when still dhimmis. The resentment reached its height in Persia, whose more ancient and venerable culture was acknowledged even by the Arabians. The soil of Khurāsān in the north-east proved especially fertile for the germination of Shīʿite-ʿAbbāsid seed. The Shīʿah doctrine struck a responsive chord in Khurāsānian hearts. Under the guise of Shīʿah Islam, old Iranianism was reasserting itself.

Only one element was still missing — leadership, leadership under which Shīʿite, ʿAbbāsid, Persian and other anti-Umayyad forces could coalesce and march against the common foe. That leadership was at last supplied by abu-al-ʿAbbās ʿAbdullāh, a great-great-grandson of al-ʿAbbās. His success in securing control of the entire anti-Umayyad machine was largely due to the clever use of propaganda. For headquarters the ʿAbbāsids had chosen a seemingly innocent and aloof village south of the Dead Sea,[2] al-Ḥumaymah, but in reality a strategic place for reaching caravans, travellers and pilgrims from all over the world of Islam. In it would-be missionaries were indoctrinated and from it sent on their secret mission. At al-Ḥumaymah the earliest and one of the most subtle and successful propaganda acts of political Islam was played. Nothing was comparable to it until the rise of the Fāṭimids.[3]

Revolt breaks out

Action began in Khurāsān. It was June 747. The seditious movement was headed by the ʿAbbāsid agent abu-Muslim al-Khurāsāni, himself a freedman of obscure origin.[4] The banner he unfurled was black, a colour he had adopted for his garments in mourning over the murder of a descendant of ʿAli in Khurāsān. That became the distinctive colour of the rising dynasty. At the head of an army composed of Yamanite Arabs (of the Azd tribe)

[1] See above, pp. 474, 485.

[2] Yaʿqūbi, vol. ii, pp. 356-7; *Fakhri*, pp. 192-3; Ṭabari, vol. iii, p. 34; Yāqūt, vol. ii, p. 342; Musil, *Northern Heǧâz*, pp. 56-61 and map in pocket.

[3] See below, p. 577.

[4] *Fakhri*, p. 186.

and Iranian peasants, abu-Muslim made a successful entry into the capital Marw. The Umayyad governor of Khurāsān, Naṣr ibn-Sayyār, appealed in vain to Marwān, pointing out the threatening danger.[1] He even had recourse to poetry:

I see the coal's red glow beneath the embers
And 'tis about to blaze!
The rubbing of two sticks enkindles fire,
And out of words come frays.
"Oh! is Umayya's House awake or sleeping?"
I cry in sore amaze.[2]

But the caliph had enough trouble to keep him busy at home. Here the rebellion fomented by Yamanites had spread from Palestine to Ḥimṣ. In al-'Irāq the Khārijites were again on the march.[3] Personally Marwān was no mean soldier. For his perseverance in warfare he had won the title of al-Ḥimār (ass), a label that then bore no stigma. He was credited with the change from fighting in lines (*ṣufūf*), a practice hallowed by association with the Prophet's method of battling, to that of cohorts (*karadīs*),[4] small units more compact and consequently more mobile. But now he stood helpless in a situation that was hopeless. Clearly the Umayyad sun was fast approaching its setting.

Final blow

The fall of Marw was followed by that of Nihāwand and other Persian cities, which opened the way to al-'Irāq. Here al-Kūfah, its chief city and the hiding-place of abu-al-'Abbās, fell without determined opposition. On October 30, 749, in its principal mosque homage was paid to him as caliph.[5] Throughout the eastern provinces the white flag was in retreat before the black. Marwān resolved on a last, desperate stand. With 12,000 troops [6] he moved from Ḥarrān and was met (January 750) on the left bank of the Greater (Upper) Zāb, an affluent of the Tigris, by the opposition under the leadership of 'Abdullāh ibn-'Ali, an uncle of the new caliph. The battle raged for nine days. The will to win was no more on the Syrian side. Gone were its days of high morale and inspiring leadership. Its defeat was now decisive.

[1] Ṭabari, vol. ii, pp. 1953 *seq.*; Dīnawari, pp. 359 *seq.*
[2] Nicholson, *Literary History*, p. 251; *Fakhri*, p. 194.
[3] Ṭabari, vol. ii, pp. 1943-9.
[4] See above, p. 478.
[5] Ya'qūbi, vol. ii, pp. 417-18; Ṭabari, vol. iii, pp. 27-33; Mas'ūdi, vol. vi, pp. 87, 98.
[6] Ṭabari, vol. iii, p. 47 (cf. p. 45); see above, p. 478, n. 6.

One after the other of the Syrian towns opened their gates to 'Abdullāh with his Khurāsāni-'Irāqi troops. Only Damascus put up the semblance of a fight. A few days of siege were enough to reduce the proud capital (April 26, 750). 'Abbāsid cavalry were stabled in its great mosque for seventy days. The victorious army pushed south to Palestine. Thence a detachment was rushed after the fleeing caliph. Outside a church at Būṣīr,[1] Upper Egypt, Marwān was overtaken and killed (August 5, 750). His head and caliphal insignia were sent to abu-al-'Abbās.[2]

What to do with the rest of the Umayyads was the next chief concern of 'Abbāsid policy. Extermination was the fate agreed upon and the execution was entrusted to 'Abdullāh. The implacable commander-in-chief shrank from no measure calculated to wipe out of existence the kindred enemy. Even tombs in Damascus, Qinnasrīn and other burial-places were violated, their corpses crucified and other remains thrown out. The body of Hishām was disentombed from al-Ruṣāfah, lashed eighty times and then burned to ashes.[3] Only the tombs of Mu'āwiyah and the pious 'Umar were spared. On June 25, 750, 'Abdullāh invited eighty Umayyad princes to a banquet at abu-Fuṭrus, ancient Antipatris, on the 'Awjā' River near Jaffa; and as they started the feast, his executioners started to mow them down, one by one. Over the still warm bodies of the dead and the dying leathern covers were spread, and the general with his lieutenants continued in the enjoyment of the repast to the accompaniment of human groans.[4] Agents and spies scoured Moslem lands hunting down fugitive scions of the fallen family. Several "sought refuge in the bowels of the earth",[5] as its surface became unsafe for them.

A dramatic escape

One person escaped the general massacre, 'Abd-al-Raḥmān ibn-Mu'āwiyah, grandson of the Caliph Hishām. This nine-

[1] Also Abūṣīr, probably Būṣīr al-Malaq in the Fayyūm. Consult Sāwīrus ibn-al-Muqaffa', *Siyar al-Baṭārikah al-Iskandarānīyīn*, ed. C. F. Seybold (Hamburg, 1912), pp. 181 *seq.*; Ṭabari, vol. iii, pp. 49-50.

[2] Mas'ūdi, vol. vi, p. 77.

[3] Mas'ūdi, vol. v, p. 471; cf. Ya'qūbi, vol. ii, pp. 427-8. See *Fakhri*, p. 204.

[4] Ya'qūbi, vol. ii, pp. 425-6; Mas'ūdi, vol. vi, p. 76; ibn-al-Athīr, vol. v, pp. 329-30; Mubarrad, p. 707; *Aghāni*, vol. iv, p. 161, cf. pp. 92-6; *Fakhri*, pp. 203-4; Theophanes, p. 427. Compare the story of Jehu's extermination of Ahab's house (2 K. 9: 14-34) and the destruction of the Mamlūks of Egypt by Muḥammad 'Ali (below, p. 692); Jurji Zaydān, *Ta'rīkh Miṣr al-Ḥadīth*, 3rd ed., Cairo, 1925, vol. ii, pp. 160-62.

[5] Ibn-Khaldūn, vol. iv, p. 120.

teen-year-old youth first hid himself in a Bedouin camp on the left bank of the Euphrates in North Syria. The camp was one day startled by the sight of approaching black standards. ʻAbd-al-Raḥmān dashed into the river. His brother, six years his junior, followed. The ʻAbbāsid pursuers were on their heels. Taking their promise of amnesty seriously, the younger yielded and returned from midstream, only to be slain. The elder kept on and gained the opposite bank.[1]

Disguised, ʻAbd-al-Raḥmān trudged on his way southward. In Palestine he was joined by his faithful and able freedman Badr. A price was set on the head of the fugitive prince and he barely escaped assassination at the hands of the governor of North Africa. Friendless and penniless he threaded his way through the length of North Africa. After five years of wandering he landed in Spain (755), conquered and held by his ancestors. There he established himself in the following year as the undisputed master of the peninsula. For capital he chose Cordova, reputedly a Carthaginian foundation, which blossomed into the seat of a new kingdom and a brilliant culture. ʻAbd-al-Raḥmān endeavoured to fashion his state after that of Damascus. He inaugurated an enlightened, beneficent régime, which on the whole conducted itself in the best tradition of its Damascene predecessors. Fourteen years before his arrival the Syrian army of twenty-seven thousand sent by Hishām under Balj ibn-Bishr al-Qushayri against the Berbers in Spain had established itself in military fiefs throughout the principal districts of the Mediterranean Spanish border.[2] The contingents from Damascus, Ḥimṣ, Qinnasrīn, Jordan and Palestine were installed in Elvira, Seville, Jaen, Malaga and Medina Sidonia respectively. The colonists gave their new places of settlement Syrian geographic names. Climatic and other physical similarities helped to make the newcomers feel at home. As the Syrians conquered the land, Syrian songs, poetry and art conquered the people of the land. From Spain and Portugal several of these cultural elements were later introduced into the New World. Arab geographers began to refer to Spain as a Syrian province, but the battle of the Zāb reduced Syria itself to an ʻAbbāsid province.

[1] *Akhbār*, pp. 52-4; ibn-al-Athīr, vol. v, p. 377.
[2] *Akhbār*, p. 31; cf. ibn-al-Qūṭīyah, pp. 14-15; Marrākushi, p. 9.

CHAPTER XLI

SYRIA AN 'ABBĀSID PROVINCE

WITH the Umayyad fall the hegemony of Syria in the world of Islam ended and the glory of the country passed away. The 'Abbāsids chose al-'Irāq for headquarters. Al-Kūfah, close to the Persian border, was the new capital. The Syrians awoke after the humiliating defeat at al-Zāb to the realization that the centre of Islamic gravity had left their land and shifted eastward. As a last resort they set their hopes on an expected descendant of Mu'āwiyah, a Sufyāni,[1] to appear Messiah-like and deliver them from their victorious 'Irāqi rivals. To the present day this expectancy is vaguely alive in the hearts of Syrian Moslems.

A new era

Meantime abu-al-'Abbās was busy consolidating his newly acquired domain. In the inaugural address previously delivered at al-Kūfah he had assumed the title of al-Saffāḥ (bloodshedder),[2] which gave a hint of the new policy. The incoming dynasty was to depend more than the outgoing on the use of force in the execution of its plans. For the first time the leathern bag ready to receive the head of the executioner's victim found a place near the imperial throne. The new caliph surrounded himself with theologians and legists, giving the infant state an atmosphere of theocracy as opposed to the secular character (*mulk*) of its defunct predecessor. On ceremonial occasions he hastened to don the mantle (*burdah*) of his distant cousin, the Prophet.[3] The well-geared propaganda machine which had worked to undermine public confidence in the old régime was now busy

[1] Ṭabari, vol. iii, p. 1320; ibn-Miskawayh, *Tajārib al-Umam wa-Ta'āqub al-Himam*, ed. de Goeje and de Jong, vol. ii (Leyden, 1871), p. 526; Yāqūt, vol. iv, p. 1000; *Aghāni*, vol. xvi, p. 88; H. Lammens, *Études sur le siècle des Omayyades* (Beirut, 1930), pp. 391-408.

[2] Ṭabari, vol. iii, p. 30, l. 20; ibn-al-Athīr, vol. v, p. 316.

[3] Genealogical tree showing the kinship between the 'Abbāsids and Muḥammad (see facing page):

entrenching the new régime in public esteem. Authority, the zealous propagandists proclaimed, should forever remain in the ʿAbbāsid house, to be finally yielded to Jesus (*ʿĪsa*), the Messiah.[1] To this was later added the warning that should the ʿAbbāsid caliphate be destroyed, the entire universe would be disorganized.[2] Anti-Umayyad, pro-ʿAbbāsid ḥadīths were fabricated wholesale. Even Umayyad names were effaced from inscriptions on buildings [3] and the style of Umayyad pulpits in mosques was modified.

The real difference between this and the preceding caliphate, however, lay in the fact that the ʿAbbāsid was oriented Persia-ward. Persian protocol pervaded the court, Persian ideas dominated the political scene and Persian women prevailed in the royal harem. It was an empire of Neo-Moslems in which the Arabs formed but one of the component parts. If the Umayyad was in a sense a successor state of the East Roman Empire, the ʿAbbāsid was in a wider sense a successor state of the empire of the Chosroes. The ʿAbbāsid régime called itself *dawlah*, new era, and a new era it was. The ʿIrāqis felt relieved from Syrian tutelage. The Shīʿites felt avenged. Persians found high posts in the government open to them; they introduced and occupied a new office, the vizirate, highest after the caliphate. Khurāsānians flocked to man the caliphal bodyguard. The Arabian aristocracy was eclipsed. Arabian-

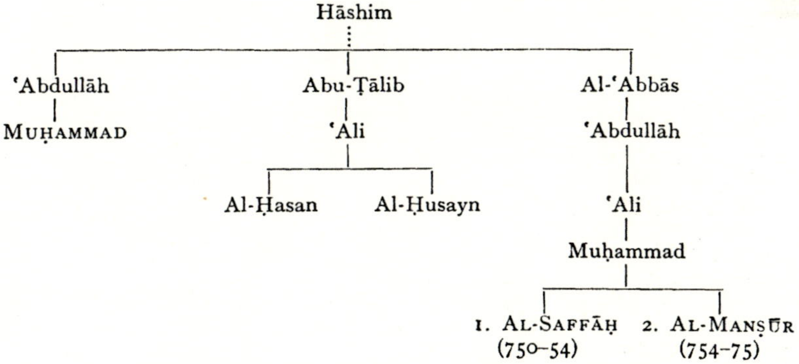

[1] Ṭabari, vol. iii, p. 33; ibn-al-Athīr, vol. v, p. 318.
[2] See below, p. 557.
[3] Ṭabari, vol. iii, p. 486; see above, pp. 512-13.

ism fell but Islam under a new guise, that of Persianism, marched triumphantly on.

Third in chronological order, after the Orthodox (*Rāshidūn*) and the Umayyad, the caliphate founded by al-Saffāḥ (750–54) and his brother abu-Ja'far al-Manṣūr (754–75) was the longest-lived and the most celebrated of all the caliphates. All the thirty-five caliphs who succeeded the second caliph were his lineal descendants. Al-Manṣūr chose for capital the site of a Christian Persian-named village Baghdād (given by God) [1] on the lower west bank of the Tigris. The Dār al-Salām (abode of peace), as the city was officially named, was built with a double surrounding wall of brick, a deep moat and a third inner wall rising to a height of ninety feet. Lying in that same valley which had furnished sites for some of the mightiest cities of antiquity, the city of al-Manṣūr soon fell heir to the power and prestige of Ctesiphon, Babylon, Nineveh and other capitals of the ancient Orient. Scene of the legendary adventures brilliantly commemorated by Shahrazād in *The Thousand and One Nights* and seat of the two luminous reigns of Hārūn al-Rashīd (786–809) and al-Ma'mūn (813–33), Baghdād has lived in legend and in history as the peerless symbol of the glory of Islam. The reigns of these two caliphs endow the whole dynasty with a halo that has not yet faded away. The dynasty enjoyed its prime between the reigns of the third caliph, al-Mahdi (775–85), and that of the ninth, al-Wāthiq (842–7).[2]

[1] Al-Ya'qūbi, *Kitāb al-Buldān*, ed. M. J. de Goeje (Leyden, 1892), p. 235; Balādhuri, p. 294.

[2] Genealogical tree of the 'Abbāsid caliphs under whom the empire reached its prime:

Al-'Abbās

1. Al-Saffāḥ (750) 2. Al-Manṣūr (754)

3. Al-Mahdi (775)

4. Al-Hādi (785) 5. Al-Rashīd (786)

6. Al-Amīn (809) 7. Al-Ma'mūn (813) 8. Al-Mu'taṣim (833)

9. Al-Wāthiq (842) 10. Al-Mutawakkil (847)

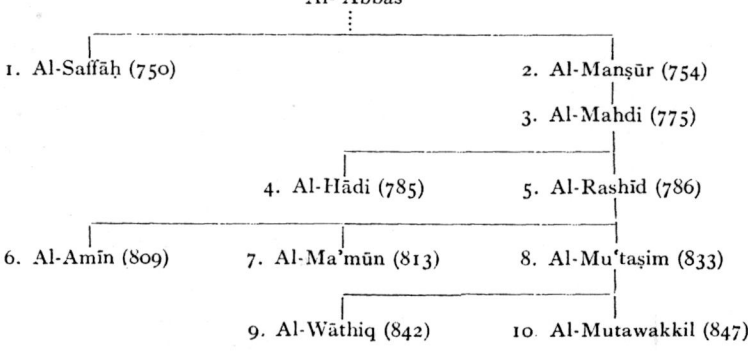

After al-Wāthiq the state starts on its downward course until al-Mustaʿṣim (1242–58), thirty-seventh of the line, when it is utterly destroyed by the Mongols. For over five centuries the successors of al-Saffāḥ and al-Manṣūr reigned, though they did not always rule.

Traitors and suspects disposed of

The first governor of ʿAbbāsid Syria was none other than ʿAbdullāh, hero of al-Zāb. At the death of al-Saffāḥ he disputed with his other nephew al-Manṣūr the caliphate, relying on a huge disciplined army presumably massed for use against the Byzantines. After butchering 17,000 Khurāsānian troops, whom he did not trust, he moved with the rest of his men, mostly Syrians, eastward.[1] He was met by abu-Muslim at Naṣībīn (November 754) and defeated. After seven years' imprisonment he was ceremoniously conducted into a house the foundations of which had been reportedly laid on salt surrounded by water. He was soon buried under its ruins.[2] Abu-Muslim was then virtually independent governor of Khurāsān, the idol of his people and the ruthless suppressor of all personal and official enemies. So successful was he that ʿAbbāsid suspicions were aroused. On his way back he was induced to stop and see the caliph at al-Madā'in (Ctesiphon). In the course of an audience with al-Manṣūr, the Persian, to whose sword after that of ʿAbdullāh the ʿAbbāsids owed their throne, was treacherously put to death.[3]

The turn of the ʿAlids came next. These had assumed that the ʿAbbāsids were fighting their battles but were now disillusioned. To abu-al-ʿAbbās and his cohorts, "the people of the house" (*ahl al-bayt*) meant their own family and not that of ʿAli and Fāṭimah. The ʿAlids persisted in claiming for their imāms the sole right to preside over the destinies of Islam, thus reducing the ʿAbbāsid caliphs to the position of usurpers. Their movement again went underground but never missed an opportunity to rise in open revolt. The renowned Mālik ibn-Anas, founder of the one of the four orthodox systems of jurisprudence that is still dominant throughout North Africa, absolved the Shīʿah from their oath of allegiance to the ʿAbbāsids. An early revolt headed by two great-grandsons of

[1] Ṭabari, vol. iii, pp. 101-2.
[2] Ṭabari, vol. iii, p. 330; Yaʿqūbi, vol. ii, p. 443.
[3] Ṭabari, vol. iii, pp. 105-17; Dīnawari, pp. 376-8.

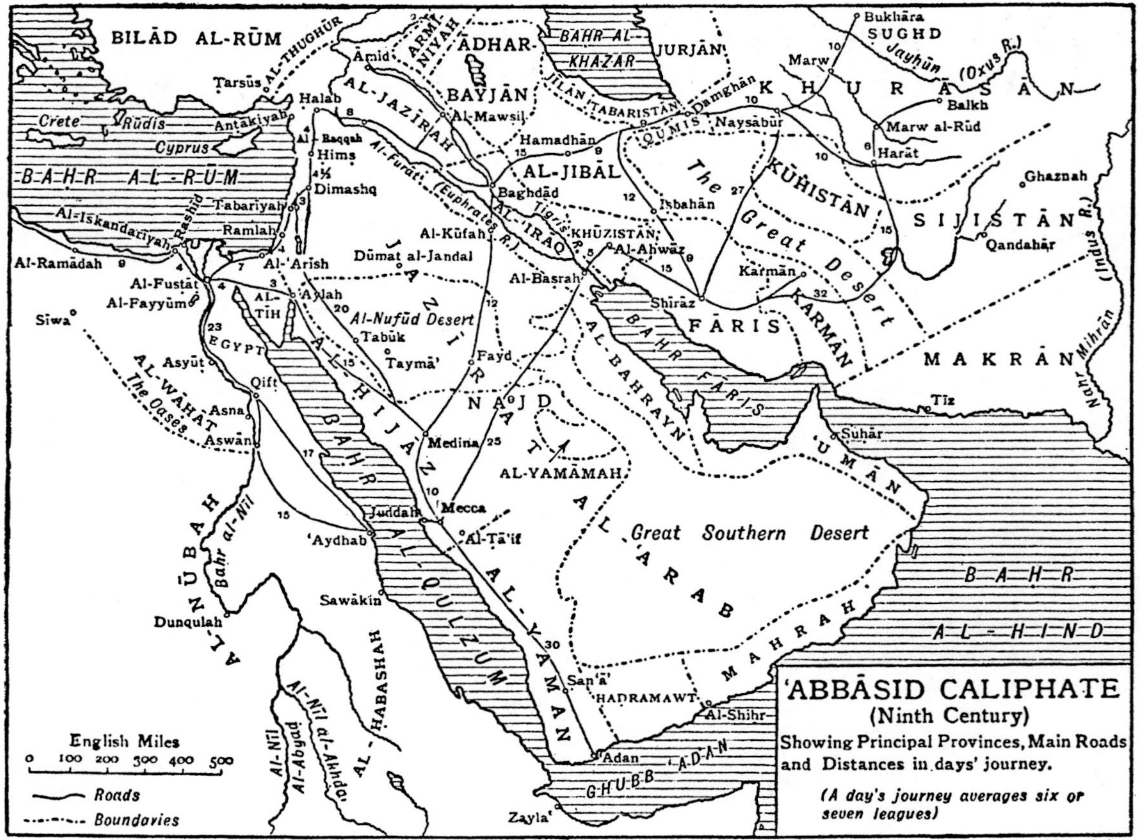

From Hitti, "History of the Arabs"

al-Ḥasan, Muḥammad and Ibrāhīm, was ruthlessly crushed.[1] Muḥammad, surnamed al-Nafs al-Zakīyah (the pure soul), was gibbeted in Medina (December 762). His brother Ibrāhīm was decapitated (February 763) near al-Kūfah and his head was dispatched to the caliph.[2]

One more group of Shī'ite collaborators had to be liquidated, the Barmakids. This was the Persian vizirial family exalted by al-Manṣūr. Descended from a Buddhist high priest (*barmak*), the members of this family achieved such distinction and displayed such generosity in the use of their wealth that the word *barmaki* has come down to the present day as meaning generous. Their prestige was too much for the strong-willed Hārūn, who in and after 803 annihilated them and confiscated their estate, said to have amounted to 30,676,000 dinars in cash exclusive of furniture and real estate.[3]

With the removal of the capital to distant Baghdād the hereditary Byzantine enemy ceased to be of major concern. The disturbances accompanying the removal gave the emperors a chance to push the imperial border farther east along the empire boundary of Asia Minor and Armenia. Al-Manṣūr and

[1] Genealogical tree of the descendants of 'Ali:

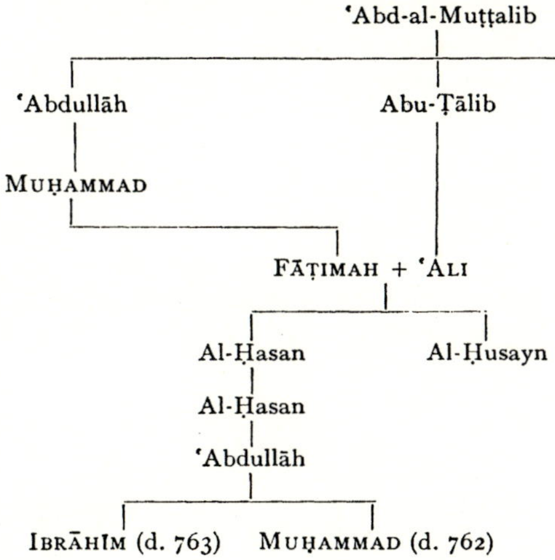

[2] Ṭabari, vol. iii, pp. 245-65, 315-16; Mas'ūdi, vol. vi, pp. 189-203; Dīnawari, p. 381.

[3] *'Iqd*, vol. iii, p. 28; Ṭabari, vol. iii, p. 680; Ṭabari, vol. iii, pp. 676-7; Mas'ūdi, vol. vi, pp. 387-94; *Fakhri*, p. 288. Cf. ibn-Khaldūn, vol. iii, pp. 223-4; *Kitāb al-'Uyūn*, pt. 3, pp. 306-8.

his successors took pains to fortify the *thughūr* of Syria and the seaports of Lebanon.[1] In 782 [2] when still a prince, Hārūn led his forces as far as Byzantium and exacted from the regent Irene a heavy tribute. As caliph he conducted from his favourite residence al-Raqqah in North Syria a series of raids into the "land of the Romans".[3] In 838 his son al-Muʿtaṣim made one last incursion into that land. Therewith the more than a century and a half long struggle between the caliphal and the Byzantine states came to an end.

Unrest in Syria, Lebanon and Palestine

The Syrians lost no time, after the loss by their country of its privileged position, in expressing their opposition by word and deed. Their attitude became worse as the days went by and left them excluded from government offices. A rejoinder by one of them to al-Manṣūr's remark that the people were lucky to escape the plague in his days, typifies the then prevailing sentiment: "God is too good to subject us to the pest and your rule at the same time".[4] In the case of the Christians the situation was aggravated by unfair extortion and increased taxation. Two full centuries had to elapse before the subjects of banu-Umayyah were reconciled to being subjects of banu-al-ʿAbbās.

Their first governor, ʿAbdullāh, found himself on assuming office in 750 confronted with several uprisings in Ḥawrān, al-Bathanīyah and Qinnasrīn led by ex-generals in Marwān's army. The rebels of Ḥimṣ and Tadmur were headed by a descendant of Muʿāwiyah, Ziyād, who was accepted as the expected Sufyāni. His camp near Salamyah counted 40,000.[5]

The polarization of Moslem Syria by the Arab dualism of Qays and Yaman, who appear under a multiplicity of names, was now intensified. The ʿAbbāsids in general favoured and used the Qaysites. Especially under Hārūn al-Rashīd, whose governor in Damascus was Ibrāhīm, a nephew of ʿAbdullāh,[6]

[1] Balādhuri, p. 163; see above, p. 442.

[2] *Kitāb al-ʿUyūn*, pt. 3, p. 278, dates the expedition 163 (A.D. 780), Yaʿqūbi (vol. ii, pp. 478, 486) 164 and Ṭabari (vol. iii, pp. 503-4) 165.

[3] Ṭabari, vol. iii, pp. 696, 709-10; Yaʿqūbi, vol. ii, p. 519, l. 14, p. 523, l. 2; Dīnawari, pp. 386-7; Masʿūdi, vol. ii, pp. 337-52. The ruins of al-Raqqah, which owes its foundation to Seleucid II, show the grand scale on which it was rebuilt by al-Rashīd and fortified by al-Ma'mūn.

[4] Ibn-ʿAsākir, vol. iii, p. 392.

[5] Ibn-al-Athīr, vol. v, pp. 331 *seq.*

[6] The precarious position in Syria necessitated the appointment of members of the ʿAbbāsid family. Ibrāhīm's father was Ṣāliḥ, brother of ʿAbdullāh. At times over different parts of Syria different governors were appointed; Yaʿqūbi, vol. ii, p. 461.

was strife bitter. In Damascus, Ḥawrān, al-Balqā', the Jordan and Ḥimṣ blood was shed.[1] For two years the district of Damascus was the scene of relentless warfare supposedly because a water-melon was filched from a Yamanite garden by a member of the opposing party.[2] The caliph, after considering leading a punitive expedition in person, entrusted it in 795 to a Barmakid general who completely disarmed the warring factions, " leaving not a lance or horse ".[3] The convulsions accompanying the struggle for the throne between al-Amīn and al-Ma'mūn, sons of Hārūn, had repercussions in Syria. Syrian troops finding themselves (811/12) encamped with Khurāsānians at al-Raqqah deserted wholesale as a ringleader harangued, " Down with the black banner! . . . To your homes! To your homes! Death in Palestine is preferable to life in Mesopotamia." [4] In the turbulent days of al-Amīn another Sufyāni, 'Ali by name, unfurled the white banner. A ninety-year-old learned man, the pretender won a host of followers, including the governor of Sidon, seized Ḥimṣ and besieged Damascus, which he captured after expelling the 'Abbāsid agent.[5]

In 829 al-Ma'mūn visited Syria and made a fresh survey of its lands with a view to increasing the revenue from it.[6] Four years later he visited Damascus to test the judges there and enforce his decree that no judge who did not subscribe to the Mu'tazilite view of the creation of the Koran could hold office.[7] Several of his predecessors had visited Syria on their way to the pilgrimage or to battle against the Byzantines. They were all kept informed by their governors and a special agent of information (*ṣāḥib al-barīd*, postmaster), who was in reality chief of secret police.[8] The Mu'tazilite doctrine, which the caliph espoused, was in direct opposition to the later orthodox view. The rationalistic movement had its inception under the Umayyads.[9]

Palestine was the scene of the next major outbreak. Here A veiled rebel

[1] Dīnawari, p. 383; ibn-al-Athīr, vol. vi, pp. 86 *seq.*, 129, 519.
[2] Abu-al-Fidā', vol. ii, p. 14; ibn-al-Athīr, vol. vi, p. 87.
[3] Ṭabari, vol. iii, p. 639.
[4] Ṭabari, vol. iii, pp. 844-5.
[5] Ya'qūbi, vol. ii, p. 532; ibn-al-Athīr, vol. vi, p. 172; Ṭabari, vol. iii, p. 830.
[6] Ibn-'Asākir, vol. iv, pp. 107-8. For his visit to Jerusalem see above, pp. 512-13.
[7] Ya'qūbi, vol. ii, p. 571.
[8] Hitti, *History of the Arabs*, p. 325.
[9] See Hitti, *History of the Arabs*, p. 429.

a Yamanite Arab of obscure origin unfurled the white banner (840/41). Curiously enough he always appeared in public veiled, hence his nickname al-Mubarqaʿ. His followers, said to have numbered a hundred thousand, were recruited mainly from the rural district and peasant class, indicating economic as well as political motivation. To them he was a Sufyāni. Taking advantage of the ploughing season, the ʿAbbāsid general at the head of a thousand troops sent by the Caliph al-Muʿtaṣim attacked their headquarters and carried the veiled rebel to Sāmarra, temporary ʿAbbāsid capital.[1]

Damascus a temporary capital

In the reign of al-Mutawakkil, al-Muʿtaṣim's son, the fire of revolt blazed again in Damascus (854/5). The people slaughtered their ʿAbbāsid governor and were subsequently put to the sword for three consecutive days by a Turkish general sent by the caliph at the head of a band of seven thousand horse and three thousand foot, who also plundered the whole city.[2] That Damascus should shortly after that be chosen as the residence of the caliph seems incredible. In 858 al-Mutawakkil transferred his seat to it possibly to escape the arrogant domination of his praetorian guard, consisting mostly of turbulent, undisciplined Turks who were originally mercenaries and slaves taken into the service by his predecessor. The humid climate of the city, its violent wind and abundant fleas drove the capricious caliph out in thirty-eight days.[3]

Anti-Christian legislation

The pattern of behaviour set by Syrian rebels in the early ʿAbbāsid period was followed for years to come. At this time, however, a new element was introduced, intensification of discontent on the part of Christians due to harsh conditions imposed on them. Before al-Mutawakkil we hear of only one serious uprising by the Christians of Lebanon. It occurred in 759–60 when Ṣāliḥ ibn-ʿAli, brother of ʿAbdullāh, was governor. Driven to arms by fresh exactions and encouraged by the presence of a Byzantine fleet in the waters of Tripoli, a band burst from its headquarters in al-Munayṭirah,[4] high in the Lebanon, and plundered several villages in al-Biqāʿ. Their leader was a youthful mountaineer of huge physique who

[1] Ṭabari, vol. iii, pp. 1319-22; ibn-ʿAsākir, vol. v, pp. 311-12.
[2] Ibn-ʿAsākir, vol. vi, pp. 47-8.
[3] Ṭabari, vol. iii, pp. 1435-6; Yaʿqūbi, vol. ii, p. 601; ibn-ʿAsākir, vol. iv, pp. 288-9.
[4] See below, p. 622.

audaciously styled himself king. Drawn into an ambuscade near Ba'labakk the Lebanese band was cut down by 'Abbāsid cavalry. In retaliation Ṣāliḥ uprooted the mountain villagers, many of whom took no part in the revolt, and had them dispersed all over Syria.[1] The protest addressed to the governor by a celebrated legist, al-Awzā'i of Ba'labakk and Beirut,[2] is worthy of recording:

The expulsion from Mt. Lebanon of dhimmis who were not a party to the rebellion whose perpetrators you have either killed or sent back home has no doubt been a subject of your knowledge. How then could the many be punished for the crime of the few and how could they be expelled from their homes and lands so long as God Himself hath decreed, "Nor doth any sinning one bear another's burden"?[3] Surely no decree has a greater claim on our final acceptance and permanent obedience. And no command is more worthy of observance and consideration than that of the Messenger of Allah, who proclaimed: "He who oppresses one bound to us by covenant and charges him with more than he can do, verily I am the one to overcome him by argument".[4]

Before al-Mutawakkil his grandfather Hārūn had re-enacted some of the anti-Christian and anti-Jewish measures introduced by 'Umar II.[5] In 807 he ordered all churches erected since the Moslem conquest demolished. He also decreed that members of tolerated sects should wear the prescribed garb.[6] But evidently much of this legislation was not enforced.[7] In 850 and 854 al-Mutawakkil revived the discriminatory legislation and supplemented it by new features which were the most stringent ever issued against the minorities. Christians and Jews were enjoined to affix wooden images of devils to their houses, level their graves even with the ground, wear outer garments of honey colour (yellow), add two honey-coloured patches on the sleeves, one sewn on the back and the other on the front, and ride only on mules and asses with wooden saddles marked by two pomegranate-like balls on the cantle.[8] On account of this distinctive dress the dhimmis came to be mock-

[1] Ibn-'Asākir, vol. v, p. 341.
[2] See below, p. 555.
[3] Koran 6:164.
[4] Balādhuri, p. 162; cf. tr., p. 251.
[5] See above, pp. 487-8.
[6] Ṭabari, vol. iii, pp. 712-13; ibn-al-Athīr, vol. vi, p. 141.
[7] Cf. Laurence E. Browne, *The Eclipse of Christianity in Asia* (Cambridge, 1933), pp. 46 *seq.*
[8] Ṭabari, vol. iii, pp. 1389-93, 1419.

ingly called "spotted" (*arqaṭ*).[1] Basing their contention on a koranic charge that the Jews and the Christians had corrupted the text of their scriptures,[2] the contemporary jurists further emphasized that no testimony of a Jew or Christian was admissible against a Moslem. No other major persecution occurred until the days of the Fāṭimid Caliph al-Ḥākim (996–1021).

Subsequent to the promulgation of these laws by al-Mutawakkil a violent outbreak took place in Ḥimṣ in which Christians and Moslems participated. It was repressed after a vigorous resistance (855). The leaders were decapitated or flogged to death and then crucified at the city gate, all churches, with the exception of one which was added to the Great Mosque, were demolished and all Christians banished from the tumultuous city, which was evidently still predominantly Christian.[3]

Normally the major disability under which dhimmis laboured was the capitation tax (*jizyah*). This was in theory the price paid for freedom of residence and worship and for the right of receiving protection of life and property. The contract was, therefore, cancelled in case of refusal to pay the tax, rising in revolt, espionage in behalf of a foreign state or offering asylum to an enemy of the state. Other grounds were gradually added to include fornication with a free Moslem woman, leading a Moslem to apostasy and violating the sanctity of God, His Messenger or His Book. A Moslem could not embrace Christianity or Judaism without risking his life. A dhimmi, if considered undesirable, could be expelled from Moslem territory. Most Moslem schools of jurisprudence would not administer capital punishment for the homicide of a dhimmi by a Moslem. A non-Moslem was not denied the right of presenting himself before a Moslem court, if he chose so to do. If one party in a case was a Moslem, it had, of course, to go to a Moslem judge. When a case involved members of two differing dhimmi communities, one Christian and the other Jewish, Moslem law took no cognizance of it unless the parties failed to agree on the choice of the tribunal. If a husband embraced Islam and the wife was Scripturary, the marriage remained

[1] Jāḥiẓ, *Bayān*, vol. i, p. 79, l. 28.
[2] Sūrs. 2:70; 5:16-18.
[3] Ṭabari, vol. iii, pp. 1422-4; ibn-al-Athīr, vol. vii, pp. 59-60; Ya'qūbi, vol. ii, p. 599. See above, p. 511.

valid; but if the wife embraced Islam, the husband had to follow suit within three months, in which all conjugal relations were interrupted, or be divorced. A dhimmi could not inherit from a Moslem.

Islamization

Thus far Syria seems to have maintained its general Christian character, but now the situation began perceptibly to change. Of the Christian banu-Tanūkh in the vicinity of Aleppo five thousand had already obeyed the behest of the 'Abbāsid Caliph al-Mahdi and embraced Islam.[1] The Tanūkhs who entered Lebanon east of Beirut in the early ninth century were one of the first Moslem Arab families to establish themselves in the mountain. In that thinly populated district still known as al-Gharb these Tanūkhs carved for themselves a principality over which they ruled for centuries. The 'Abbāsids used them as a check against the Maronites of northern Lebanon and against the Byzantines coming by sea. The Crusaders found them in Beirut and its vicinity. Before the Tanūkhs the eponymous founder of the Arislān family, which traces its descent to the Lakhmids, had established himself in al-Gharb.[2] A disciple of al-Awzā'i, his descendants still form the high aristocracy of the Druzes. It may be assumed that after al-Mutawakkil many Christian families in Syria, exclusive of Lebanon, flocked to the fold of Islam. They were actuated mainly by the desire to escape the humiliating disabilities and tribute and to acquire social prestige or political influence. The Christian ranks had earlier been thinned by migration into Asia Minor and Cyprus. The second phase of Moslem conquest, the conquest of Islam as a religion, was thus insured. The first was the conquest of Moslem arms accomplished in less than a decade in Syria.

The conquest of Arabic

The third phase was the linguistic.[3] The linguistic victory was the slowest and the last. In this field of struggle the subject peoples of Syria and other lands offered the greatest measure of resistance. They showed themselves more ready to give up political and even religious loyalties than linguistic ones. The literary Arabic won its victory before the spoken did. Syrian

[1] Ibn-al-'Ibri, *Chronicon Syriacon*, ed. and tr. P. J. Bruns and G. G. Kirsch (Leipzig, 1789), vol. ii (text), p. 133; vol. i, pp. 134-5 (tr.); see above, p. 486.

[2] *Maḥāsin al-Masā'i fi Manāqib al-Imām abi-'Amr al-Awzā'i*, ed. Shakīb Arislān (Cairo), pp. 19-20; Shidyāq, pp. 646-7.

[3] See above, pp. 484-5.

scholars under caliphal patronage began to compose in Arabic long before Syrian peasants adopted the new tongue.[1] The oldest dated Christian manuscript in Arabic that has come down to us was composed by abu-Qurrah (d. 820) and copied in 877 at St. Sāba, near Jerusalem.[2] It is preserved in the British Museum. The author, a disciple of St. John of Damascus, was Melkite bishop of Ḥarrān. Islamization no doubt facilitated and accelerated Arabicization, and transition from one Semitic tongue to another did not present too many linguistic difficulties.

By the early thirteenth century, toward the end of the 'Abbāsid era, the victory of Arabic as the medium of everyday communication was virtually complete. Linguistic islands remained, occupied by non-Moslems: Jacobites, Nestorians and Maronites. Throughout the Crusading period many such islands existed. When around 1170 Benjamin of Tudela [3] visited Mount Sinai he found on its summit a Syrian place of worship and at its base a village whose inhabitants spoke the "Chaldean language". In Maronite Lebanon the native Syriac put up a desperate and prolonged fight. It lingered there until the late seventeenth century.[4] Indeed Syriac is still spoken in three villages in Anti-Lebanon: Ma'lūla, Bakh'ah and Jubb'adīn[5]. It is still used in the Maronite and other liturgies of the Syrian Churches. In their ritual the Maronites also use *garshūni*,[6] Arabic written in Syriac script. No such attachment was shown by Greek-speaking Syrians to their mother tongue, while only one Arabic inscription in Greek characters has been found. It is a biblical inscription (Ps. 78: 20-31, 56-61) evidently from the end of the eighth century and was discovered in the Umayyad Mosque.[7]

As non-Arabians were Islamized and Arabicized they

[1] See below, p. 550.

[2] Theodorus abu Ḳurra, *De cultu imaginum*, ed. and tr. I. Arendzen (Bonn, 1897); Qusṭanṭīn al-Bāsha, *Mayāmir Thāwadūrus abi-Qurrah* (Beirut, 1924?).

[3] *Itinerary*, vol. i (London, 1840), p. 159.

[4] Consult Hitti, *al-Lughāt al-Sāmīyah al-Maḥkīyah fi Sūrīya wa-Lubnān* (Beirut, 1922), pp. 30-34.

[5] Consult G. Bergsträsser, *Neuaramäische Märchen und andere Texte von Ma'lūla* (Leipzig, 1915); Anton Spitaler, *Grammatik des neuaramäischen Dialekts von Ma'lūla* (Hamburg, 1938).

[6] Less correctly *karshūni*; from Syr. *garshūn*, foreign.

[7] Paul Kahle, *Die arabischen Bibelübersetzungen* (Leipzig, 1904), pp. xiv, 32-3.

attached themselves to Arabian tribes as clients [1] and were gradually assimilated. The old caste line between Arabians and non-Arabians, old Moslems and Neo-Moslems, was obliterated. All became Arabs. Later, in the Mamlūk period, the sedentary population was styled *awlād* (descendants of) *al-'Arab*, a term still in use, to distinguish it from *A'rāb*, Bedouins.[2] A large part of the Aramaic-speaking people of Syria and al-'Irāq hitherto referred to derogatorily as *Anbāṭ* (Nabataeans)[3] or *'ulūj* (foreigners, speaking an unintelligible language) was no more in existence. Aram, as the native name of Syria, gave way to a new one al-Sha'm, " the left ", because it lay to the left of the Ka'bah, in contrast to al-Yaman, which lay to its right.[4] Thus was the entire Semitic world Arabicized under the 'Abbāsids. For the first time the consciousness of unity engendered by the use of a common tongue and the profession of a common faith prevailed.

Syriac did not disappear without leaving its indelible imprint over the Syro-Lebanese Arabic. It is primarily this imprint that distinguishes this dialect from those in neighbouring lands. The traces are clear in the morphology, phonetics and vocabulary. The domestic and agricultural vocabulary is especially rich in Syriac borrowings.[5] The month names come directly from Syriac, which received most of them from Akkadian.[6]

[1] See above, p. 485.
[2] See below, p. 641, n. 1.
[3] Mas'ūdi, *Tanbīh*, pp. 78-9.
[4] Mas'ūdi, vol. iii, pp. 139-40.
[5] For illustrations consult Michel T. Féghali, *Étude sur les emprunts syriaques dans les parlers du Liban* (Paris, 1918); do., *Le Parler de Kfar'abīda* (Paris, 1919); Yūsuf Ḥubayqah in *al-Mashriq*, vol. xxxvii (1939), pp. 290-412; Ighnāṭiyūs Afrām in *Majallat al-Majma' al-'Ilmi al-'Arabi*, vol. xxiii (1948), pp. 161-82, 321-46, 481-506; vol. xxiv (1949), pp. 3-21, 161-81, 321-42, 481-99; vol. xxv (1950), pp. 3-22, etc.; Anīs Furayḥah, *Mu'jam al-Alfāẓ al-'Āmmīyah fi al-Lahjah al-Lubnānīyah* (Jūniyah, 1947). For ecclesiastical loan words see above, pp. 525-6.
[6] Beginning with December and January: *kānūn* I and II, firepot; *shubāṭ*, striker, fatal; *ādhār*, cloudiness; *nīsān*, banner, warfare; *ayyār*, seed produce; *ḥazīrān*, harvest; *tammūz*, son of fresh water (see above, p. 117, n. 1); *āb*, bulrushes; *aylūl*, jubilation; *tishrīn* I and II (Oct. and Nov.), dedication (to the sun-god).

CHAPTER XLII

SYRIAN CONTRIBUTION TO ARAB RENAISSANCE

Translations from Greek

MORE than any other one people the Syriac-speaking Christians contributed to that general awakening and intellectual renaissance centred in ʿAbbāsid Baghdād which became and remained the chief glory of classical Islam. Between 750 and 850 the Arab world was the scene of one of the most spectacular and momentous movements in the history of thought. The movement was marked by translations into Arabic from Persian, Greek and Syriac. The Arabian Moslem brought with him no art, science or philosophy and hardly any literature; but he did bring along from the desert a keen intellectual curiosity, a voracious appetite for learning and a number of latent talents. In the Fertile Crescent he fell heir to Hellenistic science and lore, which was unquestionably the most precious intellectual treasure at hand. In a few decades after the foundation of Baghdād (762) the Arabic-reading public found at its disposal the major philosophical works of Aristotle and the Neo-Platonic commentators, the chief medical writings of Hippocrates and Galen, the main mathematical compositions of Euclid and the geographical masterpiece of Ptolemy. In all this the Syrians were the mediators. The Arabians knew no Greek, but the Syrians had been in touch with Greek for over a millennium. For two centuries before the appearance of Islam Syrian scholars had been translating Greek works into Syriac. Long before ʿUmar II transferred the philosophical school of Alexandria to Antioch an intense wave of translation had swept the monasteries of the Syrian Church. The people who had opened the treasures of Greek science and philosophy to the Persians were now doing the same to the Arabs. The same people who before Islam were instrumental in cultivating the main elements of Greek culture, spreading them eastward and propagating them in the schools of Edessa (al-Ruhā'), Nisibis (Naṣībīn), Ḥarrān and Jundi-Shāpūr were now busily engaged in passing those elements on to the Arabic-reading world. As in Roman days they had functioned as agents of material civilization transmitting the products of the East to the West,[1] so were they now the agents of Western culture in Eastern society.

Especially did the clergy among them realize the importance of Aristotelian logic and Neo-Platonic philosophy for theological controversies, then the breath of intellectual life. Even the Gospels whose original Aramaic was lost [2] had to be done from Greek. The Septuagint itself was translated into Syriac. Edessa, whose school opened in 373, was the chief centre of intellectual Syriac activity. One of its professors made the first translation of Porphyry's *Isagoge*, the recognized manual on logic commonly prefixed to Aristotle's *Organon*. This work of Aristotle was done later by another Syrian, George, who in 686 was installed bishop of the Arab tribes.[3] His parish comprised the Tanūkh, the Taghlib and other tribes of the Syro-Mesopotamian desert. Another Syrian, who flourished on the eve of the Moslem conquest, wrote a commentary on Aristotle's *Hermeneutica*. Syriac commentaries served as models for Arabic ones. When in 439 the Emperor Zeno closed the Edessene institution, its ejected teachers migrated across the eastern border to Ḥarrān, then under Persian rule, and opened or reopened a Christian academy there. Other victims of Byzantine policy which sought rigid religious uniformity throughout the empire found asylum in Persian territory.

Besides philosophy and theology medicine and astronomy attracted Syrian attention. Astronomy, viewed from the astrological standpoint, was allied to medicine. In 555 Kisra Anūsharwān established at Jundi-Shāpūr an academy of medicine and philosophy, many of whose distinguished professors were Christians using Syriac as a medium of instruction. One of these was Jūrjīs (George) ibn-Bakhtīshū' (" Jesus hath delivered "), dean of the academy, whom al-Manṣūr in 765 summoned for medical advice. Invited by the caliph to adopt Islam, Jūrjīs replied that he preferred the company of his fathers, be they in heaven or in hell.[4] Jūrjīs became the founder

[1] See above, pp. 297-8, 353-5. [2] See above, p. 168.

[3] Assemani, vol. i, pp. 494-5; Rubens Duval, *La Littérature syriaque* (Paris, 1907), pp. 353, 377; Barhebraeus, *Chronicon ecclesiasticum*, ed. and tr. J. B. Abbeloos and T. J. Lamy (Louvain, 1872), vol. i, cols. 303-6.

[4] Al-Qifṭi, *Ta'rīkh al-Ḥukamā'*, ed. J. Lippert (Leipzig, 1903), pp. 158-60; *Fihrist*, p. 296; ibn-al-'Ibri, pp. 213-15; ibn-abi-Uṣaybi'ah, vol. i, p. 125.

of a family of physicians which for six or seven generations almost monopolized the entire court medical practice. His son Bakhtīshū' (d. 801) was the chief physician of the Baghdād hospital under al-Rashīd.

Ḥunayn ibn-Isḥāq

Yūḥanna (Yaḥya) ibn-Māsawayh (Latin Mesuë), a Christian pupil of another Bakhtīshū', supposedly translated for al-Rashīd several manuscripts, mainly medical, which the caliph had brought back from raids into Asia Minor.[1] Yūḥanna's pupil Ḥunayn ibn-Isḥāq (Johannitius, 809–73) stands out as one of the greatest translators and noblest characters of that age. A member of the Eastern Syrian Church, Ḥunayn was born in al-Ḥīrah and appointed by al-Ma'mūn chief of Bayt al-Ḥikmah (house of wisdom), that combination of academy, library, museum and bureau of translation which the caliph had established. In his work Ḥunayn was assisted by his son Isḥāq [2] and his nephew Ḥubaysh ibn-al-Ḥasan.[3] The father was more proficient in Greek and evidently did the initial draft of the translation into Syriac, which his collaborators rendered into Arabic. Most of Aristotle's and Galen's works [4] were thus made available to the Arabic student. Ḥunayn is said to have also translated Hippocrates' medical treatises and Plato's *Republic*. A comparison of these translations shows that in all cases the Syriac was closer to the Greek and that the Arabic was a paraphrase of the Syriac. Ḥunayn was more than a translator. Al-Mutawakkil appointed him his private physician and once committed him to jail for refusing to concoct a poison for an enemy.

A pupil of Ḥunayn, Yaḥya ibn-'Adi (d. 974), revised a number of the existing versions and prepared fresh translations of Aristotle's *Poetics* and of Plato's *Laws* and *Timaeus*. Yaḥya belonged to the Western Syrian community, which produced other scholars who followed their co-religionists of the Eastern community and improved on their works. Another contemporary of Ḥunayn was Qusṭa ibn-Lūqa of Ba'labakk (d. *ca.*

[1] Ibn-al-'Ibri, p. 227; ibn-abi-Uṣaybi'ah, vol. i, p. 175; Qifṭi, p. 380.

[2] Ibn-Khallikān, vol. i, p. 116.

[3] *Fihrist*, p. 297; ibn-al-'Ibri, p. 252; ibn-abi-Uṣaybi'ah, vol. i, pp. 187, 203.

[4] Ḥunayn used the Syriac translations of some Galenic works already done by Job of Edessa (Ayyūb al-Ruhāwi, *ca.* 760–835). See Job of Edessa, *Book of Treasures*, ed. A. Mingana (Cambridge, 1935), pp. xix-xx; Barhebraeus, vol. iii, cols. 181-2.

912), who distinguished himself as translator of mathematical and philosophical works. Qusṭa knew Greek, Syriac and Arabic. He journeyed to Byzantine lands in quest of manuscripts on which he worked at Baghdād. He died in Armenia, where

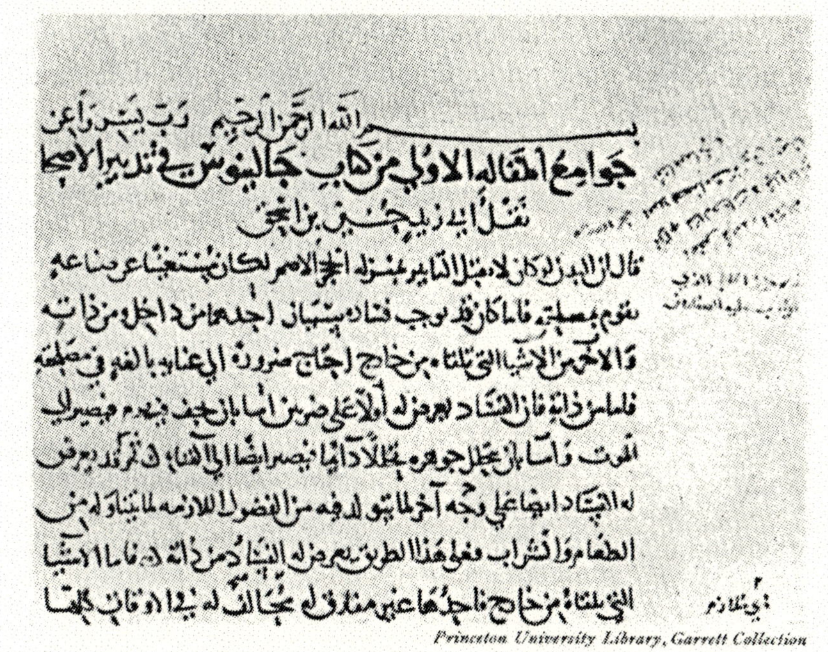
بسم الله الرحمن الرحيم رب يسر واعن
جوامع المقالة الاولى من كتاب جالينوس في تدبير الاصحا
نقل ابي زيد حنين بن اسحق

Princeton University Library, Garrett Collection

GALEN IN ARABIC, MANUSCRIPT

First lines of a chapter in Ḥunayn ibn-Isḥāq's translation of Galen, *Kitāb al-Ṣinā'ah al-Ṣaghīrah*, copied A.H. 572 (A.D. 1176/7). The MS. antedates any Greek or Latin MSS. extant and contains sections not yet edited or translated into any modern European language

he was honoured by a monumental tomb, leaving sixty-nine original works and seventeen translations.[1]

The Syrians were indifferent to Greek poetry and drama and so were the Arabs. A Maronite astrologer in the service of al-Mahdi, Thāwafīl (Theophile) of Edessa by name, made translations of Homer's *Iliad* and *Odyssey*, which did not survive.[2]

[1] *Fihrist*, p. 295; Qifṭi, pp. 262-3; G. Gabrieli in *Rendiconti della Reale Accademia dei Lincei*, ser. 5, vol. xxi (Rome, 1912), pp. 361-82.

[2] Assemani, vol. i, pp. 521-2; ibn-al-'Ibri, p. 220, where he is made a member of the Lebanese Church; cf. Ghazīri, p. 44; above, p. 522; Dibs, *Ta'rīkh Sūrīyah*, vol. iii, p. 297.

Ṣābians

Not only Christian but pagan Syrians made a major contribution to Arab intellectual life. These were the Ṣābians, more correctly pseudo-Ṣābians,[1] whose seat was Ḥarrān. Being star-worshippers and heirs of the Babylonian tradition, the Ṣābians had interested themselves in astronomy and allied sciences from time immemorial. As lovers of Hellenistic science they stood on a par with their Christian compatriots. Outstanding among their scholars was Thābit ibn-Qurrah (*ca.* 836–901). He and his disciples are credited with translating the bulk of Greek astronomical and mathematical works, including those of Ptolemy and Archimedes.[2] Moreover, they revised earlier translations. Ḥunayn's translation of Euclid, for instance, was revised by Thābit.[3] Thābit was succeeded by a son, two grandsons and one great-grandson — all of whom made names for themselves. His son Sinān was forced by a caliph to accept Islam.[4] Ḥunayn's son Isḥāq was also converted to Islam.[5]

It may be assumed that other mathematical and astronomical elements were transmitted by Aramaeans and Syrians living on Babylonian territory. Algebra (*al-jabr*), for example, appears as a full-fledged science from the pen of the renowned al-Khwārizmi (d. 850). The Babylonians had a term for this science and it is the same word, *gabru*. The assumed Syriac links here are missing.[6]

Original contribution

Clearly the bulk of Syriac literature consisted of translations and commentaries and was lacking in originality and creativeness. Only a few representative pieces have survived. In one field, however, the ascetic mystical, Syrian divines were more than copyists and imitators. It is in this same field that the parallelism to Sufi material is striking. Isaac of Nineveh, who

[1] Hitti, *History of the Arabs*, p. 358.
[2] *Fihrist*, pp. 267, 268; ibn-abi-Uṣaybiʻah, vol. i, pp. 218-20.
[3] Ibn-Khallikān, vol. i, pp. 177, 298.
[4] *Fihrist*, p. 302; ibn-abi-Uṣaybiʻah, vol. i, pp. 220-21.
[5] Al-Bayhaqi, *Ta'rīkh Ḥukamā' al-Islām*, ed. Muḥammad Kurd-ʻAli (Damascus, 1946), p. 19.
[6] The scientific terms borrowed from Greek and Latin directly or through Syriac and still current in Arabic may be illustrated by *falsafah* (philosophy), *jighrafīyah* (geography), *mūsīqa* (music). Other Latin and Greek words were Arabicized at various times: *kūrah* (district), *iskilah* (port), *nūti* (sailor, cf. Eng. nautical), *sayf* (Gr. *ksiphos*, sword). Persian loan words in Arabic may be illustrated by *bustān* (garden), *daydab* (sentry), *sarāwīl* (trousers), *ṣawlajān* (pall-mall, sceptre).

flourished in the late sixth century, emphasizes in his epistles and discourses the contemplative life, which he considers the second soul and the spirit of revelation, and asserts that it cannot be born in the womb of reason. He therefore admonishes his followers to seek solitude and while therein to think there is no other in the created world except the person himself alone and God on whom he thinks.[1] Another Syrian Christian mystic, Simon of Ṭaibūtheh (d. *ca.* 680), taught that at least a part of knowledge is apprehended not by words but through the inward silence of the mind and that that type of knowledge is the highest of all for it reaches the hidden Godhead.[2]

Moslem contribution: abu-Tammām

The finest talent of Moslem Syria of this period expressed itself through the medium of poetical composition. Two of its sons, abu-Tammām and al-Buḥturi, achieved the distinction of becoming court poets to ʿAbbāsid caliphs.

Ḥabīb ibn-Aws [3] abu-Tammām (*ca.* 804–*ca.* 850) was born in a place called Jāsim, Ḥawrān, of a Christian father who was a druggist. On his embracing Islam the young man attached himself to the Ṭayyi' tribe. Like other literati of his land he roamed through the world of Islam, visiting Egypt, where he worked as a water carrier, al-Ḥijāz, Armenia, Persia and al-ʿIrāq, before he settled in Baghdād. He joined the Caliph al-Muʿtaṣim in his new capital Sāmarra and accompanied him on his victorious expedition against ʿAmmūrīyah (Amorium, 838), which he celebrated in an ode [4] that is still committed to memory by Arab youth. True to type, he enjoyed the cup, the lute and the damsel and paid little heed to the dictates of religion.[5] His claim to glory rests not only on his original compositions but also on his compilation of *al-Ḥamāsah*,[6] which contains masterpieces of Arabic poetry from pre-Islamic days to his time. We owe this treasure of Arabic literature to the

[1] For more on Isaac consult Assemani, vol. i, pp. 444-63.

[2] Margaret Smith, *An Early Mystic of Baghdad* (London, 1935), p. 101, n. 2.

[3] A corruption of Tadūs (Theodosius?); ibn-Khallikān, vol. i, p. 214; al-Suyūṭi, *Ḥusn al-Muḥāḍarah*, vol. i, p. 267.

[4] *Dīwān abi-Tammām*, ed. Shāhīn ʿAṭīyah (Beirut, 1889), pp. 15-18; cf. al-Ṣūli, *Akhbār abi-Tammām*, ed. Khalīl M. ʿAsākir *et al.* (Cairo, 1937), pp. 109-13.

[5] Masʿūdi, vol. vii, p. 151.

[6] Al-Tibrīzi, *Sharḥ Dīwān al-Ḥamāsah*, 3 vols. (Būlāq, 1296); G. G. Freytag, *Hamasae carmina*, 2 vols. (Bonn, 1847–51); Friedrich Rückert, *Hamâsa*, 2 vols. (Stuttgart, 1846).

simple fact that the author on one of his journeys was marooned, because of excessive snow which blocked the roads, in the home of a cultured gentleman in Hamadhān (Ecbatana) whose library possessed collections of anthologies by Arabs of the desert and of other lands. Abu-Tammām used his leisure hours in perusing the collections.[1] His last days he spent in al-Mawṣil, where he was buried.

Al-Buḥturi

His younger contemporary abu-ʿUbaydah al-Walīd al-Buḥturi (*ca.* 820–97) was born in Manbij (Hierapolis) and belonged to the Buḥtur clan of the Ṭayyi' tribe.[2] He was reportedly discovered by abu-Tammām, who heard him in Ḥimṣ recite an original poem and recommended him to the people of Maʿarrat al-Nuʿmān, who engaged him at a salary of 4000 dirhams. Al-Buḥturi admired abu-Tammām and followed in his steps. In Baghdād he became the laureate of al-Mutawakkil and his successors, by one of whom, al-Muʿtazz, he was especially favoured. So avaricious was al-Buḥturi that he would wear dirty garments and almost starve his slave and brother to death.[3] Typical of his class, this poet employed his talent to extort remuneration from influential and wealthy personages under threat of changing his encomiums to lampoons. His *Dīwān* [4] offers illustrations of persons whom he both eulogized and satirized. It also reveals his interest in wine [5] and his ability to describe palaces, pools and wild animals [6] — a rather rare feature in Arabic poetry. Besides his *Dīwān* al-Buḥturi compiled a book of *Ḥamāsah*,[7] which was never regarded with the same esteem by Arab philologists as that of his predecessor. Arab critics have through the ages held al-Buḥturi as one of the trio which tops the list of ʿAbbāsid poets, the other two being abu-Tammām and al-Mutanabbi'.[8] "Probably most European critics would find Buḥturi less brilliant than Mutanabbī, yet far more poetical than Abū Tammām." [9]

Dik al-Jinn

Of a much lower calibre was ʿAbd-al-Salām ibn-Raghbān (777–849), nicknamed Dīk al-Jinn (the cock of the jinn) on

[1] Ibn-Khallikān, vol. i, p. 468.
[2] Yāqūt, *Udabā'*, vol. vii, p. 226.
[3] *Aghāni*, vol. xviii, p. 170.
[4] Vol. i (Constantinople, 1300), pp. 75, 87, 117-19.
[5] Vol. ii, pp. 176, 189.
[6] Vol. i, pp. 108, 16, 51, 111.
[7] Ed. R. Geyer and D. S. Margoliouth (Leyden, 1909).
[8] See below, p. 567.
[9] D. S. Margoliouth, art. "al-Buḥturi", *Encyclopaedia of Islām*.

account of his ugly features and green eyes. A native of Ḥimṣ, Dīk never left his homeland. He was probably descended from a Christian converted to Islam at the battle of Mu'tah.[1] Dīk is of special interest because in his verses, only a few of which have survived, he championed the cause of the vanquished peoples against the Arabian pretensions and asserted the superiority of the Syrians, by which he meant Arabicized Syrians, over the Arabians. He may therefore be considered a harbinger of that interesting intellectual movement termed Shuʿūbīyah,[2] which assumed political aspects in Persia and other lands. Dīk was a moderate Shīʿite and a poor one at that. He squandered his patrimony in pleasure and dissipation. In a fit of jealousy he fatally stabbed his wife, originally a Christian slave of his, and was thereafter convinced of her innocence and visited and tortured by her phantom, as pathetically described in his own verses.[3]

Al-Awzāʿi

In the non-poetical realm one man stands out, the theologian and jurist ʿAbd-al-Raḥmān ibn-ʿAmr al-Awzāʿi.[4] Born in Baʿlabakk in 707, he flourished in Beirut, where he died in a public bath in 774. His shrine (*maqām*[5]) is still standing in the sands south of the city. He had a reputation for learning, asceticism and moral courage[6] and was described by a biographer as the " imām of Syria, than whom no one more erudite existed in that land ".[7] Al-Awzāʿi taught that if a dhimmi fought in a Moslem army he was entitled to the same share of booty as a Moslem.[8] When al-Manṣūr visited Syria he heard al-Awzāʿi preach and greatly admired him. The legal system worked out by this jurist had a vogue in Syria for about two centuries before it was supplanted by the Ḥanafite and Shāfiʿite systems, and in al-Andalus and al-Maghrib for about forty years before it was replaced by the Mālikite.[9]

[1] *Aghāni*, vol. xii, p. 142; ibn-Khallikān, vol. i, p. 525. See above, p. 409.

[2] " Pertaining to the peoples ", i.e. non-Arabians, from a koranic verse 49 : 13.

[3] Ibn-Khallikān, vol. i, pp. 526-7; *Aghāni*, vol. xii, pp. 143-6.

[4] So called after either a Yamanite tribe or a suburb of Damascus; Yāqūt, vol. i, pp. 403-4; ibn-al-Athīr, *al-Lubāb fi Tahdhīb al-Ansāb* (Cairo, 1357), pp. 74-5; Ṭabari, vol. iii, p. 2514; abu-al-Fidā', vol. ii, p. 7.

[5] See above, p. 433, n. 4.

[6] See above, p. 543.

[7] Ibn-Khallikān, vol. i, p. 493. For more on him consult *Maḥāsin al-Masāʿi*, ed. Arislān.

[8] Al-Ṭabari, *Ikhtilāf al-Fuqahā'*, ed. Joseph Schacht (Leyden, 1933), pp. 121, 141.

[9] Ṣāliḥ, p. 23.

Not much is known about the Awzāʿi system, but probably it bore no traces of the Roman law which had prevailed in Syria, where he laboured, and which was taught on a grand scale in Beirut,[1] where he lived. Criminal law in Islam and civil law as it related to marriage, inheritance, usury and other matters are divinely revealed. Only in contractual transactions (*muʿāmalāt*) are there similarities between the two systems. In Arabic and Latin legal terminology certain terms signify the same thing: *fiqh* and jurisprudence, *fatwa* and opinion, *ijmāʿ* and consensus, *ʿādah* and custom, *maṣlaḥah ʿāmmah* and public interest; but that does not necessarily imply dependence. Loan words or Arabicized Greek and Latin words are not found. Nor do we know of any Roman or Byzantine law book translated into Arabic.

[1] See above, pp. 325 *seq.*

CHAPTER XLIII

SYRIA AN ADJUNCT OF MINOR STATES

THE first sign of internal decay in the ʿAbbāsid régime was the rise of the Turkish bodyguard under the immediate successors of al-Ma'mūn (d. 833). Like the Janissaries in Ottoman history this corps became too powerful for the caliph and at times held him in abject submission to its will.[1] Except for short intervals thereafter the ʿAbbāsid power was steadily on the decline. The caliphate was committing gradual suicide preliminary to its receiving the *coup de grâce* at the hands of Hūlāgu and his Mongol hordes (1258). As it was disintegrating petty dynasties, mostly of Arab origin, were parcelling out its domains in the west; while other dynasties, mostly Turkish and Persian, were performing the same operation in the east.

The Ṭūlūnids

First among those with which Syria was concerned was the Ṭūlūnid dynasty (868–905). This short-lived dynasty was founded by Aḥmad ibn-Ṭūlūn (868–84), whose father was a

A COIN OF IBN-ṬŪLŪN

Obverse and reverse of a gold dinar of Aḥmad ibn-Ṭūlūn struck at Miṣr (Cairo) A.H. 270=A.D. 883/4

Turk sent from Bukhāra as a present to al-Ma'mūn.[2] Aḥmad began his unusual career when his stepfather, newly appointed fief holder and governor over Egypt, sent him ahead of him as his deputy. No sooner had the ambitious young man arrived than he planned to take advantage of the distance that separated

[1] See above, p. 542.

[2] Ibn-Khaldūn, vol. iii, p. 295; vol. iv. p. 297.

him from the central government and practise independence.[1] On authorization from the caliph he increased his troops, reportedly to a hundred thousand, and marched against a rebel in Syria — the land of rebels, against ʿAbbāsid rule. This gave ibn-Ṭūlūn an entrée into that neighbouring country. On the death of its governor in 877 the time was deemed ripe for full occupation. The Egyptian army marched through al-Ramlah in the south to Damascus, Ḥimṣ, Ḥamāh and Aleppo in the north without opposition. Only Antioch closed its gates and was reduced after a short siege.[2] In A.H. 266 (879/80) Aḥmad proclaimed himself ruler of both lands. The practical test of independence had come in 875 when the Caliph al-Muʿtamid, hard pressed for cash, demanded but did not receive it from his Egyptian viceroy.

This was a turning-point in the history of Egypt. It then and there embarked upon its career as an independent state, a position which it maintained with one important interruption for centuries to come. Syria throughout this long period went with Egypt, as it did in Pharaonic days. The old connection, severed about a thousand years before, was thus re-established. The land of the Nile profited by the change, at least to the extent of having its entire revenue spent within its territory, but the position of its Syrian adjunct was not improved.

A typical military dictator, Aḥmad ruled with an iron hand. He built a powerful military machine on which he depended for the maintenance of his throne. Its core was a bodyguard of 24,000 Turkish and 40,000 Negro slaves from each one of whom he exacted an oath of allegiance. As if to justify his usurpation of power in the eyes of his subjects, he launched a programme of public works that had no parallel since Pharaonic days. He adorned his capital al-Fusṭāṭ and its new quarter al-Qaṭā'iʿ [3] with magnificent buildings, one of which was a hospital and the other a mosque. The hospital [4] cost 60,000 dinars and was the first of its kind in Egypt. The income of special property in Syria was set aside for its maintenance. The mosque, which

[1] Yaʿqūbi, vol. ii, pp. 615 *seq.*; Ṭabari, vol. iii, p. 1697.

[2] Ibn-Khaldūn, vol. iv, pp. 300-301; Kindi, ed. Guest, pp. 219 *seq.*

[3] "The Wards"; Maqrīzi, vol. i, pp. 313 *seq.*

[4] Ar. *bīmāristān*, see below, p. 642, n. 1. Ibn-Taghri-Birdi, *al-Nujūm al-Zāhirah fi Mulūk Miṣr w-al-Qāhirah*, ed. T. G. J. Juynboll, vol. ii (Leyden, 1855), p. 11; Kindi, p. 216.

still bears his name, is considered one of the grandest monuments of Moslem Egypt. Its structure cost twice that of the hospital [1] and follows in certain particulars the style of the school of Sāmarra, where Aḥmad had spent his youth. Its minaret is the oldest surviving in Egypt. This introduction of an ʿIrāqi pattern, however, did not oust the older Syro-Hellenic one and did not far extend its sway. The Mosque of ibn-Ṭūlūn remains as the only great example of that style.

On the Syrian shore ʿAkka was fortified by ibn-Ṭūlūn and a naval base was established in it. So strong was the tower that topped its double wall that three centuries later it thwarted for almost two years the combined efforts of two Crusading monarchs and in 1799 proved impregnable against the assaults of Napoleon's field artillery.[2] The Syrian geographer al-Maqdisi [3] reports that his own grandfather was summoned from Jerusalem to perform the unusual task of constructing a harbour in the water, which he did by fastening strong beams side by side and placing rocks on them. A gate was built in the middle and long chains were laid which ships entering the harbour at night could pull and thus signal their arrival.

Khumārawayh

Aḥmad was succeeded by his extravagant and dissolute twenty-year-old son Khumārawayh (884–95), one of thirty-three children of whom seventeen were boys.[4] Khumārawayh erected a palace with a "golden hall", whose walls were covered with gold and decorated with bas-reliefs of himself, his wives and songstresses.[5] The garden was rich in exotic trees planted around gilded water tanks, and in flowers growing in beds shaped to spell Arabic words. The palace had also an aviary, a zoological enclosure and a pool of quicksilver. The dynast could lie on leather cushions, moored on the surface of this pool by silken cords fastened to silver columns, and rock himself cosily to sleep.[6]

Under Khumārawayh the Ṭūlūnid domain extended from Barqah to the Euphrates and even beyond to the Tigris. On his accession in 892, al-Muʿtaḍid, the ablest and most energetic

[1] Ibn-Taghri-Birdi, vol. ii, p. 8; ibn-Khallikān, vol. i, p. 97.
[2] See below, p. 690.
[3] Pp. 162-3; quoted by Yāqūt, vol. iii, pp. 707-8.
[4] Ibn-Taghri-Birdi, vol. ii, p. 21; Suyūṭi, vol. ii, p. 11.
[5] Ibn-Taghri-Birdi, vol. ii, pp. 57-8; Maqrīzi, vol. i, pp. 316-17.
[6] Ibn-Taghri-Birdi, vol. ii, pp. 58-9; Maqrīzi, vol. i, p. 317.

ʿAbbāsid caliph of the period of decay, recognized the *status quo* and confirmed the Egyptian sovereign and his heirs in the possession of this vast territory for thirty years in return for an annual tribute of 300,000 dinars. The caliph even sought and secured the hand of Khumārawayh's beautiful daughter Qaṭr-al-Nada (dewdrop). The father settled on her a dowry of a million dirhams — so the story goes — and presented her with a thousand mortars of gold and other objects " the like of which had never been given before ".[1]

Khumārawayh's extravagance left the treasury empty. His addiction to pederasty, according to one report,[2] so enraged his slaves that they fell upon him one night in his villa outside Damascus and slaughtered him. His body was carried to Egypt for burial, and as it was being lowered into its grave, seven Koran readers chanting on the adjacent tomb of his father happened to be repeating : " Seize ye him and drag him into the mid-fire of hell ".[3] His young son and successor Jaysh (895–6) was murdered six months later by his own troops, who were alienated for lack of funds.[4]

The Qarmaṭians

The turbulent reign of Jaysh's brother Hārūn (896–904) was rendered more turbulent by the advent of the Qarmaṭians (Carmathians). This extreme Shīʿite sect, related to the Ismāʿīlite and Fāṭimid, received its name from an ʿIrāqi peasant Ḥamdān Qarmaṭ.[5] Fundamentally its organization was that of a secret, communistic society, with initiation as a requisite for admission. About 890 Ḥamdān occupied his new headquarters near al-Kūfah. Nine years later his followers were masters of an independent state on the western coast of the

[1] Ibn-Khallikān, vol. i, p. 310. Cf. ibn-Khaldūn, vol. iv, pp. 307-8 ; Ṭabari. vol. iii, pp. 2145-6 ; ibn-Taghri-Birdi, vol. ii, p. 55.

[2] Ibn-ʿAsākir, vol. v, p. 178.

[3] Sūr. 44 : 47.

[4] Subjoined is a tree of the Ṭūlūnid dynasty :

1. Aḥmad ibn-Ṭūlūn (868–84)
- 2. Khumārawayh (884–95)
  - 3. Jaysh (895–6)
  - 4. Hārūn (896–904)
  - Qaṭr-al-Nada
- 5. Shaybān (904–5)

[5] Consult Bernard Lewis, *The Origins of Ismāʿīlism* (Cambridge, 1940), pp. 19-22. *Qarmaṭ* is probably Aramaic for " secret teacher ".

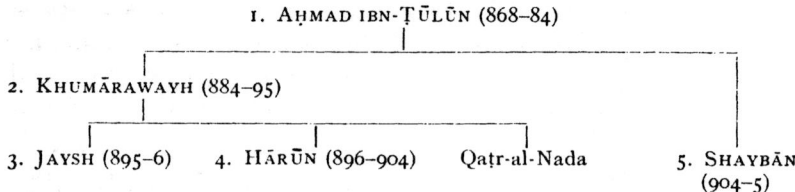

Persian Gulf. From these two centres they spread devastation in all directions. Throughout the Umayyad period Moslem Syria followed the orthodox Sunnite line; but the imposition of the hated 'Abbāsid régime opened the way for the introduction of 'Alid doctrines which now prepared the people for the reception of Qarmaṭian views. Just as in Byzantine Syria the people endeavoured to assert their nationality by espousing Christian doctrines considered heretical by Byzantium, so were they now ready to adopt ultra-Shī'ite, anti-'Abbāsid beliefs. The Qarmaṭian move against Syria was led by ibn-Zikrawayh.[1] After defeating the Ṭūlūnid garrison he laid siege to Damascus, reduced Ḥimṣ, destroyed a large number of the people of Ḥamāh and Ma'arrat al-Nu'mān and almost annihilated the population of Ba'labakk. Salamyah, later an Ismā'īlite-Assassin centre, surrendered. From many Syrian pulpits his name was cited in the Friday prayers as that of the expected Mahdi

In 902 the caliph sent against the Qarmaṭians an able general who, after defeating them and securing the allegiance of the Syrian vassals, set out for the conquest of Egypt. Meantime Hārūn was assassinated and succeeded by his uncle Shaybān (904–5).[2] In 904 the 'Abbāsid general reached the Ṭūlūnid capital al-Qaṭā'i', razed it to the ground, cut off twenty Ṭūlūnid heads and carried the remaining male members of this house in chains to the imperial capital. In the following year the last Sufyāni on record unfurled the white flag in Syria and he too was captured and sent to Baghdād.[3] The people who had once been described as acknowledging no other authority than that of the banu-Umayyah[4] had evidently at long last become demoralized and reconciled to alien rule.

The Ikhshīdids

The general who in the name of the Ṭūlūnids defended Damascus against the Qarmaṭians was a Turk from Farghānah, Ṭughj by name,[5] whose son Muḥammad managed to inherit the Ṭūlūnid legacy. After a brief interval of precarious 'Abbāsid sway in Egypt and Syria, Muḥammad established himself at al-Fusṭāṭ in 935 as the ruler of Egypt.[6] Four years later the Caliph al-Rāḍi, in response to Muḥammad's request, bestowed

[1] Ṭabari, vol. ii, pp. 2221-2.
[2] Kindi, pp. 247-8.
[3] Ṭabari, vol. iii, p. 2277.
[4] Maqdisi, pp. 293-4.
[5] Ibn-Sa'īd, *al-Mughrib fi Ḥula al-Maghrib*, ed. K. L. Tallqvist (Leyden, 1899), p. 5.
[6] Miskawayh, vol. i, pp. 332, 366, n.; ibn-Taghri-Birdi, vol. ii, p. 270.

upon him the old Iranian princely title al-Ikhshīd, thereby raising him above his peers. In the nineteenth century an Ottoman sultan conferred on his Egyptian viceroy a similar Persian title, Khedive. Following the Ṭūlūnid precedent, al-Ikhshīd began to cast covetous eyes on Egypt's northern neighbour, most of which was held and successfully defended by an adventurer ibn-Rā'iq.[1] Upon ibn-Rā'iq's death in 941 the vice-royalty of al-Ikhshīd over Syria and Egypt, together with Mecca and Medina, was recognized by the caliph and the Buwayhid overlords of Baghdād. For centuries hence the fortunes of al-Ḥijāz were linked with those of Egypt. In 944 the Ikhshīd obtained from the imperial government hereditary rights for his family in the lands he acquired.

A Negro ruler

Before he had time enough to warm his throne, al-Ikhshīd had his authority challenged in North Syria by the rising power of the Ḥamdānids, represented by their illustrious son Sayf-al-Dawlah, who installed himself in Aleppo. The armed conflicts took place mostly during the reigns of al-Ikhshīd's two sons. Unūjūr,[2] who was born in Damascus, where his father had died, succeeded Sayf in 946 under the tutelage of a Negro eunuch named abu-al-Misk Kāfūr (musky camphor).[3] Sayf-al-Dawlah's attempts to overrun all Syria were frustrated by this able regent, who defeated the Ḥamdānid troops in two engagements and compelled Sayf to recognize Egypt's overlordship. Kāfūr continued to hold the reins of government during the reign of Unūjūr's brother abu-al-Ḥasan 'Ali (960–66).[4] 'Ali was buried

[1] For the battles with him consult the contemporary historian Kindi, pp. 288-291; Miskawayh, vol. i, p. 414; ibn-Sa'īd, pp. 37 *seq.*; ibn-al-Athīr, vol. viii, p. 272.

[2] Unjūr, Anjūr; cf. ibn-Sa'īd, p. 45; ibn-Taghri-Birdi, vol. ii, p. 315; Kindi, p. 294; ibn-Khaldūn, vol. iv, p. 314; ibn-al-Athīr, vol. viii, p. 343; Miskawayh, vol. ii, p. 104. See also F. Wüstenfeld, *Die Statthalter von Ägypten zur Zeit der Chalifen*, pt. iv (Göttingen, 1876), p. 37.

[3] Ibn-Khallikān, vol. ii, p. 186.

[4] Ṭughj
|
1. MUḤAMMAD AL-IKHSHĪD (935–46)
|
2. ABU-AL-QĀSIM UNŪJŪR (946–60) | 3. 'ALI (960–66) | * * 4. ABU-AL-MISK KĀFŪR (966–8)
3. 'ALI → 5. AḤMAD (968–9)

The stars indicate a master-slave relationship.

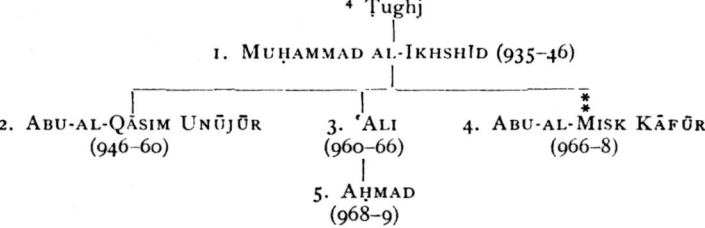

in Jerusalem, where his brother and father were interred. For two years after that the Negro ruled as a sovereign over a state which included besides Egypt and Syria a part of Cilicia with its chief city Tarsus.[1] Originally a harelipped Abyssinian slave whom al-Ikhshīd had bought from an oil dealer for eighteen dinars, Kāfūr was the first illustration in Islamic history of sovereigns who rose to high eminence from the lowliest origins. His enfranchisement, according to a story, was due to the fact that he kept his eyes fastened on his master while the eyes of all other slaves and servants had turned toward an elephant and a giraffe which the master had just received as a present. This slave could not miss for an instant the opportunity of serving his master if need be, and his extraordinary vigilance was amply rewarded.[2]

Kāfūr's name, like that of his adversary Sayf, has been immortalized by the greatest poet of the age, al-Mutanabbi', in verses which almost every school child in the Arab world today commits to memory. The verses were first composed in praise of the Egyptian potentate and later — after his failure to reward the poet with the high office to which he aspired — in ridicule of him.[3]

Fall of the Ikhshīdids

Kāfūr was succeeded by Aḥmad abu-al-Fawāris (968–9), an eleven-year-old lad unable to cope with the problems of the day. The Ḥamdānids were threatening from the north, the resurgent Qarmaṭians from the east and, more dangerously, the Fāṭimids[4] from the west. The Fāṭimid caliphate, which arose in Tunis in 909, had for years carried on secret correspondence with 'Alids and other sympathizers in Egypt. It was now time to act. In 969 its dashing general Jawhar had no difficulty in routing the Ikhshīdid army and entering al-Fusṭāṭ (July 6). The name of the Caliph al-Mu'izz was forthwith introduced into the public prayers and struck on the new coins. The Ikhshīdid vassal in Damascus, a cousin of abu-al-Fawāris, made a faint attempt to save Syria. Jawhar sent against him a general who defeated his troops at al-Ramlah and took him prisoner. Thereupon were Palestine and Central Syria incorporated into the emerging Fāṭimid empire.[5]

[1] Ibn-Khallikān, vol. ii, pp. 185-9; ibn-Khaldūn, vol. iv, pp. 314-15; ibn-Taghri-Birdi, vol. ii, p. 373.

[2] Ibn-Sa'īd, pp. 46-7.

[3] See below, pp. 567-8.

[4] See below, pp. 577 *seq.*

[5] Kindi, pp. 297-8.

The Ikhshīdid dynasty (935–69), like its predecessor the Ṭūlūnid (868–905), had an ephemeral existence. They followed the same pattern of behaviour, the pattern that typifies the case of many other states which, in this period of disintegration, broke off from the imperial government. Both made lavish use of state moneys to curry favour with their subjects and thereby ruined the treasuries. Neither of them had any national basis in the land over which it tried to rule; neither could rely upon a strong coherent body of supporters of its own race among its subjects. Being intruders the rulers had to recruit their bodyguards, which were also their armies, from alien sources. Such a rule could be maintained only so long as the arm which wielded the sword remained strong.

The Ḥamdānids: Sayf-al-Dawlah

The banu-Ḥamdān, successors of the Ikhshīdids in northern Syria, took their name from Ḥamdān ibn-Ḥamdūn of the Taghlib tribe, which was once Christian and produced the famous Umayyad poet al-Akhṭal.[1] Ḥamdān made his military and political debut in the late ninth century when he took possession of the fortress of Mārdīn.[2] His successors, after several conflicts and reconciliations with the caliphs, extended their sway into al-Mawṣil, a large part of Mesopotamia and northern Syria. The most distinguished among them was abu-al-ʿAli Ḥasan, who in 944 wrested from the Ikhshīdid vassal Aleppo, Antioch and Ḥimṣ [3] and subsequently received from the caliph the honorific title of Sayf-al-Dawlah (the sword of the state, i.e. the ʿAbbāsid, 944–67). By the bestowal of such high-sounding titles the caliphs meant to leave the impression that the recipient — in reality independent — was under their control. Sayf and his successors were tolerant Shīʿites and preserved the caliph's name in the Friday prayer. Sayf chose Aleppo [4] for capital perhaps because of its ancient citadel and its proximity to the frontier fortresses which he intended to defend against the new wave of Byzantine inroads. For the first time since Amorite days [5] the northern metropolis became the seat of an important government. In it the new ruler erected a magnificent palace with three baths and running water. A stream

[1] See above, pp. 439, 494.
[2] Ṭabari, vol. iii, p. 2141.
[3] Ibn-Saʿīd, p. 41.
[4] Ḥalab, called al-Shahbā' (grey) possibly because of its whitish stones.
[5] See above, p. 68

surrounded the palace and a garden and racecourse adjoined it.[1]

Sayf's domain covered North Syria, a section of Cilicia and a large part of northern Mesopotamia. He even established a foothold in Armenia with the aid of Kurdish supporters;[2] his mother was a Kurd. By marrying a daughter of al-Ikhshīd he hoped to be left in peaceful possession of his territory. Damascus he failed to reduce.[3] A frontier province, his principality consumed much of its time and energy struggling with the Byzantines. Sayf was the first after a long interval to take up the cudgels seriously against the Christian enemies of Islam. This Ḥamdānid-Byzantine conflict may be considered a significant chapter in the prehistory of the Crusades. As a warrior the Ḥamdānid prince had a worthy peer in the Byzantine emperor Nicephorus,[4] with whom the historians record about ten engagements. Success was not always on Sayf's side. In 962 he even temporarily lost his own capital after a brief siege in which his palace, symbol of his glory, was destroyed.[5] The repercussion was felt in Baghdād, where a demonstration staged by the people, who demanded that the caliph in person lead an expeditionary force, resulted in nothing more than tears from the caliph's eyes.[6] The death of Sayf in 967[7] and the ensuing internal discord enabled Nicephorus and his successors to push their advance, occupy a large part of North Syria and impose an ephemeral Byzantine suzerainty over the Ḥamdānid realm. In 968 Nicephorus again captured Aleppo and added Antioch, Ḥimṣ and the towns between. His successor John Zimisces[8] reduced six years later not only the coastal towns of Beirut, Jubayl, ʿArqah, Ṭarṭūs, Jabalah and al-Lādhiqīyah but such inland places as Ṣihyawn and Baʿlabakk. Antioch remained in Byzantine hands for over a century (968–1084).

Aleppo was not recaptured by the Ḥamdānids until 975. Its citadel held out for two more years. Sayf's son Saʿd-al-Dawlah had his hands full fighting a cousin claimant in Ḥimṣ before he

[1] Ibn-al-Shiḥnah, *al-Durr al-Muntakhab fi Ta'rīkh Ḥalab* (Beirut, 1909), pp. 60-61, 133.

[2] Miskawayh, vol. ii, p. 161.

[3] Ibn-Saʿīd, p. 42.

[4] Nicephorus II Phocas (963–9), Niqfūr of Arabic chronicles.

[5] Ibn-al-Athīr, vol. viii, pp. 401-2; Miskawayh, vol. ii, pp. 192-4.

[6] Miskawayh, vol. ii, p. 201, n.

[7] For a collection of Arabic texts relative to Sayf consult Marius Canard, *Sayf al Daula* (Algiers, 1934).

[8] Ar. ibn-al-Shumushqīq; ibn-al-Qalānisi, pp. 12-14.

felt secure in his succession. Meantime a disloyal vassal in Aleppo had signed a treaty with the Byzantines agreeing to the payment of tribute, which Sa'd refused to acknowledge. In 985 Sa'd besieged Qal'at Sam'ān,[1] then in Byzantine hands, sacked it and killed its monks or sold them into slavery. In the reign of Sa'd's successor Sa'īd-al-Dawlah (991–1001)[2] a new foe was looming on the southern horizon, the Fāṭimids. Hard pressed, the Ḥamdānid prince appealed to the Emperor Basil for aid. The Byzantine ruler rushed with 17,000 men to Aleppo and the enemy dispersed for the time being. But Sa'īd had afterwards to acknowledge Fāṭimid suzerainty. Being young he had a regent over him whose daughter he married. The regent now coveted the throne for himself and poisoned both his son-in-law and daughter. For two years after that he held the regency in the name of the Fāṭimid caliphs over Sa'īd's two sons 'Ali and Sharīf (1001–3). In 1003 he sent the two young princes to Cairo with the Ḥamdānid harem and appointed his own son co-regent. This was the last episode in the life of the Ḥamdānid dynasty, which was the second and last Arab dynasty to rise on Syrian soil.

The glamorous circle of Sayf-al-Dawlah

The life-cycle of the Ḥamdānid dynasty did not suffer in essence from that of its two predecessors, the Ikhshīdid and the Ṭūlūnid. A dominant leader carves a principality for himself, is followed by incompetent successors; the state moneys are squandered; discord within and foes without bring the story to an end. In this case the munificence of Sayf in his patronage of science and art was the first great drain on the treasury.

Sayf surrounded himself in his gorgeous palace with a circle of literary and artistic talent that could hardly be matched except by that of the Baghdād caliphs in their heyday. It comprised the renowned philosopher and musician al-Fārābi, the distinguished historian of Arabic literature al-Iṣbahāni, the eloquent

[1] See above, pp. 364-5.

[2] 1. Sayf-al-Dawlah abu-al-Ḥasan 'Ali (944–67)

2. Sa'd-al-Dawlah abu-al-Ma'āli Sharīf (967–91)

3. Sa'īd-al-Dawlah abu-al-Faḍā'il Sa'īd (991–1001)

4a. Abu-al-Ḥasan 'Ali (1001–3) 4b. Abu-al-Ma'āli Sharīf (1001–3)

preacher ibn-Nubātah (d. 984),[1] the philologist ibn-Khālawayh, the grammarian ibn-Jinni (d. 1002),[2] the warrior-poet abu-Firās and, above all, the illustrious bard al-Mutanabbi'.

Sayf-al-Dawlah — may God favour him, gratify his wishes and make Paradise his abode! — was the luminous spot of his age and the pillar of Islam. By him the frontiers were guarded and the state affairs well managed. . . . It is said that after the caliphs no monarch gathered around him so many shaykhs of poetry and stars of learning. After all, a monarch is like a market, people bring to him what is in demand by him. Sayf himself was a literateur, a poet and a lover of poetry.[3]

Abu-al-Ṭayyib Aḥmad ibn-al-Ḥusayn received his surname al-Mutanabbi' (prophecy claimant, 915–65 [4]) because in his youth he claimed the gift of prophecy, attempted an imitation of the Koran and was followed by a number of admirers, especially in al-Lādhiqīyah and the Syrian Desert. The Ikhshīdid governor of Ḥimṣ cast him into prison, where he remained for almost two years and from which he went out cured from his prophetic illusion but not from his vanity, self-assertiveness and self-admiration, which accompanied him throughout his life. Here is his own estimate of his work: Al-Mutanabbi'

My deep poetic art the blind have eyes to see,
  My verses ring in ears as deaf as deaf can be.
They wander far abroad while I am unaware,
  But men collect them watchfully with toil and care.

. . . .

The desert knows me well, the night, the mounted men,
  The battle and the sword, the paper and the pen![5]

The man who sang his own praise in such glowing terms had a humble origin. He was born in al-Kūfah of a father who worked as water carrier. When still a lad he moved with the

[1] His *Khuṭab* (sermons) have appeared in several Cairo and Beirut editions.
[2] Son of a Turkish slave, noted for his commentary on al-Mutanabbi'.
[3] Al-Tha'ālibi (d. 1037), *Yatīmat al-Dahr fi Shu'arā' Ahl al-'Aṣr* (Damascus, 1303), vol. i, pp. 8-9.
[4] The thousandth anniversary of his death was celebrated in Syria in 1935 (A.H. 1354); see *Al Mutanabbi: Recueil publié à l'occasion de son millénaire* (Beirut, 1936); cf. R. Blachère, *Un Poète arabe: Abou-ṭ-Ṭayyib al-Motanabbî* (Paris, 1935), pp. 66 *seq*.
[5] Al-Wāḥidi, *Sharḥ Dīwān al-Mutanabbi*, ed. Fr. Dieterici (Berlin, 1861), pp. 483-4; Nicholson, p. 307.

family to Syria. After roaming about in quest of a patron he settled in Aleppo as the laureate of Sayf-al-Dawlah; the two names have ever since remained inseparably linked. The proud poet insisted on reciting his compositions in the princely presence while sitting and without bowing down to kiss the ground. Throughout his audiences with Kāfūr he would keep his shoes on and his sword in his belt.[1] On the way back and forth he would ride with two of his slaves fully armed. The reason given for deserting the Syrian court in favour of the Egyptian is that the poet had an argument with Sayf's teacher ibn-Khālawayh, who struck him with a key on the face. Disappointed in his Egyptian patron al-Mutanabbi' stole away to Baghdād and Persia. On his way back he was killed with his son by a marauding band of Bedouins who made away with the autograph copy of his *Dīwān*.[2]

Outstanding among the odes in his *Dīwān* are those depicting the glories of Sayf's campaigns against the Byzantines. It is a question whether or not those panegyrics did not contribute more than the exploits themselves to making Sayf the myth he is in Arabic annals. In them the poet appears as the consummate phrasemaker in the Arabic language. Nuggets of wise sayings add to the value of the composition; the poet personally lived a moral life in contrast to members of his class in his day. In places the style appears bombastic and ornate, the rhetoric florid and the metaphor overdone — but not to the Easterner. Such is the hold that this poet has had upon the imagination of Arabic speakers that he is still generally considered the greatest in Islam. In him and his two predecessors, abu-Tammām and al-Buḥturi, Arabic poetry reached its full maturity, if not its zenith. With few exceptions the decline after this was steady.

Abu-Firās

Al-Mutanabbi' had a close competitor in abu-Firās al-Ḥārith ibn-abi-al-'Alā' al-Ḥamdāni (932–68), a cousin of Sayf-al-Dawlah and his comrade at arms. For one verse his patron is said to have bestowed on abu-Firās a fief near Manbij, the annual income of which amounted to a thousand dinars. In 962 the gallant poet was taken as a prisoner to Constantinople

[1] Ibn-Khallikān, vol. i, p. 64.

[2] Besides Dieterici's edition there is one by Naṣīf al-Yāziji, *al-'Urf al-Ṭayyib fi Sharḥ Dīwān abi-al-Ṭayyib* (Beirut, 1882).

and was ransomed after four years.[1] Some of his most touching poems were composed in captivity.[2] An ode of his extolling the 'Alids and berating the 'Abbāsids is still a favourite in Shī'ite circles.[3] It was he who, after the death of Sayf, claimed independent control over Ḥimṣ and fell fighting against troops sent by Sayf's son.[4]

Lesser lights in the poetical firmament of this age included the versatile Kushājim and the euphuistic al-Wa'wā'. Of Hindu origin,[5] Kushājim (d. *ca.* 971) owes his curious name to a combination of the first letters of the Arabic words for writer, poet, literateur, polemicist and astrologer—all of which he supposedly was. A native of al-Ramlah, he embarked on his career as a cook for Sayf-al-Dawlah. Some of the poetry he composed describes different dishes and drinks.[6] To his many accomplishments he added that of medicine and wrote a book on zoology. Al-Wa'wā' (d. 999), a Damascene of Ghassānid origin, is remembered by an ode in which he describes a damsel crying and biting her lip in the following terms: "She caused pearls to rain from narcissus, watered with them the roses and bit the jujubes with her hailstones".[7]

Other than poets

The court of Sayf-al-Dawlah was graced by other than poets. A historian of literature and music, al-Iṣbahāni, and a philosopher-musician, al-Fārābi, are worthy of note. Abu-al-Faraj al-Iṣbahāni (Iṣfahāni, 897–967), a lineal descendant of the last Umayyad caliph but of Shī'ite leanings, was born in Iṣbahān. From his royal relatives in Spain he received gifts in recognition of books dedicated to them. Sayf bestowed on him a thousand gold pieces for an autograph copy of his monumental *Kitāb al-Aghāni*[8] (book of songs), which is much more than what it professes to be. It is related that a contemporary learned

[1] Ibn-Khallikān, vol. i, pp. 225-6.

[2] Consult his *Dīwān*, ed. Nakhlah Qalfāṭ (Beirut, 1900); tr. in part, Rudolph Dvořák as *Abû Firâs: ein arabischer Dichter und Held* (Leyden, 1895). See also Tha'ālibi, vol. i, pp. 22-62.

[3] For text consult his *Dīwān*, ed. Sāmi al-Dahhān (Beirut, 1944), vol. iii, pp. 348-56; Canard, pp. 325-33.

[4] See above, pp. 565-6.

[5] Mas'ūdi, vol. viii, p. 318.

[6] Mas'ūdi, vol. viii, pp. 394-5, 399-400. See also his *Dīwān* (Beirut, 1313), pp. 44-5, 50, 51, 83, 84, 85, 179-80.

[7] Al-Wa'wā', *Dīwān*, ed. J. Krachkovsky (Leyden, 1914), pp. 47, 137; Kutubi, vol. ii, p. 182.

[8] 20 vols. (Būlāq, 1285); R. E. Brünnow edited vol. xxi (Leyden, 1888) and I. Guidi issued the index (Leyden, 1900).

vizir who ordinarily carried along with him on his travels thirty camel loads of reading matter happened on a copy of *al-Aghānī* and was ever thereafter content with it alone as a companion.[1]

Al-Fārābi

Muḥammad abu-Naṣr al-Fārābi (Alpharabius) was a Turk from Fārāb, Turkestan.[2] He lived in Syria as a Sufi, satisfied with an honorarium of four dirhams per day from Sayf. In 950, aged eighty, he died at Damascus, to which he had accompanied his patron. Al-Fārābi was one of the earliest Moslem thinkers to attempt a harmonization of Greek philosophy and Islam. His system was a syncretism of Aristotelianism, Platonism and Sufism. His people conferred on him the unique title of " the second teacher " after Aristotle, who was the first. He became the intellectual ancestor of ibn-Sīna and all other subsequent Moslem philosophers. His major works are *Risālat Fuṣūṣ al-Ḥikam* (epistles containing bezels of wisdom),[3] *Risālah fi Ārā' Ahl al-Madīnah al-Fāḍilah*[4] (treatise on the opinions of the inhabitants of the superior city) and *al-Siyāsah* (*Siyāsāt*) *al-Madanīyah* (political economy).[5] In the last two the author presents his conception of an ideal city, which he conceives as a hierarchical organism analogous to the human body. His city is clearly modelled after Plato's *Republic*.

More than a philosopher, al-Fārābi was a fair physician and mathematician, an occult scientist and an excellent musician. His three works on music, headed by *Kitāb al-Mūsīqi al-Kabīr* (the great book of music),[6] mark him as one of the greatest, if not the greatest, of all Arabic music theorists. Indeed he was a practitioner, too. He was able — so goes the story — to play a lute of his own manufacture in the Ḥamdānid salon and make his listeners laugh, cry or go to sleep — as he wished.[7]

Al-Maqdisi, geographer

While the Ḥamdānids ruled in North and the Fāṭimids in

[1] Ibn-Khallikān, vol. ii, p. 11.

[2] Ibn-abi-Uṣaybi'ah, vol. ii, p. 134; Qifṭi, p. 277; ibn-Ḥawqal, p. 390.

[3] Published by Friedrich Dieterici in his *Die Philosophie der Araber im IX. und X. Jahrhundert n. Chr.*, vol. xiv (Leyden, 1890), pp. 66-83.

[4] Published at Cairo, 1323, and also by Dieterici, *Philosophie der Araber*, vol. xvi (Leyden, 1895), who also translated it as *Der Musterstaat von Alfārābi* (Leyden, 1900).

[5] (Ḥaydarābād, 1346.)

[6] Extracts by J. P. N. Land appeared in *Actes du sixième congrès international des orientalistes*, pt. 2, sec. 1 (Leyden, 1885), pp. 100-168. Fr. tr. by Rodolphe d'Erlanger, *La Musique arabe*, vols. i, ii, al-Fārābī (Paris, 1930–35).

[7] Ibn-Khallikān, vol. ii, p. 501.

South Syria there flourished in Palestine one of the most original and meritorious geographers, al-Maqdisi (Muqaddasi, 946–*ca.* 1000). Born in Jerusalem (*Bayt al-Maqdis*) under the Ikhshīdids, he started at the age of twenty travels that took him through all Moslem lands excluding Spain, India and Sijistān. In 985 he embodied the information he thus gathered in a book entitled *Aḥsan al-Taqāsīm fi Ma'rifat al-Aqālīm* (the best of classification for the knowledge of climates).[1] In its composition, as he says in the introduction, he was guided primarily by personal observation and experience rather than by books. His predilection seems to have been in favour of the Shī'ah and the Fāṭimids. At his time the Shī'ah did represent the intellectual and progressive wing of Islam.

Thanks to the works of al-Maqdisi and other geographers who began to flourish in this age, our knowledge of the economic and social conditions of tenth century Syria reaches a height unattained before. No Latin, Greek or Semitic geographer ever left us material comparable to this Arabic material in quality and quantity. Al-Maqdisi surveys trade, agriculture, industry and general education. He refers, among many other things, to iron ores in the " mountains of Beirut ",[2] the abundant trees and hermits in Lebanon,[3] the sugar and glassware products of Tyre, the cheese and cotton goods of Jerusalem and the cereals and honey of 'Ammān.[4] He characterizes Syria as a " blessed region, the home of cheap prices, fruits and righteous people ".[5] Al-Maqdisi's Persian contemporary ibn-al-Faqīh[6] emphasizes the ascetics and woods in Lebanon and makes special mention of its apples. Another Persian, ibn-Khurdādhbih (d. *ca.* 912), enumerates the districts of Syria, indicating the roads and the distances between cities.[7] 'Arqah, Tripoli, Beirut and other coastal and inland towns were still strongly fortified. On the whole the general impression one receives from a perusal of these and other contemporaneous sources is favourable so far as the standard of living is concerned. People generally lived a happy, useful life — judged by the authors' standards. Christians and Jews do not seem to have been worse off under

[1] Ed. M. J. de Goeje (Leyden, 1877).

[2] P. 184; al-Idrīsi, *Nuzhat al-Mushtāq, Dhikr al-Sha'm*, ed. J. Gildemeister (Bonn, 1885), p. 16. See above, pp. 35, 277; below, p. 656.

[3] P. 188. [4] P. 180. [5] P. 179. [6] Pp. 112, 117.

[7] Pp. 74 *seq.*, 95 *seq.*

the petty dynasts of Egypt and Syria than under the ʿAbbāsids. Most of the scribes in Syria, if not all of them, and most of the physicians were still Christians.[1] In 992 Syria was visited by an earthquake which, however, did not do as much damage as that of 859/60, in which al-Lādhiqīyah and Jabalah were almost wiped out of existence and Antioch lost fifteen hundred buildings.[2] In the preceding century Syria had suffered from at least two earthquakes, in 738 and 746.

Dark ages begin

Black clouds, however, were thickening in the horizon; times of trouble lay ahead. After the mid-tenth century Fāṭimid armies of Berbers and Egyptians resumed their incursions from the south; fanatic Qarmaṭian hordes of ʿIrāqis and Persians were again overrunning the land from the north-east. Saljūq and other unruly Turkish tribes were soon to follow, pouring in from the north. Clearly the dark ages in the history of Syria had begun. A state bordering on anarchy prevailed. Pillage, fire and slaughter marched in the wake of the invaders. Leading cities — Aleppo, Damascus, Jerusalem — were tossed like a ball from one alien hand to another. Toward the end of the eleventh century Frankish and other Crusading bands were winding their way from the north-west into the torn, tortured land. Before the Crusades were over, waves of Mongol tribes were rolling over Syria from north to south. The slave dynasty of nondescript Mamlūks was superseded in its rule, or rather misrule, by the Ottoman Turks. The blackout continued throughout until the middle of the nineteenth century.

[1] Maqdisi, p. 183, ll. 4, 7-8.

[2] Ṭabari, vol. iii, pp. 1439-40.

CHAPTER XLIV

BETWEEN SALJŪQS AND FĀṬIMIDS

THE major powers that arose with the dismemberment of the ʿAbbāsid state were not those treated in the preceding chapters but the ones to be treated now, the Saljūqs and the Fāṭimids. These two powers parcelled out Syria between them; the Saljūqs held its northern part and the Fāṭimids the southern. The former were Turks, the latter allegedly Arabs.

Ṭughril in Baghdād

The eponymous founder of the Saljūq house was a Turkoman chief of the Ghuzz tribe in Turkestan who, with his rough nomadic clan, moved to the region of Bukhāra,[1] where they evidently embraced Islam. His grandson Ṭughril pushed his conquests westward through Persia and in 1055 stood at the head of his band at the very gate of Baghdād. There was but one course for the powerless Caliph al-Qā'im to follow, to exchange one master for another — the Shīʿite Persian Buwayhids for the Sunnite Turkish Saljūqs.[2] The new Saljūq ruler assumed the title of *sulṭān* (he with authority). He is the first Moslem ruler whose coins bear this title. With his successors the designation became regular. In the wake of Ṭughril's victory hordes of Turks, Saljūq and others, were funnelled into Western Asia and spread all over that region. Gradually they were Islamized and Arabicized.

Under Ṭughril's nephew and successor Alp Arslān (hero-lion, 1063–72) and the latter's son Malikshāh (1072–9), the Saljūq domain attained its greatest dimensions, from the borders of Afghanistan to the frontiers of the Byzantine empire in western Asia Minor. In 1070 Alp advanced against the Mirdāsids in North Syria and occupied Aleppo, leaving the Mirdāsid governor as his vassal.[3] Alp's general Atsiz, a Turkoman from Khwārizm, pushed into Palestine and captured al-

[1] Ibn-al-Athīr, vol. ix, pp. 321-2.

[2] Ibn-Khallikān, vol. i, pp. 107-8; ibn-Taghri-Birdi, ed. Popper, vol. ii, pt. 2, p. 225.

[3] Ibn-al-Athīr, vol. x, pp. 43-4; see below, pp. 580-81.

Ramlah, Jerusalem and other towns as far south as ʻAsqalān, whose Fāṭimid garrison held out.[1] In 1076 he occupied Damascus and exasperated its people with his exactions. Alp's son Tutush recaptured Damascus two years later and killed Atsiz.[2] In 1071 Alp won a decisive victory over the Byzantines at Manzikert, north of Lake Van, and took the emperor himself prisoner. All Asia Minor then lay open to the Turks. Hordes of them rushed into Anatolia and northern Syria. Turkish generals penetrated as far as the Hellespont. With one stroke the traditional frontier separating Islam from Christendom was pushed four hundred miles west. For the first time Turks gained a foothold in that land — a foothold that was never lost.

The fragmentation of the vast sultanate soon followed. Different Saljūq amīrs received different subdivisions. That of Asia Minor (Rūm) was held by a cousin of Alp, Sulaymān, who in 1077 established himself in Nicaea (Nīqiyah, Iznīq), not far from Constantinople. In 1084 the capital shifted south-east to Iconium (Qūniyah, Koniah). In the same year Antioch was recovered for Islam from the Byzantines by the Saljūqs.[3] No hold on Asia Minor could be secure as long as Byzantines remained entrenched in the rear. It was a son of Sulaymān, Qilij Arslān, whom the first bands of Crusaders encountered (1096) as they crossed Asia Minor *en route* to Syria.[4] One of the various Turkish states which followed the Saljūqs of Rūm about 1300 was that of the Ottomans, traditionally another branch of the Ghuzz.[5]

The Saljūqs of Syria

The Saljūq dynasty of Syria was founded by Alp's son Tutush, who in 1094 gained possession of Aleppo.[6] The city was still the leading one of North Syria and a worthy seat of a principality. Tutush fell in battle the following year and his son Riḍwān (1095–1113) became after him lord of Aleppo while another son, Duqāq, established himself over Damascus.[7] The two amīrs were soon involved in a family war [8] and a couple of years later Duqāq was forced to recognize the overlordship of

[1] Ibn-ʻAsākir, vol. ii, p. 331; ibn-Khaldūn, vol. v, pp. 145-6.
[2] Ibn-Khallikān, vol. i, p. 168. [3] See above, p. 565. [4] See below, p. 591.
[5] See below, p. 661. [6] Ibn-al-Athīr, vol. x, pp. 157-8.
[7] Ibn-Khallikān, vol. i, p. 168.
[8] Ibn-al-Qalānisi, pp. 130-32; ibn-al-Athīr, vol. x, p. 168; ibn-Khaldūn, vol. v, p. 148.

his brother. In 1096 a brother-in-law of Tutush who held Jerusalem as fief surrendered it to the Fāṭimids. It was Fāṭimid rule which the Crusaders found on their arrival in the Holy Land. Riḍwān was a partisan of the Ismā'īli Assassins and the Aleppines were then evidently mostly Shī'ites and Ismā'īlites.[1] But the Sunnites hated him. For a month he ordered the name of the Fāṭimid caliph, also of the Ismā'īli denomination, recited in the Friday prayer, but then reverted to the 'Abbāsid name. Riḍwān was one of those with whom the Crusaders were repeatedly involved in battle in North Syria. He maintained his hold on Aleppo against the Frankish attacks but his attempt at relieving Antioch, besieged in 1098, failed.[2]

Riḍwān was succeeded in 1113 by his sixteen-year-old son Alp Arslān, a feeble-minded debauchee, who was assassinated by his regent in Aleppo shortly after his installation.[3] A brother, Sulṭān Shāh, ruled under a regent for three years. In 1117 a Turkoman officer in the Saljūq army, Īl-Ghāzi ibn-Urtuq got possession of Aleppo.[4] The seat of the branch of the Urtuqid dynasty which he established lay at Mārdīn. He was a redoubtable warrior against the Crusaders.

The Atābegs

In 1128 Aleppo was annexed by another warring Turk, 'Imād-al-Dīn (pillar of the faith) Zangi,[5] of al-Mawṣil, whose father was once a slave in the service of Malikshāh and later a

[1] Ibn-al-Athīr, vol. x, p. 349; ibn-al-Qalānisi, p. 142; ibn-Khaldūn, vol. v, pp. 153-4.

[2] See below, p. 592.

[3] Ibn-al-Qalānisi, pp. 189, 198; Kamāl-al-Dīn, "Muntakhabāt min Ta'rīkh Ḥalab", in *Recueil des historiens des croisades: historiens orientaux*, vol. iii (Paris, 1884), pp. 602-3, 605-6.

A genealogical table of the Saljūqs of Syria (1094–1117):

1. Tutush ibn-Alp Arslān (1094–5)

2. Riḍwān (at Aleppo, 1095–1113) | 2. Duqāq (at Damascus, 1095–1104)

3. Alp Arslān (1113–14) | 4. Sulṭān Shāh (1114–17)

[4] Ibn-al-Qalānisi, p. 199.

[5] Founder of the Atābeg dynasty of al-Mawṣil and Syria. The *atābegs* (Tur. *ata*, "father" + *beg*, "prince", cf. Atatürk) were originally guardians or tutors of the young Saljūq princes and finally replaced them in supreme power. Abu-Shāmah, *al-Rawḍatayn fi Akhbār al-Dawlatayn*, vol. i (Cairo, 1287), p. 24.

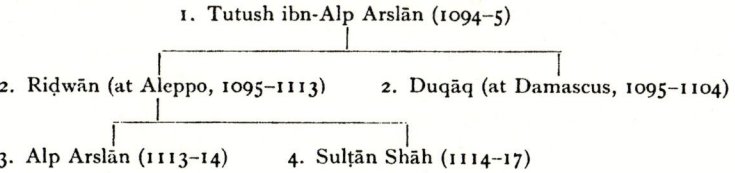

lieutenant in Tutush's army.[1] In the following years Ḥamāh, Ḥimṣ, Ba'labakk and Damascus were added to the Zangid realm. Zangi was the anti-Crusading hero who in 1144 wrested Edessa from Frankish hands [2] and inaugurated the series of victories which were continued by his son Nūr-al-Dīn and his son's successor Ṣalāḥ-al-Dīn (Saladin).[3] He was the builder of medieval al-Mawṣil. Another Turkish Atābeg was Ṭughtagīn,[4] a freedman of Tutush, who had entrusted him with the education of his son Duqāq. Following the norm of other regents, Ṭughtagīn usurped the sovereign power and was recognized as the ruler of Damascus shortly after the death in 1104 of his protégé, whose mother he had married.[5] In 1116 the Great Saljūq sultan in Baghdād appointed Ṭughtagīn governor of Syria with the right to regulate taxes and levy armies. Ṭughtagīn allied himself with Īl-Ghāzi and they jointly warred against the Franks.[6] Both were heavy drinkers; Īl-Ghāzi would at times remain under the influence of alcohol for "twenty days" at a stretch. Once Īl-Ghāzi sent him a Frankish prisoner, lord of Ṣihyawn, with the hope that he would scare the prisoner and exact a higher ransom. But Ṭughtagīn, who was then drinking heavily in his tent, simply drew his sword and decapitated the unfortunate lord, explaining later that he had no better way of scaring him.[7] In 1112 Tyre, then under the Fāṭimids, appealed to Ṭughtagīn for aid against the Crusaders. The relief he brought was temporary. The seaport was entered in 1124 by the Crusaders.[8]

The line started by Ṭughtagīn bore the name of his son and

[1] Kamāl-al-Dīn in *Recueil*, vol. iii, pp. 703 *seq.*; ibn-al-Athīr, "Ta'rīkh al-Dawlah al-Atābakīyah", in *Recueil*, vol. ii, pt. 2, pp. 10 *seq.*

[2] Kamāl-al-Dīn in *Recueil*, vol. iii, pp. 685-6; ibn-al-Athīr in *Recueil*, vol. ii, pt. 2, pp. 118-19; ibn-Khallikān, vol. i, p. 344; Dhahabi, vol. ii, pp. 38, 40; abu-Shāmah, vol. i, pp. 33-4, 36-7.

[3] See below, pp. 600 *seq.*

[4] Turkish for "warrior falcon", the Daldequin of Western historians. His Arabic honorific title was Ẓahīr-al-Dīn, "the supporter of religion". Most of these Turkish generals assumed pompous Arabic titles: Īl-Ghāzi (champion of his people) took "Najm-al-Dīn" (the star of religion), Tutush took "Tāj-al-Dawlah" (the crown of the state) and Riḍwān, "Fakhr-al-Mulūk" (the pride of kings).

[5] Ibn-al-Qalānisi, p. 190; ibn-Khallikān, vol. i, p. 169; ibn-Khaldūn, vol. v, p. 155; ibn-Taghri-Birdi, vol. ii, pt. 2, p. 388.

[6] Kamāl-al-Dīn in *Recueil*, vol. iii, pp. 620 *seq.*

[7] Usāmah, pp. 119-20; tr., pp. 149-50.

[8] Ibn-Taghri-Birdi, vol. ii, pt. 2, pp. 336-7.

successor Būri.[1] It was superseded in 1154 by the Zangid atābegs, whose achievements will be recorded later.[2]

The Fāṭimids established

The rise of the Fāṭimid caliphate, like that of the ʿAbbāsid,[3] was closely related to Syria. An insignificant out-of-the-way town, Salamyah,[4] south-east of Ḥamāh, became in the late ninth century the residence and seat of activity of the head of the Ismāʿīli Assassins. His name was Muḥammad al-Ḥabīb (the beloved) and he was supposed by his followers to be the great-grandson of the Imām Ismāʿīl ibn-Jaʿfar al-Ṣādiq, himself a descendant of ʿAli and Fāṭimah through al-Ḥusayn.[5] True to Ismāʿīlite principles al-Ḥabīb had his secret agents throughout the Moslem world working for the undermining of Sunnite power and the re-establishing of the true Islam of Shīʿism. After the ʿAbbāsid [6] this was the most effective and formidable propagandist machine in the political history of Islam.

An able agent (*dāʿi*) of his, named abu-ʿAbdullāh al-Ḥusayn al-Shīʿi, a native of al-Yaman, met in Mecca and converted several Berber pilgrims of the Quṭāmah (Qiṭāmah) tribe in North Africa. In 893 he accompanied them to Tunis, shrewdly worked himself into a position of leadership and persistently fought to displace the century-old Aghlabid régime. When sure of success he invited the head of the sect from Salamyah, now ʿUbaydullāh son of Muḥammad al-Ḥabīb. At Sijilmāsah the disguised ʿUbaydullāh was detected and imprisoned by the Aghlabid governor (905). In 909 al-Shīʿi succeeded in dethroning the Aghlabid ruler, freeing ʿUbāydullāh and establishing him in Raqqādah as the new master of the realm.[7]

[1] Table of the Būrids, atābegs of Damascus (1103–54):

1. Ṭughtagīn (1103–28)

2. Būri (1128–32) 3. Ismāʿīl (1132–4) 4. Maḥmūd (1134–8)

5. Muḥammad (1138–9)

6. Abaq (1139–54)

[2] Pp. 599-600.

[3] See above, p. 530.

[4] This form is older and more correct than Salamīyah; a corruption of Greek Salamias; cf. Canard, p. 235; Dussaud, *Topographie*, pp. 201, 244, 252.

[5] See above, p. 539, n. 1.

[6] See above, p. 530.

[7] Maqrīzi, vol. ii, pp. 10-11; ibn-Khaldūn, vol. iv, pp. 31 *seq*.

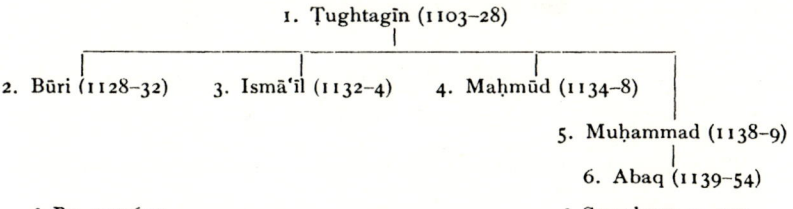

'Ubaydullāh proclaimed himself the expected Mahdi. A new caliphal dynasty was born, the Fāṭimid, also called the 'Alid and the 'Ubaydite ('Ubaydīyah). This was no mean dynasty. Its rise constituted a deliberate challenge to the current leadership of Islam by the 'Abbāsids. At its height it controlled all North Africa, western Arabia and Syria. It was the only major Shī'ite caliphate and the last of the medieval caliphates of Islam.

History has shrouded the pedigree of 'Ubaydullāh with a veil of mystery. He was presumably born in Salamyah — not far from Ḥimṣ, which had supplied the Roman throne with some of its occupants [1] — and so was his son and successor.[2] Critics point out that his line of noble ancestry is variously given and therefore not genuine. Some go as far as saying that the real Mahdi was killed in the Sijilmāsah jail and that the 'Ubaydullāh who emerged thence was but a Jew who impersonated him and played the Mahdi rôle. Others assert that 'Ubaydullāh, far from being an 'Alid or even an Arab, was in fact a descendant of the Persian 'Abdullāh ibn-Maymūn al-Qaddāḥ, the second founder after Ismā'īl of the Ismā'īlite sect,[3] which had by now become a curious mixture of extreme Shī'ite heretical views, Persian mystic concepts, Syrian gnostic elements and rationalistic views. Pro-'Abbāsid historians generally denounce the legitimacy of the Fāṭimid claim. Among modern European scholars several accept the genuineness of the ancestry.[4]

Their vast domain

'Ubaydullāh (909–34) founded a new capital south-east of al-Qayrawān and named it after himself al-Mahdīyah. His third successor al-Mu'izz (952–75) moved in 973 to Egypt, where his victorious general Jawhar had laid (969) the foundation of a new capital Cairo (al-Qāhirah, the triumphant), destined to become the most populous city of the African continent. In it he built the great university-mosque al-Azhar (the bright one), the oldest extant institution of higher learning

[1] See above, p. 340.

[2] Ibn-Ḥammād, *Akhbār Mulūk bani-'Ubayd*, ed. M. Vonderheyden (Algiers, 1927), pp. 6, 18; ibn-Khallikān, vol. i, p. 488.

[3] Ibn-Khallikān, vol. i, p. 487; ibn-Taghri-Birdi, vol. ii, pt. 2, p. 112.

[4] P. H. Mamour, *Polemics on the Origin of the Fatimi Caliphs* (London, 1934), pp. 16 *seq.*, 43 *seq.*, 124 *seq.*; W. Ivanow, *Ismaili Tradition concerning the Rise of Fatimids* (Oxford, 1942), pp. xvii-xix, pp. 27 *seq.*, 127 *seq.* (Eng.); cf. Lewis, p. 22.

and still one of the largest educational institutions in the world. Originally a Christian slave probably from Sicily, Jawhar was bought in al-Qayrawān by a Moslem master and rose to the dizzy height of an empire builder.[1] He it was who in 969 drove the Ikhshīdids from Egypt and Syria.[2]

But in Syria Jawhar had many other opponents to contend with. There were the Qarmaṭians, under al-Ḥasan ibn-Aḥmad al-Aʿṣam, receiving aid and encouragement from the ʿAbbāsids. For a time it looked as if al-Aʿṣam would have the upper hand. He occupied Damascus, forced the Fāṭimids to retreat from all the land and ventured to pursue them to their own capital Cairo.[3] Then there were the Byzantines, eager to take advantage of any fresh opportunity and renew their assault on the land they once ruled. Nor were the Turks quiescent. A general of theirs, Aftakīn (Alaftakīn), gained possession of Damascus and started a series of raids on the whole country. It was natural for the Turks and Qarmaṭians to join hands against a common foe. In 977 the second Egyptian Fāṭimid caliph al-ʿAzīz took the field in person and inflicted a crushing defeat on the allied forces outside al-Ramlah.[4] Al-ʿAzīz extended his domain in Syria, especially along the coast, but failed to reduce Aleppo, mainly because of Byzantine intervention.[5] Under him the Fāṭimid empire reached its farthest limits. His sovereignty was recognized from the Atlantic to the Red Sea and in al-Ḥijāz, al-Yaman, Syria and even al-Mawṣil.[6] For fast communication with Syria he used carrier pigeons, a hundred and twenty of which were once used for carrying plums from Damascus to his palace in three or four days. His favourite concubine was a Christian, one of whose brothers the caliph appointed bishop over Cairo and the other over Jerusalem. His vizir was a Christian, ʿĪsa ibn-Nasṭūrūs, whose deputy in Syria was a Jew, Manashsha (Manasseh) ibn-Ibrāhīm. Both were charged with favouritism toward their co-religionists. As the caliph was one day galloping on a fast mule, a woman cast in his way a placard which read: " By Him who glorified the Christians through ʿĪsa and the Jews through Manashsha and

[1] Ibn Khallikān, vol. i, pp. 209-13; Maqrīzi, vol. i, pp. 352, 377 *seq.*

[2] See above, p. 563.

[3] Ibn-Khaldūn, vol. iv, pp. 50-51.

[4] Ibn-al-Qalānisi, pp. 18-19; ibn-Khaldūn, vol. iv, p. 52.

[5] Ibn-al-Qalānisi, p. 29.

[6] Ibn-Taghri-Birdi, vol. ii, pt. 2, p. 10; ibn-Khallikān, vol. iii, p. 54.

mortified the Moslems through you, how about having pity on the Moslems and removing the disabilities under which I have been labouring ? " [1]

Precarious hold

The Fāṭimid hold on Syria was rather precarious and unstable. Not only was it contested by Qarmaṭians, Saljūqs, other Turks and Byzantines but occasionally by natives too, and Bedouins from the desert. In the second year of al-Ḥākim's reign (996–1021) [2] a sailor from Tyre, ʿAllāqah, had the nerve to strike money in his name and declare his city independent. For a time he defied the Egyptian army and with the aid of a Byzantine flotilla stood against the Egyptian fleet. But at last he had to surrender his besieged city and suffer flaying and crucifixion.[3] His skin was filled with hay and exhibited in Cairo.

The Mirdāsids

During al-Ḥākim's reign the Bedouins from the Syrian Desert were encouraged by the prevailing disorders to begin serious raids against Syria. In 1023 Ṣāliḥ ibn-Mirdās, chief of

[1] Cf. Ibn-al-Qalānisi, p. 33; ibn-Taghri-Birdi, vol. ii, pt. 2, p. 4; Suyūṭi, vol. ii, p. 14; abu-al-Fidā', vol. ii, p. 138.

[2] Table of Fāṭimid caliphs:

1. Al-Mahdi (909–34)
2. Al-Qā'im (934–46)
3. Al-Manṣūr (946–52)
4. Al-Muʿizz (952–75)
5. Al-ʿAzīz (975–96)
6. Al-Ḥākim (996–1021)
7. Al-Ẓāhir (1021–35)
8. Al-Mustanṣir (1035–94)
   - 9. Al-Mustaʿli (1094–1101)
     - 10. Al-Āmir (1101–30)
   - (Muḥammad)
     - 11. Al-Ḥāfiẓ (1130–49)
       - (Yūsuf)
         - 14. Al-ʿĀḍid (1160–71)
       - 12. Al-Ẓāfir (1149–54)
         - 13. Al-Fā'iz (1154–60)

[3] Ibn-al-Qalānisi, pp. 50-51; ibn-Khaldūn, vol. iv, pp. 56-7.

the Kilāb tribe, wrested the capital of North Syria from Fāṭimid control. The Mirdāsid line held Aleppo, with varying fortunes, for over half a century (1023–79). They allied themselves with the Kalb and the Ṭayyi' tribes. The Kalb blockaded Damascus (1025) and the Ṭayyi' set al-Ramlah on fire (1024). Brigandage, highway robbery and lawlessness which started with the Saljūqs were still thriving throughout the land. But Aleppo itself seems to have maintained its prosperous look. The Persian Ismā'īli traveller Nāṣir-i-Khusraw,[1] who visited it in 1047, refers to merchants there from al-'Irāq, Egypt and Asia Minor and to the customs levied by the Mirdāsids on the merchandise. A letter written to a friend by a Christian Baghdādi physician, ibn-Buṭlān, who visited the city about the same time, gives a bird's-eye view of Mirdāsid Aleppo. The city was enclosed within a wall of white stone with six gates. The ancient castle stood by its wall, and the summit of its hill was crowned by two churches and a mosque. There were six other churches and a congregational mosque in the city (indicating a surprisingly large Christian population). There was also a small hospital. People drank rain water from reservoirs. One market hall had twenty cloth merchants who, for the last twenty years, had been transacting business at the rate of twenty thousand dinars a day.[2]

A blind poet-philosopher: al-Ma'arri

The spirit of the age, with its political anarchy, social decay, intellectual pessimism and religious scepticism, was reflected in the poetry of a North Syrian, abu-al-'Alā' al-Ma'arri (973–1057), whose surname reveals his birthplace, Ma'arrat al-Nu'mān. Abu-al-'Alā' was descended from the Yamanite tribe of Tanūkh. At the age of four he lost one eye as a result of a smallpox attack and later the other. This physical mishap soured him further. The blind young man acquired whatever education he could at Aleppo. Later he visited Baghdād twice.[3] While there the second time he held intercourse with rationalists, Mu'tazilites and philosophers of the Greek schools and joined the circle of a freethinker, but had to hasten back home in 1010, after nineteen months, because of the illness of his mother, who died before his arrival. In Baghdād he probably came in

[1] *Sefer Nāmeh*, ed. Charles Schefer (Paris, 1881), p. 10; tr., p. 32.
[2] Yāqūt, *Buldān*, vol. ii, pp. 306-8.
[3] Ibn-Khallikān, vol. i, p. 59; Yāqūt, *Udabā'*, vol. i, p. 162.

contact with Hindus, who converted him to vegetarianism. "For forty-five years after that he would not eat meat." [1] The remaining years of his life he lived as a bachelor in his native town and is said to have willed that the following verse of his composition be inscribed on his tombstone:

This wrong was by my father done
To me, but ne'er by me to one.[2]

The little income he lived on was earned from his lectures. When the Fāṭimid caliph al-Mustanṣir, al-Ḥākim's grandson, occupied Ma'arrah, he offered its poet all that was in its treasury, but it was refused.[3] Al-Ma'arri lived most of the time in seclusion, referring to himself as *rahīn al-maḥbasayn*, the double-prison (home and blindness) inmate. On one occasion he went out to a suburb of Ma'arrah to plead before Ṣāliḥ ibn-Mirdās the case of sixty insurgent notables of his town whom Ṣāliḥ had taken into custody; they were forthwith released.

Unlike the poets of his day al-Ma'arri did not devote his talent to eulogizing princes and potentates with a view to receiving remuneration; the ode he composed in his early career extolling Sayf-al-Dawlah was evidently never presented to the prince.[4] His later works embody his pessimistic, sceptic philosophy of life and his rational approach to its problems. He included among his correspondents the chief Ismā'īli propagandist. In his *Risālat al-Ghufrān* (epistle of forgiveness)[5] al-Ma'arri peopled the limbo with reputed heretics and free-thinkers enjoying themselves and discussing textual criticism. It was this treatise that supposedly had a stimulative effect on Dante's *Divine Comedy*.[6] His *Luzūmīyāt*[7] contains some of his most popular poems, in certain of which he anticipates 'Umar

[1] Yāqūt, vol. i, p. 170.
[2] Ibn-Khallikān, vol. i, p. 59; Nicholson, p. 317.
[3] Yāqūt, vol. i, p. 178.
[4] Al-Ma'arri, *Dīwān: Saqṭ al-Zand*, ed. Shākir Shuqayr (Beirut, 1884), pp. 4 *seq.*
[5] Ed. Kāmil Kīlāni, 2 pts. (Cairo, 1923); partially translated by R. A. Nicholson in *Journal, Royal Asiatic Society* (1900), pp. 637-720; (1902), pp. 75-101, 337-62, 813-47.
[6] Miguel Asín, *Islam and the Divine Comedy*; tr. H. Sunderland (London, 1926).
[7] *Aw Luzūm Ma la Yalzam*, ed. 'Azīz Zand, 2 vols. (Cairo, 1891–5); parts of it and of *Saqṭ* translated by Ameen F. Rihani as *The Quatrains of abu'l-Ala* (London, 1904).

al-Khayyām. In his *al-Fuṣūl w-al-Ghāyāt*[1] al-Maʿarri tried to imitate the Koran, a sacrilege in Moslem eyes. The philosophy advocated in this work is basically Epicurean. The following verses illustrate his unorthodoxy:

> We laugh, but inept is our laughter;
> We should weep and weep sore,
> Who are shattered like glass and thereafter
> Re-moulded no more![2]
>
> Take Reason for thy guide and do what she
> Approves, the best of counsellors in sooth.
> Accept no law the Pentateuch lays down:
> Not there is what thou seekest — the plain truth.[3]
>
> Ḥanīfs [Moslems] are stumbling, Christians all astray,
> Jews wildered, Magians far on error's way.
> We mortals are composed of two great schools —
> Enlightened knaves or religious fools.[4]

Al-Maʿarri was one of the few Arabic poets who rose above limitations of time and place to the realm of universal humanity. The thousandth anniversary of his birthday was celebrated in 1944, under the auspices of the Arab Academy of Damascus, in Damascus, Aleppo, al-Lādhiqīyah and Maʿarrat al-Nuʿmān. Delegates from Syria, Lebanon, Transjordan, al-ʿIrāq and Egypt participated and Orientalists from Europe and America contributed essays. The celebration in Damascus was described as the greatest in the cultural history of that city.[5] In connection with these festivities his tomb at his birthplace was renovated and made a public shrine.

The Druzes

The Caliph al-Ḥākim (996–1021) was responsible for the birth of a new sect in Islam, Druzism. The sect derives its name from a Persian Bāṭinite[6] missionary Muḥammad ibn-

[1] Ed. Maḥmūd H. Zanāti, vol. i (Cairo, 1938).

[2] Abu-al-ʿAlā', *Rasā'il*, ed. D. S. Margoliouth (Oxford, 1898), p. 131; Nicholson, p. 316.

[3] *Luzūmīyāt*, vol. i, p. 394; Nicholson, p. 323.

[4] *Luzūmīyāt*, vol. ii, p. 191; Nicholson, p. 318.

[5] *Al-Mahrajān al-Alfi li-abi-al-ʿAlā' al-Maʿarri* (Damascus, 1945), p. 9.

[6] Ar. *bāṭin*, inner, esoteric. This term was applied by orthodox Moslems to those who maintained that the Koran should be interpreted allegorically and that religious truth could be ascertained by the discovery of an inner meaning of which the outer (*ẓāhir*) was but a veil intended to keep the truth from the eyes of the uninitiate. The Ismāʿīlites and Qarmaṭians were Bāṭinites.

Ismāʿīl al-Darazi (Per. for tailor), who was the first to offer public divine veneration to this Fāṭimid caliph.[1] This doctrine of the incarnation of the deity (*Mawlāna*, our lord) in human form, the last and most important manifestation being al-Ḥākim, is basic in the Druze system. The prophets are of comparatively little consequence.

Finding no response for his new creed among the Egyptians, al-Darazi migrated to Wādi al-Taym,[2] at the foot of Mount Hermon in Lebanon, where the hardy freedom-loving mountaineers, evidently already impregnated with ultra-Shīʿite ideas, were ready to give him a hearing.[3] Here he fell in battle in 1019 and was succeeded by his rival Ḥamzah ibn-ʿAli, surnamed al-Hādi (the guide), also a Persian.[4] When al-Ḥākim was assassinated, probably as a result of a conspiracy by his own household, al-Hādi denied his death and proclaimed that he had gone into a state of temporary occultation (*ghaybah*), whence his triumphal return (*rajʿah*) should be expected.[5] Al-Muqtana Bahā'-al-Dīn (d. 1031), Ḥamzah's right hand in the propagation of the new cult, addressed epistles as far as India and Constantinople,[6] but later enunciated a new policy, that pending the " absence " of al-Ḥākim no part of the religion should be divulged or promulgated — a policy doubtless dictated by the desire for safety on the part of a small heterodox minority struggling for existence. Since then " the door has been closed " ; no one could be allowed entrance or exit. The hidden imām idea had been elaborately worked out, prior to the rise of Druzism, by a number of ultra-Shīʿite groups (*ghulāh*), chief among which was the Ismāʿīlite.

In his *al-Risālah al-Masīḥīyah* (the Christian epistle)[7] Bahā'-al-Dīn identifies Ḥamzah with the Messiah. In other epistles directed to the Christians he calls them " saints " and

[1] Ibn-Taghri-Birdi, vol. ii, pt. 2, p. 69.

[2] So called after Taym-Allāh (formerly Taym-Allāt), an Arabian tribe which, after having settled in the Euphrates region and become Christianized, moved into southern Lebanon; Ṭabari, vol. i, pp. 2489-90, 2031.

[3] Ibn-Taghri-Birdi, vol. ii, pt. 2, p. 70.

[4] Ibn-Ḥajar al-ʿAsqalāni, " Rafʿ al-Iṣr ʿan Quḍāt Miṣr ", in Kindi, ed. Guest, p. 612, calls him al-Zūzani (from Zūzan, in eastern Persia).

[5] For a translation of an excerpt of this proclamation consult Hitti, *The Origins of the Druze People and Religion* (New York, 1928), pp. 61-4.

[6] For a translation of an excerpt of his epistle to Constantine VIII consult Hitti, pp. 64-7.

[7] For a translation of an excerpt consult Hitti, pp. 68-70.

"assemblies of saints", hoping thereby to win them over to his faith. He uses parables that recall those of the New Testament. This would seem to indicate that he was a Christian apostate.[1]

Ḥamzah in behalf of al-Ḥākim absolved his followers of the cardinal obligations of Islam, including fasting and pilgrimage, and substituted precepts enjoining veracity of speech, mutual aid among the brethren in faith, renunciation of all forms of false belief and absolute submission to the divine will. The last precept, involving the concept of predestination, has continued to be a potent factor in Druzism, as in orthodox Islam. Another feature of this cult is the belief in the transmigration of souls. The idea came originally to Islam from India and received an increment of Platonic elements. The Muʿtazilites and Bāṭinites had long before the time of al-Ḥākim accepted some form of the doctrine of metempsychosis, which is still held by modern mystics of Persia and by Bahāʾis. The operation of the second precept of Ḥamzah, enjoining mutual aid, has made of the Druzes an unusually compact self-conscious community presenting more the aspects of a religious fraternal order than those of a sect, and that despite the fact that the community itself is divided into two distinctly marked classes: the initiate (*ʿuqqāl*, wise) and the uninitiate (*juhhāl*, ignorant). The sacred writings, all handwritten, are accessible to the initiated few only and the meeting-places are secluded rooms on hills outside the villages, where Thursday evening sessions are held.

As they tried to gain a permanent footing in southern Lebanon, the Druzes found themselves in conflict with an already established Islamic heterodoxy, the Nuṣayrīyah, whose followers were subsequently driven out into northern Syria, their present habitat. The Druzes had to struggle against other neighbours — Shīʿites and Sunnites. From their original home in southern Lebanon they later spread into the Shūf district, east of Beirut, where the Crusaders found them and where they still flourish. In no city were they able to thrive. The first mention of the Druze people in European literature occurs in the travels of Benjamin of Tudela[2] (*ca.* 1169), when

[1] Silvestre de Sacy, *Exposé de la religion des Druzes* (Paris, 1838), vol. i, p. 83, n. 1.

[2] Vol. i, p. 61.

they were confined to Wādi al-Taym. From al-Shūf some of them, as a result of Qaysite-Yamanite blood feuds, migrated in the early eighteenth century into Ḥawrān in Syria.[1] The influx was augmented by malcontents from Lebanon in the nineteenth century. In Ḥawrān they now number about eighty-six thousand as against seventy-nine thousand in Lebanon. Throughout their entire history they have shown remarkable vigour and exercised in Lebanese and Syrian national affairs influence quite disproportionate to their number.

The Nuṣayriyah

Another surviving offshoot of the Ismāʿīlite body is the Nuṣayrīyah. Its name is derived probably from that of Muḥammad ibn-Nuṣayr of al-Kūfah (fl. late ninth century), a partisan of the eleventh ʿAlid imām al-Ḥasan al-ʿAskari (d. 874).[2] The earliest important references to ibn-Nuṣayr and his followers occur in the writings of Ḥamzah and other early Druze polemicists. The last founder of the sect according to their manuscripts was Ḥusayn ibn-Ḥamdān al-Khaṣībi (d. *ca.* 957), an Ismāʿīlite protégé of the Ḥamdānids of Aleppo.[3]

Not much is known about this religion, which is secretive in character, hierarchical in organization and esoteric in doctrine. Its sacred writings have not been exposed to the same extent as those of the Druzes, many of which came to light as a result of communal wars in the nineteenth century. Finding itself a small heterodoxy amidst a hostile majority, the cult chose to go underground. There it has remained, a partially unsolved religious riddle of the Near East.

This much, however, is known. In company with other ultra-Shīʿites (*ghulāh*), the Nuṣayris deify ʿAli. To them he is the final and most important incarnation of the deity.[4] Their late counterparts are the Takhtajis (woodcutters) of western Anatolia, the Qizil-Bāsh (red-heads) of eastern Anatolia and the ʿAli-Ilāhis (ʿAli-deifiers) of Persia and Turkestan. The Nuṣayris are, therefore, sometimes referred to as ʿAlawites, a name which became current after the French organized the region centring on al-Lādhiqīyah into a separate state under

[1] See above, pp. 42-3.

[2] See above, pp. 450, 502. Cf. abu-al-Fidā', *Taqwīm*, p. 232, n. 3, where the founder is made Nuṣayr, a freedman of ʿAli.

[3] L. Massignon in *Actes du XVIII congrès international des orientalistes* (Leyden, 1931), p. 212.

[4] Shahrastāni, pp. 143-5.

the name Alaouite. In the Crusading chronicles they are termed Nazarei. The cult represents an imposition of extreme Shīʿite ideas directly on a pagan body. In other words it is a survival of pagan Syrian cults under the guise of a Shīʿite heterodoxy. Its adepts must have passed directly from paganism to Ismāʿīlism.[1] Later they appropriated certain superficial Christian features. For instance, they celebrate a mass-like rite, observe Christmas [2] and Easter and bear such names as Matta (Matthew), Jibrāʾīl (Gabriel), Yūḥanna (John), Hīlānah (Helen). Their initiated shaykhs, who correspond to the Druze *ʿuqqāl*, are organized in a three-class hierarchy. The rest of the community constitute the uninitiated masses. Unlike the Druzes, they admit no women into the initiated class. Their meetings are held at night in secluded places. Charges of nocturnal orgies and phallic worship have been brought against them as against other groups who practise their religion in secret.[3]

Today some three hundred thousand Nuṣayris, mostly peasants, occupy the mountainous region of northern and central Syria and are scattered as far as Turkish Cilicia.

Persecution of Christians

On the whole the Christians and Jews fared well under the Fāṭimid régime. It was only during al-Ḥākim's reign that they were re-subjected to the old humiliating disabilities initiated by ʿUmar II and al-Mutawakkil [4] and put under new ones imposed by this caliph, whose mother and vizir were Christians. To the earlier regulations governing clothing to distinguish dhimmis externally from Moslems, which he reactivated, al-Ḥākim in 1009 added that when Christians were in public baths they should display a five-pound cross dangling from their necks, and Jews an equally weighty frame of wood with jingling bells.[5] In the same year he demolished several Christian churches, chief among which were Our Lady in Damascus and the Holy Sepulchre in Jerusalem. By way of implementing the koranic prohibition against wine,[6] he ordered all grapevines uprooted; any such plantation in Egypt must have been under Christian

[1] *Kitāb al-Iʿtibār*, ed. Hitti, pp. 159-60; *Arab-Syrian Gentleman*, p. 190.
[2] R. Strothman in *Der Islam*, vol. xxvii, No. 3 (1946), pp. 175-9.
[3] Conder, *Syrian Stone-Lore*, p. 423, n.
[4] See above, pp. 487-8, 542-4.
[5] Ibn-Khallikān, vol. iii, p. 5; Saʿīd ibn-Baṭrīq, p. 195; Maqrīzi, vol. ii, p. 288; ibn-Ḥammād, p. 54.
[6] For a translation of his edict consult Hitti, *Origins*, pp. 59-60.

cultivation. The caliph invited those of the dhimmis who were unwilling to abide by his regulations to profess Islam or else migrate to the land of the Romans. It seems that in his time, almost four centuries after Muḥammad, the Christians in Egypt and Syria equalled, if not outnumbered, their Moslem compatriots. Twenty years later al-Ḥākim's son and successor al-Ẓāhir, following a treaty with the Byzantine emperor, restored

A COIN OF AL-ẒĀHIR

Obverse and reverse of a gold dinar of the Fāṭimid caliph al-Ẓāhir struck at Ṣūr (Tyre) A.H. 424 = A.D. 1032/3

the destroyed churches, including the Holy Sepulchre. But the fact remains that the destruction of this shrine of Christendom was a contributory cause of the Crusades.

The behaviour of the blue-eyed Ḥākim, who was enthroned when eleven years old and died at the age of thirty-six, shows strange contradictions. He built an academy in Cairo only to destroy it with its professors three years later. He legislated against sexual immorality and went so far as prohibiting the appearance of women in the Cairo streets. He issued edicts against banquets and music and included certain dishes and chess playing. So freakish was his behaviour that anti-Fāṭimid writers charged him with abnormal psychology.[1] Freakish behaviour of Christian saints, Moslem dervishes and Hindu fakirs is familiar in Oriental annals.

More interested in luxurious living than state administration, al-Ḥākim's successors were unable to maintain order at home or sovereignty abroad. In 1023 Aleppo, capital of North Syria, was wrested away by the Bedouin Mirdāsids; in 1071

[1] Ibn-Khallikān, vol. iii, pp. 4-7; ibn-Khaldūn, vol. iv, pp. 59-61; ibn-Taghri-Birdi, vol. ii, pt. 2, pp. 62 *seq.*; Suyūṭi, *Ḥusn*, vol. ii, pp. 14-15; ibn-al-Qalānisi, pp. 66-7, 79-80; Maqrīzi, vol. ii, pp. 285-9; ibn-Ḥammād, pp. 54-5.

Jerusalem, metropolis of southern Syria, fell into Saljūq hands and five years later Damascus followed suit.[1] In 1098 Jerusalem was recaptured from the Urtuqid vassals of the Saljūqs, only to fall the following year into the hands of a strange and unexpected enemy — the Crusaders.

[1] See above, pp. 573-4, 580-81.

COAT OF ARMS OF THE KINGDOM OF JERUSALEM
On a field of silver a cross potent between four crosslets, gold

CHAPTER XLV

MEETING OF EAST AND WEST: THE CRUSADES

ON November 26, 1095, Pope Urban II, a Frenchman by birth, delivered a fiery speech at Clermont in south-eastern France urging the believers to " enter upon the road to the Holy Sepulchre, wrest it from the wicked race and subject it " to themselves. Judged by its results this was perhaps the most effective speech in history. " *Deus lo volt* " (God wills it) became the rallying cry and was reiterated throughout Europe, seizing high and low as if by a strange psychological contagion.

Complexity of motivation

The response, however, was not all motivated by ideology supplied by the Church. Besides the devout there were the military leaders intent upon new conquests for themselves; the merchants, especially of Genoa, Venice and Pisa, whose interest was more commercial than spiritual; the romantic, the restless, the adventurers ever ready to join a spectacular movement; the criminals and sinful who sought penance through pilgrimage to the land " where His feet once stood "; and the economically and socially depressed individuals to whom " taking the cross " was more of a relief than a sacrifice.[1]

[1] For more on conditions in Europe consult August C. Krey, *The First Crusade* (Princeton, 1921), pp. 24-43.

Other factors, of international character, were involved. The pope's choice of southern France as stage for his initial appeal was not without design. That part of Europe had been overrun by Moslem hordes from Spain.[1] In fact for the past four and a half centuries Islam had been on the offensive against Christendom, first through the Byzantine Empire and then through Spain, Sicily and Italy.[2] It was time for a Christian reaction. Moreover, the year before Urban made his public appeal, the Byzantine emperor Alexius Comnenus, whose Asiatic possessions had been overrun by Saljūqs almost as far as Constantinople,[3] had solicited papal aid against the Moslem invasion. The pope viewed the solicitation as providing an opportunity for healing the schism between the Greek Church and Rome, effected forty years earlier, and establishing himself as head of Christendom.

The first Crusade

By the spring of 1097 some hundred and fifty thousand men, mostly Franks and Normans, had responded. Constantinople was the rendezvous. They bore the cross as a badge; hence the designation Crusaders. The first of the campaigns was thus launched. Its route lay across Asia Minor, then the domain of Qilij Arslān. In June of that year Nicaea, Saljūq headquarters, was captured. In the next month Dorylaeum (modern Eski-Shehr) fell.[4] This victorious march restored to the Byzantine emperor, who had exacted from almost all the Crusading leaders an oath of feudal allegiance, the larger portion of Asia Minor.

The first Latin principality

After crossing the Taurus, the leaders began squabbling among themselves and planning local conquests each for himself. Baldwin, one of the leaders of the Lotharingians from the Rhineland, swung eastward into a territory occupied by Christians. Here al-Ruhā' (Edessa), then under Armenian rule, was occupied early in 1098.[5] The first Latin state was

[1] See above, pp. 463 *seq.*

[2] For the Aghlabid conquest of Sicily from Tunis consult Hitti, *History of the Arabs*, pp. 602, 605, 617, 622.

[3] See above, pp. 573-4.

[4] *Gesta Francorum et aliorum Hierosolymitanorum*, ed. Heinrich Hagemeyer (Heidelberg, 1890), pp. 197, 208; Fulcher, *Historia Hierosolymitana*, ed. Hagemeyer (Heidelberg, 1913), p. 192; ibn-al-Qalānisi, p. 134; tr. H. A. R. Gibb, *The Damascus Chronicle of the Crusades* (London, 1932), p. 42. For a general bibliography on the Crusades consult Claude Cahen, *La Syrie du Nord à l'époque des croisades* (Paris, 1940), pp. 3-104.

[5] Matthew of Edessa, *Chronique*, ed. E. Dulaurier (Paris, 1858), p. 218.

thus founded as the county of Edessa, with Baldwin as its prince. This future king of Jerusalem married an Armenian princess and settled temporarily in the north. Another Crusading chief, Tancred, one of the leaders of the Normans of southern Italy and Sicily, had turned westward into Cilicia, whose population was likewise Armenian with an admixture of Greek. He occupied Tarsus and its territory.

Meantime the bulk of the Crusading army was pouring into Syria, its main objective. North Syria, as noted above, was under virtually independent Saljūq amīrs; South Syria was under the Fāṭimid caliphs.[1] The whole land had for years been a bone of contention between Sunnite Turks and Shīʿite Egyptians. Other parts were held by local Arab chieftains. Tripoli and its territory, for instance, had been since 1089 under the Shīʿite banu-ʿAmmār;[2] Shayzar on the Orontes had been since 1081 under the banu-Munqidh.[3] Local feuds, fraternal jealousies, problems of dynastic succession had engendered a chronic state of political instability. The population itself was far from being able to present a common front. Schismatic communities honeycombed the land: Druzes in southern Lebanon, Nuṣayris in the northern mountains of Syria, Ismāʿīlites and later Assassins inland from the Nuṣayris.[4] Among the Christians the Maronites of northern Lebanon were still speaking Syriac.[5]

Antioch, the second principality

Antioch was the first Syrian city in the way of the Crusading army. It was held by a Saljūq amīr, Yāghi-Siyān,[6] who had received his appointment from the third Great Saljūq (after Ṭughril and Alp Arslān), Malikshāh of Baghdād. As the cradle of the first organized Christian church,[7] this city was of special significance to the Crusaders. The siege was long and arduous (October 2, 1097 to June 3, 1098). Attempts at relief by Riḍwān of Aleppo and Duqāq of Damascus were repelled.[8] The operations were directed by Bohemond, kinsman of Tancred and leader of the Normans, and supported by the Italian fleet,

[1] See above, pp. 579-80.
[2] Consult G. Wiet in *Mémorial Henri Basset* (Paris, 1928), vol. ii, pp. 279-84; ibn-Taghri-Birdi, vol. ii, pt. 2, p. 267.
[3] See below, p. 621.
[4] See above, pp. 583, 586.
[5] See above, p. 521.
[6] Name erroneously transcribed in ibn-al-Athīr, vol. x, p. 187; abu-al-Fidā', vol. ii, p. 220; ibn-Khaldūn, vol. v, p. 20.
[7] Acts 11:26.
[8] See above, pp. 574-6.

which, on this and later occasions, supplied food and siege engines against fortified towns on or near the coast. But it was treachery on the part of a disgruntled Armenian commander of one of the towers that sealed the fate of the city.[1]

No sooner, however, had the besiegers made their entry than they found themselves besieged. Karbūqa, a Saljūq adventurer who had wrested al-Mawṣil from the Arab banu-ʿUqayl,[2] had just arrived from his capital with reinforcements. The suffering from plague and starvation in the course of the twenty-five days that ensued was perhaps the worst ever experienced by Franks [3] in Syria.[4] Only a miraculous event could raise their morale and save the day. The event took the shape of the discovery of the " holy lance ", which had pierced the Saviour's side as He hung upon the cross and which had lain buried in an Antiochian church. In a bold sortie the Crusaders repelled the besiegers. Bohemond, the shrewdest and ablest of all the Christian leaders, remained in charge of the newly acquired principality, Antioch and its territory. The Byzantine emperor expected the re-annexation of Antioch to his empire but was disappointed. Even more disappointed was Raymond of Toulouse, wealthy leader of the Provençals, whose men had made the sensational discovery and who sought the lordship of Antioch. Another legend connected with the struggle for Antioch relates to Saint George, regarded by local tradition as a native of al-Ludd (Lydda),[5] who had been put to death under Diocletian (303) and now came to the aid of the harassed Crusaders.[6]

Along the coast

Count Raymond pushed southward. Maʿarrat al-Nuʿmān, native town of al-Maʿarri, was committed to the flames and

[1] Kamāl-al-Dīn in *Recueil*, vol. iii, pp. 580 *seq.*; ibn-al-Qalānisi, p. 135.

[2] At first tributary to the Ḥamdānids (see above, p. 564), the ʿUqaylids succeeded them in al-Mawṣil.

[3] Ar. *Ifranj*, a word which since the Crusades has become synonymous with Europeans.

[4] They even dug up and devoured dead bodies of beasts; William of Tyre, vol. i, p. 271; ibn-al-Qalānisi, p. 136.

[5] William of Tyre, vol. i, p. 332; Ṣāliḥ, p. 16.

[6] Introduced into Europe by the Normans, Saint George was adopted in the fourteenth century as patron saint of England. In the Syrian churches, where his name was connected with the conquest of a dragon and the delivery of a royal princess, he vied for first place in popularity with Saint Sergius (see above, p. 391). The bay of Beirut, on the shore of which he supposedly slew the monster, still bears his name (Khalīj Mār Jurjis). Ludolph von Suchem, ***Description of the Holy Land***, tr. Aubrey Stewart (London, 1895), p. 135.

its population was destroyed.[1] Following the Orontes valley, he reached and occupied Ḥiṣn al-Akrād,[2] commanding the strategic pass between the coastal plains and those of the Orontes. Strongly fortified 'Arqah, birthplace of a member of the Syrian dynasty of Roman emperors [3] and now in the amīrate of Tripoli, resisted the siege from February to mid-May. In March, Baldwin's brother, Godfrey of Bouillon (capital of Lower Lorraine), who had marched south by the coast and laid siege to Jabalah, joined Raymond. Under pressure from his own men, who were impatient to reach Jerusalem, and through inducement by presents from ibn-'Ammār, amīr of Tripoli, Raymond lifted the siege. Anṭarṭūs,[4] where he hit the shore, offered no resistance. Communication with the Italian fleet was hereafter possible. The coastal route was followed, the same route trodden by Alexander [5] and other conquerors. Al-Lādhiqīyah was avoided presumably because it was being occupied by naval forces of the Byzantines, who had become alienated from the Latins.[6] In al-Batrūn the Crusaders established contacts with the Maronites, " a stalwart race, valiant fighters ", who provided greatly needed guides.[7] Following Tripoli's precedent, the amīr of Beirut offered money and a bountiful supply of provisions.[8] The gardens of Sidon, where the Crusaders pitched their tents by the running water, provided a welcome resting-place for a few days. 'Akka was reached as early as May 24. Evidently garrisons existed only in a few of the major cities, and the foreign warriors neither molested the natives nor were molested by them. The march must have looked more like a promenade. Passing through Caesarea and Arsūf, they swerved inland through al-Ramlah and on June 7 stood facing the main goal of the entire expedition, the holy city.

[1] Ibn-al-Athīr, vol. x, p. 190, copied by abu-al-Fidā', vol. ii, p. 221. Cf. *Gesta Francorum*, p. 387; Kamāl-al-Dīn in *Recueil*, vol. iii, pp. 586-7.

[2] Literally " castle of the Kurds ", today Qal'at al-Ḥiṣn; Crac des Chevaliers of the Franks. This " Crac " was originally " Crat ", a corruption of " Akrād ", and is not the same word that appears in Crac de Montréal or Crac des Moabites (below, p. 596, n. 4). Crac des Chevaliers rose on the site of an early fortress built by an amīr of Ḥimṣ in 1031 who planted in it a military colony of Kurds.

[3] See above, p. 344.

[4] Tortosa of the Latin chronicles; see below, p. 609.

[5] See above, p. 232.

[6] Cahen, p. 222.

[7] William of Tyre, vol. ii, p. 459; vol. i, p. 330; Ludolph von Suchem, p. 135.

[8] William of Tyre, vol. i, p. 331.

The Crusaders then numbered some forty thousand, of whom about a half were effective troops.[1] The Egyptian garrison may be estimated at a thousand. At the end of a month's siege conducted by Godfrey, Raymond and Tancred, the city was stormed (July 15) and its population, regardless of age and sex, was subjected to an indiscriminate slaughter. An Arab source[2] puts the number of victims above 70,000, an Armenian[3] at 65,000 and a Latin refers to " heaps of heads and hands and feet to be seen throughout the streets and squares ".[4] A third Latin state, by far the most important, came into existence in Syria. At its head stood Godfrey, a devout leader and hard fighter. Allegedly reluctant to wear a crown of gold where the Saviour had worn a crown of thorns, Godfrey chose the title " defender of the Holy Sepulchre ".[5]

Jerusalem seized

Godfrey's reign was short, lasting but one year. In it he had a successful encounter with the Egyptians near 'Asqalān which contributed to rendering the Latin position in Jerusalem more secure. This seaport, however, remained the seat of a Fāṭimid garrison and the base of its fleet.[6] Jaffa (Yāfa), which lay in ruins when the Crusaders passed by, was now occupied and special privileges were given therein to the Pisans. Haifa (Ḥayfa) was occupied with the aid of a Venetian fleet.[7] Meantime Tancred was penetrating inland to the Jordan region. Without a hold on the hinterland, as well as the coast, the position of Latin Jerusalem would remain precarious. Baysān, on the route between the Mediterranean and Damascus, was one of his early acquisitions. Nābulus voluntarily submitted. Tancred took up his residence in Tiberias as Godfrey's vassal. In March 1101 he relinquished his fief to succeed his uncle Bohemond of Antioch, who had been taken captive by a Turk while on a campaign in the north.

Baldwin, first king

Godfrey's brother Baldwin, count of Edessa, was called and installed king on Christmas day 1100. He was the real founder

[1] Cf. " Annales de Terre sainte ", *Archives de l'orient latin*, vol. ii (Paris, 1884), pt. 2, p. 429; Raimundus de Agiles, " Historia Francorum qui ceperunt Jerusalem ", in Migne, *Patrologia Latina*, vol. clv, p. 657; William of Tyre, vol. i, p. 349.

[2] Ibn-al-Athīr, vol. x, p. 194.

[3] Matthew of Edessa, p. 226.

[4] Agiles, p. 659; cf. William of Tyre, vol. i, pp. 370-72.

[5] Agiles, p. 654.

[6] Ibn-Muyassar, *Akhbār Miṣr*, ed. Henri Massé (Cairo, 1919), pp. 39 *seq.*

[7] Ibn-al-Qalānisi, p. 139; ibn-Khallikān, vol. i, p. 101.

of the Latin kingdom. His immediate task was to reduce the coast towns and thus insure sea communication with the homeland and forestall hostile action by the Egyptian fleet. In the seamen of the Italian republics he found eager and greedy allies. These men insisted on a share of the booty, special quarters in the captured towns under the jurisdiction of their own republics and the right of importing and selling merchandise without the payment of taxes [1] — thus enjoying privileges associated with the capitulations. Accordingly Arsūf and Caesarea (Qaysārīyah) were seized in 1101 with the aid of the Genoese and agreed to pay tribute pending a period of truce.[2] Strongly walled ʻAkka capitulated three years later as a result of attacks by Pisan and Genoese ships. In 1110 Beirut was besieged by land and sea for eleven weeks ending May 13, on which it was stormed and many of its inhabitants were slaughtered. The adjacent pine grove, still standing, provided wood for constructing towers, hurling missiles and scaling the city walls.[3] In the same year Sidon was occupied with the aid of a Norwegian fleet of fifty-five ships.[4]

Baldwin extended his kingdom southward, too, with a view to capturing at least part of the Red Sea and Indian Ocean trade. South of the Dead Sea he built (1115) a formidable fortress, al-Shawbak,[5] to guard the caravan route from Damascus to Egypt and al-Ḥijāz. His successors followed the same policy of tightening their grip on the land by constructing castles. Al-Shawbak and al-Karak were the two most strategically located among the seven fortresses in that region.[6] On Baldwin's death in 1118, the kingdom had attained its highest limits, from al-ʻAqabah to Beirut. Secure on its peninsula, Tyre remained in Moslem hands till 1124,[7]

[1] William of Tyre, vol. i, pp. 434, 455.

[2] Albert of Aix, "Historia Hierosolymitanae expeditionis", Migne, vol. clxvi, p. 575.

[3] W. B. Stevenson, *The Crusaders in the East* (Cambridge, 1907), pp. 58-9; William of Tyre, vol. i, pp. 484-5; ibn-al-Qalānisi, pp. 167-8; Ṣāliḥ, pp. 28-9.

[4] Ibn-al-Athīr, vol. x, pp. 336-7; ibn-al-Qalānisi, p. 171.

[5] Called by the Latins Mons Regalis (Mont Royal, Montréal). According to early chronicles Crac de Montréal refers to its sister to the north-east, Crac des Moabites (biblical Kir of Moab), Ar. al-Karak, planted *ca.* 1140. This "Crac" is a corruption of Ar. *karak*, from Aram. *karkha*, town.

[6] For more on these castles consult Camille Enlart, *Les Monuments des croisades*, 2 vols. (Paris, 1925–8).

[7] See above, p. 576.

and ʿAsqalān as late as 1153. In breadth the kingdom did not reach far beyond the Jordan.

Expansion in the north

The Latin countries to the north were likewise expanding. Raymond,[1] who had had his eye on Tripoli (Ṭarābulus) ever since he passed there, returned after the capture of Jerusalem and laid siege to the town. In order to isolate it he built in 1103 a castle, Château Pèlerin,[2] on an adjacent hill named Mons Pelegrinus (pilgrims' hill). The site soon became the centre of a Latin quarter. The siege dragged slowly on despite reinforcements from the neighbouring mountain.[3] Tripoli had a population of 20,000 and its main industries were glass and paper. At intervals adjacent towns were reduced, mostly with the aid of a Genoese fleet. Al-Marqab marked the northern limit of the county of Tripoli, Jubayl the southern limit. Tripoli itself did not fall until 1109, four years after Raymond's death. Evidently the city had become a centre of Shīʿite learning under the banu-ʿAmmār with schools and libraries, all of which were now obliterated.[4] Al-Maʿarri was among the notables who had used the Tripoli library.

Farther north al-Lādhiqīyah was seized by Tancred in 1103 and Apamea three years later. Both were added to the principality of Antioch, which at times included parts of Cilicia.

At the death of Baldwin II (1118–31) the Latin kingdom with its fiefs stood complete. All three Latin states in the north — Tripoli, Antioch and Edessa — owed nominal allegiance to the king of Jerusalem. The success was remarkable and must have inspired the Franks with confidence and an optimistic outlook. But in reality the prospects were not so bright. Except in the very north and south, the area was limited to the littoral — a narrow Christian territory set against a dark background of Islam. Not a town was more than a day's march from the enemy. Inland cities, such as Aleppo,[5] Ḥamāh, Ḥimṣ, Baʿlabakk,[6] Damascus, were never conquered, though

[1] Because he was called Raymond of Saint-Gilles, the Arabs referred to him as Ṣanjīl or ibn-Ṣanjīl.

[2] Repaired by the Turks, this Qalʿat Ṭarābulus was used by them as a prison, and in the second world war as an anti-aircraft station by the British.

[3] Ibn-Khaldūn, vol. v, p. 186.

[4] Ibn-al-Qalānisi, p. 163; ibn-al-Athīr, vol. x, pp. 333-4; Sibṭ ibn-al-Jawzi, *Mirʾāt al-Zamān*, ed. James R. Jewett (Chicago, 1907), p. 17; William of Tyre, vol. i, pp. 477-8.

[5] William of Tyre, vol. ii, p. 22.

[6] William of Tyre, vol. ii, p. 413.

occasionally attacked. At times they paid tribute; Damascus paid it to Baldwin II in 1126.[1] The fertile Biqā' lay within the territory of this city. In their own states the Franks were but

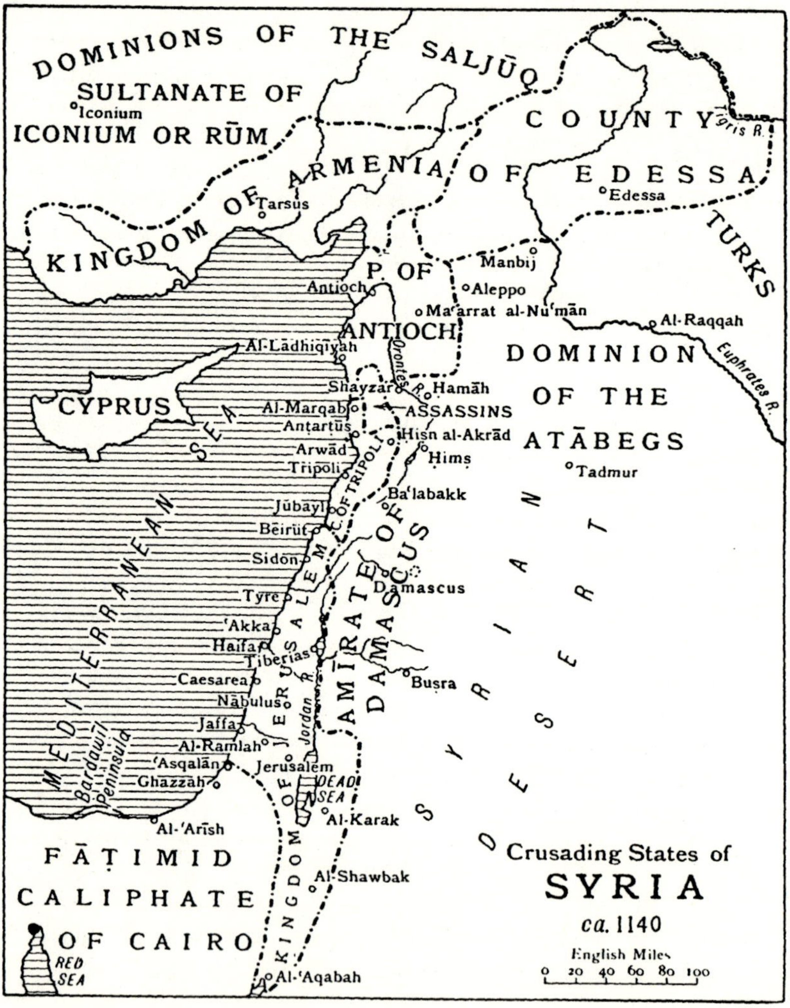

Crusading States of SYRIA ca. 1140

thinly dispersed. Even in Jerusalem and other occupied cities they never formed more than a minority. After the capture of Jerusalem a number of them, considering their vows fulfilled,

[1] In the year beginning Sept. 1156 its ruler Nūr-al-Dīn paid 8000 dinars; ibn-al-Qalānisi, p. 336.

sailed back home. Clearly such exotic states could hold their own only as long as they received a constant supply of fresh recruits from home and the forces of opposition were not unified under strong leadership.

Moslem reaction Zangi

With the rise of the blue-eyed Turkish Atābeg Zangi (1127–1146), lord of al-Mawṣil and Aleppo,[1] the elements of unification and leadership began to make their appearance. With Zangi a series of anti-Crusading heroes commenced. His were the first hammer-strokes under which the Latin states were to crumble away. The first blow fell on al-Ruhā', northern bulwark of these states. A four-week siege in 1144 ended in its capture from Joscelin II.[2] First among the states to rise, al-Ruhā' was the first to fall. Its fall marks the beginning of the turn of the tide in favour of Islam. On the European side it provoked the so-called second Crusade (1147–9).

The usual classification of the Crusades, however, into a fixed number of campaigns is artificial, as the stream was somewhat continuous and the line of demarcation not sharply drawn. A more satisfactory division would be into first a period of Latin conquest extending to 1144; second a period of Moslem reaction inaugurated by Zangi and culminating in the brilliant victories of Ṣalāḥ-al-Dīn; and third a period of petty wars, coinciding roughly with the thirteenth century, in which the Ayyūbids and the Mamlūks figured and which ended in driving all Crusaders out of the land.

Nūr-al-Dīn

The championship of the Islamic cause passed from Zangi to his son Nūr-al-Dīn (the light of the faith) Maḥmūd. More capable than his father, Nūr in 1154 wrested Damascus from a successor of Ṭughtagīn,[3] thereby removing the last barrier between Zangid territory and Jerusalem. For many years past Damascus had been a virtual ally of Jerusalem.[4] Ṣarkhad (Ṣalkhad), Buṣra, Bāniyās under the Ismā'īlites and other towns in the Damascene territory at times sought Latin aid in their wars against other Moslems.[5] The banu-Faḍl of the

[1] See above, p. 576.
[2] Abu-Shāmah, vol. i, pp. 36-7; ibn-al-Athīr in *Recueil*, vol. ii, pt. 2, pp. 118 *seq.*
[3] See above, p. 576; ibn-al-Athīr, vol. xi, pp. 130-31.
[4] Ibn-al-Qalānisi (who at this time held a high position in the Damascus government), pp. 308-9; William of Tyre, vol. ii, pp. 76-7, 105-6, 147-8, 224; abu-Shāmah, vol. i, p. 77.
[5] Ibn-al-Qalānisi, pp. 289-90, 314, 316; abu-al-Fidā', vol. iii, pp. 2-3.

Ṭayyi', perhaps the most influential of the tribes in the Syrian Desert, allied themselves at times with the Franks and at other times with the Fāṭimids.[1] Latin Jerusalem had in its service a body of light cavalry, called Turcopuli (sons of Turks),[2] recruited from Moslems, besides an infantry corps of Armenians and a contingent of Maronite archers.[3] With the seizure of Damascus the Nūrid realm extended from al-Mawṣil to Ḥawrān. The crescent was extending its horn southward.

Realizing the decrepit condition of the Fāṭimids and the advantage of placing Jerusalem where it could be crushed between an upper and a lower millstone, Nūr dispatched an able lieutenant of his, Shīrkūh, to Egypt. Here he succeeded in 1169, through diplomatic and military victories, in receiving the vizirate under the Caliph al-'Āḍid (1160–71). Two months after his investiture Shīrkūh died and his mantle fell on his brother's son Ṣalāḥ-al-Dīn (the rectitude of the faith, Saladin) ibn-Ayyūb.[4]

Enter Ṣalāḥ-al-Dīn

Al-Malik al-Nāṣir (the defender-king) al-Sulṭān Ṣalāḥ-al-Dīn Yūsuf was born in Takrīt on the Tigris in 1138 of Kurdish parents. When a year old he moved with the family to Ba'labakk, over which his father Ayyūb (Job) was appointed commander by Zangi. The interests of the young man were evidently theological, rather than military. Only reluctantly did he accompany his uncle in 1164 on his first Egyptian campaign.[5] The trip, however, marked the beginning of a new career, a career devoted to the pursuit of three objectives: replacing Shī'ite with Sunnite Islam in Egypt, uniting Egypt and Syria under one sceptre and pressing the holy war against the Franks. The first proved to be the easiest to realize. As al-'Āḍid lay on his deathbed in 1171, Ṣalāḥ as vizir simply substituted in the Friday prayer the name of the contemporary 'Abbāsid caliph al-Mustaḍī'. Thus came to its end the Fāṭimid caliphate. Incredible as it may seem, the momentous change

[1] Ibn-Khaldūn, vol. vi, pp. 6 *seq.*; A. S. Tritton in *Bulletin, School of Oriental and African Studies*, vol. xii (1948), p. 567.

[2] 'Imād-al-Dīn, p. 425; Usāmah, p. 51; tr. p. 79.

[3] Cf. Jacques de Vitry, *The History of Jerusalem*, tr. Aubrey Stewart (London, 1896), p. 79.

[4] Abu-Shāmah, vol. i, pp. 160-61; Sibṭ ibn-al-Jawzi, p. 175.

[5] Ibn-al-Athīr, vol. xi, p. 223; abu-Shāmah, vol. i, p. 155; abu-al-Fidā', vol. iii, p. 47.

was effected without even "the butting of two goats".[1] Thereby Ṣalāḥ became the sole ruler of Egypt. The second ambition of his life was realized when his Syrian suzerain Nūr-al-Dīn passed away. A few minor engagements snatched Syria from the hands of the eleven-year-old son of Nūr, Ismā'īl.[2] With the first two goals attained, the third entered the range of vision.

As adjuncts of Egypt, Cyrenaica and al-Ḥijāz immediately became parts of the newly rising Syro-Egyptian domain. Ṣalāḥ's elder brother Tūrān-Shāh added Nubia and al-Yaman. The 'Abbāsid caliph granted Ṣalāḥ in 1175 at his own request a diploma of investiture over all these lands, thereby giving away what in reality was not his to give but what it was flattering to him not to refuse. The incorporation of al-Mawṣil and its Mesopotamian dependencies rounded out the sultanate.[3] Nūr-al-Dīn's dream of enveloping the Franks and crushing them to death was becoming a reality through the achievements of his more illustrious successor.

The decisive encounter: Ḥiṭṭīn

At last Ṣalāḥ was free to concentrate on "the infidels". The hour of peril for the Latin kingdom struck when, after a six-day siege, Tiberias fell and the Moslem army moved to the adjacent Ḥiṭṭīn (Ḥaṭṭīn).[4] There the battle was joined July 3 to 4, 1187. The heat was intense. Exhausted from the long march and crazed with thirst, the heavy-armoured Franks were surrounded by light-armoured Moslems and subjected to an incessant shower of arrows the like of which they never experienced before. Of the 20,000 knights [5] and footmen only a few remained alive through apostasy or escape; the rest were slaughtered or captured. The prisoners' procession was headed by none other than the king of Jerusalem, Guy de Lusignan. He was received in a way worthy of his high office by a magna-

[1] Ibn-al-Athīr, vol. xi, p. 242; abu-al-Fidā', vol. iii, p. 53; cf. abu-Shāmah, vol. i, pp. 200-201.

[2] Ibn-al-Athīr, vol. xi, pp. 274-5.

[3] Ibn-al-Athīr, vol. xi, pp. 319-21.

[4] The "horns" (*qurūn*) of Ḥiṭṭīn tower 1700 feet above the Sea of Galilee and represent the crater of an extinct volcano. Tradition assigns the Sermon on the Mount to this site.

[5] Templars and Hospitallers. The Templars, so called because their first residence was near the site of Solomon's Temple, were organized about 1119 to protect pilgrims on their way to the Holy Land. The Hospitallers, or Knights of St. John of Jerusalem, sprang from an earlier organization established to maintain hostels (not hospitals) for pilgrims and later devoted to military pursuits. Both orders took monastic vows.

nimous and chivalrous sultan. But his companion Reginald of Châtillon, lord of al-Karak,[1] merited and received a different treatment. In violation of treaty relations, he had more than once attacked pilgrim and commercial caravans as they passed by his castle on the main route south of Jerusalem. The sultan's sister was once in such a caravan. As adventurous as he was unscrupulous, Reginald had with his Red Sea fleet harassed both the Nubian and the Arabian coasts; he even landed on the holy soil of al-Ḥijāz and moved toward Medina. When within a short day's march from the holy city itself, he was driven back by Egyptians transported on a hurriedly constructed fleet. It was rumoured that he aimed at removing the Prophet's body to al-Karak and charging a heavy fee for Moslem pilgrims to view it.[2] Ṣalāḥ had sworn to slay him with his own hand and the time had come for the fulfilment of his oath. The drink of cold water taken by the chained captive in his captor's tent did not guarantee impunity according to Arab hospitality rites, as it was not offered but requested Guy shook in his boots as Ṣalāḥ slew his captive but was reassured by him: " A king does not kill a king ".[3]

The destruction on the day of Ḥiṭṭīn of the Frankish army, which comprised besides the capital's garrison contingents from the other states, sealed the fate of the Latin kingdom. After a week's siege Jerusalem capitulated on October 2. Ṣalāḥ's treatment of the Frankish populace stood in sharp contrast with the treatment accorded the Moslems eighty-eight years earlier. Those who could ransom themselves individually did so; the poor were allowed forty days to collect a lump sum for ransom and the rest were sold as slaves. The lands of the evacuated Franks were purchased by troops and native Christians.[4] From Jerusalem the tide of conquest continued, engulfing such fortifications as al-Shawbak and al-Karak in the south, Kaw-

[1] See above, p. 596, n. 4.

[2] Ibn-Jubayr (pp. 58-60) witnessed in Alexandria the remnant of his army, chained on to camels and facing the tails, as they were led to execution to the sound of drums. Abu-al-Fidā', vol. iii, pp. 68-9.

[3] Abu-Shāmah, vol. ii, pp. 75 *seq.*, who gives an eye-witness' report; ibn-al-Athīr, vol. xi, pp. 352-5; Bahā'-al-Dīn ibn-Shaddād, *Sīrat Ṣalāḥ-al-Dīn* (Cairo, 1317), pp. 27, 60-65; tr. '*Saladin*': *or, What Befell Sultan Yūsuf* (London, 1897), pp. 42-3, 110-17; 'Imād-al-Dīn al-Iṣfahāni, *al-Fatḥ al-Qussi fi al-Fatḥ al-Qudsi*, ed. C. de Landberg (Leyden, 1888), pp. 22-8; Ernoul and Bernard le Trésorier, *Chronique*, ed. M. L. de Mas Latrie (Paris, 1871), pp. 172-4.

[4] Ibn-Khaldūn, vol. v, p. 311.

kab,[1] al-Shaqīf [2] and Ṣihyawn (Saone) to the north. ʻAsqalān, ʻAkka, Ṣafad, Ṭarṭūs, Jabalah, al-Lādhiqīyah, all fell before the end of 1189.[3] Only Tyre, Tripoli and Antioch, other than smaller towns and castles, remained in Frankish hands.[4]

The loss of the holy city aroused Europe and inspired the "Third Crusade". In it participated the three mightiest sovereigns of Western Europe, Frederick Barbarossa of Germany, Philip Augustus of France and Richard I Cœur de Lion of England. Legend and history have collaborated to make this campaign, with Richard and Ṣalāḥ as its chief heroes, one of the truly spectacular and romantic periods in Occidental and Oriental annals. ʻAkka, centre of activity

The king of Germany took the land route and was drowned crossing a river in Cilicia. Discouraged, many of his followers returned home. ʻAkka was decided on by the Syrian Latins as providing the key for the restoration of the lost domain. Against it marched all available warriors augmented by the new arrivals from Europe. King Guy led the attack despite the fact that he had pledged his honour to Ṣalāḥ after Ḥiṭṭīn never again to bear arms against him. The city was besieged. Ṣalāḥ rushed to its rescue and pitched his camp facing the enemy.

> About the trench was fought the battle
> 'Twixt God's men and the pagan cattle.[5]

The Franks had the decided advantage of a fleet and up-to-date siege artillery. For two years (August 27, 1189 to July 12, 1191) the operations, considered among the major ones in the military annals of the Middle Ages, dragged on. The Moslem governor of Beirut used native Christian mariners dressed like Franks and accompanied by pigs to carry food by sea to the besieged city.[6] Spectacular feats of valour are recorded on

[1] A newly built Crusading castle north of Baysān by the Jordan. Its full name was Kawkab al-Hawā' (the star of the sky), Belvoir in Latin sources.

[2] The Belfort of Latin chronicles. Hanging like an eagle's nest on a precipitous rock 1500 feet above al-Līṭāni River (Leontes), this fortress commands the mountain pass from Damascus to Sidon. Its full name, Shaqīf (Syr. for huge rock) Arnūn (Syr. for rushing stream, cf. Arnon, above, p. 167), suggests its ancient origin. Arnūn is considered by some a corruption of Arnold.

[3] Al-Maqrīzi, *Kitāb al-Sulūk li-Ma'rifat al-Mulūk*, ed. M. Muṣṭafa Ziyādah, vol. i, pt. 1 (Cairo, 1934), pp. 99-101.

[4] Ibn-Shaddād, pp. 65 *seq.*; ʻImād-al-Dīn, pp. 136 *seq.*; Ernoul and Bernard, pp. 179 *seq.*, 251.

[5] Ambroise, *The Crusade of Richard Lion-Heart*, tr. Merton J. Hubert, John L. La Monte (New York, 1941), p. 145.

[6] Abu-Shāmah, vol. ii, p. 161.

both sides. A Damascene coppersmith forewent the sultan's in favour of Allah's reward for having burned three of the besiegers' towers with explosives he compounded.[1] One flint stone taken from Sicily by Richard for his mangonels reportedly destroyed thirteen 'Akkans and was exhibited to Ṣalāḥ as a curiosity. Swimmers and carrier pigeons were employed between Ṣalāḥ and the beleaguered town. The dead body of such a swimmer was washed out and the 'Akkans received the money and letters he carried, prompting Ṣalāḥ's biographer [2] to remark: "Never before has it been known that someone received a trust in his lifetime and delivered it after his death" Finally, after Ṣalāḥ had sought but did not receive aid from the caliph, the garrison surrendered.

Included in the conditions of surrender were the restoration of the "true cross", captured at Ḥiṭṭīn, and the release of the garrison on the payment of 200,000 gold pieces.[3] But the money was not paid in a month and the Lion-Hearted ordered the twenty-seven hundred captives slaughtered.[4]

Rich in romantic ideas, Richard proposed a marriage between his sister and Ṣalāḥ's younger brother al-Malik al-'Ādil with the understanding that the couple would receive as a wedding present both 'Akka and Jerusalem and therewith the Christian-Moslem conflict would end [5] Al-'Ādil's son, al-Malik al-Kāmil, was in May 1192 ceremoniously knighted by Richard. His uncle Ṣalāḥ had been years before similarly admitted to the honours of Christian knighthood. Richard and Ṣalāḥ exchanged gifts but never met. On November 2, 1192, peace was concluded on the general basis that the coast belonged to the Latins and the interior to the Moslems and that the Christian pilgrims should not be molested. Palestine was partitioned. Richard bade Syria farewell and returned home:

> Ah, Syria, I now commend
> You to the Lord God! May He lend
> Me time enough, if He so will
> That I may yet relieve your ill!
> For still I think to succour you.[6]

[1] Ibn-Khaldūn, vol. v, p. 321. [2] Ibn-Shaddād, p. 120.

[3] Abu-Shāmah, vol. ii, p. 188; 'Imād-al-Dīn, p. 357; ibn-al-'Ibri, pp. 386-7; abu-al-Fidā', vol. iii, pp. 83-4.

[4] Benedict of Peterborough, ed. W. Stubbs (London, 1867), vol. ii, p. 189; ibn-Shaddād, pp. 164-5.

[5] Cf. abu-al-Fidā', vol. iii, p. 84. [6] Ambroise, p. 447.

Early in March of the following year Ṣalāḥ died of fever, aged fifty-five. His tomb, still standing by the Umayyad Mosque, is one of the most revered shrines in the Syrian capital.

More than a warrior and champion of orthodox Islam, Ṣalāḥ was a builder and a patron of learning. He founded schools, seminaries and mosques in both Egypt and Syria and included

The American Numismatic Society

A COIN OF ṢALĀḤ-AL-DĪN

Obverse and reverse of a silver dirham of Ṣalāḥ-al-Dīn struck at Dimashq (Damascus), A.H. 573 = A.D. 1177/8

in his cabinet two learned vizirs, al-Qāḍi al-Fāḍil [1] and 'Imād-al-Dīn al-Iṣfahāni.[2] His private secretary and biographer was Bahā'-al-Dīn ibn-Shaddād.[3] The vast collection of treasures of the Fāṭimid court [4] which fell into his hands on the overthrow of the caliphate, he distributed among his men, leaving nothing for himself. One of those treasures was a seventeen-dirham sapphire as weighed by the historian ibn-al-Athīr [5] in person. Styled *al-jabal* (the mountain), this stone, " which shone at night like a lamp ", supposedly once belonged to the Saljūqs, the 'Abbāsids — of whom al-Rashīd one day dropped it into the Tigris — and the Chosroes.[6] Nūr-al-Dīn's estate Ṣalāḥ passed on to the deceased ruler's son. The estate he himself left amounted to forty-seven dirhams and one gold piece,[7] but the memory he left is still a priceless treasure in the heritage of

[1] Ibn-Khallikān, vol. i, pp. 509 *seq.*; al-Subki, *Ṭabaqāt al-Shāfi'īyah al-Kubra* (Cairo, 1324), vol. iv, pp. 253-4.

[2] Ibn-Khallikān, vol. ii, pp. 495 *seq.*; Suyūṭi, *Ḥusn*, vol. i, p. 270. His *al-Fatḥ* was drawn upon in the composition of this chapter.

[3] Ibn-Khallikān, vol. iii, pp. 428 *seq.* His *Sīrah* has been extensively used in this chapter.

[4] Maqrīzi, vol. i, pp. 414-16; ibn-Taghri-Birdi, ed. Popper, vol. iii, pt. 1, pp. 85-6.

[5] Vol. xi, p. 242.

[6] Ibn-al-Athīr, vol. vi, p. 74; vol. x, p. 266; Mas'ūdi, vol. vii, p. 376; Ṭabari, vol. iii, pp. 602, 1647.

[7] Abu-al-Fidā', vol. iii, p. 9.

the Arab East. The memory of his chivalry is almost equally cherished in Europe, where it has touched the fancy of English minstrels as well as modern novelists.[1]

After Ṣalāḥ-al-Dīn's death

With the death of the great hero of Islam the third period in Crusading history begins, that of dissension and petty wars covering a century. Throughout the thirteenth century European public sentiment remained indifferent to these campaigns. Only those of St. Louis, king of France, in the middle of that century, could be compared with the first Crusade as being motivated by religious considerations. Several of the Crusades of this period were directed against Egypt with the expectation of reaching the Red Sea and participating in the opulent commerce of the Indian Ocean and on the pretext that the occupation of Dimyāṭ (Damietta) or Alexandria, for instance, might result in an exchange for Jerusalem. The Moslems also had lost the spirit of the *jihād.* What was equally serious they had lost the unified leadership and a united domain. Syria was partitioned among Ṣalāḥ's three sons, but shortly thereafter Ṣalāḥ's younger brother al-ʿĀdil acquired sovereignty over Egypt and most of Syria.[2] Throughout his rule al-ʿĀdil (*ca.* 1199–1218, the Saphadin [3] of Latin chronicles) tried to maintain cordial relations with the Franks. This policy aimed at peace and the furtherance of trade with the Italians.

From al-ʿĀdil sprang a variety of Ayyūbid branches which reigned in Egypt, Damascus and Mesopotamia. Other branches arose in Ḥimṣ, Ḥamāh and al-Yaman.[4] In the course of the ensuing dynastic turmoils one after another of Ṣalāḥ's conquests — Beirut, Ṣafad, Tiberias, even Jerusalem (1229) — reverted to Frankish hands. Jerusalem was turned over by al-Kāmil (1218–38), son of al-ʿĀdil, to Frederick II, king of Sicily, in accordance with a ten-year treaty in which al-Kāmil was guaranteed Frederick's aid against his enemies, most of whom were Ayyūbids.[5] Al-Kāmil's nephew, however, al-Malik al-Ṣāliḥ Najm-al-Dīn, utilized in 1244 a contingent of Khwārizm

[1] A Damascene poet who knew Ṣalāḥ personally attacked the character of the lame Ṣalāḥ; ibn-ʿUnayn, *Dīwān*, ed. Khalīl Mardam (Damascus, 1946), pp. 6, 210-11; another contemporary poet ibn-al-Sāʿāti, *Dīwān*, ed. Anīs K. al-Maqdisi, vol. i (Beirut, 1938), pp. 19-21, devotes several odes to the glorification of the hero.

[2] See below, p. 627.

[3] From his honorific title Sayf-al-Dīn (the sword of religion). Ibn-Khallikān, vol. ii, p. 446.

[4] See below, pp. 627-9.

[5] Abu-al-Fidā', vol. iii, p. 148; ibn-al-Athīr, vol. xii, p. 315.

Turks, dislodged from their Central Asian abode by Chingīz Khān, to restore the city to Islam. But the Franks were in no position to capitalize on Moslem dissension. They themselves were in as bad a situation, with rivalries between Genoese and Venetians, jealousies between Templars and Hospitallers and quarrels among the leaders. In these quarrels it was no more unusual for one side to secure Moslem aid against the other than it was for the Moslems to secure Christian aid against other Moslems.[1]

St. Louis

The mid-thirteenth century was marked by the advent of Louis, king of France and leader of the "sixth Crusade" (first directed against Egypt). Louis spent four years in Syria (1250–1254), where he fortified Jaffa, Caesarea, 'Akka and Sidon.[2]

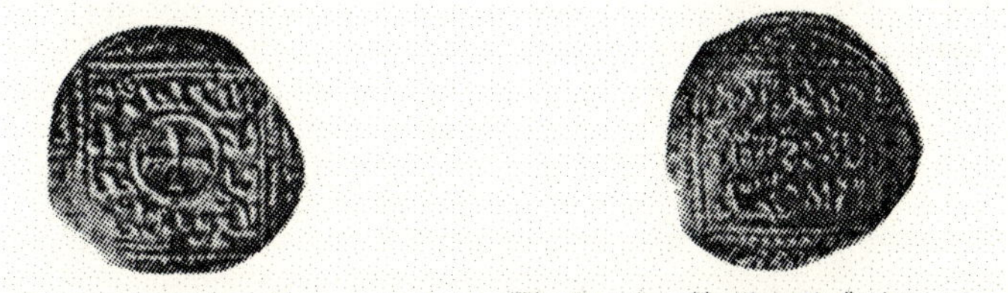

The American Numismatic Society

A CRUSADING COIN

Obverse and reverse of a silver bezant with Arabic inscription struck by the Crusaders at 'Akka about A.D. 1250. The obverse bears the mint, the date and the legend: "One God, one faith, one Baptism"; the reverse: "The Father, the Son, the Holy Ghost, one God".

Ruins of the castle in Sidon, garrisoned by Templars, where he stayed, are still standing. Of all the Crusading leaders his, by far, was the purest, the noblest character — that of a real saint.

Baybars, leader of the counter-Crusade

A new and unexpected danger, however, was now threatening from the East: the Tartars. Mongol hordes were flooding northern Syria and advancing southward. Concurrently Ayyūbids were giving way to Mamlūks.[3] Fourth among these was al-Malik al-Ẓāhir Baybars (1260–77), who inaugurated the series of sultans who dealt the final blows to Latin Syria. Baybars checked in Palestine the Mongols' first advance,[4] recovered their Syrian conquests, reunited Egypt and Syria and was then able to pursue the holy war. From 1263 to 1271

[1] See above, p. 599.
[2] Joinville, pp. 223-331.
[3] See below, p. 629.
[4] See below, p. 631.

he conducted almost annual raids against the Frankish establishments. One after the other they yielded. Even the Templars and the Hospitallers, who, entrenched in strong castles, formed the bulwark of the Latin states, were unable to withstand his reiterated blows. In 1263 Baybars occupied al-Karak and demolished the venerated church of Nazareth (al-Nāṣirah). Two years later he captured Caesarea by surprise, and after a forty-day siege received the surrender of Arsūf from the Hospitallers.[1] In 1266 Ṣafad capitulated and its garrison of two thousand Templars were executed, despite amnesty granted by him.[2] The walls of the city still bear the inscription of "the Alexander of his age and the pillar of his faith"; the bridge he built across the Jordan shows a lion on each side of his inscription. In 1268 Jaffa was seized, Shaqīf Arnūn capitulated, and what is more significant, Antioch surrendered. Of Antioch's garrison and people 16,000 were put to the sword and reportedly 100,000 were led to captivity. A young boy fetched twelve dirhams and a young girl five. The city itself, with its ancient citadel and world-renowned churches, was given to the flames, a blow from which it has never recovered.[3]

The fall of Antioch, second of the Latin states to be founded, had its demoralizing effect. A number of minor Latin strongholds were thereupon abandoned. In 1271 the tenacious Ḥiṣn al-Akrād, principal retreat of the Hospitallers and the most admirable of all medieval castles in preservation, surrendered after a short siege (March 24 to April 8). For many years this castle, which belonged to the count of Tripoli and could house as many as two thousand at a time, watched the passage connecting the northern Lebanon littoral with Syria, just as al-Shaqīf watched the southern passage. It headed the list of the mountain-type castles set to dominate the passes that led from the Moslem hinterland to the Frankish seaboard. Other forts of the same type were Miṣyāf,[4] al-Qadmūs, al-Kahf and

[1] Ibn-al-Furāt, *Ta'rīkh*, ed. Costi K. Zurayq, vol. vii (Beirut, 1942), p. 82.

[2] Al-Maqrīzi, *Kitāb al-Sulūk fi Ma'rifat Duwal al-Mulūk*, tr. M. Quatremère, *Histoire des sultans mamlouks* (Paris, 1854), vol. i (pt. 2), pp. 29-30; abu-al-Fidā', vol. iv, p. 3.

[3] Ibn-al-'Ibri, p. 500; Maqrīzi, tr. Quatremère, vol. i (pt. 2), pp. 52-4; abu-al-Fidā', vol. iv, pp. 4-5.

[4] Also Maṣyāf, Maṣyād, Maṣyāt, Maṣyāth; see art. Maṣyād, *Encyclopaedia of Islām*; Usāmah, p. 148; tr., p. 177; Dussaud *et al.*, *Syrie antique*, pl. 128. Ismā'īlites still live there.

al-Khawābi, all of which belonged to the Assassins, allies of the Hospitallers. These fortifications, of which Miṣyāf was the strongest, lay in the Nuṣayrīyah region and were now reduced. Both Anṭarṭūs [1] (Tortosa), principal fortress of the Templars,[2] and al-Marqab,[3] garrisoned by Hospitallers, hastened to make peace. These two castles represented the coastal type planted

Photo taken 1923

ḤIṢN AL-AKRĀD, CRAC DES CHEVALIERS, ONE OF THE STRONGEST AND LARGEST OF THE CRUSADER CASTLES

This castle stood sentinel over the Ḥimṣ-Tripoli road

to control the maritime road and ports and to defend them against the fleet centred in Egypt. Of the Ṭarṭūs castle not much is left, but al-Marqab is still perched like a dreadnought on a hill. The famous geographer al-Idrīsi,[4] who visited Syria shortly before this time, cites no less than sixteen forts between Beirut and al-Lādhiqīyah. Modern research indicates that the Byzantine art of fortification lies at the base of the development

[1] Antaradus (opposite the isle of Aradus), modern Ṭarṭūs; Ṭaraṭūs in Yaqūt, vol. iii, p. 529.

[2] Their chief inland stronghold was Chastel Blanc, now Burj Ṣāfīta, a Greek Orthodox church.

[3] "Watchtower", Castrum Mergathum, Margat.

[4] Ed. Gildemeister, pp. 16-23.

of the military Crusading architecture in both its Christian and Moslem aspects.[1]

The Assassins

The Assassins were a Neo-Ismā'īlite order inaugurated by al-Ḥasan ibn-al-Ṣabbāḥ, who in 1090 set up his headquarters in a fortress, Alamūt,[2] in the Alburz Mountain. They acquired their name from Arabic *ḥashīsh*,[3] the intoxicating hemp (marijuana), to which they supposedly resorted when they operated. The order was a secret organization headed by a grand master below whom stood priors followed by propagandists. Near the bottom were the *fidā'is* [4] ready to execute at all cost the grand master's orders. The *fidā'is* made free and treacherous use of the dagger against Christians and Moslems alike; they made assassination an art.

About the same time that the Crusaders were entering Syria from the north-west the Assassins were entering it from the north-east. Their first important convert was the Saljūq amīr Riḍwān [5] (d. 1113); their first stronghold was Bāniyās.[6] By 1140 they had acquired several strongholds in mountainous North Syria, a procedure in which they followed their Persian kinsmen. Qadmūs was the first to be acquired (1133). William of Tyre [7] estimates their number at 60,000. To the Europeans the Syrian grand master was the *vieux de la montagne*. His seat was at Miṣyāf.[8] For thirty years, beginning about 1162, Rāshid [9]-al-Dīn Sinān held this high office. It was his men who made two unsuccessful attempts on the life of Ṣalāḥ-al-Dīn; [10] Rāshid was bribed by a Damascene vizir loyal to the memory of Nūr-al-Dīn. Ṣalāḥ attacked Miṣyāf but did not reduce it. He in turn was suspected of having used Assassins

[1] Paul Deschamps, *Le Crac des Chevaliers* (Paris, 1934), vol. i, pp. 43 *seq.*; cf. T. E. Lawrence, *Crusader Castles* (London, 1936), vol. i, pp. 13-15.

[2] The fortress hangs like an eagle's nest, which is probably the meaning of the word, on the rough road between the Caspian shores and the Persian highlands.

[3] Indian *bhang* (Ar. *banj*). References to a drug that acted as an antidote for sorrow and "robber of the mind" occur in Babylonian literature.

[4] Variant *fidāwi*, one ready to offer his life for a cause. Cf. ibn-Baṭṭūṭah, vol. i, pp. 166-7.

[5] See above, p. 575.

[6] See above, p. 599.

[7] Vol. ii, p. 691; cf. Burchard of Mount Zion, tr. Aubrey Stewart (London, 1896), p. 105, where their number is made 40,000.

[8] Benjamin of Tudela (*ca.* 1169), vol. i, p. 59, makes Qadmūs the seat.

[9] (Not Rashīd); abu-al-Fidā', vol. iii, p. 89; ibn-Khallikān, vol. ii, p. 521.

[10] Abu-al-Fidā', vol. iii, pp. 60, 61.

against Conrad of Montferrat, titular king of Jerusalem, who was killed in 1192 by a band disguised as Christians.[1] Another prominent Frank for whose death the Assassins were responsible was Count Raymond II of Tripoli (*ca.* 1152). Sinān's successor was visited by a Frankish count in his mountain castle with its high turrets guarded by white-clad Assassins. On a signal from the master two of the sentinels threw themselves from their turrets to be torn to pieces on the rocks below.[2] The story shows that religious zeal rather than intoxicating drugs motivated the blind obedience and unquestioning loyalty of the Assassins.

In 1172 the Old Man of the Mountain sent envoys to the king of Jerusalem to discuss the possibility of conversion on the part of his men to Christianity. This was in line with the practice of dissimulation (*taqīyah*) authorized by ultra-Shīʿite tenets. Fearing the loss of tribute which the Assassins were then paying the Templars, these knights murdered the envoys.[3] When in ʿAkka St. Louis received an Assassin delegation with presents, including ornaments and beasts of crystal, amber, a ring and a shirt. The shirt meant that Louis was as close to Rāshid as his own body. Louis reciprocated.[4] Two knights who spoke Arabic served as interpreters. Before Louis' departure from France the Assassins had made an attempt on his life, indicating that their field of operation extended as far as Western Europe. Eastward they operated as far as Mongolia, where they tried to assassinate one of the Great Khāns. With Baybars' destruction of their Syrian nest, which for years had hatched intrigue and murder, the Syrian Assassin power was forever crushed.

The last of the Crusading colonies

The work begun by Baybars against the Franks was continued by his equally energetic and zealous successor Qalāwūn (1279–90). His title al-Malik al-Manṣūr (the victorious king) was well deserved. On April 15, 1282, Qalāwūn renewed the truce negotiated by Baybars with the Templars of Anṭarṭūs for another period of ten years and ten months. A treaty with similar terms was signed three years later with the princess of

[1] Ibn-al-Athīr, vol. xii, p. 51; Jacques de Vitry, pp. 116-17; Ambroise, pp. 334-5.

[2] Marinus Sanuto, "Liber secretorum", in Bongars, *Gesta Dei per Francos* (Hanau, 1611), vol. ii, p. 201.

[3] William of Tyre, vol. ii, pp. 392-4; Burchard, pp. 105-6.

[4] Joinville, pp. 250 *seq.*

Tyre, who then held Beirut.[1] After a siege of thirty-eight days ending May 25, 1285, al-Marqab yielded. Its outer walls still show numberless arrowheads imbedded between the stones. The Ayyūbid historian-amīr abu-al-Fidā',[2] then a lad of twelve years, had his first military experience on this occasion. Its Hospitallers were escorted to Tripoli.[3] Four years later this town, the largest still in Frankish hands, was captured and levelled to the ground. So oppressive was the odour from the corpses lying thick on the islet outside the port that abu-al-Fidā'[4] could not stand it. Tripoli was rebuilt several years later not on its former site but several miles from the sea, where it now stands.

Amidst preparations against 'Akka, the only place of military importance left, Qalāwūn died and was succeeded by his son al-Ashraf (1290–93). Al-Ashraf invested 'Akka for

From Henri Lavoix, "Monnaies à légendes arabes frappées en Syrie par les Croisés"

A FRANKISH DINAR STRUCK AT 'AKKA IN 1251

Bearing Arabic inscription

over a month, using ninety-two catapults, before he stormed it on May 18, 1291. He slaughtered its Templar defenders in violation of a safe-conduct he had granted them. Abu-al-Fidā'[5] took part in the siege. The city was practically wiped out of existence.[6]

[1] Maqrīzi has preserved the texts of both treaties, ed. Quatremère, vol. ii (pt. 3), pp. 172-6, 177-8, tr. pp. 22-31, 212-21; cf. treaties preserved in ibn-al-Furāt, vol. vii, pp. 204-6, 262-72.

[2] Vol. iv, p. 22.

[3] Ibn-al-Furāt, vol. viii, pp. 17-18.

[4] Vol. iv, p. 24; cf. ibn-al-Furāt, vol. viii, pp. 80-81. Idrīsi, p. 18, reports four islands in the port of Tripoli. Those visible today can hardly be so called.

[5] Vol. iv, pp. 25-6; Maqrīzi, tr. Quatremère, vol. ii (pt. 3), pp. 125-9.

[6] Rebuilt in the eighteenth century, its citadel was later used by the British as a prison and blasted by Zionist terrorists in May 1947.

ʿAkka's capture sealed the fate of the few remaining coastal towns. Tyre was abandoned on the same day and Sidon on July 14. Beirut capitulated on July 21 and Anṭarṭūs on August 3. ʿAthlīth (Castrum Peregrinorum, Château Pèlerin), deserted by its Templars, was demolished about mid-August.[1]

Service des Antiquités de Syrie

THE ISLET OF ARWAD

The Templars of Arwād held out for eleven years more. Over the gateway of the ruins of this islet's castle the Lusignan coat of arms — a lion and a palm — is still visible. With the fall of Arwād the curtain fell on the last scene of the most spectacular drama in the history of the conflict between East and West.

[1] Ṣāliḥ, p. 42; abu-al-Fidā', vol. iv, p. 26; Sanuto in Bongars, vol. ii, pp. 231 *seq.*

CHAPTER XLVI

CULTURAL INTERACTION

RICH in picturesque and romantic incidents, the Crusades were rather disappointing in intellectual and cultural achievement. On the whole they meant much more to the West in terms of civilizing influences than they did to the East. They opened new horizons — industrial, commercial and colonial — before the eyes of Europeans. The states they built in Syria correspond to modern colonial empires, and the merchant or pilgrim rather than the returned soldier was the principal culture carrier. In the East they left a legacy of ill will between Moslems and Christians the effects of which are still noticeable.

The impact on the West: science and literature

Islamic culture in the Crusading epoch was already decadent in the East. For some time it had ceased to be a creative force.[1] In science, literature, philosophy all its great lights had been dimmed. Moreover, the Franks themselves were on a lower cultural level. Nationalistic animosities and religious prejudices thwarted the free play of interactive forces between them and the Moslems and left them in no responsive mood. No wonder, then, that we know of only one major scientific work done from Arabic into Latin throughout the whole period, al-Majūsi's[2] *Kāmil al-Ṣināʿah al-Ṭibbīyah*, or *al-Kitāb al-Maliki* (the perfect in the medical art, or the royal book). This was done at Antioch in 1127 by a Pisan named Stephen. A minor work translated also in Antioch (1247) was *Sirr al-Asrār* (*Secretum secretorum*), a pseudo-Aristotelian treatise on occult science which had a wide vogue in the late Middle Ages. Systematic hospitalization in the Occident probably received a fresh stimulus from the Orient. A number of hospices and hospitals, chiefly lazar-houses,[3] begin to spring up in twelfth century Europe. Syrian leper houses may thus be considered ancestors of European hospitals.

[1] See above, p. 572.
[2] His first name ʿAli ʿAbbās, Latinized Haly Abbas; he died in 994.
[3] Cf. above, pp. 497-8.

In literature the influence was even slighter and more difficult to detect. Stories, some of which were of Persian and Indic origin, were transmitted and appear strangely altered in the *Gesta Romanorum* and other collections. Chaucer's *Squieres*

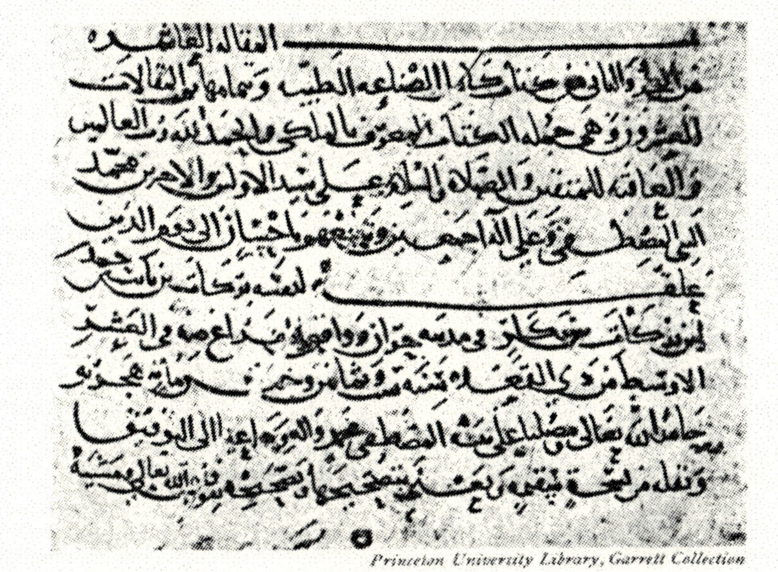

Princeton University Library, Garrett Collection

COLOPHON OF AL-MAJŪSI'S GREAT WORK ON MEDICINE, MANUSCRIPT

This *al-Kitāb al-Maliki* by 'Ali ibn-al-'Abbās al-Majūsi, copied A.H. 586 (A.D. 1190), is one of only two known complete copies. It was the only major scientific work done into Latin by the Crusaders and taken back to Europe

Tale has an *Arabian Nights* antecedent; Boccaccio's *Decameron* contains a number of tales derived orally from Oriental sources. The Holy Grail legend preserves elements of undoubted Syrian origin.

Military art

In Syria the Franks learned the use of the crossbow,[1] the wearing of heavier mail by knight and horse, the employment of the tabor and naker[2] in military bands, the conveying of military intelligence by carrier pigeons and the use of fire for signalling at night.[3] They also acquired the practice of

[1] See Ludolph von Suchem, p. 135. [2] Ar. *ṭunbūr* and *naqqārah*.

[3] Consult Ṣāliḥ, pp. 60-61; al-Ẓāhiri, *Zubdat Kashf al-Mamālik*, ed. P. Ravaisse (Paris, 1894), pp. 116-17; Qalqashandi, vol. viii, pp. 392-4; 'Umari, pp. 196-7. Cf. Suyūṭi, *Ḥusn*, vol. ii, p. 186.

celebrating victory by illumination and were introduced to the knightly sport of tournament. In fact the whole institution of chivalry was promoted on Syrian soil. Contact with Moslem knights encouraged the use of armorial bearings and heraldic devices. The double-headed eagle, of Sumerian antiquity, was used by Zangi on his coins and by the Urtuqids as a badge. It passed on to the knights of the Round Table and to Byzantium and was adopted in 1345 by German emperors. The heraldic idea finally reached the United States, which uses an eagle as its emblem. The fleur-de-lis, known to the Elamites and Assyrians, appears for the first time in Moslem heraldry as the blazon of Nūr-al-Dīn, Zangi's son. It frequently occurs on Ayyūbid and Mamlūk coins. Adopted by the Franks, it passed on to France and later to Canada. The rosette was popular with the Ayyūbids and the Mamlūks. Many Mamlūks bore names of animals, the corresponding images of which they blazoned on their shields. Baybars' crest was a lion.[1] "Azure" (Ar. *lāzaward*) and other heraldic terms testify to the enduring effect of Moslem knighthood.

ARMS OF FRANCE

Early coats of arms of France showed many fleurs-de-lis on a blue field

The order of Templars, which, like that of the Hospitallers, was the nearest approach to harmonizing war and religion — an old achievement in Islam — followed in its organization a pattern similar to that of the Assassins. At the bottom of the Christian order stood the lay brothers, esquires and knights, corresponding to the *lāṣiqs* (associates), *fidā'is* and *rafīqs* (comrades). The knight wore a white mantle with a red cross mark, the *rafīq* a white mantle with a red cap. In the higher brackets the counterparts of the prior, grand prior and grand master were the *dā'i*, *dā'i kabīr* (superior propagandist) and

[1] L. A. Mayer, *Saracenic Heraldry* (Oxford, 1933), pp. 7, 26, 107.

shaykh al-jabal (old man of the mountain).[1] Then there was another secret order, *futūwah*, in which Arab chivalry sought to express itself. The order was reformed and patronized by the ʿAbbāsid al-Nāṣir (1180–1225), who might have been impressed by the Crusading orders. The initiate was also called *rafīq* and wore distinctive trousers (*sarāwīl*). Ṣalāḥ-al-Dīn's brother al-ʿĀdil and al-ʿĀdil's sons wore such trousers. Syria had an active branch that went by the name Nubuwīyah.[2]

Architecture

Most conspicuous among all Crusading remains in Syria are the many castles still crowning its hills. Then come the churches. In the churches the Franks employed the familiar Romanesque and Gothic styles but the Byzantine and Syrian motifs of decoration. The Church of the Holy Sepulchre and the Dome of the Rock were imitated in several ecclesiastical buildings of the "round temple" type in England, France, Spain and Germany. Many of the Crusader churches have since been converted into mosques. Among these are the great cathedral of Notre-Dame in Tyre, where the historian William of Tyre [3] was archbishop (1175–85); the church of Sidon erected by the Hospitallers, now al-Jāmiʿ al-Kabīr (the great mosque); the cathedral of St. John of Beirut, now the ʿUmari Mosque, constructed in 1110 by King Baldwin; [4] and the cathedral of Our Lady in Anṭarṭūs, the most beautiful and best preserved of all, which was an object of pilgrimage. The structure was begun in 1130 and housed a picture supposedly painted by Luke and an altar over which Peter allegedly celebrated the first mass.[5] A recent minaret was added to this edifice, which no doubt stood on the site of an early Christian church. Al-Balamand (Belmont), near Tripoli, now a Greek Orthodox monastery, was built by Frankish monks in 1157.[6]

Agriculture and industry

For long generations before the Crusades pilgrims frequented the Holy Land and traders visited the eastern shores of the Mediterranean. The Crusading movement accelerated forces already in operation and popularized in Europe Oriental pro-

[1] See above, p. 610.

[2] Ibn-al-Athīr, vol. xii, p. 268; *Fakhri*, p. 434; ibn-Jubayr, p. 280.

[3] Vol. ii, p. 411; Enlart, vol. ii, pp. 353 *seq.*

[4] Ṣāliḥ, p. 58; Enlart, vol. ii, pp. 69 *seq.*

[5] Joinville, p. 328; Jacques de Vitry, pp. 20-21; Dussaud *et al.*, *Syrie antique*, pls. 117, 118; Enlart, vol. ii, pp. 403 *seq.*

[6] Enlart, vol. ii, pp. 45 *seq.*

ducts, some of which must have been previously known. The problem of tracing origins is further complicated by the fact that while the Syrian bridge was open for traffic two other bridges, the Sicilian and the Spanish, were in operation too, thus making it difficult to determine the exact route taken by any particular commodity.

While in Syria the Franks were introduced to or acquired a taste for certain native and tropical products with which the

From Enlart, " Les Monuments des Croisés " (Lib. Orientaliste, Paul Geuthner, Paris)

THE CRUSADER CATHEDRAL OF NOTRE-DAME AT ANṬARṬŪS (TORTOSA, MODERN ṬARṬŪS), A RESTORATION

marts of Syria were then stocked. Among those products were sesame, carob (Ar. *kharrūb*),[1] millet, rice (*arizz*), lemons (*laymūn*), melons, apricots [2] and shallots.[3] Apricots were at times called the plums of Damascus. The Syrian capital specialized in sweet scents and damask rose (*Rosa damascena*). Attars (Ar. *'iṭr*) and fragrant volatile oils, of Persian origin, incense and other aromatic gums of Arabia, together with other spices, perfumes and sweetmeats became favourites. Cloves and

[1] Originally Assyrian; see above, p. 138, n. 5.
[2] From Ar. *baraqrūq*, originally L. *praecoquum*, early ripe.
[3] Shallots and scallions received their name from Ascalon ('Asqalān).

similar *aromatics*, pepper and other condiments, alum, aloes and several drugs found their way into the European kitchen and store, first in the East and subsequently in the West. Fantastic ideas were readily accepted about the precious spices originating in Paradise and floated down the Nile to be fished out at its mouth.[1] In Egypt ginger (*zanjabīl*) was added to the Crusader menu. More important than all these articles was sugar (*sukkar*), with the cane of which the Franks familiarized themselves on the Lebanese maritime plain. Arab traders had introduced sugar-cane from India or south-eastern Asia, where it must have originally grown wild. Hitherto honey was the ingredient used by Europeans for sweetening foods and medicines. Tyre and its environs, home of William[2] (d. *ca.* 1190), greatest among the historians of the Crusades, was especially rich in sugar-cane plantations. With sugar went a variety of soft drinks, sweetmeats and candy (*qandah*). In Europe windmills make their appearance in 1180 in Normandy, where they were called *turquois* (Turkish). Water wheels (sing. *nā'ūrah*, noria) antedate windmills in Europe, but those near Bayreuth, Germany, follow the Syrian type. This contrivance had existed in Syria since Roman days.

In matters of fashion, clothing and home furnishing new desires were likewise sharpened if not created. The Franks became convinced that not only native foods but native clothes were preferable. Men began to grow beards, wear flowing robes and cover the head with a scarf (*kūfīyah*). Women wore Oriental gauze ornamented with sequins (*sikkah*) and sat on divans (*dīwān*), listening to the lute (*al-'ūd*) and rebab (*rabābah*); they even veiled in public.[3] Warriors, pilgrims, sailors and merchants returned with rugs, carpets and tapestries, which had been fixtures in Near Eastern homes from time immemorial. Fabrics such as damask, muslin, baldachin,[4] sarcenet (Saracen stuff), atlas (*aṭlas*), taffeta,[5] velvet, silk, satin[6] came to be appreciated as never before. Camlets (*khamlah*) and furs

[1] Joinville, p. 104. Old French *épices* (spices) came to mean bribe for the judge.

[2] Vol. ii, p. 6; Joinville, p. 310.

[3] Ibn-Jubayr, p. 333.

[4] These three words perpetuate the names of three cities: Damascus, al-Mawṣil (Mosul) and Baghdād.

[5] Ar. *tafta*, from Per. *tāftah*.

[6] From Ar. *zaytūni*, a corruption of Chinese Ts'ien-t'ang, a city in China from which this silk originally came.

acquired wider vogue. Damascene and Cairene jewels were in great demand. Ṣalāḥ-al-Dīn's brother al-ʿĀdil reportedly used jewelry to bribe Frankish wives to hold back their husbands from warfare. Oriental luxuries became Occidental necessities. Mirrors of glass replaced those of steel. The rosary, of Hindu origin, was used by Syrian Christians and then Sufi Moslems before it got into the hands of Roman Catholics. Pilgrims sent back home reliquaries of native workmanship which served as models for European craftsmen. Arras and other European centres began to imitate wares, rugs and fabrics of Oriental manufacture. With cloth and metallic wares went dyestuffs and new colours such as lilac (*laylak*), carmine and crimson (*qirmizi*). Oriental work in pottery, gold, silver, enamel and stained glass was also imitated.[1]

International exchange

In the twelfth and thirteenth centuries maritime activity and international trade were stimulated to a degree unattained since Roman days. The introduction of the compass, of which presumably the Moslems made the first practical use, was a great aid in navigation. Before the Moslems the Chinese had discovered the directive property of the magnetic needle. Among the Europeans Italian sailors were the earliest users of the compass.[2] The enhanced flow of trade necessitated new demands, one of which was for ready cash on the part of pilgrim and Crusader. This demand helped establish a money economy and increase the supply and circulation of currency. Banking firms were organized in the Italian city republics with branch offices in the Levant. The need was also felt for letters of credit.[3] The *Byzantinius Saracenatus*, bearing Arabic inscription, was perhaps the earliest gold coin struck by the Latins. The first consuls reported in history were Genoese accredited to ʿAkka in 1180. They presided over local Genoese courts, witnessed seal contracts, wills and deeds, identified new arrivals of their nationals, settled disputes and on the whole performed duties analogous to those of modern Western consuls in the Near East.

Social contacts

During the Crusades the periods of peace, it should be

[1] See below, p. 639.

[2] Consult George Sarton, *Introduction to the History of Science*, vol. iii (Baltimore, 1947), pp. 714-15.

[3] Eng. "cheque" goes back to Ar. *ṣakk*.

remembered, were of longer duration than the periods of war. Thus ample opportunity was provided for forging amicable and neighbourly bonds between Easterners and Westerners. Once the language barrier was removed the Frank must have discovered that after all the Moslem was not the idolater he was thought to be and that he shared in the Judaeo-Christian and Greco-Roman heritage of the European. We hear of many Crusaders, Reginald of Châtillon and William of Tyre for example, who mastered Arabic,[1] but of no Arabs who spoke French or Latin. The tolerance, breadth of view and trend toward secularization which usually result from mingling of men of different faiths and cultures seem in this case to have accrued to the Western rather than the Eastern society. Certain shrines in the Holy Land were venerated by Christians, Moslems and Jews alike. On the social and economic level Christians and Moslems mixed freely,[2] traded horses, dogs and falcons, exchanged safe-conducts and even intermarried. A new progeny from native mothers arose and was designated Pullani.[3] Among modern Lebanese and Palestinians, especially in Ihdin (Lebanon) and Bethlehem, are quite a few with blue eyes and fair hair. Certain Christian families, such as the Faranjīyah (Frankish), the Ṣalībi (Crusading), the Duwayhi (from de Douai ?), the Bardawīl (Baldwin)[4] and the Ṣawāya (Savoie ?) have preserved traditions or names suggesting European origins. The villages of Sinjīl (Saint-Gilles) and al-Raynah (Reynaud) in Palestine perpetuate two Frankish names.

Usāmah's testimony

In his memoirs Usāmah ibn-Munqidh (1095–1188) gives the clearest first-hand picture of interracial association. A friend of Ṣalāḥ-al-Dīn, Usāmah defended his picturesque ancestral castle on the Orontes, Shayzar, against Assassins and Franks. Never did this castle fall into Crusading hands. He himself fraternized with Franks in time of peace. To him the comparatively free sex relations among the Franks, " who are void of all zeal and jealousy ",[5] was simply shocking. Their methods of ordeal by

[1] See above, p. 611.

[2] Ibn-Jubayr, pp. 287-8, 298, 302; Usāmah, *I'tibār*, pp. 131, 134; *Arab-Syrian Gentleman*, pp. 161, 163-4.

[3] Poulains, " kids ", " young ones ".

[4] Marino Sanuto, *Secrets for True Crusaders to Help Them to Recover the Holy Land*, tr. Aubrey Stewart (London, 1896), " Sabaquet Baridoil, where King Baldwin died ". This is Sabkhat Bardawīl on the Mediterranean coast of Sinai.

[5] *I'tibār*, p. 135; *Arab-Syrian Gentleman*, p. 164.

water and duel [1] were far inferior to the Moslem judicial procedure of the day. Especially crude by contrast was their system of medication. Two members of a Frankish family at al-Munayṭirah were properly treated by a native Christian physician until a European was summoned. The latter laid the ailing leg of one of the patients on a block of wood and bade a knight chop it off with one stroke of the axe. He then shaved the head of the other patient, a woman, made a deep cruciform incision on it and rubbed the wound with salt — to drive off the devil. Both patients expired on the spot. The native physician, himself the narrator of the story, concludes with these words: "Thereupon I asked them whether my services were needed any longer, and when they replied in the negative I returned home, having learned of their medicine what I knew not before".[2]

Effects on Syria

In general the effects of the Crusades on Syria were disastrous. Fearing the return of the Franks, some of whom had simply moved across the water to Cyprus, the Mamlūks undertook the dismantling of ʿAkka, Arsūf, Caesarea, Tyre, Tripoli and other ports.[3] The Ayyūbids had destroyed ʿAsqalan.[4] After ʿAkka Tyre had become the most flourishing city of Frankish Syria. Ibn-Jubayr [5] found it unsurpassed as a fortified town; abu-al-Fidāʾ,[6] a century later, found it in ruins and desolation. Dissident Moslem elements, comprising Shīʿites, Ismāʿīlites and Nuṣayrīyah, who then, according to ibn-Jubayr,[7] outnumbered the Sunnites and had on varied occasions compromised their loyalty by aiding Franks, were now decimated; their remnant sought refuge in Central Lebanon and al-Biqāʿ. Earlier al-Ashraf had exacted from the Druzes outward conformity to Sunnite Islam, but the conformity did not last long. Baybars had forced the Nuṣayris to build mosques in their villages, but he could not force them to pray in them. Instead, they used the buildings as stables for their cattle and beasts of burden.[8] In pursuit of the "scorched earth" policy Mamlūk

[1] *Iʿtibār*, pp. 138-9; *Arab-Syrian Gentleman*, pp. 167-8.
[2] *Iʿtibār*, pp. 132-3; *Arab-Syrian Gentleman*, p. 162.
[3] Consult abu-al-Fidāʾ, *Taqwīm*, p. 239; ibn-Baṭṭūṭah, *Tuḥfat al-Nuẓẓār fi Gharāʾib al-Amṣār*, vol. i, pp. 129-30; cf. Idrīsi, p. 11.
[4] Consult ibn-Baṭṭūṭah, vol. i, p. 126.
[5] P. 304. [6] *Taqwīm*, p. 243. [7] P. 280.
[8] Ibn-Baṭṭūṭah, vol. i, p. 177.

sultans methodically ravaged Lebanon. Especially disastrous was al-Nāṣir's campaign of 1306, which resulted in the virtual annihilation of the people of Kisrawān.[1] The Shī'ites of that region were replaced by Kurds and Turkomans; Maronites from the north pushed on later to fill the vacancy. The defence of Beirut against recurring sea incursions was entrusted in 1294 by the sultans to the Buḥtur family, who were installed amīrs of al-Gharb. To this family the chronicler Ṣāliḥ ibn-Yaḥya[2] belonged. Lebanon then became less oriented westward; it assumed the general aspect that it has maintained till modern times. In fact all Syria had in it by then almost every element of civilization it possessed until the early nineteenth century, when a fresh wave of Western ideas and cultural elements began to break on its shore.

Native Christians suffered no less than schismatic Moslems. A measure of hostility was engendered between the Syrian Christians and their Moslem neighbours that was hardly attained before and that is not yet entirely abated. Alarmed by the actively helpful attitude of the Christians of Edessa and Antioch, the Moslem rulers of Jerusalem extorted "all the money and goods in the possession of the Christian inhabitants"[3] of the city and drove them out with the exception of the aged, the sick, the women and the children. When the Crusaders entered the city, they found few survivors. In Lebanon the Maronites were accorded by the Latins all the ecclesiastical and civil rights that pertained to members of the Roman Catholic Church.[4] After the capture of Beirut in 1191 by Ṣalāḥ-al-Dīn thousands of Maronites migrated to Cyprus, where four thousand of their descendants still live. The Armenian and Jacobite communities entered into closer friendly relations than ever before with the Latins, but the *rapprochement* led to no union.

The *jihād* spirit which animated the Mamlūks in their counter-Crusades seems now to have been canalized against Copts and Syrian Christians. Toward the end of his reign Qalāwūn (1279–90) issued edicts excluding his Christian subjects from governmental offices. In 1301 Sultan al-Nāṣir[5]

[1] Ṣāliḥ, p. 136. Native tradition derives the name of this district from a Mardaite leader; Shidyāq, p. 201.

[2] P. 63.

[3] William of Tyre, vol. i, p. 334.

[4] See above, p. 522. Consult Pierre Dib, *L'Église maronite* (Paris, 1930), pp. 186-90.

[5] On him see below, p. 634.

reactivated the old anti-dhimmi laws enjoining Christians and Jews to wear distinctive dress and refrain from horse and mule riding;[1] Sultan al-Ṣāliḥ did likewise in 1354.[2] Al-Nāṣir went beyond that: he ordered the abolition of a national Coptic feast[3] and padlocked many Christian churches in Egypt. This wave of anti-Christian feeling is further reflected in the contemporaneous literature. Speeches, *fatwas* (legal opinions) and *khuṭbahs* (sermons) inflamed the populace. The writings of the Syrian theologian ibn-Taymīyah (1263–1328) embody the reactionary spirit of the age.[4] Born in Ḥarrān, ibn-Taymīyah, an ardent follower of ibn-Ḥanbal, flourished in Damascus, where he lifted his voice high in condemnation of saint worship, vows and pilgrimage to shrines. His principles were later adopted by the Wahhābis who today dominate the religious and political life of Najd and al-Ḥijāz. His tomb and that of ibn-ʿAsākir can be seen on the campus of the Syrian University.

Another type of literature flourished now which may be termed counter-propaganda. It extolled the virtues of Jerusalem, recommended pilgrimage to it and insisted that the Prophet had proclaimed prayer in its mosque a thousand times more meritorious than in any other, excepting the two of Mecca and Medina. Even a preacher of the Umayyad Mosque in Damascus, ibn-al-Firkāḥ[5] (d. 1329), subscribed to these views. Alongside this genre arose the *sīrah*, a form of historical romance extolling the exploits, real or imaginary, of some Arab hero. Ṣalāḥ-al-Dīn, Baybars and ʿAntarah became the heroes of such romances. ʿAntarah was a pre-Islamic poet-warrior, but his romance (*Sīrat ʿAntar*), judged by its latest historical allusions, was conceived in Syria in the early twelfth century. Story-tellers in the cafés of Cairo, Beirut, Damascus and

[1] See above, p. 542.

[2] Qalqashandi, vol. xiii, pp. 377-81; ibn-Taghri-Birdi, ed. Popper, vol. v, p. 133.

[3] Maqrīzi, vol. i, p. 69.

[4] On them consult Kutubi, vol. i, pp. 48-9; Henri Laoust, *Essai sur les doctrines sociales et politiques de Taki-d-Dīn Aḥmad b. Taimīya* (Cairo, 1939), pp. 634-9.

[5] "Bāʿith al-Nufūs li-Ziyārat al-Quds al-Maḥrūs", tr. Charles D. Matthews, *Palestine — Mohammedan Holy Land* (New Haven, 1949), pp. 1 *seq.* Ibn-al-Jawzi (d. 1200) of Baghdād wrote a treatise *Faḍāʾil al-Quds* (the excellences of Jerusalem), described in Philip K. Hitti, Nabih A. Faris and Buṭrus ʿAbd-al-Malik, *Descriptive Catalogue of the Garrett Collection of Arabic Manuscripts in the Princeton University Library* (Princeton, 1938), No. 586.

Baghdād drawing their tales from it and *Sīrat al-Ẓāhir* (Baybars) attract larger audiences than when reciting tales from the *Arabian Nights*.

Feudalism

The Frankish states of Syria were established on feudal principles that prevailed in Europe, but some of the fief holders were natives. As a Moslem land Syria had a feudal system of its own since the days of conquest. Conquerors — whether caliphs, sultans or amīrs — granted fiefs (sing. *iqṭā'*) to their generals and high officials, who in turn parcelled out the land locally among subordinates and tenants. At the lowest level serfs and slaves tilled the soil. The collection of land-tax (*kharāj*)[1] from non-Moslems was leased out to influential persons. The 'Abbāsid caliphs replaced farming to the highest bidder by hereditary farming, the farmer paying a fixed and constant rent. The Fāṭimids and Mamlūks continued the Islamic usage.[2] In medieval Europe, however, an aristocracy of landowners had risen which occupied fortified homes in country places, established reciprocal relationship with the royalty and exercised direct control over those below them. No such aristocracy arose in Arab Islam. The fief holders as a rule lived in cities and were content with deriving the necessary income from their country possessions. The feudal organization introduced by the Franks left no traces on the local tenure of the land aside from making the military fief for a time, under the Ayyūbids, the principal form of agrarian relationship. Nor did Frankish monarchy leave permanent effect on the political institutions of Syria; but the Church which stood beside the monarchy is still represented by the Latin patriarchate of Jerusalem.

Missionary activity

An interesting by-product of the Crusades was the initiation of Christian missionary work among Moslems. Convinced, by the failure of these wars, of the futility of the military method in dealing with Moslems, men like Raymond Lull (d. 1314) began to advocate concentration on peaceful methods. A Catalan, Raymond was the earliest European to emphasize Oriental studies as an instrument of pacific campaign in which persuasion should replace violence. He himself studied Arabic

[1] See above, p. 423.

[2] Qalqashandi, vol. xiii, pp. 123 *seq.*, 139 *seq.* Consult A. N. Poliak, *Feudalism in Egypt, Syria, Palestine, and the Lebanon* (London, 1939), pp. 18 *seq.*

from a slave. With Raymond the Crusading spirit turned into a new channel: converting the Moslem rather than exterminating him.

The Carmelite order, still active in Syria, was founded in 1157 by a Crusader in that country and named after one of its mountains. Early in the thirteenth century two other monastic orders, the Franciscan and the Dominican, were founded and their representatives were stationed in many Syrian towns. In the last years of that century Beirut had a large Franciscan church.[1] In 1219 the founder of the Franciscan order, St. Francis of Assisi, visited the Ayyūbid court in Egypt and held a fruitless religious discussion with al-Kāmil. A Dominican bishop, William of Tripoli, wrote one of the most learned treatises in medieval times on the Moslems (*Tractus de statu Saracenorum*), bringing out points in which Islam and Christianity agree and advocating missionaries rather than soldiers for the recovery of the Holy Land. Like William of Tyre he was native born but of European parentage.

[1] Ṣāliḥ, p. 149; Enlart, vol. ii, p. 79.

CHAPTER XLVII

AYYŪBIDS AND MAMLŪKS

THE sultanate built by Ṣalāḥ-al-Dīn, extending from the Nile to the Tigris, was partitioned among his heirs, none of whom inherited his genius. His son al-Malik al-Afḍal (the superior king) succeeded to his father's throne in Damascus, but in 1196 he was succeeded by his uncle al-ʿĀdil of Egypt. In 1250 the Damascus branch was incorporated with that of Aleppo, which was swept away after a decade by the Mongol avalanche of Hūlāgu.[1] Ṣalāḥ-al-Dīn's second son, al-ʿAzīz (the mighty, 1193–8), followed his father on the Egyptian throne but al-ʿAzīz' son was supplanted in 1198 by the same al-ʿĀdil, who in both cases took advantage of the dissension among his nephews. It was these dynastic feuds which afforded the Franks an opportunity to regain some of their lost territory.

[1] Genealogical tree of the Ayyūbids of Damascus:

- Ayyūb
  - Ṣalāḥ-al-Dīn
    - 1. Al-Afḍal (1186–96)
  - 2. Al-ʿĀdil Sayf-al-Dīn (1196–1218)
    - 3. Al-Muʿaẓẓam Sharaf-al-Dīn (1218–27)
      - 4. Al-Nāṣir Ṣalāḥ-al-Dīn (1227–8)
    - 5. Al-Ashraf Mūsa (1228–1237)
    - 6. Al-Ṣāliḥ Ismāʿīl (1237, again 1240–1245)
      - 9. Al-Ṣāliḥ Najm-al-Dīn of Egypt (1240, again 1245–9)
        - 10. Al-Muʿaẓẓam Tūrān-Shāh of Egypt (1249–50) —— 11. Al-Nāṣir Ṣalāḥ-al-Dīn of Aleppo (grand-nephew of al-Afḍal) (1250–60)
    - 7. Al-Kāmil Muḥammad of Egypt (1237–8)
      - 8. Al-ʿĀdil of Egypt (1238–40)

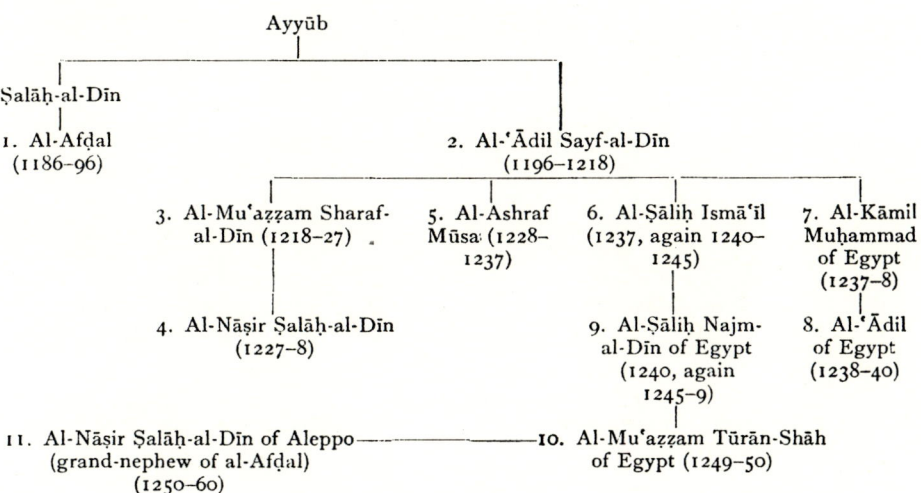

In 1200 al-'Ādil appointed one of his sons over Mesopotamia. The third son of Ṣalāḥ, al-Ẓāhir, succeeded his father at Aleppo.[1] The Ḥamāh petty branch, founded by a nephew of Ṣalāḥ-al-Dīn, survived the Mongol invasion of 1260, which two years earlier had annihilated the 'Abbāsid caliphate in Baghdād, and continued under the Mamlūks until 1341, thus outlasting all other branches of the house.[2] It numbered in its line the historian-king abu-al-Fidā' (d. 1332).[3] A minor branch, that of Ḥimṣ, was descended from an uncle of Ṣalāḥ- al-Dīn. It was destroyed by the Mamlūk Baybars in

[1] Tree of the Ayyūbids of Aleppo:

Ṣalāḥ-al-Dīn
|
1. Al-Ẓāhir Ghiyāth-al-Dīn
(1186–1216)
|
2. Al-'Azīz Ghiyāth-al-Dīn
(1216–36)
|
3. Al-Nāṣir Ṣalāḥ-al-Dīn
(1236–60)

[2] There was a brief interval (1298–1310) in which other governors ruled under the Mamlūks.

[3] Tree of the Ayyūbids of Ḥamāh:

Nūr-al-Dīn Shāhanshāh
(brother of Ṣalāḥ-al-Dīn)
|
1. Al-Muẓaffar I Taqi-al-Dīn
(1178–91)
|
2. Al-Manṣūr Nāṣir-al-Dīn
(1191–1220)
|
- 3. Al-Nāṣir Ṣalāḥ-al-Dīn (1220–29)
- 4. Al-Muẓaffar II Taqi-al-Dīn (1229–44)
  - 5. Al-Manṣūr Sayf-al-Dīn (1244–84)
    - 6. Al-Muẓaffar III Taqi-al-Dīn (1284–98)
  - (al-Muẓaffar 'Ali)
    - 7. Al-Mu'ayyad abu-al-Fidā' (1310–32)
      - 8. Al-Afḍal Muḥammad (1332–41)

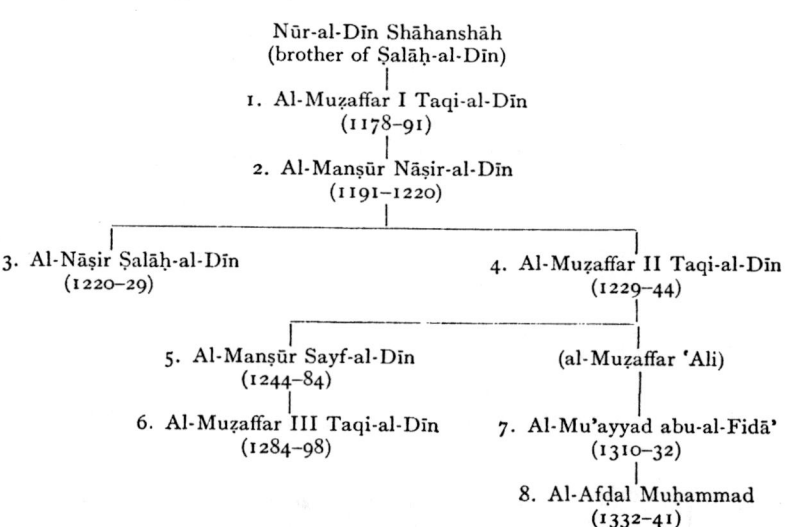

1262.[1] Another minor branch, that of Ba'labakk, traced its descent from Tūrān-Shāh, brother of Ṣalāḥ-al-Dīn.[2]

Of the many Ayyūbid branches the Egyptian was the chief. Several in this line held both Cairo and Damascus. One of them was al-Ṣāliḥ Najm-al-Dīn Ayyūb,[3] who died in November 1249 leaving a widow Shajar-al-Durr (the tree of pearls). Formerly a Turkish or Armenian slave in the harem of the Baghdād caliph al-Musta'ṣim, Shajar was freed by al-Ṣāliḥ after having borne him a son. For three months she kept the news of her husband's death a secret, pending the return of his son Tūrān-Shāh from a trip to Mesopotamia. Tūrān proved to be *persona non grata* to the slaves (*mamlūks*) and was murdered with the connivance of his stepmother. The daring and energetic woman thereupon proclaimed herself queen of the Moslems;[4] a six-year-old scion of the Damascus Ayyūbids, al-Ashraf Mūsa, was accorded the honour of joint sovereignty with her. For eighty days Shajar, the only Moslem woman to rule a country in North Africa and Western Asia, continued to exercise sole sovereignty over the lands which had produced Zenobia and Cleopatra. She had coins struck in her name[5] and had herself mentioned in the Friday prayer. When her former caliph-master addressed a scathing note to the amīrs of Egypt: "If ye have no man to rule you, let us know and we will send you one",[6] they chose her commander-in-chief 'Izz-

Ayyūbids supplanted by Mamlūks

[1] Tree of the Ayyūbids of Ḥimṣ:

Shīrkūh (Ṣalāḥ-al-Dīn's uncle)
|
1. Al-Qāhir Nāṣir-al-Dīn (1178–85)
|
2. Al-Mujāhid Ṣalāḥ-al-Dīn (1185–1239)
|
3. Al-Manṣūr Nāṣir-al-Dīn (1239–45)
|
4. Al-Ashraf Muẓaffar-al-Dīn (1245–62)

[2] For the names of this and the Karak branch consult E. de Zambaur, *Manuel de généalogie et de chronologie* (Paris, 1927), p. 98.

[3] Consult genealogical tree, above, p. 627.

[4] Abu-al-Fidā', vol. iii, p. 190; Maqrīzi, *Khiṭaṭ*, vol. ii, p. 237.

[5] With the exception of certain coins struck in India and Fārs, hers are the only ones bearing a Moslem woman's name.

[6] Suyūṭi, *Ḥusn*, vol. ii, p. 39.

al-Dīn Aybak [1] for sultan and she did the next best thing — married him. Aybak spent the first years of his reign crushing the legitimist Ayyūbid party of Syria who considered themselves successors to their Egyptian kinsmen, deposing the child joint-king al-Ashraf and disposing of his own general who had distinguished himself against Louis IX. On hearing that he was contemplating another marriage, the queen had him murdered at his bath after a ball game. Her turn then came. Battered to death with wooden shoes by the slave women of her husband's first wife, her body was cast from a tower in the citadel of Cairo.[2]

Baḥri Mamlūks

Aybak (1250–57) was the first of the Mamlūk sultans. The series is unique in dynastic annals, for, as the name [3] indicates, this dynasty — if it could be so called — was a dynasty of slaves, slaves of varied races and nationalities constituting a military oligarchy in an alien land. When one of them died, quite often it was not his son but a slave or a mercenary of his who had won distinction and eminence who succeeded him. Thus the bondman of yesterday would become the army commander of today and the sultan of tomorrow. For almost two and three-quarter centuries the slave sultans dominated by the sword one of the most turbulent areas of the world. Generally uncultured and bloodthirsty yet they endowed Cairo with some architectural monuments of which it still rightly boasts. Two other services to the cause of Islam were rendered by them: they cleared Syria and Egypt of the remnant of the Crusaders and they definitely checked the redoubtable advance of the Tartar Mongol hordes of Hūlāgu and of Tīmūr (Tamerlane).[4] But for that, the entire course of culture and history in Western Asia and Egypt might have been different.

Originally purchased in the slave markets of Moslem Russia and the Caucasus to form the personal bodyguard of the Ayyūbid al-Ṣāliḥ,[5] the first Mamlūks started a series which is somewhat arbitrarily divided into two dynasties, Baḥri (1250–

[1] He was a Turk, as the name, *ay* moon + *beg* prince, indicates. Maqrīzi, tr. Quatremère, vol. i (pt. 1), p. 1.

[2] Qal'at al-Jabal. Ibn-Khallikān, vol. iv, p. 64; ibn-al-Athīr, vol. x, pp. 60, 160.

[3] *Mamlūk*, "possessed", "slave", especially applied to one who is not black.

[4] See below, p. 655. Arab historians use *Tatar* and *Mughūl* indiscriminately.

[5] Abu-al-Fidā', vol. iii, p. 188; ibn-Khaldūn, vol. v, p. 373.

1390) and Burji (1382–1517). The Baḥris received their name from the Nile,[1] on an islet in which their barracks stood. They were mostly Turks and Mongols; the Burjis were largely Circassians.[2] Their rise was followed a decade later by the advent of the Mongols. Once more Syria became a battlefield of two contending powers.

Mongol invasions

Fresh from the destruction of the caliphate of Baghdād and the Assassin nest of Alamūt, the Mongol horde under Hūlāgu, grandson of Chingīz Khān, made its ominous appearance in North Syria. Aleppo was the first victim. Fifty thousand of its people were put to the sword — giving a taste of what was to come. Ḥārim and Ḥamāh came next. A general was dispatched to besiege Damascus, while Hūlāgu returned to Persia because of the death of his brother, the Great Khān. Latin Antioch turned into a Mongol satellite. Louis IX and the pope thought an alliance with the invaders would help in the struggle against the Moslems. Shamanism was the official religion of the newcomers — as it was of their cousins the Turks — but among them were some Christian descendants of converts by early Syrian missionaries.[3] It was a Christian general, Kitbugha, who overran and devastated most of Syria. The reigning Mamlūk was Quṭuz (1259–60), who had executed Hūlāgu's envoys.[4] The issue was settled at 'Ayn Jālūt (Goliath's spring), near Nazareth. In this battle Baybars led the vanguard under Quṭuz and administered a crushing defeat to the intruders. Kitbugha's body was left on the field.[5] The remnant of his army was pursued and chased out of Syria. In recognition of his military service Baybars expected to receive Aleppo as a fief but the sultan disappointed him. On the way homeward from Syria a fellow-conspirator addressed the sultan and kissed his hand while Baybars stabbed him in the neck. The murderer succeeded the murdered.

Fourth in the series, Baybars [6] was the first great sultan, the

[1] Colloquially referred to as *baḥr*, sea.

[2] Ibn-Khaldūn, vol. v, p. 369, and Suyūṭi, *Ḥusn*, vol. ii, p. 80, designate them as the " Turkish dynasty ".

[3] See above, pp. 518-19.

[4] The letter they carried is preserved in Maqrīzi, tr. Quatremère, vol. i (pt. 1), pp. 101-2.

[5] Abu-al-Fidā', vol. iii, pp. 209-14; Maqrīzi, ed. Quatremère, vol. i (pt. 1), pp. 98, 104 *seq.*; ibn-Khaldūn, vol. v, p. 544.

[6] For table of Baḥri Mamlūks, see below, p. 633.

real founder of Mamlūk power. His first laurels he won on the battlefield against the Mongols but his crown of glory was won against the Crusaders.[1] More than a military figure he was a great administrator. He dug canals, improved harbours and connected his two capitals in Egypt and Syria by a swift postal service modelled on the Persian-ʿAbbāsid system. He could play polo in both cities during the same week.[2] He launched public projects, renovated mosques — including the Dome of the Rock — restored citadels — among which was that of Aleppo — and established religious and charitable endowments.[3] His mausoleum in Damascus is now used as a library bearing his epithet, al-Ẓāhirīyah. This library houses one of the oldest manuscripts on paper, *Masāʾil* (questions of) *al-Imām Aḥmad ibn-Ḥanbal*, bearing the date A.H. 266 (879/80).[4]

The Mongol peril was only temporarily averted. Pushed by forces not fully determined from their abode in Central Asia, where they had roamed as far as the borders of the Chinese empire, the Mongols came in waves reminiscent in certain features of the Semitic and the Teutonic waves of earlier days. Hūlāgu's son and successor Abāqa, who chose Tibrīz for capital, renewed the attack on Syria. The Mongols were then flirting with Christianity, and Abāqa entered negotiations with the pope, Edward I of England and other European rulers urging a fresh Crusade to drive the Mamlūks out of Syria. Though superior in number and reinforced by Armenians, Georgians and Persians the Mongol army was badly beaten in 1280 at Ḥimṣ.[5] After straddling the fence for a time the Mongols jumped to the Islamic side and there remained. This invasion took place in the reign of Qalāwūn (1279–90), the outstanding Mamlūk figure after Baybars. Like his predecessor, Qalāwūn was a Turkish slave whose title al-Alfi (thousander) indicates the high price, a thousand dinars, paid for him.[6]

The adoption of Islam as the state religion by the seventh Īl-Khān Ghāzān Maḥmūd, who was brought up as a Buddhist, did not spare Syria further invasions, two of which followed.

[1] See above, pp. 607-8.

[2] Ibn-al-Furāt, vol. vii, p. 82.

[3] An imposing list of his public works appears in Kutubi, vol. i, pp. 113-15.

[4] Cf. Hitti, *History of the Arabs*, p. 347.

[5] Abu-al-Fidāʾ, vol. iv, pp. 15-16; Maqrīzi, tr. Quatremère, vol. ii (pt. 3), pp. 36-40; ibn-Khaldūn, vol. v, pp. 545-6.

[6] Suyūṭi, *Ḥusn*, vol. ii, p. 80; Maqrīzi, tr. Quatremère, vol. ii (pt. 3), p. 1.

THE BAḤRI MAMLŪKS

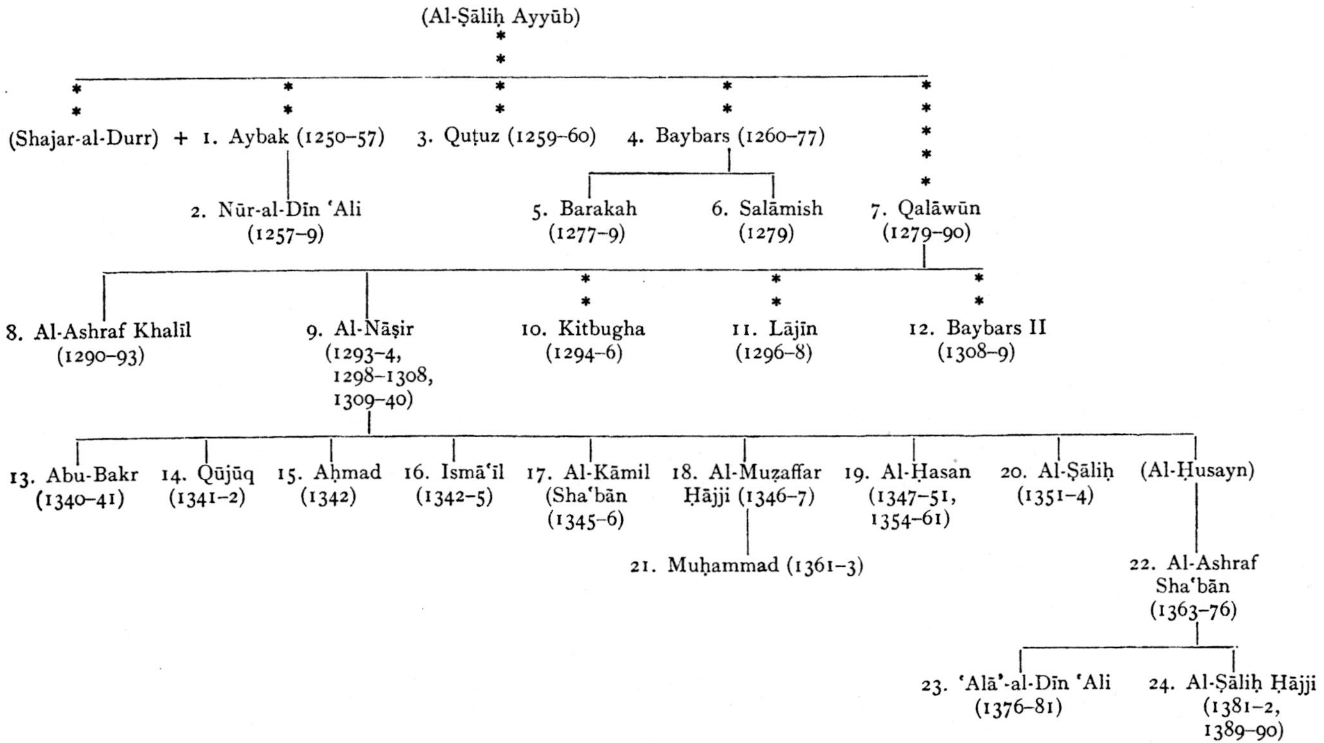

Note.—Starred lines indicate a master and slave relationship.

They were the last in this series. The first took place late in 1299, when the invading host, said to have numbered a hundred thousand including Armenians, Georgians and Franks from Cyprus, routed an Egyptian army of about one-third that number east of Ḥimṣ.[1] The reigning Mamlūk was Qalāwūn's son and second successor al-Nāṣir, who held the distinction of ruling thrice (1293–4, 1298–1308, 1309–40), covering a period longer than any other ruler's in Mamlūk annals. Continuing their victorious march, the Mongols wrought havoc and destruction throughout North Syria, and early in 1300 occupied Damascus, whose citadel held out. A large part of the city, including its suburb al-Ṣāliḥīyah, was utterly destroyed. A revolt in Persia prompted Ghāzān's return, but his troops penetrated as far south as Gaza. The Egyptian army then took the offensive, rolled them back and in 1303 severely defeated them on the historic battlefield of Marj al-Ṣuffar,[2] south of Damascus. Abu-al-Fidā',[3] who was later restored by his friend al-Nāṣir to his ancestral princedom in Ḥamāh, scouted in his native town for the Egyptian army and reported the Mongol movements. Thus was the fourth attempt to Mongolize Syria frustrated. The Mamlūks had beaten the most persistent and dangerous enemy Egypt had to face since the beginning of Islam.

As in the case of the Crusades,[4] the Mongol invasions had disastrous consequences for the minorities. The Druzes of Lebanon, whose 12,000 bowmen harassed the Egyptian army on its retreat before the Mongols in 1300, were brought to a severe reckoning. The Armenians saw their unhappy land repeatedly devastated in and after 1302 by al-Nāṣir. His Christian and Jewish subjects suffered.

Burji Mamlūks

Al-Nāṣir was followed in a period of forty-two years (1340–1382) by twelve descendants, none of whom distinguished himself in any field of endeavour. The last among them was al-Ṣāliḥ Ḥājji (1381–2, 1389–90), an incompetent child whose reign was first interrupted and then terminated by a Circassian, Barqūq. Barqūq founded a new line called Burji (1382–1517), after the towers (Ar. *burj*, sing.) of the citadel in Cairo, where they were first quartered as slaves.[5] With the exception of two

[1] Ṣāliḥ, p. 174; Maqrīzi, tr. Quatremère, vol. ii (pt. 4), p. 146.
[2] See above, p. 414.
[3] Vol. iv, p. 50. Ibn-Khaldūn, vol. v, pp. 548-9.
[4] See above, pp. 622 *seq.*
[5] Maqrīzi, *Khiṭaṭ*, vol. ii, p. 241.

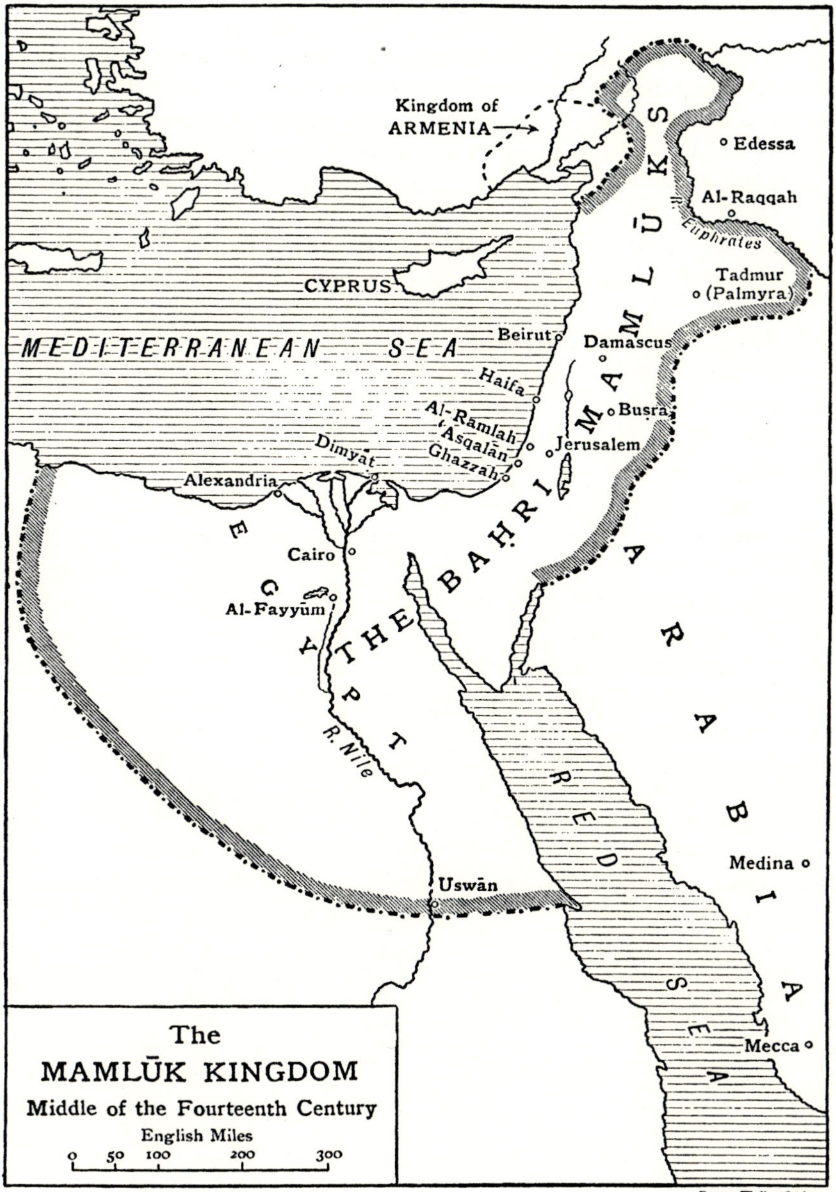

From Hitti, "History of the Arabs"

Greeks the Burjis were all Circassians. They rejected even more emphatically than their predecessors the principle of hereditary succession. Of the twenty-three Burji sultans fourteen were of almost no consequence. One year, 1421, saw the installation of three of them in succession. Rare indeed among them was he who met a natural death. Qā'it-bay's reign (1468–95) was the longest and in certain respects the most successful.[1]

The new régime was no improvement on the old. Corruption, intrigue, assassination and misrule continued to flourish. Several of the sultans were inefficient and treacherous; some were immoral, even degenerate; most were uncultured. Only one, Barqūq, claimed descent from a Moslem father.[2] Barsbāy (1422–38), originally a slave of Barqūq, knew no Arabic.[3] He had no scruples about beheading his two physicians for their failure to cure him of a fatal malady. Another slave of Barqūq, Īnāl (1453–60), could not sign his name on the official document except by tracing it over a secretary's writing, according to his contemporary ibn-Taghri-Birdi.[4] The *ghilmān*

[1] List of Burji Mamlūks:

1.	Al-Ẓāhir Sayf-al-Dīn Barqūq (interrupted by the Baḥri Ḥājji, 1389–90)	1382
2.	Al-Nāṣir Nāṣir-al-Dīn Faraj	1398
3.	Al-Manṣūr 'Izz-al-Dīn 'Abd-al-'Azīz	1405
	Al-Nāṣir Faraj (again)	1406
4.	The Caliph (see below, p. 657) al-'Ādil al-Musta'īn	1412
5.	Al-Mu'ayyad Shaykh	1412
6.	Al-Muẓaffar Aḥmad	1421
7.	Al-Ẓāhir Sayf-al-Dīn Ṭaṭar	1421
8.	Al-Ṣāliḥ Nāṣir-al-Dīn Muḥammad	1421
9.	Al-Ashraf Sayf-al-Dīn Barsbāy	1422
10.	Al-'Azīz Jamāl-al-Dīn Yūsuf	1438
11.	Al-Ẓāhir Sayf-al-Dīn Jaqmaq	1438
12.	Al-Manṣūr Fakhr-al-Dīn 'Uthmān	1453
13.	Al-Ashraf Sayf-al-Dīn Īnāl	1453
14.	Al-Mu'ayyad Shihāb-al-Dīn Aḥmad	1460
15.	Al-Ẓāhir Sayf-al-Dīn Khushqadam	1461
16.	Al-Ẓāhir Sayf-al-Dīn Yalbāy	1467
17.	Al-Ẓāhir Timurbugha	1467
18.	Al-Ashraf Sayf-al-Dīn Qā'it-bāy	1468
19.	Al-Nāṣir Muḥammad	1495
20.	Al-Ẓāhir Qānṣawh	1498
21.	Al-Ashraf Jān-balāṭ	1499
22.	Al-Ashraf Qānṣawh al-Ghawri	1500
23.	Al-Ashraf Ṭūmān-bāy	1516–17

[2] Suyūṭi, *Ḥusn*, vol. ii, p. 88.

[3] His was not a unique case; consult al-Isḥāqi, *Akhbār al-Uwal fi Man Taṣarraf fi Miṣr min al-Duwal* (Cairo, 1296), p. 210.

[4] Vol. vii, p. 559.

(boy slaves) institution, for the practice of unnatural sex relations, was again in full bloom as in 'Abbāsid days. Several Mamlūks, beginning with Baybars, were charged with pederasty. Not only the sultans but the amīrs and the entire oligarchy were more or less corrupt. The tenure of even the ablest official seldom lasted more than three years; one judge was appointed and dismissed ten times.

Administration of Syria

Though the Mamlūk régime was unique, the Mamlūk administration was but a continuation of the Fāṭimid-'Abbāsid system. Syria was divided into half a dozen provinces (sing. *niyābah*) following the general division under the Ayyūbids. These were Aleppo, Ḥamāh, Damascus, Tripoli, Ṣafad and al-Karak. Originally slaves of some sultan, the governors of the provinces were generally recruited from the military class (*arbāb al-suyūf*, lords of the sword) [1] as opposed to the learned class (*arbāb al-aqlām*, lords of the pen). In general they were independent of one another, each with a court reproducing on a small scale that of Cairo. The animosities and disturbances in the federal capital were often reflected in the provincial ones. The change of a Mamlūk sultan usually provoked a rebellion on the part of a governor in Damascus or some other Syrian province.[2] The Gharb of Lebanon was enfeoffed to its native chiefs, the Buḥturids of the Tanūkh.[3]

Because of its historic background Damascus, where Baybars — organizer of the Mamlūk sultanate — often held his court, had an advantage over its sister provinces. One of its governors, Tangiz (1312–39), was acknowledged as regent over Syria during al-Nāṣir's third reign. His province (*mamlakat Dimashq*,[4] kingdom of Damascus) included the whole of Palestine, with the exception of the petty provinces of Ṣafad and al-Karak, and extended north to Beirut, Ḥimṣ and Tadmur. Tangiz brought water to Jerusalem and restored the tower (*burj*) of Beirut, where he also built hostels (sing. *khān*) and public baths.[5] After an unusually long and beneficent reign

[1] Qalqashandi, vol. ix, p. 253.

[2] For more on government of Syria consult Gaudefroy-Demombynes, pp. xix *seq.*, 29 *seq.*; Walther Björkman, *Beiträge zur Geschichte der Staatskanzlei im islamischen Ägypten* (Hamburg, 1928), pp. 101 *seq.*, 157 *seq.*; 'Ali Ibrāhīm Ḥasan, *Dirāsāt fi Ta'rīkh al-Mamālīk al-Baḥrīyah* (Cairo, 1944), pp. 248-53.

[3] Ṣāliḥ, pp. 81 *seq.*

[4] 'Umari, p. 176; cf. Ẓāhiri, p. 131.

[5] Ibn-Baṭṭūṭah, vol. i, p. 121; Ṣāliḥ, pp. 155-6.

he fell into disgrace and was put to death in a prison in Alexandria.[1]

Famine and plague

Almost the entire Mamlūk era was punctuated with periods of drought, famine and pestilence. Earthquakes added their quota to the general devastation. The pages of the chronicles of the era are covered with reports of woe and disaster.[2] The leading historian of the age, al-Maqrīzi,[3] devotes an entire work to the famines of Egypt to the year 1405, in which he wrote. Ibn-Taghri-Birdi[4] reports at least four plagues of great severity in the fourteenth century (1348–9, 1359–61, 1362–3, 1389). In the fifteenth century no less than fourteen serious outbreaks are recorded in different chronicles, averaging one every seven years. The "black death" (*al-fanā' al-kabīr*), which in 1348 to 1349 wrought havoc in Europe, lingered in Egypt for seven years. Its victims in the capital, according to the estimates of ibn-Iyās,[5] reached the incredible figure of 900,000. Gaza reportedly lost in one month 22,000 and Aleppo an average of five hundred per day. A large number of the victims were foreigners and children who had not acquired a sufficient degree of immunity. Owing to these calamities and Mamlūk misgovernment, the entire population of Egypt and Syria, it is estimated, was reduced to about one-third of its former size.

Trade and industry

The economic situation was aggravated by taxation and policies which were unsound if not predatory. The wars against Franks and Mongols led to the imposition of burdensome taxes in both Egypt and Syria, including thirty-three and one-third per cent on rents, which caused endless complaints. Not only horses and boats but necessities of life, such as salt and sugar, were heavily taxed. Some sultans monopolized certain commodities and manipulated prices to their advantage. Others

[1] Ibn-Iyās, *Badā'i' al-Ẓuhūr fi Ta'rīkh al-Duhūr*, vol. i (Cairo, 1893), p. 172; Maqrīzi, *Khiṭaṭ*, vol. ii, pp. 54-5.

[2] E. G. Ṣāliḥ, pp. 144, 242; ibn-al-Furāt, vol. viii, p. 209, 212; ibn-Taghri-Birdi, vol. vii, pp. 528-42; do., *Ḥawādith al-Duhūr fi Mada al-Ayyām w-al-Shuhūr*, ed. William Popper (Berkley, 1942), pp. 11, 37, 312, 319. For the Ayyūbid period consult Maqrīzi, *Sulūk*, ed. Ziyādah, vol. i, pt. 1, pp. 130-33, 156-8, 248.

[3] *Ighāthat al-Ummah bi-Kashf al-Ghummah*, eds. Muḥammad M. Ziyādah and Jamāl-al-Dīn M. al-Shayyāl (Cairo, 1940).

[4] Vol. v, pp. 70-76, 154, 185, 408, 507.

[5] Vol. i, p. 191; cf. ibn-Taghri-Birdi, vol. v, p. 71.

debased the currency and contributed to the inflationary spiral.[1] As the people became impoverished, the rulers waxed rich. Without an abundance of wealth the sultans could not have erected those architectural monuments of which Egypt still rightfully boasts.[2]

Happily some of the economic loss was offset by increased trade subsequent to the Crusading enterprise. The concessions offered by al-ʿĀdil [3] and Baybars to the Venetians and other European merchants stimulated exchange of commodities and made Cairo a great *entrepôt* of trade between East and West. Syrian silk shared with perfumes and spices first place in the export trade. Glass and manufactured articles stood next on the list.[4] Damascus, Tripoli, Antioch and Tyre were among the leading centres of industry. Some of the silk in the Syrian market was imported from China; spices came from Arabia and other tropical lands; pearls were brought from the Persian Gulf to the ports of Jaffa and Tripoli.[5] When a governor of Damascus sent his agent to the Shūf district of Lebanon to explore the possibility of the use of mulberry branches for arrows, the Lebanese were greatly disturbed.[6] In the bazaars of Aleppo, Damascus, Beirut one could buy ivory- and metal-work, dyed cloth, carpets and enamelled pottery. The neighbourhood of Beirut produced olive oil and soap [7] as it does today. Pans of saltworks are still visible in ʿAthlīth and other places along the coast.[8]

Syrians did not depend entirely on foreigners for their export trade. As early as Ṣalāḥ-al-Dīn's day their merchants took up residence in Constantinople, where the emperor in compliance with Ṣalāḥ's request built a mosque for them and their Egyptian colleagues in reciprocation for privileges enjoyed by Byzantine merchants in Syria and Egypt. No other foreign merchants were permitted permanent residence in the Byzantine capital. A German clergyman, Ludolph von Suchem, who visited the Holy Land in 1336 to 1341, was most favourably

[1] Maqrīzi, *Ighāthah*, pp. 70-72; ibn-Taghri-Birdi, *Ḥawādith*, pp. 310-12.

[2] See below, p. 648.

[3] See above, p. 606.

[4] See E. Rey, *Les Colonies franques de Syrie* (Paris, 1883), pp. 204, 214-34.

[5] Hilmar C. Krueger, "The Wares of Exchange in the Genoese-African Traffic of the Twelfth Century", *Speculum*, vol. xii (1937), pp. 64, 71.

[6] Ṣāliḥ, p. 225.

[7] Ṣāliḥ, p. 229.

[8] Conder, p. 451.

impressed by the signs of prosperity in Damascus,[1] "the glorious city of Acre" and other Syrian towns.

The streets within the city [Acre] were exceeding neat, all the walls of the houses being of the same height and all alike built of hewn stone, wondrously adorned with glass windows and paintings, while all the palaces and houses in the city were not built merely to meet the needs of those who dwelt therein, but to minister to human luxury and pleasure. . . . The streets of the city were covered with silken cloths, or other fair awnings, to keep off the sun's rays. At every street corner there stood an exceeding strong tower, fenced with an iron door and iron chains. All the nobles dwelt in very strong castles and palaces along the outer edge of the city. In the midst of the city dwelt the mechanic citizens and merchants, each in his own special street according to his trade.[2]

Ibn-Jubayr,[3] who visited Damascus under Ṣalāḥ-al-Dīn, styles it "the bride of the cities" in which he sojourned and describes in detail the timepiece in its mosque which in the day showed progress of time by the operation of two brass falcons and at night by a scheme of special lights. The same timepiece was noted by Benjamin of Tudela.[4]

In Lebanon

With remarkable dexterity the feudal chiefs of Lebanon practised the Machiavellian art of political manœuvring long before the Florentine statesman lived. Through the turmoils that saw the installation over them of Fāṭimids, Ayyūbids, Franks, Mamlūks and Tartars they played the game. When the Crusaders occupied Beirut and Sidon the banu-Buḥtur amīrs of al-Gharb held some of the adjacent territory as fiefs and offered military service to the Franks.[5] Those amīrs did not hesitate to enter into the same relationship with the Mamlūks.[6] The Buḥturid fiefs comprised such small villages as Shimlān, ʿAynāb and Bayṣūr never mentioned before in history and still in existence.[7] In the struggle between Tartars and Mamlūks those amīrs had at times representatives in both camps — a feat that insured their being on the winning side no matter which it was.[8] The policy of watchful waiting and double crossing was practised on those shores in the fourteenth century before Christ; [9] it continued to be practised until the days of Fakhr-al-Dīn and al-Amīr Bashīr.[10]

[1] Pp. 129-32. [2] Ludolph von Suchem, p. 51. [3] Pp. 260, 270-71.
[4] Vol. i, pp. 84-5. [5] Ṣāliḥ, pp. 74-5, 83-4, 111-12; cf. above, p. 599.
[6] Ṣāliḥ, p. 81. [7] Ṣāliḥ, pp. 81, 128, 197, 198-9, 234-5; see above, p. 637
[8] Ṣāliḥ, pp. 93-4, 242-8. [9] See above, p. 71. [10] See below, pp. 665-6.

Although a number of Arab tribes had penetrated into the mountain, mainly from the south,[1] parts of it remained wooded. Bears and boars, even lions and onagers were, as late as the fourteenth century, encountered.[2] Syria also had such animals as attested by Usāmah,[3] who cites wild asses, gazelles, lions, boars, hyenas and leopards. Wild fruits and edible plants together with an abundance of fresh water made the mountain a favourite haunt for ascetics and hermits of both religions. A late twelfth century author [4] devotes chapters to such men and women in the mountains of Lebanon and Syria. Ibn-Jubayr [5] notes with pleasant surprise the kind treatment accorded by neighbouring Christians to these solitaries. Sufi literature has preserved many legendary tales about such men. A Moslem Lebanese ascetic, who one day missed his one-loaf ration coming from an undetermined source, sought alms from the nearest farm-house. The Christian farmer gave him two barley loaves but the dog pursued the ascetic and did not cease barking until he had deprived him of both loaves and his garment. When the ascetic remarked how greedy the dog was, God put in the canine mouth words to this effect: I guard my master's home and flocks and often go without food when there is none for him or me. But you, deprived but one day of your ration, insisted on coming to us and seeking aid. Who of the two then is more greedy, you or I? [6]

Cultural activity: hospitalization

Despite its political turmoils and economic periods of depression Syria enjoyed under the Nūrids and Ayyūbids, in particular under Nūr-al-Dīn and Ṣalāḥ-al-Dīn, the most

[1] See above, p. 483; Lammens, *Syrie*, vol. ii, pp. 8-14. In the literature of the period the Arabians domiciled in Syria and Egypt became known as *awlād* (descendants of) *al-'Arab* (ibn-Taghri-Birdi, vol. v, p. 367, l. 10; see above, p. 547); *'Arab* was used especially for Bedouins (ibn-Taghri-Birdi, *Ḥawādith*, p. 13, l. 3, p. 47, l. 15, p. 193, l. 21), though the koranic word for them, *'Urbān*, was not entirely abandoned (ibn-Taghri-Birdi, *Ḥawādith*, p. 12, l. 20, p. 190, l. 3, p. 692, ll. 15, 17; do., vol. vi, p. 749, ll. 1, 3; al-Jabarti, *'Ajā'ib al-Āthār fi al-Tarājim w-al-Akhbār* (Cairo, 1297), vol. i, p. 379, l. 9; p. 417, l. 30; ibn-al-Furāt, vol. vii, p. 178, l. 11; Qalqashandi, vol. xiii, p. 5, vol. ix, p. 254; Ẓāhiri, p. 136.

[2] Ṣāliḥ, pp. 113, 193; ibn-Baṭṭūṭah, vol. i, p. 185.

[3] *I'tibār*, pp. 220, 218, 193, 223-4, 144-5, 126, 103-12; *Arab-Syrian Gentleman*, pp. 248-9, 246-7, 223, 251-2, 231, 173-4, 133-42.

[4] Ibn-al-Jawzi, *Ṣifwat al-Ṣafwah*, vol. iv (Ḥaydarābād, 1356), pp. 314-21, 323-7. See above, p. 571.

[5] P. 287.

[6] Al-Makki, *Nuzhat al-Jalīs wa-Munyat al-Adīb al-Anīs* (Cairo, 1293), pp. 58-9.

flourishing era in its artistic and educational activity. Its capital Damascus still bears evidences of the architectural works of these two rulers. Nūr renovated the walls of the city with its towers and gates and erected public buildings, some of which remained in use until recent times. Especially significant was the hospital bearing his name,[1] now used as a commerce school building.[2] The funds for this structure came from the ransom of a Frankish prisoner.[3] Ibn-Jubayr,[4] who visited the hospital in 1184, found it with an endowment yielding fifteen dinars daily and staffed with wardens keeping a record of the cases and expenses and with physicians attending the patients and prescribing foods and free medicines. The historian ibn-al-Athīr received treatment in this institution and when he protested that he could well afford to pay for the drugs he was told that no one ever spurned Nūr's bounty. According to this historian,[5] Nūr built other hospitals and hostels throughout the domain The site of the hospital in Aleppo [6] was determined by slaughtering a sheep and hanging four parts of it in four quarters of the city. The quarter where the meat in the morning "smelled better" than the others was chosen. The same experiment was ascribed to al-Rāzi, who chose the site for Baghdād hospital about two and a half centuries earlier.[7] The Egyptian official and author al-Ẓāhiri [8] visited the Damascus hospital around 1428 accompanied by an amiable Persian pilgrim who, attracted by the comforts accorded the patients, feigned illness and was admitted. On feeling his pulse and examining him thoroughly, the head physician realized there was nothing wrong with the gentleman but nevertheless prescribed fattened chickens, fragrant sherbets, fruits, savoury cakes and other delicacies.

[1] Al-Māristān al-Nūri; ibn-Jubayr, p. 283. Ar. *māristān*, of which the older form is *bīmāristān* (ibn-Khallikān, vol. ii, p. 521), comes from a Persian word meaning home for the sick. Ibn-Jubayr refers to an older hospital which was evidently built by the Saljūq Duqāq ibn-Tutush (above, p. 574) rather than al-Walīd (above, pp. 497-8).

[2] Ṣalāḥ-al-Dīn al-Munajjid in *al-Mashriq*, vol. xlii (1948), p. 251. For a description of the building consult Ernst Herzfeld, "Damascus: Studies in Architecture", *Ars Islamica*, vol. ix (1942), pp. 2-18; J. Sauvaget, *Les Monuments historiques de Damas* (Beirut, 1932), pp. 49-53.

[3] Maqrīzi, vol. ii, p. 408. [4] P. 283. [5] Vol. xi, p. 267.

[6] Ibn-al-Shiḥnah, pp. 230-31; for more on this hospital consult Ahmed Issa, *Histoire des bimaristans à l'époque islamique* (Cairo, 1928), pp. 203-5.

[7] Ibn-abi-Uṣaybi'ah, vol. i, pp. 309-10.

[8] Pp. 44-5.

When the time came, however, he wrote a new prescription: " Three days are the limit of the hospitality period ".

This hospital was equipped with a library and served as a medical school. Ibn-abi-Uṣaybiʿah [1] has preserved the name of its first physician-professor, abu-al-Majd ibn-abi-al-Ḥakam, and a long sketch of the life of its distinguished dean under the Ayyūbid al-ʿĀdil, Muhadhdhab-al-Dīn ibn-al-Dakhwār (1169/1170–1230). There is evidence to show that physicians, pharmacists and oculists were examined and given certificates (sing. *ijāzah*) before being allowed to practise their professions. In the manuals for the guidance of *al-muḥtasib*, the official responsible for law enforcement, his duties with respect to phlebotomists, cuppers, physicians, surgeons, bone-setters and druggists are clearly set, indicating a certain measure of state control.[2] One of ibn-al-Dakhwār's brilliant students was ibn-al-Nafīs,[3] who, after serving as the dean of the Qalāwūn [4] hospital in Cairo, returned to Damascus, where he died in 1288/9. He was a physician " who would not prescribe medicine when diet sufficed ". In his *Sharḥ Tashrīḥ al-Qānūn*, a commentary on ibn-Sīna's major work, ibn-al-Nafīs contributed a clear conception of the pulmonary circulation of the blood three centuries before the Portuguese Servetus, to whom the discovery is usually credited. Syrian oculists (sing. *kaḥḥāl*) produced the only two major Arabic works of the thirteenth century: *al-Kāfi fi al-Kuḥl* (the sufficient work on collyrium) by Khalīfah ibn-abi-al-Maḥāsin, who flourished in Aleppo about 1256, and *Nūr al-ʿUyūn wa-Jāmiʿ al-Funūn* (the light of the eyes and compendium of arts) by Ṣalāḥ-al-Dīn ibn-Yūsuf, who practised in Ḥamāh about 1296. So confident was Khalīfah of his surgical skill that he did not hesitate to remove a cataract from a one-eyed man.[5] All these men, however, lived in the late twilight of Islamic science.

Medicine

To this period belongs the most distinguished historian of medicine the Arab world produced, Muwaffaq-al-Dīn Aḥmad ibn-abi-Uṣaybiʿah (1203–70). Himself a physician and son of a Damascene oculist, ibn-abi-Uṣaybiʿah studied under ibn-al-

[1] Vol. ii, pp. 155, 239-43.
[2] Ibn-al-Ukhūwah, *Maʿālim al-Qurba fi Aḥkām al-Ḥisbah*, ed. Reuben Levy (Cambridge, 1938), pp. 159-70 (text), 54-9 (tr.).
[3] Subki, vol. v, p. 129.
[4] See above, p. 632.
[5] Consult Sarton, vol. ii, pp. 1101-2.

Dakhwār and in Cairo and botanized with the celebrated Spanish Moslem ibn-al-Bayṭār. His masterpiece, *'Uyūn al-Anbā' fi Ṭabaqāt al-Aṭibbā'*[1] (sources of information on the classes of physicians), almost unique in Arabic literature, is an elaborate collection of some four hundred biographies of Arab and Greek physicians, many of whom were also philosophers, astronomers, physicists and mathematicians. The nearest approach to this work was that of a contemporary Egyptian, al-Qifṭi[2] (1172–1248), who spent the latter part of his life at Aleppo, where he acted as vizir to its Ayyūbid rulers. One of the sources of ibn-abi-Uṣaybi'ah[3] on Greek philosophy was an Egyptian of Damascene origin, abu-al-Wafā' Mubashshir ibn-Fātik,[4] who in 1053 compiled a book entitled *Mukhtār al-Ḥikam wa-Maḥāsin al-Kalim* that was translated into Spanish in the first half of the thirteenth century and then into Latin, French and English. The English edition, *Dictes and Sayings of the Philosophers*, issued in 1477 by William Caxton, was the first book printed in that language with a date and place of printing. For over four centuries the literary descendants of this Arabic work continued to influence the thoughts and writings of Western Europeans.

Madrasahs

Together with the hospitals went schools and mosques. The Nūrids introduced into Syria the type of schools styled *madrasahs* (collegiate mosques). The madrasah was not an intellectual descendant of al-Ma'mūn's Bayt al-Ḥikmah (house of wisdom) established in 830 in Baghdād — which was a general academy of sciences and arts — but rather of the Niẓāmīyah founded in Baghdād in 1067 and named after the Persian vizir of the early Saljūq sultans. The madrasahs were mosque schools, theological seminaries and law academies founded by the state to inculcate and propagate orthodoxy. In them the doctrines approved by Sunnite religion and Moslem scholasticism were studied and taught. Teachers and students received their pay from endowments (sing. *waqf*[5]) connected with the institutions and as a rule lodged in them. The teachers

[1] First edited by "Imru'-al-Qays ibn-al-Ṭaḥḥān" [August Müller], 2 vols. (Cairo, 1882), then republished with additional pages, corrections and index by August Müller, 2 vols. (Königsberg, 1884).

[2] *Ikhbār al-'Ulamā' bi-Akhbār al-Ḥukamā'* (*Ta'rīkh al-Ḥukamā'*), ed. Julius Lippert (Leipzig, 1903).

[3] Vol. i, pp. 9, 16, 21, 28, 30, 38, 41, 43, 47, 50.

[4] Yāqūt, *Irshād*, vol. vi, p. 241; Qifṭi, p. 269.

[5] See above, p. 478.

were jurisconsults (*faqīhs*), theologians (*'ulamā'*) and traditionists. No civil career was normally open to an aspirant who did not receive his training in a madrasah. Realizing the value of such institutions for the state, the Nūrids and after them the Ayyūbids made full use of them. Nūr-al-Dīn built such schools not only in Damascus but in Aleppo, Ḥimṣ, Ḥamāh and other Syrian towns.[1] Three of his schools in Damascus are the oldest monuments of their kind that have come down to us. They follow the cruciform style of Persian origin. In one of them, al-Madrasah al-Nūrīyah, described by ibn-Jubayr[2] as " one of the finest school buildings in the world ", Nūr was buried. The simple inscription on the stone is still legible : " This is the tomb of the martyr Nūr-al-Dīn ibn-Zangi, may God have mercy on him ". The mausoleum is still held in reverence by the Damascenes. Its dome is of the type termed *muqarnaṣ*,[3] often described as stalactite but in reality corbelled. Through this building the connection between the school, mausoleum (*turbah*) and mosque was established in Syria.

Nūr was equally munificent in mosque building. That of Ḥamāh still bears his name, al-Nūri. It was provided with running water, as all his large mosques, hospitals and madrasahs were. Besides, he reconstructed mosques in several cities including Aleppo, whose citadel he renovated. His inscription on a western tower of the citadel is still visible. Nūr's inscriptions are a landmark in Arabic palaeography signalizing the age in which the old angular Kufi gave place to the common rounded *naskhi*.

The Ayyūbids followed in the Nūrids' footsteps. Ṣalāḥ-al-Dīn's brother al-'Ādil resumed the building of a school begun by Nūr and was buried in it. This is the 'Ādilīyah, now housing the Arab Academy of Damascus.[4]

Ṣalāḥ-al-Dīn vied with Nūr-al-Dīn in architectural and educational patronage. His contemporary ibn-Jubayr[5] found in Damascus twenty schools, a hundred public baths, forty lavatories

[1] Ibn-Khallikān, vol. ii, p. 521 ; ibn-al-Athīr, vol. xi, p. 267. For more on the schools in Aleppo consult J. Sauvaget, *Alep* (Paris, 1941), pp. 122-4, 148.

[2] P. 284. Consult al-Nu'aymi, *al-Dāris fi Ta'rīkh al-Madāris*, ed. Ja'far al-Ḥasani (Damascus, 1948), pp. 606-7.

[3] Defined in Arabic dictionaries as " scale-shaped ". The word is an adaptation of the same Greek word whence " cornice " comes ; Herzfeld in *Ars Islamica*, vol. ix (1942), p. 11.

[4] Nu'aymi, p. 359.

[5] Pp. 283, 288.

THE ANCIENT CITADEL OF ALEPPO (QAL'AT ḤALAB), RESTORED BY NŪR-AL-DĪN (d. 1174)

To the left of the entrance is a Byzantine tower repaired and now used as a Moslem minaret

(sing. *dār li-al-waḍū'*, place for ablution) and a large number of dervish "monasteries",[1] most of them with running water. It

From Dussaud, Deschamps and Seyrig, "La Syrie" (Paul Geuthner, Paris)

KHĀN AL-ṢĀBŪN (THE SOAP CARAVANSARY), ALEPPO

An elegant structure of the Mamlūk period

was Ṣalāḥ who introduced the dervish sanctuary and the madrasah into Egypt, the madrasah to combat the widely spread

[1] Sing. *khānaqāh*, from Per.

Shīʿite doctrine.[1] In Jerusalem he built a hospital, a school and a monastery all bearing his name, al-Ṣalāḥi.[2] These were the three types of institutions favoured by the Nūrids.

Mamlūk architecture and decoration

The Ayyūbid school of Syrian architecture was continued in Mamlūk Egypt, where it is still represented by some of the most exquisite monuments Arab art ever produced. Strength, solidity and excessive decoration characterize this school. Its decorative motifs assume infinite grace on its durable material of fine stone. In the thirteenth century Egypt received fresh Syro-Mesopotamian influences through refugee artists and artisans from Damascus, Baghdād and al-Mawṣil who had fled Mongol invasions. The influence is apparent in schools, mosques, hospitals, dervish monasteries and palaces. The far-famed al-Qaṣr al-Ablaq (the multicoloured palace), built by the Mamlūk al-Nāṣir in 1314, was modelled after a palace in Damascus. The ornamentation of Ayyūbid and Mamlūk monuments enhanced their architectural beauty. Among the Ayyūbid innovations was a tendency toward elaboration in detail, greater elegance of proportion and increase in the number of stalactites. There was also a breakaway from the tradition of the plain square towers. In the Baḥri Mamlūk period the elaborate type of minaret evolved from the Ayyūbid. The finest minarets, however, belong to the Burji period, in which Arab architecture — as represented in the mosques — achieved its greatest triumphs.[3]

Exquisite specimens of iron-work, copper-work, glassware and wood-carving have come down to us from the Ayyūbid-Mamlūk age. Especially noteworthy among copper utensils are vases, ewers, trays, chandeliers, perfume burners and Koran cases, all with rich decoration.

In spite of the dazzling profusion of its motives, this decoration, with its powerful Kufic script, its running patterns of conventionalized foliage, its interlacing patterns, rosettes, arabesques and occasional heraldic motives, retains a vigour and sureness of touch that make it

[1] Ibn-Khallikān, vol. iii, p. 521; Suyūṭi, vol. ii, pp. 156, 158; cf. Maqrīzi, vol. ii, p. 363.

[2] Ibn-Khallikān, vol. iii, p. 516; Maqrīzi, vol. ii, p. 415.

[3] René Grousset, *The Civilizations of the East*, vol. i, *The Near and Middle East*, tr. Catherine A. Phillips (New York, 1931), p. 235; M. van Berchem, *Matériaux pour un corpus inscriptionum Arabicarum*, pt. 2, vol. i (Cairo, 1922), pp. 87 *seq*.

not only a delight to the eye, but also — and this is, in our opinion, the secret of Arab decoration — a delight to the intelligence.[1]

Damascus was especially noted for its " gold-like " basins and ewers inlaid with figures, foliage and other delicate designs

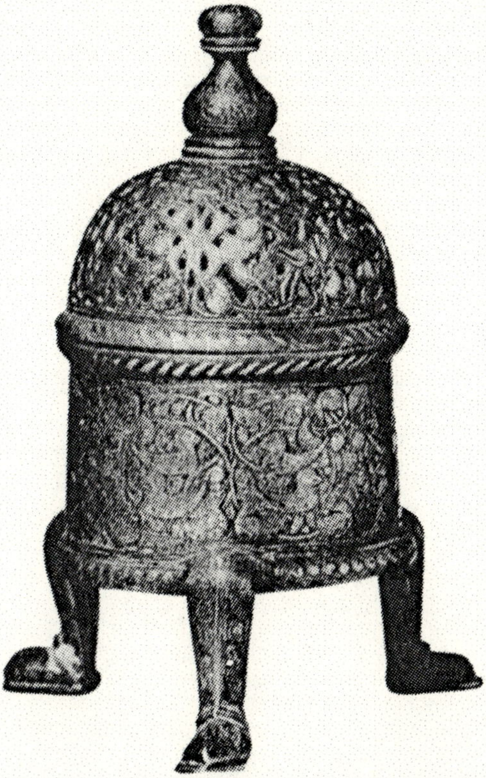

Courtesy of the Walters Art Gallery, Baltimore

A BRASS INCENSE BURNER MADE IN MAMLŪK SYRIA, SECOND HALF OF THE THIRTEENTH CENTURY

Inlaid with silver its lower part is decorated with units of scrolling stems symmetrically composed and coalescing with water-fowls

in silver. An Italian traveller[2] who visited the city in 1384/5 noted that " if the father should be a goldsmith, the sons can never thereafter be engaged in any other craft than this . . . so that by force of circumstances they are obliged to be perfect

[1] Grousset, p. 234.

[2] Simone Sigoli in Cesare Angelini, *Viaggi in Terrasanta* (Florence, 1944), p. 227.

masters of their craft ". Bronze ornaments from doors of mosques bear witness to the good taste of the age. The wood carvings with their floral and geometrical designs indicate freedom from the formulas of Fāṭimid art. A bottle in the Arab

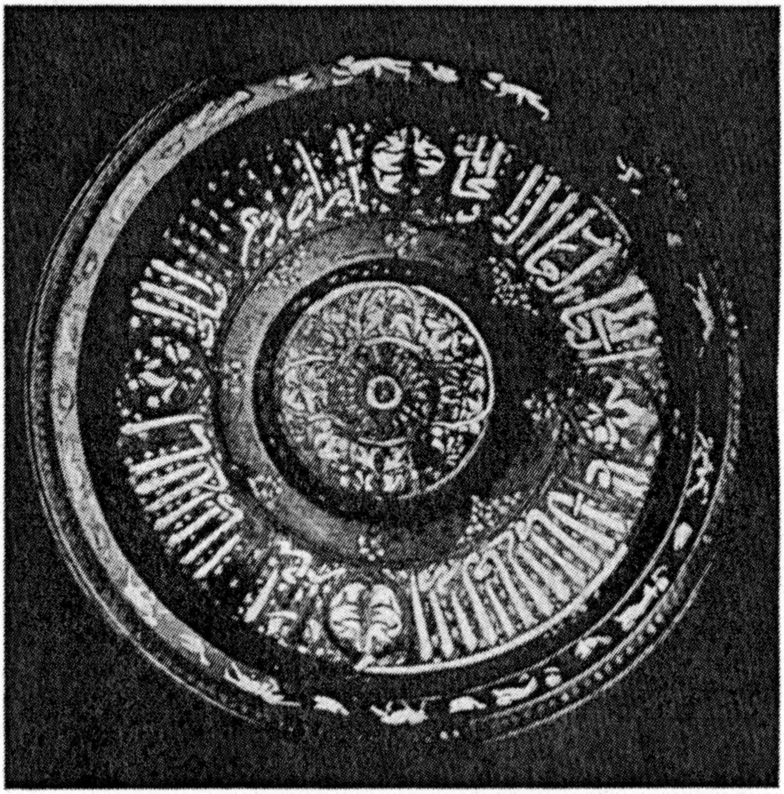

From René Grousset, " The Civilizations of the East ", vol. i, " The Near and Middle East " (Alfred A. Knopf, New York)

COPPER TRAY WITH METAL INLAY REPRESENTING MAMLŪK ART OF THE FOURTEENTH CENTURY IN DAMASCUS

Museum at Cairo bearing the name of al-Nāṣir Ṣalāḥ-al-Dīn, sultan of Damascus and Aleppo (1250–60), is one of the oldest specimens of enamelled glass. Mosque lamps preserved in this and other museums prove that Syria was still ahead of any European land in the technique of glass manufacture.[1]

[1] Sarton, vol. iii, p. 173.

Viewed intellectually the entire Ayyūbid-Mamlūk period was one of compilation and imitation rather than of origination. Nevertheless Damascus and Cairo, especially after the destruction of Baghdād and the disintegration of Moslem Spain, remained the educational and intellectual centres of the Arab world. The schools, founded and richly endowed in these two cities, served to conserve and transmit Arab science and learning. **Intellectual endeavour**

In Sufism certain significant developments took place. Aleppo under al-Malik al-Ẓāhir, son of Ṣalāḥ-al-Dīn, was the scene of the activity of an extraordinary Sufi, Shihāb-al-Dīn al-Suhrawardi (1155–91), founder of the doctrine of illumination (*ishrāq*) [1] and of a dervish order. According to this doctrine light is the very essence of God, the fundamental reality of all things and the representative of true knowledge, perfect purity, love and goodness. Clearly such theories combine Zoroastrian — more especially Manichaean — Neo-Platonic and Islamic ideas. Plotinus and Manes were the ancestors of al-Ishrāq.[2] Al-Suhrawardi was himself born in Persia. The Neo-Platonic ideas filtered at least in part through Christian, mainly Syrian, sources. The conception of God in terms of light is found in the Koran (24 : 35). Long before al-Suhrawardi, al-Ghazzāli devoted a whole treatise, *Mishkāt al-Anwār* (the niche for lights),[3] to this idea. To al-Ghazzāli, too, God is the one real light, from which all other lights are but rays or reflections. Before him Christian mystics had hinted at a spiritual light permeating the universe and itself a radiation of divinity and the essence of all things. During al-Ghazzāli's sojourn in Syria he must have come in contact with mystical teachings of Christians belonging to the Greek Church. His main endeavour was to reconcile orthodox Islam with Sufi mysticism. Al-Suhrawardi contributed several works [4] of which *Ḥikmat al-Ishrāq* [5] (the wisdom of illumination) is the most important. Intoxicated with his mystical fervour this young Sufi so incensed the conservative theologians that on their insistence he **Illuministic Sufism**

[1] Consult Ḥājji Khalfah, vol. iii, pp. 87 *seq.*

[2] Consult Arthur J. Arberry, *An Introduction to the History of Ṣūfism* (London, 1942), p. 32.

[3] (Cairo, 1322); tr. W. H. Gairdner (London, 1924).

[4] For a list consult ibn-Khallikān, vol. iii, pp. 257-8; ibn-abi-Uṣaybi'ah, vol. ii, pp. 170-71. One of his odes quoted in ibn-Khallikān is still chanted, especially in Sufi circles.

[5] (Teheran, 1316).

was starved or strangled to death on orders from the defender of the faith Ṣalāḥ-al-Dīn.[1] Hence his epithet *shaykh maqtūl* (the murdered master). His tomb lies near the post-office building of Aleppo.

Ibn-ʿArabi

Another Ishrāqi Sufi of foreign birth who spent his last days in Syria was Muḥyi-al-Dīn ibn-ʿArabi (1165–1240).[2] Ibn-ʿArabi was more of a pantheistic philosopher; in fact he is considered the greatest speculative genius of Islamic mysticism. Probably to escape restrictions then imposed on liberal thought in his native Spain, where al-Ghazzāli's works had been burned, ibn-ʿArabi, following a pilgrimage to Mecca in 1202, made Damascus his home. There his tomb, enshrined in a mosque built by the Ottoman sultan Salīm I, is still visited. The true mystic in ibn-ʿArabi's judgment has but one guide, the inner light, and will find God in all religions.[3] Raymond Lull [4] and other Christian mystics bear traces of ibn-ʿArabi's influence. In his *al-Futūḥat al-Makkīyah* [5] (Meccan revelations) and *al-Isrāʾ ila Maqām al-Asra* [6] (the nocturnal journey toward the station of the Most Magnanimous), ibn-ʿArabi develops the favourite theme involving Muḥammad's ascension to the seventh heaven.[7] A considerable number of details relating to scenes, episodes, topography and architecture in Dante's *Divine Comedy* have their precedents in these two works of ibn-ʿArabi and other Islamic writings.[8]

Biography

One of the earliest professors in Dār al-Ḥadīth (school of tradition) al-Nūrīyah of Damascus was ibn-ʿAsākir [9] (1105–1176), author of *al-Taʾrīkh al-Kabīr* (the great history), in which he sketched the lives of almost all personages who had ever been connected with that city. Of the eighty volumes of this work few have survived.[10] As a biographer, ibn-ʿAsākir was eclipsed by another product of the Damascene schools,[11] Shams-al-Dīn

[1] Ibn-Shaddād, pp. 302-3; Suhrawardi, *Thalāth Rasāʾil*, ed. and tr. Otto Spies and S. K. Khatak (Stuttgart, 1935), p. 98; ibn-Khallikān, vol. iii, p. 260.

[2] A. E. Affifi, *The Mystical Philosophy of Muḥyid Dín-Ibnul ʿArabi* (Cambridge, 1939), pp. 3, 5, 47, 108, 183-4.

[3] Ibn-ʿArabi, *Tarjumān al-Ashwāq*, ed. and tr. Nicholson (London, 1911), pp. 19, 67.

[4] See above, p. 625. [5] 2nd ed., 4 vols. (Cairo, 1293). [6] (Cairo, 1252).

[7] Koran 17:1. [8] See above, p. 582.

[9] Kutubi, vol. i, p. 333; Yāqūt, *Irshād*, vol. v, pp. 139-46; Subki, vol. iv, pp. 273-7. Nuʿaymi, pp. 100, 104, 105.

[10] Ed. ʿAbd-al-Qādir ibn-Badrān, 7 vols. (Damascus, 1329–51).

[11] See above, p. 644.

(sun of the faith) Aḥmad ibn-Khallikān, foremost among all Moslem biographers. Born in Irbil (Arbela), ibn-Khallikān was appointed in 1261 chief judge of Syria.[1] This high position he held in Damascus, with a seven years' interval, until shortly before his death in 1282. Ibn-Khallikān produced the earliest dictionary of national biography in Arabic, *Wafayāt al-A'yān wa-Anbā' Abnā' al-Zamān* [2] (obituaries of eminent men and sketches of leading contemporaries), a collection of biographies. The author took pains to establish the correct orthography of names, fix dates, trace pedigrees, ascertain the significant events and on the whole produce as accurate and interesting portrayals as possible. A continuation of this work was penned by al-Kutubi (the bookseller, *d.* 1363) of Aleppo under the title *Fawāt al-Wafayāt*.[3]

A more prolific but less thorough biographer than ibn-Khallikān was Ṣalāḥ-al-Dīn Khalīl ibn-Aybak, known as al-Ṣafadi after his birthplace (1296–1363).[4] Son of a Turkish slave, al-Ṣafadi studied in Damascus under the grammarian abu-Ḥayyān al-Tawḥīdi and later associated with the traditionist-historian al-Ḥāfiẓ al-Dhahabi (1274–1348)[5] and the canon lawyer Tāj-al-Dīn al-Subki (*ca.* 1327–70).[6] So voluminous was al-Dhahabi's history of Islam that it deterred copyists, baffled book collectors and consequently failed of survival. Al-Ṣafadi held the post of treasurer of Damascus. The work for which he is best known is *al-Wāfi bi-al-Wafayāt* [7] (adequate treatment of obituaries) in thirty volumes, in the extant part of which the lives of some fourteen thousand rulers, judges and literati are portrayed. This is the largest biographical dictionary in Islam. Ibn-Khallikān's *Wafayāt* has 865 biographies, al-Kutubi's *Fawāt* 506 and ibn-abi-Uṣaybi'ah's *'Uyūn* about 400. In the introduction to his dictionary al-Ṣafadi worked out a manual of

[1] Subki, vol. v, pp. 14-15; Suyūṭi, vol. i, pp. 265-6.

[2] Several editions. The one used here is in 3 vols. (Cairo, 1299); tr. de Slane, 4 vols. (Paris, 1843–71).

[3] 2 vols. (Cairo, 1283). For a criticism of ibn-Khallikān's approach as compared with Plutarch's consult Gustave E. von Grunebaum, *Medieval Islam* (Chicago, 1946), pp. 279-80.

[4] Subki, vol. vi, pp. 94-103.

[5] Of his many works only *Duwal al-Islām*, 2 vols. (Ḥaydarābād, 1337), was used above.

[6] His *Ṭabaqāt al-Shāfi'īyah al-Kubra*, 6 vols. (Cairo, 1324), was drawn upon in the writing of this section.

[7] Ed. H. Ritter, vol. i (Istanbul, 1931).

historical method, " the first of its kind produced anywhere in the world ".[1] Al-Ṣafadi supplements the works of his predecessors, particularly ibn-Khallikān and Yāqūt. Originally a Greek slave, Yāqūt wrote an important dictionary of learned men, *Muʿjam al-Udabāʾ* (*Irshād*), but he is better known for his geographical dictionary, *Muʿjam al-Buldān*.[2] This masterpiece of literature was completed in 1228 at Aleppo and dedicated to its vizir al-Qifṭi.[3] Yāqūt died in that city.

History and geography

Closely related to biography and geography is history. Among the Syrian historians cited in the foregoing pages are abu-Shāmah (1203–68),[4] whose chief work, *Kitāb al-Rawḍatayn fi Akhbār al-Dawlatayn*,[5] was mainly the history of Nūr-al-Dīn and Ṣalāḥ-al-Dīn, and abu-al-Fidāʾ (1273–1332), one of the last Ayyūbid rulers of Ḥamāh,[6] whose *Taʾrīkh* [7] condenses and continues the more voluminous history of ibn-al-Athīr (d. 1234). Abu-al-Fidāʾ was born in Damascus, whither his parents had fled from the Mongols. So popular was his history that it was continued, summarized and abridged by later writers. Equally worthy was his contribution to geography. In the introduction to his *Taqwīm al-Buldān* [8] (tables of the lands) he argues for the sphericity of the earth and cites the loss or gain of one day as one travels around it. This Syrian author may perhaps be considered " the greatest historiogeographer of the period irrespective of nationality or religion ".[9] A contemporary and fellow-countryman of abu-al-Fidāʾ, Shams-al-Dīn al-Dimashqi (Damascene, d. 1326/7), produced a cosmographical treatise, *Nukhbat al-Dahr fi ʿAjāʾib al-Barr w-al-Baḥr* (choice piece of the age relative of the marvels of land and sea),[10] which is poorer than the *Taqwīm* in its mathematical aspects but richer in its physical, mineral and ethnic information. Another, ibn-Faḍl-Allāh al-ʿUmari, who, after serving as chancellor in the Mamlūk court, at Cairo returned to his birthplace in Damascus, where he

[1] Sarton, vol. iii, p. 309.
[2] Ed. F. Wüstenfeld, 6 vols. (Leipzig, 1866–73).
[3] See above, p. 644.
[4] Kutubi, vol. i, pp. 322-5.
[5] 2 vols. (Cairo, 1287–8).
[6] See above, p. 628.
[7] 4 vols. (Constantinople, 1286).
[8] Ed. M. Reinaud and MacGuckin de Slane (Paris, 1840); tr. M. Reinaud, vols. (Paris, 1848).
[9] Sarton, vol. iii, p. 308.
[10] Ed. A. F. Mehren (St. Petersburg, 1865); Fr. tr. by Mehren (Copenhagen, 1874).

died of the plague (1349), produced two important works: *Masālik al-Abṣār fi Mamālik al-Amṣār* (paths of the eyes through the kingdoms of the main towns) [1] and *al-Ta'rīf bi-al-Muṣṭalaḥ al-Sharīf* (acquainting [the reader] with the noble epistolary style),[2] a manual for administrators and diplomats.

The names of the two leading historians in the Mamlūk period, the Egyptian al-Maqrīzi and the Tunisian ibn-Khaldūn, are connected with Syria. Al-Maqrīzi (1364–1442), whose valuable *al-Khiṭaṭ* [3] was repeatedly cited in the above pages, was of Ba'labakkan ancestry and held a professorship in Damascus. As chief judge of Egypt, his younger contemporary ibn-Khaldūn (1332–1406) in 1401 accompanied the Mamlūk sultan al-Nāṣir Faraj to Damascus on his campaign against Tīmūr and was received as an honoured guest by the dreadful Mongol. Ibn-Khaldūn's *Muqaddamah* (prolegomena),[4] which is the first volume in his comprehensive history,[5] entitles him to the distinction of being the greatest philosopher of history Islam produced. In his attempt to interpret historical happenings and national traits on economic, geographic, physical and other secular bases, ibn-Khaldūn had no predecessor in Islam and remains without a worthy successor.

This array of biographers, geographers, historians and encyclopaedic scholars, beginning with ibn-'Asākir and ending with ibn-Khaldūn, makes Syria and Egypt of the Ayyūbid and Mamlūk period without peer among the lands of Islam.

Tīmūr

The onslaught on Syria by Tīmūr Lang (Tamerlane) was the last in the Mongol series. Tīmūr claimed descent from Chingīz Khān.[6] Like a cyclone he and his hordes swept from Central into Western Asia leaving havoc and ruin in their wake. For the fourth or fifth time Syria lay prostrate at Mongol feet.[7] For three days in October 1400 Aleppo was given over to plunder. Its citadel was perhaps for the first time taken by

[1] Ed. Aḥmad Zaki, vol. i (Cairo, 1924). For a critical appreciation consult 'Abd-al-Laṭīf Ḥamzah, *al-Ḥarakah al-Fikrīyah fi Miṣr fi al-'Aṣrayn al-Ayyūbi w-al-Mamlūki al-Awwal* (Cairo, 1947), pp. 324-7.

[2] (Cairo, 1314).

[3] 2 vols. (Cairo, 1270).

[4] Earlier than the Cairo (1284) edition is that of M. Quatremère, 3 vols. (Paris, 1858); tr. de Slane, 3 vols. (Paris, 1862–8, ed. Boutboul, Paris, 1934–8).

[5] Vol. vi (Cairo, 1284), pp. 379 *seq.*, contains his autobiography, the best source of his life.

[6] Cf. ibn-'Arab-Shāh, *'Ajā'ib al-Maqdūr fi Akhbār Tīmūr* (Cairo, 1285), p. 6.

[7] See above, pp. 631-2.

storm, the invader having sacrificed of his men enough to fill the moat with their corpses. Some twenty thousand of the city's inhabitants were slaughtered; severed heads were built into a platform ten cubits high by ten in circumference.[1] The city's priceless schools and mosques built by Nūrids and Ayyūbids were forever destroyed. The routing of the Egyptian army of Sultan Faraj opened the way to Damascus. Its citadel held out for a month. In violation of the capitulation terms the city was plundered and committed to the flames. Thirty thousand of its men, women and children were shut up in its great mosque, which was then set on fire. Of the building itself only the walls were left standing. The cream of Damascene scholars, craftsmen, artisans, armourers, steel workers[2] and glass manufacturers were carried away to Tīmūr's capital, Samarqand, there to implant these and other minor arts. Damascus lost its leadership in damascening. From the pen of ibn-Taghri-Birdi,[3] whose father was chief armour-bearer of Faraj, we have a graphic description of the entire Syrian campaign. This was perhaps the heaviest blow that the city, if not the whole country, ever suffered.

By 1402 the wild conqueror had crushed the Ottoman army at Ankara, captured Brusa and Smyrna and taken Bāyazīd I prisoner.[4] Fortunately for the mamlūks Tīmūr died in 1404. His successors exhausted themselves in internal struggles which made possible the reconstitution of the Ottoman power in Asia Minor and later the rise of the Ṣafawid dynasty in Persia.

Ottomans against Mamlūks and Ṣafawids

Rivalry between the Mamlūk and the Ottoman sultanates for supremacy in Western Asia asserted itself in the second half of the fifteenth century. The Ṣafawid state became involved in the early sixteenth. Ottoman-Mamlūk relations were strained in the days of Khushqadam (1461–7), who unlike his Turkish and Circassian Mamlūk predecessors was a Greek,[5] and Muḥammad II, conqueror of Constantinople. But hostilities did not break out till 1486, when Qā'it-bāy contested with the Otto-

[1] Ibn-Taghri-Birdi, vol. vi, pt. 2, 52; cf. ibn-Iyās, vol. i, p. 327.

[2] Iron ore came presumably from neighbouring Lebanon; see above, pp. 35, 277, 571.

[3] Vol. vi, pt. 2, p. 5, l. 14, pp. 50 *seq.* Cf. Mīrkhwānd, *Ta'rīkh Rawḍat al-Ṣafā'* (Teheran, 1270), Bk. VI; Maqrīzi, vol. ii, p. 241.

[4] Ibn-'Arab-Shāh, p. 6; ibn-Iyās, vol. i, p. 334; vol. iii, p. 48.

[5] Ibn-Taghri-Birdi, vol. vii, p. 685.

man Bāyazīd II the possession of Adana, Tarsus and other border towns. Towards the end of his reign this Mamlūk sultan sent a message to the pope threatening reprisals on the Christians of Syria as Ferdinand was destroying the last Islamic power in Spain. Shortly after that hostilities began between Ottomans and Persians resulting in the swift destruction of the Ṣafawid army and the occupation of Mesopotamia by Salīm I (1512–20). The Ṣafawids were ardent Shīʻites and established their rite as the state religion. Salīm charged that the Mamlūk Qānṣawh al-Ghawri (1500–16) had entered into treaty relations with the Ṣafawid Shah against him and had harboured various political refugees.

Marj Dābiq: a decisive victory

Meantime Qānṣawh had moved northward under the pretext of acting as an intermediary between the two contestants.[1] In his train were the chief judges of his realm and the puppet caliph al-Mutawakkil. This caliph was a descendant and successor of al-Mustanṣir (uncle of the last ʻAbbāsid caliph in Baghdād), whom Baybars had in 1261 installed in Cairo merely to confer legitimacy upon his crown and give his court an air of primacy in Moslem eyes.[2] Qānṣawh sent a special envoy to Salīm, who thought of no better way of insulting him than to shave his beard and send him back, on a lame donkey, with a declaration of war. The two armies were locked in battle on August 24, 1516, on the blood-stained field of Marj Dābiq, north of Aleppo. The seventy-five-year-old Qānṣawh, who had begun his career as a slave of Qā'it-bāy, fought valiantly but hopelessly. He could not depend upon the loyalty of his Syrian governors nor could he match his troops with the redoubtable Janissaries[3] with their superior equipment. Khā'ir Bey, the treacherous governor of Aleppo, who was entrusted with the command of the left wing, deserted with his men at the first charge.[4] The Turkish army employed artillery, muskets and other long-range weapons which the Egyptian army, comprising Bedouin and Syrian contingents, was unfamiliar with or dis-

[1] Al-Qaramāni, *Akhbār al-Duwal wa-Āthār al-Uwal* (Baghdād, 1282), pp. 219-20.

[2] Maqrīzi, tr. Quatremère, vol. i (pt. 1), pp. 146-68; ibn-Khaldūn, vol. v, pp. 382-3; abu-al-Fidā', vol. iii, p. 222; Suyūṭi, *Ḥusn*, vol. ii, pp. 49-52; ibn-Iyās, vol. i, pp. 100-101.

[3] Tur. *yeni-cheri*, new troops, name given to the regular infantry recruited mainly from young captured Christians and largely responsible for the Ottoman conquests.

[4] Ibn-Iyās, vol. iii, pp. 46, 51.

dained to use, clinging to the antiquated theory that personal valour is the decisive factor in combat. Gunpowder [1] and "heavy guns mounted on wagons drawn by horses" [2] were also used by the Turks. In the heat of the battle Qānṣawh was stricken with apoplexy and fell from his horse. Salīm's victory was complete. He seized the caliph and later took him to Constantinople, but the claim that the caliph transmitted to the Ottoman sultan the dignity of his office is a nineteenth century fiction. In the citadel of Aleppo Salīm found Mamlūk treasures estimated in millions of dinars. In mid-October he moved on to Damascus. Syria passed quietly into Ottoman hands, where it was to remain for four full centuries. Its people, as on many a previous occasion, welcomed the new masters as deliverers from the old.

Mamlūk rule abolished

From Syria the Ottoman army streamed south into Egypt, where Ṭūmān-bāy, a slave of Qānṣawh, had been proclaimed sultan. The two armies met on January 22, 1517, outside Cairo. "Plastered with shots and bullets" [3] the Egyptian army was soon routed. Ṭūmān-bāy fled to a Bedouin camp where he was betrayed and later (April 17) hanged at one of Cairo's main gates.[4] Egypt was no more a sovereign state. Al-Ḥijāz, with its two holy cities, automatically became a part of the rising Ottoman empire. In the first Friday congregational services Egyptian preachers invoked Allah's blessing on the conqueror in these words:

> O Lord! uphold the sultan, son of the sultan, ruler over both lands and the two seas, conqueror of both hosts, monarch of the two 'Irāqs, minister of the two Holy Cities, the victorious king Salīm Shāh. Grant him, O Lord, Thy precious aid; enable him to win glorious victories, O Ruler of this world and the next, Lord of the universe.[5]

A new era dawned upon the Arab world: that of domination by the Ottoman Turks.

[1] Evidently a Chinese invention, gunpowder was introduced by the Mongols about 1240 into Europe, where its use for projective purposes through firearms was later developed; cf. Sarton, vol. iii, pp. 722-3. The first mention of artillery (*madāfi'*) in Syrian history is perhaps in Yaḥya, p. 229, where Genoese seamen bombard Beirut in 1382.

[2] Qaramāni, p. 220.

[3] Ibn-Iyās, vol. iii, p. 97.

[4] Ibn-Iyās, vol. iii, p. 115; Suyūṭi, vol. ii, p. 90; Qaramāni, p. 220; cf. Sa'd-al-Dīn, *Tāj al-Tawārīkh*, vol. ii (Constantinople, 1280), p. 361.

[5] Ibn-Iyās, vol. iii, p. 98.

PART V

UNDER THE OTTOMAN TURKS

CHAPTER XLVIII

SYRIA A TURKISH PROVINCE

FROM modest beginnings in the early fourteenth century the petty Turkish state in western Asia Minor rose in the course of the following two centuries to a dominant position in Western Asia, south-eastern Europe and north-eastern Africa. Its rise was one of the major facts in modern history. The term Turk appears for the first time about A.D. 500 as name of a nomadic people in Central Asia.[1] In the sixth century Turkish peoples succeeded in establishing nomadic states extending from Mongolia and the northern frontier of China to the Black Sea. If the Arabians were parasites of the camel, the Turks were parasites of the horse. They drank its milk, ate its flesh and rode on it to victory. They used stirrups and bows and arrows. Mobility was the chief advantage they possessed over their foes. In Turkestan they came in contact with Indo-European peoples, and it was in this region that the Arab conquerors of the late seventh and early eighth centuries first encountered Turkish-speaking people.[2] When at last those of them to be designated Ottoman reached Asia Minor, they found the country already partly Turkicized by their Saljūq cousins.[3] Both Saljūqs and Ottomans traditionally belonged to the Ghuzz tribe or federation of tribes.

The Ottoman state

The eponymous founder of the Ottoman state and dynasty was a semi-historical leader ʻUthmān[4] (1299–1326), whose name, assuming its genuineness, indicates that by that time his clan was beginning to be or was Islamized.[5] With the adoption of Islam thousands of religious, scientific and literary terms from Arabic, and some from Persian, found their way into the

[1] See above, p. 437. [2] See above, pp. 458 *seq.*
[3] See above, pp. 573 *seq.*
[4] On him consult Mehmed Fuad Köprülü, *Les Origines de l'empire ottomane* (Paris, 1935), pp. 87 *seq.*; Paul Wittek, *The Rise of the Ottoman Empire* (London, 1938), pp. 7-9; Joseph von Hammer, *Geschichte des osmanischen Reiches*, vol. i (Pest, 1827), pp. 40 *seq.*
[5] On the early religion of the Turks, see above, p. 631.

Turkish language. With little written literature [1] of its own this language in the meantime adopted the Arabic characters, which remained in use until the reforms of Muṣṭafa Kemāl in 1928. For about sixty-six years after its foundation in about 1300 the Ottoman state was a frontier amīrate with Brusa (Bursa) as capital after 1326.[2] From 1366 to 1543 it was a kingdom with Adrianople (Edirne) as capital.[3] The conquest of Constantinople in 1453 by Muḥammad II the Conqueror (al-Fātiḥ, 1451–1481) marks the emergence of the empire. Thus did this Moslem Turkish state fall heir to the Byzantine empire, to which it later successively added several states of the Arab caliphate. The Ottoman empire attained its height under Sulaymān I the Magnificent (al-Qānūni, the lawgiver, 1520–66), son of the conqueror of Syria and Egypt, Salīm I. Under Sulaymān the greater part of Hungary was reduced, Vienna was besieged, Rhodes was occupied and North Africa, exclusive of Morocco, acknowledged the political authority of the Sublime Porte (*al-Bāb al-ʿĀli*) in Constantinople.[4] The failure of the second

[1] Syriac script was used by Turks in Central Asia; see above, pp. 169, 518.

[2] Genealogical table of the first Ottoman rulers:

1. ʿUthmān I (1299)
|
2. Ūrkhān (1326)
|
3. Murād I (1359)

[3] 3. Murād I (1359)
|
4. Bāyazīd I (1389–1401)
|
Sulaymān (claimant, 1403–10) — 5. Muḥammad I (1403) (sole ruler 1413) — Mūsa (claimant, 1410–13)
|
6. Murād II (1421)
|
7. Muḥammad II (1451)

[4] 7. Muḥammad II (1451)
|
8. Bāyazīd II (1481)
|
9. Salīm I (1512)
|
10. Sulaymān I (1520)
|
11. Salīm II (1566)
|
12. Murād III (1574)

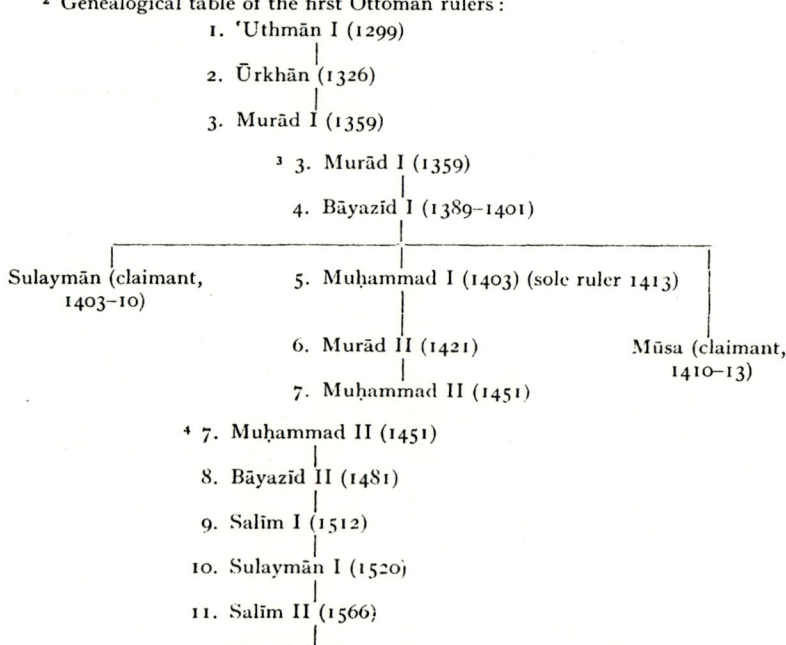

attempt to capture Vienna in 1683 marked the beginning of the end. The empire under Sulaymān extended from Budapest on the Danube to Baghdād on the Tigris and from the Crimea to the first cataract of the Nile. No such state was built by Moslems in modern times. It was also one of the most enduring Moslem states. From 1300 to 1922, when the empire came to an end, thirty-six sultans, all in the direct male line of ʿUthmān, ruled.[1]

Administrative divisions of Syria

It was Sultan Salīm I (1512–20) who incorporated the Arab world in the Ottoman empire.[2] After his decisive victory at Marj Dābiq he triumphantly entered Ḥamāh and Ḥimṣ, both of which capitulated. Salīm then received the submission of Tripoli, Ṣafad, Nābulus, Jerusalem and Gaza, " none of which

[1]
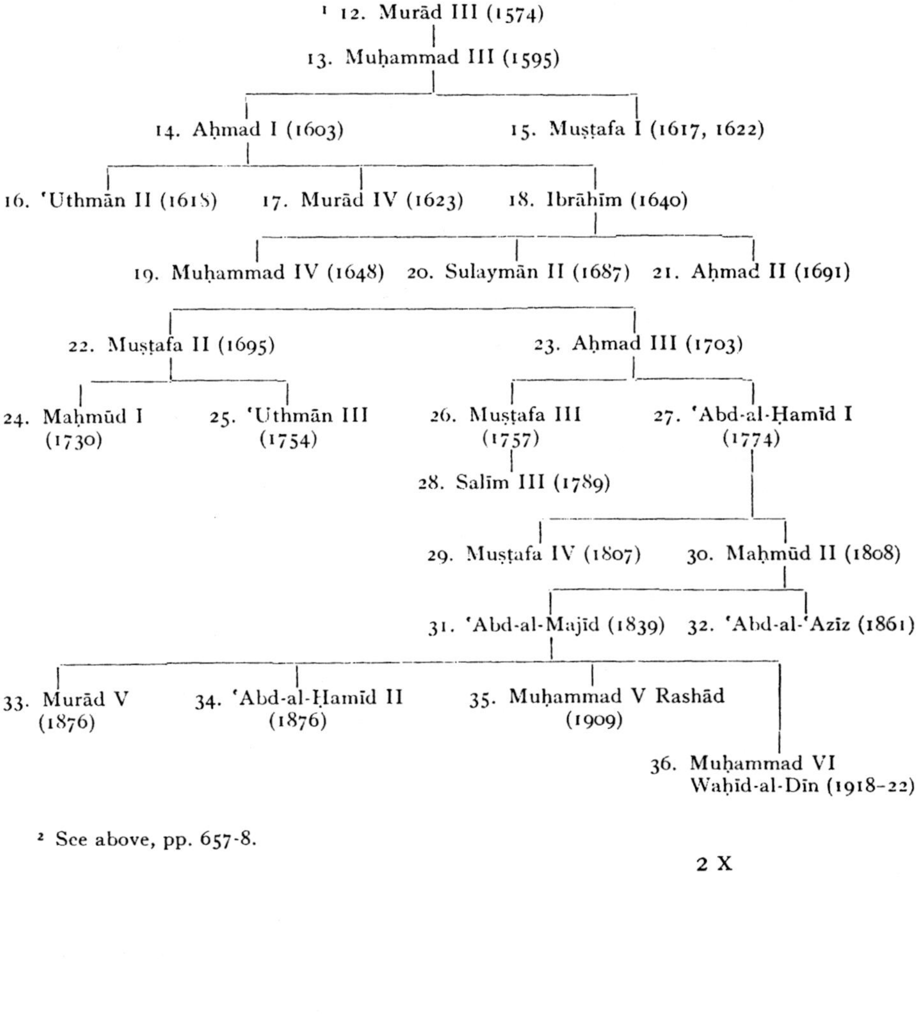

[2] See above, pp. 657-8.

put up any resistance whatsoever ".[1] On his way back from Egypt he lingered long enough in Syria to consolidate his position and organize the new domain. For purposes of taxation he empowered a commission to draw up a cadastre of the whole land, reserving a large portion of the fertile plain of al-Biqā' and the rich valley of the Orontes to the crown.[2] The Mamlūk procedure of farming out (*talzīm*) tax collection to the highest bidder was, of course, retained. The Ḥanafite rite of jurisprudence, preferred by the Ottomans, was given official status in Syria.[3] An Aleppine jurist, Ibrāhīm al-Ḥalabi (d. 1594), wrote *Multaqa al-Abḥur* (confluence of the seas), which was first published in Constantinople and became a handbook of Ḥanafi law throughout the empire.

The Mamlūk administrative divisions [4] were in general maintained, with some change in nomenclature. The *niyābah* now became *walāyah* (pronounced in Turkish *vilāyet*), and the *nā'ib* became a *wāli*.[5] The honorary title placed after the *wāli's* name was pasha; this made pashalik synonymous with walāyah. The walayāh of Aleppo embraced at one time seven sanjāqs.[6] The walāyah of Damascus, augmented by the addition of Jerusalem, Ṣafad and Gaza, was put under Jān-Birdi al-Ghazāli, the treacherous Mamlūk nā'ib of Ḥamāh who had followed his colleague of Aleppo in betraying al-Ghawri.[7] This made al-Ghazāli the virtual viceroy of Syria. But all other administrative divisions were entrusted to Turks. Later Syria was divided into three walāyahs: Damascus, with ten sanjāqs, chief among which were Jerusalem, Nābulus, Gaza, Tadmur, Sidon and Beirut; Aleppo, with nine sanjāqs embracing North Syria; and Tripoli, with five sanjāqs including Ḥimṣ, Ḥamāh, Jabalah and Salamiyah. Sidon was made a walāyah in 1660 to act as a check on Lebanon.[8]

[1] Ibn-Iyās, ed. Paul Kahle and Muḥammad Muṣṭafa, vol. v, p. 149.

[2] For more on taxes consult Ömer Lûtfi Barakan, *Kanunlar* (Istanbul, 1945), pp. 206 *seq*.

[3] Ibn-Iyās, vol. v, p. 238; al-Ghazzi, *al-Kawākib al-Sā'irah bi-A'yān al-Mi'ah al-'Āshirah*, ed. Jibrā'īl Jabbūr (Beirut, 1945), p. 210. [4] See above, p. 637.

[5] *mutaṣarrifīyah* and *mutaṣarrif* did not come into use till later.

[6] Von Hammer, vol. ii, p. 477, n.d. Tur. *sanjāq* (Ar. *sanjaq*) is a translation of Ar. *liwā'*, banner. All these technical terms were evidently used earlier by the Saljūqs.

[7] Farīdūn Bey, *Majmū'ah Munsha'āt al-Salāṭīn*, 2nd ed. (Istanbul, 1274), p. 455; Ibn-Iyās, vol. v, pp. 156, 157; Sa'd-al-Dīn, vol. ii, pp. 364-5.

[8] Consult Lammens, *Syrie*, vol. ii, p. 60; *Relazioni dei consoli veneti nella Siria*, ed. G. Berchet (Turin, 1866), pp. 89, 126.

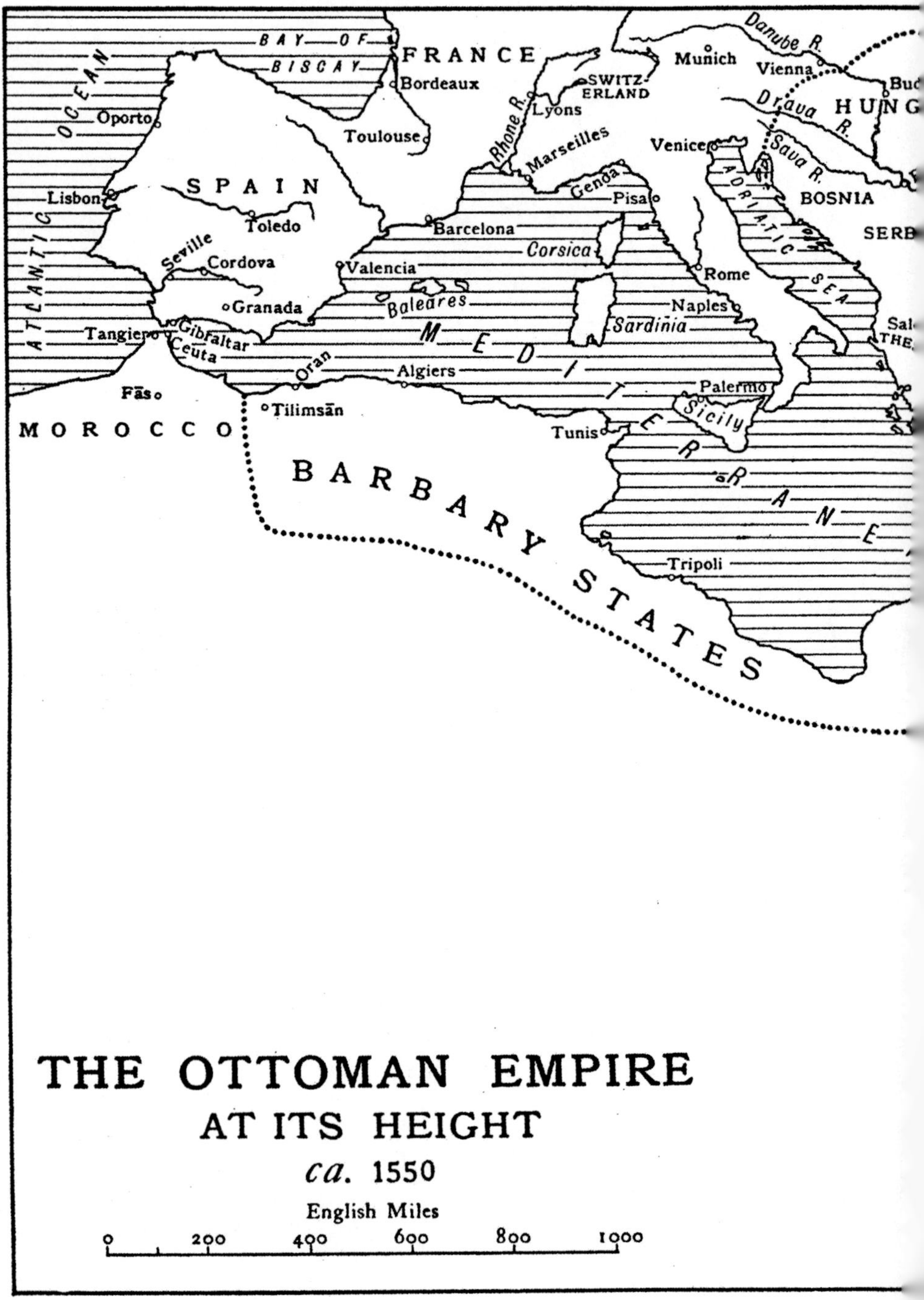

THE OTTOMAN EMPIRE AT ITS HEIGHT

ca. 1550

ARAL SEA
Oxus R.
Volga R.
Don R.
Azov
COSSACKS
CASPIAN SEA
MOLDAVIA
Odessa
CRIMEA
LACHIA
harest
be R.
GARIA
anople
NIA
BLACK SEA
Constantinople
Batum
Trebizond
GEORGIA
Tiflis
Baku
ARMENIA
Erzerum
Tibrīz
Ankara
Sivas
Brusa
ANATOLIA
Diyār Bakr
PERSIA
Al-Mawṣil
Koniah
Smyrna
ens
Tarsus
Alexandretta
Tigris R.
Iṣbahān
Antioch
Aleppo
Al-Lādhiqīyah
Rhodes
Tadmur
Baghdād
Tripoli
Hims
Euphrates R.
ete
Cyprus
Beirut
Damascus
Sidon
Shīrāz
SEA
'Akka
Al-Baṣrah
PERSIAN GULF
Alexandria
Jerusalem
Gaza
ARABIA
Cairo
EGYPT
AL-ḤIJĀZ
RED SEA
Medina
1st Cataract
Mecca
Juddah
Nile R.
HADRAMAWT
AL-YAMAN
SUDAN
ADEN
Adan
GULF OF
ETHIOPIA

[facing p. 664

In 1724 Ismā'īl Pasha al-'Aẓm, founder of a prominent Damascene family, was entrusted with the walāyah of Damascus. His son As'ad, who began his career as governor of Sidon and then of Ḥamāh, was one of the best known wālis of Damascus under the Ottomans. He was also in charge of the holy pilgrimage and must have amassed a large fortune. His palace in Ḥamāh, now housing a native school, is one of the show places of the city on the Orontes. More sumptuous is that of Damascus built about 1749 and considered the most beautiful Arab monument of the century. Its style, woodwork and mosaic exemplify the finest in Islamic art at its decline. Its marble was imported from Italy. Partly destroyed in the uprising against the French mandate in 1925, it was renovated and occupied by the Institut Français de Damas. Other members of this Syrian family were appointed over Damascus, Sidon or Tripoli, but unlike the Lebanese governors they remained loyal to the Ottoman sultan despite the fact that several of them were degraded and had their property confiscated. Ismā'īl spent some of his last days in jail and As'ad was treacherously killed in the bath by orders from Constantinople.[1]

Special position of Lebanon

Lebanon, however, with its hardy Druze and Maronite mountaineers, deserved a different treatment. Expediency dictated that its native feudal lords be recognized,[2] especially since the real danger came from Egypt and Persia. While in Damascus Salīm received a delegation of Lebanese amīrs headed by Fakhr-al-Dīn I al-Ma'ni [3] of al-Shūf, Jamāl-al-Dīn (Arislān ? [4]) of al-Gharb and 'Assāf al-Turkumāni of Kisrawān.[5] Fakhr-al-Dīn who, according to a Lebanese chronicler,[6] had advised his men at Marj Dābiq, " Let's wait and see on what the victory will be and then join it ", now appeared before the Ottoman sultan, kissed the ground and delivered a most eloquent prayer :

O Lord, perpetuate the life of him whom Thou hast chosen to administer Thy domain, made the successor (*khalīfah*) of Thy covenant,

[1] Muḥammad Kurd-'Ali, *Khiṭaṭ al-Sha'm*, vol. ii (Damascus, 1925), pp. 289, 290-91 ; Ḥaydar al-Shihābi, *Ta'rīkh*, ed. Na''ūm Mughabghab (Cairo, 1900), p. 769. *Les Guides bleus : Syrie — Palestine — Iraq — Transjordanie* (Paris, 1932), pp. 124, 303-4.

[2] See above, pp. 637, 640.

[3] On the origin of this family see Shidyāq, pp. 247-8.

[4] Ḥaydar, p. 561. For the Arislān family see above, p. 545. Jamāl belonged to the Yamanite faction, the Tanūkhs to the Qaysite.

[5] See above, p. 623.

[6] Ḥaydar, p. 560.

empowered over Thy worshippers and Thy land and entrusted with Thy precept and ordinance; he who is the supporter of Thy luminous law, the leader of the pure and victorious nation, our lord and master of our favours, the commander of the believers.[1] . . .

Impressed by his eloquence and seeming sincerity, Salīm confirmed Fakhr-al-Dīn and the other Lebanese amīrs in their fiefs, allowed them the same autonomous privileges enjoyed under the Mamlūks and imposed on them a comparatively light tribute[2] Fakhr-al-Dīn was recognized as the leading chieftain of the mountain (*sulṭān al-barr*). Thereafter the Ottoman sultans dealt with their Lebanese vassals either directly or through a neighbouring Syrian wāli. As a rule these vassals acted independently, transmitted their fiefs to their descendants, offered no military service to the sultan, exercised the right of life and death over their subjects, exacted taxes and duties and at times even concluded treaties with foreign powers.

Al-Ghazāli

Al-Ghazāli signalized his loyalty to the new régime by apprehending the Buḥturid Tanūkh[3] leaders of al-Gharb, who remained loyal to the Mamlūks, and jailing them in the citadel of Damascus. He decapitated both ibn-al-Ḥanash, the Arab chieftain of Sidon and al-Biqā' who refused to submit,[4] and ibn-al-Ḥarfūsh, head of a Shī'ite family in al-Biqā', and forwarded their heads, together with other Bedouin heads from the mountain of Nābulus, to Constantinople. But he who betrayed his first masters could not long remain loyal to the new ones. Taking advantage of the death of Salīm in 1520, al-Ghazāli proclaimed himself in the Umayyad Mosque an independent sovereign under the title al-Malik al-Ashraf (the most noble king), struck coins in his own name and tried to induce his former colleague Khā'ir Bey, whom Salīm had rewarded with the vice-royalty of Egypt, to follow his example. But Aleppo did not openly support al-Ghazāli and Sulaymān sent against him an army which, on January 27, 1521, destroyed the Syrian rebels and killed al-Ghazāli at al-Qābūn, near Damascus. The punishment the Syrian capital and its environs received was

[1] Ḥaydar, p. 561; cf. Duwayhi, p. 152; Shidyāq, p. 251.

[2] Kisrawān's share was only 4200 gold piastres; Duwayhi, p. 152; 'Īsa I. al-Ma'lūf, *Ta'rīkh al-Amīr Fakhr-al-Dīn al-Thāni* (Jūniyah, 1934), p. 9, n. 1.

[3] See above, pp. 545, 637, 640. One of these princes had visited Salīm in Damascus and offered him Arab steeds; ibn-Sabāṭ, supplement to Ḥaydar, p. 596, and to Ṣāliḥ, p. 269. Cf. Shidyāq, p. 246.

[4] Ḥaydar, p. 596.

even more severe than that meted out earlier by Tīmūr.[1] About a third of the city and its villages was utterly destroyed.[2] Ever since then the name of the Janissaries has become associated in the Syrian mind with destruction and terror.

The system of administration

Ottoman political theory, at least as understood by the average wāli, held that the conquered peoples, especially if non-Moslems, were flocks (raia, raya [3]) to be shepherded for the benefit of the conqueror. The terminology, borrowed from the vocabulary of Bedouin life in Arabia, expressed traditional concepts in the minds of the descendants of Central Asiatic nomads. As human cattle the conquered were to be milked, fleeced and allowed to live their own lives so long as they gave no trouble. Mostly peasants, artisans and merchants, they could not aspire to military or civil careers. But the herd needs watchdogs. These were recruited mainly from war prisoners, purchased slaves and Christian children levied as a tribute and then trained and brought up as Moslems. All recruits were put through a rigorous system of training in the capital covering many years. They were subjected to keen competition and careful screening; the mentally bright among them were further prepared for governmental positions and the physically strong for military service. The toughest were drafted into the infantry corps termed Janissary. The governing and the military class in the empire came at first almost exclusively from this source.[4] Grand vizirs, vizirs, admirals, generals, provincial governors were once slaves and so they remained. Their lives and property were always at the disposal of their sultan master, who never hesitated to exercise his right of ownership. History does not record the creation of a parallel machine. It left the house of ʿUthmān as the only aristocracy in the empire, wielding absolute power in the administration of the state and for its defence.

Another basis of classification was religious affiliation. From time immemorial Near Eastern society was stratified in terms of belief rather than of race and within the religious

[1] See above, p. 656.

[2] Ibn-Iyās, vol. v, pp. 363, 371, 376-8, 418-19; Qaramāni, pp. 316-17.

[3] From Ar. *rayāʿa*, pl. of *raʿīyah*, herd. In 1856 the term was replaced by the less obnoxious one *tabaʿah*, followers, subjects.

[4] Albert H. Lybyer, *The Government of the Ottoman Empire* (Cambridge, 1913), pp. 45 *seq.*; Barnette Miller, *The Palace School of Muhammad the Conqueror* (Cambridge, 1941), pp. 6 *seq.*, 81, 95.

community the family rather than the territory was the nucleus of organization. Hence in the minds of the people religion and nationality were inextricably interwoven. Each of the religious groups of the Ottoman empire was termed a millet.[1] The two largest millets were those of Islam and the Rum (Greek Orthodox).[2] Armenians and Jews were also classified as millets. According to this system all non-Moslem groups were organized into communities under religious heads of their own who also exercised certain civil functions of importance. This amounted to a provision for the government of subject minorities. Europeans — Venetians, Dutch, French and English — domiciled in the land were likewise treated as millets. In 1521 Sulaymān signed with the Venetians a treaty, set out in thirty chapters,[3] which confirmed privileges previously enjoyed under the Byzantines. The French obtained their first capitulations fourteen years later [4]; the English followed in 1580. Originally intended as concessions from a strong sovereign, rather than exactions from a weak one, the capitulations gave extraterritorial privileges to foreigners and lingered as a humiliating institution until the dissolution of the empire.

Abuses and attempts at reform

The Ottoman wāli was no improvement on his predecessor the Mamlūk nā'ib, who likewise was recruited from the slave class. Besides, he was farther removed from the central government and therefore freer from its control. But that did not make much difference, as corruption in the capital was as rife as in the provinces. Wālis often bought their appointments there and entered upon their duties with the main desire of promoting their own interests. Not a few returned to Constantinople to face execution and confiscation of property. Exploitation went hand in hand with instability. In the first hundred and eighty-four years of its career as an Ottoman city Damascus witnessed no fewer than a hundred and thirty-three

[1] From Ar. *millah*, religion, nationality.

[2] The Turks took Arabic *rūm*, a contraction of the word for Romans, and applied it to all Ottoman subjects of the Greek Orthodox faith irrespective of nationality or language. The term is retained to the present day despite the fact that the Greek Orthodox owe no allegiance to Rome. The Saljūqs designated their sultanate in Anatolia " Rūm " (see above, p. 574) because it was conquered from the Eastern Roman Empire.

[3] Late Lat. *capitula*, chapters, whence " capitulations ".

[4] For the terms consult I. de Testa, *Recueil des traités de la porte ottomane*, vol. i (Paris, 1864), pp. 15 *seq.*

wālis, of whom only thirty-three held their office as long as two years each.[1] Aleppo evidently did not fare much better. A Venetian consul there reports nine pashas in three years.[2] At times pashas engaged in bloody conflicts against one another with utter disregard of the central government. Occasional visits by Janissaries added to the misery of the people, most of whom, however, were manifestly reconciled to their fate. The general attitude seems to have been one of passivity, frustration, distrust of leadership and pessimism as to the result of effort. The old spirit of rebellion which had often flared under ʿAbbāsid and Fāṭimid misrule was by this time apparently dead. Clearly the dark ages which began under the Saljūq Turks [3] were getting darker under the Ottoman Turks. While Europe was entering upon her age of enlightenment, Syria was groping in Ottoman darkness.

The need for introducing drastic reforms and curbing abuses of officials was early felt by Muṣṭafa Köprülü, grand vizir from 1689 to 1691, whose promulgation of new regulations for the better treatment of non-Moslems foreshadowed the attempted reforms of the three bold sultans, Salīm III (1789–1807), Maḥmūd II (1808–39) and ʿAbd-al-Majīd I (1839–61). All these reform regulations, however, remained ink on paper. Those of Salīm, entitled *Niẓām-i Jadīd* (new regulations), were opposed by the Janissaries and corrupt officials. Those of ʿAbd-al-Majīd, entitled *Khaṭṭ-i Sharīf* (the noble rescript) of Gül-Khāné (1839), and *Khaṭṭ-i Humāyūn* (imperial rescript, 1856), aimed at removing the disabilities under which the raya laboured, guaranteeing the lives, property and honour of all subjects irrespective of creed and race, abolishing the farming out of taxes and considering all people of whatever tongue or millet equal before the law. But no effective implementation was provided for these *tanẓīmāt* (reform regulations), which were, moreover, premature.[4] Powerful conservative theologians opposed them, foreigners who enjoyed extra-territoriality did not like them and even Jewish and Christian money-changers (sing. *ṣarrāf*) objected to the features involving non-farming out of

[1] Lammens, *Syrie*, vol. ii, p. 62.

[2] *Relazioni*, p. 121.

[3] See above, p. 572.

[4] For Turkish text consult Luṭfi, *Ta'rīkh* (Constantinople, 1303), vol. vi, pp. 61-64; Enver Z. Karal, *Osmanli Tarihi*, V, *Nizam-i Cedit ve Tanzimat Devirleri* (Ankara, 1947), pp. 266-72; for French see de Testa, vol. v, pp. 140-43, 132-7.

taxes. The reforming attempts of Salīm, who had not been immured as had his predecessors,[1] cost him his throne. His second successor Maḥmūd, greatest among modern sultans, rendered a national service when, on a memorable day of June 1826, he ordered the guns trained on the barracks where the Janissaries were mustered and wholly destroyed them. It was this Maḥmūd who adopted the fez (*ṭarbūsh*) as a headgear and, interestingly enough, was called the *giaur* [2] sultan by his subjects.

Abortive constitutional measures

The next champion of the cause of liberalism and reform was a grand vizir, Midḥat Pasha. Midḥat began his career at the age of twenty-two as a government official in Damascus. For years thereafter he worked ardently but secretly with a few kindred souls to provide his country with a constitutional régime. The first results became apparent when Murād V issued on July 15, 1876, a proclamation in which the word for constitution [3] was used for the first time in an official document. After a three-month reign Murād became insane and was succeeded by his brother ʻAbd-al-Ḥamīd II, who on December 23 solemnly proclaimed the promulgation of a constitution and the institution of a representative parliament. The draft was proposed by Midḥat as grand vizir and modelled on the French and Belgian constitutions. The new document proclaimed that all subjects were to be known as Ottomans and be personally free and that Islam was the religion of the state. It provided for the protection of all recognized religions, guaranteed the freedom of the press within the limits of the law and established the principle of popular representation through a parliament of two chambers, one of deputies and one of senators, the deputies to be elected for four years and to represent each a constituency of 50,000. ʻAbd-al-Ḥamīd, as later events showed, aimed by the introduction of this liberal measure at warding off threatening encroachment on his sovereignty and at winning Western European sympathy, rather than at the amelioration of the

[1] His predecessor ʻAbd-al-Ḥamīd I (1774–89) refused to observe the usual practice of confining the heir apparent in a carefully guarded kiosk in the seraglio. "Seraglio" comes from It. *serraglio*, an enclosure of palisades, and was confused with Tur. *sarāy*, palace, from Per. *serāy*, building, inn.

[2] From Per. *gaur*, infidel; applied derogatorily by Turks to non-Moslems, especially Christians.

[3] Ar. *qanūn asāsi*, used again by his successor ʻAbd-al-Ḥamīd; *ʻIlmīyah Sālnāmehsi* (Constantinople, 1334), pp. 20-50.

condition of his people. In the following February he banished Midḥat and the following year he dissolved the parliament. Under pressure from England, however, Midḥat was recalled and appointed governor of Syria, soon thereafter to be banished to al-Ṭā'if in al-Ḥijāz, where he was presumably assassinated by agents of the Porte in 1883.[1]

Social and economic aspects

Neither the political nor the ethnic structure of Syria was seriously affected by the Ottoman conquest. The only radical change in the Ottoman period was incidental and involved the desert population.[2] Turks came and went as officials but there was no Turkish colonization of the land. At heart they and their Syrian subjects always remained strangers to one another A few thousand Moslem Circassians drifted into North Syria and Transjordan after the Russo-Turkish war of 1877, and several thousand Armenian refugees found haven in Lebanon after the first world war. Arabic remained the language of the people. It borrowed only a few Turkish words, mostly relating to politics, army and food.[3]

Syrian economic life underwent a steady decline for which Ottoman maladministration, however, was not entirely to blame. The Ottoman conquest of the Arab East coincided with changes in the international trade routes that left that region economically insignificant. The foundation of the prosperity of those lands, as repeatedly noted above,[4] rested on trade, especially India-to-Europe trade. The discovery in 1497 of the sea route from Europe to India around the Cape of Good Hope by the Portuguese navigator Vasco da Gama, the rounding of the southern tip of South America in 1520 by another Portuguese Ferdinand Magellan with the ensuing discovery of the Philippine Islands, the memorable westward voyage in 1492 of the Genoese Christopher Columbus which discovered America, these and related events changed the course of the great trade routes. The centre of world activity and civilization consequently shifted westward. In the inauguration of the age of exploration and discovery that therewith dawned the Arab

[1] His life was published by his son Ali Haydar Midhat Bey, London, 1903.

[2] See above, p. 483.

[3] E.g. *bāsha* (Tur. *pāsha*); *bayraq* (Tur. *bayrāq*), flag; *balṭah*, axe; *jāwīsh* (Tur. *chāwush*), sergeant; *burghul* (Tur. *bulghur*), crushed wheat; *qāwarmah* (Tur. *qāwurmah*), minced and spiced cooked meat. Certain Turkish words borrowed by Arabic were of Persian or Greek origin.

[4] Pp. 296, 353 *seq.*, 620, 639.

peoples had no share. Their ships were swept from the eastern seas by the Portuguese commander Affonso de Albuquerque, who between 1503 and 1515 gave his countrymen control over the Persian Gulf and the Indonesian trade. The Portuguese were thus able to circumvent the Mediterranean corsairs and to by-pass Arab lands, whose population belonged to a different faith and whose merchants levied high tariffs on transit merchandise. The Mediterranean, hitherto a middle sea, was no longer filling that position; it had to wait three and a half centuries, till the opening of the Suez Canal, before it could resume its place as a highway and a battlefield.

Syrian merchants had hereafter to depend more upon the overland trade. As the terminus of the route leading to Baghdād and al-Baṣrah, Aleppo began to flourish as a centre of internal trade for the empire and of international trade between Europe and Asia. It eclipsed for the time being Damascus, as the ports of Alexandretta and Tripoli eclipsed Beirut.[1] In fact it remained until the mid-seventeenth century the principal market of the entire Near East.[2] A sizable Venetian colony grew in Aleppo. Their consular reports refer to arrivals at both Aleppo and Damascus of caravans with spices from India. Spices were in special demand for preserving meat in those pre-refrigeration days.

Venetian traders in the Syrian cities and ports soon had a competitor in the French, whose earliest consulate was established in Aleppo. A French consul there in 1683 thought that the city was "the largest, most beautiful and richest in the entire Ottoman empire after Constantinople and Cairo".[3] The capitulations granted Francis I by Sulaymān in 1535 [4] laid the basis of French trade and led to French supremacy in the Levant. In 1740 Maḥmud I signed a treaty with Louis XV putting not only French pilgrims to the Holy Land but all other Christians visiting the Ottoman empire under the protection of the French flag. These concessions served as the basis of the French claim to protect all Catholic Christians of Syria.[5]

[1] On these seaports consult F. Charles-Roux, *Les Échelles de Syrie et de Palestine au XVIIe siècle* (Paris, 1928), pp. 5 *seq.*

[2] Sauvaget, *Alep*, p. 201.

[3] D'Arvieux, *Mémoires* (Paris, 1735), vol. vi, p. 411.

[4] See above, p. 668.

[5] De Testa, vol. i, pp. 186 *seq.*; F. Charles-Roux, *France et chrétiens d'orient* (Paris, [1939]), pp. 68-77.

Besides Aleppo the French had settlements (factories) in Alexandretta, al-Lādhiqīyah, Tripoli, Sidon, Acre and al-Ramlah. English merchants followed the French and both gradually replaced the Venetians and Genoese in the Syrian cities and ports. The foundation of the Levant Company in 1581 under Queen Elizabeth started the migration of English businessmen to Syria. Again Aleppo was the centre.[1] Consular reports reveal some fifty British merchants there in 1662. Shakespeare [2] cites the case of a sailor's wife whose " husband's to Aleppo gone ". The entire European colony numbered about two hundred.[3] These traders tried to satisfy the Western taste for Eastern luxuries promoted during the Crusades. Through their activity the old land routes were reactivated. The list of native products was headed by silk from Lebanon, cotton from Palestine, wool and oil. Competition with the sea traders was keen but the Portuguese insistence on high, almost monopolistic, prices gave the traders in Syria their chance.

The merchants of each nation had a khān (hostel) of their own allocated by the government. A typical khān was a two-story quadrangular structure enclosing a courtyard. The ground floor was used for the merchandise, the upper as lodging quarters for the merchants. They were mostly bachelors and wore native clothes. As a measure of safety they were not permitted out in Aleppo after sunset. Thanks to the capitulations they enjoyed the privilege of exemption from the jurisdiction of local courts. Several of these khāns are still standing. That built under Fakhr-al-Dīn II (d. 1635) in Sidon for the French is today occupied by the Sisters of St. Joseph.

No enduring benefits evidently accrued to Syria from this new development in its trade, which was largely in European hands. The population of the land continued on its downward course in wealth and in numbers. Volney,[4] who visited Aleppo in 1784 or 1785, estimates that of the three thousand two hundred taxable villages in the walāyah of Aleppo at the beginning of the Ottoman period there were only about four hundred left, which seems incredible. He did not think the city had more

[1] Alfred C. Wood, *A History of the Levant Company* (Oxford, 1935), pp. 11 *seq.*, 75 *seq.*

[2] *Macbeth*, act I, sc. 3.

[3] Grant, *Syrian Desert*, p. 93.

[4] *Voyage en Syrie et en Égypte*, 2nd ed. (Paris, 1787), vol. ii, p. 135.

than a hundred thousand inhabitants,[1] though consular reports of the late sixteenth century make its population two to four times as many.[2] A leading Turkish historian [3] states that as late as about 1740 the tax-gatherer's office in Aleppo was still greatly coveted because its holder could amass enough to buy a vizirate on his return to the capital.

On the heels of European businessmen came missionaries, teachers, travellers and explorers. The door was thus opened to modern influences, one of the most pregnant facts in the history of Ottoman Syria. The missionaries were Jesuits, Capuchins, Lazarites and members of other Catholic orders. Their activity was centred in the native Christian communities and resulted in the founding of the Uniat Churches — Syrian and Greek — in the seventeenth and eighteenth centuries.[4] Lebanon under Fakhr-al-Dīn II and his successors especially welcomed Western cultural influences.[5] In one of its villages, ʽAyn Ṭūrah, the Jesuits, who had been operating in the land since 1625,[6] established in 1734, in collaboration with the Maronites, what may be called the first important modern school. When forty years later their order was temporarily suppressed, the Lazarites occupied their posts.

Cultural aspects

Intellectually the period was one of sterility. Oppressive rule, high taxation, economic and social decline are not conducive to creative or original work in art, science or literature. The era of compilation, annotation, abridgment and imitation which had its beginnings centuries before continued with fewer and poorer productions. Throughout the Ottoman age no Syrian poet, philosopher, artist, scientist or essayist of first order made his appearance. Illiteracy was widespread, almost universal. Judges were appointed whose mastery over the written word was deficient. A few intellectuals, like the historian Naʽīma of Aleppo (*ca.* 1665–1716), were attracted to the imperial capital and fully Ottomanized.

Among the Arabic chroniclers and biographers utilized in the composition of this chapter were Aḥmad ibn-Sinān al-

[1] Volney, vol. ii, p. 139.

[2] *Relazioni*, pp. 59, 102.

[3] Jawdat, *Ta'rīkh*, vol. iii (Constantinople, 1309), p. 269.

[4] See above, pp. 520, 523. Consult *Lubnān* (Beirut, 1334), pp. 300 *seq.*

[5] See below, p. 683.

[6] For some of their early reports consult Antoine Rabbath, *Documents inédits pour servir à l'histoire du christianisme en orient*, vol. i (Paris, 1905), pp. 30 *seq.*

Qaramāni (1532–1610),[1] who was in the government service at Damascus; Najm-al-Dīn al-Ghazzi (1570–1651),[2] traditionist and professor in Damascus; and Muḥammad al-Muḥibbi (1651–1699), who also held a professorial chair in Damascus. All three were of Damascene nativity. Damascus was evidently an intellectual centre until the beginning of the eighteenth century and Aleppo a financial centre. Al-Muḥibbi was educated in Constantinople and acted for some time as assistant judge in Mecca. His principal work is a collection of twelve hundred and ninety biographies of celebrities who died in the eleventh Moslem century (1591–1688). Damascus provided the locale in which al-Maqqari of Tilimsān (d. 1632) compiled between 1628 and 1630, from material brought with him from Morocco, the voluminous work considered the chief source of information for the literary history of Spain.[3] Another Damascene of note was ʿAbd-al-Ghani al-Nābulusi (1641–1731), a Sufi and traveller, most of whose works are still unpublished.[4]

Three chroniclers cited in this chapter were Maronite Lebanese. Patriarch Isṭifān al-Duwayhi (1625–1704), when sixteen years old, went to the Maronite seminary in Rome, which was founded in 1584 by Pope Gregory XIII for training Maronite students for clerical life. Al-Amīr Ḥaydar al-Shihābi (*ca.* 1761–1835)[5] had his villa at tiny Shimlān, overlooking Beirut. Ṭannūs al-Shidyāq (d. 1859), a native of al-Ḥadath, near Beirut, and a judge under the Shihāb amīrs, compiled the annals of the feudal families of Lebanon.

The Maronite seminary in Rome afforded these Christians of Lebanon a unique educational facility. Some of the brightest among their youth were picked for training in it and either returned to their homeland to occupy high ecclesiastical positions or remained in Rome to teach and write. One of the earliest distinguished graduates was Jibrāʾīl al-Ṣahyūni (Latinized Sionita, 1577–1648), who, after teaching Syriac and Arabic in Rome, transferred to the chair of Semitic languages at the

[1] For his biography consult al-Muḥibbi, *Khulāṣat al-Athar fi Aʿyān al-Qarn al-Ḥādi-ʿAshar* (Cairo, 1284), vol. i, pp. 209-10. [2] Muḥibbi, vol. iv, pp. 189-200.

[3] *Nafḥ al-Ṭīb min Ghuṣn al-Andalus al-Raṭīb*, ed. R. Dozy *et al.*, 3 vols. (Leyden, 1855–60).

[4] *Dhakhāʾir al-Mawārīth fi al-Dalālah ʿala Mawāḍiʿ al-Ḥadīth*, 4 vols. (Cairo, 1934).

[5] On his life consult Ḥaydar, *Lubnān fi ʿAhd al-Umarāʾ al-Shihābīyīn*, ed. Asad Rustum and Fu'ād A. al-Bustāni (Beirut, 1933), vol. i, pp. v-viii.

Sorbonne in Paris. There he collaborated in the compilation of the polyglot Bible. He was succeeded in his work on the polyglot by his fellow-Lebanese, Ibrāhīm al-Ḥāqilāni (Ecchelensis, 1600–64), who had also studied at Rome and was professor of Arabic and Syriac in the college of the Propaganda there. In 1646 al-Ḥāqilāni was appointed to a chair at the Collège de France. The Paris polyglot was the first to include Syriac and Arabic versions. Another product of the Maronite seminary, and perhaps the most distinguished of them all, was Yūsuf Sam'ān al-Sam'āni (Assemani, 1687–1768), to whose efforts the Vatican library owes many of the finest manuscripts in its Oriental collection. The researches of al-Sam'āni on these manuscripts in Syriac, Arabic, Hebrew, Persian, Turkish, Ethiopic and Armenian, for the sake of which he undertook two trips to the East, were embodied in his voluminous *Bibliotheca Orientalis* (4 volumes, Rome, 1719–28), still a major source of information on the Churches of the East. In 1736 al-Sam'āni was delegated by the pope to the Maronite synod held at al-Luwayzah in Lebanon, through which the Maronites were brought into closer contact with the papal see.[1] It was the work of these Rome-educated Maronite scholars that made modern Europe for the first time fully conscious of the importance of Near Eastern languages and literatures, especially in their Christian aspects.

The printing press

The monastery of Qazḥayya in Lebanon had the privilege of being the seat of the first press in the Arab East. The press, whose origin is unknown but which was perhaps introduced from Rome by one of those Lebanese scholars, produced in 1610 the Psalms in the Syriac language and in Arabic written in Syriac characters.[2] Syriac was then still in use among Maronites as attested by travellers and resident Europeans. D'Arvieux,[3] who visited North Lebanon in 1660, reports that the bishop of Ihdin spoke perfect Arabic and Syriac. By the end of the century Syriac as a spoken language was probably dead. Volney's [4] inquiries revealed its use in only two villages in Anti-Lebanon, in one of which it is still spoken.[5]

[1] On al-Sam'āni's contribution to effect *rapprochement* between the Maronites and Rome consult Dibs, vol. ix, pp. 483-7; Rabbath, vol. i, pp. 181-2.

[2] Garshūni, see above, p. 546. Consult Louis Cheikho, "Ta'rīkh Fann al-Ṭibā'ah fi al-Mashriq", *al-Mashriq*, vol. iii (1900), pp. 251-7, 355-62.

[3] Vol. ii, p. 407. [4] Vol. i, pp. 331-2. [5] See above, p. 546.

The first Arabic press with Arabic characters in the East made its appearance in 1702 at Aleppo. Its origin too is shrouded in mystery. It followed by one hundred and eighty-eight years the Arabic press at Fano, Italy, the first of its kind in the world.[1] This Italian press owed its invention probably to papal interest and may have been the ancestor of the Aleppine press. Other establishments followed in Lebanon. Their output was mostly religious and linguistic, supplementing the work of the schools. Slowly but surely the implementation for embarking on a new cultural life was being forged.

[1] Consult Hitti, "The First Book Printing in Arabic", *The Princeton University Library Chronicle*, vol. iv (1942), pp. 5-9.

CHAPTER XLIX

THE MA'NS AND THE SHIHĀBS: LORDS OF LEBANON

THE preliminary exposure of the entire Syrian country to Western cultural influences, treated in the preceding chapter, and the emergence of Lebanon as a separate political entity, to be treated in this one, are two of the most significant developments in the Ottoman period. Around these two developments and the general misrule of the Ottoman government most of the events in the history of this entire period may be grouped.

With the Ottoman conquest the Ma'ns began to replace the Tanūkhs [1] as masters of central and southern Lebanon. To the north of them were the 'Assāfs, whose chief was confirmed by Salīm over Kisrawān with the addition of Jubayl.[2] The height of the 'Assāf power was reached under the long amīrate of Manṣūr (1522–80), whose authority extended from near Beirut to 'Arqah north of Tripoli. The 'Assāfs had their seat at Ghazīr, where some of their buildings' remains can still be seen. In 1590 the political heritage of this family passed to its rivals the banu-Sayfa (Sīfa ?) of Tripoli, who were responsible for the murder of the last 'Assāfid ruler.[3] The Sayfas were of Kurdish origin. In the case of all these feudal families the head amīr would usually parcel out the fief among subordinate amīrs, *muqaddams* (front men) or shaykhs. The Shihābs, for instance, successors of the Ma'ns, had under them in the early eighteenth century the Janbalāṭs [4] over al-Shūf, the abu-al-Lam's over al-Matn, the Talḥūqs over the Upper Gharb, the Arislāns over the Lower

[1] Some of their buildings are still standing in 'Abayh, where the shrine of al-Sayyid 'Abdullāh al-Tanūkhi (d. 1480) is frequented by Druze pilgrims.

[2] See above, p. 665.

[3] Duwayhi, p. 181; Ḥaydar, *Ta'rīkh*, p. 60; Shidyāq, p. 181.

[4] A Kurdish family from the Aleppo region whose original name was Jānbūlād; Shidyāq, p. 130. The Janbalāṭs are now Druzes and bear the honorific hereditary title of shaykh. The Shihābs bear the title of amīr; some of them are still Moslems but the majority are Maronites.

Gharb and the Khāzins over Kisrawān.[1] As for the Maronites, they had their own muqaddams, one of whose functions was to raise and transmit the tribute due the Ottoman government. Prominent among the muqaddams were those of Basharri, al-Batrūn and Jubayl.[2] As Druzes and Maronites the Lebanese were mostly subject to their own laws administered by the religious heads of their respective communities under the millet system.

That Lebanon under its local feudal lords fared better than Syria under its Turkish governors is indicated by the increase in its population through natural causes and immigration. The comparative safety and stability it enjoyed attracted Sunnites from al-Biqā' to Sāḥil 'Alma and neighbouring villages and Shī'ites from Ba'labakk to Jubayl and other places in Kisrawān. Maronites from the Tripoli district expanded southward to the foothills north of Jūniyah, and Druzes expanded northward to Brummāna and other villages in al-Matn.[3]

The struggle for power on the local and national levels, by peaceful and forceful methods, occupied no small part of the time and energy of the amīrs, muqaddams and shaykhs. At times these feudal chiefs found themselves in armed conflict with their suzerain in Constantinople. In 1584, while a convoy of Janissaries was passing through Lebanon, they were attacked and robbed of large sums of money which represented taxes from Palestine and Egypt on their way to the treasury in the capital. Enraged, the sultan sent a punitive expedition against Yūsuf Sayfa — in whose district the robbery took place — and destroyed many of his villages by fire. Then another expedition was directed against the Druzes to the south on the charge that they were the ones who perpetrated the crime. The Turkish commander — Ibrāhīm Pasha, wāli of Egypt — slaughtered five to six hundred of the Druze delegation which went to meet him at 'Ayn Ṣawfar [4] and reportedly 60,000 of the people, whom he first disarmed. The amīr of Jabal al-Durūz (mountain of the

[1] The abu-al-Lam's were raised from muqaddams to amīrs by a Shihāb governor in 1711 (Shidyāq, p. 67); originally Druzes they are now entirely Maronites. The Talḥūqs came to Lebanon from North Africa in the retinue of the Fāṭimids (cf. Shidyāq, p. 155) and are now Druze shaykhs. The Khāzins are Maronite shaykhs; Shidyāq, pp. 71 *seq.*

[2] For more on the muqaddams consult Shidyāq, pp. 217-23.

[3] Duwayhi, p. 153; Shidyāq, p. 215.

[4] Duwayhi, p. 178; Ḥaydar, *Ta'rīkh*, pp. 618-19.

Druzes, as that part of Lebanon was then called) was then Qurqumāz (Qurqumās), who in 1544 had succeeded his father Fakhr-al-Dīn I. Qurqumāz took refuge in Qal'at Nīḥa (Shaqīf Tīrūn), near Jazzīn. While there he died, perhaps poisoned by an agent of the Porte. His father before him was treacherously killed by the wāli of Damascus. Qurqumāz left a twelve-year-old son, named Fakhr-al-Dīn after his grandfather, and a widow who hid him with the Khāzins in Kisrawān.[1]

Fakhr-al-Dīn II

Young Fakhr-al-Dīn succeeded his father in 1590. Under him the Ma'nid power reached its zenith. He was undoubtedly the ablest and most fascinating figure in the history of Ottoman Lebanon if not of all Syria. He embarked on his career with three ambitions burning in his heart: building up a greater Lebanon, severing the last links between it and the Porte and setting it on the road of progress. All three no doubt represented tendencies among his people. By intermarriage, bribery, intrigue, treaties and battles — the recognized media of the day — he sought to achieve his political purposes.

After receiving from the sultan the sanjāqs of Beirut and Sidon, Fakhr moved against his neighbour Yūsuf Sayfa, whose daughter he had married, and wrested control of northern Lebanon from his hands after several engagements. The Shī'ite banu-Ḥarfūsh of Ba'labakk and the Bedouin chiefs of the Biqā' and of the region south as far as Galilee submitted to the rising lord of Lebanon. Sultan Aḥmad I was too busy fighting Hungarians and Persians to bother with a Lebanese vassal. Besides, he had in 1606 a rebel on his hands, 'Ali Jānbūlād,[2] Kurdish chief who usurped the walāyah of Aleppo. Fakhr lost no time in entering into an alliance with the Aleppo dictator According to George Sandys,[3] English traveller who visited Lebanon in 1610, the sea-coast from the Dog River to Mount Carmel and the cities of Ṣafad, Bāniyās, Tiberias and Nazareth were included in Fakhr's territory. The southward expansion brought under his command castles which since Crusading days dominated strategic roads and sites. The addition of the rich al-Biqā' increased his income enough to enable him to organize a trained, disciplined army, with a core of professional soldiers,

[1] Shidyāq, p. 81; Ma'lūf, p. 48.

[2] An ancestor of the Lebanese Janbalāṭs; see above, p. 678, n. 4.

[3] *A Relation of a Journey*, 2nd ed. (London, 1621), pp. 211-12.

to replace the old irregulars whose chances of standing against Janissaries were nil.[1] The income left was enough to employ spies in his rivals' and enemies' courts and to bribe Ottoman officials.[2]

Another source of revenue was the trade he encouraged especially with the Florentines, whose ships provided Lebanese silk, soap, olive oil, wheat and other cereals with a lucrative foreign market. In 1608 the lord of Lebanon signed with Ferdinand I, the Medici grand duke of Tuscany, whose capital Florence was, a treaty containing a secret military article clearly directed against the Porte.[3] Thereupon the sultan, prompted by his Damascus wāli Ḥāfiẓ Pasha, resolved to take action against his audacious vassal and put an end to his separatist and expansionist policy. An army was sent against him in 1613 from Damascus but could not accomplish much in the mountains. But when a fleet of sixty galleys appeared to blockade the coast, prudence dictated retirement on Fakhr's part. Three ships which happened to be at the port of Sidon carried him with one of his wives and a retinue to his friends and allies in Italy.[4] His son ʿAli, assisted by his brother Yūnus, was entrusted with the amīrate.

Fakhr remained in Europe five years (1613–18) during which he visited Leghorn, Florence, Naples, Palermo, Messina, Malta and other places of interest and became imbued with ideas which strengthened rather than weakened the earlier ones he entertained. Only one disappointment he had: his attempt to return with an expeditionary force from the European powers and the pope proved futile. While he was there the legend that the Druzes were descended from a Crusading count de Dreux was manufactured.[5]

On his return he lost no time in taking measures to regain whatever territories were lost in his absence especially to the banu-Sayfa. The death of their chief Yūsuf removed from the

[1] Muḥibbi, vol. iii, p. 267; cf. d'Arvieux, vol. i, p. 438.

[2] Cf. d'Arvieux, vol. i, p. 457.

[3] For this and other treaties with the grand dukes consult P. Paolo Carali. [Qara'li], *Fakhr ad-Dīn II e la corte di Toscana* (Rome, 1936–8), vol. i, pp. 146 *seq.*, vol. ii, p. 52; G. Mariti, *Istoria di Faccardino grand-emir dei Drusi* (Livorno, 1787), pp. 74 *seq.*

[4] Aḥmad al-Khālidi al-Ṣafadi, *Ta'rīkh al-Amīr Fakhr-al-Dīn*, ed. Asad Rustum and Fu'ād A. al-Bustāni (Beirut, 1936), pp. 17-19.

[5] Volney, vol. ii, pp. 40-41.

way his father-in-law and greatest foe. The way was open both north and south. Once again the old Lebanese state was re-established and stretched. In 1622 the Porte bestowed on him the sanjāqs of ʻAjlūn and Nābulus. Two years later it considered it expedient to recognize the *fait accompli* and acknowledge

From Giovanni Mariti, "Istoria di Faccardino grand-emir dei Drusi" (Livorno, 1787)

FAKHR-AL-DĪN AL-MAʻNI II, AMĪR OF LEBANON, 1590–1635

Fakhr lord of *ʻArabistān*, from Aleppo to the borders of Egypt. This diminutive man, whose enemies described him as so short that if an egg dropped from his pocket to the ground it wouldn't break,[1] was the only one able to maintain order, administer justice and insure regular taxes [2] for himself and the sultan.

The year after his elevation to the governorship of Syria his men engaged Muṣṭafa Pasha, wāli of Damascus, in a battle at ʻAnjar in al-Biqāʻ and captured him. But Fakhr immediately

[1] Maʻlūf, p. 211. Sandys, p. 210: "His name is Faccardine; small of stature, but great in courage and achievements: about the age of forty; subtill as a foxe, and not a little inclining to the Tyrant. He never commenced battell, nor executeth any notable designe, without the consent of his mother."

[2] Ar. colloquial *mīri*, from *al-māl al-amīri*, money due the government.

released the prisoner.[1] During the next eleven years the amīr was free to pursue the third ambition of his life — modernizing Lebanon. In his public and private projects he employed architects, irrigation engineers and agricultural experts he brought from Italy. Documents show that he invited missions from Tuscany to introduce the Lebanese farmer to improved methods of tilling the soil and made requests for cattle to improve the local breed.[2] He embellished and fortified Beirut, where he built an elaborate residence with a magnificent garden. Maundrell [3] in 1697 visited this garden in which stood several pedestals for statues " from whence it may be inferr'd, that this emir was no real mahometan ". His unfinished palace in Sidon stood opposite the khān built there for the French.[4] In this period the Capuchin mission entered Sidon and established centres in Beirut, Tripoli, Aleppo, Damascus and in certain villages of the Lebanon.[5] The Jesuits and Carmelites entered the country about the same time.[6] In the interest of agriculture he encouraged migration of Christians from North to South Lebanon. According to Volney,[7] Christian families migrated to Lebanon " daily " from Syria to escape Turkish rule. He also welcomed to Lebanon his friends the Janbalāṭs of Aleppo. He admitted into his intimacy European missionaries, merchants and consuls, all of whom enjoyed the capitulations initiated by Sulaymān. Consular reports show he protected European merchants in Sidon against pirates.[8] Throughout his career he had for counsellors Maronites, first among whom was abu-Nādir al-Khāzin, who also commanded his troops. He raised the status of this family, which had protected and reared him as an orphan, from that of commoners to that of shaykhs by once addressing its head in a letter " dear brother " (*al-akh al-'azīz*) — such was the protocol of the day.[9] Under the hereditary governorship of Kisrawān by this family, Kisrawān became a

[1] Ma'lūf, p. 232; cf. Duwayhi, pp. 198-9.

[2] Carali, vol. ii, p. 52.

[3] P. 54. The ascription by Volney, vol. ii, p. 172 of the planting of the pine grove outside of Beirut to Fakhr is erroneous, as the grove has stood there since the Crusades. He very likely reforested the place.

[4] See above, p. 673. The ancestral seat of the Ma'ns was in Ba'aqlīn; their remains survive there and in neighbouring Dayr al-Qamar.

[5] Consult Rabbath, vol. ii, pp. 464-72.

[6] See above, p. 674; Duwayhi, p. 203.

[7] Vol. ii, p. 68.

[8] *Relazioni*, p. 163.

[9] Ma'lūf, p. 71.

flourishing Christian district.[1] For a time he had the distinguished scholar al-Ḥāqilāni [2] as agent in Italy. Through him he deposited money in a Florentine bank which his descendants a century later tried, through the aid of the other scholar al-Samʿāni, to recover, but in vain.[3]

Fakhr's sympathetic attitude toward the Christians made some ascribe Christianity to him. According to Sandys,[4] "he was never knowne to pray, nor ever seen in a Mosque". D'Arvieux [5] thought that the amīr had the religion of his people, "who had no religion". It is likely that he and the other Maʿns professed Islam before the Ottoman authorities and the outside world and practised Druzism with their people. A document claims that in 1633 he was baptized by a Capuchin father who was his physician.[6]

The amīr's social and economic programme did not make him neglect the military needs of his realm. The revenue from the increased trade, especially from the seaports of Tripoli and Sidon, sufficed for both demands. The cultivation of mulberry trees was then flourishing. The annual income of his amīrate was estimated at nine hundred thousand gold pounds, of which forty-three thousand went to the imperial treasury. With up-to-date material from Tuscany he equipped an army of forty to a hundred thousand, mostly Maronites and Druzes, and renovated some of the old castles. A castle crowning a hill in Tadmur still bears his name. This increased scale of armament, his negotiations with Europeans and his sympathy with Christianity attracted once more the suspicious eye of the sultan to him. In 1633 Murād IV ordered his wāli in Damascus, Kūchūk Aḥmad Pasha, to march against Fakhr-al-Dīn at the head of a vast army mustered from Anatolia and Egypt. Meantime a fleet under Jaʿfar Pasha began to operate against the coastal castles and ports. Fakhr-al-Dīn's subordinates, the Sayfas, Ḥarfūshes and Yamanites, began to desert him. His gallant son ʿAli, who held Ṣafad, fell in battle at Wādi al-Taym at the

[1] Shidyāq, p. 85.

[2] See above, p. 676; Carali, vol. i, pp. 402-3.

[3] Carali, vol. ii, pp. 315-18, 378-88.

[4] P. 210.

[5] Vol. i, p. 367.

[6] Carali, vol. ii, pp. 640 *seq.* A cross is said to have been found in his clothes at his death; Maʿlūf, p. 275; cf. F. Wüstenfeld, *Fachr ed-Dīn der Drusenfürst und seine Zeitgenossen* (Göttingen, 1886), pp. 167-8.

foot of Mount Hermon.[1] The amīr's requests for aid from his Italian allies went unheeded. For months he hid in Qal'at Nīḥa and then in an almost inaccessible cave in the mountain outside of Jazzīn, where he was at last discovered and led in chains with three of his sons to Constantinople (about February 10, 1635).[2] Eloquence, which once saved his grandfather's amīrate,[3] saved his neck — but only for a short time. Pleaded he before the sultan:

> Verily I am a misunderstood man. No troops did I ever muster except by order of your vizirs and representatives; no castles did I build except for the defence of the realm; and no men did I kill except those who rebelled against the Ottoman state. I captured the rebels' fortresses only to deliver them to the Ottoman government. Moreover I insured the safety of the pilgrims' road [to Mecca] against Bedouin aggression; I delivered the taxes to the imperial treasury at the times they were due; and I enforced the noble Islamic law [*sharī'ah*] with strict adherence to its ordinances and regulations.[4]

The banished amīr lived on borrowed time until news was received by the Porte that his relatives and followers were not obeying the new authority established. On April 13, 1635, he was beheaded with three of his sons who accompanied him and his body was exhibited for three days in a mosque.[5] The independent greater Lebanon of which he dreamed and which he successfully initiated was again attempted by a successor of his, al-Amīr Bashīr al-Shihābi,[6] but was not fully realized until 1943.

Period of anarchy

Lebanon entered upon a period of anarchy following the removal of Fakhr-al-Dīn from the political scene. 'Ali 'Alam-al-Dīn,[7] whom Kūchūk Aḥmad in the name of the sultan appointed over southern Lebanon, followed a partisan policy, confiscated the Ma'ns' property and persecuted them. In the course of a dinner to which he was invited at 'Abayh, he had his men fall upon his hosts, the Tanūkhs, and slaughter them. Those who were not there were pursued until the entire family was exterminated.[8] The opposition was headed by

[1] Muḥibbi, vol. i, p. 386.
[2] Duwayhi, pp. 204-5; Shidyāq, pp. 330-35; Ma'lūf, pp. 272-82; Carali, vol. ii, pp. 340-56.
[3] See above, pp. 665-6.
[4] Ma'lūf, p. 273; cf. Shidyāq, p. 336.
[5] Carali, vol. ii, pp. 355-6.
[6] See below, pp. 691 *seq.*
[7] Originally Tanūkhs, the 'Alam-al-Dīns headed the Yamanite faction and were therefore opposed to their Qaysite kinsmen; Shidyāq, p. 114.
[8] Ḥaydar, *Ta'rīkh*, p. 719; Shidyāq, pp. 114-15.

Mulḥim son of Yūnus and nephew of Fakhr-al-Dīn,[1] who for years contested the control of the region and succeeded in regaining a precarious hold under suspicious Ottoman supervision. The régime was continued under Mulḥim's son Aḥmad, who in 1697 died childless. The Maʿn family thereby became extinct.

The Shihābs succeed the Maʿns

At a national conference held at al-Sumqānīyah, near Baʿaqlīn, the Lebanese notables elected al-Amīr Bashīr al-Shihābi of Rāshayya as their governor (*ḥākim*), and communicated their decision to the wāli of Sidon with the assurance that they would pay through him the taxes, some of which were evidently still due Aḥmad.[2] Evidently the Lebanese spirit of home rule was not entirely dead. Turkey, herself in danger of being destroyed by European powers, was content so long as the taxes were guaranteed.

The Shihābs now entered upon the political heritage of the Maʿns. They held the reins of government until 1841, using the old techniques: bribing Ottoman officials, rising against weak sultans, playing one chief or one party against another and thus maintaining their hold on the mountain. They never adopted the Druze creed of their people, although their Druze people may have so considered some of them. Centuries of tight-rope walking made Lebanese politicians adept in the practice of dissimulation.

On representations from Ḥusayn, a young son of Fakhr-al-Dīn who had been taken to Constantinople, Ottomanized and sent as ambassador to India, Bashīr[3] was made regent pending the attainment of majority by al-Amīr Ḥaydar al-Shihābi of Ḥāṣbayya, son of Aḥmad Maʿn's daughter. Ḥaydar's amīrate (1707–

[1] Genealogical tree of the Maʿn family:

1. Fakhr-al-Dīn I (d. 1544)
|
2. Qurqumāz (Qurqumās, 1544–85)
|
3. Fakhr-al-Dīn II (1590–1635) — Yūnus
Yūnus
|
4. Mulḥim (1635–57)
|
5. Aḥmad (d. 1697)

[2] Ḥaydar, *Lubnān*, pp. 3-4; Shidyāq, pp. 358-9; Maʿlūf, p. 401.

[3] Usually referred to as Bashīr I to distinguish him from his illustrious successor Bashīr II; see below, p. 691.

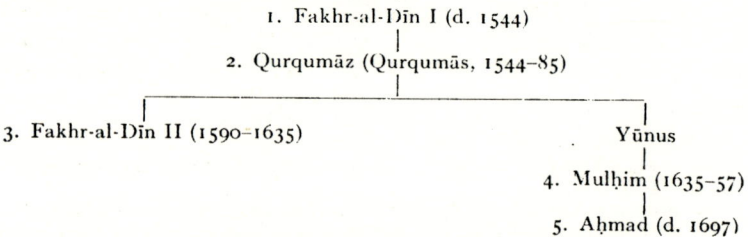

1732) was signalized by the utter destruction of the Yamanite party at the battle of 'Ayn Dārah in 1711.[1] Some members of the defeated faction migrated to Ḥawrān, where they laid the basis of a new Druze community.[2] The unpopular 'Alam-al-Dīns were tracked down and exterminated. For the valour they displayed in this battle the abu-al-Lam's were made amīrs.[3] With the Yamanite power crushed, Ḥaydar was free to reorganize the feudal system with his partisans — Janbalāṭs, abu-al-Lam's and al-Khāzins — at the helm. The Yamanite Arislāns he made share their district with the Talḥūqs.[4] His son and successor Mulḥim (1732–54) added al-Biqā' and Beirut [5] to his domain but kept his residence at Dayr al-Qamar. This made him clash with the 'Aẓm wālis of Sidon and Damascus.[6]

After the crushing of the Yamanites a new alignment in Lebanese party politics resulted in two factions: Janbalāṭi and Yazbaki. The Janbalāṭs had then become one of the most powerful and wealthy Druze families. The Yazbakis received their name from a leader of the 'Imād family, which was also Druze and came originally from the Mawṣil district.[7] The alignment went beyond the aristocracy and involved the Maronites. The feud which began in the last decades of the eighteenth century lingered until the first decades of the twentieth. Mulḥim abdicated in 1754 and his two brothers contested the amīrate after him. One, Manṣūr, leaned toward the Janbalāṭs; the other, Aḥmad, favoured the Yazbakis. Aḥmad was the father of the historian Ḥaydar, repeatedly cited in this chapter. The period of civil disturbance lasted until Yūsuf, son of Mulḥim, attained majority and succeeded to the amīrate.[8] At a national assembly held at al-Bārūk in 1770 Manṣūr announced that he was tired of the affairs of the state and ready to abdicate in favour of his nephew Yūsuf, who was thereupon proclaimed governor of the mountain.[9] The wāli of Damascus was notified accordingly. The district over which Yūsuf ruled extended from Tripoli to Sidon.

[1] Shidyāq, pp. 364-5. [2] See above, p. 43. [3] See above, p. 679, n. 1.
[4] See above, p. 679, n. 1. [5] Ḥaydar, *Lubnān*, pp. 37, 40.
[6] See above, p. 665. [7] Shidyāq, p. 162.
[8] Sa'd al-Khūri, a Maronite from Rashmayya and member of a family that has given the Republic of Lebanon two of its presidents, was his guardian; Ḥaydar, p. 783; Shidyāq, p. 377. Yūsuf raised the family rank to that of shaykh; Ḥaydar, *Ta'rīkh*, p. 849.
[9] Ḥaydar, *Ta'rīkh*, p. 807; Shidyāq, pp. 386-7.

Al-Shaykh Ẓāhir al-ʻUmar

By this time two other persons were on the scene to share the limelight with the Shihābi amīr: Ẓāhir al-ʻUmar and Aḥmad al-Jazzār. With their rise Palestine begins to compete with Lebanon for a front place in the historical parade. Aleppo and Damascus keep in the background. The urban and country population in and around these two cities must have been low in number and in morale.

A Bedouin whose father was made by Bashīr I shaykh under the governor of the Ṣafad district, young Ẓāhir al [Āl]-ʻUmar, entered the political arena about 1737 by adding Tiberias to his Ṣafad domain.[1] With the aid of the Shīʻites of Upper Galilee, who were especially oppressed by Turkish officials and ready to follow any leader who promised relief, Ẓāhir resolved to rid the region of its rulers. Nābulus and Nazareth submitted. Acre was the next large prize that fell into his hands (1750).[2] The city had been partly in ruins since Crusading days and the usurper fortified it, made it his residence and used it for exporting silk, cotton, wheat and other Palestinian products to foreign markets. A benevolent dictator, Ẓāhir stamped out lawlessness, encouraged agriculture and assumed a tolerant attitude toward his Christian subjects. His biographer[3] reports on the testimony of an eye-witness that as Ẓāhir was once passing on horseback by the Virgin Mary's church in Nazareth, he alighted, knelt and vowed to keep an oil lamp burning in the church in case of victory. "Even a woman could travel around carrying gold in her hand without fear of being molested by anyone."[4] His financial obligations to the Ottoman government he regularly met, for he realized that to the government it made no great difference who the agent was, Turk or Arab, so long as the cash was forthcoming.

At this time Turkey was embroiled in a bitter struggle with Russia under Catherine and its prestige throughout the East was at a low ebb. In Egypt ʻAli Bey dared defy the sultan and send his agent abu-al-Dhahab[5] to seize Damascus and other

[1] Volney, vol. ii, p. 85; Shidyāq, p. 360; Ḥaydar, *Ta'rīkh*, p. 801; Mikhā'īl N. al-Ṣabbāgh (al-ʻAkkāwi), *Ta'rīkh al-Shaykh Ẓāhir al-ʻUmar al-Zaydāni*, ed. Qusṭanṭīn al-Bāsha (Ḥarīṣa), pp. 31-3 (where the dates are not accurate).

[2] Volney, vol. ii, p. 89; Ṣabbāgh, pp. 41-4.

[3] Ṣabbāgh, p. 48.

[4] Ṣabbāgh, p. 50.

[5] A slave of ʻAli, abu-al-Dhahab (the father of gold) was so generous with the distribution of gifts that he acquired this epithet; Jabarti, vol. i, p. 417.

Syrian towns which he did in 1771. Ẓāhir had entered into alliance with 'Ali, whose aim was to resuscitate the old Mamlūk rule. With the co-operation of a Russian fleet which bombarded Sidon, Ẓāhir occupied this city in 1772.[1] The Russians also bombarded Beirut and plundered it. Yūsuf Shihāb allied himself with the wāli of Damascus against the new upstart. A squadron was sent from Constantinople to lend its aid. With the co-operation of the land forces it seized Sidon in 1775 and blockaded Ẓāhir in his strongly fortified capital. Turkish bullets proved ineffective against Acre's walls but Turkish gold had its effect upon its garrison, bringing about Ẓāhir's death. In the Syrian army which tried to defend Sidon against Ẓāhir was one Aḥmad al-Jazzār, before whose adventures those of Ẓāhir pale.

Aḥmad Pasha al-Jazzār

A Christian Bosnian by birth, Aḥmad committed a sex crime when a boy, fled to Constantinople, sold himself to a Jewish slave dealer and landed in the possession of 'Ali Bey in Cairo. His master used him as an executioner. The technique he developed and the delight he took in his work earned him the surname of *al-jazzār* (the butcher), a surname in which he ever thereafter took pride and which he successfully endeavoured to live up to. From Egypt he fled to Syria, where for the military service he rendered against Ẓāhir he was rewarded with the governorship of Sidon.[2] For a short time he held Beirut but refused to acknowledge the authority of Yūsuf. Beirut's population then, according to Volney,[3] who passed through it, was only about six thousand.

Al-Jazzār extended his authority southward and succeeded Ẓāhir in Acre. He further fortified the city by forced labour from neighbouring villages, built a small fleet, organized a cavalry corps of eight hundred Bosnians and Albanians and an infantry corps of some one thousand Maghribis. The partial monopoly he exercised over the trade of his district enabled him to defray all necessary expenses and live in luxury. The large mosque he built in Acre is still standing. His ambition carried him beyond the confines of Palestine and the littoral of Lebanon. In 1780 he received a firman making him wāli over Damascus. For almost a quarter of a century after that he ruled as virtual

[1] Ṣabbāgh, p. 115; Shidyāq, p. 389; Ḥaydar, *Lubnān*, p. 93.
[2] Ḥaydar, *Ta'rīkh*, pp. 811, 827.
[3] Vol. ii, p. 170.

viceroy of Syria and arbiter of Lebanese affairs. No major setback marred his career, ended in 1804 by natural death, a rather unique record in the Syrian annals of the period. The Turks had their hands full with a new and powerful internal enemy, the Wahhābis of Arabia, and that was part of the explanation.

The high-water mark in al-Jazzār's career was attained in 1799, when he checked the advance of Napoleon. The French

From F. B. Spilsbury, "Picturesque Scenery in the Holy Land and Syria" (London, 1803)

AḤMAD PASHA AL-JAZZĀR OF ACRE CONDEMNING A CRIMINAL

invader had conquered Egypt and marched triumphantly along the Palestinian coast until he reached the gates of al-Jazzār's capital. With the aid of the English fleet under Sir Sidney Smith, al-Jazzār successfully defended Acre from March 21 to May 20, when Napoleon was forced to retreat with an army decimated by plague. French inscriptions can still be read on tombstones marking soldiers' burials on Mount Carmel.

A usurper dictator, the lord of Acre ruthlessly cut down his enemies and rivals, crushed the Shīʿite and Bedouin partisans of his predecessor and on the whole terrorized Syria and Lebanon. His name still lives there as a synonym of cruelty. A native chronicler, Mushāqah,[1] reports that his grandfather, an official in the government, witnessed one day more than forty outside the city wall arrayed for execution by impalement. The last four were spared on the intercession of this official. The same author reports that once when al-Jazzār's suspicions were aroused against his harem, he had all thirty-seven of them dragged, one after the other, to a burning pyre by his eunuchs.[2] In Lebanon he pitted one party against another, patronized the Janbalāṭs and, following a battle in Qabb Ilyās in 1788 in which Yūsuf was routed, requested the people to elect Bashīr al-Shihābi.[3] Yūsuf was hanged in the prison of Acre.[4]

Bashīr's position as governor-general of Lebanon was at **Bashīr II**
first precarious. The sons of his predecessor, Yūsuf, were actively conspiring against him and his patron al-Jazzār was turning against him for failing to support him in the struggle against Napoleon. Forced to retire, he fled in 1799 to Egypt on one of Sidney Smith's ships.[5] The British then became his friends.

[1] Mīkhā'īl Mushāqah, *Mashhad al-'Ayān bi-Ḥawādith Sūrīya wa-Lubnān*, ed. Mulḥim K. 'Abduh and Andarāwus H. Shakhāshīri (Cairo, 1908). A valuable but poorly edited source.

[2] Mushāqah, p. 54.

[3] Genealogical tree of the Shihābs:

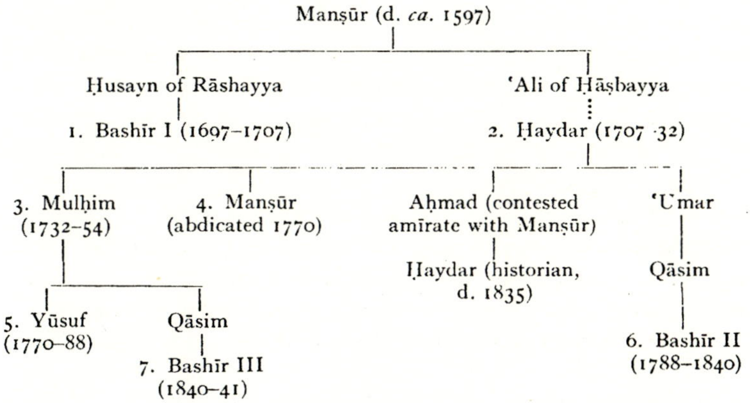

[4] Consult Ḥaydar, *Ta'rīkh*, p. 856; Mushāqah, p. 46; Shidyāq, pp. 419-20, 427.

[5] Ḥaydar, *Lubnān*, pp. 201 *seq.*

After a few months' absence he returned to crush his domestic foes and consolidate his domain. Yūsuf's sons were blinded before they were punished by death. Al-Biqā' was re-attached to Lebanon, the desires of the Damascus wāli notwithstanding. His policy toward the Turks was now one of firmness and friendliness. Early in 1810, when the Wahhābis of Najd, emerging from the desert, burst through the Syrian frontier and were threatening 'Ajlūn and southern Ḥawrān, Bashīr was there with 15,000 Lebanese to help drive them back.[1] At the head of his victorious men he paid Damascus a visit. He was no longer a local chieftain but was playing a part in Syrian affairs and in disputes between rival wālis of Damascus and Tripoli. This, however, forced another period of exile on him (1821–2), which he spent again in Egypt.[2] There he struck up a significant friendship with Muḥammad 'Ali, viceroy of the country and founder of its royal family.

When a few years later Muḥammad 'Ali launched his campaign against Turkey through Syria, Bashīr cast his lot with him. The Egyptian viceroy had expected—by way of compensation for the services he had rendered his Turkish suzerain on the battlefield of Greece in the war of its people for independence, and the battlefield of Arabia where the Wahhābis were crushed—at least the addition of Syria to his vice-royalty. But his expectation was not fulfilled. Lebanese troops stood side by side with the Egyptians in the siege of Acre in 1831.[3] Thanks to Bashīr's co-operation the task of Ibrāhīm Pasha, son of Muḥammad 'Ali and commander of the Egyptian expedition, was rendered comparatively easy. Ibrāhīm captured Damascus, routed the Turkish army at Ḥimṣ, crossed the Taurus and struck into the heart of the land of the Turks. He came close to administering the final blow to the "sick man of Europe". He was then forced to withdraw by England, Austria and Russia. In Syria his régime was ended in 1840. Muḥammad 'Ali's ambition to establish an Arab empire with himself at its head turned out to be a daydream. As yet there was no foundation in the consciousness of the people for such a state.[4] It was eighty-five

[1] Ḥaydar, *Lubnān*, pp. 556-7.

[2] Ḥaydar, *Lubnān*, pp. 724-8.

[3] Mushāqah, p. 101; Shidyāq, pp. 567-8; Ḥaydar, *Lubnān*, pp. 832 *seq.*

[4] Cf. Asad J. Rustum, *The Royal Archives of Egypt and the Origins of the Egyptian Expedition to Syria* (Beirut, 1936), pp. 47 *seq.*, 83 *seq.*

years before another potentate entertained such ambitious schemes. This was al-Sharīf Ḥusayn of Mecca, whose attempt was equally premature.

On the expulsion of Ibrāhīm the Turks called Bashīr to account. A British ship took him early in the autumn of 1840 to Malta.[1]

The exile in Malta was allowed to transfer to Constantinople, where he died in 1850. His remains were translated in

From Dussaud, Deschamps and Seyrig, "La Syrie" (Paul Geuthner, Paris)

THE PALACE OF AL-AMĪR BASHĪR II, BAYT AL-DĪN

Built in 1811, in the Arab style of the preceding centuries, this palace is now a museum

October 1947 to the grounds of the princely palace he erected in his days of glory at Bayt al-Dīn. No other such picturesque and sumptuous villa exists in the mountain. Water Bashīr brought to it in a nine-mile aqueduct from 'Ayn Zaḥaltah, whose spring is fed by snow and rain falling on a cedar-covered hill. The Lebanon of Bashīr prospered no less than that of Fakhr-al-Dīn. Bashīr built roads, renovated bridges and set

[1] Mushāqah, pp. 132-4; Shidyāq, pp. 620-21.

Beirut on its way to becoming what it is today, the gateway of Lebanon and Syria. The city was avoided by the Ma'ns and Shihābs partly because of its exposure to piratical and other hostile attacks. Fakhr and Bashīr fought not only for an independent but also for a greater Lebanon, one that would embrace with the mountain the coastal towns and the eastern plain. Both encouraged foreign trade relations. Both welcomed political refugees and religious minorities. Bashīr offered refuge to a number of Druze families from Aleppo and to Greek Catholics. In contrast to his unprepossessing Ma'nid predecessor, the Shihābi had pronounced physical features. His eagle eyes, tiger face and wavy beard inspired awe and reverence. He was doubtless a Christian but did not consider it *politique* to profess his faith. His father was the first Shihābi to forsake Islam in favour of Maronitism. If Fakhr-al-Dīn was the first modern Lebanese, Bashīr was the second. In the Ma'nid tradition the Shihābi opened the door still wider to Western cultural, particularly educational, influences. To his people he is known as Bashīr al-Kabīr (the great), a name that has become legendary in their mountain saga. Anecdotes extolling his equity, sternness, wisdom and ability are still told and retold around fireplaces.

In 1840 another Bashīr,[1] who had taken part in the rising of the Lebanese against Ibrāhīm Pasha when he tried to disarm and overtax them,[2] and who had co-operated with the Ottomans and the British in expelling him, was appointed governor of Lebanon. The Ottomans, who were carrying out a policy of centralization initiated by Maḥmūd the reformer, were now convinced more than ever that the only way of keeping the mountain under control was to sow the seeds of discord and stir up strife between its Christian and Druze population. Hitherto, as noted above,[3] the alignment in the mountain ran across the denominations and arrayed Qaysites against Yamanites, or Yazbaki against Janbalāṭi. The civil strife between Christians and Druzes thus engendered began in 1841 and culminated in the massacre of 1860, which brought about European inter-

[1] See above, p. 691, n. 3.

[2] For the rebels' manifesto consult Fīlīb and Farīd al-Khāzin, *Majmū'at al-Muḥarrarāt al-Siyāsīyah*, vol. i (Jūniyah, 1910), pp. 3-5.

[3] P. 687.

vention.[1] A French army occupied Lebanon for about a year. The estimated number of Christians massacred in 1860 is 11,000, and of those who perished by destitution 4000.[2]

An internationally recognized autonomous Lebanon

By the organic statute of 1861, revised in 1864, an autonomous system of government was allowed the mountain under a Christian governor-general (*mutaṣarrif*) of the Catholic faith designated by the Porte and approved by the signatory powers.[3] This chief executive was appointed for a renewable term of five years and assisted by an elective administration council of twelve representatives from the different religious communities. Sub-governors (sing. *qā'im-maqām*) administered the seven districts into which the new province, Mutaṣarrifīyat Jabal Lubnān, was divided after being stripped of Beirut, Sidon, Wādi al-Taym and eastern al-Biqā'. The government maintained its own judiciary and preserved order by a local militia. No Turkish troops were quartered in it, no tribute was sent to Constantinople and no military service was required of its citizens.

This autonomous Mount Lebanon, though stripped of certain strategic areas that lay within its natural boundary, entered upon an era of relative tranquillity and prosperity that was hardly matched in any other province of the empire. New roads were opened, high villages were converted into summer resorts and a narrow-gauge railway was constructed connecting Beirut with Damascus. The handicap under which its people had through the ages laboured, difficulty of internal communication, which was partly responsible for their political failure to form a united state, was being slowly overcome. Summer resorts capitalized on the beauty nature generously lavished on the mountain. The scantiness of its natural resources found part compensation in the facilities it enjoyed for overseas trade, and the poverty of its soil served to stimulate its sons, as it did their ancestors, to become the principal traders and colonists of the Levant. The saying became current: Happy is he who possesses even a goat's enclosure in the Lebanon. The increasing

[1] William Miller, *The Ottoman Empire and its Successors, 1801–1927* (Cambridge, 1936), pp. 300-303; J. F. Scheltema, *The Lebanon in Turmoil* (New Haven, 1920), is a rather inaccurate translation of a good Arabic source.

[2] Colonel Churchill, *The Druzes and the Maronites under the Turkish Rule from 1840 to 1860* (London, 1862), p. 219; cf. Khāzin, vol. ii, p. 99.

[3] To the representatives of France, England, Russia, Prussia and Austria, who signed the 1861 statute, the representative of Italy was added in 1864.

prosperity was reflected in overpopulation, especially among the Christian elements, which sought relief through emigration. The fertility of the women of the mountain was in striking contrast with the barrenness of its soil.[1] Beginning with the eighties of the last century, Lebanese emigrants have sought new abodes for themselves and their families in Egypt, America, Australia and other parts of the civilized world. In the United States alone it is estimated that no less than a quarter of a million are of Lebanese descent.[2]

The series of mutaṣarrifs opened with an especially able man, Dā'ūd Pasha, who restored to the Lebanon a part of its lost territory, established for the Druzes a school in 'Abayh that still bears his name and struggled against the feudal lords in the south and the clerical party in the north. The latter was led by Yūsuf Karam, who after a number of military engagements was banished to Italy, where he died. The second successor of Dā'ūd, Rustem Pasha, subsequently ambassador in London, was an equally firm and economical administrator.[3] The privileged position enjoyed by Lebanon was abolished by the Turks in the first world war. Its charter served as a model for Crete and on the whole it was " the most successful example of autonomy applied to a Turkish province ".[4]

[1] Miller, p. 300.

[2] Cf. *Arabic-Speaking Americans* (Institute of Arab American Affairs) (New York, 1946), p. 4; Philip K. Hitti, *The Syrians in America* (New York, 1924), pp. 62-5. In America the Lebanese are still generally known as Syrians.

[3] List of mutaṣarrifs: Dā'ūd (1861–8), Franco, Naṣri (1868–73), Rustem (1873–83), Wāṣa (1883–92), Na''ūm (1892–1902), Muẓaffar (1902–7), Franco, Joseph (1907–12), Koyoumjian, Ohannes (1912–15). Of these Dā'ūd and Koyoumjian were of Armenian, Franco and Rustem of Italian, Wāṣa of Albanian and Muẓaffar of Polish origins.

[4] Miller, p. 306.

CHAPTER L

THE CONTEMPORARY SCENE

THE contemporary period in the life of the Arab East as exemplified by Syria and Lebanon is distinguished by the emergence and operation of potent forces that involve and relate to Western penetration and imperialism, the rise of local nationalism, the struggle for independence and the inception and spread of the Pan-Arab movement. These forces are dynamic and interactive. They are responsible for the most significant happenings of the last century and a half.

Political penetration

The nineteenth century opened with three major European powers competing for preponderant influence in a shrinking Ottoman empire that had been on the defensive for about a century. These were France, Russia and Great Britain. Austria had somewhat retreated; Prussia was still a second-rate power; Italy was non-existent. France's interest rested on economic considerations, a policy of prestige, the time-honoured capitulations and the traditional friendly relations with the Catholic and Maronite minorities. Especially significant were the capitulations of 1740 which placed all pilgrims to the Holy Land under French protection.[1]

The humiliating defeat administered by Russia to Turkey and signalized by the treaty of Kuchuk Kainarji (1774) practically substituted Russian influence for French. Russian interest dates from the days of Peter the Great and Catherine[2] and stems from the country's landlocked position and consequent desire to seek warm water seaports and from her professed sympathy with the Greek Orthodox community. The treaty of Kuchuk Kainarji recognized the czars as the protectors of that community. Conflicting claims on the part of France and Russia for the protection of the holy places was one of the causes of the Crimean War (1854–6). England, not a territorial neighbour of Turkey, had since the sixteenth century developed special

[1] See above, pp. 667-8.

[2] See above, pp. 688-9.

interest because of her overland trade relations with India and the Far East, as well as the Near East.[1] With the beginning of the disintegration of the Ottoman empire England's interest transcended commercialism into imperialism; she neither wanted to see Turkey dismembered nor wished Russia installed on the Bosphorus. It was this rivalry between the great powers that gave Turkey a new lease of life and insured her prolonged existence. The so-called Near Eastern question was in the last analysis the problem of expanding at the expense of the Ottoman empire and filling up the vacuum created by the gradual disappearance of this once mighty power.[2]

Before the close of the nineteenth century a new Western power had begun to loom on the Ottoman horizon: Germany. Her *Drang nach Osten* policy, initiated by Kaiser Wilhelm, soon gave her the ascendancy in Turkish Affairs. This was the time of ʻAbd-al-Ḥamīd II (1876–1909), one of the most reactionary rulers to ascend the throne of ʻUthmān. In the Kaiser the sultan found a new and welcome friend. The German emperor and empress visited Constantinople in 1898 and proceeded to Jerusalem and Damascus, where he laid a wreath at the tomb of Ṣalāḥ-al-Dīn. In a fiery speech he assured the sultan and with him "the three hundred million Moslems who revere him as the caliph" that the German emperor was, and would remain at all times, their friend.[3] Subsequently the concession for the Baghdād railway, bisecting North Syria, was given to a German company.[4] Thus was Berlin to be connected with Baghdād. This railway was one of the factors leading to the first world war. Meantime German officers were sent to reorganize the Ottoman army.

The Ḥamīdian régime

The point of departure in ʻAbd-al-Ḥamīd's policy was that the state should be more Asiatic than European. By way of implementation he resorted to an antiquated institution, the caliphate, which he tried to revivify. In the hope of retaining the loyalty of the non-Turkish Moslem elements in the empire and winning over all Moslems outside its boundaries, he tried

[1] See above, p. 673; M. V. Seton-Williams, *Britain and the Arab States* (London, 1948), pp. 1-5, 101 *seq.*

[2] Miller, p. 1.

[3] George Antonius, *The Arab Awakening* (Philadelphia, 1939), p. 77.

[4] Edward Mead Earle, *Turkey, the Great Powers and the Bagdad Railway* (New York, 1923), pp. 67-71.

to assert the earlier political power of the caliphate with its ideal of Pan-Islam. Gradually he succeeded in reducing his ministers to the position of secretaries and in concentrating the administration of the realm in his own hands. He put the press under strict censorship, abolished whatever measure there was of freedom of speech and spread an elaborate system of delation and espionage over the whole empire. In constant fear for his throne and life, he withdrew more and more into a life of seclusion behind the walls of his Yildiz palace. Wholesale arrests and executions coupled with the massacre of the Armenians won him the title of the " red sultan ".

In pursuance of his Pan-Islamic policy the sultan-caliph completed in 1908 the Ḥijāz railway, which connected Constantinople with Medina, passing through Syria from north to south, at a cost of £3,000,000, a third of which was raised by voluntary contributions from Moslems all over the world. It was this al-Ḥijāz railway whose bridges Lawrence helped to blow up in the first world war.[1] The engineers were Germans and the official in charge was a Syrian, Aḥmad 'Izzat Pasha, the sultan's private secretary. Another Syrian, abu-al-Huda al-Ṣayyādi, exercised a strange influence over the caliph as his imām.

After thirty years of dictatorial reign 'Abd-al-Ḥamīd awoke one July day in 1908 to find himself helpless in the face of a revolution led by officers in his own army. This was the work of the Committee of Union and Progress, the striking arm of a secretly organized society known as the Young Turks. The Young Turks were successors of the Young Ottomans, to whom Midḥat [2] belonged. The society had its inception at Geneva in 1891 through the activity of youthful reformers and students and was later moved to Paris. Its aim was to achieve a constitution of the Western type with an elective parliament and to break down the barriers of the millet system, thereby bringing about a homogeneous democratic state. On July 24, 1908, 'Abd-al-Ḥamīd reluctantly announced the restoration of the constitution of 1876 [3] and the following day ordered the abolition of espionage and censorship and the release of all political

[1] T. E. Lawrence, *Seven Pillars of Wisdom* (New York, 1938), pp. 198-203, 207-11.

[2] See above, pp. 670-71.

[3] See above, p. 671.

prisoners. On December 10 he opened the parliament with a flourish and declared in a speech from the throne that the earlier parliament was only temporarily suspended pending the adequate preparation, through education, of the citizenry. Meantime a wave of optimism and enthusiasm had engulfed the entire nation. In Beirut, Damascus, Aleppo, Jerusalem and other towns of the empire the proclamation of the constitution was hailed with bonfires, orations and fireworks. The nightmare, it was believed, was gone. A new day had dawned. "Turkey, it appeared, had been converted overnight into a Utopia."[1] But 'Abd-al-Ḥamīd had no more intention of preserving the constitution of 1908 than that of 1876. Caught intriguing with the reactionaries and staging a counter-revolution in April 1909, he was replaced by his doddering brother, Muḥammad Rashād. Authority remained in the hands of the committee.

Union and Progress

The new régime had more patriotic zeal than experience or political sagacity. Its policy of Ottomanization — reducing all racial and religious elements in the state into a common Ottoman denominator — was bound to fail. The Arabs interpreted the new *ḥurrīyah* (liberty) to mean freedom to realize their own national aspirations and to promote their own cultural individuality including language. Soon separatist movements began to assert their claims. With the failure of Ottomanization the Young Turks turned to the discredited Ḥamīdian policy of Pan-Islam. Domestic troubles were aggravated by international complications culminating in the war with Italy (1911–12), which caused Turkey the loss of Tripoli and Cyrenaica, her last foothold in Africa, and in the Balkan wars (1912–13), which stripped Turkey of almost the last vestiges of her suzerainty in that area. With all that the triumvirate of Enver, Ṭal'at and Jemāl was unable to cope. In the world war that ensued Turkey cast her lot with the Central Powers and her performance in the struggle demonstrated the utter failure of Ottomanism and the bankruptcy of Pan-Islam. It led to the emergence of a new Turkey, a national Turkey less hampered by religious and ethnic complications. The architect of this state was a member of the Young Turks party, an officer who had participated in

[1] Harry Luke, *The Making of Modern Turkey* (London, 1936), p. 144.

their revolution. His name was Muṣṭafa Kemāl. His were the only thoroughgoing reforms that reached the masses.

Cultural penetration

Of all the eastern provinces of the empire Lebanon was the one least affected by the disabilities imposed by the Ḥamīdian régime. The measure of self-government it enjoyed after 1861 safeguarded the continued flow of ideas and other cultural elements from Western sources, a flow that had its beginnings in the earliest days and that was reinforced by Fakhr-al-Dīn and Bashīr.[1] The military occupation of Syria by Ibrāhīm Pasha (1831–40),[2] whose father was the first to establish vital contacts between Egypt and the West, opened the Syrian door wider for Western cultural influences. Ibrāhīm removed certain disabilities relating to dress and mounts under which the Christians in Syria had been labouring for ages.[3] It was then that the Jesuit order returned to Lebanon after a period of suspension[4] and American missionary enterprise found a firm lodging. In 1948 the Protestant Church of Syria celebrated its hundredth anniversary. In 1834 the American Press was established in Beirut. The Imprimerie Catholique of the Jesuits followed nineteen years later. Both presses are still going concerns. Translations of the Bible into modern Arabic were issued by both establishments. Jesuit educational activity, which was inaugurated in the early seventeenth century,[5] culminated in the founding in 1874 of the Université Saint-Joseph in Beirut, where the American mission had established in 1866 a college now known as the American University of Beirut. These two universities remain the leading institutions of learning in that part of the world. Native schools, presses, newspapers, magazines and literary societies began to flourish. Translations from French and English became numerous and popular.[6] Of all the new ideas thus imported nationalism and political democracy were unquestionably the most potent, the most dynamic.

Nationalism and the struggle for independence

The Arab nationalist awakening had its inception as a purely intellectual movement centring on the study of the Arabic language, history and literature. Its pioneers were mostly Syrian intellectuals, more specifically Christian Lebanese

[1] See above, pp. 683, 693-4. [2] See above, p. 692.
[3] See above, pp. 542-5, 587-8. [4] See above, p. 674. [5] See above, p. 674.
[6] A. H. Hourani, *Syria and Lebanon* (Oxford, 1946), pp. 35-7.

educated at the American University of Beirut.[1] In their hands classical Arabic began to be moulded into a new instrument capable of expressing modern thought. The concept of nationalism, with its stress on secularism and material values, ran counter to the most cherished ideals and traditions of Islam, which at least in theory recognizes no bond other than that of religion. The adoption of nationalism of the latter-day type by the Arabic-speaking peoples and the insurrection of the Sharīf of Mecca, Ḥusayn, in 1916 against the Ottoman Turks shattered any remaining hopes of Pan-Islamic unity and substituted for it Pan-Arab unity, one based on language and secular culture rather than on religion. Lebanon's response to Western Christian stimuli was accelerated by the migration of thousands of its sons to the New World,[2] whence by their writings and return visits they kept the flame of liberty, independence and democracy burning. The Arab congress held in Paris in 1913 was called by Shukri Ghānim, brother of the Syrian deputy to the 1876 Constantinople parliament, and had a preponderantly Syrian membership. Its demands were moderate, including decentralization with administrative and cultural autonomy.

The Syrian intellectuals and champions of Arab nationalism found in neighbouring Egypt a more congenial atmosphere for their activity. Receiving its stimuli mainly from American ideology, the movement drew its inspiration from the past glory and cultural achievements of the Arabic-speaking peoples and looked forward to a consolidated Arab world. It started from a wide base, general Arabism of the non-provincial type. Soon, however, it suffered fragmentation. As the political aspects developed, they became diversified and localized. Egyptian nationalist aspirations parted company with Pan-Arabism in the early 'eighties, when opposition to British occupation became their chief immediate concern. Arab nationalism in Egypt thus asssumed regional colouring to be able more effectively to arouse local public opinion in its drive against the British. In Syria Arab nationalism concentrated its force against Ottoman domination and Turkification and, after the institution of the French mandate in 1919, on opposition to French rule. It

[1] Antonius, pp. 43, 51-5; Hans Kohn, *A History of Nationalism in the East* (London, 1929), pp. 268 *seq.*; Martin Hartmann, *The Arabic Press of Egypt* (London, 1899), pp. 3-13.

[2] See above, p. 696.

acquired fresh strength from the blood of patriots executed by Jemāl Pasha in the course of the first world war.[1] In Palestine, the southern part of Syria amputated and mandated to Great Britain, Arab nationalism was nourished throughout by hostility to the British and to Zionism — which in 1948 eventualized in the birth of Israel — as an intruding nationalist movement of Central and Western European Jews.

In 1921 Transjordan, with a biblical name but no real historical existence, was in turn amputated from Palestine and placed under the Amīr ʻAbdullāh, since 1946 king, who was then threatening to avenge the loss of the Syrian throne temporarily occupied by his brother Fayṣal, later king of al-ʻIrāq.[2] The new amīrate served a good purpose as a buffer state between the British mandated territory and the restless Bedouins of the desert. In 1949 it became the Hāshimite Kingdom of the Jordan.

The fragmentation of nascent Arab nationalism ran parallel to the fragmentation of the Arab territory which, until the first world war, was united under Ottoman rule. Between the first and second world wars the many Arabic-speaking lands of the Ottoman empire fell apart and developed into different states and quasi-nations. Community of language, religion and economic interest, however, operated to bring them together again. After 1940 the movement toward Pan-Arabism was again reactivated and intensified, eventuating in the creation of the Arab League. Reaction against political Zionism as a disruptive, expansive force contributed to this result. Both Syria and Lebanon have been members of the League since its organization in 1945.

Democracy

With the urge for nationalist assertion and the spread of education went an increased desire for more democratic practices in social and political life. Discontent among the farming class provided fertile soil for the reception and germination of new democratic ideas. In the mid-nineteenth century the feudal organization of the two leading Lebanese communities was beginning to show signs of breaking down. But the structure of the Druze feudalism proved to be more substantial than that

[1] For their number and reasons for condemnation consult *La Vérité sur la question syrienne* (Commandement de la IVème armée) (Constantinople, 1916), pp. 158-68.

[2] Hans Kohn, *Nationalism and Imperialism in the Hither East* (London, (1932), pp. 162-4, 177-8; Antonius, pp. 304-5.

of the Maronite; it has survived in a weakened form till the present day. In Syria, too, the feudal organization has not entirely disappeared. In northern Lebanon an agrarian insurrection against the Khāzins [1] and other feudal lords was in full swing when the civil war with the Druzes broke out.[2] Its leader was a farrier from Rayfūn named Ṭāniyūs Shāhīn, who in 1859 succeeded in forming a peasant commonwealth with himself at its head.[3] The Maronite clergy, recruited mostly from the common people, espoused the popular cause. When Dā'ūd Pasha assumed the governorship of the mountain the democratic section of the Maronite community withheld the payment of taxes to a foreigner who was favoured by the local aristocracy. The Maronites had demanded a native governor-general. Yūsuf Karam was the hero of the insurrection.[4] With the winning of the fight against the French for independence the Syrians and Lebanese adopted on a larger scale than ever before Western democratic concepts and institutions and adapted them to their particular needs. Lebanon was first among the Arabic-speaking states to institute a republican form of government. Syria followed. The Republic of Lebanon was fully achieved and generally recognized in 1943; that of Syria two years later.

The exposure of Syria, Lebanon and Palestine in the course of the nineteenth century to fresh economic, scientific and political ideas was more intensive and continuous than that of the seventeenth.[5] It partook more of the character of the exposure of the entire Arab world many centuries earlier to European cultural influences of the Greek variety.[6] In the contemporary period, too, the process of cross-fertilization was general; it embraced the entire Near East, in fact practically all Asia and Africa. Once more the people of the eastern Mediterranean became oriented westward as in Phoenician, Roman and Byzantine days. The resultant conflict between the traditional, static, religious point of view and the modern, scientific, secular point of view was felt most in Moslem communities. Nor was the conflict limited to the higher levels. The entire area, like most other parts of the nineteenth century

[1] See above, pp. 683-4. [2] See above, pp. 694-5.
[3] Anṭūn D. al-'Aqīqi, *Thawrah wa-Fitnah fi Lubnān* (Beirut, 1938), pp. 83-90.
[4] See above, p. 696. [5] See above, p. 683.
[6] Discussed above, pp. 548 *seq.*

SYRIA AND LEBANON ON THE EVE OF THE SECOND WORLD WAR

With Adjoining Countries

world, was enmeshed in the economic net spread by the industrialization of Western Europe. Native handmade products competed at a decided disadvantage with imported wholesale machine-produced goods, resulting in the dislocation of the local economy.

It was this impact of Western Europe upon the Arab East in the nineteenth century that gave the East the shock that fully awakened it from its medieval slumber. With the awakening the Middle Ages of Syria and Lebanon draw to an end and the dawn of the modern era breaks. The entire period has been one of transition. The emergence of nationalism as a dominant force in the life of the people, the adoption of political democracy, the trend toward secularization and modernization — all these constitute a new chapter in the history of Lebanon and Syria. The definitive history of that chapter is still to be written.

INDEX

Titles of books, as well as Arabic and other Semitic words and technical terms occurring in the text, in italics. Main references indicated in heavy type.

When in the text reference is made to a book for the first time, the title in full — including author, edition (if any), place and date of publication — is given in the footnotes and then indexed. Thereafter, the title is given in an abridged form unless the author's life is sketched and the book is cited again, in which case the title is given in full and indexed for the second time. Books printed in Moslem presses often bear the *hijrah* date, which began A.D. 622.

In pronouncing Arabic words the accent generally falls on the long vowel bearing the macron (–); the ' stands for a glottal stop; the ' for a deep guttural that has no correspondent in English; such dotted letters as *ṣ* and *ṭ* are emphatically sounded; *aw* and *ay* are diphthongs.

The author's thanks are due to Mrs. R. Bayly Winder and Mr. Richard W. Downar, who assisted in the compilation of this index.

Abāḍites, 402. *See also* Ibāḍites
Abana, 41, 472. *See also* Barada
Abāqa, 632
'Abar Nahara, 220
'Abayh, 696
'Abbās, al-Saffāḥ, abu-al-, 530, 531, 532, **534** *seq.*
'Abbāsid: caliphate, 4; cavalry, 532, 543; régime, 535; era, 546; misrule, 669
'Abbāsids, **529** *seq.*
'abd, 488
Abd-Ashirta, 71, 72, 155
'Abd-al-Ḥakam, ibn-, *Futūḥ Miṣr*, 427 n. 2
'Abd-al-Ḥamīd II, **670-71**, 698-700
'Abd-al-Ḥamīd al-Kātib, 493
Abd-Khiba, 161
'Abd-al-Laṭīf Ḥamzah, *al-Ḥarakah al-Fikrīyah*, 655 n. 1
'Abd-al-Majīd I, 669
'Abd-al-Malik, Umayyad: 449, 462, 473; dinars of, 474; tutor under, 496
Abd-Melkarth, 142
'Abd-Rabbihi, ibn-, *al-'Iqd*, 404 n. 4
'Abd-al-Raḥmān I, 515, 532-3
'Abd-al-Raḥmān ibn-'Abdullāh al-Ghāfiqi, 468-9
'Abd-al-Raḥmān ibn-al-Ash'ath, 458
'Abdullāh, son of Ḥusayn, 703
'Abdullāh ibn-'Ali, **531-2**, 540
'Abdullāh al-Ḥusayn al-Shī'i, abu-, 577. *See also* Shī'i, abu-'Abdullāh al-Ḥusayn, al-
'Abdullāh ibn-Maymūn al-Qaddāḥ, 578. *See also* Qaddāḥ, 'Abdullāh ibn-Maymūn, al-
'Abdullāh ibn-al-Zubayr, **451-3**
Abel, F.-M., *Géographie de la Palestine*, 38 n. 4
Abgar, 247, 282, 517
Abgars, the, 308
Abi-Milki, 74
'Abīd ('Ubayd?) ibn-Sharyah, 479, **492-3**
Abraham, 60, 68
Absha, 76
Abulustayn, 443
Abūṣīr, 127
Abydos, in Asia Minor, 446, 447
Abydos, in Egypt, 28, 137
Abyssinian: language, 62
Acheulean: culture, 7 n. 1
Acre: 31, 253; reached by Tigranes, 249; shipyards in, 426, 489; walls of, 689. *See also* 'Akka
Actium, 283
Adad, 77, 172. *See also* Hadad
Adad-nirari I, 152, 162
Adana, 657
Addu, 172. *See also* Hadad
Adhanah, 442
Ādharbayjān, 429, 477
'Adhrā', 414
Adhruḥ, 410, 432
'Āḍid, al-, Fāṭimid, 600
'Ādil, al-: 620, 628; concessions by, 639. *See also* Malik al-'Ādil, al-
'Ādilīyah, 645
'Adlūn: caves of, 9
Adonis, 117, 256
Adonis-Ishtar, 19
Adrianople, 662
Adrianus, rhetorician, 321
Aegean: 247; area, 180
Aelia Capitolina, 340. *See also* Jerusalem

Aelius Gallus, 378
Aemelius, of Apamea, 324, 399
Afāmiyah, 239, 521. *See also* Apamea
'Affūlah, 26
Afghanistan, 458
Afqah, 117 n. 3, 121
Africa: 5; peoples of, 4; northern, 64; sailing around, 100; colonies in, 102; west coast of, 107
African: elephants, 265
Aftakīn, 579
Aga-Oglu, Mehmet, *Persian Bookbindings*, 518 n. 4
Agenor, 103, 105
Aghāni, al-, 405, 444, 479, 480, 505, **569-70**
Aghlabid: dynasty, 145
'Agli-bōl, 400
Agrippa I, 309
Agrippa II, 309
Ahab, 38, 140, 166, 167, **192**
Ahaz, 196
'ahd, 422
Aḥīqār, 168, 226
Aḥīrām: inscription, 112, 113; sarcophagus of, 125; throne of, 205
ahl al-bayt, 537
ahl al-dhimmah, 422. *See also dhimmis*
ahl al-kitāb, 420, 485
Aḥmad I, 680
Aḥmad 'Izzat, 699
Aḥmad al-Jazzār, 688. *See also* Jazzār, Aḥmad, al-
Aḥmad ibn-Ṭūlūn, 557. *See also* Ṭūlūn, ibn-
Ahmed Issa, *Histoire des bimaristans*, 642 n. 6
Ahmose I, 149
Ahrūn, 497
Ahur Mazda, 224
Ai, 179
Aila, 190, 383, 410. *See also* Ezion-geber
'Ā'ishah, daughter of Muḥammad, 431
'Ajlūn, 682, 692
Ajnādayn, 414
Akhbār Majmū'ah, 464 n. 1
Akhlamu, 162, 163
Akhṭal, al-, 439, 440, **494**
'Akka: 31, 81 n. 6, 91; fortified, 559; capitulates, 596; consuls in, 620. *See also* Acre
Akkadian: 61, 67; cuneiform, 113; words, 138; dynasty, 147. *See also* Assyro-Babylonian
Akkadians, 62. *See also* Babylonians
'Akkans, 604
Akko, 81. *See also* 'Akka
Alalakh, 114, 152. *See also* Tell al-'Aṭshānah
'Alam-al-Dīns, 687
Alamoundaros, 403. *See also* Mundhir, al-, Ghassānid
Alamūt, 631
Albania, 106
Albanians, 689
Albright, William F., *From Stone Age to Christianity*, 21 n. 3; *Archaeology and the Religion of Israel*, 99 n. 3
Albuquerque, Affonso de, 672
Alburz Mt., 610
āleph, 110
Aleppo: 31, 68, 155, 156, 158, 253; earthquake in, 41; as a trade route, 138; Great Mosque of, 511; capital, **564-6**; citadel of, 646; consulate in, 672; business centre, 673. *See also* Ḥalab
Alexander I Balas, 256
Alexander II Zabinas, 256
Alexander the Great: 5, 57, 60, 84, **231** *seq.*; conquest of, 106, 125, 144, 228, 369; "sarcophagus of", 235; successors of, 264
Alexander Jannaeus, 246, 377
Alexander Severus, 308, **344-5**
Alexandretta, 31, 32, 232, 672
Alexandria: foundation of, 233; siege of, 244; museum of, 258
Alexandrian: coins, 394
Alexandros of Palmyra, 390
Alexius Comnenus, 591
'Ali, abu-, 37 n. 2. *See also* Qādīsha River
'Ali, Orthodox caliph: 428, **429-34**; Mashhad of, 433
'Ali, son of Fakhr-al-Dīn II, 681
'Ali, Sufyāni, 541
'Ali Bey, of Egypt, 688-9
'Ali Ibrāhīm Ḥasan, *Dirāsāt fi Ta'rīkh*, 637 n. 2
'Ali Jānbūlād, 680
'Ali-Ilāhis, 586
'Alid: rulers, 435; opposition, 436; doctrines, 503, 561
'Alids: 430, 453, **529** *seq.*, 537; subsidy for, 438
Aliyan Baal, 115, 116, 117, **118**, 120, 122, 329
'Allāqah, 580
Allath, 401

Allāt, 385
Allenby, 60, 134
Alp Arslān, 573
Alpharabius, 570. *See also* Fārābi, al-
Alpine: 26; type, 146
Alps, 107
Amanus: 31, 60, 82, 139, 448; cedars from, 138
'Amawās, 424 n. 2. *See also* 'Amwās
Amaziah, king of Judah, 386
Ambroise, *Crusade of Richard*, 603 n. 5
Amelikites, 28
Amenemhab, 130, 131
Amenemhet III, 127, 128
Amenhotep II, 152
Amenhotep III, 71, 72, 150, 152
Amenhotep IV, 72, 132, 150, 152
America, 696
American: influence, 5; mission, 701
American Press of Beirut, 701
American University of Beirut: 701, 702; Museum, 13
'āmil, 477
amīr, 477
amīr [al-baḥr], 426 n. 5
amīr al-mu'minīn, 451
'Āmir ibn-Sharāḥīl al-Sha'bi, 491-2
Amki, 71. *See also* 'Amq, al-
'Ammān: 253 n. 1; honey of, 571
'Ammār, banu-, 592, 597
'Ammār, ibn-, 594
Ammianus Marcellus, **356**, 357
Ammon, country: 144, 187; kingdom, 179; deities of, 191; pays tribute, 196; envoys from, 199
Ammon, deity, 233
Ammonites, 186, 198
'Ammūriyah, 446, 553. *See also* Amorium
Amon, deity, 131, 133, 134
Amon-Re, 131
Amorion, 446. *See also* Amorium
Amorite: 66; language, 62, 77; dynasties, 68; land, 70; state, 71; term, 75; physiognomy, 76; religion, 77; institutions, 78; ceramics, 87; names, 149
Amorites: 37, 64, **65** *seq.*, 75, 123; Central Syrian, 74; high places of, 78
Amoritic, 65, 67
Amorium, 446
Amos, **213**, 215
'Amq, al-, 39
'Amr ibn-al-'Āṣ: 60, 411, 412, 435; arbiter, 432
'Amrīt, 65. *See also* Marathus
Āmu Darya, 458 n. 5. *See also* Oxus
Amurru, country: 65, 71, 156; sea of, 139
Amurru, deity, 77
'Amwās: 424; plague of, 425
Amyūn, 521
Anat, 119, 120, 329
'Anat-har, 149
Anat-Ishtar, 120
Anatolia: eastern, 154; climate of, 443
Anatolian: people, 154
Anbāṭ, 547
Ancient East: 188; trade of, 388
Ancyra, 395. *See also* Ankara
Andalus, al-, 555
Andrae, Tor, *Mohammed*, 524 n. 5
'Anjar, 166, 253, 682. *See also* Chalcis, in Coele-Syria
Ankara, 154, 395. *See also* Ancyra
Anṣār, 453
Anṭākiyah, 424. *See also* Antioch
Antaradus, 83, 609 n. 1. *See also* Tortosa
'Antarah, 624
Anṭarṭūs: 594, 609, 611; Our Lady in, 617, 618
Ante-Nicene Fathers, 336
Anti-Lebanon: 34, **41-2**, 60, 289; settlement in, 47; crests of, 47; villages in, 546
Anti-Taurus, 443
Antigonus, 237, 255, 376
Anṭilyās: 13; caves of, 12
Antioch: 31, 267, **302-7**, 449; earthquakes in, 40; founded, 237, **251** *seq.*; library in, 258; camp in, 264; mint in, 267; people of, 268; population of, 278; lilies of, 295; chalk in, 296; armament factories in, 296; troupes from, 302; musicians of, 310; Church of, 335; intellectual capital, 357; Christian city, 373; earthquakes of, 373; sacked by Persians, 373; sack of, 392; theology from, 523; reduced, 549; principality, 592-3, 597; fall of, 608
Antiochian: coins, 394
Antiochians, 254, 305
Antiochus I, 264
Antiochus III, 108, **241-3**, 264, 265, 266, 268, 272
Antiochus IV Epiphanes: 198, 247, 252, 253, 264, 277, 283; coin of, 243
Antiochus VII Sidetes, 263
Antiochus VIII Grypus, 263
Antiochus X Eusebes, 249

Antiochus XIII Asiaticus, 249
Antiochus of Ascalon, 255-6
Antipater, Maccabean, 283
Antipater, Macedonian general, 237
Antipater, Tyrian philosopher, 323
Antipater of Hierapolis, 321, 322
Antipater of Sidon, 259-60
Antoninus Pius, 302, 311
Antonius, George, *Arab Awakening*, 698 n. 3
ʿ*anwatan*, 414
Apamea: 252, 264, 267, 293, **307**, 521; depot for war elephants, 239, 265; wine of, 296. *See also* Afāmiyah
Aphrodite, 119, 173, 256
Aphrodite-Astarte, 136
Apocrypha, 257
Apollinaris, bishop, 371
Apollo: 106, 273, 295, 303; in Daphne, 254; statue of, 427
Apollodorus, engineer, 354
Apophis I, 149
Apostles, 336, 365
Apostolic Fathers, 336
Appian, 267
ʿAqabah, al-, 39, 383 n. 2, 388. *See also* Elath
ʿAqīqi, Anṭūn D., al-, *Thawrah*, 704 n. 3
Aqṣa Mosque, **513**
Aquitania, 347
Arab: world, 4; administration, 422; armada, 446, 447; prisoners, 448; coinage, 457; science, 497; caliphate, 662; empire, 692; congress, 702; nationalism, 703-4
Aʿrāb, 547
Arab Academy of Damascus, 583
Arab East, 697, 706
Arab League, 703
Arab Moslem: civilization, 420
Arab Museum at Cairo, 650
ʿArab-Shāh, ibn-, ʿ*Ajāʾib al-Maqdūr*, 655 n. 6
ʿArabah, al-, 39, 190. *See also* Wādi al-ʿArabah
ʿArabi, ibn-, **652**
ʿArabi, ibn-, *al-Futuḥāt*, 652 n. 5; *al-Isrāʾ*, 652 n. 6
Arabia: 241; horse introduced into, 52; camel in, 52; cradle of Semites, 62; exodus from, 64; spices from, 99, 353; Christians in, 333
Arabia Felix, 270, 308, 378. *See also* Yaman, al-
Arabia Petraea, 382
Arabian: horse, 52; peninsula, 62; myrrh, 106; cavalry, 265; merchandise, 270; products, 271; soldiers, 424; philosophy, 490; medicine, 490; aristocracy, 535
Arabian Desert, 31, 34, 43
Arabian Moslems, 420, 485, 530, 548
Arabian Nights, 615, 625. *See also The Thousand and One Nights*
Arabians: 59, 64; distinguished from Arabs, 62 n. 1
Arabic: tongue, 4; colloquial, 18; literature, 28; language, 61, 62, 64, 443; writings, 103; alphabet, 384; replaces other languages, 473; books, 490; Bedouin, 496; writing, 526; conquest of, 545-6; Syro-Lebanese, 547; press, 677; -speaking peoples, 702; -speaking lands, 703
Arabism, 702
ʿ*Arabistān*, 682
Arabs: 4; plants introduced by, 47
Aradians, 83
Aradus: 82, 83, 84, 130, 238; coin of, 227, 231; surrenders, 232; mint in, 267; caravans from, 271. *See also* Arwād
Aragon, 466
Aral Sea, 472
Aram, 58
Aram Damascus, **164**, 168
Aram Naharaim, 164
Aramaean: invaders, 139; states, 164; culture, 164; merchants, 168; deities, 191
Aramaean-Phoenician: culture, 226
Aramaean Syria, 254
Aramaeans: 4, 58, 64, 97, **162** *seq.*; borrow alphabet, 110
Aramaic: -speaking peoples, 59; language, 61, 62, 162, 164, **168-70**; alphabet, 169; inscriptions, 169; official language, 220; persistence, 256-7; literature, 257; tongue, 288; lingua franca, 384; loan words from, 525
Aramaic Syria, 256
arbāb al-aqlām, 637
arbāb al-suyūf, 637
Arbela: battle of, 234
Arberry, Arthur, J., *Introduction to the History of Ṣūfism*, 651 n. 2
Arcadius, 351, 357
Archelaus, 284
Archigenes, 321
Archimedes, 552
Ardata, 74
Aretas, 377

Arethusa, 252. *See also* Rastan, al-
Arian Christianity, 468
Arianism, 350, 371
Arislān, family, 545
Arislān, Shakīb, ed., *Maḥāsin al-Masā'i*, 545 n. 2
Arislāns, 678
Aristobulus, 246
Aristotle: 237, 356; philosophic works of, 548, 550
Arius, 357, 358
arizz, 618
Ark, the, 203
Arka, 82, 344. *See also* 'Arqah
Armalah, Isḥāq, *al-Malakīyūn*, 523 n. 2
Armenia: 282, 462, 520, 539; province of, 477
Armenian: conquests, 280
Armenian Church, 520
Armenians: 27, 96, 154, 632, 634; in Lebanon, 37; millet, 668
Armenoid, 26, 76
Arnon, 167
Arpad, 140
'Arqah, 71 n. 4, 344, 594
arqaṭ, 544
arrādah, 478
Arrapkha, 150. *See also* Kirkūk
Arsaces, 239
Arṣu, 401
Arsūf, 596
Artaxerxes, Sāsānid, 345
Artaxerxes I, 222
Artaxerxes III, 225
Arvad, 130. *See also* Aradus
Arvieux, d', 676, 684
Arvieux, d', *Mémoires*, 672 n. 3
Arwād, 71, 613. *See also* Aradus
arz al-Rabb, 51
'Āṣ, 'Amr, ibn-al-, *see* 'Amr ibn-al-'Āṣ
'Asākir, ibn-: tomb of, 624
'Asākir, ibn-, *al-Ta'rīkh*, 414 n. 1; 652 n. 10
A'ṣam, al-Ḥasan ibn-Aḥmad, al-, 579
Ascalon: 30, 82, 185; Philistine city, 181; onion of, 294; wrestlers from, 301; wines from, 353; henna from, 383. *See also* 'Asqalān
Ash'ari, abu-Mūsa, al-, 432
Ashdod: 182, 185; Philistine city, 181; envoys from, 199
Ashdodites, 185
Asherah, 119, 175
Ashira, 175. *See also* Asherah
Ashirat, 77
Ashraf, al-, Mamlūk, 612, 622
Ashraf Mūsa, al-, Ayyūbid, 629
Ashtart: 119, 136; temple of, 187
Ashtoreth, 119
Ashur, deity, 213
Ashur-bani-pal, 144
Ashur-nasir-pal, 139
'āshūrā', 450
'Āṣi, al-, 31, 39, 40. *See also* Orontes
Asia: 5; peoples of, 4
Asia Minor: 231, 239, 243; foothold in, 443
Asiatic: animals, 53
Asín, Miguel, *Islam and the Divine Comedy*, 582 n. 6
Asmā', daughter of abu-Bakr, 453
'Asqalān: 30, 82 n. 7; encounter near, 595. *See also* Ascalon
'Assāfs, 678
Assassin: sect, 60
Assassins: 592, **610-11**; Syrian branch of, 32; organization of, 616
Assemani, 676. *See also* Sam'āni, Yūsuf Sam'ān, al-
Assemani, *Bibliotheca Orientalis*, 517 n. 2
Assur, 66
Assyria, 91, 145
Assyrian: language, 62; monuments, 98; conquest, 107; inscriptions, 134; parallel, 329
Assyrians: 58, 59, 616; in Lebanon, 37
Assyro-Babylonian: 61; civilization, 144; records, 163. *See also* Akkadian
Astarte, 119, 185
Aswad al-Du'ali, al-, 491
Aswān, 170. *See also* Uswān
Atābegs, **575** *seq.*
Atargatis: 121, **173-4**, 385; temple of, 256, 313
'Athar-'atheh, 401
Athenaeus, 302
Athenaeus, *Deipnosophists*, 259 n. 3
Athenian: money, 208
Athīr, ibn-al-, 642
Athīr, ibn-al-, *al-Lubāb*, 555 n. 4
'Athlīth, 613
'Ātikah, 481
Atlantic: 457; discovery of, 109; eastern, 184
aṭlas, 619
Atsiz, 573, 574
Attic: sculpture, 227; jars, 276, 383
Attis, 160
Augustine, 463
Augustus Caesar, 282, 283, 289, 290, 332
Auranitis, 42 n. 3, 293. *See also* Ḥawrān
Aurelian, 395, 396

Aurignacian, 12, 13
Australia, 5, 696
Austria, 692, 697
Autran, C., *Phéniciens*, 79 n. 2
Avaris, 149, 178
Avidius Cassius, 292
Avignon, 469
'awāṣim, 442
awlād al-'arab, 547, 641 n. 1
Awlās, 442
Awrās Mt., 462
'awsaj, 412
Awzā'i, al-, 492, 543, **555-6**
Aya Sofya, 314. *See also* Santa Sophia
Aylah, 410. *See also* Aila
'Ayn Dārah, 687
'Ayn Jālūt, 631
'Ayn al-Tamr, 462
'Ayn Ṭūrah, 674
'Ayntāb, 334 n. 3
Ayyūb al-Anṣāri, abu-, 444
Ayyūbid: branches, 606; coins, 616
Ayyūbid-Mamlūk: age, 648, 651
Ayyūbids, 599, **627** *seq.*, 645
Azariah, 198. *See also* Uzziah
Azd, tribe, 530
Azhar, al-, 578
Aziru, 71, 72, 74, 75, 155
'Azīz, al-, Ayyūbid, 627
'Azīz, al-, Fāṭimid, 579
'Azīzu, 401
'Aẓm, Ismā'īl, al-, 665
Azraq, al-, palace, 507
Azraqis, al-, 455

bā', 476
ba'al, 115
Ba'al, 77
Baal: 105, 121, 127, 244, 310; vessels of, 201; attributes of, 204; becomes Zeus, 254
Baal, king of Tyre, 142, 144
Baal II, 202
Baal of Apamea, 307
Baal of Gaza, 347
Baal-Lebanon, 102
Baal Marqod, 347
Baal-Shamain, 174
Baal-Shamīn, 400
Baalat, 119
Baalat Gubla, 119
Ba'albak, 310. *See also* Ba'labakk
Baalism, 194, 211, 256
Baanes, 414, 415
Babylon: 220, 241, 271; Amorites in, 66; under Chaldaeans, 201; fall of, 218; prisoners carried to, 226; treasures of, 234
Babylonia: ploughs from, 17, 85
Babylonian: language, 62, 138; influence, 87; balance, 226
Babylonians, 59, 62, 65
Bacchus, 313
Bactria, 236, 247, 265. *See also* Balkh
bādiyah, 440, 496, 507, 509
Bādiyat al-'Irāq, 43. *See also* Samāwah, al-
Bādiyat al-Jazīrah, 43. *See also* Mesopotamian Desert
Bādiyat al-Sha'm, 43 n. 5. *See also* Syrian Desert
Badr: battlefield of, 433
Baedeker, *Palestine and Syria*, 247 n. 2
Baghdād: 4, 60, 539; site of, 536; railway, 698
Baghdādi, al-, *Mukhtaṣar al-Farq*, 453 n. 4; *Uṣūl al-Dīn*, 498 n. 6
Bahā'-al-Dīn, al-Muqtana, 584
Bahā'-al-Dīn ibn-Shaddād, 605
Bahā'-al-Dīn ibn-Shaddād, *Sīrat Ṣalāḥ-al-Dīn*, 602 n. 3
Bahā'is, 585
Bahā'ism, 60
Baḥrayn, al-, 477
Baḥri Mamlūks, **630-31**, 633
Bakh'ah, 546
Bakhtīshū', 550
Bakhtīshū', Jūrjīs, ibn-, 549
Bakirki, 522
Bakr, abu-, 410, 419, **428**
Baktāshi, 448
Ba'labakk: 39, 172, **310-16**; Sun temple in, 40; settlement in, 288; church in, 517. *See also* Heliopolis
Balādhuri, al-, 419, 427
Balādhuri, al-, *Futūḥ al-Buldān*, 404 n. 3; *Ansāb al-Ashrāf*, 449 n. 6
Balamand, al-, 617
balāṭ, 448 n. 2
balāṭ al-shuhadā', 469
Baldwin I, 382, 591, 592, **595-6**
Baldwin II, 597, 598
Balearic, 105, 107
Balj ibn-Bishr al-Qushayri, 533
Balkh, 236, 460. *See also* Bactria
Balmarcodes, 347. *See also* Baal Marqod
Balqā', al-, 403, 541
Baluchistan, 458
Bambyce-Hierapolis, 256
Bāniyās, in Palestine, 242 n. 2, 610. *See also* Paneas

Bar-Rakkab, 171
Barada, 41, 42, 472
Barbate River, 464
Barcelona, 105
Bardesanes, 370
Bargylus, 32. *See also* Jibāl al-Nuṣayrīyah
Barhebraeus, *Chronicon ecclesiasticum*, 549 n. 3. *See also* 'Ibri, ibn-al-
barīd, 438, 474
Barlaam, 500
barmaki, 539
Barmakids, **539**
Barqūq, 636
Barrois, A.-G., *Manuel d'archéologie*, 83 n. 1
Barsauma, bishop, 372
Barsbāy, 636
Barthold, W., *Turkestan*, 460 n. 3
Bārūk, al-, 51, 687
Bāsha, Quṣṭanṭīn, al-, *Mayāmir Thāwadūrus*, 546 n. 2
Bashan: 42 n. 3, 75, 165; oaks of, 275. *See also* Ḥawrān
Bashīr al-Shihābi I, 686
Bashīr al-Shihābi II, 685, **691-4**
Bashīr al-Shihābi III, 694
Basil the Great, 355
Basilides, 318
Baṣrah, al-: 429, 431, 436, 437; order restored in, 455; province of, 477; intellectual centre, 491
Baṣri, al-, *Futūḥ al-Sha'm*, 414 n. 1
Bassianus, 308
Batanaea, 324. *See also* Bashan
Bathanīyah, al-, 540
bāṭin, 583 n. 6
Bāṭinite, 583
Bāṭinites, 585
Baṭn al-Sirr, 412
Batrūn, al-: 12, 17, 594; bishop of, 521
Baṭṭāl, 'Abdullāh, al-, 448
Baṭṭūṭah, ibn-, *Tuḥfat al-Nuẓẓār*, 430 n. 1
Bay of Biscay, 471
bay'ah, 428, 440
Bāyazīd II, 657
Baybars: 5, **607-9, 631-2**; concessions by, 639
Bayhaqi, al-, *Ta'rīkh Ḥukamā'*, 552 n. 5
Baylān, 31. *See also* Beilan
Baysān, 26, 81 n. 4, 253, 281, 368, 414, 595. *See also* Beth-shean
Bayt al-Dīn, 603
Bayt al-Ḥikmah, 550
Bayt Jibrīn, 28, 253. *See also* Beth Gubrin and Eleutheropolis
Bayt al-Mā', 254 n. 2. *See also* Daphne
bayt al-māl, 513
Bayt Mirsim, 84
Becker, Carl H., *Islamstudien*, 524 n. 1
Bedouin: hospitality, 44
Bedouins, 44, 61, 128, 154
Beeliada, 204
Beer-sheba, 38
Beilan, 31. *See also* Baylān
Beirut: 4, 74; rainfall in, 45; temperature in, 46; coin of, 255; settlement in, 288; villages of, 487; iron in mountains of, 571; besieged, 596; cathedral of, 617; sanjāq of, 680; added, 687; population of, 689
Beirut-Damascus: railway, 42, 695
Bel: **400**; temple of, 396
Belfort, 39, 603 n. 2. *See also* Qal'at al-Shaqīf
Belisarius, general, 358, 372, 402
Belmont, 617. *See also* Balamand, al-
Beloch, Julius, *Die Bevölkerung der griechish-römischen Welt*, 279 n. 2
Belvoir, 603 n. 1. *See also* Kawkab al-Hawā'
Ben-Hadad I, 166, 170
Benedict of Peterborough, 604 n. 4
Benjamin: tribe, 191
Benjamin of Tudela, 546, 585, 640
Benjamin of Tudela, *Itinerary*, 197 n. 2
Berbers: 437, **462-4**, 475; Islamized, 438; in Spain, 533
Berchem, M. van, *Matériaux*, 648 n. 3
Bergsträsser, G., *Neuaramäische Märchen*, 546 n. 5
Beroea, 253. *See also* Aleppo
Berytus: 253, 273, 274, **308-10**; actors from, 301; law school of, **325-7, 359-62**; fabrics from, 353; earthquakes in, 361. *See also* Beirut
bēth, 110
Beth Gubrin, 28
Beth-pelet, 182
Beth-shean: 26, 81, 120, 179, 182, 187, 253, 318; temple of, 120; pole at, 121; snake worship at, 123. *See also* Baysān
Beth-shemesh: 112; ovens at, 207
Bethlehem, 621
Bevan, Edwyn R., *House of Seleucus*, 239 n. 6
Bewer, Julius A., *Literature of the Old Testament*, 212 n. 2

Bezold, C., *Tell el-Amarna Tablets*, 72 n. 3
Bible: polyglot, 676; translations of, 701
Bibliotheca Orientalis, 676
bilād al-Rūm, 426. *See also* Asia Minor
Bilqīs, 190
bīmāristān, 558 n. 4
Biqā', al-: **39-40**, 66, 127, 128, 598, 664; added, 687. *See also* Coele-Syria
Biqa'-Jordan-'Arabah, 39
Bīr al-Kāhinah, 462
Bi'r al-Sab', 38. *See also* Beer-sheba
Bīrūni, al-, *Ṣifat al-Ma'mūr*, 34 n. 5
Bisharri, 50, 679
Bithynia, in Asia Minor, 322
Björkman, Walther, *Beiträge*, 637 n. 2
Blachère, R., *Un Poète arabe*, 567 n. 4
Black Sea, 184
Black Stone, 452
Blanckenhorn, Max, *Handbuch der regionalen Geologie*, 32 n. 1
Boak, E. R., *History of Rome*, 347 n. 1
Boğazköy, 152, 154, 157
Bohemond, 593, 595
Book of the Dead, 212
Bosnians, 689
Bosphorus, 349, 444, 698
Bostra, 293. *See also* Buṣra
Bouchier, E. S., *Syria as a Roman Province*, 259 n. 3
Braidwood, Robert J., *Mounds in the Plain of Antioch*, 20 n. 4
Breasted, James H., *Ancient Times*, 91 n. 3; *Ancient Records of Egypt*, 127 n. 2; *Edwin Smith Surgical Papyrus*, 148 n. 4; *History of Egypt*, 149 n. 3
Bréhier, Louis, *Les Origines du crucifix*, 348 n. 3
Briggs, M. S., *Muhammadan Architecture*, 512 n. 2
Brissa, 201. *See also* Wādi Barissa
British, 703
British Museum, 158
Bronze Age: 23, 25; Middle, 87; Late, 87
Browne, Laurence E., *Eclipse of Christianity*, 543 n. 7
Brünnow, Rudolf E., and Domaszewski, Alfred v., *Die Provincia Arabia*, 378 n. 3
Brusa, 662
Buddha, 461
Budge, E. A. Wallis, and King, L. W., *Annals of the Kings of Assyria*, 163 n. 1
Buḥtur: family, 623
Buḥturi, al-, **554**
Buḥturi, al-, *Dīwān*, 554 n. 4; *Ḥamāsah*, 554 n. 7
Buḥturid Tanūkh, 666
Buisson, du Mesnil, du, *Inventaire des inscriptions palmyréniennes*, 400 n. 5
Bukhāra: 460, 557, 573; raided, 437
Bukhāri, al-, *al-Jāmi'*, 505 n. 1
Burckhardt, John L., *Travels*, 382 n. 3
burdah, 534
Būrids, 577 n. 1
burj, 634
Burji Mamlūks, 631, **634** *seq.*
Burrows, Millar, *What Mean these Stones*, 28 n. 3
Bursa, 662. *See also* Brusa
Bury, J. B., *History of the Later Roman Empire*, 353 n. 1; *Administrative System*, 481 n. 9
Būṣīr, Upper Egypt, 532
Busr ibn-abi Arṭāh, 427
Buṣra: 293 *n.* 4, 382, 383, 409; cathedral of, 403, 512
Buṭlān, ibn-, 581
Butler, Howard C., *Syria*, 348 n. 1; *Early Churches in Syria*, 367 n. 1
Buwayhid: overlords, 562
Buwayhids, 573
Byblus: 14, 18, 26, 34, 88, 97; alphabetic text from, 112; sacred prostitution in, 118; surrenders, 232; mysteries of, 256
Byzantine: 284; roads, 43; army, 47; fleet annihilated, 427; settlers, 463; coinage, 473; weight, 475; models, 479; castle, 510; school, 512
Byzantine empire, 489, 591, 662
Byzantine Syria, **349** *seq.*, 355, 359, 363, 561
Byzantines: autocratic, 370; hostile relations with, **442** *seq.*; attacks against the, 461
Byzantium: 349, 444; eunuch system from, 528

Cadiz, 102. *See also* Gades
Cadmus, 106, 109, 255
Caesarea, on the sea: 284, 316, 358, 359, 415; dancers from, 301; purple from, 353; reduced, 416-17; seized, 596. *See also* Qaysārīyah
Caesarea Philippi, 242 n. 2, 316. *See also* Bāniyās, in Palestine
Caetani, Leone, *Annali dell' Islām*, 403 n. 5

Cahen, Claude, *La Syrie du Nord*, 591 n. 4
Cairo: colonies in, 5; a new capital, 578; an entrepôt, 639
Caligula, 296, 302, 333
Callinicus, 445
Cambridge Ancient History, 232 n. 1
Cambyses, 224
Canaan: **79** *seq*., 153; land of, 28; kings of, 72; language of, 81; city-states of, 81-3; people of, 84; religion of, 118; imparts to Israel, 203
Canaanite: language, 61, 62; pantheon, 77; settlements, 82; houses, 83; society, 86; merchants, 88; wool, 91; captives, 93; maiden, 93; inscriptions, 112; scribes, 113; religion, 116; "high places", 120, 123; temples, 120, 123; incense stands, 121; jars, 127; names, 149; settlements, 163; cult, 191; fashions, 206; lamp, 207
Canaanites: 3, 64, **78** *seq*., 85; glass of, 91; garments of, 93; sacred pillar of, 121; chariots of, 184
Canada, 616
Cantineau, J., *Le Nabatéen*, 384 n. 3
Cape of Good Hope, 100, 671
Capuchin: mission, 683
Capuchins, 674
Caracalla: 302, 311, 322, 337, **341-3**; inscription, 134; coins of, 390
Carali, P. Paolo, *Fakhr ad-Dīn*, 681 n. 3
Carchemish: 25, 26, 131, 155, 156, 158, 163; battle of, 201; defeat at, 217. *See also* Jarābulus
Carmathians, 560. *See also* Qarmaṭians
Carmel: 60, 181; skeletons of, 11; cave, 13, 15, 19. *See also* Mt. Carmel
Carmelite: order, 626, 683
Carrhae, 282. *See also* Ḥarrān
Carthage, 95, 102, 105, **107-8**, 232, 462
Carthagena, 104, 105
Carthaginian: inscription, 104; sailors, 107
Carthaginians, 107
Cary, M., and Haarhoff, T. J., *Life and Thought in the Greek and Roman World*, 284 n. 9
Casius, 32, 82. *See also* Mt. al-Aqra'
Caspian Sea, 34, 52
Cassiterides, 103
Cassius, 282
Castrum Peregrinorum, 613. *See also* 'Athlīth
Catherine, of Russia, 688, 697
Cato, 108
Caxton, William, 644
Central Asia: 46, 60, 64, 457, 489, 632; silk route from, 271; Islam in, 460, 461
Central-Asiatic: merchandise, 270; nomads, 667
Central Syria: 26, 75, 97, 563; Amorites in, 65, 70-71; elephant in, 88
Ceuta, 464
Ceylon, 489, 518
Chabot, J.-B., *Choix d'inscriptions*, 389 n. 5
Chalcedon, 443
Chalcis, in Coele-Syria: 166, 253, 287, 378; capital, 247. *See also* 'Anjar
Chalcis ad Belum, 351, 374. *See also* Qinnasrīn
Chalcolithic: 23, 24; man, 14; Age, 23, 29; culture, 23; towns, 25; agriculture, 26
Chaldaean: Empire, 57; hegemony, **144**. *See also* Neo-Babylonian
Chaldaeans, 70, 163, 217
Chaldaeans, Uniat, 517
Charles Martel, 468, 469
Charles-Roux, F., *Les Échelles*, 672 n. 1; *France*, 672 n. 5
Château Pèlerin, 597
Chebar, 222
Cheikho, L., *al-Naṣrānīyah*, 525 n. 2
Chesney, Francis R., *Expedition for the Survey of the Euphrates*, 41 n. 4
Chiera, Edward, *Sumerian Religious Texts*, 66 n. 1
Childe, V. Gordon, *New Light*, 6 n. 1
China: 38; confines of, 4, 457, 476; wheat of, 25; silk from, 298; silkworms from, 353; missionaries to, 371; Syrian monks in, 518; frontier of, 661
Chinese: ancient civilization, 6; silk, 275, 353, 383; records, 382; magnetic needle, 620; empire, 632
Chinese Turkestan, 488
Chingīz Khān, 607
Chosroes I Anūsharwān, 372, 373, 374
Chosroes II, 409
Christ: 5, 39, **328** *seq*.; Crucifixion of, 41; Resurrection of, 41; dialogue of, 197; birth of, 284; nature of, 370; humanity of, 371; divinity of, 500
Christian: 3; hermits, 37; church of Syria, 59; assemblies, 330; sophists, 359; places of worship, 365; art,

368-9; influence, 499; anti-, 542-3; manuscript in Arabic, 546; pilgrims, 604; mystics, 651; children levied, 667; money-changers, 669; subjects, 688; elements, 696
Christian Church: in Syria, 369
Christian Lebanese, 701
Christianity: **328** *seq.*; birthplace of, 3; official religion, 350; apology for, 500
Christians: **328** *seq.*; Syriac-speaking, 548; doctrines, 561; as scribes, 572; persecution of, 587-8
Christians of St. John, 485
Christians of St. Thomas, 518
Christology, 517, 519
Christopher Columbus, 671
Chrysopolis, 447. *See also* Scutari
Chrysostom, 355, 373. *See also* John Chrysostom
Chrysostomus, Joannes, *Opera omnia*, 369 n. 2
Church of the East, 371, **517** *seq.*
Church Fathers, **335-6**
Church of the Holy Sepulchre, 350, 409, 587, 588, 617
Church of the Nativity, 366, 367
Churchill, Colonel, *Druzes*, 695 n. 2
Cicero, 255, 256, 259, 260
Cilicia: 21, 31, 189, 264, 592; ores of, 138; satraps of, 225; overrun, 249; privacy in, 280; Roman province, 281; under Ikhshīdids, 563
Cilician: Gates, 60, 231, 442; coast, 102; passes, 290
Circassians, 636, 671
Clay, Albert T., *Amurru: Empire of the Amorites*, 66 n. 3
Cleopatra, 95, 283
Clermont, 590
Coele-Syria: 39 n. 5, 64, 71, 144, 267, 287, 305; Alexander in, 234; expedition to, 243; Ituraeans in, 247; productivity of, 292; under Nabataeans, 378. *See also* Biqā', al-
Collège de France, 676
Collinet, Paul, *Histoire de l'École de Droit de Beyrouth*, 325 n. 6
Cologne, 298
Combier, Charles, *Aperçu sur les climats de la Syrie*, 47 n. 2
Committee of Union and Progress, 699-700
Commodus, 302
Companions, 492, 494
Conder, C. R., *Tell Amarna Tablets*, 72 n. 3; *Syrian Stone-Lore*, 79 n. 2
Conrad of Montferrat, 611
Constans II, 427
Constantine IV, 444
Constantine the Great, 284, **349-50**, 358
Constantinople: 462; new capital, 349; campaign against, 440; attacks on **443-8**; rendezvous, 591
Cooke, G. A., *Text-Book of North-Semitic Inscriptions*, 102 n. 3
Coon, Carleton S., *Races of Europe*, 154 n. 2
Copper Age, 23, 29
Coptic-Ethiopic Church, 520
Copts, 479, 518
Corcyra, 97
Cordova, 105, 466
Cordova Mosque, 516
Corinthian: 254; capitals, 313
Cornelius Palma, 382
Cornwall, 103
Corpus Inscriptionum Latinarum, 308 n. 10, 311 n. 3, 348 n. 2
Corpus Inscriptionum Semiticarum, 382 n. 5
Corsica, 105
Cos, 261
Council of Chalcedon, 372, 523
Council of Ephesus, 371
Council of Nicaea, 358, 371
Cowper, B. H., *Syriac Miscellanies*, 363 n. 1
Crac des Chevaliers, 594, 609. *See also* Ḥiṣn al-Akrād
Crac de Montréal, 596 n. 5
Crassus, 281, 282
Creswell, K. A. C., *Early Muslim Architecture*, 510 n. 2
Cretaceous, 34, 35, 39, 43
Cretan: ceramics, 87
Crete: 59, 97, 105, 149, 182, 445; Minoan, 28, 137
Crimea, 663
Crimean War, 697
Croesus, 217
Crowfoot, J. W., *Early Churches in Palestine*, 365 n. 4
Crowfoot, J. W., and Crowfoot, Grace M., *Early Ivories*, 192 n. 4
Crusader: churches, 617
Crusaders: 59, 591; contact with Maronites, 594
Crusades: 5, 84, **590** *seq.*; cultural achievement of, 614; effects of, 622
Crusading: castles, 32, 40; times, 53; monarchs, 559; leaders, 591; colonies, 611

Ctesiphon, 60, 282, 373, 537. *See also* Madā'in, al-
Cumont, Franz, *Les Religions orientales*, 334 n. 1; *Études syriennes*, 334 n. 3
Cyaxares, 217
Cybele, 160
Cyprian, 463
Cypriote: ceramics, 87; weapons, 88; pottery, 116
Cyprus: 114, 115, 142, 427, 445; colonies in, 102, 220; quinquereme in, 267; expedition against, 420
Cyrenaica, 107, 601, 700. *See also* Libya
Cyrrhus, 252, 292, 521. *See also* Qūrus
Cyrus, 217, 221, 234
Cyzicus, 445

dabbābah, 478
Dagon, 77, 185
Ḍaḥḥāk ibn-Qays al-Fihri, al-, 452
Ḍahr al-Qaḍīb, 32
dā'i, 577, 616
Dakhwār, ibn-al-, 643
Dalman, Gustaf, *Arbeit und Sitte*, 92 n. 1; *Petra*, 378 n. 3
Dalton, O. M., *Byzantine Art*, 354 n. 6
Damascene: caliph, 4; jewels, 620; craftsmen, 656
Damascus: 4, 26, 42, 60, 127, 167, 308, 431; water system of, 42; rainfall in, 46; region, 64, 71; inlaying in, 147; Aramaean capital, 168; Persian headquarters, 232; under Nabataeans, 247; plum tree from, 294; alabaster of, 296; armament factories in, 296; sword blades from, 353; under Nabataeans, 378; silk from, 383; pillaged, 409; surrenders, 414-15; reoccupied, 416; the glory that was, **457** *seq.*; capital, **469** *seq.*; life in, 479; canals of, 489; patriarchate in, 523; tombs in, 532; temporary capital, 542; hospital in, 642; basins from, 649; Ottoman city, 668
Damashunas, 155
Damietta, 606. *See also* Dimyāṭ
ḍammah, 476
Daniel, 116
Daphne: 106, 254, 295, **302-5**; games at, 263, 278; oracle of, 303
Dār al-Ḥadīth al-Nūrīyah, 652
Dār al-Salām, 536. *See also* Baghdād
dār al-ṣinā'ah, 426 n. 1
Darazi, al-, 584
Darb al-Ḥadath, 443
Dardanelles, 446
Darius III, **232-4**
Darius the Great, 169, 220, 231, 234
Dāthin, 411
Dā'ūd Pasha, 696, 704
David, 38, 166, 184, **187-9**, 375
dawlah, 535
Day, Alfred Ely, *Geology of Lebanon*, 32 n. 1
Daybul, al-, 461
Dayr al-Qal'ah, 347
Dayr al-Qamar, 687
Dayrāni, Afrām, al-, *al-Muḥāmāh*, 522 n. 7
Dead Sea: 23, 24, 39, 40, **41**, 190; asphalt of, 296, 383
Debevoise, Neilson C., *Political History of Parthia*, 241 n. 1
Deborah, 180
Decalogue, 210
Decameron, 615
Decapolis, 252, 281, **317-18**, 380
Delos, 273, 274, 347
Delta, 99, 102, 382
Demetrius I Soter, 269
Demetrius II Nicator, 245
Deschamps, Paul, *Le Crac*, 610 n. 1
Deuteronomy, 200
Dhahab, abu-al-, 688
Dhahabi, al-, *Duwal al-Islām*, 455 n. 3; 653 n. 5
dhimmah, 486
dhimmi, **544-5**
dhimmis, 422
dhimmis, **485** *seq.*, 587
dhurah, 17, 48
Diana, 303
Diaspora, 222, 340
Diatessaron, 369
Dib, Pierre, *L'Église maronite*, 623 n. 4
Dibon, 196
Dibs, Yūsuf, al-, *Ta'rīkh Sūrīyah*, 522 n. 7
Diehl, Charles, *Byzance*, 481 n. 9
Dietrich, Albert, *Phönizische Ortsnamen*, 104 n. 4
Dīk al-Jinn, 554-5
Dimashq, 26, 424. *See also* Damascus
Dimashqi, al-, *Nukhbat al-Dahr*, 447 n. 7; 654 n. 10
Dimyāṭ, 606
dīnār, 423 n. 2
Dīnawari, al-, *al-Akhbār al-Ṭiwāl*, 431 n. 4

Dindorf, Ludwig, *Historici Graeci minores*, 284 n. 2
Dio Cassius, 340, 342
Diocletian, 304, 308, 332, 593
Diodorus the Peripatetic, 255
Diodorus Siculus, 104, 106, 383, 386
Diogenes Laertius, 342
Diogenes Laertius, *Lives of Eminent Philosophers*, 255 n. 2
Dionysius, Seleucid official, 278
Dionysus, 109, 333
Diringer, David, *Alphabet*, 110 n. 2
dīwān, 429, 619
Dīwān, of al-Mutanabbi', 568
dīwān al-khātim, 478
Diyār Bakr, 520
Djehuti, 131
Dog River: 142; inscription at, 201
Doliche, 334. *See also* 'Ayntāb
Dome of the Rock, 189, 457, **511-13**, 632
Dominican: order, 626
Domitian, 330, 332
Dorylaeum, 448. *See also* Eski-Shehr
Dougherty, Raymond P., *Nabonidus and Belshazzar*, 218 n. 2
Druze: occupation of Ḥawrān, 42; community, 60; feudalism, 703
Druzes: 37, 121, **583-6**, 592, 622; laws of, 679
Druzism, 583, 585, 684
Dubertet, Louis, *Contributions à l'étude géologique*, 32 n. 4
Dübner, Fred., *Theophrasti Characteres*, 324 n. 1
Duchesne, André, *Historiae*, 468 n. 2
Duke Eudes, 468
Dūmat al-Jandal, 412. *See also* Jawf, al-
Dunand, 112, 113
Dunand, Maurice, *Fouilles de Byblus*, 18 n. 4
Duqāq, 574-5, 592
Dur Sharrukin, 368
Dura-Europus: **271-2, 391-2**; fresco from, 173; Aramaic in, 256; agora of, 268; earliest synagogue at, 365; church of, 368; frescoes of, 398
Dusares, 348, 385. *See also* Dūshara
Dūshara, 348, 384. *See also* Dusares
Dussaud, René, *Topographie historique de la Syrie*, 32 n. 3; *Les Arabes en Syrie*, 403 n. 3; and Frédéric Macler, *Mission dans les régions désertiques de la Syrie*, 299 n. 2; *Voyage archéologique*, 381 n. 1
Duval, Rubens, *La Littérature syriaque*, 549 n. 3
Duwayhi, al-, 522, 675
Duwayhi, al-, *Ta'rīkh al-Ṭā'ifah al-Mārūnīyah*, 521 n. 3
Dvořák, Rudolph, *Abû Firâs*, 569 n. 2

Earth Mother, 160
East: Moslem, 4; Arab, 5
East Canaanite, 77
East Roman Empire: successor state of, 535
East Semitic, 67
East Syrian Church, **517** *seq.*
Easter, 145
Ebal, 38
Ecbatana, 234. *See also* Hamadhān
Ecchelensis, 676. *See also* Ḥāqilāni, Ibrāhīm, al-
Ecclesiastes, 257
Eden, 295
Edessa: 100, 170, 253, 271, **369-70**, Arab dynasty in, 247; armament factories in, 296; seat of Christianity, 335; church in, 439; school of, 548; wrested, 576; first Latin state, 591; county of, 592. *See also* Ruhā', al-
Edessan: Church, 369
Edirne, 662. *See also* Adrianople
Edom: 41 n. 7, 179, 187, 190, 375; ore deposits of, 23; iron of, 184; pays tribute, 196; envoys from, 199
Edomites: 177, 186; revolt of, 96; driven, 247
Egypt: 7, 64, 70; cave-dwellers of, 17; pre-dynastic, 24; ploughs from, 85; linen in, 100, 207, 295; papyrus from, 114, 298; cultural superiority of, 135; reduced, 233; conquest of, 244; caravans from, 271; subdued, 418; province of, 477; patriarch in, 523
Egyptian: culture, 59, 135; court, 74; ceramics, 8; glass, 91; monuments, 93, 98; artists, 93; hieroglyphic, 110, 111, 156; motifs, 116; influence, 125; war chariots, 130; soldiers, 131; lists, 127; border, 128; residents in Syria, 135; thought, 137; foreign policy, 149; treaty, 160; forces, 199; oppressors, 213; balance, 226; fleet, 446, 596; expedition, 692
Egyptians: 59; pre-dynastic, 14
Eighteenth Dynasty, 93, 156
Ekron: Philistine city, 181; captured, 199
El, Ugaritic, 119
El Wer, 174

Elagabalus, 308, 312, **343-4**
Elam, 68
Elamites, 616
Elath, 190. *See also* Ezion-geber
Elephantine, 170
Eleutheropolis, 253. *See also* Bayt Jibrīn
Eleutherus, 31. *See also* Nahr al-Kabīr, al-
Elijah, 38, 194
Elishah, 194
Elohim, 191
Eltekeh, 199
Emesa, 238, 248, 287, **307-8**, 340, 343, 344. *See also* Ḥimṣ
Emmaus, 316
Emmaus, 'Amwās, 316
Engberg, Robert M., and Shipton, Geoffrey M., *Notes on the Chalcolithic and Early Bronze Age Pottery*, 25 n. 8; *Hyksos Reconsidered*, 146 n. 1
England, 4, 692
English: merchants, 173
Enlart, Camille, *Les Monuments des croisades*, 596 n. 6
Ennion, 298
Enoch, 257
Enver, 700
Enver Z. Karal, *Osmanli Tarihi*, 669 n. 4
Ephemeris epigraphica, 293 n. 2
Ephraem Syri, *Opera*, 524 n. 5
Ephraim, tribe, 191
Ephraim, the Syrian, 364, **369-70**. *See also* Ephraem Syri
Epiphanes, 247, 278. *See also* Antiochus IV
Epiphania, 253. *See also* Ḥamāh
Erech, 65
Erlanger, Rodolphe d', *La Musique arabe*, 570 n. 6
Erman, Adolf, *Literature of the Ancient Egyptians*, 128 n. 2
Erotimus, 377. *See also* Ḥārithath II
Esarhaddon, 134, 142, 144, 226
Esau, 157, 177
Esdraelon, 31, 38, 424. *See also* Marj ibn-'Āmir
Esh-baal, 204
Eshmum-'azar, 124, 125
Eski-shehr, 448, 591. *See also* Nicaea
Ethbaal, king of Sidon, 142, 192
Ethbaal III, 202
Ethiopia, 169
Ethiopian: forces, 199
Ethiopic: 257; language, 61
Etruscans, 121
Euclid, 552
Eudoxia, 357
Euphrates: 24, 39, 152; middle, 66; upper, 129; canal of, 222
Europa, 105, 106
Europe: 5, 10, 106; peoples of, 4; early culture of, 5
European: influence, 5; alphabets, 110; powers, 686
Eusebius, historian, 320, 333, **358**, 360
Evagrius of Samosata, 361
Evangels, 494
Exodus, **178**
Ezekiel, 100, 157, 202, 216
Ezion-geber, 99, **189-90**
Ezra, 197, 221, **222-3**

Faḍālah ibn-'Ubayd al-Anṣāri, 443, 444
Faḍl, banu-, 599
fahd, 480
Faḥl, 474 n. 3. *See also* Fiḥl
Fakhr-al-Dīn I al-Ma'ni, 84, 665, 680
Fakhr-al-Dīn II, 673, 674, **680-85**
Fakhkhārīyah, al-, 150. *See also* Washshukanni
falsafah, 552
Fano, 677
Faqār, dhu-al-, 433
faqīhs, 645
Far East, 169
Far Eastern: products, 271
Fārābi, al-, 566, **570**
Fārābi, al-, *Risālat Fuṣūṣ*, 570 n. 3; *Risālah fi Ārā'*, 570 n. 4; *al-Siyāsah*, 570 n. 5
Faraj, Mamlūk, 656
Farazdaq, al-, 494
Farghānah 460, 488
Farīdūn Bey, *Majmū'ah*, 664 n. 7
Farmā', al-, 244 n. 1. *See also* Pelusium
Farmer, Henry G., *History of Arabic Music*, 504 n. 1
fata al-'Arab, 444
Fāṭimah, daughter of Muḥammad, 429
Fāṭimid: sect, 560; caliphate, 563; suzerainty, 566; empire, 579; hold on Syria, 580; art, 650; misrule, 669
Fāṭimids: **573** *seq.*; established, 577
fatwa, 556, 624
Fawāris, abu-al-, Ikhshīdid, 563
fay', 423
Fayṣal, son of Ḥusayn, 703

Féghali, Michel T., *Études sur les emprunts syriaques*; *Le Parler de Kfar'abīda*, 547 n. 5
Fertile Crescent: 62, 64, 150; horn of, 6, 43, 59
Fidā', abu-al-, 612, 622, 628
Fidā', abu-al-: *Taqwīm al-Buldān*, 40 n. 2; 654 n. 8; *Ta'rīkh*, 401 n. 9; 654 n. 7
fidā'is, 610, 616
Fifteenth Dynasty, 149
Fiḥl, 252 n. 2, 414. *See also* Pella
Fihrist, al-, 498
Filasṭīn, 424. *See also* Palestine
fiqh, 491, 556
Firās, abu-, 568-9
Firās, abu-, *Dīwān*, ed. Qalfāṭ, 569 n. 2; ed. al-Dahhān, 569 n. 3
Firkāḥ, ibn-al-, 624
First Dynasty, 76, 136
fityān, 433
Fitzgerald, G. M., *Sixth Century Monastery*, 368 n. 1
Flavia Neapolis, 316. *See also* Neapolis
Florence, 681
Florentines, 681
Fortuna, 316
Fountain of Wisdom, 499
France: 4, 591, 697; conquests in, 4; caves in, 10; station in, 12
Francis I, 672
Franciscan: order, 626
Frankish: monarchy, 625
Franks: 591, 593, 601, 614; fleet of, 603; churches of, 617; acquire new tastes, 618
Frederick II, king of Sicily, 606
French: mandate, 665; capitulations, 668; supremacy, 672; pilgrims, 672; merchants, 673; army, 695; influence, 697
Fulcher, *Historia Hierosolymitana*, 591 n. 4
Furāt, ibn-al-, *Ta'rīkh*, 608 n. 1
Furayḥah, Anīs, *Mu'jam al-Alfāẓ*, 547 n. 5
Furzul, 154
Fusṭāṭ, al-: 561, 563; capital, 558
Futrus, abu-, 532
futūwah, 433, 617

Gabinius, 281
Gadara: 260-61; springs of, 325
Gades, 102, 103, 104. *See also* Cadiz
Galen: 342; works of, 550; manuscript in Arabic, 551
Galicia, 466
Galilean: hills, 49
Galilee: **38**, 267, 688; Upper, 38; Lower, 38; offered choice, 246; tetrarchy of, 284; wine of, 296
Gallienus, 392
Garland, of Meleager, 261
Garrod, Dorothy A. E., and Bate, D. M. A., *Stone Age*, 9 n. 2
Garrod, Miss, 10, 14
garshūni, 546
Garstang, 20
Garstang, John, *Heritage of Solomon*, 83 n. 1; *Hittite Empire*, 155 n. 2
Garstang, John, and Garstang, J. B. E., *Story of Jericho*, 16 n. 1
Gashmu, 223, 386
Gath, 181
Gaudefroy-Demombynes, *La Syrie*, 58 n. 9
Gaul, 104, 107
Gaulanitis, 41 n. 7. *See also* Jawlān, al-
Gaza: 77, 82, 185, **359**; ear-rings from, 104; Philistine city, 181; siege of, 233; defeat at, 237; musicians from, 301; wines from, 353; silk from 383. *See also* Ghazzah
Geber, 498. *See also* Jābir ibn-Ḥayyān
Gedrosia, 274
Gelb, Ignace J., *Hurrians*, 74 n. 2; *Hittite Hieroglyphic Monuments*, 158 n. 2
Genoa: merchants of, 590
Genoese: 607; fleet, 597; consuls, 620
Georgians, 632, 634
Gerasa: 252, 300, 317, 318; potters in, 296; churches of, 366. *See also* Jarash
Gerizim, 38
German: officers, 698
Germanicia, 442. *See also* Mar'ash
Germany, 4, 698
Gerrha, 271, **272-3**, 382
Gerrheans, 272
Gesenius, 114
Gesta Francorum, 591 n. 4
Gesta Romanorum, 615
Geta, 322, **341-3**
Gezer: 26, 82, 179, 190; shrine, 25; Semites in, 78; calendar, 91, 207; temple, 120; "high place" of, 123
Gezerite: cave-dwellers, 24
Ghānim, Shukri, 702
ghanīmah, 423
Gharb, al-, 545, 666

Ghassān: kings of, 402
Ghassānid: court, 404-6
Ghassānids, 372, **401** *seq.*
Ghassūlian: culture, 24-6
Ghawri, al-, 664. *See also* Qanṣawh
ghaybah, 584
Ghazīr, 678
Ghazīri, Bernard G., *Rome et l'Église syrienne-maronite*, 522 n. 8
Ghazzah, 77. *See also* Gaza
Ghazzāli, al-, 515
Ghazzāli, al-, *Iḥyā'*, 504 n. 1; *al-Munqidh*, 516 n. 1; *Mishkāt al-Anwār*, 651 n. 3
Ghazzi, al-, 675
Ghazzi, al-, *al-Kawākib*, 664 n. 3
ghilmān, 636
ghulāh, 434, 584, 586
ghūṭah, 472
Ghūṭah, al-, 42
Ghuzz, 574
giaur, 670
Gibb, H. A. R., *Damascus Chronicle*, 591 n. 4
Gibbon, Edward, *History of the Decline and Fall*, 342 n. 2
Gibeah, 85, 186
Gibraltar, 464, 469
Gideon, 180
Gilboa, 187
Gilead, 41, 127, 166, 173, 289
Glueck, Nelson, *Explorations in Eastern Palestine*, 380 n. 7; *Other Side of the Jordan*, 385 n. 3
Gnostic: sect, 170, 334
Godfrey of Bouillon, 594, 595
Goeje, M. J., de, *Mémoire sur la conquête*, 409 n. 3
Golden Horn, 446
Golden Rule, 329
Goliath, 182
Gomorrah, 41
Gontrand, 354
Good Shepherd, 368
Gordon, Cyrus H., *Ugaritic Handbook*, 58 n. 1; *Loves and Wars*, 116 n. 1
Goshen, 178
Gospels: 327, 328; original Aramaic of, 549
Gouraud, 134
Gozan, 21, 169. *See also* Tell al-Ḥalaf
Granada, 295
Grant, Christina P., *Syrian Desert*, 289 n. 3
Grant, Elihu, *Rumeileh*, 148 n. 2; *People of Palestine*, 207 n. 8
Great Britain, 104, 197, 399, 697
Great Khāns, 611
Greco-Latin: civilization, 349
Greco-Macedonian: cities, 252; elements, 262, 288; colonies, 267, 287
Greco-Roman: world, 233, 270; colonies, 299; cults, 334, 337; models, 368; influences, 378; heritage, 621
Greco-Syrian: synthesis, 254; poets, 259-61; bowl, 276; cities, 281
Greece: influence from, 59; laurel from, 106; pottery from, 298
Greek: translation from, 4, **548** *seq.*; philosophy, 4, 254, 548 *seq.*; thought, 4; science, 4, 497, 548 *seq.*; learning, 4; architecture, 106; colonization, 107; inscriptions, 109, 134; earthenware, 227; trading settlements, 228; cities, 231, 249; states, 231; civilization, 243; gymnasium, 244; culture, 251; settlements in Syria, 251; soldiers, 251; settlers, 253-4, 265; language, 256, 288; colonists, 256; commercial activity, 270; constitution, 281; tongue, 285; veterans, 288; polytheists, 331; imports, 383; fire, 445, 447; logic, 491; churches, 500; replaces Syriac, 523
Greek Anthology, 225 n. 2
Greek Church, 591
Greek Fathers, 501
Greek Orthodox: **523**; millet, 668; community, 697
Greeks: 3; borrow alphabet, 109; weapon of, 265
Gregory XIII, 675
Gregory of Nazianzus, 360
Gregory Thaumaturgus, 360
Grousset, René, *Civilizations of the East*, 648 n. 3
Grunebaum, Gustave E. von, *Medieval Islam*, 653 n. 3
Gubla: 68, 72, 74, 84, 126, 127, 128; ships of, 127; prince of, 134; tamarisk in, 136; jars from, 137. *See also* Jubayl
Gublites, 72
Gudea, 138
Guides bleus, 665, n. 1
Gül-Khāné, 669
Gulf of Alexandretta, 24, 30, 31, 70
Gulf of al-'Aqabah, 44, 99, 190
Gulf of al-Kuwayt, 44
Guthrie, Kenneth S., *Numenius of Apamea*, 324 n. 2
Guy de Lusignan, 601, 602, 603

Ḥabābah, 480
Ḥabīb, Muḥammad, al-, 577
Hadad: 77, 160, **172-4**, 310; cult of, 155
Hadad Rammanu, 308, 334. *See also* Hadad-Rimmon
Hadad-Rimmon, 172
Hadadezer, 166
Haddad, George, *Aspects of Social Life in Antioch*, 302 n. 7
Hādi, Ḥamzah ibn-ʻAli, al-, 584
ḥadīth, **491-2**
Hadrian, 292, 302, 304, 308, 340
Ḥāfiẓ al-Dhahabi, al-, 653. *See also* Dhahabi, al-
Ḥāfiẓ Pasha, wāli, 681
Hagar, 177
Haifa: 31; occupied, 595. *See also* Ḥayfa
Ḥajar, ibn-, *al-Iṣābah*, 432 n. 2
Ḥajjāj ibn-Yūsuf, al-: 452, **453** *seq.*, 473, 489: reforms of, 475-6; orations of, 493
Ḥājji Khalfah, *Kashf al-Ẓunūn*, 498 n. 4
ḥakam, 432
ḥakīm, 498
Ḥākim, al-: 544, 580, 583, 584, 588; reactivates earlier regulations, 587
Ḥalab, 68, 253. *See also* Aleppo
Ḥalabi, Ibrāhīm, al-, *see* Ibrāhīm al-Ḥalabi
Ḥalafian: culture, **21**, 26
Ḥalīmah, 402
Hall, H. R., *Ancient History*, 17 n. 2
Ḥalpa, 155. *See also* Aleppo
Halys River, 154
Ḥamād, al-, 43
Hamadhān, 234, 554. *See also* Ecbatana
Ḥamāh: 39, 71, 156, 158, 167, 253; king of, 167; state of, 187
Ḥamāsah, al-, 553
Ḥamdān, banu-, 564. *See also* Ḥamdānids
Ḥamdān ibn-Ḥamdūn, 564
Ḥamdān Qarmaṭ, 560
Ḥamdānid-Byzantine: conflict, 565
Ḥamdānids, 562, **564** *seq.*
Ḥamīdian: régime, 698-700
Hamilcar Barca, 105
Hamites, 14, 26, 463
Hamitic: language, 61
Ḥammād, ibn-, *Akhbār Mulūk*, 578 n. 2
Ḥammād al-Rāwiyah, *Dīwān*, 495 n. 7
Hammer, Joseph von, *Geschichte*, 661 n. 4
Hammurabi: 66, 68; laws, 210, 368
Ḥamzah ibn-ʻAli al-Hādi, 584, 585. *See also* Hādi, Ḥamzah ibn-ʻAli, al-
Ḥanafite: system, 555
ḥanīf, 387
Ḥanīfah, abu-, 501
Hannibal, 105, **107-8**, 243
Ḥāqil, 34
Ḥāqilāni, Ibrāhīm, al-, 676, 684
Har, 149
Haran, 68, 150. *See also* Ḥarrān
Harāt, 518
Ḥarfūsh, ibn-al-, 666
Ḥārim, 631
Ḥārith, al-, 377. *See also* Ḥārithath
Ḥārith ibn-Jabalah, al-, 402, 507
Ḥārithath, 377. *See also* Ḥārith, al-
Ḥārithath II, 377
Ḥarithath III, **377-80**
Ḥārithath IV, **378-9**, 381, 382
Harmhab, 136
Harper, George M., *Village Administration in the Roman Province*, 299 n. 1
ḥarrahs, 43
Ḥarrān: 68, 163, 164, 175, 177, 217, 282, 403, 531; star worshippers of, 486; school of, 548
Harrer, Gustave A., *Studies in the History of the Roman Province*, 286 n. 2
Harris, Zellig, *Grammar of the Phoenician Language*, 74 n. 7
Hartmann, Martin, *Arabic Press*, 702 n. 1
Hārūn, Ṭūlūnid, 560, 561
Hārūn al-Rashīd, 433, 447
Ḥasan, al-, 429, **435-6**, 439
Ḥasan ʻAli, abu-al-, Ikhshīdid, 562
Ḥasan, al-ʻAskari, al-, 586
Ḥasan al-Baṣri, al-, 491, 493
Ḥāṣbayya, 40
Hāshimite Kingdom of the Jordan, 703
Hāshimites: subsidy for, 438
ḥashīsh, 610
Hasmonean, 245, 246
Ḥassān ibn-al-Nuʻmān al-Ghassāni, 462
Ḥassān ibn-Thābit, 405
Ḥassān ibn-Thābit, *Dīwān*, 405 n. 2
Hathor, 127
Ḥaṭṭīn, 601. *See also* Ḥiṭṭīn
Hattushilish, 156, 162
Ḥawqal, ibn-, *al-Masālik*, 58 n. 9
Ḥawrān: **42-3**, 127, 293, 692; plateau, 49; annexed, 289; remains in, 406

Ḥawrōn, deity, 136
Ḥaydar al-Shihābi, governor, 686
Ḥaydar al-Shihābi, historian, 675, 687
Ḥaydar al-Shihābi, *Ta'rīkh*, 665 n. 1; *Lubnān fi 'Ahd*, 675 n. 5
Ḥaydarābād, 461. *See also* Nīrūn, al-
Ḥayfa, 31, 595. *See also* Haifa
Ḥayyān, ibn-, *see* Jābir ibn-Ḥayyān
Hazael, 140, 167
Ḥazm, ibn-, *al-Fiṣal*, 499 n. 4
Hazor, 82, 147, 179
Hebrew: prophets, 41, 213, 215; language, 61, 62; nation, 68; Patriarchs, 153; conquest, 179; monarchy, 186, 189; names, 204, 222, 246; religious art, 204; sacred music, 205; synagogues, 206; craftsmen, 207; ritual, 208; coin, 209; contribution, 209; sage, 211; poetry, 211; prophetism, 212
Hebrew-Aramaean: relationship, 164
Hebrew Bibles, 169
Hebrews: 64, 114, **176** *seq.*; as Bedouins, 203
Hebron, 157, 177
Hegira, 428
hekāl, 189
Helen of Troy, 94, 95
Helena, Constantine's mother, 350
Heliopolis, in Syria: 310-16; flute players from, 301, 310; oracle of, 311; temple of, 311. *See also* Ba'labakk
Hellas, 257
Hellenic: cultural influence, 236; community, 268
Hellenic East, 256
Hellenism: champion of, 244; introduced, 251; pagan, 349
Hellenistic: period, 4; days, 95; age, 251 *seq.*, 276; culture, 254, 417; kings, 265, 286; states, 273; monarchies, 277; science, 552
Hellenistic East, 275
Hellenistic Syrian: tradition, 276
Hellenization: policy of, 239; veneer of, 253; degrees of, 254; of Orient, 256
Hellespont, 238, 395, 574
Heracles, 136. *See also* Herakles
Heraclius: 404, 411, 412, 415, 416, 417; recovers Syria, 409
Herakles, 104. *See also* Melkarth
Herat, 518. *See also* Harāt
Hercules, deity, 116, 232
Hermeneutica, 549
Hermias, 278
Herod Antipas, 284
Herod the Great, 283, 284, 289, 294, 307, 309
Herod the tetrarch, 380
Herodian: family, 254, 283, 316
Herodotus, 58, 103
Herzfeld, Ernst H., *Archeological History of Iran*, 386 n. 9
Hesiod, 103
Hezekiah, **198-200**
Hierapolis, 95, 172, 173, 373. *See also* Manbij
Hieromax, 260. *See also* Yarmūk
ḥijāb, 481
Ḥijāz, al-: 58, 406; pilgrimage to, 436; irrigation in, 438; province of, 477; railway, 699
Ḥijr, al-, 380, 385. *See also* Madā'in Ṣāliḥ
hijrah, 428
Hilarion of Gaza, 364
Hill, George F., *Catalogue of the Greek Coins of Phoenicia*, 225 n. 1
ḥilm, 439
Himalayas, 461
Ḥimṣ: 41, 248, 307; occupied, 395; mosque in, 418; district of, 439; registers of, 484; Great Mosque of, 511, 544; rebels of, 540; outbreak in, 544. *See also* Emesa
Hindu, 620
Hindu Kush, 241
Hindus, 582
Hippo, 102
Ḥīrah, al-, 404
Hiram, 84, 99, 188, 189
Hirth, F., *China and the Roman Empire*, 353 n. 4
Hishām, 527-8
Ḥiṣn al-Akrād, 594, 608
Hitti, Philip K., *History of the Arabs*, 24 n. 2; *Arab-Syrian Gentleman*, 53 n. 6; *Origins of the Islamic State*, 404 n. 3; *al-Lughāt al-Sāmīyah*, 546 n. 4; *Syrians in America*, 696 n. 2
Ḥiṭṭīn, 601-2
Hittite: 27, 74; advance, 72; army, 75; weapons, 88; motifs, 116; princess, 136; state, 155; chariotry, 156; kingdom, 157; language, 157; literature, 158; religion, 158
Hittite-Assyrian: culture, 171
Hittiteland, 85, 139
Hittites: 59, 71, 75, **154-61**; pass horse on, 52; use of iron by, 184

Hivites, 153
Hogarth, D. G., *Nearer East*, 42 n. 4
Hollow Syria, 39 n. 5, 60, 187. *See also* Biqā', al-
Holy Cities, of al-Ḥijāz, 495
Holy Family, 60
Holy Land: shrines in, 621
Holy Sepulchre, 366. *See also* Church of the Holy Sepulchre
Homer, 103
Homer: *Iliad*, 88 n. 2; 237
Homo sapiens, 6, 11
Honorius, 351, 354
Hooton, Ernest A., *Up from the Ape*, 11 n. 1
Hophra, 202, 217
Horace, 319
Horites, 146, 153. *See also* Hurrians
Horus, 333
Hosea, 215
Hospitallers, 601 n. 5, 607, 608, 612, 616
Hourani, A. H., *Syria*, 701 n. 6
Hrozny, Friedrich, *Die Sprache der Hethiter; Hethitische Keilschrifttexte*, 158 n. 1; *Code hittite*, 158 n. 3
Hubal, 385
Ḥubaysh ibn-al-Ḥasan, 550
Huda, al-Ṣayyādi, abu-al-, 699
Hūlāgu, 557, 627, 630, **631**
Ḥūlah, al-, 39
Ḥumaymah, al-, 530
Ḥunayn, musician, 505
Ḥunayn ibn-Isḥāq, 550
Hungary, 399, 662
Huntington, Ellsworth, *Palestine*, 47 n. 3
Ḥurr ibn-'Abd-al-Raḥmān al-Thaqafi, al-, 468
Hurrian: **150-54**; swords, 116; language, 152; tablets, 153
Hurrians: 26, 79; in Syria, 65; physical features of, 154
Ḥusayn, al-, 429, **436**, **450-51**
Ḥusayn, al-Sharīf, 693, 702
Ḥūwārīn, 404
Ḥuwayṭāt, 388
Hyksos: 83, **146-50**, 157; introduce horse, 52; period, 93, 135; swords, 116; rise of, 126; out of Egypt, 129
Hyrcanus, 246
Hyrcanus II, 281, 283

Iamblichus, Neo-Platonist, 325, 355. *See also* Jamblichus
Ibāḍites, 502
Iberian: peninsula, 103, 457, 463; stock, 105
Ibrāhīm al-Ḥalabi, 664
Ibrāhīm Pasha, son of Muḥammad 'Ali, **692** *seq.*, 701
Ibrāhīm Pasha, Turkish commander, 679
'Ibri, ibn-al-, *Mukhtaṣar al-Duwal*, 441 n. 4; *Chronicon Syriacon*, 545 n. 1
Ibshīhi, al-, *al-Mustaṭraf*, 422 n. 2
Ice Age, 10
Iconium, 574
'Idhāri, ibn-, *al-Bayān al-Mughrib*, 462 n. 4
Idrīsi, al-, *Ṣifat al-Maghrib*, 103 n. 1; *Dhikr al-Andalus*, 464 n. 2
Idumaea, 267
Ifrīqiyah: 437, 458, 462; province of, 477
Ifrīqīyah, 437. *See also* Ifrīqiyah
Ignatius, bishop of Antioch, 336
Ihdin, 621, 676
Ījī, al-, *Kitāb al-Mawāqif*, 499 n. 2
Ikhnaton, 72, 75, 155
Ikhshīd, al-, 562
Ikhshīdids, **561** *seq.*
Īl-Ghāzi ibn-Urtuq, 575, 576
Īl-Khān Ghāzān Maḥmūd, 632
Iliad, 551
Īliyā', 435. *See also* Jerusalem
Illyria, 106
Illyrius, 106
'Ilmīyah Sālnāmehsi, 670 n. 3
'Imād-al-Dīn al-Iṣfahāni, 605
imām, 450
Imprimerie Catholique of Beirut, 701
Imtān, 354
Īnāl, 636
India: 4, 52, 150, 247; southern, 59; influence from, 59; elephants from, 265; products of, 273; sugar from, 275; rice from, 275; jewels from, 298; spices from, 353; missionaries to, 371; conquest in, **461**; Christianity in, 518; caravans from, 672
Indian: campaign, 235; merchandise, 270; products, 271; craftsmen, 515
Indian Ocean: 247; trade, 596
Indians, 4
Indo-European: nomads, 52; influence, 59; civilization, 146; era, 218
Indo-Europeans, 146, 150
Indo-Iranian: influence, 59
Indo-Iranians, 146
Indonesian: trade, 672
Indra, 150
Indus, 238, 471
Ionia, 100

Ionian: cities, 218
Ipsus, 265, 266
'*Iqd, al-*, 479
Iqrītish, 445. *See also* Crete
iqṭā', 625
Iram, 383
Īrān, 458
Iranian: 226, 227, 241; peasants, 531
Iranians, 460
'Irāq, al-: 43; declares for al-Ḥasan, 435
Irish, 104
irjā', 501
Irqat, 71. *See also* 'Arqah
'*Īsa*, 535
'Īsa ibn-Nasṭūrūs, 579
Isaac, 164, 177
Isagoge, 549
Isaiah, 199, **214**
Isaurian: dynasty, 447
Iṣbahān, 453
Iṣbahāni, al-, 566, **569-70**
Iṣbahāni, abu-al-Faraj, al-, *al-Aghāni*, 404 n. 1; 569 n. 8
Iṣfahāni, al-, 569. *See also* Iṣbahāni, al-
Iṣfahāni, Ḥamzah, *al-Ta'rīkh*, 401 n. 9
Isḥāq, Ḥunayn, ibn-, *see* Ḥunayn ibn-Isḥāq
Isḥāq, son of Ḥunayn ibn-Isḥāq, 552
Isḥāqi, al-, *Akhbār al-Uwal*, 636 n. 3
Ishmael, 177
Ishrāq, al-, 651
Ishtar, 68, 69, 117, 119
Isis, 333
Iskandar dhu-al-Qarnayn, 236. *See also* Alexander the Great
Iskandarūnah, 30, 232. *See also* Alexandretta
Islam: 3; spread of, 4; slaves in, **488-9**; interaction with, 523-6; classical, 548
Islamic: literature, 28; conquests, 419; law, 488
Islamization, 463, 545
'*iṣmah*, 503
Ismā'īl ibn-Ja'far al-Ṣādiq, 577
Ismā'īli-Assassins, 577
Ismā'īlism, 587
Ismā'īlite: sect, 560, 578
Ismā'īlites, 592
Israel: 148; children of, 157; kingdom of, **191-9**; prophets of, 211; birth of, 703
Israelites: early, 61; influx of, 75; carried into captivity, 197
Issus: 30; battle of, **231-2**
Iṣṭakhri, al-, *Masālik al-Mamālik*, 32 n. 3
Isthmus of Suez, 31
Iṣṭifān al-Duwayhi, *see* Duwayhi, al-
Italian: troops, 285, 286; colonists, 317; republics, 596, 620; sailors, 620
Italians, 274
Italy: 4, 107, 697; trees introduced into, 294; pottery from, 298
'*iṭr*, 618
Ittobaal, 113
Ituraeans: 246; state of, 247; Judaized, 288
Ivanow, W., *Ismaili Tradition*, 578 n. 4
'Iyāḍ ibn-Ghanm, 418
Iyās, ibn-, *Badā'i' al-Zuhūr*, 638 n. 1; *Ḥawādith al-Duwhūr*, 638 n. 2
'Izz-al-Dīn Aybak, 629-30

Jabal 'Āmil, 411
Jabal al-Durūz, 42, 679
Jabal Lubnān: Mutaṣarrifīyah, 695
Jabal Ramm, 383
Jabal al-Shamāli, al-, 38. *See also* Ebal
Jabal al-Shaykh, al-, 41 n. 6, 472. *See also* Mt. Hermon
Jabal al-Ṭubayq, 52 n. 3, 53
Jabalah, 603, 604
Jabalah ibn-al-Ayham, 404, 405, 444
Jabarti, al-, '*Ajā'ib al-Āthār*, 641 n. 1
Jabbūr, Jibrā'īl, '*Umar ibn-abi-Rabī'ah*, 494 n. 7
Jābir ibn-Ḥayyān, 498
Jābiyah, al-: 403; camp in, 418, 419; conference of, 422, 424
Jabneh, 136
jabr, -al, 552
Jabrites, 499
Jacob, 164, 177
Jacob Bardaeus, 372, 520
Jacobite: scholars, 520
Jacobite Church, **371-2**, 520
Jacobites, 439
Jacobitism, 520
Ja'far, al-Manṣūr, abu-, 536. *See also* Manṣūr, al-
Ja'far al-Ṣādiq, 498
Jaffa: 131, 595; rafts to, 189; destroyed, 339; seized, 608
Jafnah ibn-'Amr, 401
Jafnid: dynasty, 401
jāhilīyah, 490
Jāhilīyah, 496
Jāḥiẓ, al-, *al-Tāj*, 480 n. 6; *al-Bayān*, 493 n. 6

Jamblichus, historian, 320
Jamblichus, Neo-Platonist, **325**
Jāmiʿ al-Kabīr, al-, 511
Jamīl al-ʿUdhri, 495
Jān-Birdi al-Ghazāli, 664
Janbalāṭi, 687, 694
Janbalāṭs, 678, 683, 687, 691
Janissaries, 667
Jannābatayn, 414 n. 2
Jarābulus, 25, 158. *See also* Carchemish
Jarājimah, **448-9**. *See also* Jurājimah
Jarash, 252 n. 4, 300, 318. *See also* Gerasa
Jarbāʿ, al-, 410
Jarīr, 494
Jarmaq, al-, 38
Jaussen and Savignac, *Mission archéologique*, 384 n. 2
Jawdat, *Taʾrīkh*, 674 n. 3
Jawf, al-, 412. *See also* Dūmat al-Jandal
Jawhar, general, 563, **578-9**
Jawlān, al-, 41, 43
Jawzi, abu-al-Faraj, ibn-al-, *Sīrat ʿUmar*, 475 n. 4; *Naqd al-ʿIlm*, 502 n. 1; *Ṣifwat al-Ṣafwah*, 641 n. 4
Jawzi, Sibṭ, ibn-al-, *see* Sibṭ ibn-al-*Jawzi*
Jaxartes, 235, 460
Jayḥūn, 458 n. 5. *See also* Oxus
Jaysh, 560
Jazīrah, al-: 424; province of, 477. *See also* Mesopotamia
Jazīrat Ṭarīf, 464
Jazīrat ibn-ʿUmar, 271
Jazzār, Aḥmad, al-, **689-91**
Jebusites, 146, 188
Jeffery, Arthur, *Foreign Vocabulary*, 525 n. 8
Jehoahaz, 167
Jehoiachin, 202, 222
Jehoiakim, 201
Jehovah: 41, 116, 191, 199, 213; worship of, 197; code from, 210; religion of, 211; identified with Zeus, 244
Jehu, 167, 194
Jemal Pasha, 700, 703
Jeremiah, 201, **214-15**, 222
Jericho: 18, 26, 81, 147, 179; shrine, 15, 16, 19; pottery, 20; walls of, 40; pre-Israelite, 88; balm of, 107; burial customs in, 123
Jeroboam I, 191
Jeroboam II, 167, 196, 213
Jerusalem: 14, 38, 82; rainfall in, 46; fortifications of, 198; siege of, 199, 339; fall of, 202; royal palace of, 204; destruction of, 217; visited by Alexander, 234; aristocracy of, 244; captured by Maccabeans, 245; charter to, 268; hippodrome in, 283; cross restored to, 409; reduced, 416-17; patriarchate in, 523; cotton goods of, 571; seized, 595
Jesuit: order, 683, 701
Jesuits, 674, 683
Jesus: **328** *seq.*; language of, 168; figure of, 368; one person of, 372
Jew, 3
Jewish: high priest, 95; colony, 221; commonwealth, 245-6; aristocracy, 287; resistance, 338; art, 368; anti-, 543
Jewish Palestine, 257
Jews: 27; in Babylon, 221; modernized, 244; under Seleucids, 274; census of, 287; keep Hebrew, 288; millet, 668
Jezebel, 192, 194
Jibāl al-Nuṣayrīyah, 32
jihād, 606, 623
Jilʿād, 43 n. 2. *See also* Mt. Gilead
Jilliq, 403
Jinni, ibn-, 567
Jisr Banāt Yaʿqūb, 9
jizyah, 423, 544
Joannes Maro, 521. *See also* Yūḥanna Mārūn
Job, 115, 211
Job of Edessa, *Book of Treasures*, 550 n. 4
Johannitius, 550. *See also* Ḥunayn ibn-Isḥāq
John the Baptist, 380
John Chrysostom, 335, **356-8**, 369, 370
John of Ephesus, *Ecclesiastical History*, 403 n. 1
John Hyrcanus I, 246, 274
John Zimisces, 565
Joinville, *Histoire de Saint Louis*, 34 n. 4
Jonathan, 204
Jonathan, high priest, 269
Jones, A. H. M., *Greek City*, 302 n. 5
Jordan River: 39, 49; bed, 9; valley, **40**, 46, 47, 188
Josaphat, 500
Joscelin II, 599
Joseph, 149, 177
Josephus, 140, 274, 284, 293, 302, **319**, 383

Josephus, *Antiquities*, 58 n. 6; 318 n. 3; *Jewish War*, 318 n. 3
Joshua, 176, 179
Josiah: reforms of, 200
Jubayl, 14, 34, 53, 68, **126**. *See also* Byblus
Jubayr, ibn-, 622, 640, 641, 642, 645
Jubayr, ibn-, *Riḥlah*, 472 n. 5
Jubb'adīn, 546
Judaea: 38, 340; revolt in, 245; tribute from, 268; procurator of, 287
Judaeo-Christian: literature, 138; heritage, 621
Judah: conquest of, 144; "lion of", 190; tribe, 191; kingdom of, 191, **198-202**; pays tribute, 196; last days of, 201; laid waste, 202
Judaism: cradle of, 3
Judas Maccabeus, 245
Judges, the, **180**, 186, 375
Judhāmah, 411
juhhāl, 585
Julia Domna, 307, 311, **340-44**
Julia Maesa, 343, 391
Julian, count of Ceuta, 464
Julian, emperor, 305, 351
Julius Caesar: 283, 302; in Syria, 282
jund, 424, 484
Jundi-Shāpūr: school of, 548; academy of, 549
Jūniyah, 30
Jupiter, 233, 334
Jupiter Capitolinus, 340
Jupiter Damascenus, 172, 308, 514
Jupiter Dolichenus, 334
Jupiter-Hadad: temple of, 313
Jupiter Heliopolitanus, 172, 312, 348
Jurājimah, **448-9**, 461
Jurassic, 32, 34, 35
Jurjūmah, al-, 448
Justin, emperor, 402-3
Justin Martyr, 316, **336**, 386
Justinian I, 358, 366, 373, 513
Justinian II, 449, 462
Justinian Code, 4, **326**
Juttah, 38
Juvenal, 302, 321

Ka'b ibn-Ju'ayl, 494
Ka'bah, al-, 429
kabīrah, 498
kabsh, 478
Kābul, 235, 458
Kadesh-barnea, 178
Kafarḥayy, 521
Kāfi fi al-Kuḥl, al-, 643
Kafr Yūba, 27
Kāfūr, Ikhshīdid, 562-3
Kahf, al-, 608
kaḥḥāl, 643
kāhin, 525
kāhinah, 462
Kahle, Paul, *Die arabischen Bibelübersetzungen*, 546 n. 7
Kaiser Wilhelm, 698
Kalb, tribe, 431, 452, 581
Kaldu, 163. *See also* Chaldaeans
kāmil, 496
Kāmil al-Ṣinā'ah, 614
Kammerer, A., *Pétra et la Nabatène*, 378 n. 5
Kanatha, 317, 347. *See also* Qanawāt
Kanopus, 136
kānūn I, 547 n. 6
Kar-Esarhaddon, 142
Kara Tepe, 112
karadīs, 531
karak, 596 n. 6
Karak, al-, 43, 596, 602, 608. *See also* Le Crac
Karbalā', **450-51**
Karbūqa, 593
Karmān: 453; province of, 477
ka(r)mu, 17
Kasār 'Aqīl, 13
Kasārah, 46
Kāshghar, 461
Kashmir, 52
Kassites, 52, 146, 150
Kawkab al-Hawā', 602-3
Keller, Albert G., *Homeric Society*, 106 n. 5
Kenites, 179, 190
Kennedy, Alexander B. W., *Petra*, 380 n. 4
Khabiru, **75**, 126, 146, **160-61**
Khābūr, al-, 21, 65, 150, 164
Khaḍrā', al-, 472
Khā'ir Bey, 657, 666
Khālawayh, ibn-, 567
Khaldūn, ibn-, 449, **655**
Khaldūn, ibn-, *Kitāb al-'Ibar*, 103 n. 1; 655 n. 5; *Muqaddamah*, 441; n. 2; n. 4
khalī', 480
Khālid, son of Yazīd I, 498
Khālid ibn-al-Walīd, 5, **412** *seq.*
Khalīfah ibn-abi-al-Maḥāsin, 643
Khalīl ibn-Aḥmad, al-, 491
Khallikān, ibn-, 491, 493, **653-4**
Khallikān, ibn-, *Wafayāt al-A'yān*, 455 n. 3; 653 n. 2

khamlah, 619
khān, 637
Khān al-Ṣābūn, 647
Khānates, 460
kharāj, 422, 423, 475, 625
Khārijite, 433
Khārijites: 453, **501-2**, 531; eliminated, 455
kharrūb, 618
Khaṣībi, Ḥusayn ibn-Ḥamdān, al-, 586
khaṭīb, 493
Khaṭṭ-i Humāyūn, 669
Khaṭṭ-i Sharīf, 669
Khatti: 154; princess of, 160
Khattians, 154, 155, 157
Khattic, 154
Khattushash, 154, 155
Khawābi, al-, 609
Khāzin, Fīlīb and Farīd, al-, *Majmū'ah*, 694
Khāzins, al-, 679, 687, 704
Khaznah, al-, 378, 379
Khedive, 562
Kheta, 156
Khirbat al-Mafjar, **505-7**
Khirbat al-Munyah, 507
Khirbat al-Tannūr, 385
Khīva, 460. *See also* Khwārizm
Khufu, 127
Khumārawayh, **559-60**
Khurāsān: 457, 458, 475; subjugated, 437; revolt in, 530-31
Khurāsāni-'Irāqi: troops, 532
Khurāsānian: troops, 537
Khurāsānians, **530** *seq.*, 535, 541
Khurdādhbih, ibn-, 571
Khurdādhbih, ibn-, *al-Masālik w-al-Mamālik*, 447 n. 6
khūri, 526
khuṭbah, 441, 624
Khwārizm, 460
Khyan, 149
Kilāb, tribe, 581
Kilwah, 52
Kindi, al-, *Ta'rīkh Miṣr*, 487 n. 1
King 'Abdullāh's Road, 289 n. 4
King's Highway, 289
Kirjath-sepher, 85, 206. *See also* Bayt Mirsim
Kirkūk, 150
Kirmān, 456 n. 2. *See also* Karmān
Kirmil, 82 n. 2. *See also* Mt. Carmel
Kisra Anūsharwān, 549. *See also* Chosroes I
Kisrawān, 35, 623, 678, 683
Kitāb al-'Ayn, 491
Kitāb al-Mulūk, 493
Kitāb al-Ṣinā'ah, 551
Kitbugha, 631
kittān, 91
Knudtzon, J. A., *Die el-Amarna Tafeln*, 71 n. 3
Koeppel, Robert *et al.*, *Teleilāt Ghassūl*, 23 n. 1
Kohn, Hans, *History of Nationalism*, 702 n. 1; *Nationalism and Imperialism*, 703 n. 2
Koniah, 574. *See also* Iconium
Köprülü, Mehmed Fuad, *Les Origines de l'empire ottomane*, 661 n. 4
Koran: writing of, 406; offer of, 420; canonization of, 429; manuscripts of, 432; corruption of, 455; readers, 497, 560; vigils in, 525; light in, 651
Kraeling, Carl H., *Gerasa*, 252 n. 5
Kraeling, Emil G. H., *Aram and Israel*, 162 n. 1
Krey, August C., *First Crusade*, 590 n. 1
Kūchūk Aḥmad, 684
Kuchuk Kainarji, 697
Kūfah, al-: 384, 429, 430, 436, 437, 450, 454; new capital, 431, 529; mosque at, 433; order restored in, 455; province of, 477; intellectual centre, 491
Kufic: 384; inscriptions, 512
kūfīyah, 619
kuḥl, 76
Kurd-'Ali, Muḥammad, *Khiṭaṭ*, 665 n. 1
Kurdish: bowmen, 265
Kurdistan, 519
kurdūs, 478
Kushājim, 569
Kushshar, 154
kuttāb, 497
Kutubi, al-, 653
Kutubi, al-, *Fawāt*, 495 n. 3

La'ash, 170
lāban, 32
Labdah, 341. *See also* Leptis
Lachish: 26, 82, 147, 179, 227; inscription, 112; captured, 199; vats at, 206; olive pits at, 207
Lādhiqīyah, al-: 32, 239; tobacco from, 48; burned, 446; avoided, 594; seized, 597. *See also* Laodicea
Lady of Gubla, 127
Lagash, 138
Laja', al-, 42
Lajjūn, 129 n. 3. *See also* Megiddo

Lake Tiberias, 39. *See also* Sea of Galilee
Lakhmids, 402
Lammens, Henri, *La Syrie*, 292 n. 5; *La Vie universitaire*, 325 n. 6; *Tasrīḥ al-Abṣār*, 449 n. 7; *Études sur le siècle des Omayyades*, 534 n. 1
Lamʿs, abu-al-, 678, 687
Langdon, Samuel H., *Babylonian Wisdom*, 329 n. 2
Laodicea: 32, 252, 267, **307**; jockeys from, 301; a "village", 302. *See also* Lādhiqīyah, al-
Laodicea-Berytus, 253, 254
Laoust, Henri, *Essai*, 624 n. 4
Larsa, 66
Last Supper, 215
Latakia, 48, 239. *See also* Lādhiqīyah, al-
Latin: official language, 285; literature, 289, 319; provinces, 347; churches, 500; principality, 591; kingdom, 596, 597; states, 608; strongholds, 608; patriarchate, 625
Latin Syria, 607
Lawrence, T. E., *Crusader Castles*, 610 n. 1; *Seven Pillars*, 699 n. 1
Laws, of Plato, 550
Layla, of Majnūn, 495
laylak, 620
laymūn, 618
Lazarites, 674
lāzaward, 616
Le Crac, 43 n. 4. *See also* Karak, al-
Le Strange, Guy, *Palestine under the Moslems*, 426 n. 2; *Lands of the Eastern Caliphate*, 442 n. 2
Lebanese: 5; ancient, 3; maritime plain, 38; early, 50, 96; landscape, 86; emigrants, 102, 696; type among, 154; authors, 257; amīrs, 666; scholars, 676; silk, 681; farmer, 683; politicians, 686, 687; troops, 692
Lebanese Phoenicia, 373
Lebanon: 3, 12, 152; caves of, 7, 9, 38; name, 32, 58; strata of, 37; Republic of, 42, 51; crests of, 49; cedar of, **50-51**, 98, 127, 274; sheep in, 53; Amorites in, 65; northern, 71, highlands of, 79; rural, 86; forests of, 98, 275, 426; French occupation of, 134; cedar from, 188, 189; wood from, 269; mines of, 277; slopes of, 310; wine from, 487; patriarch in, 523; unrest in, 540 *seq.*; Christians of, 542; hermits in, 571; feudal chiefs of, 640; Arab tribes in, 641; ascetics of, 641; special position of, 665 *seq.*; refugees in, 671; silk from, 673; emergence of, 678; safety in, 679; modernizing of, 682; terrorized, 691; governor of, 694; autonomous, **695-696**; prosperity in, 695-6; Republic, 704
Lebanon Mts.: 49; relief of, 52
Lebanons: bulls in, 139
Leo the Isaurian, 446, 524
Leon, in Spain, 466
Leontes, 39. *See also* Līṭāni, al-
Leontius, professor, 360, 361
Leptis, 341
Levant Company, 673
Levi, tribe, 180
Leviathan, 116
Lewis, Bernard, *Origins of Ismāʿīlism*, 560 n. 5
Lewy, H., *Die semitischen Fremdwörter*, 103 n. 2
Libanius, rhetorician, 303, 355
Libya, 100, 102
Libyan: desert, 233
Lidzbarski, Mark, *Handbuch der nordsemitischen Epigraphik*, 171 n. 6; *Ephemeris*, 174 n. 3
Liḥyān, 375
Lion-Hearted, 604. *See also* Richard I Cœur de Lion
Līṭāni, al-, 39
Logos, 371
Longinus, 324, 393, 395, **399-400**
Lord's Prayer, 525
Lorey, E. D., and Berchem, M. van, *Les Mosaïques de la mosquée des Omayyades*, 515 n. 6
Louis IX, 631. *See also* St. Louis, king of France
Louis XV, 672
Lubnān al-Sharqi, 41 n. 5. *See also* Anti-Lebanon
Lucian, 116, 173, **322-3**
Lucian, *De Dea Syria*, 95 n. 4
Luckenbill, Daniel D., *Ancient Records of Assyria*, 39 n. 1; *Annals of Sennacherib*, 88 n. 1
Ludd, al-, 593
Lugal-zaggisi, 65
Luke, 617
Luke, Harry, *Making of Modern Turkey*, 700 n. 1
Lukkām, al-, 31 n. 1, 448. *See also* Amanus
Luli, 142

Lusignan, 613
Luṭfi, *Ta'rīkh*, 669 n. 4
Luwayzah, al-, 676
Lyall, Charles J., *Translations of Ancient Arabian Poetry*, 405 n. 1
Lybyer, Albert H., *Government of the Ottoman Empire*, 667 n. 4
Lycus, 30. *See also* Nahr al-Kalb
Lydda, 181, 593. *See also* Ludd, al-
Lydia, 217
Lydians, 52
Lyons, 341, 347
Lysimachus, 239

ma warā' al-nahr, 458
Ma'arrat al-Nu'mān, 554, 581, 583, 593
Ma'arri, al-, **581-3**, 597
Ma'arri, al-, *Dīwān*, 582 n. 4; *Risālat al-Ghufrān*, 582 n. 5; *Luzūmīyāt*, 582 n. 7; *al-Fuṣūl*, 583 n. 1
Ma'bad, 504
Macalister, R. A., *Excavation of Gezer*, 25 n. 3
Maccabean: brothers, 245; battles, 266; uprising, 274; family, 283
Maccabees, 246
Macedonia, 238
Macedonian: empire, 237; soldiers, 251; settlers, 253-4, 265; nobility, 264; veterans, 288
Macedonians: 59, 70, 231, 236; weapon of, 265
Macrinus, prefect, 343, 344
Madā'in, al-, 537
Madā'in Ṣāliḥ, 380. *See also* Ḥijr, al-
Madonna, 333
Madrasah al-Nūrīyah, al-, 645
madrasahs, 644
Magellan, Ferdinand, 671
Maghārat al-Amīrah, 17 n. 6
Maghārat al-Ṭābūn, 10
Maghārat al-Wādi, 13 n. 1, 14
Maghrib, al-, 510, 555
Maghribis, 689
Magians, 486. *See also* Zoroastrians
Magnesia, 95, 243, 265, 280
Mahdi, 453, 503, 578
Mahdi, al-, 'Abbāsid caliph, 536, 544
Mahdīyah, al-, 578
Maḥmūd I, 672
Maḥmūd II, 669-70, 694
Mahon, 105
mā'idah, 467
Majd ibn-abi-al-Ḥakam, abu-al-, 643
Majnūn Layla, 495
Majūs, 486. *See also* Magians
Majūsi, al-: 614; manuscript of, 615
Makki, al-, *Nuzhat al-Jalīs*, 641 n. 6
Malabar, 518
Malaga, 105, 466
Malak-bel, 400
Malalas, 373
Malalas, *Chronographia*, 256 n. 4
Malatia, 172
Malaṭīyah, 442. *See also* Malaṭyah
Malaṭyah: 172; fortifications of, 442. *See also* Malatia
Malchus I, 378. *See also* 'Obīdath III
malik, 402, 441
Mālik, 378. *See also* Māliku
Malik al-'Ādil, al-, Ayyūbid, 604, 606
Malik al-Afḍal, al-, Ayyūbid, 627
Mālik ibn-Anas, 537
Malik al-Kāmil, al-, Ayyūbid, 604, 606
Malik al-Ṣāliḥ Najm-al-Dīn, al-, Ayyūbid, 606
Malik al-Ẓāhir, al-, 607. *See also* Baybars
Mālikite: system, 555
Malikshāh, 573, 592
Māliku, 378
Maliku II, 381
Malkat, 120
Mallon, Alexis *et al.*, *Teleilāt Ghassūl* I, 23 n. 1
Malta, 106, 107, 114
Ma'lūf, 'Īsa I., al-, *Ta'rīkh al-Amīr*, 666 n. 2
Ma'lūla, 546
Mamlūk: coins, 616; architecture, 648; rule abolished, 658
mamlūks, 629
Mamlūks, 5, 57, 599
Mamour, P. H., *Polemics*, 578 n. 4
Ma'mūn, al-, 487, **541**
Manāh, 385
manārah, 515 n. 7
Manashsha (Manasseh) ibn-Ibrāhīm, 579
Manasseh, 200
Manbij, 373, 424. *See also* Hierapolis
Manchu: in Syriac characters, 518
Mandaic, 170
Mandeans, 485
Manetho, 146, 148
Mani, **370-71**
Manichaean, 651
Manichaeism, 370
manjanīq, 468
Ma'ns: **678** *seq.*; become extinct, 686
Manṣūr, al-: 536; visits Syria, 555
Manṣūr ibn-Sarjūn, 414, 425

Manzikert: decisive victory at, 574
maqām, 433 n. 4, 555
Maqdisi, al-, 448, 559, **571**
Maqdisi, al-, *Aḥsan al-Taqāsīm*, 41 n. 6; 571 n. 1
Maqna, 410
Maqqari, al-, *Nafḥ al-Ṭīb*, 464 n. 1; 675 n. 3
Maqrīzi, al-, **655**
Maqrīzi, al-, *al-Mawā'iẓ, w-al-I'tibār*, 487 n. 1; 655 n. 3; *Kitāb al-Sulūk*, ed. Ziyādah, 603 n. 3; tr. Quatremère, 608 n. 2; *Ighāthat al-Ummah*, 638 n. 3
maqṣūrah, 441
Maradah, 448. *See also* Mardaites
Mar'ash, 442, 443
Marathon, 224
Marathus: 65 n. 2; surrenders, 232; caravans from, 271. *See also* 'Amrīt
Marcion, 336
Marcus Aurelius, 292, 305
Mardaites, **448-9**
Mārdīn, 520, 564, 575
Marduk, 212
Mari, **65-9**, 152
Ma'rib, dam, 401
Marino Sanuto, *Secrets for True Crusaders*, 621 n. 4
Marinus of Tyre, 320
Marisa, 274
māristān, 642 n. 1
Mariti, G., *Istoria di Faccardino*, 681 n. 3
Marj ibn-'Āmir, 31, 424. *See also* Esdraelon
Marj Dābiq: 665; decisive victory at, 657
Marj Rāhiṭ, 414, 452
Marj al-Ṣuffar, 414, 634
Mark Antony, 282, 283, 390
markabah, 146 n. 4
Maron, 521. *See also* Mārūn
Maronite: community, 60; archers, 600; seminary, 675; scholars, 676; minorities, 697; feudalism, 704
Maronites: 37, 439, **521-2**; migrate to Cyprus, 623; laws of, 679
Marqab, al-, 609
Marrākushi, al-, *al-Mu'jib fi Talkhīṣ*, 466 n. 6
Marseilles, 104
Marsīn, 21
Martu, 65, 66, 77
MAR-TU, 65
Mārūn, **521-2**
Marw: 458, 531; churches in, 518
Marwān I, ibn-al-Ḥakam, 452, 484, 497
Marwān II, 478, 489, 529, **531-2**
Marwānid: branch, 445
Marwānids, 449
Masā'il al-Imām Aḥmad, 632
Māsarjawayh, 497
Māsawayh, ibn-, 550
mashhad, 433 n. 4
Mashrafīyah, 409
Masjid al-Aqṣa, al-, 513. *See also* Aqṣa Mosque
Maslamah ibn-'Abd-al-Malik, 447, 448, 449
Masorites, 526
Maspero, G., *Études égyptiennes*, 131 n. 4
Massilia, 104. *See also* Marseille
Maṣṣīṣah, al-, 442
Mas'ūdi, al-, 522
Mas'ūdi, al-, *Murūj al-Dhabab*, 401 n. 9; *al-Tanbīh w-al-Ishrāf*, 455 n. 2
Matāwilah, 37, 503. *See also* Shī'ites
Matn, al-, 35, 678
Matthew of Edessa, *Chronique*, 591 n. 5
Matthews, Charles D., *Palestine*, 624 n. 5
Mattiwaza, 152, 160
Maundrell, 683
mawāli, 454, 474, 485, 530
Māwardi, al-, *al-Aḥkām al-Sulṭānīyah*, 423 n. 1
mawla, 474, 475, 488
Mawṣil, al-: 519, 564; built, 576
Maximus, Tyrian philosopher, 323
maydān, 448
Maydānī, al-, *Majma' al-Amthāl*, 405 n. 5
Mayer, L. A., *Saracenic Heraldry*, 616 n. 1
Maysūn, 425, 438
McCown, Chester C., *Ladder of Progress*, 28 n. 3
McCown, Theodore D., and Keith, Arthur, *Stone Age*, 11 n. 1
Mecca: nursery of song, 504; pilgrimage from, 511; Mosque of, 516
Medes, 201, 217, 218
Media, 150, 197
Median: cavalry, 265
Medina: 430, 435; nursery of song, 504; Mosque of, 516
Medinese: dissidents, 451
Mediterranean: Eastern, 6, 146; climate, 12; basin, 25, 105; region, 45; littoral, 48, 94; pines, 49; coast, 79;

western, 103; traffic, 127; termini of routes, 139; type, 146; civilization, 295; trade, 353, 389
Meek, Theophile, *Hebrew Origins*, 176 n. 3
Megiddo: 26, 28, 81, 82, 84, 179; plain of, 60; ivory, 91, 93; battle of, 129, 132; fall of, 130; stables at, 189; battlefield of, 200; caravans from, 271
Meiser, Karl, *Studien zu Maximos*, 324 n. 1
Mekal, 123
Mélanges de l'Université Saint-Joseph, 173 n. 1
Meleager, 260-61
Melitene, 442. *See also* Malaṭyah
Melkarth, 104, 105
Melkites, **522-3**
Memphis, in Egypt, 100, 127, 142
Menander of Laodicea, 320
Mercer, S. A. B., *Tell el-Amarna Tablets*, 71 n. 3
Merenptah, 178, 181
Merib-baal, 204
Merovingians, 354
Mesha, 123, 194
Mesolithic: **14**, 15, 16, 17, 18; sculpture, 28; art, 19; culture, 20; ibex, 52
Mesopotamia: 26; lower, 7, 29; art in, 21; horse in, 52; Amorites in, 66; lamp from, 207
Mesopotamian: plains, 31; pottery, 20; society, 66
Mesopotamian Desert, 43. *See also* Bādiyat al-Jazīrah
Mesopotamians, 145
Messiah, 584
Messianic: prophets, 214
Messina, 681
Mesuë, 550. *See also* Māsawayh, ibn-
Micah, 215
Middle Ages, 4
Middle Egypt, 149
Middle Kingdom, 127
Middle Stone Age, **14**
mi'dhanah, 515 n. 7
Midḥat Pasha, 670-71, 699
Midian, 178
Midianite: 52; priest, 178
Midianites, 179, 180
miḥrāb, 516
Miletus, 382
Milk-qart, 119, 136, 170, 232. *See also* Melkarth
millah, 668 n. 1
Miller, Barnette, *Palace School*, 667 n. 4
Miller, William, *Ottoman Empire*, 695 n. 1
Mīna al-Bayḍā', al-, 89, **115**
Minorca, 105
Minos, 106
Mirdāsids, 573, **580-81**, 588
mīri, 682 n. 2
Mīrkhwānd, *Ta'rīkh*, 656 n. 3
Miskawayh, ibn-, *Tajārib al-Umam*, 534 n. 1
Miskīn al-Dārimi, 495
Miṣyāf, 608, 609, 610
Mitanni: **150-52**, 157; land, 131; kingdom, 152; throne of, 160
Mitannian: princess, 136; kings, 150
Mitannians, 160
Mithra, 150, **333-4**
Mithradates the Great, 249, 250, 282
Mithraism, 333
miṭlāq, 436
Moab: 41, 144, 179, 187, 289, 375; deities of, 191; pays tribute, 196; envoys from, 199
Moabite Stone, 195
Moabites, 186
Molech, 119. *See also* Moloch
Moloch, 118. *See also* Melkarth
Mommsen, Theodor, *History of Rome*, 280 n. 4; *Provinces of the Roman Empire*, 293 n. 1
Mongol: in Syriac characters, 518; hordes, 557, 607; tribes, 572
Mongolia, 271, 276, 661
Mongolians, 59
Monophysite Church, 372
Monophysites, **371-2**
Monophysitism, 403
Monothelites, 448
Mons Pelegrinus, 597
Mons Regalis, 596 n. 6
Montet, 112
Montet, Pierre, *Byblos et l'Égypte*, 53 n. 1; *Les Reliques de l'art syrien*, 137 n. 1
Moon-God, 18
Mopsuesta, 442. *See also* Maṣṣīṣah, al-
Morgenstern, Julian, *Ark*, 182 n. 3
Mosaic: code, 210
Moses: 60, 83, 176, 178; laws of, 210; a henotheist, 213
Moslem: 3; pilgrims, 199, 289; art, 369; pilgrimage road, 382; dynasties, 440; heraldry, 616; dissident elements, 622
Moslem Syria, 561

Mosul, 519. *See also* Mawṣil, al-
Mot, 115
Mother Earth, 118
Mother Goddess, 89
Mt. 'Ajlūn, 43
Mt. al-Aqra', 32. *See also* Casius
Mt. Athos, 224
Mt. Ba'li-ra'si, 140
Mt. Carmel: 82; caves of, 9, 10, 38. *See also* Carmel
Mt. Casius, 256, 305
Mt. Gerizim, 197, 198, 274
Mt. Gilead, 43
Mt. Hermon: 35, 40, 41, **42**, 472, 685; timber from, 98
Mt. Hirmil, 248
Mt. Lebanon: 449, 695; copper in, 296; dhimmis of, 543
Mt. Seir, 41, 177
Mt. Silpius, 357
Mt. Sinai, 546
Mt. Tabor, 38
Mousterian: 10; lower, 11; culture, 18
Mouterde, René, *Le Nahr el-Kelb*, 142 n.4
Mshtta, 507. *See also* Mushatta, al-
mu'addib, 496
mu'āmalāt, 492, 556
Mu'āwiyah I: 411, **425** *seq.*, **431** *seq.*, 449; fleet of, 445; issues coins, 474
Mu'āwiyah II, 445
Mubarqa', al-, 542
Muḍarites, 469
Mughīrah ibn-Shu'bah, al-, 436
Muhallab, al-, 455
Muḥammad: **410**; in Buṣra, 403
Muḥammad II the Conqueror, 662
Muḥammad 'Ali, **692**
Muḥammad al-Ḥabīb, *see* Ḥabīb, Muḥammad, al-
Muḥammad ibn-al-Ḥanafīyah, 453
Muḥammad ibn-Nuṣayr, 586. *See also* Nuṣayr, Muḥammad, ibn-
Muḥammad ibn-al-Qāsim al-Thaqafi, 461
Muḥammad Rashād, 700
Muḥammad ibn-Ṭughj, 561
Muḥibbi, al-, 675
Muḥibbi, al-, *Khulāṣat al-Athar*, 575 n. 1
muḥtasib, al-, 643
Mu'izz, al-, 'Abbāsid, 563
Mu'izz, al-, Fāṭimid, 578
Mūjib, al-, 167. *See also* Arnon
Mukhtār al-Ḥikam, 644
Mukrān, 461
Mulḥim, Ma'ni, 687
mulk, 441, 534
Müller, W. Max, *Asien und Europa*, 163 n. 4
Multān, 461
Multaqa al-Abḥur, 664
Munayṭirah, al-, 542, 622
Mundhir, al-, Ghassānid, **403-4**
Mundhir, al-, III, 402
Munqidh, banu-, 592
muqaddams, 678
muqarnaṣ, 645
muqātilah, 424
Muqtana Bahā'-al-Dīn, al-, 584. *See also* Bahā'-al-Dīn, al-Muqtana
Murād IV, 684
Murād V, 670
Murji'ites, **501**
Murshilish I, 155, 161
murū'ah, 496
Mūsa ibn-Nuṣayr, **464** *seq.*
Muṣ'ab ibn-al-Zubayr, 452
muṣawwirūn, 505
Mushāqah, Mīkhā'īl, *Mashhad al-'Ayān*, 691 n. 1
Mushatta, al-, 507, 508, 509
Mushrifah, al-, 68. *See also* Qaṭna
mushrikūn, 524
Musil, Alois, *Arabia Deserta*, 391 n. 3; *Palmyrena*, 391 n. 3; *Arabia Petraea*, 409 n. 2; *Northern Ḥeğâz*, 410 n. 2; *Ḳuṣejr 'Amra*, 507 n. 3
Muslim al-Khurāsāni, abu-, 531
Muslim ibn-'Uqbah, 451
Muṣṭafa Kemāl, 662, 701
Mustanṣir, al-, Fāṭimid, 582
Mu'tah, 409-10
Mu'tamid, al-, 558
Mutanabbi', al-, 563, **567-8**
mutaṣarrif, 695
mutaṣarrifīyah, 664 n. 5
Mu'taṣim, al-, 540
Mutawakkil, al-: 542; laureate of, 554
Mutawakkil, al-, puppet caliph, 657
Mu'tazilite: view, 541
Mu'tazilites, **498-9**, 581, 585
Mu'tazz, al-, 554
Muwaqqar, palace, 507, 509
Muwatallish, 156
Muyassar, ibn-, *Akhbār Miṣr*, 595 n. 6
Muzāḥim, 497
Mycenaean: ceramics, 87; weapons, 88; ivory, 89; pottery, 116

Naaman the Syrian, 172
Nabataea: 377, 381, 382, 399; produce of, 383

Nabataean: engineers, 377; kings, 377; coinage, 378; colonists, 383; culture, 383; script, 384; merchants, 384; religion, 384; influence, 386; pottery, 388; sites, 388; origin of diacritical points, 526
Nabataean Arabia, 277
Nabataeans: 64, 247, **375** *seq.*; architecture of, 387-8
Nābighah al-Dhubyāni, al-, 405
Nābighah al-Dhubyāni, al-, *Dīwān*, 405 n. 1
Nabonidus, 218
Nabopolassar, 201, 217
Nābulus: 198, 253, 316; submits, 595. *See also* Shechem
Nābulusi, al-, *Dhakhā'ir*, 675 n. 4
Nadīm, al-, *al-Fihrist*, 370 n. 2
Nādir al-Khāzin, 683
Nāfi' ibn-al-Azraq, 455
Nafīs, ibn-al-, 643
Nafs al-Zakīyah, al-, 539
nafūrah, 295
Naharin, 129, **130**, 131, 132, 150, 164
Nahr Ibrāhīm, 12, **117**, 121
Nahr al-Jawz, 12
Nahr al-Kabīr, al-, 31, 32, 60, 127
Nahr al-Kalb: 30; caves of, 12; inscriptions, 134
nā'ib, 664
Nā'ilah, 431
Na'īma of Aleppo, 674
Naironi, Fausto (Murhij), *Dissertatio*, 522 n. 6
Najaf, al-, 433
Najd, 495
Namārah, al-, 384
Namrūn, ibn-, 522
Naples, 347, 681
Napoleon: 5, 60, **690-91**; artillery of, 559
Naram-Sin, 139, 161
Narbonne, 468
Nasafi, al-, *'Umdat 'Aqīdat Ahl*, 502 n. 5
Naṣībīn, 100, 253, 548. *See also* Nisibis
Nāṣir, al-, Mamlūk, 623-4
Nāṣir-i Khusraw, *Sefer Nameh*, 581 n. 1
naskhi, 645
Naṣr ibn-Sayyār, 460, 461, 531
naṣṣ, 503
Naṭūfian: **14-15**, 20; culture, 16; horse, 52
Naṭūfians, 16
Naukratis, 136
nā'ūrah, 40 n. 1, 619
Nawbakhti, al-, *Firaq al-Shī'ah*, 498 n. 6
Naysābūr, 460
Nazareth: caves of, 10; church of, 608, 688
Neanderthal: type, 11; man, 11
Neapolis, 253, 316. *See also* Nābulus
Near East: 5, 10, 11, 16, 23, 704; prehistory of, 10; wheat of, 25; cereals from, 48; plough in, 145
Near Eastern: 25; history, 61; market, 276; question, 698
Nebuchadnezzar; 5, 134, 202, 217, 218, 221; in North Syria, 144; general, 201; palace of, 235
Necho: 100, 200, 201, 217; defeated, 201
Nefertiti, 132
Negeb, 38
Nehemiah, 184, 197, 209, 221, **222-3**
Neo-Babylonian: 200; Empire, 57, 201; inscription, 134; suzerainty, 217; age, 226
Neo-Babylonians, 163
Neolithic: 7, 25, 26; age, 16; culture, **20**; period, 23; dolmens, 28
Neo-Moslem, 475, 485
Neo-Moslems: 490; empire of, 539
Neo-Platonic: philosophy, 4, **323** *seq.*; doctrine, 371; commentators, 548
Neo-Platonism, **324**
Neo-Pythagoreanism, 325
Nero, 331
Nestorian: term, 517; monastery, 518
Nestorian Church, **371**, 520
Nestorianism, 520
Nestorians, **371-2**
Nestorius, 357, 371
New Empire, 77
New Kingdom, 129
New Stone Age, 7, 14
New Testament: dualism in, 226
New World: 702; plants from, 48
New York: colonies in, 5
Nicaea, 350, 574, 591
Nicator, 253. *See also* Seleucus I
Nicene Creed, 350
Nicene and Post-Nicene Fathers, ed. Philip Schaff, 358 n. 1; 370 n. 1
Nicephorium, 234. *See also* Raqqah, al-
Nicephorus, 565
Nicholson, Reynold A., *Literary History*, 405 n. 3
Nicolaus of Damascus, 284, 294

Nile: 30; valley, 50, 127
Nineveh: 24, 67, 144; fall of, 200
Nīqiyah, 574. *See also* Nicaea
Niqmad, 115
Nīrūn, al-, 461
Nīshāpūr, 197, 460. *See also* Naysābūr
Nisibis: 100, 253, 271, 369; school of, 548. *See also* Naṣībīn
niyābah, 634, 664
Niẓām-i Jadīd, 669
Niẓāmīyah, al-, 644
Noah, 50, 61
Nöldeke, Th., *Die Ghassânischen Fürsten*, 401 n. 9
Normandy, 619
Normans, 591
North Africa, 438
North Arabians: 154; receive alphabet, 169; deity, 178
North Syria: 16, 26, 29, 75, 76, 95, 138-9; art in, 21; cultural focus, 23; glazed paintings from, 28; mountains of, 138
North Syria-Mesopotamia, 21
North Syrian: pottery, 20, 21; Neolithic, 23
North Syrians, 16
Norwegian: fleet, 596
Nu'aymi, al-, *al-Dāris*, 645 n. 2
Nubātah, ibn-, 567
Nu'mān, al-, Ghassānid, 404
Numenius, of Tyre, 324
Numidia, 338
Nūr-al-Dīn, son of Zangi: 576, **599-600**, 642; blazon of, 616; schools built by, 643
Nūr al-'Uyūn wa-Jāmi' al-Funūn, 643
Nūrids: 644, 648; mosques built by, 656
Nuṣayr, Muḥammad, ibn-, 586
Nuṣayri: sect, 60
Nuṣayris, 592, 622
Nuṣayrīyah: 31, 32, **586-7**; conflict with, 585
Nuṣayrīyah Mts., 32, 34. *See also* Jibāl al-Nuṣayrīyah
Nuwayri, al-, *Nihāyat al-Arab*, 444 n. 1
Nuzi: 150; documents, 91; archives, 153; tablets, 161
Nuzi Akkadian, 79

Obermann, Julian, *New Discoveries at Karatepe*, 112 n. 3
'Obīdath, 377
'Obīdath III, 378, 381
Obodas I, 377. *See also* 'Obīdath
O'Callaghan, Roger T., *Aram Naharaim*, 164 n. 2
Ochus, 225. *See also* Artaxerxes III
Odyssey, 551
Og, 75
Old Kingdom, 53, 126
Old Man of the Mountain, 611
Old Stone Age, 7, 14
Old Testament, 116, **209-10**
Olmstead, A. T., *History of Assyria*, 144 n. 1; *History of the Persian Empire*, 226 n. 2
Olympian: games, 302
Ömer Lûtfi Barakan, *Kanunlar*, 664 n. 2
Omri: 166, 192, 386; house of, 194
Ophir, 99
Oppenheim, Max F. von, *Der Tell Halaf*, 21 n. 2
Organon, 549
Oriental: despotism, 224; garb, 236: monarchs, 262; perfumes, 262; religions, 335
Oriental Church: schism in, 371
Origen, 336, 345
Orleans, 354
Orontes: 31, 32, 49, 60; valley, 232. *See also* 'Āṣi, al-
Orthodox Church, 523
Orthodox Syrians, 520
Osiris: 135; cult, 136
Osiris-Isis, 19
Ostia, 347
Ottoman: fleet, 84; era, 486; state, 661 *seq.*; sultans, 666; political theory, 667; officials, 686
Ottoman Empire: 662, 663, 696; disintegration of, 698
Ottoman Turks, 669
Ottomanism, 700
Ottomans: 574; against Ṣafawids, 656
Oxus: 238, 458, 460; crossed, 437

Padan Aram, 164, 177
Pahlawi: 472; alphabet, 169
Palaeolithic: artifacts of, 9; middle, 10, 11, 12; late, **12-13**; early, **7**, 9, 13, 14; man, 13; culture, 16
Palaestina Prima, 351
Palaestina Secunda, 351
Palaestina Tertia, 351
Palermo, 105, 681
Palestine: 3, 14, 16, 23, 25; highlands of, 5; tells of, 7; caves of, 9; pottery, 20, 21: metal implements of, 23;

name, 31, 58; earthquake, 41; wheat from, 49; Amorites in, 65; pre-Israelite, 75, 83, 92; western, 81; guilds in, 87; coins in, 208; copper in, 296; unrest in, 540 *seq.*; cotton from, 673; amputated, 703
Palestine-Lebanon: coast, 46
Palestinian: sites, 23; town, 28; coast, 46, 60; plants, 50; highlands, 52, 82; bronze, 76; synagogue, 365
Palestinians, 25
Palmyra: 26, 40, 44, 271, 382, **388** *seq.*; temple of, 173, 514; Aramaic in, 256; goldsmiths in, 296; last days of, 395; ruins of, 396-9; frescoes of, 398
Palmyrene: **388** *seq.*; tribes, 271; language, 399; script, 399; archers, 399; gods, **400-401**
Pamphilus, 360
Panammu I, 171, 172
Panammu II, 167, 171
Pan-Arab: movement, 696; unity, 702
Pan-Arabism, 703
Paneas, 242. *See also* Bāniyās, in Palestine
Pan-Islam, 700
Pan-Islamic: policy, 699; unity, 702
Panjāb, 218, 235, 458
Pannonia, 347
Papinian, **326-7**, 341, 342
Paradise, 227, 295
Paris: colonies in, 5
Parker, Richard A., and Dubberstein, Waldo H., *Babylonian Chronology*, 237 n. 5
Parmenio, 232, 233
Parthia, 247, 311, 382
Parthian: dynasty, 239, 392; conquests, 280; king, 282; empire, 389
Parthians: 239, 249; extend empire, 247; in Syria, 282
Passover, 198
Paton, David, *Early Egyptian Records*, 128 n. 3
Paton, Lewis B., *Early History of Syria*, 79 n. 2
Patton, John H., *Canaanite Parallels*, 115 n. 3
Paul, 105, **331**, 332, 335, 337, 380
Pax Romana, 290
Peet, T. Eric, *Rhind Mathematical Papyrus*, 148 n. 5
Pekah, 167, 196
Pella, 252. *See also* Fiḥl
Pelusium, 244. *See also* Farmā', al-
Pentateuch, 197
Pentecost, 386
Pepi I, 127
Pergamum, 239, 277
Perizzites, 146
Persepolis, 220, 234, 235
Persia: 64, 231; influence from, 59: eunuch system from, 528
Persian: hegemony, 57; navy, 224; officials, 225; influence on Judaism, 226; loan words, 227; residency, 227; empire, 231; army, 232; office of vizir, 264; kings, 264; bowmen, 265; trees, 275; rule, 295; incursions, 417; mourners, 451; craftsmen, 515; translations from, 548; pilgrims, 642
Persian Gulf: 60, 70, 168, 266, 377, 639; posts, 100; pearls from, 383
Persian Moslems, 530
Persians: 4, 59, 217, 236; a world power, 218
Peshitta, 369
Peter the Great, 697
Petra: 35, 43, 64, 247, 272, 297, **376-7**, 380, 382, 383, 389; caravans from, 271
Petrie, 104
Petrie, Flinders, *Ancient Gaza*, 104 n. 3; *Wisdom Literature*, 137 n. 3
Pfister, R., *Textiles de Palmyre*, 389 n. 6
Pharaoh: representative in Syria, 135
Pharaohs, 28, 148, 264, 297
Pharaonic: reports, 91; domination, 126
Pharisees, 338
Pharpar, 472. *See also* Barada
Philadelphia, 253. *See also* 'Ammān
Philip I Philadelphus, 249
Philip II, Seleucid, 249
Philip the Arab, 311, 317, 345
Philip Augustus, 603
Philip of Macedon, 231
Philippopolis, 316. *See also* Shabbah, al-
Philistia: 31, 38, 59, 181; pays tribute, 196
Philistine: pottery, 85; power, 182; smiths, 184; cities, 199, 316; coast, 271
Philistines, 58, 77, 97, **180-85**
Philo of Alexandria, 340
Philo of Byblus, 114, 116, 320
Philodemus, 260
Philostratus, sophist, 342
Philostratus and Eunapius, *Lives of the Sophists*, 321 n. 2

Philoteria, 252
Phoenicia: 81, 114, 125, 127; quinquereme in, 267; songs from, 302
Phoenicia Libanesia, 308
Phoenicia ad Libanum, 351
Phoenicia Prima, 351
Phoenicia Secunda, 351
Phoenician: 91, 127; coast, 41, 126, 127; language, 61; metal, 88; ivory, 91; sources, 95; colonies, 97, 102, 104, 220, 273; ships, 98, 100, 106, 223; bireme, 99; merchants, 99, 109, 274; inscriptions, 102, 104, 114; writing, 102, 109; characters, 105; colonization, 105; miners, 106; middleman, 109; alphabet, **110-13**; literature, 114; burials, 125; advent, 126; princess, 136; cities, 139, 247, 254, 274, 276; city-states, 140, 167, 186, 225; architects, 189; fleet, 224; national spirit, 232; cultural, 254; wave, 274; city-state, 287; purple, 295
Phoenician Syria, 254
Phoenicians: 3, 64, **79** *seq.*, 100; career of, 5; vine introduced by, 50; cotton of, 91; maritime activity, 97; sea traffic of, 100; nautical achievement, 100; in the Atlantic, 103; posts of, 105; spice trade of, 106; ramming, 267; lose mother tongue, 288
Phoenix, on Lycian coast, 427
Phrygians, 156, 160
Picard, Leo, *Structure and Evolution of Palestine*, 12 n. 4
Pillars of Hercules, 100, 103, 107
Pirenne, Henri, *Mahomet et Charlemagne*; *Histoire de l'Europe*, 421 n. 1
Pisa: merchants of, 590
Pisans, 595
Platonists, 256
Pliny, 95, 294, 295, 317
Pliny, *Natural History*, 32 n. 2
Plotinus, **324-5**
Plutarch, 256
Poebel, Arno, *Historical Texts*, 65 n. 1; *Das appositionelle Pronomen*, 171 n. 5
Poetics, 550
Pognon, H., *Inscriptions sémitiques de la Syrie*, 170 n. 3
Poidebard, Antoine, *Un Grand Port disparu*, 84 n. 3; *La Trace de Rome*, 391 n. 4
Poitiers, 468
Polar Star, 98
Poliak, A. N., *Feudalism in Egypt*, 625 n. 2
Pompeii, 168
Pompey: 60, 250, 280, 281, 378; in Rhodes, 259
Pontius Pilate, 284, 287, 328
Pontus, 249, 250, 282
Porphyry, Neo-Platonist, **324-5**, 355, 356
Portuguese: 672; navigators, 100
Poseidon, 103
Posidonius, 252, 258-9, 267
Post, George E., *Botanical Geography*, 50 n. 7; *Flora of Syria*, 207 n. 4
Probus, 319
Procopius, historian, 358, 372
Propaganda, college, 676
Prophet, the, **409-10**. *See also* Muḥammad
Protestant: hymnals, 501
Protestant Church of Syria, 701
Proverbs, 115
Provincia Arabia, 289
Provincia Syria, 281
Prussia, 697
Ptolemaic: house, 249
Ptolemais, 249, 253. *See also* Acre
Ptolemies: 270, 273, 274; industry under, 275
Ptolemy, geographer, 317, 548, 552
Ptolemy I, 237, 238, 258
Ptolemy II Philadelphus, 253
Ptolemy Euergetes, 239, 240
Puchstein, O., *Erster und zweiter Jahresbericht über die Ausgrabungen in Baalbek*; *Führer durch die Ruinen von Ba'albek*, 312 n. 3
Pullani, 621
Punic, 105, 114, 341, 463
Puteoli, 347, 382, 383
Pylae Syriae, 31. *See also* Baylān
Pyrenees, **457** *seq.*

Qabb Ilyās, 691
qabr, 384
qadar, 499
Qadarites, 499
Qaddāḥ, 'Abdullāh ibn-Maymūn, al-, 578
Qadesh, city: 60, 84, **130**, 147, 156; prince of, 129
Qadesh, goddess, 123
qāḍi, 477 n. 1
Qāḍi al-Fāḍil, al-, 605
Qādīsha River, 37
Qadmūs, al-, 608, 610

Qāhirah, al-, 578. *See also* Cairo
Qā'im, al-, 'Abbāsid caliph, 573
qā'im-maqām, 695
Qā'it-bay, 636
Qalānisi, ibn-al-, *Dhayl Ta'rīkh Dimashq*, 447 n. 7
Qal'at al-Baḥr, 84
Qal'at al-Maḍīq, 239. *See also* Afāmiyah
Qal'āt Nīḥa, 680, 685
Qal'at Sam'ān, 364, 365
Qal'at al-Shaqīf, 39 n. 5. *See also* Belfort
Qalāwūn, 611, 612, 632
Qalqashandi, al-, *Ṣubḥ al-A'sha*. 441 n. 3
Qanawāt, 317 n. 8. *See also* Kanatha
qandah, 619
Qannūbīn, 521
Qanṣawh, 657-8. *See also* Ghawri, al-
Qaramāni, al-, 674-5
Qaramāni, al-, *Akhbār al-Duwal*, 657 n. 1
Qarmaṭian: hordes, 572
Qarmaṭians: **560-61**, 563, 580; in Syria, 579
Qarqar, 140, 166, 167, 192
Qaryatayn, al-, 480, 510
qāshāni, 512
Qāsimīyah, al-, 32, 38, 39
qaṣr, 507 n. 2
Qaṣr al-Ablaq, al-, 648
Qaṣr al-Ḥayr, **509-10**
Qaṣr al-Ṭūba, 509
Qasṭal, al-, palace, 507
Qaṭā'i', al-, 558, 561
Qaṭana, 68. *See also* Qaṭna
Qaṭar ibn-al-Fujā'ah, 456
Qaṭna, 68, 71, 127, 147, 153. *See also* Qaṭana
Qaṭr-al-Nada, 560
Qayrawān, al-: 469; established, 437
Qays, party, 540
Qays ibn-al-Mulawwaḥ, 495
Qays al-Ruqayyāt, ibn-, *Dīwān*, 495 n. 6
Qaysārīyah, 416. *See also* Caesarea, on the sea
Qaysite: party, 452
Qaysites, 528, 594, 694
Qazḥayya, 676
qiblah, 511
Qifṭi, al-, 644
Qifṭi, al-, *Ta'rīkh al-Ḥukamā'*, 549 n. 4; 644 n. 2
Qilij Arslān, 574, 591
Qinnasrīn: 402, 416, 424, 520; tombs in, 532. *See also* Chalcis ad Belum
qirmizi, 620
Qiṭāmah, 577. *See also* Quṭāmah
Qizil-Bash, 586
qmḥw, 17
Qubbat al-Ṣakhrah, 511
Qubbat al-Silsilah, 513
Qubrus, 426. *See also* Cyprus
Quḍā'ah, tribe, 411
Queen Elizabeth, 673
Quirinius, 286, 293
Qulbān Qarāqir, 412. *See also* Qurāqir
Qūniyah, 574. *See also* Iconium
Qurāqir, 412
qurbah, 488
Qurnat al-Sawdā', al-, 32
Qurqumāz, Ma'ni, 680
qurrā', 497
Qurrah, abu-, 546
Qurrah, Thābit, ibn-, 552. *See also* Thābit ibn-Qurrah
Qūrus, 252. *See also* Cyrrhus
Quṣayr 'Amrah: 507, 509; frescoes of, 505
Qusṭa ibn-Lūqa, **550-51**
Quṭāmah, 577
Qutaybah, ibn-, *al-Ma'ārif*, 401 n. 9; *'Uyūn al-Akhbār*, 493 n. 1; *Kitāb al-Shi'r*, 494 n. 3
Qutaybah, pseudo-ibn-, *Qiṣṣat Fatḥ al-Andalus*, 466 n. 5
Qutaybah ibn-Muslim al-Bāhili, **458-61**
Qūṭīyah, ibn-al-, *Ta'rīkh Iftitāḥ al-Andalus*, 466 n. 5
quṭn, 91
Quṭuz, 631

rabābah, 619
Rabbath, Antoine, *Documents inédits*, 674 n. 6
Rabbath-Ammon, 253. *See also* 'Ammān
Rabbil II, 381, 382
Rabel, 381. *See also* Rabbil II
Rachel: tribe, 178
Rāḍi, al-, 561
Rā'iq, ibn-, 562
ra'īyah, 667 n. 3
raj'ah, 584
Rakkab-El, 174
Ramesids, 148
Ramlah, al-, 25, 511, 563, 594
Rammanu, 77. *See also* Hadad

Ramses II: 134, 136, 156, 178; stele of, 142
Ramses III, 163, 181, 182
Raphia, 242, 264, 265, 266
Raqīm, al-, 376
Raqqādah, 577
Raqqah, al-: 234 n. 4; caliph's residence in, 540
Ra's al-Shamrah: 9, 18, 85, **115** *seq.*, 152; smelting iron in, 87; scales and weights in, 87; text, 94; cuneiform, 110; tablets, 112. *See also* Ugarit
Ra's al-Shaq'ah, 247 n. 2. *See also* Theouprosopon
Rashap, 77, 120, 123
Rāshayya, 686
Rāshid-al-Dīn Sinān, 610
rāshidūn, 428, 536
Rastan, al-, 252. *See also* Arethusa
Ravenna, 354
Rayfūn, 704
Raymond II of Tripoli, 611
Raymond Lull, 625-6, 652
Raymond of Toulouse, 593, 594, 595, 597
Rayy, al-, 453
Records of the Past, 200 n. 2
Red Sea: 31, 39, 100, 184; trade, 189; fleet, 602
Reginald of Châtillon, 602
Rehoboam, 191, 198
Renaissance, 204
Republic, 550
Resapha, 391. *See also* Ruṣāfah, al-
Reshuf, 174
Rey, E., *Les Colonies franques*, 639 n. 4
Rezin, 167, 196
Rezon, 166, 191
Rhine Province, 11
Rhodes: 97, 382, 427; Stoic school in, 259
Rhodian: jars, 276
Rhotert, Hans, *Transjordanien: vorgeschichtliche Forschungen*, 52 n. 4
Rib Addi, 72, 74, 75
Riblah, 144, 201, 202
Richard I Cœur de Lion, 603
Riḍwān, 574-5, 592, 610
Rihani, Ameen F., *Quatrains of abu'l-Ala*, 582 n. 7
Rimmon, 172
Risālah al-Masīḥīyah, al-, 584
Roderick, Visigoth, 464, 505
Rogers, Robert W., *Cuneiform Parallels*, 368 n. 3
Roman: period, 4; law, 4, 300; genius, 4; roads, 43; legions, 249; officials, 281; governors, 285; interest in Syria, 288; administration, 289, 290; colonies, 289; policy, 289; trader, 297; franchise, 337; imports, 383; law, 492; fortresses, 507; columns, 516
Roman Catholic: 523; rite, 520
Roman Catholic Church, 359
Roman Catholics, 517
Roman Hellenism, 284
Roman Palestine, 284
Roman Syria, 292, 299, 302, 319
Romanization, 337, 380
Romans: 4, 59, 107, 108, 272; annex Syria, 249-50; as polytheists, 331
Rome: 107, 108, 244, 249; empire of, 4; influences from, 59; embassy from, 243; civil war in, 282
Romer, Alfred S., *Man and the Vertebrates*, 11 n. 1
Rostovtzeff, M., *Social and Economic History of the Hellenic World*, 245 n. 1; *Excavations at Dura-Europos*, 268 n. 1; *Caravan Cities*, 268 n. 2; *Social and Economic History of the Roman Empire*, 297 n. 1
Rouen, 354
Round Table, 616
Rowe, Alan, *Topography and History of Beth-shan*; *Four Canaanite Temples*, 120 n. 9
Roxana, 236
Rückert, Friedrich, *Hamâsa*, 553 n. 6
Rūdis, 427. *See also* Rhodes
Ruhā', al-, 253 n. 3, 548. *See also* Edessa
Rum: millet, 668
Rūm, 444, 574
Ruqqād, al-, 415, 416
Ruṣāfah, al-, 391, 403, 510, 532
Ruska, Julius, *Arabische Alchemisten*, 498 n. 3
Russia, 298, 688, 692, 697
Russian: fleet, 689; influence, 697
Russo-Turkish: war, 671
Rustah, ibn-, *al-A'lāq al-Nafīsah*, 489 n. 5
Rustem Pasha, 696
Rustum, Asad J., *Royal Archives*, 692 n. 4
Ryckmans, G., *Les Noms propres sud-sémitiques*, 392 n. 2

Sā'āti, ibn-al-, *Dīwān*, 606 n. 1
Ṣabbāgh, Mikhā'īl, al-, *Ta'rīkh al-Shaykh Ẓāhir*, 688 n. 1

Ṣābi'ah, 485
Ṣābians, 485, **552-3**
sabīl, 513
ṣabr, 496
Sachs, Curt, *History of Musical Instruments*, 206 n. 1
Sacy, Silvestre de, *Exposé de la religion*, 585 n. 1
Sa'd-al-Dawlah, Ḥamdāni, 565-6
Sa'd-al-Dīn, *Tāj al-Tawārīkh*, 658 n. 4
Sadducees, 338
Saeki, P. Y., *Nestorian Documents*, 518 n. 1
Ṣafa, al-: 42 n. 5, 403; inscriptions at, 299
Ṣafad: earthquake in, 41; capitulates, 608
Ṣafadi, al-, *al-Wāfi*, 653 n. 7; *Ta'rīkh al-Amīr*, 681 n. 4
Ṣafawid: state, 656
Ṣafawids: state religion by, 657
Sahar, 174
Sahara, 15, 45
ṣāḥib, 477
ṣāḥib al-barīd, 541
ṣāḥib al-kharāj, 477
Sāḥil 'Alma, 34, 679
Sahure, 76, 127
Ṣahyūni, Jibrā'īl, al-, 675
Sa'īd, ibn-, *al-Mughrib*, 561 n. 5
Sa'īd ibn-Baṭrīq, 522
Sa'īd ibn-Baṭrīq (Eutychius), *al-Ta'rīkh al-Majmū'*, 517 n. 1
Sa'īd ibn-Misjaḥ, 504
ṣā'ifah, 443
St. Anthony, 364
St. Augustine, 102
St. Ephraim, 524. *See also* Ephraim the Syrian
St. Francis of Assisi, 626
St. George, 593
St. George Bay, 32
St. Jerome, 353, **358-9**
St. John the Damascene, 414, 438, 440, 484, **499-51**, 524, 546
St. Louis, king of France, 606, **607**, 611
St. Sāba, monastery, 499, 546
St. Sergius, 391
Saïte: renaissance, 137
Sakje Geuzi, 21, 26
Saladin: 5, 576. *See also* Ṣalāḥ-al-Dīn
Ṣalāḥ-al-Dīn: 382, 513, 576, **600** *seq.*; coin of, 605; tomb of, 698. *See also* Saladin
Ṣalāḥ-al-Dīn ibn-Yūsuf, physician, 643
Ṣalāḥi, al-, 648
Salamis, 224
Salamīyah, 577 n. 4. *See also* Salamyah
Salamyah, 540, 561, 577, 578, 664
Ṣāliḥ ibn-'Ali, 542, 543
Ṣāliḥ Ḥājji, al-, 634
Ṣāliḥ ibn-Mirdās, 580-81, 582
Ṣāliḥ Najm-al-Dīn Ayyūb, al-, 229
Ṣāliḥ ibn-Yaḥya, 623
Ṣāliḥīyah, al-, 272. *See also* Dura-Europus
Salīm I, 657-8, 663
Salīm III, 669-70
Saljūqs: **573** *seq.*, 580; of Syria, 574-6
Ṣalkhad, 383, 599
Sallāmah, 480
Salm, 175
salūqi, 480
Salūqiyah, 239. *See also* Seleucia, on the Orontes
Sam'āni, al-Qāḍi, al-, *al-Ansāb*, 492 n. 1
Sam'āni, Yūsuf Sam'ān, al-, 676
Samār Jubayl, 521
Samaria: 38, 166, 191, 267, 283: siege of, 142; palace of, 192; refortified, 196; pays tribute, 196
Samaritan: hills, 49; temple, 274
Samaritanism, 60
Samaritans: 38, **197-8**; chastised, 234 attacked, 246; ill-treatment of, 287
Samarqand, 460, 656
Sāmarra, 21
Samāwah, al-, 45. *See also* Bādiyat al-'Irāq
Samḥ ibn-Mālik al-Khawlāni, al-, 468
Samos, 105
Samosata, 116, 173, 443. *See also* Sumaysāṭ
Sampsigeramus, 308, 390
Samuel, 50, 186
Sanballat, 223
Sanchuniathon, 114
Sandys, George, 684
Sandys, George, *Relation of a Journey*, 680 n. 3
sanjāq, 31 n. 2, 664 n. 6
Ṣannīn, 32
Sanskrit: alphabet, 169; linguistics, 491
Santa Sophia, 314, 448. *See also* Aya Sofya
São Paulo: colonies in, 5
Saphadin, 606. *See also* Malik al-'Ādil, al-, Ayyūbid
saqqāṭah, 510

Sarābīṭ al-Khādim, 110
Saracen, 500
Saragossa, 466
sarāwīl, 617
Sardinia: 105, 107; colonies in, 102
Sargon I, 65, 139
Sargon II, 142, 156, 197, 199, 214
Sarjūnids, 438
Ṣarkhad, 599. *See also* Ṣalkhad
ṣarrāf, 669
Sarton, George, *Introduction to the History of Science*, 620 n. 2
Sarūm, 521
Sasanians, 272
Sāsānid: dynasty, 372, 392
Saturn, 145
Saul: 38, 166, 182, 184, **186-7**; home of, 85
Sauvaget, J., *Les Monuments historiques*, 642 n. 2
Ṣawāri, dhu (or dhāt)-al-, 427
Sāwīrus ibn-al-Muqaffa', *Siyar*, 532 n. 1
Sayce, A. H., *Records of the Past*, 71 n. 3
Ṣaydā', 81 n. 8. *See also* Sidon
Sayf-al-Dawlah, Ḥamdāni, 562, **564** *seq.*, 582
Sayfa (Sīfa?), 678, 681, 684
Sayḥūn, 235 n. 1, 458 n. 5. *See also* Jaxartes
Says, 509. *See also* Usays
sayyid, 436
Schaeffer, Claude F. A., *Cuneiform Texts of Ras Shamra*, 9 n. 6; *Ugaritica*, 18 n. 3
Scheil, V., *Recueil de lois assyriennes*, 174 n. 1
Schiffer, Sina, *Die Aramäer*, 163 n. 4
Schumacher, Gottlieb, *Northern 'Ajlūn*, 28 n. 2
Scilly Isles, 103
Scripturaries, 485, 486
Scutari, 447. *See also* Chrysopolis
Scythopolis, 253, 281, 368. *See also* Beth-shean
Sea of Galilee: 10, 275, 377; cave near, 12
Sea of Marmora, 444
Sea People, 116, 126
Sebaste, 316
Second Isaiah, 214, 215
Seleucia, on the Orontes: 252, 267; founded, 239
Seleucia-Ctesiphon, 517
Seleucia-on-the-Tigris, 241, 270, 271, 279, 282
Seleucid: kingdom, 57, 241, 246; era, 237; house, 247; institutions, 262 *seq.*; army, 264, 265; depot, 265; fleet, 266; empire, 267; policy, 270; trade, 273; throne, 273; anarchy, 280; colonies, 288
Seleucid Syria, 275, 278, 301
Seleucids: 270, 274; tithes, 268
Seleucis, 267
Seleucus, Chaldaean, 258
Seleucus I Nicator, 234, **237-9**, 256, 262, 265, 267, 272
Seleucus II Callinicus, 239
Seltzer, C. Carl, *Racial Characteristics of Syrians; Contributions to the Racial Anthropology of the Near East*, 154 n. 1
Semiramis, 343
Semites: 14, 25, 26, **61**, 62; advent of, 57; first, 61; original home of, 64; sacrifice by, 123; Hellenized, 258
Semitic: emigrants, 17; mother tongue, 18; invasion, 24; languages, 61-2, 64; migration, 62; -speaking people, 62; tongue, 64; traits, 64; people, 65; invaders, 66; immigrants, 103; place names, 104, 105; fertility cult, 116; princes, 149; features, 154; empires, 218; culture, 251, 420; names, 253; gardening, 295
Semple, Ellen C., *Geography of the Mediterranean Region*, 40 n. 3
Seneca, *Questiones naturales*, 41 n. 2
Sennacherib: 87, 91, 99, 142, 199; returns to Nineveh, 200
Senwosret I, 127, 128
Septimius Ḥayrān, 392
Septimius Severus, 302, 305, 307, 311, 341-2
Septuagint, 57, 171
Sergiopolis, 391. *See also* Ruṣāfah, al-
Sergius, patriarch, 417
Sergius, patrician, 411, 412
Seth, 148
Seti I, 134
Seton-Williams, M. J., *Britain*, 698 n. 1
Severus, Jacobite patriarch, 360, 372
Seville, 466
Seyrig, Henri, *Antiquités syriennes*, ser. 2, 398 n. 1; ser. 1, 510 n. 2
Shafaṭ-ba'al, 112
Shāfi'ite: system, 555
Shahbah, al-, 317. *See also* Philippopolis
shahīd, 436

Shahrastāni, al-, *al-Milal w-al-Niḥal*, 456 n. 1
Shajar-al-Durr, 629
Shalmaneser I, 152
Shalmaneser III: 139, 140, 167; obelisk of, 194
Shalmaneser V, 140, 196
Sha'm, al-, 58, 547
Shāmah, abu-, 654
Shāmah, abu-, *al-Rawḍatayn*, 575 n. 5; 654 n. 5
Sham'al: 144, 167, 170; relief from, 368
Shamanism, 631
Shamash, 174, 210, 400
Shāpūr I, 305, 392
Shaqbah, al-, 14
Shaqīf, al-, 603, 608. *See also* Qal'at al-Shaqīf
Shaqīf Arnūn, 608
Shaqīf Tīrūn, 680. *See also* Qal'at Nīḥa
Shara, dhu-al-, 384. *See also* Dūshara
Sharḥ Tashrīḥ al-Qānūn, 643
Sharon, 31, 38, 196
Sharuhen, 147, 149
Shāsh, al-, 461
shātiyah, 443
Shawbak, al-, 596, 602
Shay'-al-Qawm, 401
shaykh al-jabal, 617
Shayzar, 253, 415, 592, 621
Shechem, 82, 147, 161, 191, 198, 253, 274, 316. *See also* Nābulus
Shem, 61
shī'ah, 430
Shī'ah, al-: **502** *seq.*; pilgrimage in, 433
Shī'ah Islam, 450
Shihāb-al-Dīn al-Suhrawardi, 651. *See also* Suhrawardi, al-
Shihāb al-Zuhri, ibn-, 491
Shihābs: **678** *seq.*; succeed the Ma'ns, 686
Shiḥnah, ibn-al-, *al-Durr al-Muntakhab*, 565 n. 1
Shī'i, abu-'Abdullāh al-Ḥusayn, al-, 577
Shī'ism, 451
Shī'ite: 436; partisans, 433; ultra-, 561
Shī'ites: 37, 441, **502** *seq.*; avenged, 535
Shīrkūh, 600
Shishak, 198. *See also* Shishonk
Shishonk, 198
Shubbiluliuma, 74, 152, 155, 160
Shūf, al-, 639
Shukri Ghānim, *see* Ghānim, Shukri
Shuraḥbīl ibn-Ḥasanah, 411
Shu'ūbīyah, 555
Shuwayr, al-, 46
Sibṭ ibn-al-Jawzi, *Mir'āt al-Zamān*, 597 n. 4
Sicily: 97, 592; colonies in, 102
Sīdi 'Uqbah, 438
Sidon: 39, 41, 74, 83, **84**; fossil fishes in, 34; mollusc of, 94; submits to Sennacherib, 142; deities of, 191; in ashes, 225; palace in, 227, 683; coin of, 228; surrenders, 232; mint in, 267; glass of, 276; dyes in, 295; purple from, 383; garden of, 594; church of, 617
Sidonian: glass manufacturer, 298
Sidonians, 88, 274
Ṣiffīn, **431-2**
Sihon, 179
Ṣihyawn: 603; lord of, 576
Sijilmāsah, 577, 578
Sijistān, 458
sikkah, 619
Siloam, 199
Simeon Stylites, **365-6**, 372
Simon, Maccabean, 245
Simon Bar Kokba, 340
Simon of Ṭaibūtheh, 553
Simyra, 72, 74, 82, 130
Sin, 175
Sinai: 30, 31, 58; coast of, 60; mines of, 110; dealings with, 112
Sinaitic: peninsula, 64; script, 110
Sinān, son of Thābit ibn-Qurrah, 552
Sinjirli, 142, 167, 170, 172. *See also* Sham'al
Sinuhe, 128
Sīr Darya, 235 n. 1. *See also* Jaxartes
sīrah, 624
Sīrat 'Antar, 624
Sīrat al-Ẓāhir, 625
Sirr al-Asrār, 614
Sisters of St. Joseph, 673
Sistine Madonna, 205
Sīwah, 233
Sixth Dynasty, 53
Smith, George A., *Historical Geography*, 42 n. 5
Smith, Sidney, *Babylonian Historical Texts*, 218 n. 2
Smith, Sir Sidney, 690, 691
Snefru, 127
Sodom, 41
Solomon: 157, **189-92**; fleet of, 190

Song of Songs, 115
Sophronius, patriarch, 418
Sorbonne, 676
South Arabia: frankincense of, 60, 298, 382; spice-producing, 377
South Arabian: pantheon, 77; tribes, 425
South Arabians, 76
South Arabic: script, 110
South Palestine, 76
South Syria: 26; satrapy, 267
Sozomen, 359
Spain: 64, 438; conquests in, 4; combs in, 91; colonies in, 97, 102; lead from, 100; settlements in, 107; conquest of, **463** *seq.*
Spanish-Roman, 467
Sparta, 95
Spitaler, Anton, *Grammatik,* 546 n. 5
Squieres Tale, 615
Starcky, Jean, *Palmyre,* 391 n. 2
Steindorff, George, and Seele, Keith C., *When Egypt Ruled the East,* 130 n. 1
Stephen, Pisan, 614
Stevenson, W. B., *Crusaders in the East,* 596 n. 3
Stoic: philosophy, 4
Stoicism, 329
Stone Age: implements, 13; culture, 20; camel in, 52; in Syria, 147
Strabo, 103, 104, 105, 278, 279, 295, 308, 316, 323, 378, 383, 385, 386
Strabo, *Geography,* 17 n. 1
Strait of Gibraltar, 103
Straton's Tower, 283. *See also* Caesarea, on the sea
Strzygowski, Joseph, *Orient oder Rom*; *Origin of Christian Church Art*; *L'Ancien Art chrétien de Syrie,* 368 n. 2
Subarians, 150
Subartu, 150
Subki, al-, *Ṭabaqāt al-Shāfiʿīyah,* 605
Sublime Porte, 662
Suchem, Ludolph von, 639
Suchem, Ludolph von, *Description of the Holy Land,* 593 n. 6
Suez Canal, 672
Sufi: institution, 525
Sufism, 651
ṣufūf, 531
Sufyāni, 540-41, 561
Sufyānids, 449
Suhrawardi, al-, *Ḥikmat al-Ishrāq,* 651 n. 5
Sukenik, E. L., *Ancient Synagogues in Palestine,* 365 n. 2
sukkar, 619
Sulaymān, Saljūq, 574
Sulaymān, Umayyad caliph, **445-6,** 466, 467
Sulaymān I the Magnificent: 662, 663; capitulations granted by, 672
ṣulḥan, 415, 423
Ṣūli, al-, *Akhbār abi-Tammām,* 553 n. 4
sulṭān, 573
Sulṭān Shāh, 575
Sumaysāṭ, 116, 442. *See also* Samosata
Sumer, 29
Sumerians: 62; dynasties, 65; poet, 66; poem, 78; words, 138
Sumerians, 65, 138
Sumero-Babylonian: culture 59; influence, 79
Sumero-Hurrian: dictionary, 153
Sumqānīyah, al-, 686
Sun-Goddess, 19
Sunnis, 491
Sunnite: view, 502
Ṣūr, 81 n. 7. *See also* Tyre
Surayj, ibn-, 504
Sūri, 59 n. 1
Suryān, 520
Suryāni, 59 n. 1
Susa, 220, 234, 236
Suwa, 412
Suyūṭi, al-, *Ḥusn al-Muḥāḍarah,* 497 n. 2
Sydney: colonies in, 5
Syri, 346
Syria: 3, 4, 5, 9, 24, 64; southern, 3, 75, 76, 77; people of, 4; historical importance of, 5; pre-history of, 6; history of, 7, 61; eastern, 7, 47, 49; modern, 17; northern, 23, 79, 126; illiterate culture of, 24; glacial epoch in, 34; structure of, 39; earthquakes in, 40, 572; winds in, 45; floral regions in, 49; horse introduced into, 52; camel in, 52; donkey in, 53; name, 57-8; determining factors, 59; overrun by Amorites, 66; present-day, 85; early, 106; immigrants from, 109; incorporated in Egyptian empire, 129; in Egyptian empire, 135; metallurgy in, 147; use of iron in, 184; satraps of, 225; war elephants in, 266; Hellenistic kings of, 270; trade of, 270; prosperity of, 273; agricultural products of, 274; plants introduced into, 274; forests,

275; population of, 279; a Roman province, 280 *seq.*; conquest of, 280; kingdom of, 281; imperial province, 286; legate of, 286; Greek settlements in, 289; at its height, 290; leading province, 292; population of, 292; spices in, 294; linen from, 295; gypsum in, 296; frankincense from, 297; glass from, 353; bishops, 355; an 'Abbāsid province, 534 *seq.*; hegemony of, 534; unrest in, 540 *seq.*; dark ages in, 572; administration of, 637-8, 663 *seq.*; ascetics of, 641; Turkish province, **661** *seq.*; Catholic Christians of, 672; terrorized, 690
Syria-Palestine: 4, 12, 18, 128, 218; Mesolithic culture of, 20; copper of, 23; papyrus introduced into, 277; province of, 477
Syria-Palestine-Lebanon, 29, 129
Syria Prima, 351
Syria Secunda, 351
Syriac: language, 4, **170-71**; -speaking peoples, 59; asserted itself, 369; characters, 384; liturgy, 522, 523; loan words from, 525; vowel pointing, 526; in Lebanon, 546; borrowings, 547; translations from, 548; commentaries, 549; used by Maronites, 676
Syriac Bible, 335
Syrian: capital, 4; diet, 25; littoral, 31; climate, 45; highlands, 45; vegetation, 48; Republic, 58-9; ports, 60, 70; culture, 61, 226; industries, 87; tribute bearers, 93; civilization, 103, 105, 109, 226; fellah, 123; shields, 133; sea, 135; influence on Egypt, 135; girls in Egypt, 136; products, 136; tassels, 137; language, 171; goddess, 173; coast, 181; sphinx, 204; shepherds, 206; landscape, 208; monarchy, 237, 238; kingdom, 239; academy, 256; trade, 273; manufacturers, 275; roads, 290; gardening, 295; plants, 295; wines, 296; cinnabar, 296; traffic, 297; styrax, 297; glassmaker, 298; weavers, 298; imports, 298; musicians, 302; goddess, 310; Roman citizen, 337; soldiers, 338; dynasty at Rome, 340 *seq.*; sun-god, 344; settlements, 347; merchants, 347, 348, 353, 672; religious penetration, 349; emigrants, **353-5**; basilica, 367; minaret, 516; churches, 520; songs, 533; peasants, 546; contribution to Arab renaissance, **548** *seq.*; missionaries, 631; intellectuals, 702
Syrian Christian Church, **517** *seq.*
Syrian Christianity, 335, 524
Syrian Christians, 329
Syrian Desert: **43-4**, 49, 60, 77, 282, 388; lions in, 346
Syrian Gates, 31, 60
Syrian Latins, 603
Syrian Monophysites, 372
Syrian Saddle: 31, 60, **70**, 176; significance of, 24
Syrians: 4, 5; early, 3; Christian, 4; history of, 17; migrate into Egypt, 137; educated, 257; Semitized, 288; in Constantinople, 639
Syro-Arab: states, 375, 381
Syro-Arabs, 438
Syro-Hellenic: pattern, 559
Syro-Persian: elements, 262
Syro-Phoenicia, 305

Ṭabari, al-, 427
Ṭabari, al-, *Ta'rīkh*, 404 n. 1; *Ikhtilāf al-Fuqahā'*, 555 n. 8
Ṭabarīyah, 424. *See also* Tiberias
Tacitus, 356
Tadmur: 26, 348, **388**; rebels in, 540. *See also* Palmyra
Taghlib, tribe, 439, 494
Taghri-Birdi, ibn-, 656
Taghri-Birdi, ibn-, *al-Nujūm al-Zāhirah*, ed. Popper, 447 n. 7; ed. Juynboll, 558 n. 4
Taharqa, 199. *See also* Tirhaka
Tāj-al-Dīn al-Subki, 653. *See also* Subki, al-
Takhtajis, 586
takīyah, 448, 514
Ṭal'at, 700
Ṭalḥah, claimant, 431
Talḥūqs, 678, 687
ta'līf al-qulūb, 438
talzīm, 664
Tamar in Idumaea, 389
Tamerlane, 630, 655. *See also* Tīmūr
Tammām, abu-, **553-4**
Tammām, abu-, *Dīwān*, 553 n. 4
Tammuz, 117, 120
Tammuz-Astarte: cult, 160
Tancred, 595
Tangier, 462
Tangiz, 637
Ṭāniyūs Shāhīn, 704
Ṭanjah, 462. *See also* Tangier

Ṭannūs al-Shidyāq, 675
Tanūkh, banu-, 545
Tanūkh, tribe, 581. *See also* Tanūkh, banu-
Tanūkhs, 545, 678, 685
tanẓīmāt, 669
Taoist, 518
taqīyah, 611
Ṭarābulus, 82 n. 3, 225. *See also* Tripoli
ṭarbūsh, 670
Ṭarīf, 463
Tarifa, 464. *See also* Jazīrat Ṭarīf
Ṭāriq, **463** *seq.*
Tarn, W. W., *Hellenistic Civilization*, 255 n. 1; *Hellenistic Military and Naval Developments*, 266 n. 5
Tarshish, 104
Tarsus: 104, 442, 563, 657; occupied, 592
Tartars, 607, 640
Tartessus, 104. *See also* Tarshish
Ṭarṭūs, 83, 609. *See also* Tortosa
Tāshkand, 461. *See also* Shāsh, al-
Taurus Mts.: 58, 60, 70, 277, 443, 448, 591; crossed 692
Ṭawānah, al-, 462. *See also* Tyana
Tawmāt Nīḥa, 35
Tayādhūq, 497
Taymā', 175, 218, 272
Taymīyah, ibn-, 624
Ṭayyi', tribe, 581, 600
Teima, 218. *See also* Taymā'
Tell al-'Ajjūl, 147. *See also* Gaza
Tell al-'Amārnah: 71, 75, 82, 84; letters, 113; correspondence, 132; tablets, 150
Tell al-'Aṭshānah, 114, 152. *See also* Alalakh
Tell al-Duwayr, 26, 179, 227. *See also* Lachish
Tell al-Fūl, 85. *See also* Gibeah
Tell al-Ḥalaf: 21, 150, 169; dromedary in, 53
Tell al-Ḥarīri, 66. *See also* Mari
Tell abu-Hawām, 88
Tell al-Jazar, 25. *See also* Gezer
Tell al-Judaydah: 18, 28; pottery, 20
Tell al-Mutasallim, 26, 81 n. 5. *See also* Megiddo
Tell al-Naṣbah: bee-keeping in, 208
Tell Rifaḥ, 242. *See also* Raphia
Templars, 601 n. 5, 607, 608, 611, 616
Temple of Solomon: 189, 296, 386; ritual of, 204; rebuilt, 221, 283; treasures of, 222; altar of, 244; burned, 339
Ten Commandments, 210
Tennes, 225
Tertiary, 30, 34
Tertullian, 463
Teshub, 159, 160, 334
Testa, I. de, *Recueil*, 668 n. 4
Tethys, 34
Tha'ālibi, al-, *Yatīmat al-Dahr*, 567 n. 3
Thābit ibn-Qurrah, 552
Thales, 114
Thammūd, 375
Thapsacus, 234
Thāwafīl of Edessa, 551
Thayyim, son of Sa'd, 347
Thebes, in Egypt: temple at, 131
Thebes, in Greece, 106
Theodorus, brother of Heraclius, 412, 416
Theodorus abu Ḳurra, *De cultu imagi-num*, 546 n. 2
Theodosian Code, 327
Theodosius II, 359, 371
Theodosius the Great, 304, 351
Theophanes, 447
Theophanes, *Chronographia*, 402 n. 6
Theophrastus, *De historia plantarum*, 96 n. 3
Theos Epiphanes, 244. *See also* Antiochus IV
Theouprosopon, 247. *See also* Ra's al-Shaq'ah
Thermopylae, 224, 243
Thousand and One Nights, The, 536
Thrace, 106
thughūr, 443, 540
Thureau-Dangin, F., *Die sumerischen und akkadischen Königsinschriften*, 65 n. 3
Thutmose I, 129, 131, 136, 152
Thutmose III, 5, 70, 72, 82, 84, 86, 123, 129, 130, 131, 132, 137, 139, 149, 152
Thutmose IV, 92, 136
Tiberias: 40, 316; built, 284
Tiberius, 287
Tiberius II, 404
Tibrīz, 632
Tibrīzi, al-, *Sharḥ Diwān al-Ḥamāsah*, 553 n. 6
Tiglath-pileser I, 139, 162, 388
Tiglath-pileser III, 140, 167, 168, 196
Tigranes, 249, 250
Tigranocerta, 249
Tigris: 21; forded by Alexander 234

Tigro-Euphrates: valley, 50; region, 62
Timaeus, 550
Tīmūr, 630, 667
Ṭiqṭaqa, ibn-al-, *al-Fakhri*, 427 n. 1
Ṭirāz, 479
Tirhaka, 144, 199
Tirzah, 191, 192
Titus: destroys Jerusalem, 339-40
Tjeker, 181
Toledo: 466; cathedral of, 467
Torrey, Charles C., *Our Translated Gospels*, 168 n. 3
Tortosa, 83. *See also* Antaradus
Toulouse, 468
Tours: battle of, 468-9
Toynbee, Arnold J., *Survey*, 59 n. 3; *Study of History*, 103 n. 3
Trachonitis, 293, 308. *See also* Ḥawrān
Trajan: 297, 302, 330, 390; forum of, 354
Transjordan: 41, 43, 179, 267, 293, 703; cities of, 7; dolmens in, 28; rainfall in, 46; plateau, 49; annexed, 289; under Nabataeans, 380
Transoxiana, 437, **458** *seq.*
Trinity, 479
Tripoli: 31, 84, 253, 612; Phoenician capital, **224-5**
Tripolis, 225. *See also* Tripoli
Tristram, H. B., *Land of Israel*, 41 n. 4; *Survey of Western Palestine*, 49 n. 2
Tritton, A. S., *Caliphs and their Non-Muslim Subjects*, 422 n. 1
Tryphon, 273, 280
ṭūb, 137 n. 4
Ṭughj, 561
Ṭughril: in Baghdād, 573
Ṭughtagīn, 576
Ṭukhāristān, 460
Tulaylāt al-Ghassūl: 23, 24; mural paintings, 28
Ṭūlūn, ibn-: **557** *seq.*; coin of, 557
Ṭūlūnids, **557** *seq.*
Tūmān-Bāy, 658
Tunis, 102, 437 n. 7, 577
Tunisia, 437 n. 7
Tūrān, 458
Tūrān-Shāh, brother of Ṣalāḥ-al-Dīn, 601, 629
turbah, 645
Turcopuli, 600
Turkestan, 247, 437, 458, 518
Turkey, 686, 688, 698
Turkification, 702
Turkish: mountains, 32; dynasties, 458; tribes, 572; words from, 671; army, 692; troops, 695
Turks: 5, 59, 460; contact with, 437; praetorian guard of, 542; hordes of, 573
Turville-Petre, F., *Researches in prehistoric Galilee*, 9 n. 4
Tuscany, 681, 684
Tushratta, 150, 152
Tutankhamon, 133
Tutush, 574
Twelfth Dynasty, 127, 148
Twentieth Dynasty, 99
Tyana, 462
Tyre: 39, 41, 83, **84**, 102, 108, 260-61; silk in, 92; mollusc of, 94; capture of, 144, 199; reduction of, 217; resists, **232-3**; temple of, 234; mint in, 267; glass of, 276; dyes in, 295; circus players from, 301; fabrics from, 353; purple from, 383; dockyards in, 426; glassware of, 571; Notre-Dame in, 617. *See also* Ṣūr
Tyrian: purple, 94, 95; masons, 188; architects, 204
Tyrian Baal, 192
Tyrians, 189

ʻUbaydah, Nabataean, 377. *See also* ʻObīdath
ʻUbaydah ibn-al-Jarrāḥ, abu-, 411, 415, 418, 425
ʻUbaydite: dynasty, 578. *See also* Fāṭimid
ʻUbaydullāh, son of Muḥammad al-Ḥabīb, 577-8
ʻUbaydullāh, son of Ziyād, 450
ubhul, 51
Ubi, 71
ʻūd, al-, 619
Udaynath, **391-3**
Ugarit: 9, 23, 25, 26, 84, **115** *seq.*; temple at, 77, 113, 120; ceramics, 87; devastated, 181; literature, 204. *See also* Ra's al-Shamrah
Ugaritic: literature, 115; text, 116
Ukhūwah, ibn-al-, *Maʻālim al-Qurba*, 643 n. 2
ʻulamā', 645
Ullaza, 74
Ulpian, **326-7**
ʻulūj, 547
ʻUmān, 455, 477
ʻUmar, Orthodox caliph: 418, 419, 426, **428-9**; covenant of, 422; sends teachers, 497

'Umar, son of Sa'd ibn-abi-Waqqāṣ, 450
'Umar II ibn-'Abd-al-'Azīz: 447, 468, 475, 484, 493, 524, **527**; disabilities imposed by, 487-8, 543; transfers schools, 498, 548
'Umar al-Khayyām, 582-3
'Umar ibn-abi-Rabī'ah, 494-5
'Umari, al-, 487, 654
'Umari, al-, *al-Ta'rīf bi-al-Muṣṭalaḥ*, 474 n. 4, 655 n. 2; *Masālik al-Abṣār*, 487 n. 2; 655 n. 1
Umayyad: empire, 4; caliphs, 391; glory, 467; mosque, 472; poetry, 496; fall, 527 *seq.*
Umayyad Mosque of Damascus, 511, **513-16**
Umayyad Syria, 484
Umayyads: poets of, 494
Umayyah, banu-, 561. *See also* Umayyads
Umm al-Biyārah, 376
Umm al-Jimāl, 367
Umm Qaṭafah: caves of, 9
umm walad, 488
'Unayn, ibn-, *Dīwān*, 606 n. 1
Uni, 127
Uniat, churches, 674
Union and Progress, *see* Committee of Union and Progress
Unis, 127
United States, 197
Université Joseph, 701
Unūjūr, 562
'Uqayl, banu-, 593
'Uqbah ibn-Nāfi', **437-8**
'uqqāl, 585, 587
Ur: 177; tombs of, 138
Urban II, 590
Urdunn, al-, 424
Urfa, 253 n. 3. *See also* Ruhā', al-
Urmiyah, 150, 519
Urtuqid: dynasty, 575
Urtuqids, 616
Urusalim, 161. *See also* Jerusalem
Usāmah ibn-Munqidh, **621-2**
Usāmah ibn-Munqidh, *Kitāb al-I'tibār*, 53 n. 6
Uṣaybi'ah, ibn-abi-, **643-4**
Uṣaybi'ah, ibn-abi-, *'Uyūn al-Anbā'*, 497 n. 5; 644 n. 1
Usays, 509
Uswān, 170, 396. *See also* Aswān
Uthāl, ibn-, 439, 497
'Uthmān, founder of Ottoman state: 661; house of, 667
'Uthmān, Orthodox caliph, 426, 428, **429-30**
Utica, 95
'Uyūn w-al-Ḥadā'iq, al-, 511 n. 1
'Uzza, al-, 385, 402
Uzziah, 198

Valerian, 332, 392
Van Dyck, Cornelius, *al-Mir'āt*, 59 n. 3
Varuna, 150
Vasco da Gama, 671
Venetian: merchants, 95; fleet, 595; colony, 672
Venetians: 607; millet, 668
Venice: 354; merchants of, 590
Venus: temple of, 316
Vergil, 319
Verus, emperor, 302
Vespasian, 316, 339
Via Maris, 289
Vienna, 662, 663
Virgin, the, 37
Virolleaud, Charles, *La Légende phénicienne*, 116 n. 1
Visigothic: kingdom, 464
Visigoths, 468
Vitellius, 287, 294
Vitry, Jacques de, *History of Jerusalem*, 600 n. 3
Vogüé, de, *Inscriptions sémitiques*, 392 n. 1
Volney, 676, 683
Volney, *Voyage en Syrie*, 673 n. 4
Vulgate, 61, 170, 359

Waḍḍāḥ al-Yaman, 481
Waddington, W. H., *Inscriptions grecques*, 385 n. 1
Wādi al-'Arabah, 380, 411. *See also* 'Arabah, al-
Wādi Barissa, 201
Wādi Mūsa, 376
Wādi al-Naṭūf, 14
Wādi al-Sirḥān, 380, 412. *See also* Baṭn al-Sirr
Wādi al-Taym, 584, 586, 695
Wafā' Mubashshir ibn-Fātik, abu-al-, 644
Wahab-Allāth: 393; coins of, 394
Wahb ibn-Munabbih, 493
Wahb ibn-Munabbih, *al-Tījān*, 493 n. 1
Wahhābis, 624, 690, 692
Wāḥidi, al-, *Sharḥ Dīwān al-Mutanabbi'*, 567 n. 5

walāyah, 664
wāli, 664
Walīd I, al-: 449, **457** *seq.*, 462; segregates the diseased, 497
Walīd II, al-, 461, 480, **528**
Walīd, Khālid, ibn-al-, *see* Khālid ibn-al-Walīd
Waltzing, J. P., *Étude historique sur les corporations professionnelles*, 347 n. 3
waqf, 478, 644
Wāqidi, al-, *al-Maghāzi*, 410 n. 2
Wāqūṣah, al-, 415
Washshukanni, 150
Wāṣil ibn-'Aṭā', 498
Wāsiṭ, 455
Wāthiq, al-, 536
Wa'wā', al-, 569
Wa'wā', al-, *Dīwān*, 569 n. 7
Weissbach, Franz H., *Die Denkmäler*, 134 n. 3
Wellhausen, J., *Skizzen und Vorarbeiten*, 410 n. 1; *Das arabische Reich*, 425 n. 1
Wenamon, 134, 181
Wensinck, A. J., *Handbook*, 504 n. 1
West: 5; Christian, 4
West Canaanite, 77
West Goths, 468. *See also* Visigoths
West Semitic, 67
West Syrian Church, **519-21**
Western: ideas, 623; cultural influences, 674, 678, 694, 701
Western Aramaic, 399
Western Asia: 21, 23, 77, 138; silver in, 87; powers of, 125; silkworm of, 275
Western Europe: 706; megalithic structures of, 28
Western Lebanon, 31, 49
Western Semitic, 79
Wiegand, Theodore, *Baalbek*, 312 n. 3
William of Tripoli, 626
William of Tyre, 617, 619
William of Tyre, *History*, 58 n. 7; 610
Winckler, Hugo, *Keilinschriftliches Textbuch*, 168 n. 1
Winnett, F. V., *Study of the Lihyanite and Thamudic Inscriptions*, 403 n. 3
Witiza, 464
Wittek, Paul, *Rise of the Ottoman Empire*, 661 n. 4
Wood, Alfred C., *A History of the Levant Company*, 673 n. 1
Woolley, 114
Works of Gregory Thaumaturgus, tr. S. D. F. Salmond, 360 n. 1
Wright, William, *Apocryphal Acts*, 524 n. 4
Wüstenfeld, F., *Die Statthalter von Ägypten*, 562 n. 2; *Fachr ed-Dīn*, 684 n. 6

Xerxes, 224, 231

Yāfa, 131 n. 3, 595. *See also* Jaffa
Yāghi-Siyān, 592
Yaḥdun-Lim, 67
Yahweh: 204; sanctuary, for 188; cult of, 194; worship of, 201; mouth of, 214
Yahwism, 188, 194
Yaḥya ibn-'Adi, 550
Yakin-el, 142
Yamāmah, al-, 453
Yaman, party, 540, 687
Yaman, al-; 58, 270; province of, 477. *See also* Arabia Felix
Yamanites, 452, 469, 528, 684, 687, 694
Yamkhad, 68, 155
Yantin-'Ammu, 68
Ya'qob-har, 149
Ya'qūb al-Barda'i, 372 n. 4, 403. *See also* Jacob Bardaeus
Ya'qūbi, al-, 510
Ya'qūbi, al-, *Ta'rīkh*, 414 n. 1; *Kitāb al-Buldān*, 536 n. 1
Yāqūt, 472
Yāqūt, *Mu'jam al-Buldān*, 41 n. 7, 654 n. 2; *Mu'jam al-Udabā'*, 496 n. 5; 654
Yarīm-Lim, 155
Yarkhi-bōl, 400
Yarmūk: 260; battle of, 47, **415-16**
Yazbaki, 687, 694
Yazīd I, son of Mu'āwiyah, 440, **444**, 450, 452, 480, 504
Yazīd II, 449
Yazīd III, 489, 529
Yazīd ibn-abi-Sufyān, 411, 412
Yāziji, Nāṣīf, al-, *al-'Urf al-Ṭayyib*, 568 n. 2
Yildiz, 699
Young Ottomans, 699
Young Turks, 699, 700
Yuhanan, A., *Death of a Nation*, 519 n. 1
Yūḥanna Mārūn, 521
Yūḥanna ibn-Māsawayh, 550. *See also* Māsawayh, ibn-
Yūsuf, abu-, 486

Yūsuf, abu-, *Kitāb al-Kharāj*, 423 n. 1
Yūsuf Karam, 696, 704
Yūsuf Sayfa, 679, 680

Zāb, the Greater (Upper), 531
Zabadāni, al-, 42, 60
Zabbā', al-, 393. *See also* Zenobia
Zabbay, 394
Zabda, 393, 394, 395
Zabdibōl: inscription of, 398
Zacharias of Gaza, 360, 361
Zagros, 150
Zahi, 130, 132
ẓāhir, 583
Ẓāhir, al-, Fāṭimid: coin of, 588
Ẓāhir al-'Umar, **688-9**
Ẓāhiri, al-, 642
Ẓāhiri, al-, *Zubdat Kashf*, 615 n. 3
Ẓāhirīyah, al-, 632
Zaḥlah, 154, 166
zakāh, 474, 525
Zakar-Baal, 134-5, 139
Zakir, 170, 174
Zama, 108
Zambaur, E. de, *Manuel*, 629 n. 2
Zangi, 'Imād-al-Dīn: **575-6**, **599**; coins of, 616
zanjabīl, 619
zāwiyah, 513
Zayd ibn-Ḥārith, 409, 410
Zaydān, Jurji, *Ta'rīkh Miṣr*, 532 n. 4
Zaytūnah, al-, palace, 510
Zedekiah, 202
Zeller, Eduard, *Die Philosophie der Griechen*, 325 n. 1
Zeno, emperor, 369, 549
Zeno, Stoic philosopher, 236, 255
Zeno of Sidon, 255
Zenobia, **393-6**
Zerubbabel, 222, 223
Zeus, 105, 198, 244, 323, 334
Zeus Olympius, 244
Ziklag, 181
Zikrawayh, ibn-, 561
Zimri-Lin, 67, 68
Ziyād, Sufyāni, 540
Ziyād ibn-Abīh, **436-7**, 493
Zobah, 165, 166
Zoroaster, 224, 361
Zoroastrianism, 216, 224, 370
Zoroastrians, 486
Zubayr, al-, 431
Zumoffen, G., *La Phénicie*, 9 n. 1; *Géologie du Liban*, 34 n. 1
Zunbīl, 458
Zuṭṭīyah, al-: caves of, 9

Printed in the United States
32451LVS00004B/156

9 781931 95661